*P*INTERPRETING THE *R*OPHETIC *W*ORD

*P*INTERPRETING THE
*R*OPHETIC
*W*ORD

AN
INTRODUCTION
TO THE
PROPHETIC
LITERATURE
OF THE
OLD TESTAMENT

WILLEM A. VANGEMEREN

ZondervanPublishingHouse
Grand Rapids, Michigan

A Division of HarperCollins*Publishers*

Interpreting the Prophetic Word
Copyright © 1990 by Willem VanGemeren

Requests for information should be addressed to:

🏛 ZondervanPublishingHouse
Grand Rapids, Michigan 49530

Library of Congress Cataloging-in-Publication Data
VanGemeren, Willem.
    Interpreting the prophetic word : an introduction to the prophetic
literature of the Old Testament / Willem A. VanGemeren.
        p.   cm.
    Previously published: Grand Rapids, Mich. : Academie Books,
c1990.
    Includes bibliographical references and index.
    ISBN 0-310-21138-7
    1. bible. O.T. Prophets—Criticism, interpretation, etc.
2. Prophets.   I. Title.
BS1505.2.V336   1996
224'.06—dc 20   96–9249
                                                                          CIP

Edited by John Vriend and Dimples Kellogg

Printed in the United States of America

96 97 98 99 00 01 02 /❖ DH/ 10 9 8 7 6 5 4 3 2

Contents

FIGURES

TABLES

Preface

It is my great pleasure to present these studies on the prophetic word. In writing I have tried to avoid adapting the prophetic word to any eschatological system because it is my deep desire that the prophetic voice be heard. God's servants, the prophets, bear a harmonious testimony—along with the teaching of our Lord and the apostles—that our heavenly Father has prepared great things for those who consecrate themselves to him by forming a counterculture, his kingdom on earth. The Scriptures repeatedly call on the people of God to renew themselves with unwavering loyalty to seek God's kingdom. The Scriptures also repeatedly call on the people of God not to depend on cultural, social, political, religious, or economic structures for their identity. Our Lord invites all his disciples to follow him in the discipline of radical obedience and thus become the salt of the earth.

The different prophetic voices harmoniously witness in their diversity to the purposes of God in redemptive history. The reader of the Prophets is in danger of silencing the variety of the prophetic testimony (1) by dividing the Word in such a way that a text is understood only in relation to Christ's first or second coming, to the Millennium or the eternal state; (2) by attempting to fit the texts into an eschatological framework or by carefully avoiding or by explaining away any texts that may not quite fit; (3) by reading the New Testament back into the Old Testament as the *fulfillment* without due regard for the continuing relevance of the Prophets as Scripture in which the mission, teaching, and nature of Christ must be understood; and (4) by limiting the applicability of God's Word to any certain time or a particular people.

My prayer is that we may listen to the prophetic Word as God's revelation to his children and that we may continually remain sensitive to the movement of the Spirit of restoration so that the Father's purposes may be accomplished, our Lord and Savior may be pleased with the purity of our lives, and the Spirit of Christ may use us in building the church of the living Christ as a testimony to the world that we are the children of the kingdom of God.

This work was made possible by the encouragement of many friends, colleagues, and my present and former students. I am greatly indebted to President Luder G. Whitlock, Jr. and Dean Richard G. Watson of Reformed Theological Seminary for having provided me with a teaching schedule that freed me for writing. I recognize my assistants (Pat Apel, Mike Ericson, Richard Konieczny, Mark Snow, and Pat Williams) for their diligence and enthusiasm in proofreading and checking bibliographical details. Further, I am greatly indebted to Mrs. Jane Sheppard for her cheerful diligence and care in typing the manuscript and in revising it. I thank Mr. Ed van der Maas of Zondervan Publishing House for his continual encouragement during the writing of this book.

Finally, I dedicate this book to my wife, Evona, who helped me many times both in typing and in administering our household with love, devotion, and wisdom. My three daughters are blessed to have a mom who lives in the strength of the Spirit of restoration. This work is lovingly dedicated to her.

Part 1

The Prophetic Phenomenon in Israel

Introduction to Part 1

The prophets of the Old Testament were God's ministers of the Word during the Mosaic administration. They had seen something of the glory of God and expressed in poetic form the vision of God, his kingdom, the messianic age of *shalom* ("peace"), the work of the Spirit, a new community of people, and the transformation of creation and humanity. The prophetic message of salvation (1 Peter 1:10–12) is rich, embracing the work of the triune God in restoring creation to a state of *shalom,* in which the children of God live by his order, enjoy his benefits, and will no more be oppressed by Satan, enemies, misunderstanding, or physical distress.

Our Lord explained his mission using these Old Testament writings. To his disciples he said, "Everything must be fulfilled that is written about me in the Law of Moses, the Prophets and the Psalms" (Luke 24:44). From this we learn that everything in the Old Testament has its proper focus in Jesus Christ. A Christian reading the Old Testament cannot but pay careful attention to the relationship between the Old Testament and our Lord. Each division of the Old Testament, including the prophetic writings, relates to our Lord. These Scriptures are God's Word to his people, and the authority of that Word has not been diminished since the coming of Jesus Christ. The very basis for apostolic preaching was the Old Testament.

The three divisions (the Law, the Prophets, and the Psalms) of which our Lord spoke reflect the three divisions of the Hebrew Bible (*Tanakh:* Torah, Prophets, Writings).[1] The Prophets (*nᵉbî'îm*) consist of the "Former Prophets" (*nᵉbî'îm rî'šônîm*: Joshua through 2 Kings, except Ruth) and the "Latter Prophets" (*nᵉbî'îm 'aharônîm*: Isaiah to Malachi, except Daniel and Lamentations). (See figure 1.)

The Law, the Prophets, and the Writings (including Lamentations and Daniel) form the Scriptures of the Jews and are to be treated as God's Word by Christians.[2] The Christian Bible consists of two parts: God's Word *before* the Son and God's Word *after* the Son. The two parts relate to each other similarly to the way we commonly designate 1 and 2 Samuel, Kings, and Chronicles.

God's messengers before Christ (the prophets) and God's messengers

16

after Christ (the apostles) encourage us to persevere in waiting for the new age of righteousness, justice, and absolute joy. All who respond in faith to the promises of God live both in the grateful enjoyment of his present benefits and in the hope of the realization of the fullness of the new age. The prophetic revelation—as God's Word regarding his Messiah—bridges the era between Moses and our Lord, but as God's Word regarding the salvation to come, it bridges the gap between Moses and the new creation.

| Torah | Nevî'îm (Prophets) | | Ketuvîm |
	Former	Latter	(Writings)
Genesis	Joshua	Isaiah	Psalms
Exodus	Judges	Jeremiah	Proverbs
Leviticus	1–2 Samuel	Ezekiel	Job
Numbers	1–2 Kings	*The Twelve*	*5 Scrolls*
Deuteronomy		Hosea	Song of Songs
		Joel	Ruth
		Amos	Lamentations
		Obadiah	Ecclesiastes
		Jonah	Esther
		Micah	Daniel
		Nahum	Ezra–Nehemiah
		Habakkuk	1–2 Chronicles
		Zephaniah	
		Haggai	
		Zechariah	
		Malachi	

Figure 1. The Books of the Hebrew Old Testament

CHAPTER 1

The Development of Prophetism

INTRODUCTION

The prophets opened windows to the grand plan of God by which the eye of hope may have a vision of what God has prepared for his people.

The prophets spoke *in* time as they were human beings empowered by the Holy Spirit to speak God's word in space and time. Yet the prophets spoke *out of* time as their writings reflect more than the historically and culturally conditioned collection of Israel's prophets. The Lord empowered the prophets by the Spirit to proclaim and write down the revelation he gave them as a witness for future generations.

The prophets bore a message of transformation in a historical context to people who were complacent with their abilities and achievements. They spoke of God's imminent judgment on all humanity, including Israel and Judah, because humankind rebelled against the Lord, the King of Glory. They announced the coming kingdom of the Lord, the Judgment, and the transformation of creation.

The prophetic vision of God's glorious kingdom shattered the reality of human kingdoms and structures but also shaped the vision of a remnant that lives in harmony with God. The prophets posited a sharp antithesis between God's kingdom and human kingdoms, divine revelation and human religion. The distinction between revelation and religion is fundamental in understanding the nature of the prophetic role and in interpreting the prophetic message.

REVELATION AND RELIGION

Revelation

The Lord favored Israel with his revelation. They received his oracles as well as the promises, covenants, adoption to sonship, and manifestation of his glory (Rom. 3:2; 9:4–5). His relation to Israel was full of grace and promise as he guided his people to be a royal priesthood (Ex. 19:5–6) in all their activities (personal, liturgical, economic, societal, and political).[1] He led them into his way of wisdom so that they might receive his peace and the fulfillment of his promises (Isa. 48:17–19). By loving God and by submitting to his revelation, Israel was destined to become a wise nation, guided, protected, and blessed by the Lord (Deut. 4:6–8; 26:19).

Israel was unique in their claim to divine revelation.[2] God, the King of this world, had given Israel his revelation by which they might prosper on his earth. He willed to guide his people to himself and promised to lead them into the way that would lead into an era of rest and joy (Isa. 48:17–19). All he expected was faith, devotion, and submission to his instruction. Under those conditions Israel would develop a counterculture among the nations and enjoy the benefits of God's kingdom (Deut. 30:11–14; Rom. 10:6–8).

God's revelation was his gift to Israel. He had brought them out of Egypt into Canaan. He had instructed, comforted, fed, guided, disciplined, and promised to be with Israel in prosperity and adversity. He was Israel's King and Warrior, who had solemnly sworn to take all of Israel's concerns to heart! He had also promised to take care of them in the present and to secure their future. It made no sense to seek any other god or power because Yahweh, the Creator of everything, is King, and all things are under his control. But revelation demands a response of absolute loyalty and submission to the God who has spoken. (See figure 2.) Any deviation from the way of revelation, slight as it might be, degrades revelation into *religion*.

Religion

The nations around Israel were religious. They also sought "divine" guidance. They, too, desired to live in peace and enjoy prosperity. To obtain these ends, they sought to know the will of the gods through professional diviners, magicians, enchanters, and interpreters of dreams. They made every effort to maintain harmony between the society of humans and the world of the gods.

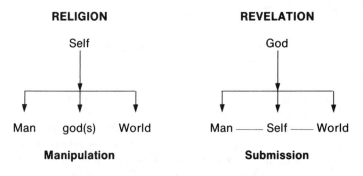

Figure 2. Religion and Revelation

Religion is a system of belief and morality that gives human beings a sense of meaning, but as a system, it is defined and developed by human beings. Religion defines for human beings how they may live at peace with their environment.[3] Religion begins and ends with man.

Religion is an attempt to *explain* what has happened, what is happening, and what may happen. In primitive societies people live in constant fear that the gods may become angry. To avoid catastrophe, they endeavor to please the gods through prescribed rituals. In the absence of revelation they depend on professional priests and diviners to ascertain what the gods desire. Whether in war or in peace, in adversity or in prosperity, they seek to know what they should do to advance their goals and to control the desired outcome. In this, humans

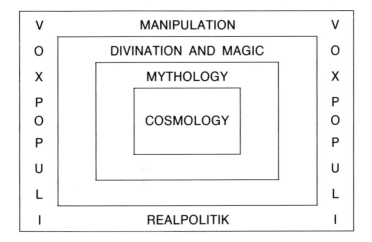

Figure 3. Religious Framework of Reference

are very religious. Though the methods and nature of these religious expressions differ from society to society, humans in the most technological and secularized society have much in common with their fellow humans in the most primitive society. Superstitions, science, techniques, and phobias bring humans to the same basic issue of life: how can I control my destiny?

Religion is *manipulative*. In their crises humans are very adept at looking for and finding salvation. "Salvation" is that complex of acts, structures, and institutions by which human beings individually and collectively define, determine, and control their happiness. (See figure 2.) Salvation is understood differently by each nation and culture, as shaped by their cosmogony, mythology, divination, and magic. (See figure 3.) *Cosmology* supplies a structure for understanding how the world came into being, how it is ordered, and how supernatural phenomena relate to it. *Mythology* supplies an interpretation of human experience and custom. It is a more comprehensive framework within which individuals and society understand themselves and in terms of which they explain all that is beyond rational explanation.[4] *Divination* and *magic* provide a bridge between the world of the supernatural and that of humans, one by which humans aim at some special insight or power in controlling their destiny.[5]

Divination[6]

Divination (the mantic) is the practice of knowing the future; it occurs in two forms: *inductive* and *intuitive*.[7] (See figure 4.) When a diviner uses an object ("omen"), divination is of the inductive type. The object or omen may be a natural event (signs in the sky), unusual phenomena (the behavior or noise of animals),[8] or a ritual involving water, oil, fire, arrows, or lots. The intuitive form of divination occurs when an individual acts as a medium to give a word from the gods.

Figure 4. Divination and Magic

The ancients developed many techniques of divination.[9] In Assyria and Babylonia the *bārû* ("seer") priests, an important caste of diviners,[10] specialized in examining the entrails of sacrificial sheep (extispicy). They looked for a sign by "seeing" the position of the internal organs (liver,[11] gall bladder, stomach, etc.).[12] The *bārû* were consulted by kings at court and by generals on the battlefield.[13] They wrote manuals and instructed novices in the art of divination.

Other forms of divination include interpreting dreams,[14] liquids,[15] and fire;[16] casting lots;[17] shooting arrows;[18] throwing sticks;[19] mediums' consulting the dead (*necromancy*);[20] using *teraphim*;[21] watching the behavior of animals;[22] and observing signs in the heavens (*astrology* or *astromancy*).[23] Regardless of the technique, the diviner believed that the gods gave humans an omen. The diviner did not claim infallibility but offered probability. Therefore, he used a variety of omens and left the final decision to the one who had sought his advice.

Intuitive divination approaches biblical prophetism but was relatively rare among the nations surrounding Israel. The tablets discovered at Mari have given us a closer look at intuitive divination.[24] Forty-six of these tablets provide some insight into two distinctive forms of "prophetism": intuitive prophets and diviner-prophets.[25] The intuitive prophets came from a seminomadic background. They were ecstatics who had their message transcribed and sent to a king or official. The diviner-prophets were professional or lay diviners. They were closely associated with the king and were expected to speak words of encouragement. The professional prophets differed from the lay, as they were permitted to "stand" or "rise"[26] when speaking. They spoke only of what they had seen; the lay prophets spoke of what they had dreamed.[27]

Literary prophecies were rare in the ancient Near East. The intuitive prophets gave isolated oracles, unlike Israel's prophets. In this regard the prophetic movement in Israel is unique.[28] The prophets of God spoke God's word at different times and "in various ways" (Heb. 1:1), but in their diversity they formed an extensive prophetic tradition.

Magic

Magic, the practice of the occult, was also widely used in the ancient Near East. In Assyria, Babylonia, Egypt, and Canaan, gods and humans alike tried to gain advantage over others by following prescribed rituals. The ancients were very adept in the magic arts and employed them as a powerful "force" in society.[29] For example, the Babylonian story of creation extols the magical powers of Ea-Enki, the patron deity of the magic spells in Babylon: "Ea, who understands everything . . . made and established against it a magical circle for all. He skillfully composed his overpowering, holy incantation. He recited it and thus caused [it] to be upon the water. He poured out sleep upon him."[30]

The magicians were often schooled, especially those in Egypt.[31] They wrote manuals prescribing rituals for casting spells and for warding off the powers of magic by using special colors, amulets, and ceremonies. (See figure 4.) Magic affected mutual relations, business, religions, and international affairs. Magic gave people special powers.[32] Through magic, people gained advantages for themselves (fertility, protection, prosperity, and peace) but also used these same skills in creating disadvantages for their enemies (infertility, destruction, adversity, and war).[33] All these practices were manipulative.

Magic could also be a destructive force when it ruptured relations. Some people lived in fear and others thought that they possessed special powers. Magic was essentially manipulative; it held the promise of individual or national success, even at the cost of others. The popularity of these practices explains the prohibitions in the Bible against engaging in cultic prostitution, wearing the symbols of the opposite sex, having tattoos, cutting one's hair, and displaying charms.[34]

Revelation Contra Religion

The people of Israel were like the nations, for they, too, shared in the primeval history of creation and rebellion. For this reason the Lord had given Israel a brief account of their prehistory in Genesis 1–11.[35] These chapters explain God's kingship over creation and human beings' acts of rebellion against him.[36] Humankind willingly and consistently rejected God's kingdom in order to establish its own kingdom.

Genesis 1–11 contrasts God's kingdom with the aggressive power of the nations. God inaugurated a rule of harmony, meaning, and joy (chaps. 1–2), but humans established self-rule by rebellion against God and by the corruption of his order (3:1–11:9). Apart from God's grace to humankind, the kingdom of humans distinguishes itself by autonomy (self-rule without regard of God), dictatorial power, and oppression, resulting in anarchy. It is of the very nature of human kingdoms to be obsolescent. Though a nation may develop and achieve the greatest cultural achievements, the kingdoms of humans must fall![37]

These eleven chapters shed light on how humankind develops its own religious structures. Religion may take many forms: animism, polytheism, monotheism, moralism, or even secularism. All these forms have one element in common: the rejection of the radical claims of revelation. Religion as a system or frame of reference helps humans to explain their world, define their place in this world, and operate with purpose. All the peoples in the ancient Near East developed religious systems. Religion is *open* to every available means (political, economic, social) to bring harmony among people, within society, and within nature,[38] but it is *closed* to revelation. At the royal courts wise men, religious leaders, and the practitioners of the occult met to give counsel to the king.[39] Diviners and magicians explained the will of the gods, based on their interpretation of dreams, omens, spells, or special rituals. They aimed at one thing: the perpetuation of human structures on earth.

Like those of the nations, their ancestors had worshiped idols (Josh. 24:2), but by grace the Lord had established a *relation* with the people of Israel, better known as *covenant*.[40] They were chosen from the nations to be his people (Ex. 19:5; Deut. 7:6; 14:2; 26:18), his kingdom (Ps. 114:2), and the recipients of his royal law (Rom. 3:2). Yahweh had set them apart from the nations so that they might establish a new order—a countercommunity founded on the charter of his revelation. As revelation opposes religion, so God's people were to distinguish themselves from the cultures of the nations by developing a counterculture. As a counterculture,[41] God's people, motivated and mobilized by the Spirit of God, were called to establish his kingdom on earth. His revelation, internalized by the Spirit, was to shatter the religious ways of the nations. Revelation cannot coexist with religion. (See figure 5.)

The Lord shatters human structures. Israel had witnessed that God is victorious over magic and mantic. In Egypt the Lord had afflicted the economic, social, and religious structures through the ten plagues. Even the Egyptian magicians had to recognize the sovereignty of Israel's God:

"The magicians said to Pharaoh, 'This is the finger of God' " (Ex. 8:19). Similarly, Balaam, the diviner from Paddan-aram had to admit,

> There is no sorcery against Jacob,
>   no divination against Israel.
> It will now be said of Jacob
>   and of Israel, "See what God has done!"
> (Num. 23:23)

RELIGION	REVELATION
Manipulation	Submission
Divination and magic	Divine guidance and protection
Realpolitik	Divine wisdom
Vox populi	Counterculture

Figure 5. Religion and Revelation

Forms of Divine Revelation

Yahweh is opposed to all human forms of religions and human attempts to control the future. He alone sovereignly rules over all things in heaven and earth (Isa. 41:4; 44:6), and he is free to reveal his will through any means, whether by lots, dreams, visions, the Urim and Thummim, or his prophets. Casting lots was one form of legitimate divination (Lev. 16:8; Josh. 18:6, 8, 10; 1 Sam. 14:41; Acts 1:26). The Lord also freely used dreams (Deut. 13:1; 1 Kings 3:5–15) and the prophets as his means of revelation. In addition, the Urim and the Thummim were stones by which the priests could consult the will of God (Ex. 28:30; Lev. 8:8; Num. 27:21; 1 Sam. 23:2, 4, 9–12; 28:6; Ezra 2:63; Neh. 7:65).

Revelation Against Religion

The many references and allusions to divination and the magic arts in the Old Testament indicate that Israel lived in a pagan context.[42] Because of the attractions inherent in divination and magic, the Lord prohibited his people from mixing paganism with Yahwism: "The nations you will dispossess listen to those who practice sorcery or divination. But as for you, the LORD your God has not permitted you to do so" (Deut. 18:14). Apart from the above forms of "legitimate"divination, he prohibited all other forms of divination and magic, whether ancient or new (Lev. 19:26–29, 31; Deut. 18:10–11; 2 Kings 9:22; Isa. 3:2–3; 8:19; Jer. 27:9; Ezek. 13:18–20).[43] The prophets, too, uniformly condemned dependency on such religious expressions. For example, Isaiah said, "When men tell you to consult mediums and spiritists, who whisper and mutter, should not a people inquire of their God? Why consult the dead on behalf of the living?" (Isa. 8:19).

Throughout Israel's history, pagan rituals, including divination and magic, held a special attraction. Saul (1 Sam. 28:3) and Josiah (2 Kings 23:24) attempted to purge those pagan practices. But other kings, such as Manasseh, encouraged all forms of paganism, which encompassed the practices of magic and mantic (2 Chron. 33:6). In the last days of Jerusalem the women of the city thought to avert the judgment of God by sewing protective charms to ward off the Babylonian threat (Ezek. 13:18–23). Of course, their efforts were of no avail!

Realpolitik and Vox Populi

Yet Israel had grave difficulty in living by the revelation of God alone. She adopted an unhealthy *syncretism* of revelation and religion.[44] Two perennial dangers reduce revelation to religion: *Realpolitik* and the *vox populi.* (See figure 5.) *Realpolitik,* or power politics, is a pragmatic application of any technique by which an individual or a group can maintain or enhance life. It is manipulative, works at the expense of others, and undermines the essential nature of revelation. *Realpolitik* gives coherence to all human structures (power, society, economics, and cult) and is readily adaptable to new situations or crises. For example, when faced with the coalition of Aram and Israel, King Ahaz of Judah looked to Assyria for a political solution (2 Chron. 28:16) and even worshiped the gods of Aram as a religious fix (v. 23). He believed in the religion of manipulation: The end justifies the means. In *Realpolitik* anything is fair in achieving the goal.

Vox populi ("the voice of the people") is a form of *Realpolitik.* In search of freedom, prosperity, and happiness, humans in any society establish a sacred alliance of relative values that form the basis of laws, social interaction, politics, economics, cultic expressions, and traditions. *Vox populi* rewards all who support the common ideals but punishes anyone who challenges them. *Vox populi* shuns the absolute demands of revelation by softening the radical nature of faith in favor of popular expectations. Israel's false prophets, the Pharisees, and the Sadducees were bound by the *vox populi.* The true prophets, our Lord, and the apostles faced the antagonism aroused against them by a human commitment to pragmatism (*Realpolitik*) and to popular views and traditions (*vox populi*).

Revelation and Wisdom

Israel did not have to search for God through religious manipulations because the Lord had given them his revelation. The revelation of Yahweh is first and foremost a revelation of who Yahweh is. He is the great King, the Creator of everything, the God of the Fathers and of promise, and the Redeemer of Israel (Ex. 3:15; 19:5; 20:2). He is also the Sovereign King over all nations (15:11–16, 18). He guides and protects his people who submit to his sovereignty, and he gives wisdom to all who seek him diligently. He rewards all who abandon the path of *Realpolitik* and the *vox populi* for the "paths of righteousness" (Ps. 23:3; see Prov. 3:5–8). But the Lord condemns anyone who relies on self, divination, magic, human structures (*Realpolitik*), and human systems of value (*vox populi,* see Prov. 6:16–19).

Daniel's situation illustrates the contrast between revelation and religion. Daniel and his friends were surrounded by practitioners of the magic and mantic arts, but they remained unwaveringly loyal to Yahweh. They trusted him for wisdom while denying that any "wise man, enchanter, magician or diviner can explain to the king the mystery he has asked about" (Dan. 2:27). God exalted Daniel to the position of overseer of all "the magicians, enchanters, astrologers and diviners" (4:7; 5:11), but he made the sages of Babylon look foolish and abased King Nebuchadnezzar to live like an animal.

Conclusion

The danger of mixing religious ways with a selective interpretation of God's revelation comes naturally in our search for peace with God, our world, and ourselves. We shall see that Israel's problems with syncretism, *Realpolitik,* and *vox populi* persist today.

In the next section we shall consider:

1. the special place of Moses as the servant of the Lord;
2. the special place of Moses as mediator-intercessor of the covenant;
3. the nature of the prophetic office as defined by the Mosaic revelation;
4. the special place of Samuel as the servant of the Lord;
5. the special place of Samuel in the definition of the prophetic role;
6. the contribution of Elijah in the definition of the prophet as a covenantal prosecutor;
7. the heritage of the classical prophets: the Mosaic revelation, the prophetic model as defined by Samuel, and the message as revealed to Elijah on Mount Sinai.

THE DEVELOPMENT OF PROPHETISM IN ISRAEL

The development of prophetism in Israel reveals the interweaving of divine and human activity. Through the prophets, people heard the "voice" of God and received a new vision for life (see chap. 12: "Living the Prophetic Word"). As spokesmen for Yahweh, the prophets viewed human activities from God's vantage point. They spoke of judgment, urged repentance, and envisioned a transformed humanity and a new world order: the kingdom of God. The prophets, as heralds of the kingdom, form one continuous stream from Moses to John the Baptist.

Moses, the beginning of the stream, is *the fountainhead* of the prophetic movement. The course of the stream through the history of redemption is altered at crucial junctures, or rapids. The prophets were God's spokespersons in crisis, as R. B. Y. Scott expressed so well: "They [the prophets] spoke in the atmosphere of moments which were critical for men because Yahweh's righteous will was present, and his claims were pressing."[45]

The first such critical era was in the days of Samuel when Israel was caught up in immorality, tribal squabbles, and syncretism. Samuel lived during what we may call the "rapids" of Israel's history, and he was instrumental in developing the prophetic *model*. Elijah faced another crisis situation: the bankruptcy of Israel's faith. His mission was to call out a remnant, and in this regard his ministry determined the message of the prophets. Elijah is the beginning of the prophetic office of *covenant prosecutor* in the sense that he accused God's people of treachery and comforted the remnant with the hope of God's kingdom. All prophets from Elijah to John the Baptist share a common message of judgment on the self-sufficient and of the hope of all who long for God's kingdom. Hence, we may think of John the Baptist as the last cataract in the prophetic stream. (See figure 6.)

Moses: The Fountainhead

Moses has a special place in redemptive history (Heb. 3:1–5). In God's administration of his people, which lasted till the coming of the Son of God, Moses was God's servant. He was also the fountainhead of the prophets. The prophetic message was rooted in the Mosaic revelation, just as the apostolic teaching (*paradosis* or "tradition") was rooted in Jesus' teaching.

Moses: The Servant of Yahweh

Moses occupied a unique position in God's covenant administration. He ministered to Israel as *the servant* of the Lord and was exalted by his special relationship with the Lord (Num. 12:6–8; Deut. 34:10–12).[46]

When Aaron and Miriam complained about Moses' exalted position as mediator between Yahweh and Israel, Moses did not respond to their charge (Num. 12:3). Instead, the Lord spoke to defend his servant,

When a prophet of the LORD is among you,

> I reveal myself to him in visions,
>   I speak to him in dreams.
> But this is not true of my servant Moses;
>   he is faithful in all my house.
> With him I speak face to face,
>   clearly and not in riddles;
>   he sees the form of the LORD.
> Why then were you not afraid
>   to speak against my servant Moses?

(vv. 6–8)

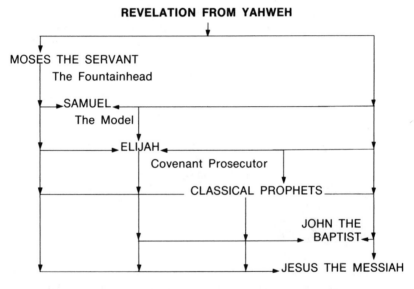

Figure 6. The Development of the Prophetic Movement

The Lord confirmed Moses' authority to be his chosen vehicle of communication: "I reveal . . . I speak to him . . ." (Num. 12:6; see Deut. 18:18). He set Moses apart as his servant (Ex. 14:31; Deut. 34:5; Josh. 1:1–2)[47]—a relationship of confidence and friendship between a superior and an inferior.[48] Moses in a unique way remained God's servant, even after his death; he served as the "head" of the covenant administration till the new covenant in our Lord Jesus (Num. 12:7; see Heb. 3:2, 5).[49]

The characteristic difference between Moses and the prophets after him lies in the directness in which the Lord spoke to his trusted servant.

Moses as the fountainhead was the first to receive, to write down, and to teach the revelation of God. This revelation extended to all facets of life, including the laws of holiness, purity, rituals, family life, work, and society.[50] Through Moses, the Lord had planned to shape Israel into "a counter-community."[51] God's revelation was to make them immune to the detestable practices of the pagans, including divination and magic.[52] The word of revelation by the power of the Spirit was to transform Israel into mature children.

The last words of the Pentateuch testify to the importance of Moses.

> Since then, no prophet has risen in Israel like Moses, whom the LORD knew face to face, who did all those miraculous signs and wonders the LORD sent him to do in Egypt—to Pharaoh and to all his officials and to his whole land. For no one has ever shown the mighty power or performed the awesome deeds that Moses did in the sight of all Israel (Deut. 34:10–12).

According to this prophetic epitaph of Moses' ministry, Moses occupied a unique place as God's friend. He had enjoyed the privilege of close communion with the Lord, "The LORD would speak to Moses face to face, as a man speaks with a friend" (Ex. 33:11).

Moses' position and revelation foreshadow the unique position of our Lord. Moses served in God's kingdom as a faithful "servant" (Heb. 3:2, 5), whereas "Christ is faithful as a son over God's house" (v. 6). Moses, like our Lord, verified the revelation of God by signs and wonders (Deut. 34:12; see also Ex. 7:14–11:8; 14:5–15:21).

Moses: The Mediator of the Covenant

Moses was the mediator of the covenant of Sinai (Ex. 19:3–8; 20:18–19). The Old Testament associates Moses with the covenant, the theocracy, and the revelation at Sinai.[53] This covenant, also known as the Mosaic (or Sinaitic) covenant, was *an administration of grace and promise by which the Lord consecrated a people to himself through the sanctions of divine law.* The Lord dealt with his people graciously, gave his promises to all who had faith in him, and consecrated them to order their lives by his holy law.[54] The covenant administration was a concrete expression of God's kingdom. The Lord was present with his people and extended his special rule over them.[55] The essence of the covenant is the promise, "I will be your God, and you will be my people" (Ex. 6:7; Deut. 29:13; Ezek. 11:20).

Although Moses did not as yet know of the revelation of God in Christ, he saw the "glory" of God (Ex. 34:29–35). The apostle Paul confirmed the grace of God in the Mosaic covenant when he wrote to the church at Rome, "Theirs is the adoption as sons; theirs the divine glory, the covenants, the receiving of the law, the temple worship and the promises. Theirs are the patriarchs, and from them is traced the human ancestry of Christ, who is God over all, forever praised! Amen" (Rom. 9:4–5).

Moses: The Eschatological Prophet

Moses, the greatest prophet before Jesus' incarnation spoke of the ministry of another prophet (Deut. 18:15–22).[56] He was God's witness to Israel that a greater fulfillment lay ahead: "Moses was faithful . . . , testifying to what would be said in the future" (Heb. 3:5). The nature of that future was nothing less than the rest that comes (4:1–13) in Jesus Christ, for whose sake Moses also suffered (11:26).

The eschatological hope of the Mosaic revelation is the presence of God among his people. Israel's eschatology begins in God's covenants with Abraham and with Israel.[57] Moses—the servant of God, the intercessor, the mediator of the covenant—pointed beyond his administration to an *era of rest*. He spoke of the enjoyment of rest and ordained that all the members of the covenant fellowship should long for the rest-to-come in the celebration of the *Sabbath* ("rest"). The Sabbath is the sign of the covenant (Ex. 31:14–17), the sign of Israel's consecration to a holy mission (v. 13), and of their being blessed with all God's gifts in creation (Deut. 26:18–19; 28:3–14).[58]

Moses painfully realized that the people could not enter into that rest because of his disobedience and because of Israel's rebelliousness (Deut. 4:21–26). Yet he spoke of a new era opened up by God's grace, freedom, and fidelity (vv. 29–31; 30:5–10, 32:39–43). Moses looked forward to an era of peace; tranquility; and the full enjoyment of God's presence, blessing, and protection in the Promised Land (12:9–10; 25:19; cf. Ex. 33:14; Josh. 1:13).[59]

This hope, grounded in Yahweh's fidelity (Deut. 4:31), is most clearly expressed in Moses' final testimony, "the Song of Moses" (chap. 32). In it he recites Yahweh's loving acts and favor to Israel (vv. 1–14), warns against Israel's rebellion and their consequent suffering (vv. 15–35), and comforts the godly with the hope of Yahweh's vengeance on the enemies and the deliverance of the remnant of Israel and of the nations (vv. 36–43). He even alludes to the greatness of Yahweh's love to Gentiles (vv. 36–43; Rom. 15:10).[60]

The eschatological significance of the Song of Moses reverberates in the prophetic messages of judgment and hope, justice and mercy, exclusion and inclusion, vengeance and deliverance.[61] Moshe Weinfeld assesses the significant place of Moses in the eschatology of the Old Testament: "The belief in a final revelation of God to save the world thus unites all Israelite sources from the prayer of Moses to the contemporary liturgy."[62] The Mosaic administration, therefore, was

31

never intended to be an end in itself. It was a stage in the progress of fulfillment of the promises, and an important stage at that![63]

Moses: The Fountainhead of the Prophetic Tradition

As fountainhead of the prophetic tradition, Moses saw more of God's glorious self-revelation than anyone else in the Old Testament (Ex. 33:18; 34:29–35). He spoke by God's authority. Whoever questioned Moses challenged the Lord. Israel could find comfort, grace, and blessing because in Moses the roles of covenant *mediator* and *intercessor* (32:1–34:10; Num. 14:13–25) came together. He prayed for Israel, spoke boldly as their advocate in the presence of the Lord, and encouraged them to look beyond himself to Yahweh.[64]

The possibility of additional revelation opens the Mosaic "canon" to more revelation from God.[65] Moses was not the end of divine revelation, but the beginning, the fountainhead, of the prophetic movement. (See figure 7.) He gave specific instructions on the office, role, and message of the prophets (*nᵉḇî'îm*).[66] The prophets comprised a class of theocratic officers by whom the Lord guided the covenant community in addition to the priests (and Levites), kings (Deut. 17:14–20), tribal and local leadership (elders, leaders, and princes).

The prophets, like the priests and kings, were called and chosen by the Lord to serve as guardians of his kingdom.[67] The prophet was an individual who, unlike the priestly caste and the royal dynasty, could not claim hereditary rights.[68] He received a distinct call, as may be inferred from the promise, "The LORD your God will raise up for you a prophet" (Deut. 18:15, 18). As officers in God's kingdom, the prophets were called to shepherd God's people. The prophets in Israel conformed to seven criteria laid down in the Mosaic revelation. (See figure 7.)

WHO IS A PROPHET OF GOD?

He is an Israelite, called by God, and empowered by the Spirit
    who serves as God's spokesperson
    who has received authority and a revelation from God
    who is a good shepherd over God's flock
    who demonstrates God's Word and mission by signs

Figure 7. Mosaic Definition of a Prophet of God

First, the prophet as an *Israelite* shared fully in the heritage of the covenant, the divine revelation, and the promises; therefore, the new revelation had to be continuous with the Mosaic revelation (Deut. 13:1–5). This was true of all prophets, including our Lord (Matt. 5:17–19).

Second, the prophet received a distinct *call* from the Lord. Like Moses, he knew without a doubt that he had been sent with a message by the great King.

Third, the Holy Spirit empowered the servant of God to withstand the pressures of his contemporaries, to speak the word of God, and to discharge his office faithfully. The power of the *Spirit,* which had characterized the ministry of Moses (Num. 11:17), was also present with the prophets.[69] Some underwent a visible change as the Spirit "lifted" them "up" (Ezek. 3:12, 14; 8:3; 11:1, 24; 43:5) or "came upon" them (1 Sam. 19:20; 2 Chron. 20:14; Ezek. 11:5). They all experienced an overwhelming sense of the Spirit's presence that left them with no doubt that God had spoken. That feeling explains the prophetic sense of an inner compulsion, as in the case of Amos.

> The Sovereign LORD does nothing
> without revealing his plan
> to his servants the prophets. . . .
> The Sovereign LORD has spoken—
> who can but prophesy?
> (Amos 3:7–8)

Fourth, the prophet declared God's word as his *spokesperson.* He did not serve himself; he served his Lord (Deut. 18:18–19; cf. Ex. 4:10–16; 7:1).

Fifth, the *authority* of the prophet lay not in his personal credentials but in the privilege of speaking in the name of the Lord (Deut. 18:19–20, 22).

Sixth, the prophet was like Moses in that he was a *good shepherd* for God's people; he loved them and interceded on their behalf.

Seventh, a true prophet might give a *sign* verifying that the Lord had sent him. The sign (*'ôt*) verified the prophet's having been sent by the Lord (Ex. 3:12; 4:8; Deut. 13:2) and witnessed to the authenticity of his message. Though the signs were diverse—a miracle (1 Kings 13:5; 2 Kings 20:9), a designation of a specified time (1 Sam. 12:16–19; Isa. 7:14–25), a special event (1 Sam. 10:3–7, 9–11; 1 Kings 13:3–5; 2 Kings 19:29), the prophet himself (Isa. 8:18; 20:3; Ezek. 24:24), or an object lesson (Ezek. 4:3)—they signified that the prophet's mission was in the service of the Lord and that the prophet was God's mouthpiece. Whether or not the prophet gave a sign, the veracity of his message was vindicated by fulfillment (1 Kings 13:26; 16:12; 2 Kings 24:2; Jer. 28:15–17; Ezek. 33:33).

God's people were responsible for "testing" the new revelation by the standard ("canon") of the older revelation and by verifying the "signs" of the prophet (Deut. 13:1–5; 18:20–22). The veracity of the prophetic word could also be verified by later generations, as Ezekiel writes, "When all this comes true—and it surely will—then they will know that a prophet has been among them" (Ezek. 33:33).

Conclusions

The prophetic tradition had its origin in the Mosaic revelation, the covenant, law, sanctions, judgments, promises, and eschatology. The Mosaic revelation embodied within it the hope that the Lord would raise up an eschatological prophet *like* Moses.[70] The final epitaph (Deut. 34:10–12) was a reminder that the godly were to live in the hope of God's raising up a prophet like Moses to do mighty wonders and be able to lead God's people into the promised rest (Heb. 3:1–4:13). The godly received encouragement in the prophetic ministry of Samuel, in the royal counselor-prophets, in Elijah, and in the literary prophets. But Moses finds his counterpart and fulfillment in Jesus, whose words and signs attest that he is greater than Moses (John 1:14–18; 21:25; Heb. 3:1–6).

Samuel: The Prophetic Role Model

The Era Between Moses and Samuel

Samuel bridges the epochs of Moses–Joshua and that of David–Solomon. After the death of Moses, the word of the Lord came to Joshua, and Israel received continual reassurance that the Lord was with them (Josh. 3:7; 4:14; 6:27). Shortly before his death Joshua challenged the leaders of Israel to remain faithful to the Lord (23:1–11) because he could not bring Israel into a state of "rest" on account of his old age (13:1). In spite of the repeated warnings by Moses (Deuteronomy), Joshua (chaps. 23 and 24), and God's servants (Judg. 2:1–5; 6:7–10), Israel rebelled against the Lord and often experienced divine abandonment. The Lord tested the loyalty of his people (2:22–3:1), but Israel failed him as individuals, as tribes, and as a nation. Since the "rest" that they began to enjoy under Joshua (Josh. 22:4) had been conditioned on covenantal fidelity (v. 5), Yahweh suspended the fulfillment of this promise of rest (Judg. 2:3, 21; Ps. 95:11). Israel reached a very low point in redemptive history. (See figure 8.)

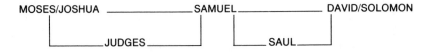

Figure 8. Samuel and the New Era

34

Samuel: The Servant of the Lord

Samuel has the distinction of being the first of the prophets (Acts 3:24). The Lord called him to be his prophet (1 Sam. 3:1–14), and as a prophet he embodied the spirit of Moses (Jer. 15:1). He was recognized as God's "servant," by whom the Lord spoke to his people individually (1 Sam. 9:6) and nationally (7:2–4; 8:1–22). Samuel's prophetic ministry was so unique that all the tribes heard about it: "And all Israel from Dan to Beersheba recognized that Samuel was attested as a prophet of the LORD" (3:20).[71]

The Lord raised up Samuel in this crisis in Israel's history.[72] He served Israel as Yahweh's "judge," "priest," and "prophet."[73] Samuel became Israel's priest after the tabernacle in Shiloh was destroyed and the ark taken by the Philistines (1 Sam. 4:1–7:1). Samuel, like Moses, interceded for Israel (7:9). He continued to do so even after Israel had initiated a wrong course (12:17, 19, 23). As the last of the judges (Acts 13:20) and the first of the prophets (3:24),[74] he served as a transition figure between the era of the judges and the kings. Samuel was a faithful judge who lived up to the theocratic ideal, shaped Israel's political life, unified the tribes, and victoriously fought the Philistines (1 Sam. 7:13b–17). But he did not give Israel her "rest."

Samuel: The Guardian of the Theocracy

Samuel became the role model for the prophets as the guardian of the theocracy. (See figure 8.) He showed a pastoral concern for all twelve tribes (1 Sam. 4:1), brought revival to Israel (7:6; 12:18–19), led Israel in worship, and guided the tribes with his counsel. He also led Israel into a period of international stability and national peace and prosperity.

In his position as God's spokesman to the people and to the theocratic king, Samuel defined the role of the prophets as guardians of the theocracy.[75] He rebuked Saul's resistance to his prophetic authority (1 Sam. 13:1–14) and declared God's judgment on Saul and his descendants (15:22–26). Also, like Moses and Joshua, Samuel exhorted Israel to remain faithful to Yahweh in his farewell speech, lest God's curses overtake them (12:1–25).

Centuries later Israel still remembered Samuel's legacy. The Chronicler comments on Josiah's celebration of the Passover, "The Passover had not been observed like this in Israel since the days of the prophet Samuel; and none of the kings of Israel had ever celebrated such a Passover as did Josiah, with the priests, the Levites and all Judah and Israel who were there with the people of Jerusalem" (2 Chron. 35:18). The psalmist places him next to Moses and Aaron as God's priest.

> Moses and Aaron were among his priests,
> Samuel was among those who called on his name;

35

> they called on the LORD
> and he answered them.
>
> (Ps. 99:6)

Elijah: The Covenant Prosecutor

Elijah the Tishbite lived during another period of crisis.[76] Ahab had married Jezebel, a Phoenician princess, who had introduced Baal worship and pagan culture into Israel. Ahab followed the political ambitions of his father, Omri, who had begun making Israel into a political-military power of international renown. Ahab's administration had opened Israel to a grand future of economic prosperity and military might, as Israel had become a "power" among the nations. The people had rejected the covenant and the way of revelation and had become enamored with a new way of life. *Realpolitik* had triumphed!

Elijah: The Beginning of the End

Elijah has a distinct role in the history of redemption.[77] Though he left no prophetic book, Elijah has a special place next to Moses. If Moses is the *fountainhead* and Samuel the *rapids* of the prophetic stream, then Elijah shaped the *course* of the classical prophets. (See figure 6.) The stories surrounding Elijah incorporated in 1 Kings 17—21 and 2 Kings 1:1—2:11 present us with one of the greatest prophets of the Old Testament.[78] (See figure 9.)

MOSES_____ SAMUEL_____ ELIJAH_____PROPHETS

People   King and people   People and leaders

Warning   Threatening   Curse inevitable

Figure 9. Elijah and the Prophets

Alone and exhausted, persecuted after the Mount Carmel experience (1 Kings 18), Elijah made his way to Mount Horeb (19:7). Overcome with despair, he had been ready to die, but was called to meet with the Lord at Mount Sinai.[79] There the great prophet of Yahweh stood by the place where Moses had received the revelation and had seen the glory of the Lord.[80] Elijah's return to Mount Sinai marked the end of one era, one that was characterized by divine patience, and the beginning of another, one that was characterized by purification. Israel had shown herself to be a nation hardened in unbelief. The situation had changed dramatically from the days when Moses repeatedly interceded on her behalf. Unlike Moses, who *interceded* on behalf of Israel (Ex. 31—34),

Elijah *accused* God's people of infidelity. The days of God's patience were drawing to an end. A new era was coming![81]

Elijah: The Message of the Classical Prophets

On Mount Sinai Elijah brought three charges and a personal lament against Israel: They "[1] have rejected your covenant, [2] broken down your altars, and [3] put your prophets to death with the sword. [4] I am the only one left, and now they are trying to kill me too" (1 Kings 19:10, 14). Yahweh came to Elijah in a voice like "a gentle whisper" (v. 12) to which the prophet responded with awe, sensing the presence of Yahweh.[82]

The theophanic phenomena (wind, fire, and earthquake) are to be interpreted in relation to the three charges and to the three instruments of Yahweh's judgment on Israel: Jehu, Hazael, and Elisha (1 Kings 19:11–17). Judgment would come through (1) internal political forces in Israel, represented by Jehu; (2) external military forces, represented by the Aramean Hazael; and (3) the prophetic ministry, symbolized by Elisha.[83] God's response (1 Kings 19:15–18) outlines Israel's history: the fall of the Omride dynasty (1 Kings 20–2 Kings 13), the troubles associated with the dynasty of Jehu (2 Kings 9:1–15:12; see Hos. 1:4–5), and the oppression by the Arameans and the ultimate fall of Israel in 722 B.C. (2 Kings 17:5–6).

Elijah is the beginning of a long line of prophets who charged God's people with breaking the covenant and pronounced God's judgment on them. Though Elijah primarily directed his message to the king, his ministry extended beyond Ahab to *all* Israel. He was God's first covenant prosecutor, for he charged Israel with its failures to conform to the covenantal expectations (1 Kings 18:21). (See figure 6.) The issue is no longer between prophet and king; it is between prophet and people, as it was in the days of Moses and Samuel.[84] The prophet no longer warns and threatens; he proclaims judgment and the reality of the covenantal curses. This is the essence of the prophetic lawsuit (rîb, *see* Appendix).

God's revelation also contains words of encouragement. In response to Elijah's lament about being the only remaining true believer, Yahweh assured him that he will "reserve seven thousand in Israel—all whose knees have not bowed down to Baal and all whose mouths have not kissed him" (1 Kings 19:18). The Lord promised to preserve for himself a remnant of godly people who submit themselves to his revelation. Yahweh declared to his servant Elijah that he is free in judgment—even to the point of holocaust, genocide, or execration—but he is also free in maintaining his covenants and the promises with the remnant.[85]

As covenant prosecutors, the prophets stood between the Lord and the people. They listened in on the divine council while observing God's movement in history. The prophet of God was both a man "in his time" and "out of his time." As a man "in his time," he delivered a prophetic message that must be understood within its historic, geographic, and cultural contexts. As a man "out of his time," he spoke of events that pertain to the establishment of God's kingdom, the judgment of the wicked, and the vindication of the godly remnant.

The Spirit of Elijah

Elijah is a significant individual in redemptive history.[86] The Holy Spirit empowered him and gave him a concern for the spiritual condition of his people. Elijah longed for a people whose heart would be loyal to the Lord as he discerned the necessity of judgment and purification (see Mal. 4:5–6). His ministry is continuous with Moses and with all the prophets who served after him as "covenant prosecutors," including the literary or classical prophets. The spirit of Elijah was with Amos, Hosea, Isaiah, Jeremiah, Ezekiel, and with all the other prophets before, during, and after the Exile. He was with John the Baptist (Mal. 4:5; Matt. 11:14; 17:10–13)[87] and the apostles, and he is still present with all who proclaim God's Word faithfully.

REVIEW

The prophetic ministry is a direct continuation of the revelation of God through Moses, the fountainhead of Old Testament revelation.[88] Moses desired for God's people to form a counterculture, a new community transformed by divine revelation and by the Spirit. The prophetic message was consistent with the Mosaic revelation, for it applied more explicitly the blessings and the curses of which Moses had spoken and supplemented the existing canonical writings with a new word from God.

All prophetic utterances were to be tested by God's revelation to Moses. The prophets applied and further developed the essential elements of the Mosaic revelation: the judgments and blessings, the call for covenantal loyalty, and the hope in the grand future prepared for the people of God. The prophets, like Moses, called for a commitment to Yahweh that must lead to "conflict with civilization."[89]

A major development took place with Samuel, who was the role model of the Old Testament prophetic movement. He declared the word of God to all Israel and anointed their first two kings. As a guardian of the theocracy, he led Israel into revival and peace. Samuel sought to guard the theocracy established by God's covenant at Mount Sinai, and he spoke God's word to king and people alike. His ministry consisted of intercession for the people, application of the curses and blessings of the Mosaic covenant, and a godly life. And yet, Samuel, too, was an eschatological prophet; he longed for greater spiritual sensitivity, discernment, and a rest that would outlast him.

The prophets after Samuel spoke God's word with little apparent result. Israel and Judah readily adopted the mantic and magical practices of the pagans. They adapted to the worship of many gods and adulterated the revelation of Yahweh. Finally, Elijah arose and brought a covenantal suit from the Lord at Mount Sinai. From that point, the prophets turned increasingly away from the kings to the people with the express purpose of calling forth a remnant.

The prophetic message of the classical prophets includes a statement of God's legal suit against his people, an announcement of judgment, a call for repentance, and a proclamation of the good news of God's deliverance. They affirmed that Yahweh is faithful in his commitment to renew the covenants, to usher in his kingdom, and to fulfill his promises. The prophets were God's appointed covenant prosecutors, but in this function they did not cease praying that God's people might turn to the Lord, undergo a transformation by the Spirit, and enjoy the blessings of the kingdom.[90]

QUESTIONS AND ISSUES:

1. Define:

classical prophet	prophetic "suit"
counterculture	*Realpolitik*
covenant prosecutor	religion
divination	remnant
eschatological prophet	revelation
eschatological rest	servant of God
guardian of the theocracy	Spirit of Elijah
magic	syncretism
Mosaic covenant	*vox populi*

2. What were God's purposes in giving his revelation?
3. What did the ancient Near Eastern peoples seek to obtain by divination and magic?
4. How does Israel's prophetic institution differ from that of intuitive diviners?
5. What perspectives did Israel gain from Genesis 1:1–11:9?
6. How was Israel to develop a counterculture?
7. What are the major developments in the history of prophetism from Moses to John the Baptist?
8. Describe the importance of Moses' place in the Sinai administration.

9. What is meant by Moses being the fountainhead of the prophets? How does this relate to his being an "eschatological prophet"?
10. What are the revealed qualities of a prophet of God?
11. What is the redemptive-historical place of Samuel?
12. How did Samuel *define* the prophetic role in relation to Moses and to the prophets after him.
13. How did Elijah shape the course of the classical prophets?
14. How did the Lord define the role and message of the prophets in his revelation to Elijah? Relate the role and message to the ministry of John the Baptist, Jesus Christ, the apostles, and the preaching of the Word.

CHAPTER 2

The Prophetic Tradition

INTRODUCTION

The prophetic tradition of Israel has a rich and colorful history.[1] In spite of the variety of prophetic phenomenon in *space* (north, south,

41

exile) and in *time* (premonarchial, monarchial, exilic, and postexilic), the prophets enjoyed the common bond with the past (the Mosaic revelation) and the future acts of God: the new era of God's coming, the transformation of all things, the judgment of the wicked, and the vindication of the righteous.

In this chapter we shall consider (1) the prophetic office, role, and message, (2) the development of the prophetic tradition in Israel and Judah, and (3) the challenge to the prophetic message and office by the false prophets.

THE PROPHETIC OFFICE, ROLE, AND MESSAGE

The prophets in Israel and Judah were office bearers in the theocracy. They fulfilled the prophetic role by listening in on the divine council and by proclaiming in words and symbols what they had heard. Because the prophetic tradition developed over many centuries, a caution against oversimplification is in order. Oversimplification has often led to a disregard of the distinctive features of the prophet as a human being in a historical context and as God's messenger sent to meet the particular needs of God's people in that context.[2] In reality, the prophetic phenomenon was diverse as to *place* (Israel or Judah), *time* (preexilic, exilic, postexilic), *message,* and *language.*[3] (See figure 10.)

OFFICE: Spokesman for God

ROLE: Member of divine council
Member of prophetic tradition
Speaker for God's kingdom
Critic of human kingdoms

MESSAGE: Judgment and deliverance
Contextually relevant
Unity and diversity: Organic relationship
                         Theocentric focus
                         Progressive revelation
                         Distinctiveness of the message
                         of each prophet

Figure 10. The Prophetic Office, Role, and Message

The Prophetic Office

The prophet (*nāḇî'*) was *a spokesman for God* with the distinct call to be the ambassador of God.[4] (See figure 10.) Every prophet was "like Moses" and conformed to the seven criteria set forth in the Mosaic revelation: (1) he was an Israelite, (2) called by the Lord and

(3) empowered by the Holy Spirit; (4) he served as God's spokesperson; (5) his authority lay in speaking in the name of the Lord; (6) he was a good shepherd over God's people; and (7) he vindicated his message by signs. (For a fuller discussion, see chap. 1: "Moses: The Fountainhead of the Prophetic Tradition.")

The Prophetic Role

The prophets were first and foremost speakers; their oracles were subsequently written down.[5] They were, by their unique call, members of the divine council, and by their place in the society of man, they were spokespersons for God.[6] (See figure 10.) In general, the prophets were more at home in the royal court than at the sites of worship. The prophets often shattered the expectations of their contemporaries by prophetic criticism (Jer. 6:27), by interpretation of the older revelation, and by new revelation. The impact of the new revelation was often so great that people rejected God's messenger (Luke 20:10–12; see Neh. 9:26; Jer. 7:25–26; Matt. 23:34; Acts 7:52; Heb. 11:36–38). But if the people had only listened to Moses, they would have been more open to the voice of God (see Luke 16:29).

Several explanations of the prophetic phenomenon in Israel do not do justice to the distinctiveness of God's prophets. For Gunkel, Hölscher, and Lindblom, the prophet was an ecstatic, a man of deep religious experience.[7] Max Weber likened the prophet to a *guru,* a charismatic man, who by his charisma eternalized his teaching among his followers.[8] Mowinckel defined the prophetic role in relation to Israel's worship. Based on the involvement of Moses and Samuel in Israel's worship (cult), he explained that the people consulted the priests for divine oracles and that thus the prophetic institution was associated with cultic sites.[9] This interpretation lacks support from the prophets themselves. Though several prophets were priests (Jeremiah and Ezekiel), they were more often found at the royal court than at worship sites.[10]

Recently, the study of the prophetic movement has received new insights from the correlation of prophetism in its ancient Near Eastern context with anthropology and sociology. The fruitfulness of this approach is clear, but there is little consensus on the social standing of the prophets in ancient Israel.[11] David L. Petersen explains the various levels of prophetic involvement as "role enactment."[12] He perceives that the words for prophet reflect the variety in prophetic role: (1) "seer" (*rō'eh*)—a public and social figure, a holy man, who was fully integrated into the structures of Israelite society, as in the case of Samuel;[13] (2) "man of God" ('*îš*

43

hā'ᵉlōhîm)—a holy, itinerant man, around whom stories were told of God's mighty acts through him, for example Elijah and Elisha;[14] and (3) "seer" (*ḥōzeh*) and "prophet" (*nābî'*)—men whose ministry conformed to the concept of "classical prophet" with a concern for moral issues.[15]

He also distinguishes between the geographic and political contexts in which the prophets ministered. The *ḥōzeh* served in Judah as heralds of the divine council.[16] The *nābî'* arose in Israel as a "covenant spokesman."[17] The former received God's message through visions and word, whereas the latter received it mainly through the word. The Judahite prophets related to the Davidic covenant and the Mount Zion traditions, whereas the Israelite prophets operated from the Sinaitic covenant.[18]

The Prophetic Message

The prophetic message is diverse, depending on the individual personality of the prophet, the temporal context, the needs of the people, and the content of the revelation.[19] Each prophet was compelled by the Spirit to bear witness to the plan of God. But each spoke from a unique vantage point and gave a unique perspective on God's plan. Each prophetic book makes a distinct contribution to the colorful mosaic of revelation because of the historical context, the psychology and background of the prophet, the response of the people, and the particular focus of its revelation.

Though the message is far from uniform, the prophets shared a common prophetic heritage.[20] As members of the divine council, the prophets contributed to the prophetic message. (See figure 10.) As human beings, the prophets shared concepts, language, and literary forms. By carefully studying the development of the prophetic writings over time, we witness a progression in the prophetic heritage from preexilic to postexilic times. This progression cannot be explained as merely a human development; it has a coherence with its dual aspects of salvation and judgment. (See figure 11.)

First, the prophetic message as God's witness to the new era of salvation reveals a marvelous unity.[21] The prophets are "consistently eschatological" in that they affirmed the end of the old era—the end of politics and religion—and the beginning of a new era.[22] The prophets spoke of the coming of God in redemption; that is, of the eternity of time when the Lord will be present with his people and will bless his loyal devotees with the eternal fulfillment of the promises.

Second, the prophets announced the Day of the Lord: the reality and radical nature of God's judgment. They declared that Yahweh holds the nations, peoples, and even Israel and Judah accountable and that the moment of accountability takes place in time. He has reserved a day for judgment and wrath on all ungodliness. This means that the intrusions of God's judgment in time—such as the fall of Samaria, Jerusalem, and Babylon—are significant foreshadowings of his final day of vengeance when he will fully establish his kingdom on this earth. Here I agree with Odendaal that "every historical coming of this day [the Day of the Lord] is always type and promise of its final coming and forms an intrusion of the consummation."[23]

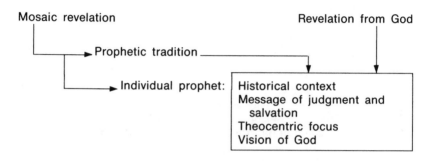

Figure 11. Aspects of the Prophetic Message

The prophetic message reveals an underlying continuity.[24] Moses was the fountainhead of the prophetic movement, and Samuel gave shape to it in relation to the monarchy.[25] Though prophetism underwent significant changes after Elijah and then again after the Exile, the prophetic heritage showed an organic and progressive development over the centuries.[26]

The prophetic message is *organic* in that the prophets, being messengers of *one* God, received revelation over a long period of time and in diverse ways, but the message of each relates to that of the others (Heb. 1:1–3). This means that each prophet witnesses in his own time to the redemptive working of God and must be heard as such. It also means that we must relate the prophetic message to the rest of the Scripture, including the words of our Lord and his apostles. Through this manifold witness, we gain a grander perspective of God's working in history.[27]

The prophetic message is *theocentric.* The prophets bear witness to God (his perfections, acts, and revelation) and to humanity's need of God's full and free salvation (forgiveness, wisdom, revelation, blessing, protection, and rule).[28] In this sense, too, the prophets complement the apostles as they speak of God's salvation in Jesus Christ (1 Peter 1:10–12).

The prophetic message is also *progressive*. It transformed gradually as changes took place in redemptive history: exile, restoration, postrestoration, and so on. The prophetic themes, vision, and prophecies have their origin and power in the Spirit of God, under whose superintendence the prophetic witness developed into a prophetic corpus. The progressive revelation of God is like a seed that germinates, grows, and develops.

The progressive development from the preexilic to the postexilic prophets aids in interpreting the prophetic word, even as the progressive development of God's revelation in Jesus Christ helps us to understand the prophets. The progressive aspect of the prophetic message may also be likened to rivulets that contribute to the prophetic stream, which rushes from the preexilic era till the advent of our Lord, *and* with the writings of the apostles form one river. The progressive dimension also explains the twists and turns in redemptive history; progression always entails elements of continuity and discontinuity. In other words, the organic and progressive message of the prophets is inner-related, distinct, full of movement, diverse, but always revealing an inner unity, being bound together by one Spirit and disclosing one plan of redemption.

PROPHETISM IN ISRAEL AND JUDAH

Introduction

The prophetic movement advanced significantly under the sponsorship of King David. Samuel anointed David to be God's "king," and the prophet Nathan gave him God's promise of a dynastic monarchy by which the Lord would establish his everlasting kingdom. He was God's "anointed" servant, called to "shepherd" God's flock (2 Sam. 5:2; 7:7). His ministry was clearly continuous with that of Moses, Joshua, and Samuel. David, too, was a theocratic officer over the twelve tribes and an intermediary between Yahweh and the nation.

Court Prophets

God spoke to David through court prophets. Nathan,[29] for example, was consulted by David regarding the building of the temple (2 Sam. 7:2), brought the word of promise (the Davidic covenant, vv. 5–16), had Solomon named Jedidiah ("friend of God," 12:25), and made sure that Solomon succeeded David as king (1 Kings 1:34). Nathan, along with Gad, also delivered God's message of judgment on David, who responded positively (2 Sam. 12:1–25; 24:11–17).

> David was receptive to the word of God through the prophets Nathan,[30] Gad,[31] and Heman.[32] He was also receptive to the word of God from priests, such as Zadok, to whom he said,

46

"Aren't you a seer?" (2 Sam. 15:27). David modeled true theocratic leadership by being sensitive to God's theocratic officers, the prophets and priests. David encouraged the worship of the Lord[33] and gave his life to amassing the material resources required for the building of the temple (1 Chron. 28:1–29:9). He regulated priestly work by instituting orders of ministry. He further designated the Levites to serve in various capacities as gatekeepers, musicians, singing prophets, treasurers, and temple officials (chaps. 23–26). Of particular interest is his appointment of Asaph, Heman, and Jeduthun to the ministry of singing prophets (25:1–5),[34] opening up the close connection between the prophets and the poets of Israel.[35]

Court prophets were God-directed advisers to and critics of the king. Like Samuel, the court prophets were guardians of the monarchy, ensuring that the king did not stray from the covenant and that he fulfilled his theocratic role as a shepherd of God's people.[36] Court prophets gave advice (including political),[37] rebuked, declared God's judgment, and kept record of the deeds of the king.[38]

The close association of king and prophet was not uncommon in the ancient Near East. In Mesopotamia, prophets, diviners, and magicians gave counsel to the king. They joined the king on his military campaigns and were all too eager to please him. The Israelite prophet, however, came with a genuine word from God, spoke on behalf of the great King, Yahweh, and did not look for the king's favor.[39]

Prophets in Israel and Judah

Long before Elijah came on the scene (1 Kings 17), prophets, both named and anonymous, had played a vital role in the history of Israel and Judah. God's word came through Ahijah and an unnamed "man of God" to Jeroboam I (11:29–39; 13:1–9; 14:2–18), through Shemaiah to Rehoboam (12:22–24), and through Jehu to Baasha (16:1–4). More significant than the names of the prophets or their prophecies is the affirmation that God's word did come true (14:17–18; 15:29–30; 21:21–22; 2 Kings 9:36; 10:10, 17; 17:21–23).

In spite of the secession (931–722 B.C.), the Lord is free in sending his prophets across human barriers. The story of the prophet who came from Judah (1 Kings 13) to Bethel illustrates the Lord's freedom. The Lord sent a southern prophet across the borders into Israel to rebuke Jeroboam. The prophet was obedient until a prophet in Bethel invited him to eat with him. He acted subversively, claiming to have received a word from God, though it contradicted God's revelation to the southern prophet. When the southern prophet was killed by a lion on his second departure from Bethel, the northern prophet interpreted this "accident" as God's judgment: "It is the man of God who defied the word of the LORD" (1 Kings 13:26).

This interaction between the northern prophet and the southern prophet and the obedience-disobedience motif is most significant. Walter Gross has demonstrated that the seeming disparity in the words of the northern prophet undergirds the importance of obedience to Yahweh, regardless of circumstances.[40] It is virtually impossible to penetrate the motivation of the northern prophet, let alone the ways of God.[41] For the writer of Kings, it was not important to the story why the Bethel prophet lied or why he changed his role from that of opponent to one of false intermediary.[42] The story has "a unified, cogent message": Yahweh's word must be fully and unconditionally obeyed.[43] The message of the story presents us with a God who brings his threats into reality. God speaks and acts, regardless of man's unresponsiveness.[44]

We raise here an issue related to the story of the kings of Israel and Judah. Why do the historical books rarely mention the writing prophets? Certainly, the authors knew about Hosea, Amos, Micah, Jeremiah, and Ezekiel, to name a few![45] For example, it would appear that they amplify the prophetic message of judgment and hope as an independent testimony to the grace of God in a time of need. The books of Kings offer a redemptive historical presentation of Israel's and Judah's failure and need of repentance. These books present the exilic community with a record of God's fulfillment of his word through the nonwriting prophets and with an implicit call to repent and trust in God's freedom and love.

The Lord used his servants the prophets as court prophets as long as the kings were sensitive to his word. But after the secession of Israel from Judah and the resultant apostasy, a rift developed between the monarchs and the prophets.[46] The prophets were forced out of the royal courts. One such lonely figure was Ahijah of Shiloh, who had announced the secession of Israel to Jeroboam I. He had witnessed the cultic, cultural, and social changes under Jeroboam (1 Kings 12:25–33), who also defied the prophetic word (13:4). Only when Jeroboam's young son, Abijah, was gravely sick did the king turn to the prophet, sending his wife in disguise lest Ahijah recognize her (14:1–2).

The history of Israel and Judah discloses the insensitivity to and outright disregard of the prophetic word. Kings of Israel and Judah resisted the prophets, had them imprisoned and even killed (see Matt. 23:37). Yet the prophets quietly served the Lord. Some enjoyed a positive response to their message, but most experienced alienation and disgrace (v. 37). (See table 1.)

TABLE 1. PROPHETS IN ISRAEL AND JUDAH

Prophet	King of Israel	King of Judah	Text
Iddo		Rehoboam, Ahijah	2 Chron. 9:29
Ahijah	Jeroboam I		1 Kings 11:26–40; 14:1–18
Shemaiah		Rehoboam	1 Kings 12:22–24
Prophet from Judah	Jeroboam I		1 Kings 13:1–34
Hanani		Asa	2 Chron. 16:7
Jehu son of Hanani	Baasha		1 Kings 16:1–4
Elijah	Ahab Ahaziah		1 Kings 17:1– 2 Kings 2:12
Anonymous prophet	Ahab		1 Kings 20:13–43
Micaiah	Ahab		1 Kings 22:1–36
Elisha	Jehoram, Jehu, Jehoahaz, Jehoash		1 Kings 19:19–21; 2 Kings 2–10; 13:14–21
Anonymous	Jehu		2 Kings 9:4
Jehaziel		Jehoshaphat	2 Chron. 20:14–17
Eliezer		Jehoshaphat	2 Chron. 20:37
Zechariah		Joash	2 Chron. 24:20
Jonah	Jeroboam II		2 Kings 14:25–27
Isaiah		Hezekiah	2 Kings 18:1/–20:21

Prophets in Israel

The prophets of God appeared at crises points in Israel's history.[47] Nine dynasties of kings succeeded each other over the two centuries of Israel's separate existence as a nation. (See table 2.) The northern kings opposed the worship of Yahweh in Jerusalem, treated any expression of allegiance to the dynasty of David as treachery, and rejected the words of God's servants. Nevertheless, the Lord sent his prophets with a message of blessing and judgment. The history of Israel vindicated the prophetic word, as dynasty succeeded dynasty. For example, Ahijah announced the rise of Jeroboam I as the first king of the ten tribes, but he also foretold the death of Jeroboam's son and the end of his dynasty (1 Kings 14:1–16).

The record of the ministry of Elijah and Elisha is at the center of the two books of Kings (1 Kings 17:1–2 Kings 8:15). These two prophets were involved with the two greatest dynasties (Omri and Jehu, 885–753

TABLE 2. KINGS OF ISRAEL AND JUDAH, 931–586 B.C.

	Israel	Prophets in Israel		Prophets in Judah	Judah
I	Jeroboam I (931–910)		931		Rehoboam (931–913)
	Nadab (910–909)				Abijah (913–911)
II	Baasha (909–886)		900		Asa (911–870)
	Elah (886–885)				
III	Zimri (885)		875		
IV	Omri (885–874)	Elijah			Jehoshaphat (873–848)
	Ahab (874–853)	Elisha			
	Ahaziah (853–852)				
V	Joram (852–841)		841		Jehoram (848–841)
	Jehu (841–814)				Ahaziah (841)
					Athaliah (841–835)
					Joash (835–796)
					Amaziah (796–767)
					Uzziah (792–740)
	Jehoahaz (814–798)	Jonah	800		
		Amos			
		Hosea			
	Jehoash (798–782)				
	Jeroboam II (793–753)				
	Zechariah (753)				
VI	Shallum (752)		750	Isaiah	Jotham (750–731)
VII	Menahem (752–742)			Micah	
	Pekahiah (742–740)				Ahaz (735–715)
VIII	Pekah (740–732)				

	Israel	Prophets in Israel		Prophets in Judah	Judah
IX	Hoshea (732–722) FALL OF SAMARIA		722		Hezekiah (729–686)
			700		
			650		Manasseh (696–642)
			625	**Nahum** **Zephaniah**	Amon (642–640) Josiah (640–609)
				J E **Habakkuk**	
			600	R E M	Jehoahaz (609) Jehoiakim (608–598)
			586	I **Ezekiel** A **Daniel** H **Obadiah**	Jehoiachin (598–597) Zedekiah (597–586) FALL OF JERUSALEM

B.C.), which together lasted more than half of Israel's history! The kings of these dynasties grasped every opportunity to make Israel a major international power, and they succeeded in bringing cultural and economic prosperity to it.

The Dynasty of Omri (885–841 B.C.)

The Omride dynasty made Israel a political power. Omri's moving of the capital to Samaria symbolized the new policy of rapprochement with other powers. Israel made alliances with any power that was advantageous to its shortsighted goal of becoming a superpower. Samaria became the symbol of *Realpolitik:* an openness to economic opportunities, cultural exchanges, and political alliances (see figure 12). *Realpolitik* operates from the assumption that the political, social, economic, and religious structures are basically good and that humans can improve their lives and society by preserving and improving the existing structures.

Elijah opposed *Realpolitik.* His opposition to Ahab was like Samuel's opposition to Saul, but more intense, because at Mount Carmel Elijah stood against the people as a whole. After the contest between religion and revelation on Mount Carmel, Elijah realized that the popular confession that Yahweh is God (1 Kings 18:39) was nothing more than an emotional expression of temporary excitement. He went alone to meet his God on Mount Sinai where Moses had received the revelation and had seen God's glory. The prophetic charges against Israel would mark a shift in redemptive history. He accused Israel, and as we have already seen (see chap. 1), this inaugurated a new era in the prophetic movement—that of the prophets as God's covenant prosecutors. From this point, the prophets announced the inevitable fall of Samaria and called on the remnant of godly people not to involve themselves with the *Realpolitik* of their day.

SAMARIA	JERUSALEM
Symbol of *Realpolitik*	Symbol of *Realpolitik* and of *vox populi*
Symbol of human kingship and power	Symbol of God's presence and protection
	Temple, Davidic king
Fall in 722 B.C.	Fall in 586 B.C.

Figure 12. Samaria and Jerusalem

The narratives from 1 Kings 17:12 to 2 Kings 8:15 bear out that curses as well as blessings were associated with the prophets of God.

Through the prophetic ministry of Elijah and Elisha, the Lord brought drought and famine, extended judgment on Omri's dynasty and on Israel. But God also revealed his love for individuals, including Gentiles (1 Kings 17:7–24; 2 Kings 5:1–15; Luke 4:25–26).

The Dynasty of Jehu (841–753 B.C.)

Israel remained unchanged as a political body when the dynasty of Omri came to an end and was succeeded by the dynasty of Jehu. Jehu inaugurated external changes by ridding Israel of Baalism, but the policy of *Realpolitik* remained essentially unchanged. The Lord afflicted them with drought and war. Israel nearly succumbed to the power of Aram (2 Kings 14:26–27; see Amos 1:3–5), but God showed his compassion to them (2 Kings 13:23). Jeroboam II brought Israel to even greater political and economic achievements, which provided the aristocracy with new opportunities for enrichment.

Despite God's goodness, patience, and compassion, the people did not repent. They devoted themselves all the more to building up treasures on earth and securing their prosperity. Everything they did was directed toward improving the structures of society, even if it meant injustice, lack of love, unrighteousness, and oppression of the socially and economically disadvantaged. In this context, a century after Elijah and Elisha, the Lord raised up two prophets, Amos and Hosea (ca. 750 B.C.). (See table 3.)

Amos and Hosea

Amos and Hosea were in continuity with the prophetic tradition established by Moses and redefined by Elijah at Mount Sinai. These two *classical*[48] (literary) prophets entered a world aflame. The poor and the godly cried out for divine justice. The rich and powerful were complacent with the social, political, and economic structures. The century-long conflict with Aram had left them more determined to develop in the humanistic and religious ways of the nations. When Aram was preoccupied with the growing Assyrian Empire, Israel pushed aggressively forward with the newly developed expansionist policy of Jeroboam II. They sought growth, development, and opportunity, but did not realize that Assyria would soon control Aram and Israel.

With the growth of Assyria, Samaria made every effort to maintain her prosperity, even if she had to reorient herself to a shifting political scene. To this end she was busily engaged in establishing alliances with Aram, Assyria, and Egypt.[49] She sought to perpetuate the structures that had propelled her to an internationally recognized power.

Amos and Hosea condemned Samaria's *Realpolitik*. They demonstrated how foolish and rebellious Israel had become. The leaders and people had not listened to the revelation of Moses. Furthermore, they

TABLE 3. PROPHETS IN ISRAEL

931 B.C.	875	800	750	722
Jeroboam I (931–910)	Omri (885–874)	Ahab (874–853)	Jehu (841–814)	Jeroboam II (793–753)	EXILE
	Syncretism ——— **Acculturation** ——————→ **Israel like the nations**			
Abijah	Elijah/Elisha		Amos/Hosea	

TABLE 4. PROPHETS IN JUDAH

931 B.C.	740	700	650	600	586
Rehoboam (931–913)	Uzziah (792–740)	Hezekiah (729–686)	Manasseh (696–642)	Josiah (640–609)	EXILE
Prophets:	Isaiah Micah			Nahum Zephaniah Habakkuk Jeremiah	
					Ezekiel
	A S S Y R I A				BABYLON

had not returned to the Lord after having been disciplined in many ways. The prophets condemned Israel's corruption, apostasy, and hardness of heart and announced her imminent exile. But Israel resisted the prophets with an optimistic belief in her manifest and glorious destiny. A generation later, Samaria fell to Assyria, and part of her population went into exile.

Shortly before Israel's end, God raised up two prophets in Judah: Isaiah and Micah (730 B.C.). They, too, condemned Samaria's power, pride, and pragmatism. After Yahweh had vindicated his word in Samaria's fall (722 B.C.), Isaiah and Micah used this tragic moment to warn the southern kingdom. Jerusalem, while more conservative, had thought herself to be secure because of the presence of God's temple. (See figure 12.) But the prophets warned that what had happened in Israel was a foreboding sign of Jerusalem's fall!

Prophets in Judah

The prophets of Judah fared little better than their northern counterparts. They, too, first spoke God's word to kings: Iddo and Shemaiah (during the reign of Rehoboam), Hanani (during the reign of Asa; 2 Chron. 16:7), Jahaziel and Eliezer (during Jehoshaphat; 2 Chron. 20:14, 35–37), and Zechariah (during Joash; 2 Chron. 24:20–22). The treatment of the prophets mirrored the shifting political scene of Judah, which unlike her northern neighbor was ruled by both godly and wicked kings. The godly kings responded to the prophetic word, even as their forefather David had, but the ungodly kings disregarded—and even despised—the prophetic word, the temple, and their theocratic mission (2 Chron. 25:19).[50]

Realpolitik and *Vox Populi*

The Judean leaders and people were entrenched in the religion of *Realpolitik* and *vox populi*. Judah, too, was rooted in the wisdom of the kingdoms of this world; her structures were intimately tied to the economic, political, cultural, and military structures of the nations. Judah, too, looked to Assyria, Egypt, Babylon, and the smaller nations to solve her problems.

Judah, like Israel, was in decline, but it took longer for Judah to come to the anguish of exile. Isaiah and Micah bridged the era between the fall of Samaria and the political vicissitudes of Jerusalem under Hezekiah (729–686 B.C.). Both prophets challenged Judah and her leadership to reject the immediate gratification of *Realpolitik,* to look to Yahweh's kingdom, and to practice righteousness, justice, and fidelity.

Popular expectations (*vox populi*) encouraged an optimistic and pragmatic way of life. The people selectively listened to the oracles of Isaiah and Micah as they warmly greeted the promise of God's presence with Judah and his abandonment of Israel (Isa. 8:6–10). However, they did not go as far as to respond to the prophetic call of absolute submission to Yahweh (vv. 19–21; Mic. 6:8). The people believed that they, their king, and the temple were invulnerable. Had not God promised to be with them, to protect and bless them? Popular expectations held on to the promises of God's presence, the inviolability of Jerusalem, and the perpetuity of God's promises to David, that is, the *theology of Zion*.[51]

Manasseh and the Last Days of Judah

Judah's pragmatic way of life was significantly advanced by Hezekiah's son, Manasseh (696–642 B.C.).[52] His practice of *Realpolitik* had made Judah a nation like the other nations. After his despicable regime of fifty-five years, Judah was left with very few distinctive marks of the Sinai or Zion traditions. Zephaniah and Jeremiah witnessed, initially with joy, the changes under Josiah, the grandson of Manasseh. But the reforms (622 B.C.) of Josiah (640–609 B.C.) were short-lived and external. After Josiah's death (609 B.C.), Judah's course followed a more definite commitment to *Realpolitik*.

The fall of Assyria changed the face of the ancient Near East. Nineveh was destroyed in 612 B.C. and the Assyrian Empire fell in 605 B.C., as Nahum had announced. For the following seventy years Babylon controlled the power structures (Jer. 29:10). The Babylonian success was first interpreted as God's judgment on Assyria (Isa. 10:5–19). But God's prophets proclaimed that Babylon was also God's instrument of judging Judah! (See table 4.)

Prophetic Responses

Habakkuk, at first, stood aghast at the prospect of the Babylonian invasion of Jerusalem. He asked how the Lord could use a wicked nation to punish Judah. The Lord assured him that everything was according to his purposes and that the righteous had to persevere in waiting for his judgment on evil and for the glorious establishment of his kingdom.

Jeremiah and Ezekiel also announced God's judgment on Judah. Jeremiah was Yahweh's spokesman during the crisis in Jerusalem. He declared that the city, the temple, and the Davidic king would fall to Babylon. He proclaimed that after Babylon's rule of seventy years (Jer. 29:10), the Lord would usher in a new era of restoration, covenant, forgiveness, temple, and the righteous rule of his Messiah (30:5–33:26).

Ezekiel was Yahweh's servant in Babylon. He explained to a small group of exiles that Yahweh was determined to bring Jerusalem down. He also pointed to the era of restoration: the consecration of everything to the Lord, the transformation of a new people by the Spirit, and the beneficent presence of Yahweh in the midst of his people.

The prophets expanded the boundaries of traditional theology when they spoke of the great acts of Yahweh in judgment and restoration. Traditional theology had confined Yahweh and his promises to their interpretation of Moses. But the prophets exploded the traditional concept of the promises and displayed them as being more magnificent and wonderful. They proclaimed that Yahweh would be faithful to the covenants and the promises and that the Spirit would inaugurate a new era: the era of the new covenant and of spiritual transformation.

The Exilic Era

The Exile was an era of desolation and at the same time, an era of restoration.[53] The fall of Jerusalem meant the desolation of the temple, alienation from the Lord, the break of the people from the Land of Promise, and the removal of the Davidic monarch. The Exile also had a positive impact in bringing about the unity of a godly remnant from both Israel and Judah. It opened up an era of spiritual transformation by the Spirit of restoration, evidenced by a renewed loyalty to Yahweh, to the canonical revelation, to his wisdom in judgment, and by a renewed hope in the full restoration.

In this transition period God had his special servant. Daniel, God's man in high office, had been exiled approximately twenty years before Jerusalem's fall and served God until after Babylon's fall! He gave inspired counsel to foreign kings, witnessed to the kingdom of the Lord, prayed for the restoration of Jerusalem, and received a revelation of the victorious progress of God's kingdom.

Daniel's kingdom vision gave him a broad perspective on his place in redemptive history. He was not entrapped by *Realpolitik* or by the *vox populi,* nor was he complacent with the Babylonian system of morality. Daniel stood head and shoulders above his contemporaries and distinguished himself by his radical love for God. This faithful servant was a man of integrity and zealous for the kingdom of God.

The Postexilic Era

The good news of the postexilic era (from 538 B.C. onward) lies in the greatness of Yahweh's love in renewing his covenants and fulfilling his promises. He had forgiven his people, restored them to the land, dwelt among them, blessed and protected them. The offerings and sacrifices, the temple service, the priesthood, and the Davidic dynasty in token form (Zerubbabel) were restored in the postexilic era.[54]

The context of the postexilic ministry of Haggai and Zechariah differed significantly from that of the preexilic prophets. Following God's judgment, they encouraged God's people with the good news that God was again present with them. They challenged God's people with the promise of an even greater era of fulfillment of the promises if they would only respond with zeal in seeking his kingdom.

Era of Fulfillment

Clearly, the era of the new covenant was already present after the Exile. God was with his people, the Spirit was present in power, the temple was restored, and Zerubbabel (of Davidic descent) was God's token of the messianic kingdom. Though the postexilic prophets confirmed the continuity of the theocratic place of king (Zerubbabel) and priest (Joshua), they also called on individuals to serve the Lord in the power of the Spirit.

The postexilic prophets together with the reforms of Ezra and Nehemiah laid a solid foundation for the renewal of theocracy. The theocracy was demonstrably present in the temple, the law of God, the work of God's Spirit, and the purification of God's people from the ways of the world. The postexilic people were no saints, but they did respond to the challenges of the prophets and the theocratic leaders. The prophetic works (Haggai, Zechariah, Malachi, and Joel) together with Chronicles and Ezra–Nehemiah attest to the radical transformation of God's people after the Exile.

Era of Hope

Even though the postexilic community experienced some realization of the promises, the reality of fulfillment was delayed. The people were disappointed with the slowness of the progress in fulfillment. The postexilic prophets encouraged them to believe that Yahweh was true to his promises of the grand restoration. The prophets also exhorted them to hasten the fulfillment. They spurred the remnant on to an even greater love and devotion to the Lord and to the establishment of a counterculture.

They also urged the godly to develop a realistic hope. The postexilic prophets were the first to deal with the dissonance between prophetic utterance and fulfillment.[55] They helped God's people understand that the fulfillment of the promises of restoration is progressive, that God is free, and that humans are responsible. They confirm that God is true to his word, but he is also free in how he fulfills his promises! The postexilic prophets gave a realistic portrayal of the progress of redemption by indicating that deliverance will come, but not without persecution, resistance by the kingdoms of this world, and apostasy from within.

They confirmed the veracity of God's promises. They encouraged the godly to persevere in fidelity to the Lord with the hope that the Lord will reward his saints with the joys of his kingdom, the messianic era, and the new creation.

Religion of Vox Populi

The prophets and the godly remnant cannot be held responsible for the subsequent degeneration of revelation to religion. The postexilic community continued to suffer from the same problems as the preexilic community. They, too, fixed God's Word by interpretation and traditions. They, too, became complacent, when their expectations of fulfillment were frustrated by subsequent happenings.[56] The gradual shift from revelation to *vox populi* also explains the rejection of our Lord by the leadership of the Jews.[57] Further, it accounts for what has happened over and over again in the history of Christianity. Christians, too, restricted the revelation of God with myopic vision and tradition. Christians, too, reduced the eternal into temporal and spatial categories. Christians, too, walked in the way of *Realpolitik* and *vox populi,* instead of keeping in step with the Spirit. Christians, too, failed in keeping alive the hope in Christ's coming and in the salvation-to-come.

TRUE AND FALSE PROPHETS

Who is a prophet of God and who is not? The above discussion of the prophetic office, role, and message began with the Mosaic criteria. Though the revealed criteria for discerning the prophets of God are clear, Israel had difficulty in distinguishing the true from the false.[58] Prophets were false when they misled people (Deut. 13:2; 18:20; Jer. 2:8; 23:27), when their morals were loose (Jer. 23:14), or when they practiced magic and divination (Isa. 8:19; Jer. 14:14).[59] But how did Israel and Judah know that someone who claimed to come with a message from God was indeed sent by the Spirit?

The false prophets belonged to the socially and religiously acceptable institution of "professional" prophets who responded to the needs of their time. They operated from within the limited perspectives of their contemporaries: *Realpolitik* and *vox populi.* These prophets encouraged the people by giving concrete solutions in crises and by speaking comforting words based on their understanding of the Word of God.

The false prophets did not realize that they posed a threat to the prophets of God and that they deceived the people of God. We know these prophets as "false," but how could God's people discern between the true and the false, between the "old" revelation and the "new," and between claim and counterclaim?

The Problem of Validation

The true prophet had a relevant message in a crisis situation. His words were all too often unpopular with his contemporaries[60] and were opposed by false prophets who tickled the people's ears with their message of hope (Ezek. 13:10). Ezekiel likens these prophets to whitewash because they did not portray the situation as it was but merely tried to make it look better (vv. 10–12, 14–15; 22:28).

Jeremiah and the False Prophets

The study of Jeremiah's interaction with the false prophets illustrates how difficult it was to identify the true prophet. Jeremiah faced many such prophets in Jerusalem. These false prophets were ideologists who operated from the belief that their interpretation of God's revelation through Moses was true and would always be true.

Theology of the False Prophets

The false prophets were zealous for the preservation of the old way but were closed to new revelation. They could find prooftexts for their theology and were thus able to bind God to Judah and her institutions. But they were unresponsive to any interpretation or new revelation that might alter their understanding of the Mosaic revelation.

They further believed that the people of Judah—as the legitimate heirs of the covenant, temple, theocracy, and Davidic monarchy—were the children of God. Their hope was fixed on institutions (God's law, the temple, the Davidic monarchy, and the privileged covenant status of Judah) rather than the living God. They considered Jerusalem, "the city of God," to be invincible.[61]

For example, Hananiah predicted *in the name of the Lord Almighty* (!) the restoration of the exiles, Jehoiachin, and the temple vessels (Jer. 28:2–4). A dispute arose when Hananiah affirmed his trust in the ancient oracles of salvation and Jeremiah spoke of God's freedom.[62] Jeremiah insisted that Jerusalem would fall.

No wonder that they treated Jeremiah's radical message concerning the destruction of the Temple and the cessation of the Davidic monarchy with contempt. Jeremiah proclaimed that Yahweh is free, and in his freedom he may even destroy his own "temple," as he had done at Shiloh (Jer. 26:6). The priests and the prophets angrily challenged him, "Why do you prophesy in the LORD's name that this house will be like Shiloh and this city will be desolate and deserted?" (v. 9). Jeremiah was a threat to their theology of the temple and ultimately to their view of God.[63]

Jeremiah challenged his contemporaries to study the prophetic word of the past and to interpret God's revelation afresh. Some of the elders did remember Micah's oracles of judgment against Jerusalem (Jer. 26:18–19). But that failed to convince the people. They resisted Jeremiah's announcement that Yahweh had ordained the fall of Judah (27:1–11) and that no diviner or prophet could avert God's judgment

(vv. 9–10, 14–15). The false prophets of Judah were no better than those of Samaria (23:13–14).

Jeremiah had no sympathy for the false prophets. He declared that the Lord would show no regard for the false messengers of peace (Jer. 8:10–17). Their message was rooted in their underlying desire for comfort, security, and prosperity.

> Greedy for gain;
> prophets and priests alike,
> all practice deceit.
>
> (v. 10)

The people were too easily taken in by these preachers of hope, tradition, and a popular view of God (*vox populi*). The false prophets did not completely reject Yahweh and his way, but they were blind to God's greatness. They all had one goal: self. Power, greed, and self-justification characterized the false prophets whose self-centered words filled the people with "false hopes" (23:16). They did not prepare God's people for the future day of accountability (vv. 20, 33–40). They deluded the people by keeping God "small," restricting him to their understanding of his revelation. Jeremiah declared, "They are prophesying to you false visions, divinations, idolatries and the delusions of their own minds" (14:14).[64]

Jeremiah's Suffering

The prophet Jeremiah suffered greatly because of the false prophets' opposition.[65] He expressed his innermost feelings when he said:

> Concerning the prophets:
> My heart is broken within me;
> all my bones tremble.
> I am like a drunken man,
> like a man overcome by wine,
> because of the Lord
> and his holy words.
>
> (Jer. 23:9).

But Jeremiah encouraged the true prophets of God to speak clearly, without fear (vv. 28–29).

Criteria of Validation

It appears from Jeremiah's interaction with the prophets of his time that the prophetic movement was a complex phenomenon. The complexity was due to the place of the prophets within the structures of society. Judean society recognized Hananiah as "the prophet" (Jer. 28:1, 15) who spoke in the name of the Lord (v. 2). Hananiah, like other false prophets, enjoyed popular support (v. 1), representing the theological perspective of his contemporaries (*vox populi*). The false prophets depended on the *vox populi* for credibility and vindication, whereas Jeremiah trusted in the Lord to vindicate him and his message.

The message of the false prophet seriously challenged the credibility of the true prophet of God.[66] The oracles of the prophets exhorted the godly to discern and submit themselves to God's revelation and prepare themselves for the new era. This they do by receiving, treasuring, and submitting themselves to the revelation of God, which shatters human visions, structures, and ways. The prophetic word afflicts the comfortable but comforts the afflicted! The true prophet proclaimed a historically verifiable message, which would be vindicated by subsequent events.[67] However, a prophet generally did not live to see the fulfillment. He was rejected by his contemporaries and suffered for his witness to God's work.

False prophets depended on traditional values and operated from a closed theological system.[68] They were in continuity with God's word to Moses (Sinai theology) and David (Zion theology). But they did not share in the fresh interpretation of God's revelation or in the development of the prophetic tradition. Further, they restricted their interpretation and application so that they could not readily adapt and apply the revelation of God to a new and concrete situation.

The rise of false prophets was inevitable because of the expectations of popular theology (*vox populi*) that defined what the prophet could or could not say.[69] It was also inevitable that the monarchy would develop a group of professional counselors.[70] The false prophets gained status by promoting the interests of the monarch and by speaking to the desires of the people. Thus when a true prophet of God spoke, his audience might misinterpret his message as being "false" when it contradicted their expectations.[71]

In retrospect, seven criteria may be applied to sift out the false prophets from the prophetic movement. These criteria apply equally to the preexilic, exilic, and postexilic prophets and to our Lord and his apostles. (See figure 13.)

> The proposed solutions to the phenomenon of false prophets and its impact on the prophetic institution have been many and diverse. Von Rad assumes that false prophets always spoke a message of salvation and were connected with Israel's cult.[72] R. P. Carroll explains it psychologically by the criterion of lack of fulfillment (or *cognitive dissonance*),[73] according to which the gap between prophecy and fulfillment created a problem for the godly who had to await fulfillment before they could discern the true prophet from a false one. Crenshaw concludes that the prophets

could not and did not find adequate ways of "self-validation" or authentication.[74] Blenkinsopp modifies Crenshaw's radical thesis by explaining that the sociopolitical conditions of the late seventh century were so complex that "the criterion of historical falsification does not do justice to the complex nature of prophecy."[75] He further concludes that this explains the failure of prophetism to keep itself alive in the postexilic era.[76] Both Crenshaw and Blenkinsopp explain the phenomenon of prophetism concretely and realistically, as prophet faced people and as prophet faced prophet.[77] Wilson correctly observes that "it is likely that the problem is even more complex than even the most perceptive interpreters have realized."[78]

TRUE PROPHETS	FALSE PROPHETS
1. Foundation: Revelation	Revelation and religion
2. Holistic proclamation	Selective proclamation
3. Independence from power structures	Dependence on power structures: *Realpolitik*
4. Members of a divine and social institution	Members of a social institution
5. Vision of the reality of the kingdom of God	Guardians of status quo
6. Theocentric ethics	Man-centered ethics
7. Suffering for the sake of God	Popularity and power

Figure 13. True and False Prophets

First, the false prophets brought together revelation and religion. This syncretistic way of life helped them gain popular recognition. In contrast, the true prophets operated solely from the framework of revelation; they were guardians of the Mosaic *revelation*.

Second, the false prophets selected themes from the revelation of God that would comfort the people of God. They believed in God's promises (the election of Israel, the covenant, the inviolability of the temple, the promises regarding David, the election of Zion), but did not apply God's warnings and threats to themselves.[79] They bound God to Judah by their interpretation, but they were closed to his revelation in the form of either reinterpretation or new revelation. Neither did they recognize God, the Creator of everything, as free in his rule over creation.[80]

Sanders asks whether the true and false prophets invoked the same theological traditions, or operated from different theological positions.[81] He concludes that while the prophets, true and false, operated from the same theological framework, the false prophets operated from a different hermeneutical framework. They had divorced "redemption" from "creation" and thereby formed a "definite" understanding of what God could and could not do, based on their interpretation of God's covenant promises and the place of the theocratic institutions in Israel. The true prophets presented God as the great King over all creation, who sovereignly rules over the nations and uses them in accordance with his free will. Fixation (of canonical interpretation) results from an "impulse to monotheize," that is, to affirm Yahweh's ontological and ethical integrity with little regard for a theological reflection on God the Creator. The Old Testament prophets were overwhelmed by the splendor and freedom of God, who may freely judge and destroy, but who may also freely create "a new thing, a new heart, a new spirit in his people, . . . transforming his people, by wounding and healing, into a new Israel."[82]

The true prophets affirmed the whole counsel of God. They opposed any human restriction on the *freedom of God,* whether in the temple, law, or monarchy. The heart of the prophetic heritage lies in the concern for the true freedom of God, as Zimmerli writes, "Prophetic proclamation thus shatters and transforms tradition in order to announce the approach of the Living One."[83]

Third, the false prophets fostered illusions by advocating *Realpolitik.* They provided solutions for the problems at hand, whether they were social, political, or economic. The true prophets maintained a relative *independence* from social structures. They became the objects of ridicule, hatred, and plots. More often than not the prophet of the Lord was a lonely individual whose behavior, clothing, and speech marked him as different from his contemporaries. He often did not enjoy simple human comforts as he suffered for the sake of Christ (Luke 20:9–15; Acts 7:52).

Fourth, the false prophets lived and worked for a human ideal, dream, vision, or institution.[84] They promoted programs and techniques, sought to eternalize the present and to institutionalize the Spirit in space and time. This conflict in ideology explains the threats made against Jeremiah: "Come, let's make plans against Jeremiah; for the teaching of the law by the priest will not be lost, nor will counsel from the wise, nor the word from the prophets. So come, let's attack him with our tongues and pay no attention to anything he says" (Jer. 18:18).

True prophets functioned as *intermediaries* between God and man. The prophetic institution was, by definition, both *divine* and *social*. It was a divine institution because the Lord commissioned his prophets with a word from above; it was a social institution because prophets spoke God's word to a people whose expectations were all too often determined by *Realpolitik,* social pressures, popular beliefs, and practices.

Fifth, the false prophets were guardians of the status quo. The covenant, the Davidic monarch, the temple, and the priesthood were "sacred" symbols of God's kingdom. Their vision of the kingdom, based on the past acts of God, provided them with a myopic vision for reconstruction.

The true prophets operated from the conviction that, while God is King, Yahweh will fully establish his kingdom by his Spirit. They rejected any human attempt at reconstructing or establishing the kingdom by *Realpolitik,* economic, social, power, cultural, and military structures.

Sixth, the false prophets taught a man-centered morality. They embraced the revelation of Moses as it was popularly interpreted (*vox populi*) and practiced forms of piety (prayer, sacrifices, and fasting).

True prophetic ethics were both *theocentric* and *eschatological*. Theocentric ethics provided a system of interpreting the law of God in the larger framework of who God is. An act was good only when done for the love of God rather than for immediate reward and recognition. Further, an act was good when it corresponded with the vision of the transformed world of righteousness, justice, love, fidelity, and peace. This is the essence of eschatological and theocentric ethics.[85]

> Koch defines this prophetic contribution by the term *monanthropology*. Monanthropology is that manner of life whereby society (and the individual) operates from an absolute faith in Yahweh (*monotheism*) so that man's way (*anthropology*) is in harmony with the ways of God. Koch considers man's activity as two levels of concentric circles. At the inner level, man shows concern for society, family, animals, and land. At the outer level, the believing community, while closest to the blessings of God, is the center of humanity and shares a responsibility for humanity at large.[86]

Seventh, false prophets gained popularity and power through a syncretistic, optimistic program of *Realpolitik*. But true prophets *suffered,* waiting for the fulfillment of God's word. During their suffering the prophets awaited Yahweh's vindication of their message (Heb. 11:32).[87] Generally, another generation would see the fulfillment of their announcements. Yet, even when the people witnessed fulfillment, they continued to view the prophets as the objects of human manipulation and suspicion.

Childs insists that the biblical books vindicate God's prophets. Micaiah was vindicated by the death of Ahab, and Jeremiah was vindicated in the fall of Jerusalem.[88] The acts of God in the history of his people bear out the veracity of his word and justify his prophets as his spokesmen. More than that, the historical pattern of proclamation and fulfillment extends the canonical significance of the prophetic word to subsequent generations. They are also responsible for hearing God's word, heeding it, and discerning the true from the false. The community at large rejected the radical message of the prophet, but the remnant listened and treasured his words as the word of God. The remnant witnessed the veracity of the true prophets in the near fulfillment and believed that the eschatological message of the true prophets would also be fulfilled.

The Prophetic Mission and Vision

The true prophets lived by the transforming power of the coming kingdom of God. The Lord called them to announce the coming kingdom and to prepare for his coming. Since God's kingdom will come by the work of the Spirit and not by human power or might,[89] the prophetic vision of God's freedom in his rule shattered human dreams and ambitions. Zimmerli wisely states,

> We must not, however, think that the prophets were simply interpreters of history. . . . Behind the word of the prophets was not the river of history, rushing with invincible force, and by its rigid laws forcing its way on and breaking down all opposition. Behind their preaching stood the Lord of freedom, in whose hands all history remains a tool which can be wielded freely by him.[90]

The true prophets were also intercessors for God's people. Moses and Samuel were remembered for their intercessory role on behalf of God's people (Jer. 15:1; see also Ex. 32:11–14, 30–34; Num. 14:13–23; Deut. 9:18–20, 25–29; 1 Sam. 7:5–9; 12:19–25; Ps. 99:6–8). This aspect helps us balance the otherwise forensic (legal) expressions of the prophetic word.

Since the prophet was both intermediary and intercessor, his role placed him in a "tension-filled life."[91] The prophets belonged to the people of God and loved God's people. As members of the divine council, they listened in to what God had planned, but as human beings, they empathized with God's people (Isa. 22:4; Jer. 8:21–9:11).

The true prophet had a theocentric *mission.* First, Yahweh's prophet was receptive to instruction.

The Sovereign LORD has given me an instructed tongue,
  to know the word that sustains the weary.
He wakens me morning by morning,
  wakens my ear to listen like one being taught.

(Isa. 50:4)

He was an obedient servant to his Lord.

The sovereign LORD has opened my ears,
  and I have not been rebellious;
  I have not drawn back.

(v. 5)

Second, the true prophet of God might suffer hardship:

I offered my back to those who beat me,
  my cheeks to those who pulled out my beard;
I did not hide my face
  from mocking and spitting.

(v. 6)

The prophet looked forward to Yahweh's vindication of him and his message (vv. 7–9). Third, the prophet invited the godly to respond to God's grace and to walk in the way of the Lord.

Who among you fears the LORD
  and obeys the word of his servant?
Let him who walks in the dark,
  who has no light,
trust in the name of the LORD
  and rely on his God.

(v. 10).

The prophets of God were members of God's council and received a *vision* of the kingdom of God (the coming of God in salvation) that transformed them into instruments for the Master's use. The word of God through his servants remains God's witness to himself; it is the spiritual force in a material world. Walther Zimmerli shows a fine appreciation for the abiding power inherent in this word.

The word of Yahweh is the real power that shapes history, remaining constant in the midst of change. . . . In its own history Israel learned by experience that it was not the policies of its kings and their armies that made history, but the word of Yahweh proclaimed by the preexilic prophets.[92]

REVIEW

The prophetic tradition developed during Israel's long history in the land, in exile, and in the postexilic era. The preexilic prophets gradually were pushed away from the structures of society in both Israel and Judah. They critically stood up against the temple, the king, the programs, and the structures of their time.[93] Although they loved the covenant, the temple, and the pure worship of God, they opposed the perversion of worship, the stagnation of God's people, and the misinterpretation of the covenant. They did not ask God's people to adopt new religious values but explained the magnificence of the older revelation in the light of the new revelation.

The prophets spoke God's word to people in crisis. During war, siege, famine, or other adverse times, they addressed living people and applied God's message to the issues at hand. Each prophet had a distinct vocabulary, individual gifts, and a unique personality. But the Spirit of God transcended the human temporal perspective.[94] In spite of the diversity in personalities, literary modes, and historical circumstances, the Spirit of God used and transformed the variety in the prophetic messages into a revelation for God's people in any age.

The prophetic tradition reveals variety and unity.[95] The tradition was comprised of various emphases, distinct contributions, and watershed-like developments. Each prophet was an individual with a distinctive call and message from God. However, this concern for distinctive characteristics should not mislead us to pay exclusive attention to the differences. R. E. Clements rightly rejects the Wellhausian assumption that the prophets were individualists.[96] The true prophets formed a tradition that was founded on the covenantal structure. Clements states, "For the prophets and the psalmists the covenant tradition formed the heart of their religion."[97] But the false prophets never developed a lasting tradition. Their false hopes were shattered in the fall of Samaria and of Jerusalem. Their interpretations proved wrong.

The prophets announced God's judgment and salvation. They declared that Israel and Judah would have to experience the Exile, through which process God would gather a remnant and constitute a new community. This new community would need continual purification in preparation for the Day of Judgment (the Day of the Lord).[98]

The postexilic events foreshadow the coming kingdom of God and of his Messiah. The messages of the postexilic prophets have much in common with the preaching of our Lord and his disciples. First, they preached the reality of *judgment* on the Day of the Lord. Second, they made an offer of *grace, salvation,* and full *participation* in the righteous kingdom of Yahweh and of his Messiah. Third, they called for a lifestyle of *discipleship, purification,* and *preparation* for the kingdom-to-come. Fourth, they announced the *presence* of Yahweh, the covenant, and his kingdom. Fifth, they also called for *perseverance* to live godly lives and to hasten the day of the establishment of the kingdom. Yahweh will bring in the new heaven and new earth. His kingdom is secure! This is the message of the classical prophets.

QUESTIONS AND ISSUES

1. Define court prophet, eschatological ethics, Sinai theology, theocentric ethics, theocentric message, Zion theology.
2. Discuss the office, role, and message of the prophets.
3. How is the prophetic message theocentric, progressive, and organic?
4. How did the Lord demonstrate his grace and patience in Israel?
5. What was the cultural context of the ministry of Elijah and Elisha, and how did they minister in this context?
6. How did God's prophets announce the end of Israel, and how did Israel respond?
7. What should Judah have learned from Israel's fall in 722 B.C.?
8. How did Judah compare with Israel in her response to God's revelation?
9. Why was the *vox populi* the great danger to Judah's spiritual health?
10. Briefly describe the context of the ministry of Isaiah, Micah, Habakkuk, Jeremiah, Ezekiel, and Daniel. How was their message conditioned by the historical context?
11. How was the postexilic era a fulfillment of the prophetic word? How did the message of the postexilic prophets differ from that of the preexilic prophets?
12. What are the seven criteria for validating the prophet, according to the Mosaic revelation? Why did the phenomenon of false prophets confound many?
13. By what seven criteria could the godly distinguish between true and false prophets? Relate these criteria to the ministry of our Lord and the apostles. How do the criteria still apply to the faithful preaching and teaching of God's Word?
14. What was the mission of the prophet and what was his vision?

CHAPTER 3

Perspectives on Prophecy

INTRODUCTION

Interpreting the prophetic word is truly exciting! We are heirs of the apostles, who in turn lead us back to the prophets. In Jesus Christ all Christians are heirs of the prophetic-apostolic tradition and are called upon to understand the oracles of God, spoken through his prophets and the apostles. In Jesus Christ we, too, become involved in understanding what God's Spirit has said concerning the salvation that is to come (1 Peter 1:10).

The legacy of the prophets and apostles gives us a perspective on the past, present, and future acts of God in Christ. The prophets and apostles received God's revelation and were faithful in proclaiming it, regardless of the consequences. By the Spirit of God, they committed his revelation to written form. The Holy Spirit still bears witness that their words are truly the Word of God and are profitable for instruction, reproof, and comfort, as the Spirit empowers his Word and applies it to our lives (2 Tim. 3:16–17; see 1 Cor. 2:10–16).

70

Regrettably, the interpretation of the prophetic legacy has been affected by division, fragmentation, expressions of distrust, and misunderstanding. Disagreements arising from exegetical, theological, or philosophical differences have often been expressed with rigidity and lack of love, and certain approaches to interpretation have too often exalted eschatology as *the* test of orthodoxy.[1]

An exploration of the prophetic word requires an openness to the whole revelation of God in both the Old Testament and the New Testament, to the cultural context of the prophets, to the prophetic language, metaphors, and forms of speech, as well as to the canonical importance of the prophetic message.

> Many years ago Bernard Ramm asked, "Can prophetic literature be interpreted by the general method of grammatical exegesis, or is some special principle necessary?"[2] In response, he gave several principles of interpretation based on the writings of Girdlestone[3] and Davidson.[4] First, the language, historical background, and literary analysis of each passage must be in accordance with the usual rules of interpretation, which includes the rule that Scripture interprets Scripture. Second, attention must be paid to the "essence" or nature of the text (i.e., is it moral, ethical, didactic, predictive, theological, conditional, or fulfilled?). The nature of fulfillment must be considered by asking if the prophecy has been fulfilled, if it is still to be fulfilled, or if it has multiple fulfillments. Third, he adhered to "literal meaning of a prophetic passage" as the "controlling guide."[5] Fourth, he asked, "What hermeneutical method does the New Testament use in employing the Old?"[6] This last principle is basic to Ramm's form of typological interpretation, that is, a Christocentric interpretation of the prophetic word.[7]
>
> More recently Joel Green addressed the problems relating to interpreting the prophetic word. He sees problems inherent in the prophetic writings (literal/figurative; the context; the cultural relatedness; the language of the future) and in the readers (problems we bring to the text).[8] According to Green one of the greatest obstacles to prophetic interpretation lies in our unwillingness to read the prophetic word as God's word given in time and space. He concludes that throughout the history of Christianity we have been preoccupied with sorting things out, but that this effort to systematize is "an extrabiblical pursuit."[9]

This study is all the more meaningful for the Christian interpreter who approaches the prophets as having a relevant message for their days and for ours.[10] But this study must be accompanied by *prayer* and an attentive listening to the *Spirit of God*. God has been patient as he has communicated his message over the centuries, revealing in different modes and emphases a colorful mosaic of his plan of redemption. So the interpreter must be *patient* and take into account the historical and cultural context to which the Lord has accommodated his revelation. Calvin loved the way in which God accommodated himself to human culture[11] and was very critical of anyone who was not patient in hearing the voice of God in the prophets.

> As far as Sacred Scripture is concerned, however much froward men try to gnaw at it, nevertheless it clearly is crammed with thoughts that could not be humanly conceived. Let each of the prophets be looked into: none will be found who does not far exceed human measure. Consequently, those for whom the prophetic doctrine is tasteless ought to be thought of as lacking taste buds.[12]

The interpretation of the prophetic word also calls for humility and illumination. *Humility* begins with the fear of the Lord. *Fear* is a biblical term for submission to God's will in contrast to self-reliance (Prov. 1:7; 3:5–7; Eccl. 12:13). Submission is an act of devotion to God, to his purpose, and to his freedom in the working out of his plan in establishing his kingdom. Humility arises from a need for divine *illumination* and expresses itself in an openness to see and hear with the heart of faith. The prophetic words will remain unheard by those who are comfortable, complacent, and proud. The reason for this is simple. The Holy Spirit is with the humble of heart in awakening their understanding and in giving them new structures for living. For them, the prophetic windows open up magnificent vistas. But rigidity and entrapment by *Realpolitik* and the *vox populi* lead to mistaking the vision of man for the vision of God. Thanks be to God that his Spirit comes to the aid of all who approach the prophetic word with a spirit of submission.

Interpretation of the prophets also involves serious *study*. Luther was right in lamenting the difficulty of dealing with them: "They have a queer way of talking, like people, who, instead of proceeding in an orderly manner, ramble off [*sic*] from one thing to the next, so that you cannot make head or tail of them what they are getting at."[13] The student of the prophetic message may more easily adapt to the strangeness of the prophetic books by steeping oneself in the historic and cultural milieu of each prophet; by appreciating the literary forms, images, and metaphors; by relating the prophetic books to the people of

God throughout the history of redemption (i.e., preexilic, exilic, postexilic, etc.); and by rooting oneself in the progress of redemption.

At this point, I interject a warning against the formal or technical analysis of the Prophets. The *technician* in us presses to find the pieces, bring them together, and be content with a consistent presentation of the prophetic message. This approach omits many pieces that do not fit the "system," or it makes them fit for the sake of consistency. The *poetic* approach allows for tensions and paradoxes because God's revelation has many facets and because humans cannot project the finished picture while they see through a glass darkly.

In this chapter we shall consider each of the ingredients for interpreting the prophetic word: (1) the cultural context, (2) the written form (literary perspective), (3) the place of the prophetic book in shaping the faith and practice of God's people (canonical function), and (4) the relation of the prophecies throughout the progress of redemption (redemptive-historical perspective). (See figure 14.)

INTERPRETING THE PROPHETS		
Prophets *Cultural Context*	**Prophetic Writings** *Literary Perspective*	**Interpreter** *Canonical Function*
Time Place Images Metaphors	Prophetic speech Literary heritage Poetic-prophetic Oracles of judgment Oracles of salvation	Rule of faith and practice Humility Illumination Study Stability/adaptability
REDEMPTIVE HISTORICAL PERSPECTIVE		

Figure 14. Ingredients for Interpreting the Prophetic Word

CULTURAL CONTEXT

The prophets were God's servants *in time* applying God's word during crises in the covenant relation between God and his people. They spoke a language their contemporaries could understand and in forms suited to their audience.[14]

The prophetic speech is poetic, imaginative, full of similes and metaphors. It is the language of pictures and windows, drawn from the cultural context of the day. Through his servants, the prophets, God the Father pulled back the curtain of the new age and allowed his children, before and after Christ, to grasp a little of the glory prepared for them. The prophets were God's messengers *out of time,* for they spoke of the visions of God.

Biblical language of God is metaphorical. Through figures of speech (as Creator, King, Father) humans express something of the reality of God in human figures. G. B. Caird develops an extensive application of metaphor to biblical language. He further views eschatological language as a special application of metaphor.[15] David Tracy wonders why so little has been made of the study of metaphor in theological discourse.[16] He argues that theological discourse is possible only after a careful reflection of the biblical usage of the metaphor.

The works of Paul Ricoeur have had a great impact on hermeneutics, including the study of *metaphor.* He defines the characteristics of metaphor as follows: (1) the transformation of a noun; (2) a transference or movement *from* something well known *to* something lesser known (*epiphor*); (3) a transposition of a name by deviation, borrowing, or substitution (*allotrios*); and (4) a typology of metaphor. The semblance (*mimesis*) between the image and the reality is such that the metaphor has only one literal meaning. The study of poetry and rhetoric assumes that we belong to this world. Any form of discourse is referential and alive.[17]

An application of the rules of metaphor to the Prophets introduces a proper caution in the interpretation of biblical images regarding the language of the new acts of God. The interpreter studies the use and the typology of the metaphor of the language of eschatology ("Day of the Lord," "deliverance," "kingdom," etc.), knowing that his understanding of the *mimesis* is limited by his belonging to this world of time and space. The goal of interpretation is not to arrive at *the* meaning of the text, but to open discourse with the text, as Ricoeur writes incisively, "The parabolic message proceeds from this *tension* between a form which circumscribes it and a process which transgresses the narrative boundaries and points to an 'other,' to a 'beyond.'"[18] Interpretation, accordingly, must pass by literary analysis in its methodology from exegesis to theological interpretation.[19]

The interpreter of the prophets must be sensitive to the historical context, language, and literary imagery. The prophets were real human beings who shared their lives with their contemporaries in a cultural context.[20] They received a vision of God but spoke of it in a language that people could understand. The prophets painted multifaceted pictures representing the acts of God from their days until the full inauguration of the kingdom of God. (See figure 14.) The prophetic word has a bearing on the historical context of the prophet, but its relevance goes far beyond what the prophet said and how it was fulfilled. Davidson comments, "Consequently, to expect fulfillment in the exact terms of the prophecy is to mistake its nature."[21] The prophetic oracles are God's word to each new generation in its own historical context. Each generation can find its identity in the history and progression of fulfillment while living in the hope of the great future God has prepared for his people. Each generation must get involved in the interpretation and application of the prophetic word so that it, too, may contribute to the progress of redemption.

Interpretation of the prophetic word requires both an understanding of the social world of Israel and a sensitivity to God's accommodation to human language and images. Isaiah, for example, announced the grandeur of salvation in the imagery of victory: light, brightness, and joy (Isa. 51:4; 58:8, 10; 59:9; 60:1, 3, 19–20). He set this metaphor within the historically conditioned language of a victorious people, who would receive recognition from the nations (11:11–16; 14:2; 49:22–26; 60:4). The nations will provide the redeemed with precious objects (60:4–16), bring tribute to Jerusalem (23:17–18; 60:13–16; 66:20), and serve them (61:4–6).

The apostle John adapted many of Isaiah's literary portraits in his magnificent description of the New Jerusalem. He portrayed the gates of the New Jerusalem as never being shut so that the glory and honor of the nations may be brought into the city. Nothing impure will ever enter that city, nor will anyone who does what is shameful or deceitful be allowed in. Only those whose names are written in the Lamb's Book of Life will enter (Rev. 21:24–27). John used the language of accommodation to express the exaltation, glory, and light in describing the blessings of the children of God.

LITERARY PERSPECTIVE

The prophet was primarily God's spokesperson, and his voice was the voice of God. He spoke with the authority of the One who sent him. The prophet was aware of his distinct call and of belonging to a prophetic tradition.[22]

The psychological dimension is always involved in the process of revelation. That the prophet was conscious during the process of receiving and transmitting the message of God is seen most clearly when he is in dialogue with the Lord.[23]

Prophetic dialogue helps us understand the reality and difficulty of the prophetic mission. It is as if the prophet allows us to "'overhear' what was initially a transaction between him and the Lord."[24] Moses began his ministry against his will. He repeatedly questioned his fitness for ministry (Ex. 3:11–5:23). In his intercession for Israel he "persuaded" the Lord to renew the covenant (32:30–34:10; Num. 14:11–25). He also protested God's judgment in not being permitted to enter the Promised Land (Deut. 1:37; 3:23–27; 31:2; 32:52; 34:4).

Though Moses' position as God's friend was special, the Lord also freely listened and graciously responded to his other servants, the prophets (Ezek. 4:7–15; Hab. 1–2). At Horeb, in the presence of the Lord, Elijah indicted Israel on three counts of covenant breach. The Lord acknowledged each charge (1 Kings 19:9–18), responding with gentleness to Elijah's cause for discouragement. When Jeremiah felt betrayed, he charged the Lord with deceiving him (Jer. 12:1–13; 20:7–18). Yet the Lord did not set his servant aside, but encouraged Jeremiah to persevere in his mission.

The Prophetic Word as Literature

The prophets, as God's spokespersons, were *communicators* of the word. (See figure 14.) They spoke the message of God in ways that their contemporaries recognized as "prophetic"; they were "poets with a 'message.'"[25] Both true and false prophets used "forms" of speech in addressing kings, leaders, and people.[26] They also creatively used Israel's cultural and revelatory heritage.[27] Both groups shared in the rich heritage of God's revelation to Israel.[28] The prophets, as heirs of the revelation from Sinai and Zion, were steeped in all the traditions of Israel: theophanic,[29] war,[30] legal,[31] wisdom,[32] and cultic.[33]

Classical prophecy was first and foremost an oral expression, the written forms being secondary,[34] but the process from oral to written form is far from clear. Certain speeches may have been written soon after the original pronouncement. Others may have circulated, possibly among a group of disciples.[35] In cases where there was a significant time lapse, the prophet could summarize his oracles, paraphrase them, and polish his work into a literary masterpiece. After the fall of Samaria and of Jerusalem, some prophetic books may have been edited under less than favorable conditions. For example, the prophecy of Jeremiah underwent several stages of collection and editing, resulting in an "anthology of anthologies" completed during the Exile.[36]

The prophets employed distinct forms of prophetic speech and rhetorical devices. They lived in a cultural milieu in which oral and literary forms were the accepted ways of communication.

> Gunkel's permanent contribution lies in his recognition of the prophets as speakers and in his categorization of the writings as containing several forms of speech. He characterized the "form" (genre) by its formal structural components (vocabulary, grammar,

and idioms) and its life situation (*Sitz-im-Leben*).[37] His work had a great impact on the form-critical study of the prophets.[38]

Claus Westermann also assumes that the prophets, as God's orators, had distinctive forms of prophetic speech.[39] He divides the contents of the prophetic books into three categories: prophetic speech, accounts, and utterances directed from man to God.[40] Wolff, Koch, and Tucker have argued that the prophets worked creatively with the forms of prophetic speech.[41]

Several other literary approaches have made a serious attempt at "listening in" on the prophetic speech. The *morphological approach* studies the *similarities* of shared imagery and forms of expression within the prophetic tradition (community).[42] Frye applied the morphological approach to poetry as a method of examining, describing, and classifying texts into *archetypes*.[43] An *archetype* is "a recurring image" or composite of the literary elements represented in different texts. The employment of repetition may best be appreciated when the text is read aloud, for Kapelrud has observed that "poetry was primarily and ordinarily oral."[44]

Rhetorical analysis has explained many seemingly strange features of prophetic speech by looking at the function of the literary units as examples of the *art* of persuasion.[45] The prophets used the art of persuasion in convincing their contemporaries of the certainty of judgment and the reality of God's salvation. Rhetorical analysis studies the relationships between the literary materials, the prophet, and his audience. Gitay's study on Isaiah 40–48 exemplifies the prophetic art of persuasion, which he defines as follows: "It is the task of this volume to call attention to new dimensions in studying the prophetical literature from the perspective of the art of speech and persuasion, new dimensions which carry significant implications for understanding the nature of prophetic activity."[46]

Jack R. Lundbom studied the rhetoric of Jeremiah, and his approach may well be applied to the study of other prophets. He defines Jeremiah's rhetoric as *"a preacher's rhetoric"* in which the prophet involved the audience and remained in dialogue with them.[47] He further concludes that the rhetoric of Jeremiah consistently goes from the ironic to the straightforward, from the figurative to the literal, from the general to the specific, and from the abstract to the concrete.[48] Rhetorical analysis aids the reader in feeling the dynamics of the prophetic proclamation as he listens to the dialogue, argumentation, and rhetorical variation of the prophet. The focus is not primarily on analysis of "forms," but on listening to the prophetic speech in its original life situation.

The results that have come from form-critical analysis, morphological analysis, and rhetorical criticism are valuable if *criticism* is understood as a form of literary analysis. Analysis may be compared to a set of glasses that help the student of the text focus on a particular aspect of that text to describe it more clearly. But it is far from easy to distinguish between the content and the form of the oracles. At times the genres fuse together, and the form and content are similarly interrelated.[49]

Alter has made a fine contribution toward the appreciation of the poetic features of biblical prophecy. He argues that poetry is very suitable in prophetic speech. It permitted the prophet to address a real audience for purposes of persuasion and yet to speak to the people of God who were generations removed from him.

> Such speech is directed to the concrete situation of a historical audience, but the form of the speech exhibits the historical indeterminacy of the language of poetry, which helps explain why these discourses have touched the lives of millions of readers far removed in time, space, and political predicament from the small groups of Hebrews against whom Hosea, Isaiah, Jeremiah, and their confreres originally inveighed.[50]

However, analysis of prophetic speech is all too often preoccupied with the form. A fixation on the form may lead to a dichotomy of judgment and hope or to an analysis of individual units of tradition without relating these units to the message of the book. Here I agree with Koch's caution:

> The longer I am engaged in the interpretation of prophetic books of the Old Testament, the more skeptical I become about literary criticism in its prevailing form. With insouciant confidence, it sifts out a profusion of non-genuine material from these writings, on the grounds of stylistic "doublets," or what it takes to be factual contradictions.[51]

Oracles of Judgment and Salvation

The prophets were given a twofold ministry. On the one hand, they were messengers of judgment and closure, proclaiming an end to an era of God's favor and blessings; on the other, they were heralds of salvation, preaching a new era of divine favor.[52] This twofold ministry is reflected in the two major forms of prophetic speech: the oracles of judgment and salvation. These categories of prophetic speech are complementary, or as Raitt puts it, they "are bound together in the unity of the divine will and the unity of the Divine Person."[53]

The prophetic covenant prosecutors addressed the people and the king alike. They were heirs of the revelation to Israel (Mount Sinai) and the revelation to David (Mount Zion). In the *oracles of judgment* the prophets accused and condemned Israel for having departed from the

Sinai revelation.[54] They also pronounced judgment on the kings of Israel and Judah for being unfaithful.

The *oracles of judgment* appear in many forms: covenant lawsuit, woe oracles, disputation speech, prophecy of disaster, and oracles against the nations (see the appendix). The judgment oracle is rooted in the covenant sanctions (Lev. 26:14–39; Deut. 4:25–29; 28:15–68; 30:17–18; 31:28–32:43), according to which God had forewarned Israel that a breach of covenant would bring his curses on them: famine, infertility, war, plagues, and exile. The prophets applied the covenant sanctions to Israel and related them to the larger prophetic motif of the Day of the Lord ("the day of vengeance"). But the prophets still called for repentance, keeping the door open for God's future acts.[55] They proclaimed the oracle of judgment in the crisis between covenant promises and divine judgment (theodicy).[56] The resolution of the tension lies in the oracle of salvation, which is the opening of a new future of divine activity.[57] This future is grounded in the promise of a new beginning.

The *oracles of salvation* announce a new era in which the eschatological salvation breaks through into human alienation. "Deliverance" is that complex of divine acts involving the renewal of God's relationship with creation and with a redeemed community.[58] The proclamation of the new era is the message that promises the free involvement of the Creator-Redeemer.[59]

The Lord had bound himself to Israel and to the dynasty of David, but he was also free to abandon Israel and her kings. The prophetic oracles of judgment spoke of *closure* to God's favor, grace, forgiveness, and longsuffering. Yet God is also free in *opening* his favor again by creating a new era of blessing and forgiveness ("the year of favor"). The eschatology of the new era is continuous with God's revelation to Moses, who had spoken of the dawn of a new era after judgment (Lev. 26:40–45; Deut. 4:30–31; 32:43). The prophetic oracles of salvation—in a variety of forms (see the appendix)—elaborate on the nature of that new era. The new era begins with the promises of the old era as given in the covenants with creation, Abraham, Moses, and David, but gloriously transforms them by the promise of God's greater involvement with his people and of their greater participation. The new era also shapes new perspectives on the messianic rule and the involvement of the Spirit.

THE CANONICAL FUNCTION

The message of the prophets opens itself up by looking at two horizons. The historical, cultural, and literary context forms the one horizon in the process of interpreting the prophetic word, whereas the relation of the message of each prophet to all parts of Scripture forms the other horizon.[60] God's revelation in response to crisis and the prophetic language (metaphors and figures of speech) must be understood in a particular historical context, and yet as his messengers they proclaim a message of judgment and salvation that is relevant for many generations.[61] Our approach to the prophets (hermeneutics) to a large extent determines how we read the prophetical books. (See figure 14.)

Hermeneutics

The complex phenomenon of interpreting the prophets in relation to each other, to the New Testament, and to the modern context is the object of *hermeneutics*.[62] Hermeneutics undertakes the *canonical function* by seeking the meaning of the prophetic book in its historical situation (cultural milieu) and by relating it to the unfolding of the plan of God.[63] Hermeneutics helps twentieth-century readers not to read the text as if it has been written only for them (existential reading) or only for Israel (nationalistic reading). In a canonical interpretation, readers ask how God's Word has been understood by his people in any age (before, during, or after the Exile; before or after the coming of our Lord) in the unfolding of the progress of redemption.

Since the focus of the prophetic message is theocentric, it is not enough to ask how the prophecies have been fulfilled.[64] The question of *how* or *when* (verification principle) operates from the assumption that the study of the prophets consists mainly of the reconstruction of a historical schema, of futuristic projections, or of a list of predictions (fulfilled and to be fulfilled).

The theocentric focus points readers to the God of the prophets. He spoke through the prophets, and they witnessed to his plan of salvation. Since the specifics of the plan always have a bearing on the general plan, the prophetic oracles may readily be applied to a new historical context. The prophetic word, as the Word of God, calls for fresh interpretation, correlation, and application as the historical conditions change.[65] There is no doubt that the message allows "great flexibility of interpretation as regards time, circumstance, and the particular form which Israel would assume in the time of its salvation."[66]

For example, the message of Hosea, originally addressed to Israel in 750 B.C., also functioned as God's Word to the godly in Judah during the Assyrian crises, the Babylonian siege, and the subsequent exile. They interpreted Hosea's oracles of judgment in the light of Samaria's fall and reread the prophecy as also given to Judah. The godly in Judah who heard the prophecy received it as God's Word to them. They believed that what had happened to Israel could also happen to them because God's nature and expectations are the same.

When it was received as God's Word by the godly remnant of Judah, the book of Hosea became the *rule of faith and practice* in addition to the

Mosaic revelation. Its status as inspired Scripture widened the original canonical function of Hosea; in other words, God's revelation in space and time extended beyond the fall of the northern kingdom (722 B.C.) to the fall of Judah (586 B.C.). Its canonical function again widened during the Exile when the godly studied the prophecy of Hosea. They drew comfort from the prophetic emphasis on the depth of Yahweh's love, received instruction as to how to find salvation in the Lord alone, and gained a perspective on God's sovereign rule over the nations. In exile they awaited the "salvation to come," being uncertain as to how or when it would come. The Spirit of God encouraged them to read, interpret, and apply the "word of the prophets" (2 Peter 1:19–21). The godly did not know the whole design of God's plan, but they persevered in hope.

The canonical function widened even more in the postexilic era. The remnant of the twelve tribes who had put their trust in the Lord had already experienced "healing" by God's renewal of the covenant, by his forgiveness, and by his blessings to the people. Yet they lived in the tension of judgment and restoration. As they read Hosea in a new canonical context, they applied his message of repentance and loyalty to Yahweh to themselves. Moreover, Hosea provided them with a framework of understanding their age in the light of the new age. They believed that the Lord had been faithful to them by permitting them to share in the new age of restoration, yet the prophet led them to long and work for an even more wonderful fulfillment of God's promises. (See figure 15.)

In the coming of Jesus, the canonical function of the prophecy broadens further. Jesus is the love of God and the Divine Warrior incarnate. He brings salvation, transformation, and also judgment. All (including Gentiles) who belong to his body, the church, are grafted into the history of redemption, into the promises and covenants of God. They, too, must read the prophecy of Hosea in the new context of Jesus' incarnation, resurrection, and glorification. Hosea still has a distinct place within the community of faith as the prophet bears witness to the severity of God's judgment and the depth of his love. (See figure 15.)

Each new event in redemptive history challenges the community of faith to reread the prophetic word. The new canonical reading of Hosea involves the interpretation of both Hosea and the New Testament. Yet this rereading cannot set aside God's witness through his prophet. Since God has spoken through his prophet *and* through his Son (Heb. 1:1–3), he expects us to listen to both his servant and the Son. Their witnesses are complementary.

A study of the messianic prophecies in the New Testament reveals an intricate picture of the apostolic application of the Old Testament.[67] Micah 5 illustrates the complexity of hermeneutics. The magnificent prophecy of the Messiah's birth in Bethlehem (Mic. 5:2) is set within the historical context of the Assyrian Empire.

> He will deliver us from the Assyrian
> when he invades our land
> and marches into our borders.
>
> (Mic. 5:6).

HOSEA AS WITNESS OF THE NEW ERA

Hosea
| God's spokesman in Israel
└►Written form: Book of Hosea
　└►Function in Judah c. 722 B.C.
　　└►Function in Judah c. 700 B.C.
　　　└►Function in Judah c. 600 B.C.
　　　　└►Function among remnant of Israel and Judah in exile
　　　　　└►Function in post-exilic era
　　　　　　└►Function in New Testament
　　　　　　　└►Function in early church
　　　　　　　　└►Function throughout church history
　　　　　　　　　└►Function in the present era

Figure 15. The Canonical Reading of Hosea

Micah brings together into one grand mosaic the birth of the Messiah, the exile of Israel, the restoration of Israel, God's judgment on Assyria and the godless nations, and the exaltation and prosperity of Israel (chap. 5).

Micah's prophecy sheds light on the progress of redemption. True, Jesus was not born during the Assyrian regime. Assyria's domination came to an end at the battle of Carchemish (605 B.C.); Babylon propelled herself to power for seventy years; and Judah went into exile from 586 B.C. to 538 B.C. A remnant of the exiles returned in 536 B.C., but they were powerless and subject to hostile acts and foreign rulers. Assyria and Babylon had come to an end, their power being continued under different names. By the advent of our Lord, the Jews had tasted some of the benefits (Assyria's fall, restoration); but still awaited others (messianic kingdom, freedom from enemies and opposition, fullness of blessings).

Fulfillment cannot be restricted to Micah's time, to the postexilic era, or even to the coming of our Lord. It unfolds and clarifies the nature and time of fulfillment in the progress of redemption. I call this process of

82

unfolding *progressive fulfillment.* The hermeneutics of progressive fulfillment looks at God's promises as a vine that grows, extends its branches in various directions, bears fruit, and keeps developing. Applying this to redemptive history, I believe that we are still at the stage of branching and budding and that the stage of the mature, productive vine takes us to the second coming of our Lord.

The promises of God cannot be reduced to predictions. A prediction limits the word to a particular fulfillment, whereas a promise unfolds progressively over time. A promise is like a rolling snowball in its momentum and significance. Beecher aptly states this point: "Every fulfilled promise is a fulfilled prediction; but it is exceedingly important to look at it as a promise, and not as a mere prediction."[68]

Micah encouraged his contemporaries—and all who read his book— to look at the Messiah as the victorious King, the world as the realm of God's rule, and God's people as sharing in the victory and glory of their great King. This prophetic word still extends hope to God's people today. The very fact that the kingdom of God has not yet been fully and visibly established on earth is a motivating factor in hoping and praying that the child born in Bethlehem, Jesus the Christ, may soon come and inaugurate the eternal kingdom on earth.

Stability and Adaptability of the Canon

The prophetic message is applicable to a wide variety of historical contexts. With the addition of each book to the canon, the people of God were forced to ask how the writing changed their perception of God and his expectation of them. The Law of Moses forms the hub of the canon, to which the Prophets, the Writings, the Gospels, the Acts, the Epistles, and the Apocalypse were gradually added. Each book expanded the horizons of the godly and challenged the previous interpretation and understanding of God, humankind, salvation, the kingdom, and the world.

This process is most evident in the New Testament. The coming of our Lord radically altered the understanding of the Old Testament. The apostles understood the canon in the light of Jesus' ministry, message, and exaltation. The traditional understanding of Moses' words and the Prophets had to undergo a radical transformation in view of the coming of our Lord.[69]

Each new event in the progress of redemption and each new revelation challenge the received traditions. Each generation has to ask itself how to adapt to the light of the Lord's revelation. But the richness and diversity of God's revelation has often exposed human unwill- ingness to adapt to new forms of revelation. The Samaritans, for example, accepted only the Torah of Moses. Similarly, the Jewish people resisted the new revelation in Jesus Christ.[70]

God's people live in the dynamic tension of continuity and disconti-nuity.[71] The very way in which the community adapts to the revelation of God determines how it is willing to evaluate its faith and practices in the light of the Word of God.

Tradition and stabilization are inevitable. Tradition always develops when the Word of God is received as canon, that is, as the rule of faith and practice within the community of God's people. The new revelation or interpretation first destabilizes the belief system and practices of the community. But gradually, when an interpretation is accorded authority, a new stability sets in. The authoritative interpretation paves the way for a tradition; accordingly, it is a shortcut between interpretation and application. The stability of the canon is directly proportional to the acceptance of a given tradition. (See figure 16.)

```
God's Word
      Interpretation
            Stability
                  Tradition
                        Fresh interpretation
                              Tension
                                    Adaptability
                                          Reduction of Tension
                                                Stability
                                                      Tradition, etc.
```

Figure 16. Stability and Adaptability in Interpretation

The interpretation of God's Word naturally forms tradition, and tradition shapes interpretation. Traditional interpretation often leads to a *reductionistic hermeneutic* that is unable to adapt to either new revelation or new insight. This was already the situation when the prophets of God encountered the rigidity and systematization of their contemporaries.[72] Recognized leaders opposed the prophets by appeal to traditional interpretations, applications, and values. The Word becomes an "it" whenever people resist the Spirit.

Even though the fixation of the "meaning" of canonical writing brings stability to the community and an expression of faith, it is not without danger. Reception of God's Word sets in motion a wave that begins with renewed understanding of spiritual things and a spiritual renewal but all too often ends with a dead tradition and an unwillingness to apply God's Word to new contexts (2 Cor. 3:6). Thus the Word becomes an "it" whenever it supports human traditions.

Fixation in hermeneutics explains the differences between the Jews and the Samaritans and between the various groups of Pharisees and sects in Jesus' day. It also explains distinctive differences between Catholics and Protestants, between Reformed and Arminian, and between pre-, post-, and amillennialists.

The Spirit of God calls on each generation to respond anew to his revelation. He is the power who applies the Word of God to each new situation in the progress of redemption. He transforms human beings, interpretations, and traditions. As long as the Spirit is operating in and through the Word, the community of God's people lives in the tension between *stability* and *adaptability*.[73]

Each prophetic writing challenges the *stability* of the community. More than that, the prophetical books individually and collectively challenge our approach to and understanding of the New Testament.[74]

In the new revelation of God in Jesus Christ, the prophetic canon underwent another challenge. The people of God in the first century had to wrestle with many questions, such as what the Spirit of God was saying in the Scriptures of the Old Testament, how those Scriptures related to the mission of Jesus of Nazareth, how the church should adapt the old revelation to the new revelation (New Testament books), and how their system of faith and ways of living should be altered in the coming of the Spirit of Christ. These issues have to do with *adaptability*.[75]

Gradually stability set in, and the tension between Old and New was reduced in favor of the New Testament writings. The voice of the prophets became silenced, and the community's understanding of the apostles determined how the prophetic word should be understood. However, reducing the Old Testament to a minor premise is dangerous. This is done when tradition encourages reading the Old Testament in the light of the New Testament only.[76] The Old Testament is also all too often reduced to a collection of morals, prooftexts, or predictions.[77] The problem with the Old Testament is not found in its content, but in humans who ignore tensions and differences in favor of a preunderstanding (*vox populi*). The ancient heresy of Marcion (second century A.D.)—with its separation of Old from New, of God from Jesus, of creation from redemption, and of material from spiritual—has persisted throughout the history of the church.[78] It is a most serious misunderstanding of the gospel, as James A. Sanders writes,

> Any attempts to do away with the Old Testament, as in the Marcionite sense, therefore, is to do away with the peculiar image of Christ. . . . The New Testament image of Christ by its own admission and insistence, depends on the Old Testament; and the New Testament claims about him submit uniquely and only to the Old Testament judgment of them.[79]

REDEMPTIVE-HISTORICAL PERSPECTIVE

The Covenants and the Promises

God's commitment to and care for his creation flows from his covenant with creation. The revelation on the Creation, the Fall, the Flood, and the Noahic covenant (Gen. 1–9) proclaims God's kingship over all creation and his commitment to bless all life. The Lord has committed himself to sustain, bless, and transform his creation, even after the rebellion at Babel (11:1–9).

God has a plan for creation, which also involves his plan of redemption. His purpose for creation is the context for redemption and for extending his blessings to his people. Creation and redemption together form the matrix for understanding God's ways in Israel and in Jesus Christ. In other words, there is no redemption unless it affects the whole of creation (Rom. 8:19–25; Col. 1:13–23). Further, there is no Redeemer unless he is the Creator (John 1:3; Col. 1:15–17). (See figure 17.)

R E D E M P T I O N

| Covenant Renewal |
| Covenant with David |
| Covenant with Moses |
| Covenant with Abraham |
| Covenant with Creation |

O F   C R E A T I O N

Figure 17. The Covenants in Creation and in Redemption

Key redemptive elements in the early stages of the history of redemption are of cosmic significance: (1) God's blessing on the family, (2) the hope in "the seed" (Gen. 3:15), (3) the hope in God's provision of rest and comfort (5:29), (4) God's blessing on the fallen creation (9:1), (5) the regularity of nature (8:22), (6) the hope in God's presence (9:27),[80] and (7) God's special relationship with men of integrity (Enoch and Noah).

The *Abrahamic covenant* contains both national and cosmic dimensions.[81] The promises pertain to Abraham's descendants. God promises to be their God and to adopt them as his children (Gen. 12:2–3; 15:5, 18; 17:2–16). He promises to protect, bless, and prosper them (12:3; 22:17–18; 26:13–14). He also promises to give them the enjoyment of the land of Canaan in peace (28:13–15; 48:15–16). He promises to make them his instrument in bringing to himself all the clans of the family of man (12:3).

The eschatological dimensions of the promises bring into view the extension of God's presence beyond the boundaries of the Promised Land and beyond the physical descendants of Abraham to a world affected by judgment and curse. The Abrahamic covenant embraces all nations, the whole earth, and the eternal fulfillment of God's promises.

The *Mosaic covenant* applies the benefits of the Abrahamic covenant to Israel and extends the promises from the individual patriarchs to the entire nation.[82] The promises gain a certain concreteness through the existence of Israel in the land. The covenant at Mount Sinai inaugurates the fulfillment of the focal promise of God's presence among his people; that is, he established his kingship in Israel in his commitment to bless and protect his people.

The revelation of the divine attributes (Ex. 34:6) guarantees the continuity of covenant and promise. The future lies in God's faithfulness rather than in Israel's fickle nature! In the Mosaic covenant Israel received the revelation of the glory and love of God, adoption, and the oracles of the Lord (Rom. 3:1; 9:3−4). In their new status of adoption, they were called out to be God's holy and glorious servants: "a kingdom of priests and a holy nation" (Ex. 19:6). But their future also depended on their response to their covenant King. The Lord promised that the fulfillment was theirs if only they would respond to him in fidelity (Isa. 48:17−19).

The *Davidic covenant* (2 Sam. 7:8−16) adapts the promises of the covenants to a theocratic kingdom characterized by bliss, harmony, and peace.[83] God's covenant with David extends into eternity and is the basis of hope that enmity will cease and that God will be forever present with his people. The temple was the symbol of this commitment (Ps. 132).

The era of David and Solomon brought about a realization of the promises, while holding out a greater fulfillment. The election of David and David's election of Zion inaugurated a new era of God's presence, peace, prosperity, and rest from the enemies. Fulfillment reached a new height in Solomon's reign: the presence of the Lord, the prosperity of Israel, the establishment of God's kingdom, the multitude of Israelites, and the special relation of Yahweh with Solomon (1 Kings 1−10).

The postexilic prophets bore witness to the inauguration of eschatology in God's judgment (exile) *and* in his salvation (postexilic restoration). They proclaimed that God's acts *in history* are to be viewed as the eschatological curses and blessings. A disregard of this lengthy period from the return from exile to Jesus' day can lead only to a radical break between the Testaments. All too often we look at the Old as a history of

revelation, Israel's failure to respond, and God's subsequent judgment.
(See figure 18.)

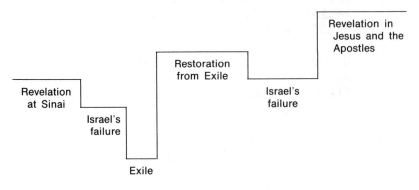

Figure 18. Old and New

Figure 18 emphasizes the importance of the postexilic era.[84] The
remnant did enjoy a restoration, a renewal of the covenants, and a
greater presence of the Spirit. They did experience a spiritual transformation, the presence of God, and the extension of his kingdom. But like
early Christianity, Judaism became stifled by cultural, political, social,
and religious rigidity. They, too, changed their focus from seeking the
kingdom of God to being complacent with human structures (synagogue, schools, teachers, temple, etc.). Living with hope was reduced to
a preoccupation with the past and present, as Yehezkel Kaufmann
reflects, "The people eagerly awaited the 'end of wonders,' but the end
never came. Then prophecy was stilled, the song of redemption frozen
on its lips, a divine enigma for the ages."[85]

Prophecy and Eschatology

In a sense the whole Bible is eschatological. The English words
"eschatological" and "eschatology" are derived from the Greek word
eschatos ("last"), but the etymology is ambiguous and slippery. I. Howard
Marshall observes, "We cannot abolish the use of the word, but we can
at least handle it with the care that we would bestow on any valuable but
slippery object."[86] The use of eschatology in this book accepts a broader
definition: biblical teaching which gives humans a perspective on their
age and a framework for living in hope of a new age.[87]

Interpretation of the prophets involves eschatology.[88] The prophets
announce the *closure* of one era and the *opening* of a new era. The *new era
in the progress of redemption* has elements of continuity with the past era
as the new acts of grace flow out of the promises of God. Yet the new

88

era has elements of discontinuity as God confirms an even grander fulfillment of his promises.

The prophets also point beyond their time to an eternity of time when God will fulfill the promises and covenants.[89] He will be with his people and rule over them with his Messiah from age to age. Beecher understood this emphasis well. Several decades ago he wrote,

> If one affirms that the promise is fulfilled in Jesus Christ, he ought not to separate that fulfillment from the rest of the eternal fulfilling movement. The idea of a long line of fulfillment is not a hypothesis offered for the solution of difficulties, but a part of the primary conception of a promise that is for eternity.[90]

The eschatological prophetic message is theocentric with its focus on the coming of the great King; the inauguration of the Davidic (messianic) era; the outpouring of the Holy Spirit; the renewal of the covenant; the renewal of the people of God; the ingathering of both Jews and Gentiles; the glory and joy associated with the presence of the Lord; the joy of God's people; the restoration of the land of Canaan, Jerusalem, and the earth; and the removal of evil, curse, death, and any other forms of divine judgment.[91]

In the coming of Jesus, the inauguration of the kingdom showed more clearly its eschatological dimension. The Gospels present the teaching and ministry of Jesus from the perspective of the risen Christ, who has come to fulfill the Law of Moses and the prophetic word. They integrate this with Jesus' teaching on the future—the Judgment, the elect, the Resurrection, the growth and joy of the kingdom with the prophetic hope. The past, present, and future come together in Jesus Christ.

The prophetic hope, rooted in the revelation to Israel with its progression in the divine covenants (creation, Abraham, Moses/Israel, David), receives its confirmation in the ministry of Jesus. In Jesus the future is full of hope because he is now seated at the right hand of the Father. The witness of the Old Testament and the New Testament finds its focus in Jesus through whom the Father will complete his plan of redemption (2 Cor. 1:20). He is the One of whom the prophets have spoken (Rom. 1:2; 16:26), and he is the Alpha and the Omega.

> Behold, I am coming soon! My reward is with me, and I will give to everyone according to what he has done. I am the Alpha and the Omega, the First and the Last, the Beginning and the End. Blessed are those who wash their robes, that they may have the right to the tree of life and may go through the gates into the city (Rev. 22:12–14).

The focus on Jesus does not negate the abiding validity of the Old Testament Law, Prophets, and Writings.[92] A restoration of the prophets as God's spokespersons to the twentieth century will also enrich the understanding of the message of Christ and his apostles. Their message on the Day of the Lord, the kingdom of God, the messianic era, the renewal of the people of God, the participation of the Gentiles with Israel in redemption, and the transformation of creation is God's word to us. The dual witness of Old and New as the Word of God for today will lead to refreshing results for our churches, evangelism, worship, and private lives.

Progressive Unfolding of the Plan of God

The prophetic kaleidoscope provides views from various angles into the progressive fulfillment of God's promises throughout the history of redemption, including the correlation of creation and redemption; the compenetration of several stages of fulfillment; the overlap of time and eternity; and the extension of the benefits of the new covenant to the saints of the Old Testament. Each prophet witnesses to the presence of judgment and salvation, to man's responsibility in the unfolding of salvation, and to Yahweh's commitment and freedom in bringing in the fullness of salvation.[93] (See figure 19.)

B.C. *and* A.D.

The differences between B.C. and A.D. are not to be minimized, even though they are too often magnified. The differences may be expressed in the words *greater, eschatological,* and *spiritual.* In Jesus the fulfillment of the prophetic hope is more real, as the nature of the hope gains greater clarity. This clarity is correlative with the greater revelation of the Father in the Son, in whom the fullness of the Godhead dwells incarnate (Heb. 1:1–2). In Jesus the eschaton (new age) is more present as evident in his miracles, the proclamation of the kingdom, and the Resurrection. The Resurrection is *the* sign of the new age (the eschaton). Another sign of the eschaton is the outpouring of the Holy Spirit. The Spirit indwells and ministers to believers in anticipation of the resurrection yet to come and the fullness of the eschatological age.[94]

The prophets present a new perspective. They proclaim that all God's people, regenerated by the Spirit of God, live between the two foci of creation and the new creation. They live in the tension between this world with its *Realpolitik* and the presence of the kingdom of God. For God's people, eschatology is always here as they experience the evidences of God's kingdom in blessing and in judgment. During the present age the world is under God's judgment, but the children of God already receive their Father's goodness as tokens of the glory awaiting them. In the tension between creation and the new creation they live *in faith,* awaiting the fullness of salvation. This means that everything is B.C. *and* A.D.[95] This means that all acts and revelations of God in Old and in New are *anno Domini* ("in the year of our Lord") and that the whole progress of redemption is *before the coming* (of Christ), that is, the era of climactic fulfillment at his second coming. Not only does this do justice to the whole of Scripture (*tota Scriptura*),[96] but it also avoids the danger of isolating the acts of God in the first advent of Christ from the involvement of the Trinity in creation and in the history of Israel. (See figure 19.)

Before the Coming (of Christ)

CREATION   NEW CREATION

Anno Domini

Figure 19. B.C. and A.D.

The New Testament confirms the prophetic hope by its witness that in Jesus Christ the promises of God are true.[97] Consequently, Jesus is the focus of hope; the reality and fulfillment of all divine promises are guaranteed in him. The salvation of which the prophets have spoken (1 Peter 1:10–12) is found in none other than Jesus Christ. However, only the Father knows the nature, manner, and time of the fullness of salvation (Acts 1:7). Since fulfillment is in Jesus Christ (2 Cor. 1:20), the complete fulfillment of the promises is the object of hope by both the Old Testament and the New Testament saints. Both Old Testament and New Testament witness to the salvation to come and to the exclusive claims of Jesus that he is the way by which the Father will fully inaugurate all the promises and covenants, including the rule of David.[98]

The Age to Come

The assumption that the New Testament is the fulfillment of the Old Testament drives a wedge between the Testaments, as both Old and New witness to the age to come. The acts of God in Egypt, in the conquest, in the Davidic-Solomonic era, in the two kingdoms, in the postexilic period, and in Christ create a hope for a greater reality, a greater salvation, and a greater establishment of God's kingdom.

The Old Testament people of God lived in the tension of present and future reality, between the past acts of God and the promise of the future acts of God. The same may be said of the New Testament writers who look forward to the age of fulfillment: the day of salvation (1 Thess. 1:10).[99] The phrase "this age" (Matt. 12:32; Luke 20:34–35; 1 Tim. 4:8) applies to life between creation and the new creation. This

91

age, in the words of Ladd, is "the age of human existence in weakness and mortality, of evil, sin, and death."[100]

The "age[s] to come" (Luke 18:30; 20:35; Eph. 2:7; Heb. 6:5) is always present, as our Father blesses and protects his children, assuring them of the nearness of the new age (i.e., eschatology). The present and the future overlap so that the future overshadows the present. It is clear that every act of special grace (covenant, promise, blessing, and fulfillment) is a *present* reality of the age to come!

The phrase "the age to come" relates to the prophetic designation "in that day," "in the last days," or "in those days" (Isa. 2:2; Jer. 33:16; Joel 2:29). The phrase the "age to come" applies to God's word of hope as God's people await a new age. Isaiah, Jeremiah, and Ezekiel comforted the godly remnant with the eschatological hope that after the Exile, the Lord will open a new era of forgiveness, covenant renewal, and restoration. For example, Isaiah made the distinction between "the former" and "the latter" (or "the new"), signifying the era before the fall of Jerusalem and the exile of her population as "the former" and the process of restoration as "the latter" (Isa. 41:4; 42:9; 43:19; 65:17; Zech. 1:4; 7:7).

The relationship between Old and New is held together by their common witness to Jesus Christ, the King of Kings and Lord of Lords. The Jesus of the Gospels, the Epistles, and the Apocalypse is the glorious Son of God, the eschatological Prophet, the hope of the ages: "I am the Root and the Offspring of David, and the bright Morning Star" (Rev. 22:16). Jesus came to bring in the consummation, establish the kingdom of God, and fulfill all the promises of God (Acts 3:19–21). Reality, fulfillment, and hope lie in our glorious Lord.

The center of the revelation of God's design in redemptive history is Jesus Christ. The central thesis of the Bible is that history is the record of the outworking of God's purposes and that redemptive history is the revelation of the outworking of God's designs. The beginning and the end have meaning in the incarnation of the Son of God (Col. 1:15–17, 19–20).[101]

The coming of Jesus at the midpoint of redemptive history guarantees the end. The end will come according to the design of God because in Jesus he guarantees victory, redemption, and the resolution of the struggle between good and evil: "For he has rescued us from the dominion of darkness and brought us into the kingdom of the Son he loves, in whom we have redemption, the forgiveness of sins" (Col. 1:13–14). The Father has appointed his Son to bring in the fullness of the new age and therefore expects that all who seek the Father will first submit themselves to his Son. But the end will be the glorious beginning of the everlasting movement of fulfillment!

REVIEW

The hermeneutic of this chapter may be summed up in twelve theses.

1. The promises of God, as confirmed in the covenants with creation, Abraham, Moses, and David, are the object of hope of God's people before and after the coming of the Messiah, our Lord. (See figure 20.)

2. The prophets develop and apply the promises of God. The Old Testament prophets have very few predictions that may be directly applied to their time or to any nation, person, or event. The prophetic message may best be seen as a collage of prophetic utterances in which each prophecy or oracle has its own setting and may not be isolated from the holistic interpretation of the book as a whole.[102] (See figure 20.)

The predictions take the form of promise, and the promises are temporal expressions of God's eternal plan. Beecher makes the point by stating that "every fulfilled promise is a fulfilled prediction; but it is exceedingly important to look at it as a promise, and not as a mere prediction."[103] Similarly, Gurdon C. Oxtoby writes,

> The essential Christian position is one of fulfillment rather than prediction. . . . *The marvel is not that any prophet foretold. The marvel is that Jesus fulfills. . . .* The wonder is in the consummation that has come about because of Christ. To glorify prediction rather than fulfillment is to misunderstand the nature of the forecast, and to miss the significance of the Christian gospel.[104] (See figure 20.)

Hope: Promises of the Father
Focus: Jesus Christ
Power: Spirit of restoration
Tota Scriptura: Old and New Testaments
Progressive fulfillment

Involvement of Father, Son, and Holy Spirit
Continuities and discontinuities
Tokens of eschatological realization in history of redemption
Freedom of God
Correlation of Creation and redemption
Involvement of humans: Submission, interpretation, application

Figure 20. Progressive Fulfillment

3. The prophetic word is God's word of hope to his people before and after Christ. The prophets bore witness in their different emphases to the grandeur of God's redemption as well as to God's wisdom in working out his promises. The sheer vastness in size of the prophetic

93

word should guard against oversimplification.[105] They called on their contemporaries to look to the Lord for the fulfillment of the promises in accordance with his immutable plan. Certainly tensions exist between the enjoyment of the covenant promises and the fullness, as Bright reminds us,

> So, like Israel of old, we have to live in tension. It is the tension between grace and obligation: the unconditional grace of Christ which is proffered to us, his unconditional promises in which we are invited to trust, and the obligation to obey him as the church's sovereign Lord.[106]

The focus of the hope in the fulfillment of God's promises is Jesus Christ, the midpoint of redemptive history.[107] The language of hope comes to expression when we recognize that the language of eschatology is the language of metaphor.[108] When we speak of what God has prepared for his people, as witnessed to by Moses and the prophets and by Jesus and his apostles, we cannot use the language of sight. We must use the language of vision, which is an extension of metaphor. Frederick Ferré has defined the language of metaphor as an expression of man's finitude and God's freedom.

> Surely it is meaningful for each man to hope that the metaphors he adopts as his own . . . are not without basis of similarity. . . . The rest he must hold only as a hope and a constant reminder of the finitude of the knower. . . . The rest . . . he must be content to "leave in God's hands."[109]

The elements of prophetic hope include (1) the anticipation of God's rule in Zion, (2) the universal acknowledgment of God's rule and the eradication of idolatry, (3) the revelation of God's glory and splendor, (4) the abolition of evil and tyranny, (5) the sanctification of God's name and the establishment of God's kingdom on earth, (6) the hope of the imminent coming of the day of salvation and judgment, and (7) the hope of salvation and fulfillment of the promises.[110]

4. The working out of God's plan is progressive as the promises become more and more specific and as they are more fully enjoyed by the godly. This means that the benefits of God conferred on the postexilic community were greater than those granted the preexilic people and also that the present benefits in Christ are greater than those of the postexilic era of restoration. Nevertheless, we keep Beecher's caution in mind.

> If one affirms that the promise is fulfilled in Jesus Christ, he ought not to separate that fulfillment from the rest of the eternal fulfilling movement. The idea of a long line of fulfillment is not a hypothesis

offered for the solution of difficulties, but a part of the primary conception of a promise that is for eternity.[111]

5. Though the promises are eternally operative and the fulfillment is progressive,[112] the interpreter of the prophetic word must carefully listen to the prophets as God's witnesses in time and space. The prophetic word is God's Word addressed to his people in a culturally and historically conditioned context. The study of the word invites our listening to the prophetic speech in another historical context. The speech forms are diverse but essentially may be classified as oracles of judgment and oracles of salvation. As forms of prophetic speech the oracles address real people living in a historical context. The horizons of this historical context are twofold. First, Elijah's charges against Israel at Mount Horeb mark the evident inauguration of the messages of judgment, in which all the prophets share as covenant prosecutors. Second, the new era after the Exile marks the era of catharsis, renewal, and eschatology.

6. The prophets consistently call on the people of God to be open to the new acts of God and to evaluate the old acts in the light of the new. This way of looking at the world is what Sanders calls "the hermeneutic of prophetic critique."[113] The prophetic message uniformly warns most strongly against human structures and institutions, especially religious ones. The contest between the power of man and the power of the Spirit always leads to human bondage because the Spirit is free. Those who are truly liberated experience the eschaton. Yet the faithful before and after Christ live in the tension of the present reality of salvation and the glorious, eternal fulfillment of the promises of God in Christ.[114]

7. The work of Christ is *continuous* with the work of God in the Old Testament but *discontinuous* with the religious structures of humankind. The coming of Christ marks the watershed in redemptive history. In Christ's coming the eschaton rushed in more evidently as the glorious Son of God became flesh. The distinction between Old and New may be explained by the difference in emphases: national and universal, material and spiritual, type and antitype, prefigurement and reality, promise and fulfillment. Yet as long as we await the universal, spiritual, and real fulfillment, we, too, live in hope of the promise that Jesus is the fulfiller of the promises of God.

The emphasis on the spiritual in the New Testament may be explained as arising from a context in which people were preoccupied with their physical existence and the material outworking of God's plan in a grand messianic age.[115] However, our Lord did refer to the physical-material fulfillment of the promises, as he taught, "Blessed are the meek, for they will inherit the earth" (Matt. 5:5; cf. Ps. 37:11; Rom. 4:13). Hence caution is in order not to generalize a hermeneutic from

Augustine's saying, "The Old is in the New revealed and the New is in the Old concealed." The argument goes like this: Since the New Testament reveals that the sacrifices and institutions in the Old Testament are types, shadows, and symbols of the ministry of our Lord, the New Testament revelation eclipses the Old Testament revelation.

A. B. Davidson represents those who read the Prophets in the light of the New: "And the thing itself being come, to which they pointed, they have now themselves fallen away."[116] This hermeneutic assumes that the New Testament addresses all concerns of the Old Testament, that New Testament scholars are in general agreement on its meaning, which they are not, and that the fulfillment is here. The danger of this separation of the Testaments lies in the shift in focus from Jesus Christ as the fulfiller to the New Testament as the fulfillment, from the church industrious to the church victorious, and from anticipation of the coming of our Lord to a glorification of Jesus' earthly and present ministry.

8. The interpretation of the prophetic word as a part of *tota Scriptura* is not just an option for those who are so inclined; it is the imperative for the church of Jesus Christ. True discipleship demands that the disciples of Christ long for the consolation of Israel and for the restoration of all things. Kirkpatrick writes that "the great lines of thought" of the Prophets come together in Christ "in a wholly new combination, the spring of fresh forces and larger hopes for the world."[117] This implies that a transformation of the prophetic message takes place in the coming of our Lord and in the apostolic mission. But the advance in the progress of redemption only enhances the place of the Prophets as the "old" becomes "new"; that is, "It is not fulfilled and exhausted, but fulfilled and illuminated."[118]

The fresh combination of the manifold teaching of the prophets and of our Lord and the apostles inspires the reader of Scripture to greater hope and longing for the coming of our Lord, who alone is the reality and who is Lord in the outworking of the Father's plan of redemption. The New Testament affirms the place for eschatological hope, as C. K. Barrett puts it,

> This conviction that God has yet greater things to do than the great things He has already done for us, that He is the God of the future as well as the past, is supplemented in NT eschatology by the equally strong conviction that God is no more confined to the future than He is to the past, and that, being *free* at all times, He has acted as decisively and as revealingly, in the mid-course of history as He will do at its end; or, in other words, that the end of history, and with it God's unique and conclusive action which declares not only His own character but also the meaning of all history, has already begun.[119]

9. The freedom of God demands that interpretation of the prophetic word, in conjunction with the teaching of our Lord and of his apostles, be conducted with the greatest humility. Even though the Lord has revealed his plan of redemption, he has not given a diagram for interpreting the unfolding or progression of this plan to his people. Torrance warns us most urgently against treating the Scriptures like calculus,

> However, there is no formal or hermeneutical way of anticipating such a disclosure in the future on the ground of what has already been disclosed, for precisely the same reason, namely, that biblical statements indicate far more than they can express. The ultimate Truth of God to which they point beyond themselves is so unlimited in his intelligibility and freedom that he breaks through the calculus of our predictions and keeps on disclosing himself in quite unexpected ways.[120]

10. The proper response to the freedom of God is the imitation of Christ, including a hungering and thirsting for the righteousness of the kingdom of God and a zeal for his kingdom and glory.[121] Redemptive theology may risk the reduction to the present and the removal of the longing for the age to come. But the context of redemption within the framework of creation intensifies the tension between creation in alienation and the promises of a holistic redemption. Thus a proper regard for creation as the sphere of God's operation leads to a longing for a restoration of order. God's new order in this world will bring harmony, the rule of God, and the everlasting bliss of the people of God. Hence, Schmid proposes to look at all theology as an expression of creation theology: "All theology is creation theology, even when it does not speak expressly of creation but speaks of faith, justification, the reign of God, or whatever, if it does so in relation to the world. And it must do that as long as it makes any claim of being responsible."[122]

11. God has revealed aspects of his plan of redemption of creation, but not the comprehensive knowledge. In Jesus Christ he has further confirmed his commitment of cosmic salvation (John 3:16). Although all lines of promise converge in Jesus Christ, we do not know how all promises will be realized in that God is free. The freedom of God and the failure of systems of human interpretation must be constant reminders not to absolutize, principalize, or systematize the glorious future into a grand scheme. So von Rad writes, "God's power in history is complete. . . . But God's sovereignty in history is hidden; it mocks the most clever and profound human criteria and confronts man with impenetrable riddles. . . . God is mobilizing history for his great future."[123] This means also that those who deny a place for ethnic Israel in the purposes of God *and* those who work out the details of this plan are

guilty of playing God. Beecher reminds us that since the promise is eternally operative and since we are not yet at the end of eternity, we are "not qualified to say whether in this particular the promise corresponds with the fulfillment."[124] John Bright correctly defines *eschatology* in the broad sense as faith in the Lord who will fulfill all his promises.[125]

12. The prophetic message has a bearing on the parameters of biblical hope and on the proper response to this hope.[126] Through the progressive revelation of God (preexilic, exilic, postexilic; in Christ, and apostolic), there is a constant factor whose significance increases with the increment of the acts of God in redemptive history. Figure 21 outlines this for us.

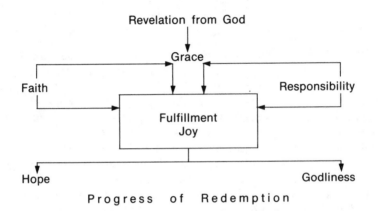

Figure 21. Revelation and Redemption

The greater the revelation, the greater the grace; the greater the grace, the greater the faith; the greater the faith, the greater the responsibility; the greater the responsibility, the greater the fulfillment; the greater the fulfillment, the greater the joy; the greater the joy, the greater the hope; and the greater the hope, the greater the desire for godliness.

The *parameter* is distinct from the *perimeter* of the prophetic message. The perimeter, as the outer boundary, pertains to the revelation of the God who acts sovereignly and freely in establishing his kingdom, regardless of man's responsiveness. He is faithful and assures the people of God in all ages that his work of redemption will come to fruition, that his acts have a purpose, and that his purpose is hidden in his secret counsel. The plan of God calls for a response from the godly community, and this response must be commensurate with the revelation given. Hence the parameter expands in proportion to the revelation and acts of the Lord.

QUESTIONS AND ISSUES

1. Define: adaptability, age-to-come, hermeneutics, metaphor, oracle of judgment, oracle of salvation, stability.
2. What attitudes does the Spirit expect of the interpreter of the prophetic word?
3. What are the "ingredients" of interpretation?
4. How is the prophetic word set in a cultural-historical context?
5. Was the prophetic person conscious at the moment of revelation?
6. What difference does it make whether we approach the prophetic literature with the assumption that the prophet was primarily an *orator* or a *writer*?
7. What is the place of literary analysis in understanding the prophets?
8. How does the canonical function of a prophetic book shift in the different historical circumstances?
9. Relate canonical function, stability, adaptability, and hermeneutics.
10. What are the dangers inherent in stability and in adaptability? Why is tension in interpretation a positive ingredient?
11. What are the four covenants? Relate these to the promises of covenant renewal in the postexilic era.
12. Explain how the correlation of creation and redemption keeps God's people from a closed system of hermeneutics.
13. How does a regard for God's acts in the postexilic era affect the relationship between Old and New?
14. What is the prophetic eschatology? Relate this to the progressive unfolding of redemption.

Part 2

The Message of the Minor Prophets

Introduction to Part 2

We shall begin our study of the prophetic word with an examination of the Minor Prophets (Hosea-Malachi). The term *Minor Prophets* is based on the size of the written oracles. The relatively small size of the writings has an advantage in that the message of these prophets may help us delve into the complexity of the many prophetic literary features, images, and motifs.

To accomplish this end we shall consider these writings in their canonical order and in their historical context. We shall also pay attention to distinctive literary features and motifs in each one. It is tempting to consider a variety of motifs, but I have chosen to select those motifs that have a bearing on the prophetic message as a whole in its rich diversity (see chap. 8: "Summary of Prophetic Motifs").

The distinctive contribution of the prophets is related to the historical *and* canonical situation. By *historical* I mean the temporal and cultural context in which the prophet spoke God's words of warning, judgment, exhortation, and hope. The minor prophets take us from 760 B.C. till well into the fifth century B.C. They announced the end of Damascus (732 B.C.), Samaria (722 B.C.), Nineveh (612 B.C.), Jerusalem (586 B.C.), and the kingdoms of their day (Aram, Israel, Assyria, Judah, etc.). The *canonical* dimension pertains to the process of collecting, writing, and transmitting the prophetic speech, permitting another generation to read these oracles as the Word of God inspired by the Spirit of God. One God spoke to many prophets over the centuries. This means that while we shall consider the diversity in prophetic motifs, the prophetic word unfolds a magnificent unity. The unifying factors are found in the interpretation and reinterpretation of the covenants and the promises of God.[1] (See table 5.)

I have made no attempt to systematize the motifs. However, it is my hope that the approach laid out in the first three chapters may encourage the student of prophecy to study more closely the unique message of the prophets and to relate the prophecies to each other and to the message of our Lord and his apostles.

TABLE 5. THE MINOR PROPHETS

Prophet		Historical Context (Time)	Canonical Context (Book)	Message
Hosea	750	Israel	Judah	Yahweh is holy in his love
Joel	425	Locust plague	Remnant	The Spirit of God is the guarantee of the fullness of restoration
Amos	760	Israel	Judah	The Day of the Lord: Desolation and restoration
Obadiah	580	Exile	Exilic/post-exilic	The kingdoms of this world will become the Lord's
Jonah	700	Evil of Nineveh	Exilic/post-exilic	The freedom of the Lord
Micah	725	Israel/Judah	Judah	The kingdom of God and of his Messiah
Nahum	630	Nineveh	Judah	Yahweh is the Divine Warrior
Habakkuk	605	Rise of Babylon	Judah	Yahweh's righteousness and the triumph of faith
Zephaniah	630	Josiah's reforms	Judah	The Day of the Lord: Vengeance, purification, and restoration
Haggai	520	New era	Remnant	Now is the day of fulfillment
Zechariah	520	New era	Remnant	Vision of Zion's glory
Malachi	460	Apathy	Remnant	Yahweh loves the $s^e gull\hat{a}$

CHAPTER 4

Hosea, Joel, and Amos

Hosea: The love of Yahweh
   Hosea and his time
   Literary form and structure
     Literary form
     Structure
   The message of Hosea
     Israel is a prostitute
     Yahweh's judgment
     Repentance and remnant
     The depth and mystery of Yahweh's love
     The hope of restoration
       The new people of God
       The renewal of the covenants
       The new leadership
     Conclusion
Joel: The Day of the Lord and the Spirit of restoration
   Joel and his time
   Literary form and structure
     Literary form
     Structure
   The message of Joel
     The Day of the Lord
     Today is the day of salvation
     The Spirit of restoration
     The democratization of the Spirit
Amos: Yahweh is the author of desolation and restoration
   Amos and his time
   Literary form and structure
     Literary form
     Structure
   The message of Amos
     Yahweh's theophany
     Judgment is determined

HOSEA: THE LOVE OF YAHWEH

Hosea and His Time

Hosea, one of the last prophets to the northern kingdom,[1] was raised in a period of opulence, prosperity, opportunism, and scheming during which the rich and powerful availed themselves of all opportunities to live luxuriously. Hosea was God's messenger (ca. 753 B.C.) to a complacent, self-indulgent, and apostate people. He had a deep sense of mission, of belonging to the prophetic tradition, and of his redemptive historical place. Hosea was also well acquainted with the history and the geography of the northern kingdom, as evident from the geographical references.[2]

Hosea was God's spokesman to the last generation of Israel. He proclaimed and witnessed the fall of Jehu's dynasty (1:4). He denounced Israel's palace intrigues, political ambitions, and attempts at political survival. Politics brought with it conspiracy, treachery, and anarchy as an international power struggle for "world domination" raged outside. He called for absolute loyalty to Yahweh and abandonment of *Realpolitik* (14:2–3). Truly, he was "the messenger of her [Israel's] end, and more importantly, the messenger of Israel's God, to whom he had to bear witness as Lord also of this end."[3]

The concurrent reigns of Uzziah of Judah (792–740 B.C.) and Jeroboam II of Israel (793–753 B.C.) rivaled the "golden age" of David and Solomon in prosperity and peace (see 2:4–17).[4] Israel had successfully recovered from the Aramean incursions (2 Kings 14:25). Trade and commerce flourished. The politicians and merchants in Samaria improved their living standards, but the workers and farmers suffered poverty, hunger, and oppression. Israel was rotting from within.

Israel had also become proud, and economic progress only added to its self-confidence. The social structure encouraged power, greed, self-indulgence, corruption of justice, luxurious living among the upper classes, and the decay of social unity. The affluent showed no sense of responsibility toward the poor. As the gap between the rich and the poor became ominously wide, the poor were reduced to the level of slaves while the aristocracy imitated royalty and adopted a lavish lifestyle.[5]

Prosperity had brought an unprecedented degree of cultural corruption. The much-sought-after political power had opened Israel to foreign cultural influence, including the demoralizing influence of Canaanite Baal worship (2:7, 17; 11:2) with its fertility cults and bacchanalian orgies (4:10–13). Sacred prostitution was rampant (Amos 2:7–8). Perversion of the Mosaic faith was seen at the sanctuaries of Dan and Bethel.

Israelite religion was syncretistic, adapting to cultural changes in the ancient Near East. It continued the multiplicity of sacrifices, offerings, and tithes (8:11, 13; 9:4; 10:1; Amos 5:22) and adapted to Assyrian religious expressions (Amos 5:16).[6] Sanctuaries were crowded with worshipers who joined the erotic, religious rites that were part of pagan rituals. Her priests were corrupt like the people (4:4–9; 5:1; 6:9). These practices led to the rapid decay of the essence of Israel's existence as the people of God. The shallowness of Israel's commitment to Yahweh posed a real threat to the nation and to society as a whole.

Hosea ministered God's word to a people who still enjoyed the benefits of the economic boom but were about to experience national crises in rapid succession (7:7; 8:4). He proclaimed that Israel's security and alliance with foreign powers would eventually lead to her destruction.[7]

Hosea began his ministry with the annunciation of Yahweh's judgment on Jehu's dynasty (1:4) shortly before 753 B.C. Within a generation Israel's power, economic and cultural superiority, and international repute eroded.[8] Israel experienced instability from within because of the rapid political changes in Samaria (7:7; 8:4). Shallum (752 B.C.) ruled for one month (2 Kings 15:8–15) and was killed by Menahem, who ruled for ten years (752–742 B.C.). Menahem strengthened his position by paying tribute (v. 19) to Tiglath-pileser III of Assyria (745–727 B.C.). Pekahiah succeeded him but was murdered by Pekah, his captain (v. 25).

Pekah (740–732 B.C.) formed a political alliance with Aram (Rezin). Together, after Ahaz had refused to join the confederacy (5:8–11), they attacked Ahaz of Judah. With Ahaz's encouragement Assyria became involved in the Syro-Ephraimite region and attacked Aram, exiled her population, reduced Damascus to rubble, and extended her military control to within Israel in 732 B.C. (2 Kings 15:29; Hos. 5:8–11).[9] Tiglath-pileser III, the Assyrian king, also set up Hoshea as king over Israel (732 B.C.) (5:13–14; 7:8–9; 8:9–10), meanwhile permitting Israel a relatively autonomous political life. Hoshea's ambitions, moreover, conflicted with Assyria's interests when he made a political alliance with Egypt (2 Kings 17:4; see Hos. 5:13; 7:11; 9:3; 11:5; 12:1). The Assyrian response came in the form of a siege of Samaria under Shalmaneser V, who destroyed Samaria and exiled her inhabitants.[10] (See table 6.)

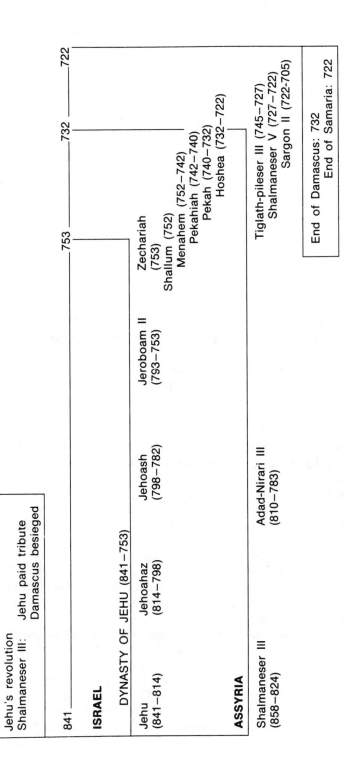

TABLE 6. THE LAST DAYS OF ISRAEL

Jehu's revolution
Shalmaneser III: Jehu paid tribute
                    Damascus besieged

841 _____ 753 _____ 732 _____ 722

ISRAEL

DYNASTY OF JEHU (841–753)

Jehu   Jehoash   Jeroboam II
(841–814)   (798–782)   (793–753)

                                Zechariah
                                (753)
                                Shallum (752)
                                Menahem (752–742)
                                Pekahiah (742–740)
                                Pekah (740–732)
                                Hoshea (732–722)

ASSYRIA

Shalmaneser III   Adad-Nirari III   Tiglath-pileser III (745–727)
(858–824)   (810–783)   Shalmaneser V (727–722)
                                        Sargon II (722–705)

End of Damascus: 732
End of Samaria: 722

The way of God with Israel is best reflected in Hosea's relationship with Gomer. Her infidelities represented Israel's apostasy, her children spoke of Yahweh's judgment, and Hosea's willingness to take Gomer back depicted Yahweh's love for Israel. Though Gomer had been unfaithful to him, he willingly accepted the ridicule and disgrace that came from taking her back. Thus Hosea unveiled the details of his married life so all Israel would stand aghast at Gomer's adultery and at Hosea's love for his adulterous wife. Yet his love for Gomer symbolically pointed to Yahweh's deep love for apostate Israel. The marriage analogy also provides psychological insight into the prophet. He must have suffered from the strains in his marriage as well as from criticism and rejection by his contemporaries (9:7–8).

Literary Form and Structure

Literary form[11]

As an ambassador of God, Hosea spoke *for* God (12:9; 13:4) and *against* the people (lawsuit or legal disputation, 2:2; 4:1; 12:2).[12] He showed clear affinities with the prophetic[13] and wisdom traditions (14:9). Some oracles have the characteristic "divine speech" (i.e., where "Yahweh speaks in the first person"), and others have the formulaic language of "prophetic speech" (third person).[14] The distinctive prophetic speech forms in Hosea are the *rîb* ("legal disputation"), with its lament, threats, and accusations (4:6–7; 5:11; 7:8–9; 8:1–14); exhortations (2:2–3; 4:15; 8:5; 14:1–2); didactic forms (2:21–22; 5:1; 8:7); precepts (6:6);[15] and salvation oracles (14:5–9).[16] His style is lively and well adapted to the life situation of the northern kingdom, as Wolff observes, "Thus Hosea's audience must have been struck by the great number of metaphors he employed. In principle he omits no sphere of life; but the imagery drawn from the vegetable and animal world and from family life clearly predominates."[17] His literary style employs proverbs, parallelism, catchwords, irony, similes, metaphors, repetition, assonance, and wordplays.[18]

Hosea's prophecies to the northern kingdom were later recorded and gathered into a collection. After the fall of Samaria, the godly community in Judah applied the prophetic message to themselves and preserved the prophetic tradition in written form.[19] Of course, the change in canonical function and historical context necessitated changes in interpretation and application, such as Hosea's condemnation of Israel's involvement with the fertility cults, pagan cultures, *Realpolitik*, adaptation to the world, and isolation from God. This also means that the typological significance of Hosea's marriage analogy has a general application to God's people. Hosea's concluding appeal calls on each new generation to assess its way in the light of God's revelation (14:9).

Hosea was God's prophet to Israel, who in his writing also spoke to Judah (1:7, 11; 4:15; 5:5, 10, 13; 6:4, 11; 11:12; 12:2) and still speaks to all who are grafted into the covenant of grace. The canonical function of Hosea extends beyond the fall of Samaria (722 B.C.) to the southern kingdom, to the postexilic era, and also to the church of Jesus Christ.

Structure[20]

A. Superscription, 1:1
  B. Part One: Yahweh and Israel, 1:2–3:5
    1. The marriage of Hosea and Gomer, 1:2–2:1
    2. Judgment and hope, 2:2–23
    3. Hosea and his wife: restoration, 3:1–5
      C. Part Two: Fourteen prophetic speeches, 4:1–14:8
        1. *Rîb* ("lawsuit") against the Israelites who lack knowledge of the Torah, 4:1–19
        2. Judgment (*mišpāt*) against the priests, king, and people, 5:1–15
        3. Warning against pragmatic repentance, 6:1–11
        4. Case against the kings and leaders, 7:1–16
        5. Case against self-reliant Israel, 8:1–14
        6. Case against pagan Israel, 9:1–9
        7. Case against unfaithful Ephraim, 9:10–17
        8. The fall of Samaria, 10:1–8
        9. Israel's fall due to its longstanding apostasy, 10:9–15
        10. Yahweh's love for Israel, 11:1–11
        11. Israel's long history of rebellion, 11:12–12:14
        12. Ephraim's helplessness, 13:1–11
        13. Ephraim's fall and Yahweh's promise to redeem, 13:12–16
        14. Call to repentance and promise of restoration, 14:1–8
        D. Epilogue, 14:9

The Message of Hosea

In spite of the certain and impending judgment of Israel's sin, Hosea magnificently *demonstrates* and *describes* the love and grace of God. This message of Yahweh's love for a rebellious people and of his chastisement, healing, and restoration is relevant for God's people in any age.

Israel Is a Prostitute

The people, whom the Lord had blessed, had rebelled against their Maker and Redeemer.

> When I fed them, they were satisfied;
>   when they were satisfied, they became proud;

> then they forgot me.
>
> (13:6; see also 5:5; 7:10)

This theme is dramatically depicted in the marriage analogy. Hosea's marriage to Gomer was by God's command. It is unclear whether Gomer was a known (temple) prostitute or simply a woman prone to infidelity.[21] The symbolic significance of Gomer lies in her role as a parody of Israel, which had become dependent on the Canaanite fertility cults[22] for purposes of cultural identity.[23] The children born to Hosea and Gomer—*Jezreel* ("bloodshed"), *Lo-Ammi* ("not my people"), and *Lo-Ruhamah* ("without compassion")[24]—were symbolic of Yahweh's wrath and judgment on the king (Jezreel) and the people (Lo-Ruhamah and Lo-Ammi) alike.

Israel cheapened grace, the covenant, and her unique covenantal relationship with Yahweh by a narcissistic way of life. She learned from the nations that everything has a price, and she exchanged her loyalty to Yahweh for the gods of prosperity, power, and sex. Israel chose an alternate lifestyle that encouraged greed, passion, riches, the fast pace of life, a disregard for human beings, and a complacency with God. Israel no longer had the distinctives of a counterculture shaped by divine revelation.[25] Yahweh gave Israel life ("what is good," 8:3; see v. 1), but they disregarded revelation as something alien (v. 12). (See figure 22.)

God's people adapted to the ways of the nations (*Realpolitik*). They were enticed by the material achievements of the nations and aimed at putting Israel on the map by over-production, export, import, political alliances, and cultural exchanges.

> For they have gone up to Assyria
> like a wild donkey wandering alone.
> Ephraim has sold herself to lovers.
>
> (8:9)

The prophet repeatedly condemned the people for having forsaken their primary allegiancë to Yahweh for an adulterous commitment to national, economic, and social interests (4:1–2; 12:8; 13:2). Their food and drink depended on the structures of their society, and the structures of society depended on their ability to keep harmonious relations with the surrounding nations. Priests, prophets, kings, and rulers had led God's people *from* the Lord *to* syncretism, acculturation, and *Realpolitik*.

The people were religious. They proliferated the religious sites and readily made their offerings to appease the deities: "Though Ephraim built many altars for sin offerings, these have become altars for sinning" (8:11). In presenting their sacrifices, the people did not realize that they placated neither God nor their conscience (9:4–5). They were intoxicated with their religiosity, and religion became the cause of their fall (4:1–19).

110

Israel became like a "spreading vine" from which the Lord expected love, devotion, and righteousness, but instead Israel produced a long history of infidelity, oppression, and injustice, which led to paganism (10:1). Though they acknowledged Yahweh, they did not know him (8:2). In vain did the Lord look for faithfulness, love, and "knowledge" (*da'at,* NIV "acknowledgment") of God (4:1). Since they did not "know" him, Yahweh rejected their sacrifices (8:13) and challenged the godly to discern and cultivate a spirit of wisdom: "For I desire goodness [*hesed*], not sacrifice; obedience (*da'at,* lit. "knowledge") to God, rather than burnt offerings" (6:6 JPS). Obedience (*da'at*) and "love in action" (*hesed,* NIV "mercy") are the basic ingredients of a vital covenant relationship, that is, conjugal fidelity.[26]

In their intoxication with cultural, material, and political achievements, they had become entrapped by the materialism of the nations. The people of Israel were ignorant of how close they were to political, military, social, and religious disaster (8:1–11).

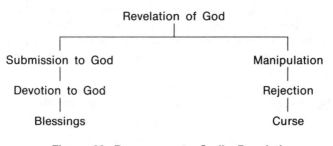

Figure 22. Responses to God's Revelation

Yahweh's Judgment

Israel must come to her senses, but how?[27] Hosea compared her to a prostitute (chaps. 1–3), a stubborn heifer (4:16; 10:11), a flighty dove (7:11–12; see 9:11), dew (13:3), and chaff (13:3). She was unreliable, worthless, rebellious, and filled with self-importance. Yahweh's remedy for Israel's "sickness" (5:13; 7:1, 9; 14:4) was separation from himself. Judgment was both imminent and just, because of the people's continual breaking of the stipulations of the covenant (12:14). The prophet likened them to people who "sow the wind and reap the whirlwind" (8:7), and he stated that from them "lawsuits spring up like poisonous weeds in a plowed field" (10:4). They had broken the covenant of the Lord and had to suffer the consequences (5:5, 7; 6:4, 7–9). A manipulative way of life leads to rejection of the revelation of God and bears the fruit of divine curse. (See figure 22.)

Hosea's message reveals the emotions of God who is free to judge and yet bound by his love for his people.[28] Israel had hurt Yahweh by her refusal to learn from God's past acts of goodness and of discipline. What else can he do for them (6:4)? His love for Israel must lead to judgment. Judgment is an act of love, because he seeks a response from his people. He is so devoted to reestablishing his covenant love that he will suffer withdrawal from the relationship for their sake. To accomplish this, he will lead them into a "desert" (2:3), and he will withdraw to his place (5:15). He wants to heal them, but they have run away from their Physician.

Yahweh, Israel's Protector, Lover, Divine Warrior, and Savior, would become Israel's greatest enemy. He loved them dearly in Egypt and the wilderness, and he planted them in the land with great expectations (13:4–8). But he would reduce Israel's national, social, religious, and economic life to nothingness! God planned Israel's judgment, exile, and desolation (8:13; 9:3, 6). Israel would suffer disgrace, humiliation, exile, bloodshed, and oppression because she resisted Yahweh's love. She, too, would experience abandonment, symbolized by the names of Hosea's children: bloodshed, no compassion, and rejected from the covenant status (1:2–9). Covenant history ends with God's judgment (9:15–17). Nobody, not even the prophet's intercession for a lesser judgment, could avert the wrath of God (9:14).

Yahweh would employ the ungodly nations,[29] after whom Israel sought to pattern herself, as his instrument of judgment.

> When I please, I will punish them;
>   nations will be gathered against them
>   to put them in bonds for their double sin.
>   (10:10)

Yahweh would also bring Israel's economy down,

> even though he thrives among his brothers.
> An east wind from the LORD will come,
>   blowing in from the desert;
> his spring will fail
>   and his well dry up.
> His storehouse will be plundered
>   of all its treasures.
>
>   (13:15)

Hosea's threatening words extend God's condemnation to his people in any age. God's children live in rebellion whenever and wherever they cheapen grace by living out their dreams, by establishing their petty kingdoms, and by maintaining structures merely to ensure their security. His words applied to Judah before her exile, to the Jews in and after the

Exile, to the Jews of Jesus' day, and to Jews and Christians in our age. The good news of the gospel is only good news as long as we live by grace, seeking favor with God and man. The gospel is not a door by which we may find security and then live in whatever way we desire. Instead, it is a passage to the "other way" in which the Christian stays in close dependence on his Savior.

Repentance and Remnant

The call to repentance went out to all, but the benefits of hope and protection are restricted to the remnant. Yahweh discloses a new possibility for the remnant, who love him with all their hearts, who seek him diligently (5:15), and who confess that Yahweh alone is the source of life (14:2–3). The Lord rejected their forms of appeasement, including the liturgy of repentance (6:1–3) so cleverly composed and orchestrated by the priests. In this liturgy, Israel readily confessed her waywardness, expecting immediate reconciliation and gratification.

> Let us acknowledge the LORD;
>   let us press on to acknowledge him.
> As surely as the sun rises,
>   he will appear;
> he will come to us like the winter rains,
>   like the spring rains that water the earth.
>   (6:3)[30]

```
Rejection of Realpolitik ────────▶ Dependence on the Lord
Rejection of fertility cults ────▶ Love for God
Rejection of cultures ───────────▶ Counterculture
Rejection of kings ──────────────▶ Submission to David
```

Figure 23. True Repentance

Throughout the prophecy the Lord opens up the way of "knowledge" of God (6:6). This way—and this way alone—leads to true repentance. (See figure 23.) True repentance includes (1) a turning away from human systems of security to the Lord and (2) a demonstration of devotion to the Lord with the same intensity as they had previously shown for the fertility gods, for social and economic advantages, and for political survival.

The new community had to return to the revelation of God (4:6) and establish God's way on earth by a radical loyalty to what is important to God.

> But you must return to your God;
>   maintain love and justice,

and wait for your God always.

(12:6)[31]

His children cannot claim him as their Father unless they, too, seek his kingdom as their sole pursuit of happiness.

> Sow for yourselves righteousness,
>> reap the fruit of unfailing love,
> and break up your unplowed ground;
>> for it is time to seek the LORD,
> until he comes
>> and showers righteousness on you.

(10:12)

Similarly, Paul challenged the Christian community to sow righteousness by doing good, sharing with the needy, walking in the Spirit, and seeking every opportunity to establish God's righteous kingdom in all areas of life (1 Cor. 9:9–11; Gal. 5:21–22; 6:7–10).

True repentance calls for submission to the Lord of the covenant (Mount Sinai revelation) *and* also to the Lord's anointed King (Mount Zion revelation). It was not enough to live by one portion of God's revelation and to reject another. God had given his revelation through Moses at Mount Sinai (12:13), and he had given his rule on earth through a Davidic king (2 Sam. 7:5–16). The revelation regarding David's unique position and Yahweh's decree to establish his kingdom on earth through David (Mount Zion theology, see Pss. 2; 72; 132) was of ultimate importance for the remnant from the north. The Lord had tolerated their secession from the Davidic dynasty (931 B.C.). But people may not enter into the era of restoration unless they completely abandon their former ways, submit to Yahweh, and express loyalty to Yahweh's Messiah: "Afterward the Israelites will return and seek the LORD their God and David their king. They will come trembling to the LORD and to his blessings in the last days" (3:5). (See figure 23.)

The Depth and Mystery of Yahweh's Love

The tender love and mercy (*ḥesed*) of Yahweh in forbearing with his covenant people[32] is woven throughout the book.[33] This is the classic message of Hosea.[34] Many passages drip with grief as God weeps over his people like a mother: "How can I give you up, O Ephraim? How can I surrender you, O Israel?" (11:8; see 6:4–6; 11:1–4, 7–8).[35]

Israel's early history reveals God's compassion, care, and love. He cared for Jacob, the patriarch, when he worked for Laban in Paddan-aram (12:12). He was with Israel in Egypt, where he adopted them as sons and carried them lovingly in his mighty arms (11:1, 3; see Ex. 19:4). He brought them out of Egypt by Moses ("a prophet," 12:13), satisfied their needs in the desert (9:10; 13:5–6), gave them his revelation (8:12; 12:13), and brought them into Canaan (2:8). (See figure 24.)

Yahweh's acts of love: Exodus—Wilderness—Revelation—Conquest

Israel's response: Love for foreign cultures—Acculturation

Figure 24. Yahweh's Acts and Israel's Response

Hosea employed the Exodus *wilderness* motif for four purposes. First, it established Yahweh's love, compassion, and fidelity. Israel had no inherent right to grace. Yahweh "found" them in a wasteland, and he treasured them like "grapes" and like "early fruit" on a fig tree (9:10). They were his elect people on whom he freely bestowed his favor. He led them out of Egypt and was present with them when they lived in their tents in the desert (12:9). He is the incomparable God who condescended to Israel and identified himself with their misery: "I am the LORD your God, who brought you out of Egypt" (12:9; 13:4).

Second, Israel's resistance to the Lord was all the more serious in that she rebelled against the God who loved her. He elected her, dealt kindly with her, and set her up to be his royal nation. He expected Israel to be a "model" nation among the nations as he sustained them with his grace and trained them (10:11) by his revelation to be a counterculture. Instead of developing the qualities of a counterculture (righteousness, justice, and love), they became a kingdom characterized by unrighteousness, unfaithfulness, and lack of love (2:2, 5; 4:1–2; 5:3; 6:4; 9:1; 10:13). The people's rebellious spirit was deeply rooted in their history, institutions, and pride. Their apostasy reached back to the wilderness (9:10; 11:2; 13:6) and was most clearly expressed in their choice of Saul of Gibeah as king, whose kingship was like that of the nations (9:9; 10:9; 13:10–12).

Third, Yahweh's promise of the renewal of his love, compassion, and fidelity will be like a second Exodus. He will appear to them again after their judgment and deliver them from the nations. Hosea reflects on the history of redemption with the anticipation that a new act of redemption will mark a new era of covenant renewal; that is, a new bonding of Yahweh with his people.[36]

Fourth, the Lord had revealed himself as holy and had consecrated Israel to be holy (Ex. 31:13; Lev. 11:45; 19:2). Israel's separation from God would lead to a state of separation in exile. But even in that despicable state of abandonment, the Lord promised to be present with them, to consecrate them, and to love them.

115

I will not carry out my fierce anger,
nor will I turn and devastate Ephraim.
For I am God, and not man—
the Holy One among you.
I will not come in wrath.

(Hos. 11:9)[37]

How can this be? Here we stand before the mystery of grace and election. Yahweh's love is rooted in salvation history, and the renewal of his love is grounded in his being, expressed in the phrase "I am the LORD your God" (12:9; 13:4).[38] He promises himself so that the people of God may know that they may find life in Yahweh alone! Yahweh freely opens up a *new era of covenant renewal* in which he gave more of himself, deepened his commitment, and made the promises more attractive. Love truly flows out of God's holiness, a holiness that loves and binds rather than repels and separates. I agree with Berkhof's comment: "The deepest expression of the unity of holiness and love is given by Hosea" (11:9).[39]

The Lord's wrath was only for a moment, compared with the depth of his love for Israel. The experience of judgment, likened to a return to the desert (2:3), was intended to bring some to their senses and to the recognition that Yahweh is Lord (v. 16; 12:9). He stood with open arms, ready to be reconciled, to forgive, and to restore all the covenantal benefits. Their Father (11:1–4) and Physician (7:1; 11:3; 14:4), he was ready to be reconciled and to heal. As their lover, he was still ready to sing his love song to his beloved.

There I will give her back her vineyards,
and will make the Valley of Achor a door of hope.
There she will sing as in the days of her youth,
as in the day she came up out of Egypt.
(2:15; see the parable of the prodigal son, Luke 15:11–32)

The book concludes with Yahweh's love song.[40] By the metaphors of "dew" and "cedar," he assured them that his love, covenant renewal, blessings, and fulfillment of the promises are still as fresh as at the Exodus, yes, even better! He brings prosperity and joy to his people.[41]

I will be like the dew to Israel;
he will blossom like a lily.
Like a cedar of Lebanon
he will send down his roots;
his young shoots will grow.
His splendor will be like an olive tree,
his fragrance like a cedar of Lebanon.
Men will dwell again in his shade.
He will flourish like the grain.

116

> He will blossom like a vine,
>> and his fame will be like the wine from Lebanon.
>>> (14:5–7; see Song 2:3; 4:8–5:1)

Israel had worshiped in groves, under pine trees and cedars, and had used wood to make idols. But no longer would they practice the fertility cults. Instead, the Lord will be their "pine tree"; that is, their only "idol."[42]

> O Ephraim, what more have I to do with idols?
>> I will answer him and care for him.
> I am like a green pine tree;
>> your fruitfulness comes from me."
>>> (14:8)[43]

Hosea's language of judgment and salvation presents the hearer with a God who loves even in judgment. The mystery of God's holiness surrounds his every act. The fool stumbles over the issue of God's wrath, grasping onto his own securities in life, not realizing how they provide him with no ground to stand upon in Yahweh's judgment. The righteous remnant perceive God's love, discerning with awe the freedom, love, holiness, and wisdom of God (14:9). They respond by imitating God in righteous living (Matt. 11:15; 13:9, 43). Great is their joy as they walk on the path of living faith!

The Hope of Restoration

Hosea spoke of the process of restoration as a "healing" love.[44] Yahweh, the faithful lover (2:14–23; 14:5–8), will renew his love for the remnant with greater zeal and commitment.[45] The restoration motif extends to the renewal of each covenant: creation (Noahic),[46] Abrahamic, Mosaic, and Davidic. The whole of creation will join in the blessings of God when he forgives his people, renews his unfailing love, and blesses them.

THE NEW PEOPLE OF GOD

The new people of God respond to God's covenant renewal with conjugal fidelity (2:20; 3:5).[47] The metaphor of marriage (2:16–23) applies to the covenant renewal or, better, the "renewal of the covenants." The Lord is the *Bridegroom* and the covenant people the *bride*. (See figure 25.) He graces them with the benefits of the covenants with creation, Abraham, Moses, and David. In this light we may appreciate the New Testament imagery of the church being the bride of Christ (Eph. 5:26–27; Rev. 21:2, 9; 22:17). The bounty resulting from the renewal of his covenant with creation will be greater than their wildest dreams (Hos. 2:21–22; 14:5–8). Eichrodt observes, "Where such an *inner rediscovery* of true communion with God occurs, Yahweh can also show himself as the bountiful Lord of heaven and earth."[48]

THE RENEWAL OF THE COVENANTS

The covenants—as administrations of grace and promise—undergo a transformation in the covenant renewal. Instead of restricting the benefits, the Lord graciously magnifies his promises and transforms Israel's doom, signified by the name *Achor* ("trouble," 2:15), into a new day of "hope," restoration, and covenant renewal (1:10–11; 2:15, 22–23). The covenant renewal is implied in the change of names. *Lo-Ammi* ("not my people") becomes "you are my people" (2:23). *Jezreel* ("bloodshed") becomes a symbol of fertility and prosperity (vv. 22–23) and of the unification of the tribes under one leader (1:11).[49] The name *Lo-Ruhamah* ("without compassion") similarly is replaced in the renewal of covenant ceremony, at which time the Lord freely promises, "I will betroth you to me forever . . . in love and compassion" (2:19).[50] Thus doom turns to blessing.

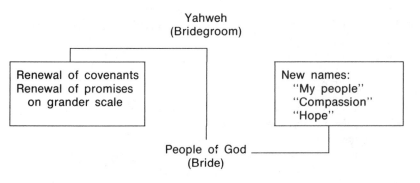

Figure 25. Renewal of Covenant

In the renewal of the covenant the Lord assures his people that creation and redemption belong together.[51] The renewal of creation opens up the fullness of redemption when heaven and earth will minister to the needs of the redeemed in fulfillment of God's manifold promises. Only when creation is in harmony (Rom. 8:22–23) will God's people be able to find rest (Hos. 2:18).[52] This involves nothing less than a restoration of a paradisiacal state of *shalom* (vv. 18, 21–23).[53]

The covenant is God's. Nothing will stand in his way in fulfilling and implementing the promises. He promises to bring the people back to the land, to "heal" them from their sins and afflictions, and to renew their happiness by providing for all their needs (1:10–11; 14:4–8). All that he has promised in the covenants—with creation, Abraham, Moses, and David—will be theirs; only more of it!

The leader under which the remnant will thrive is none other than a Davidic king. He is God's appointed means of blessing and peace (see Ps. 72). Hosea intimates that the political future of the northern kingdom lies in Judah under the house of David[54] and that a Davidic monarch will rule over all twelve tribes (1:11; 3:5).[55]

The prophetic word concerning the Davidic monarch was being fulfilled as early as ten years after Samaria's fall. A remnant from the north found asylum under the charismatic, messianic leadership of Hezekiah (729–686 B.C.) and Josiah (640–609 B.C.). These kings invited the remnant to participate in the Passover celebrations and encouraged them to declare their loyalty to Yahweh and to his king (2 Chron. 30:1, 5, 9–14, 18–19, 25; 35:17–18).

The prophetic promises also extend to all who are in Jesus Christ, to both Jews and Gentiles (Rom. 9:25–26; 1 Peter 2:10). God renews his commitment to be the covenant God of all who submit to the Messiah of God (Hos. 6:6; see Matt. 9:13; 12:7). This promise is still open to the Jews who remain in a state of rejection of the gospel (Rom. 10:1; 11:26), as well as to Gentiles. The proclamation of the gospel extends God's compassion, promises, blessings, and covenant privilege to all who seek the Messiah and await his salvation in absolute abandonment to the Father's favor (Acts 2:36–38; 4:10–12; Rom. 10:9).

Conclusion

The marriage allegory (chaps. 1–3) and the prophetic oracles point to the constancy of Yahweh's love (11:9). What is new is Hosea's proclamation of the depth of Yahweh's love for a sinful people, as Eichrodt wrote,

> For the first time in the history of Israel, *the message of the love of God* is heard in Hosea's proclamation as the center of God's action with his people. . . . Hosea breaks through this sober reticence and dares to speak of Yahweh's affection for Israel using the chief expression for the powerful passion which joins a man and wife: ('-*h-b*).[56]

Hosea opens up a new and marvelous era of covenant renewal. The wonder of grace is that in Christ, Yahweh has even further demonstrated the depth of his love. It is unfortunate that Yahweh's freedom in judgment and salvation and Israel's offense at the cross have led some to conclude that the Lord's way is closed to ethnic Israel. The gospel of Hosea does not justify this conclusion. The prophetic word, instead, warns Christians that they, too, may become the objects of wrath and condemnation if they persist in the way of pride, structures, *Realpolitik,* and *vox populi.* Hosea warns us most urgently to seek the Lord and to establish diligently God's kingdom of righteousness, love, and peace in all areas of our lives (Matt. 6:33). Then we, too, may enjoy the benefits and live with the vision of renewal, of Zion, and of God's everlasting presence.

JOEL: THE DAY OF THE LORD AND THE SPIRIT OF RESTORATION

Joel and His Time

The identity of Joel and his era remains an enigma. Next to nothing is known about Joel, the "son of Pethuel," except that he served the Lord as Yahweh's prophet (1:1).[57] The time of his ministry is equally uncertain because he did not set it in a clearly defined historical context. There is much to be said in favor of a preexilic date and a postexilic date,[58] but the prophecy itself is inconclusive. Arguments in favor of a ninth-century date are (1) its canonical place between Hosea and Amos, (2) the themes shared with the early prophets, and (3) the language and style. Joel could well be the first classical prophet.[59]

Joel may also be understood within the social, political, and religious milieu of the postexilic era. Arguments in favor of a postexilic date include (1) the significant place of the elders and priests (1:2, 13–14), (2) the centrality of the temple (1:9, 14, 16; 2:17), (3) Joel's language,[60] (4) his familiarity with other prophetic writings, (5) his awareness of the Exile (3:2), (6) the existence of a small community in postexilic Judah (2:27; 3:16),[61] and (7) the reference to the Greeks (3:6). In a postexilic dating the prophet may have been contemporaneous with Haggai and Zechariah (515 B.C.),[62] or he may be the last Old Testament prophet.[63] I assume a date shortly after Nehemiah's completion of Jerusalem's wall (445 B.C.; see 2:7, 9). While I assume a late fifth-century date of Joel (425–400 B.C.), I find Calvin's position on the matter noteworthy.

> As there is no certainty it is better to leave the time in which he taught undecided; and as we shall see, this is of no great importance. Not to know the time of Hosea would be to readers a great loss, for there are many parts which would not be explained without a knowledge of history; but as to Joel there is, as I have said, less need of this; for the import of his doctrine is evident, though his time be obscure and uncertain.[64]

Joel's message is universal. He declared to the elders,

> Tell it to your children,
> and let your children tell it to their children,

and their children to the next generation.
(1:3)

The story of the terrible locust plague (vv. 4–12) was to be retold from generation to generation. The locust plague affected all areas of life: wildlife, agriculture, husbandry, economics, social life, religious life, the priesthood, and the temple. For Joel, the locust plague serves as a metaphor for the Day of the Lord. As bad as the locust plague was, the Day of the Lord would be far worse (2:1–11)! The focus of his message is also on the Spirit of restoration as God's sign of protection from the eschatological Day of the Lord.

Literary Form and Structure

Literary Form

The first two chapters of Joel may have been used liturgically.[65] The prophet called on the people to pray for the Lord's favor in individual (1:19–20) and in communal (2:17) laments, to fast (1:14; 2:12), and to renew their devotion (2:12). The liturgy is followed by an oracle of deliverance (vv. 17–32). In the third chapter the prophet delineates the nature of the Day of the Lord in *judgment* against the nations (3:1–15) and in *deliverance* of his people (vv. 16–21).

Joel is familiar with other prophetic writings as evident in the citations,[66] the creative use of earlier prophetic utterances,[67] and a reworking of prophetic motifs. Though Joel is steeped in the prophetic tradition, his language is fresh, creative, and relevant.[68] Joel employs various literary devices: parallelism, metaphor, catchwords, rhetorical devices, repetition, and symmetry.[69]

Structure

The two parts of the prophecy (1:2–20; 2:18–3:16) reveal a clear pattern (ABC–A'C'B').[70] The lament of the locust plague (A) turns into joy for the believing community as they receive the encouraging oracle of God's blessing (A'); the catastrophe of the locust plague is a sign of an even greater calamity (the Day of the Lord, B–B'); and the call to repent is symmetrical with the promise of the outpouring of the Spirit (C–C').

Superscription, 1:1
  A. Lament over crop failures, 1:2–20
    B. Eschatological Catastrophe, 2:1–11
      C. Call to repent, 2:12–17
  A'. Blessing and joy, 2:18–27
      C'. Enabling by the Spirit, 2:28–32
    B'. Eschatological Day of the Lord, 3:1–16

The Message of Joel

Joel used the occasion of the locust plague to expound the meaning of covenant life and suffering. For Joel, suffering is a token of God's final and climactic judgment over all his opponents (3:1–15).[71] Through adversities the Lord kindly reminds his people not to take their covenant status for granted, but to prepare themselves for the Day of Judgment (2:1–2).

The Day of the Lord

The Day of the Lord is the period in which the Lord sovereignly acts in judgment and vengeance, scrutinizing everything on earth and in heaven (2:11–12). Joel proclaimed that the Day of the Lord is (1) always near, (2) characterized by great tribulation, (3) inescapable, (4) and cosmic in dimension (vv. 1–11). Its devastation is so great that it dwarfs the effects of the locust swarm—or for that matter, the traumatic effects of the exile of Israel and Judah (vv. 2–3). Joel gave a revelatory perspective on the shock that had overwhelmed the covenant community. He gave them a vision of God's sovereignty over creation and of his commitment to the new community. Joel also encouraged the godly to take heart and await the new age of blessing.

Today Is the Day of Salvation

Joel announced this dreadful day of accountability and judgment to evoke a response of greater devotion to the Lord. Return to radical discipleship opens up the eschatological era as an age of blessing and salvation instead of curse and judgment (2:12). The Lord is faithful; he is

> gracious and compassionate,
> slow to anger and abounding in love,
> and he relents from sending calamity.
>
> (2:13)

Joel further declared the constancy of God's purpose for the covenant community: "Then the LORD will be jealous for his land and take pity on his people" (2:18). The marvel is that God, before whom heaven and earth tremble in judgment, will shake heaven and earth for the purpose of blessing his people *in fulfillment* of his promises. He may delay fulfillment, but he has not lost interest in his people. Like a good ruler, he is zealous to bring prosperity and joy to his people, but while he is reducing the opposition of the enemy, his people may have to wait a time for an eternity of covenant benefits.

The promises are grounded in God's zeal for the covenant community. The Lord assures the full enjoyment of covenant life: spiritual ("my Spirit," 2:28), material ("grain, new wine and oil, enough to satisfy you

122

fully," 2:19, 23–26), and the removal of all adversities ("never again will I make you an object of scorn to the nations," v. 19; see v. 26; 3:17). These blessings are the gifts of the victorious King (2:23, 26) so that his own may rest, assured that he is with them (v. 27; 3:17), and worship his name (2:20–23).

The Lord sustains his people who persevere in faith. He may bring desolations on the earth (3:1–15). But his people need not fear his acts of sovereign judgments, for he has promised to protect them and be present with them (vv. 16–17). He has given them his word of assurance. The monergistic emphasis is reassuring, as the Lord declares, "I will drive the northern enemy far from you. . . . I will repay you. . . . I will pour out my Spirit. . . . I [will] restore the fortunes, . . . I will gather all nations" (2:20, 25, 28; 3:1–2). His sovereign and gracious acts demonstrate that he is a faithful covenant God (2:27).

The Spirit of Restoration

But how can they know that he is present in adversity? The Holy Spirit is the guarantee of God's presence in suffering, of communion with God, and of the promised restoration. He is *the Spirit of Restoration*. The prophecy of the Spirit of God is Yahweh's guarantee of restoration, of the establishment of his kingdom, and of the rest promised to his people (3:17–18, 20–21). It is regrettable that our English versions separate the promises of blessing from the ministry of the Spirit by the phrase "and afterward."

> *And afterward,*
>   I will pour out my Spirit on *all* people.
> Your sons and daughters will prophesy,
>   your old men will dream dreams,
>   your young men will see visions.
> Even on my servants, both men and women,
>   I will pour out my Spirit *in those days.*
>   (2:28–29, emphasis mine)

This rendering gives the mistaken impression (see Interpretation A in figure 26) that the Lord has two stages of fulfillment: (1) the material restoration of what was lost through the locust plague in Joel's day (vv. 17–27) and (2) the coming of the Spirit (vv. 28–32). This interpretation is insensitive to the eschatological language of verses 17–27. These verses are in the form of an assurance oracle that holds out God's absolute, free, and unrestricted goodness. No one will take away the joy of God's children when the Lord will remove all enemies (vv. 19–20, 26–27), disgrace (vv. 19, 26–27), and mourning (v. 23) from his people! Theirs is the full enjoyment of his covenant presence (v. 27), as he alone will be their God. Is this not the language of eschatology? Yet it is also the language of realized eschatology. The people of Joel's generation received the blessings of God (vv. 23–25), and they again had occasion to rejoice (vv. 23, 26). (See interpretation B in figure 26.)

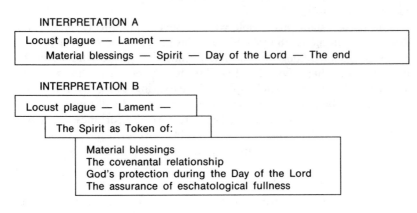

Figure 26. Interpretation of Joel 2:17–32

How then are we to understand the phrase "and afterward"? The phrase forms an inclusion with "in those days"[72] and is preferably rendered by a general temporal conjunction such as "when."[73] The coming of the Spirit is hereby linked to God's response to his people: "The LORD will be jealous for his land and take pity on his people" (2:18). The outpouring of the Spirit of God must be taken as the sign of covenant renewal (v. 27; see Ezek. 39:29), of God's promise of restoration (2:18–27), and of his vindication (3:1–6).

The Holy Spirit is God's eschatological gift to the new community before the Day of the Lord (2:28–32).[74] Through his operation the presence and blessings are both eternal and temporal. They are to be enjoyed in this age *and* in the age to come (1 Tim. 4:8). Like the temporal and material benefits, they are tokens of the new age. In other words, they are eschatological in nature. This means that in adversity, the Spirit witnesses within the heart of the believer that evil will cease and that God's full blessings will be unleashed on those who are the recipients of his grace and the heirs of the new creation (Rom. 8:18–30).

The Democratization of the Spirit

The Spirit is the Spirit of God who works within creation, including the children of the kingdom, preparing it for and advancing the restoration of all things. What Joel says about his work in "all flesh" (*kōl bāśār*, NIV "all people") is complementary to the salvation oracles of

Jeremiah and Ezekiel. Jeremiah speaks of the internalization of the law of God (Jer. 31:33–34; see Pss. 37:31; 40:8). The internalization of the law signifies the full cooperation of the children of God with the Spirit in living harmoniously with the new order of restoration. The new, regenerated heart of the faithful desires nothing less than to advance God's cause in this world. Ezekiel more clearly makes the connection between circumcision of the heart and the outpouring of the Spirit (Ezek. 36:27; see Joel 2:13). For Ezekiel, too, the Spirit signifies a greater work of God whereby he works in a greater number of people so as to enlarge his kingdom on earth. Restoration depends not on frail human leaders, institutions, or programs, but on the Spirit, who works mightily in and through humans.

HOLY SPIRIT

Leaders as guardians   People of God
of the theocracy   Internalization
        Democratization

Figure 27. The Spirit of Restoration

Joel goes on to explain the subjects of the new age of covenant renewal, of the Spirit, and of the blessings. (See figure 27.) The Spirit is given to all people (2:28, *kōl bāśār,* lit. "all flesh"). Joel clarified that the "all" is a restricted "all"; namely, "everyone who calls on the name of the LORD" and "whom the LORD calls" (v. 32). The Hebrew text shows the connection between "all people" and the further explication in verse 32 by the repetition of *wᵉhāyâ* (lit. "and it will be," NIV "and") in verses 28 and 32. I believe that verses 28–29 and 32 are best read together as bounded by four inclusions. (See figure 28.)

The Spirit was associated with leadership in the Old Testament: Moses and the seventy elders (Num. 11:25), Joshua (Deut. 34:9), kings (2 Sam. 23:2; Ps. 51:11), and the prophets (2 Kings 2:9; 2 Peter 1:21). But Joel proclaims a democratization of the Spirit; that is, a special endowment of the Spirit in every member of the people of God.[75] (See figure 27.) The assurance of the Spirit is given to all—regardless of sex, social standing, or age[76]—who find refuge in the Lord alone: "the name of the LORD. . . on Mount Zion . . . in Jerusalem" (Joel 2:32). The Lord assures his people that he is with them in blessing and protection, even when he unleashes his judgments on the nations[77] before and during the full inauguration of the Day of the Lord. They need not fear, because he "will be a refuge for his people, a stronghold" (3:16).

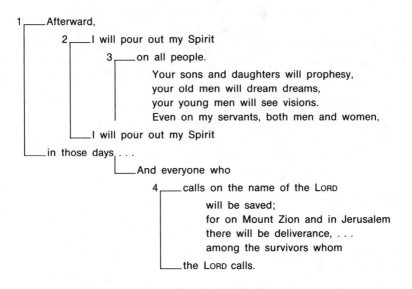

Figure 28. The Inclusions in Joel 2:28–32

The goal of Yahweh, the Divine Warrior, is the *full establishment of his kingdom on earth.* He will avenge his enemies (3:1–15), symbolized by the desolation of Egypt and Edom (v. 19). He will vindicate his people, who patiently await his victory. They will share in his triumph as he renews creation (vv. 18, 20–21). The prophecy ends with a vision of a transformed world with a river flowing in the midst of the New Jerusalem (see Ps. 46:4; Isa. 33:20–21; Zech. 14:8), the very presence of God among a forgiven people (Joel 3:18–21). This is the vision of *shalom.*

In the coming of Jesus, the prophecy of Joel has made significant progress toward a greater reality. (See figure 29.) Not only does Jesus speak of the future cataclysmic transformation and his authority to deliver and condemn, but he has also given his church the gift of the Holy Spirit as an assurance of his presence. The Spirit is the eschatological gift of the Father and the Son (Acts 2:16–39). He witnesses concerning the restoration to come and calls on all the members of the new community—male or female, slave or free, young or old, Jew or Gentile—to look forward to the redemption of creation, to the release from bondage, and to the expectation of the new heaven and new earth (see Rom. 8:18–27; Gal. 5:5). Those who call on the name of Jesus will find protection from the Day of the Lord ("the wrath to come," [see Rom. 10:11–13; 1 Thess 1:10]). They have the Spirit of God as the sign of redemption, protection, and restoration.

OLD TESTAMENT	NEW TESTAMENT
Moses	Jesus Christ
Leaders	Leaders
Regenerate saints	Regenerate saints

Increase in number
Regardless of sex, social standing, age, and ethnic origin

Figure 29. The Extension of the Work of the Spirit

Joel's prophecy continues to have the canonical function of calling God's people to pledge greater loyalty to the Lord, to look at the freedom of God in his compassion and grace, and to develop an eschatological focus in their daily lives. Joel calls us to walk in the Spirit, to pursue Christian living with an edge, and to have compassion for all who have not yet called on the name of Jesus, including the Jews.[78] The Christian community must look beyond Joel's time and beyond the present (the gift of the Spirit in Christ) to the era of restoration: the New Jerusalem. Wolff writes,

> The fulfillment exceeds the promise by far. On the other hand, the light of the promise casts its rays beyond the fulfillment that has taken place. For in the present communion with Christ, security and blessings are still largely hidden under temptations and deprivations. . . . But as far as the completely new world is concerned . . . the New Testament people of God together with the Old Testament people of God are waiting for a future event which will exceed the bounds of the old expectation (cf. Rev. 22:1–5).[79]

AMOS: YAHWEH IS THE AUTHOR OF DESOLATION AND RESTORATION

Amos and His Time

The prophet Amos was an older contemporary of Hosea.[80] He ministered God's word to Israel for several weeks in 760 B.C., shortly before an earthquake that shook Israel's national existence:[81] "The words of Amos, one of the shepherds of Tekoa—what he saw concerning Israel two years before the earthquake, when Uzziah [792–40 B.C.] was king of Judah and Jeroboam son of Jehoash (II, 793–753 B.C.) was king of Israel" (1:1).

Amos hailed from Tekoa, a rural community situated about five miles south of Bethlehem.[82] Amos was well educated and at home with the social, judicial, and international affairs of his day. He publicly spoke at Bethel (7:10–17), a major cultic site; at Samaria, Israel's capital (3:9; 4:1; 6:1); and possibly at Gilgal (5:5). He was also acquainted with the geography, history, and social and political life of the surrounding peoples: Aram, Philistia, Edom, Ammon, and Moab (1:3–2:3).[83] (For the "time" of Amos, see "Hosea and His Time.")

Amos was surrendered to God[84] and concerned about his covenantal responsibilities.[85] He was a Judean sage familiar with the wisdom traditions.[86] If the wise thought it prudent to keep silent for self-preservation (5:13), Amos could not and would not be silenced.[87] The word of God was a fire in his bosom (3:8). He dissociated himself from the "professional" prophets (7:10–13).[88] He rejected the opulent lifestyle of the rich (3:10, 12, 15; 5:11; 6:4, 8) with its taint of immoral, oppressive, and unjust acts (2:6–7; 4:1; 5:10, 12; 8:4–6).

Amos's criticism is all the more valid because he was a businessman by profession (1:1; 7:14–15).[89] He left all he had for the sake of God, who called him away from his security at the border of the Judean wilderness (7:15). He followed the call of God and went north to Israel, knowing well that he and his message would be rejected by the hardhearted aristocracy. Amos resisted the orders of Amaziah, a cultic priest at the Bethel sanctuary (vv. 12–13), opposed *Realpolitik,* and boldly proclaimed God's message of universal judgment and of salvation.

By revelation Amos received visions of God's judgment upon Israel (7:1–9:10). This message moved him deeply, as he proclaimed the imminence of the Day of the Lord to the northern kingdom. Urgency[90] characterizes his prophetic speech.

> Does a lion roar in the thicket
>   when he has no prey?
> Does he growl in his den
>   when he has caught nothing?
> Does a bird fall into a trap on the ground
>   where no snare has been set?
> Does a trap spring up from the earth
>   when there is nothing to catch?
> When a trumpet sounds in a city,
>   do not the people tremble?
> When disaster comes to a city,
>   has not the LORD caused it?
> Surely the Sovereign LORD does nothing
>   without revealing his plan
>   to his servants the prophets.

> The lion has roared—
>> who will not fear?
> The Sovereign LORD has spoken—
>> who can but prophesy?
>
>> (3:4–8)

Little did Amos know how imminent the Day of the Lord was for Israel. Israel's successes in Transjordan (6:13)—early in the reign of Jeroboam II (793–753 B.C.)—were being reduced by Aramean aggressions east of the Jordan (1:3, 13) by 760 B.C. Assyria, preoccupied with the Urartu kingdom (810–743 B.C.), was not free in continuing her dominance over Aram until the first campaign by Tiglath-pileser III in 743 B.C. The renewed military buildup between Israel and Aram by 760 B.C. was further aggravated by a massive earthquake.[91] Israel's world was beginning to crumble by 760 B.C.

Jeroboam II did not realize that Israel's end was so near. The prophet Jonah had declared God's grace in extending Israel's survival under Jeroboam II (2 Kings 14:25), but Amos announced her fall and that of Aram (1:5; 732 B.C.) and other nations. The leaders wallowed in their filthy riches ("beds inlaid with ivory") and enjoyed the finest foods (4:1; 5:11; 6:4, 6), not knowing that God's judgment was impending!

Literary Form and Structure

Literary Form

Amos was a literary giant of his time, and from his literary work we also discover a man who was a great rhetorician (2:12; 4:1; 5:14; 6:13; 7:10–11, 16; 8:5–6; 9:10).[92] His preaching is characterized by simplicity, directness, vivid imagery, and shock techniques. The book contains an autobiographical narrative (7:10–17),[93] oracles against the nations (1:3–2:16), woe oracles (5:18–20; 6:1, 3–6), vision reports (7:1–3, 4–6, 7–8; 8:1–2; 9:1–4),[94] numerical sayings (1:3, 6, 13; 2:1, 6), wordplay (5:5; 6:1, 6–7; 8:2), wisdom sayings (3:3–6, 8), irony (4:4–5; 6:12), rhetorical questions (3:3–6, 8; 5:18–20; 9:7), metaphors (2:13; 3:4–5; 4:12; 5:19, 24), similes (2:9; 5:7; 6:12), alliteration, parallelism, hymns (1:2; 4:13; 5:8–9; 9:5–6), and the messenger formula ("this is what the LORD says," 1:6, 13; 2:1, 6; 3:11–12; 5:3–4, 16; 7:17; "says the LORD," 1:5, 8, 15; 2:3; 5:17).[95] The didactic questions, woe cries, numerical sayings, and exhortations reveal Amos's affinity for the wisdom tradition of Israel.[96]

The issue of authenticity and integrity usually occupies a large part of the discussion on Amos.[97] Harrison admits the possibility of minor insertions, but he still claims that "on the basis of the available evidence there seems little doubt that Amos, with or without scribal help, was responsible for recording the oracles and visions attributed to him."[98]

Peter C. Craigie concludes that the book was preserved in Judah "as an authentic record of the prophetic voice."[99]

God's universal judgment is the central thesis of this prophetic book (1:2). The prophecy was never intended to be restricted to the historical context in Israel. The canonical function of the superscription—with its reference to the kings of Israel and Judah (v. 1)—expands the scope of the addressees from the northern kingdom to Judah. Moreover, the short hymn of Yahweh's roaring from Jerusalem sets the framework of applying the hymns, oracles, and visions to all the nations on earth. This is further supported by the oracles of judgment against the nations (1:3–2:16) that expand the scope of the message beyond Israel and Judah to the nations![100] Finally, the inclusion of the four hymns (1:2; 4:13; 5:8–9; 9:5–6), proclaiming the cosmic rule of Yahweh, also opens up the prophecy to a wider canonical setting and application.

The issue of composition becomes secondary when we read the prophecy as more than a proclamation of God's judgment against the northern kingdom. Amos sets God's judgment in the context of God's universal sovereignty.[101] The final section of hope (9:11–15) broadens the canonical function of Amos to an eschatological framework: from judgment to hope in the final restoration.[102]

Structure[103]

Superscription and thesis, 1:1–2
    A. Oracles against the nations, 1:3–2:16
        1. Aram, 1:3–5
        2. Philistia, 1:6–8
        3. Phoenicia, 1:9–10
        4. Edom, 1:11–12
        5. Ammon, 1:13–15
        6. Moab, 2:1–3
        7. Judah, 2:4–5
        8. Israel, 2:6–16
    B. Five oracles, 3:1–6:14
        1. First oracle, chap. 3
        2. Second oracle, chap. 4
        3. Third oracle, 5:1–17
        4. Fourth oracle, 5:18–27
        5. Fifth oracle, 6:1–14
    C. Five visions of judgment, 7:1–9:10
        1. Locusts, 7:1–3
        2. Fire, 7:4–6
        3. Plumbline, 7:5–9
        3a. Autobiographical parenthesis, 7:10–17
        4. Summer fruit, 8:1–14

     5. Desolate sanctuary, 9:1–10
  D. Epilogue, 9:11–15

The Message of Amos

The four hymns (1:2; 4:13; 5:8–9; 9:5–6),[104] the oracles, the visions, and the prophetic mission point to Yahweh as the sovereign, free, and all-powerful Ruler over the nations.[105]

Yahweh's Theophany

The four hymnic fragments amplify the message of Yahweh's freedom and power. In each hymn Amos impresses the reader with the *name* of Yahweh as he sets forth the power of God over creation.[106] The first hymn (1:2) summarizes the thesis of the book: the terror of Yahweh's coming into his created order. The phenomena associated with his coming (theophany) affect all creation, represented here by drought. Amos was called to announce Yahweh's awe-inspiring coming; hence his proclamation was God's instrument of judgment. In other words, Amos was called to do Yahweh's "roaring." God's word through Amos brings drought and desolation.[107] (See figure 30.)

YAHWEH'S SOVEREIGNTY OVER CREATION			
Withering of creation	Creator of mountains, wind, light and darkness	Creator of constellations, light and darkness, seas and land, destruction	Theophany: sovereign over water, sea, and land King over heaven and earth: judgment
1:2	4:13	5:8–9	9:5–6

Figure 30. The Four Hymns in Amos

The three other hymnic passages develop the effect of Yahweh's coming into his creation. Amos's favorite designations for God are Yahweh (5:8; 9:6), Yahweh Almighty (4:13; 9:5),[108] and Lord (Adonai, 9:5). He does not add to the theology of who Yahweh is, but portrays his awesome and powerful coming.

In the second hymn, Amos speaks of the desolation associated with the coming of the Almighty. Yahweh is the Creator-Ruler, who by virtue of his creative power rules over humankind.[109] He is the Creator—the One sovereign over mountains and the wind, who condescends to communicate with human beings (4:13). The prophet reminds Israel of the Lord's past commitment to them. Yahweh demonstrated his love by delivering them from Egypt, guiding them through the wilderness, giving them the land, and sustaining them with the prophetic word (2:9–11). He revealed his royal law to Israel, expecting her to separate herself from the nations, but instead Israel contaminated herself with the ways of the nations (2:6–8). Even further, people flouted the Sabbath—*the* sign of their consecration (Ex. 31:12–17)—in favor of material gain (Amos 8:5).

The Lord despised their tokens of religiosity because they corrupted true worship and love of one's fellowman (4:4–5). He hated the fertility cults and the immorality associated with pagan religious forms (2:8). As long as people followed the deceptions of paganism and hoped in productivity, prosperity, and power through their religious symbols, they would not look to the Creator-Revealer for life, health, and meaning. He alone is the giver of rain (4:7–8), crops (4:6, 9), and health and peace (vv. 10–11).[110] But Israel stubbornly refused to turn away from the path of national success.

In the third hymn, Amos describes the vastness and power of Yahweh's kingdom. His rule extends over heaven (Pleiades, Orion) and earth (darkness, dawn, sea, and dry land, 5:8)! He alone maintains order even in the opposites of heaven and earth, blackness and dawn, night and day, sea and the land. Israel rejected God's kingdom of "justice" (*mišpāt*) and "righteousness" (*ṣᵉdāqâ*, 5:7; see 5:24; 6:12). *Righteousness* is the order that characterizes God's rule over creation through his acts (blessing, lavish gifts, generosity) and brings harmony, peace, and joy. *Justice,* as it relates to God, is the aspect of righteousness that pertains to his wise and fair judgments. Amos accused the leaders of having abandoned the royal ideal by their utter disregard for justice and righteousness. The "gates" of the cities were full of cries of joy from those who had been vindicated and declared innocent (5:7). Justice and righteousness were turned into poison (6:12). When God restores order, human structures no longer hold any significance.

The fourth hymn is the most dramatic. The theophany is attended by cosmic upheaval, resulting in the undermining of human civilization. Yahweh is Lord over heaven and earth, creation, and the nations. Everything is subject to his movement in creation. He determined Israel's exile (9:3, 8–9)!

Judgment Is Determined

The five visions provide insight into God's firm determination to destroy Israel and into the prophet's role of intercessor. Amos, like Moses, asked God to forgive Israel (7:2), lest she be destroyed by natural phenomena (locusts, vv. 1–3). Amos was relieved when the Lord responded with patience (v. 3), but the Lord had not forgiven Israel. The second vision—of fire (v. 4)—did not come to pass because

Locusts	Fire	Plumbline	Fruit basket	Temple
Suspension of judgment		Judgment is inevitable		God's abandonment of Israel

Israel's guilt

Figure 31. The Five Visions of Amos

of Amos's prayer (7:5–6). Yet Israel's guilt was not dealt with, and God's sentence was only suspended. (See figure 31.)

God's decree of judgment is fixed! He forbears Israel's guilt only so long. Even before Amos can pray for relief, the Lord declares in the third vision that he will no longer be gracious ("I will spare them no longer," 7:8). Israel had fallen short of his expectations, had created anarchy in God's kingdom, and was subject to judgment. The plumb line demonstrated how far off course they were.

The interaction between Amaziah, the high priest of the royal cult at Bethel, and Amos (7:10–17) interrupts the first three and the last two visions. The seeming interruption amplifies the necessity of God's judgment. Amaziah represents the establishment that is unresponsive to God's word. Israel is beyond the point of correction. God's decree of exile stands (v. 17)!

The fourth vision, the basket of ripe fruit (8:1–3), develops the third vision (7:9) and the announcement of exile (v. 17); the "time is ripe" for judgment (8:2). The songs of the sanctuaries will change into laments because of the many dead (v. 3). The structures of Israel's society—religion, economy, and politics—will come down (vv. 9–14). Instead of their present securities, the people will be doomed to a life of endless meaninglessness, as Wolff comments, "Here there is neither life nor death but only an endless, desperate, and futile searching."[111]

The final vision (9:1–3) is climactic. Yahweh will abandon his people. They will be doomed to grope in the darkness of alienation as he remains hidden from them. No place in the depth of the earth or the height of heaven will provide them with shelter from the stormy blasts of Yahweh's judgment (vv. 3–4). His judgment is inescapable because Yahweh has decreed to haunt them: "I will fix my eyes upon them for evil and not for good" (v. 4; see 8:7).

The Day of the Lord

The prophet most clearly set before Israel the next stage of redemptive history: the Day of the Lord (*yôm Yahweh*, Amos 5:18–20).[112] He had already interceded on her behalf but to no avail. Israel had to undergo the shock of divine abandonment and learn that Yahweh could not be taken for granted. Israel had thought that ultimately their destiny was in their own hands. For them the teaching on the Day of the Lord was nothing but a "golden age," promised to them by covenant. In their pride they felt confident and superior and may well have called themselves "the foremost nation" (6:1). It is not surprising that they were blind to their sin of pride. It is a bit much, however, that in spite of their bigotry, they longed for the Day of the Lord as a deserved era of blessing and prosperity (5:18).[113] Amos spoke of the awe of this day as an inescapable doom and likened its anguish to darkness.

> It will be as though a man fled from a lion
>   only to meet a bear,
> as though he entered his house
>   and rested his hand on the wall
>   only to have a snake bite him.
> Will not the day of the Lord
>   be darkness, not light—
> pitch-dark, without a ray of brightness?
>   (vv. 19–20)

Thus the prophet announced the fall of Samaria as a temporal expression of the Day of the Lord.[114] During this time Israel would be greatly ravaged with only a remnant left.

> Fallen is Virgin Israel,
>   never to rise again,
> deserted in her own land,
>   with no one to lift her up.
>   (5:2; see v. 3)

Yahweh is the agent of desolation (1:3–5, 7–8, 9–14; 2:1–3, 4–5, 6; 3:2, 14; 4:12; 5:27; 6:8; 7:8; 8:2, 9; 9:1–4). The Exile would certainly come (4:2–3; 5:5, 27; 7:11, 17), and sinners would meet their just deserts.

> All the sinners among my people
>   will die by the sword,
> all those who say,
>   "Disaster will not overtake or meet us."
>   (9:10)

The end came in 722 B.C.[115]

The Freedom of the Lord

Yahweh is free to break the covenant relationship, as grace and promise are conditional.[116] Yahweh's power in desolation is nevertheless a constrained power.[117] He is free to have compassion on his people, and more than that, he is free to preserve a remnant.[118] Through judgment he separates the undesirable material ("the pebbles") to be cast away with the chaff, but he will keep the grain (9:8–9). He will shake the descendants of Israel so as to purify a remnant to himself.

The Remnant

Amos realized that his ministry would strike at the hearts of only a few. Most people remained unalarmed by the prophet's oracles of doom, and they sarcastically retorted, "Disaster will not overtake us or meet us" (9:10). He likened the remnant to a small part a shepherd may rescue.

135

As a shepherd saves from the lion's mouth
   only two leg bones or a piece of an ear,
   so will the Israelites be saved,
those who sit in Samaria
   on the edge of their beds
   and in Damascus on their couches.
                                                        (3:12)[119]

Though the threat of exile (4:2–3; 5:5, 27; 7:11, 17) was imminent, the Lord encouraged the remnant with the promise of restoration to the Land of Promise (9:13–15; see Jer. 24:6; 31:28; 42:10). The remnant is composed only of those who *seek* him and him alone as their Savior (5:4) and who wisely *persevere* in doing good.[120]

Therefore the prudent man keeps quiet in such times,
   for the times are evil.
Seek good, not evil,
   that you may live.
Then the LORD God Almighty will be with you,
   just as you say he is.
Hate evil, love good;
   maintain justice in the courts.
Perhaps the LORD God Almighty will have mercy
   on the remnant of Joseph.
                                                        (vv. 13–15)[121]

Yahweh expects conformity to his will ("to do right").[122] True religion consists of the love of God as evidenced in compassion for those in need (5:14–15; see Lev. 19:15; Ps. 41:1). So the prophet called on the remnant to distance themselves from the evil practices of their time (2:1–3, 6–8; 5:12), from pious acts and religious formalism (5:21–26), by letting "justice [*mišpāṭ*] roll on like a river, righteousness [*ṣᵉdāqâ*] like a never-failing stream!" (v. 24).[123] Only by seeking God's kingdom of righteousness and justice will they find joy for themselves (Matt. 6:33–34). (See figure 32.)

GOD'S KINGDOM

Nature	*Subjects*
Righteousness	Righteous
Justice	Just
Judgment on human chaos	
Restoration and transformation	

Figure 32. The Kingdom of God and the Remnant

Covenant Renewal

The remnant would enjoy the renewal of the covenants. The hope with which the prophecy concludes is tersely stated, but there is hope (9:11–15).[124] The crumbling Davidic dynasty ("David's fallen tent," v. 11) will rise with new power and inaugurate a new era of blessings. The benefits of the messianic era will extend to Israel[125] and to the nations.[126] This era is integrated in God's grand plans for transformation of creation so as to richly bless the world of creation with the full and permanent enjoyment of his people (vv. 13–15).

The application of Amos's universalistic allusion widened the door for Gentiles to enjoy a full share in the covenant privileges of the early church, when James defended the Gentile mission by quoting from Amos 9:11–12 (see Acts 15:16–17).[127] The message of Amos further extends to the coming of our Lord, who has revealed "his plan to his servants the prophets" (Amos 3:7; see Rev. 10:7; 11:18). Jesus, the Savior and Messiah of David, is also the Divine Warrior who will establish his kingdom through desolation of human kingdoms (Rev. 6:15–17; see Amos 9:1).

REVIEW

The witness of these canonical prophets transcends time and space. They were God's spokespersons to Israel and to Judah, and to God's people before and after the Exile. Though they directly addressed God's ancient covenant people, the prophets still speak to us in their writings. The historical context has changed, but their message is as valid today as it was in the eighth, seventh, or fifth century B.C.

Hosea emphasizes the triad of sin, judgment, and the wrath of God. Yet he exalts the love of the Lord, a love that goes back to his deliverance from Egypt. Rather than respond to God's love, Israel broke covenant again and again. In all his dealings, in love and in discipline, the Lord had revealed himself to be a loving husband. He was faithful, ready to be reconciled, to forgive, and to comfort. This message is vividly portrayed in the relationship of Hosea and Gomer. Their three children are symbolic of God's treatment of Israel in judgment: Jezreel—a valley known for war and bloodshed ("Achor," Hos. 2:15)—depicts Israel's suffering; Lo-Ruhamah signifies the removal of God's "compassion"; and Lo-Ammi (lit. "not my people") denotes divine abandonment. However, the Lord freely transforms the significance of each name by making a renewal of his covenants in the most grandiose manner.[128] Israel and Judah again will be known as the "people" of the Lord, the object of his love and "compassion," and he will transform the Valley of Achor ("trouble") into the "Door of Hope" (2:15).

Hope belongs to the remnant, which consists of all who submit themselves to the Lord and to his Messiah, and who practice righteousness and love. This is Hosea's kingdom message or gospel. Yahweh is free, holy, and loving. He is holy in his hatred of sin and in his judgment but also in his deep commitment ("love," *ḥesed*) to consecrate a people to himself.

The cycle of accusation, threat, judgment, and new life opens up the possibility of a new era, limited to those who seek God, commune with him, and live as a counterculture. Hosea still speaks regarding the reality of judgment and the promises of God's kingdom, covenant, and new creation to all who wait for the greater unfolding of God's love, salvation, and presence in Jesus Christ (Eph. 2:1–10; 1 Peter 2:4–12).

Joel adds to this testimony of divine love by promising us the presence of the Spirit of God. The prophet Joel may have lived as much as a century after the exile of Judah, and his message may have been given to a community of people who already sought the Lord. But God's people were still vulnerable to disasters, such as agricultural tragedies (locusts). In this context the prophet called them to greater acts of devotion in view of the greater day of trouble awaiting all of humankind. The Day of the Lord is a day of vindication that is near, certain to happen, and from which no one will escape, except for those who have found refuge in the Lord. That day has cosmic dimensions, the likes of which no one can imagine (Joel 2:10–11, 30–31; 3:14b–16).

The question "Who can endure it?" (Joel 2:11) may be answered with hope only by those who respond in faith and submission to Yahweh. Joel posits the grace and compassion of Yahweh as the ground of salvation and of the full enjoyment of deliverance: joy, fulfillment, everlasting removal of disgrace, and God's presence (vv. 19–27). By the gift of his Spirit, the Lord assures *all* who call on his name; male or female, slave or free, young or old, that he is their Protector (3:16), their King, and their Benefactor.

The Spirit of restoration is a guarantee of God's protection, care, and the glorious future prepared for all who have called on the name of the Lord. He is the sign of God's presence and of the fulfillment of the promises of full restoration. Yet Yahweh will go through with his judgment on the nations that will not submit to his will (Joel 3:1–16). Joel presents us with the great King, the Deliverer, the holy Lord of Zion who will establish an everlasting home for his people (vv. 17–21). The last words summarize the vision of the era of restoration: "The LORD dwells in Zion!" (v. 21). Where the Lord dwells, there is *shalom.*

Amos directs attention to Yahweh's power in desolation and restoration. Amos was "the first one to announce a message of Yahweh's judgment over all Israel."[129] He also extended the judgment of God to Judah and to the nations, proclaiming most clearly God's sovereignty over creation. Amos, like Joel, announced the terror of the Day of the Lord, and his message to Israel had a theocentric focus. The people had thought of this day as an extension of their prosperity and as a sanction of the *Realpolitik* of Jeroboam II. But Amos spoke of the certainty of judgment on all the nations, including Israel, while extending hope to a remnant that would persevere in doing God's will on earth. The covenant people may suffer desolation and alienation along with the nations, but they are the object of God's love and of the renewal of the covenants, including the covenant with David.[130]

QUESTIONS AND ISSUES

1. Define:
   democratization
   era of restoration
   fertility cult
   internalization
   justice (*mišpāṭ*)
   knowledge (*daʿaṯ*) of God
   love (*ḥesed*)
   remnant
   repentance
   righteousness (*ṣᵉdāqâ*)
   shalom
   theophany
2. What was the historical context of the ministry of Hosea, Joel, and Amos?
3. How does Hosea's marriage reflect Yahweh's relationship with Israel in his judgment and restoration of Israel? What are the names of Hosea's children? What is their significance? How do the changes in names typify the new relationship between Yahweh and his people?
4. What are the reasons for God's judgment, according to the oracles of Hosea, Joel, and Amos?
5. What era in Israel's history does Hosea reflect in showing Yahweh's love and Israel's unworthiness? Give examples of Yahweh's feelings for Israel in her state of condemnation. Explain why we cannot bring together the unity of Yahweh's holiness and love.
6. What expectations does God have of all who may enter into his kingdom, according to Hosea, Joel, and Amos?
7. How was God's word through Hosea and Amos vindicated in Samaria's fall (722 B.C.)?

8. Explain the nature and extent of covenant renewal in these three prophets. How are Gentiles also included in the process of covenant renewal?
9. How does Joel bring together the historical and the eschatological?
10. Were the promises in Joel 2:17–27 fulfilled before the coming of Christ? Are they fulfilled in the present age? Does Joel distinguish between material and spiritual blessings? Explain the phrase "and afterward" in 2:28 in relation to the material and spiritual aspects of covenant renewal.
11. What is the purpose of the Holy Spirit? With whom does he dwell? What is meant by internalization and democratization? How does Peter apply Joel 2:28–32 to the Pentecost experience?
12. What is the theological contribution of the hymns and visions of Amos?
13. Define God's kingdom in terms of righteousness, love, and justice. What does God expect from his children?
14. How did Amos correct the popular understanding of the Day of the Lord? What response does God expect from the remnant? What does he expect from us today?

CHAPTER 5

Obadiah, Jonah, and Micah

OBADIAH: THE KINGDOMS OF THIS WORLD WILL BECOME THE LORD'S

Obadiah and His Time

This small prophetic book tells us nothing regarding the prophetic call of Obadiah, the length of his ministry, or even the historical context within which Obadiah spoke. Who was this Obadiah? Obadiah is a common name in Israel[1] and signifies "servant (*'-b-d* = "serve" or "be in service to") of Yahweh."[2] But nothing else is known about the prophet, his parental lineage, or the town from which he hailed.

The proposed dates for his ministry range from 850 to 400 B.C.[3] It is plausible to argue for a date shortly after Jerusalem's fall (586 B.C.) when Edom rejoiced in the city's defeat. Other prophets also singled out Edom as conspirator with Babylon (Jer. 49:7–22; Ezek. 25:12–14; 35:5–6; see Lam. 4:21–22; Ps. 137:7). Moreover, the similarities between Obadiah and Jeremiah 49 suggest that the two prophets drew from a common source.[4] Possibly Jeremiah 49 is to be dated earlier than Obadiah because Obadiah contains elements of hope and encouragement, which would be appropriate for a book written in the Exile.[5] Jeremiah 49 contains no such element of hope.

In 586 B.C. God delivered Judah into the hands of Babylon under the kingship of Nebuchadnezzar (2 Chron. 36:11–21). The people of Judah were exiled to a strange land, far from their beloved Jerusalem. Psychologically, emotionally, and spiritually they had reason to despair (see Pss. 89:50–51; 137; Lamentations). In exile the people experienced alienation from God, the temple, Jerusalem, the king, the priesthood, the land, and all other covenant benefits. A godly remnant, however, did respond to the prophetic exhortations to seek the Lord. They remembered what they had lost, eagerly sought the Lord alone for their salvation, and pleaded with him to restore them as his people (Lam. 5:21).

For the remnant, the prophecy of Obadiah was God's answer to their prayers. They longed for God, awaited his love and justice, and wondered when God would judge the Edomites and the other nations.[6] They were also anxious for the establishment of God's kingdom in power, justice, righteousness, and peace. Then all wrongs would be rectified!

Literary Forms and Structure

Literary Forms

The prophecy is short but problematic. Jerome (A.D. 345–419) observed that its problems are in inverse proportion to its size.[7] Two main issues are prominent in the study of Obadiah: the literary parallels with Jeremiah and the structure of the book.[8] Both issues have been complicated by extensive treatments, but no consensus has been reached. If Allen's conclusion that Obadiah "borrowed cultic and traditional themes in developing his prophecy"[9] is correct, it is very likely that the argument of who borrowed from whom will never be resolved. Consequently, I agree with Childs that the proliferation of historical data and literary reconstruction do not significantly affect the interpretation of Obadiah.[10]

Structure

    A. Superscription, v. 1a
      B. Oracles of judgment against Edom, vv. 1b–9
        C. Reasons for Edom's fall, vv. 10–14
          D. The Day of the Lord for the nations, vv. 15–16
           E. The glory of the Lord's kingdom, vv. 17–20

The Message of Obadiah

This short prophecy is directed specifically against Edom for their pride and hatred of their "brother" Jacob (v. 10; see Amos 1:11). The Edomites boasted about the trouble that had come upon the people of Judah (vv. 11–12). They collaborated with the Babylonians by entrapping the Judeans at intersections. They openly rejoiced in Judah's trouble and encouraged the Babylonians. Great was their hatred of Judah and even greater their joy when Jerusalem was razed and desecrated by the Babylonian troops. They had no regard for the miserable lives of the Jews. The fall of Jerusalem was the fulfillment of their national dream: the end of Israel.

The spirit of bigotry manifested by Edom during Judah's crisis has no place in God's kingdom. Obadiah portrayed in vivid imagery how Edom had rejoiced, cheered, and feasted when Yahweh disgraced his own people and how she, too, would be destroyed without any compassion (vv. 10, 15–16, 18–19). God's justice will triumph in Edom's fall!

The prophecy, however, should not be restricted to Edom, because Edom is representative of all nations hostile to the Lord and to the establishment of his kingdom on earth (Isa. 34:1–2, 6; Joel 3:19; Amos 9:12).[11] Notice how Obadiah expanded the original vision concerning Edom's fall to include all nations.

> The day of the Lord is near for all nations.
> As you have done, it will be done to you;
>   your deeds will return upon your own head.
> Just as you drank on my holy hill,
>   so all the nations will drink continually;
> they will drink and drink
>   and be as if they had never been.
>   (vv. 15–16)

The promised possession of the land (vv. 19–21) is made even more concrete through an explicit description of the land, its border, and the restoration of the exiles. God's judgment on Edom typifies God's ultimate victory over the nations, as Calvin wrote,

> This then is what the Prophet now means, when he promises to the Jews the heritage which they had lost; yes, God then enlarged the borders of Judea. Hence, he shows that they should not only be

restored to their former condition, but that the kingdom would be increased in splendour and wealth, when Christ should come.[12]

The message of judgment on Judah's enemies was a message of comfort and encouragement for the captive Jews. The prophetic word assured them that Yahweh would save his people and that he would avenge their enemies.[13] In God's judgments on earth, they will witness his determination to establish his glory on earth. The nations will no longer desecrate what is holy to the Lord. (See figure 33.)

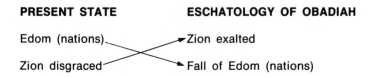

PRESENT STATE   **ESCHATOLOGY OF OBADIAH**

Edom (nations)   ➤Zion exalted

Zion disgraced   ➤Fall of Edom (nations)

Figure 33. The Comfort of Obadiah

Yahweh alone can and will transform this world and bring order out of anarchy.[14] This transformation is the essence of the kingdom of God. Childs observes, "In sum, the canonical shape of the oracles of Obadiah has interpreted the prophetic message as the promise of God's coming rule which will overcome the evil intent of the nations, even Edom, and restore a holy remnant to its inheritance within God's kingship."[15]

The kingdom of God (Zion) will be exalted when all resistance to God's lordship is put down. The Day of the Lord will bring destruction to the enemies of his children. Any intrusion of divine judgment in the history of redemption is evidence that God rules. The godly may take comfort in the hope that human powers will be brought down and that God's kingdom will come with power and salvation.[16] This happened in the history of Aram, Assyria, Babylon, and the empires that rose and fell. Their fall is to be interpreted, not as an accidental occurrence, but as an eschatological event of the greatest significance. This is what Obadiah meant when he said that Seir (the great Edomite city and counterpart of Zion) shall fall so that Zion may rise: "The kingdom will be the LORD's" (v. 21).

> Unfortunately, the history of these two "brothers" was anything but peaceful. Israel had a long history of rivalry with Edom, going back to Genesis 25.[17] The Lord had revealed to Rebekah that two nations were in her womb; from Esau and Jacob developed Edom and Israel.
>
> The wandering Israelites requested passage through the Edomite territory (Num. 20), but they were refused and had to bypass Mount Hor and go around the land of Edom (21:4). At another

point the Edomites permitted passage when the Israelites moved from the Arabah into the mountains of Edom, past Zalmonah and Punon to Oboth (Deut. 2:2–8; Num. 33:41–45). The attitude found in Scripture toward the Edomites is ambivalent; sometimes they were to be treated as brothers (Deut. 23:7), and sometimes not. In comparison, the Moabites and Amorites were explicitly forbidden to enter the assembly of the Lord, not even to the tenth generation, but Edomites were permitted to enter after the third generation (v. 8).

David subjugated the Edomites (2 Sam. 8:13–14). During Solomon's reign they created disturbances led by Hadad the Edomite (1 Kings 11:14–25). They fought against Judah during the reign of Jehoshaphat (873–848 B.C.) but were repelled and became a vassal-state of Judah (2 Chron. 20; see 1 Kings 22:47). They rebelled under his son, Jehoram of Judah (848–841 B.C.), who was unsuccessful in crushing their insurrection (2 Kings 8:20–22; 2 Chron. 21:8–10). Ezekiel describes the relationship as an "ancient hostility" (Ezek. 35:5).

Against this background we must understand the Edomite aspirations during Judah's disaster in 586 B.C., when they said, "These two nations and countries will be ours and we will take possession of them" (Ezek. 35:10). This attitude is also reflected in Psalm 137:7, where the writer prays,

> Remember, O LORD, what the Edomites did
> on the day Jerusalem fell.
> "Tear it down," they cried,
> "tear it down to its foundations!"

One might also consider the statement in 1 Esdras where Edom was credited with the burning of the temple in 586 B.C. Later, when the exiles returned from Babylon, Darius commanded that "all the country which they hold should be free without tribute; and that the Edomites should give over the villages of the Jews which they then held" (1 Esd. 4:45, 50; see Judith 7:8, 18).

The Edomites became known as Idumeans. *Idumea* and *Idumeans* applied to the Edomite territory that was carved out of southern Judah after the Judeans were exiled to Babylon. The Nabateans forced the Edomites to leave Edom and to find refuge in southern Judah.[18] In the second century Judas Maccabee "fought against the children of Esau in Idumea . . . and he gave them a great overthrow, and abated their courage, and took their spoils" (1 Macc. 5:1–3, 65). Josephus informs us that John Hyrcanus was also instrumental in subduing the Edomites, forcing them to submit to ritual circumcision and conversion to Judaism (*Ant.*

12.8.1). Herod the Great traced his ancestry back to a converted Idumean. In *The Jewish War* Josephus described how Edomites sided with the Zealots against the Jewish "establishment" and massacred more than twenty thousand of Jerusalem's inhabitants all for the sake of "liberty."[19] With the fall of Jerusalem in A.D. 70, the Edomites dropped out of recorded history.

JONAH: THE GREAT KING IS FREE IN HIS COMPASSION

Jonah and His Time

Jonah, the son of Amittai, lived in the eighth century B.C. He was born at Gath-Hepher, in the territory of Zebulun, about five miles north of Nazareth. We know from 2 Kings 14:25 that he prophesied during the reign of Jeroboam II (793–753 B.C.) of Israel.[20] In his early ministry he was probably very popular because he prophesied the victory of Israel and the expansion of its territory to the original boundaries. Thus the Lord granted a temporary stay in his judgment on Israel by permitting his people an unparalleled era of prosperity under Jeroboam II (2 Kings 14:24), but Israel and Judah took God's grace for granted.

By the time of Jonah's ministry, Assyria was preoccupied with the mountain tribes of Urartu and did not continue her westward campaigns until Tiglath-pileser III (745 B.C.) came to power. Israel rejoiced in the Assyrian preoccupation. She aggressively pursued a policy of defense by strengthening the fortified cities, building up the army, and employing international diplomacy. Had the Israelites heard of Jonah's mission to proclaim God's judgment on Nineveh, they would have treated Jonah as a national hero. But they did not realize how God was free to deal favorably with Assyria and pour out his judgment on Israel. How unfair all this seems!

Literary Form and Structure

Literary Form[21]

The prophecy of Jonah is unlike the other prophetic books. It contains no prophetic oracles[22] and gives no indication of authorship.[23] Though Jonah was an eighth-century prophet, other considerations favor a later date of the book's composition.[24] Ellison holds that a Judean prophet composed the work as an encouragement to Judah about to be exiled.[25] Craigie concludes that it may have been composed during or after the Exile.[26] Regardless of the dating of the prophecy and the original audience, Jonah is God's prophet[27] to Nineveh, and this book is God's prophetic word.[28]

The book's purpose cannot be understood without defining the literary genre of Jonah. Many proposals have been made and some are very convincing. Is the genre historical,[29] didactic,[30] allegorical,[31] satiric,[32] midrashic,[33] or parabolic?[34] I take the book to be historical with a parabolic force. A parable need not be unhistorical; its purpose lies in the perspectives it offers for wise living. First, the prophet represents the people of God who in their disobedience to the Lord fail to receive God's blessings.[35] Second, the Lord freely rules over creation and delivers Gentiles from their troubles; but God's people may be blind to his greatness and freedom.[36] Jonah failed to appreciate that the Lord may be equally forbearing with the nations. Yahweh, the great King, is free to bless, to be gracious, and to be patient with the nations. More than that, he can show compassion on pagans and even has a concern for animals: "But Nineveh has more than a hundred and twenty thousand people who cannot tell their right hand from their left, and many cattle as well. Should I not be concerned about that great city?" (Jonah 4:11).

Third, Jonah is negatively patterned after Elijah. He, like Elijah, was sent on a mission, and when his mission seemed to have failed, he, too, was ready to die (4:8; 1 Kings 19:4). But unlike Elijah, Jonah had no ground for despondency.[37] The book makes Jonah look foolish, as Allen concludes: "Jonah is made to appear a ridiculous figure whose part none would be prepared to defend."[38] The book is a prophetic *māšāl* ("proverb")[39] that draws attention to Jonah's folly and encourages a wise response by the self-righteous.

Structure

   I. Jonah's commission and flight, 1:1–2:10
      A. Jonah's commission, 1:1–2
        B. Jonah on the ship to Tarshish, 1:3
          C. The dilemma and prayer of the sailors, 1:4–8
            D. Jonah's proclamation, 1:9
          C'. Response and deliverance, 1:10–16
        B'. Jonah in the fish, 1:17–2:1

JONAH'S PRAYER, 2:2–9

        B". Jonah on land, 2:10
  II. Jonah at Nineveh, 3:1–4:11
      A. Jonah's commission, 3:1–2
        B. Jonah in Nineveh, 3:3
            D. Jonah's proclamation, 3:4
          C. The dilemma, response, and deliverance of Nineveh, 3:5–10

147

JONAH'S LAMENT, 4:1–4

B'. Jonah under the shelter, 4:5–7
C'. Jonah's dilemma and response, 4:8–9
D'. God's proclamation, 4:10–11

The Message of Jonah

Jonah, a prophet of God, was on the run from God. What a parody! The caricature of Jonah is far from positive. He took off for Tarshish by boat and was asleep during a storm. He did not identify with the anxiety of the sailors. He did not pray for them. He had no pangs of conscience about dropping out of God's mission. Unlike Elijah and Elisha, he had little sympathy for the pagans.

In the midst of the storm, while the prophet of God was asleep, the pagans were busily praying to their gods. The sailors, in dread and desperation, finally awakened Jonah and asked him to join them in prayer. Jonah even then did not confess that he was the cause of their troubles; not until he was found guilty and responsible for their adversity did he confess. Then Jonah stated proudly that he was a worshiper of the true God: "I am a Hebrew and I worship the LORD, the God of heaven, who made the sea and the land" (1:9). (See figure 34.)

JONAH'S PROCLAMATION	YAHWEH'S PROCLAMATION
God is the Creator	I love creation
God is the Judge	I have compassion

Figure 34. The Irony in the Message of the Book of Jonah

The sailors' response to the good news that Yahweh is sovereign over creation was overwhelming. They believed that this God of whom Jonah spoke has power over creation and judges those who rebel against him. They were more righteous than Jonah because they stood in awe of the Lord. Further, they received Jonah as the prophet of the Most High God when they consulted him about what they should do (1:11). They also demonstrated concern for life when they tried to save themselves by rowing out of the storm. They even prayed for God's forgiveness as they threw Jonah overboard: "Then they cried to the LORD, 'O LORD, please do not let us die for taking this man's life. Do not hold us accountable for killing an innocent man, for you, O LORD, have done as you pleased'" (v. 14).

When they had thrown him into the sea, their faith was rewarded. The sea became quiet. The sailors went merrily on their way while

Jonah's destiny remained uncertain. They sailed the quiet sea while Jonah was in the midst of the sea. Their prayers had already been answered, just as Jonah began to pray (chap. 2). They immediately presented sacrifices and voluntary offerings as thanksgiving to the Lord (1:16) while Jonah still had to be broken before he vowed to bring his offerings of thanksgiving (2:9).[40]

In this story the sailors are the heroes of faith, though they knew virtually nothing of God's perfections and acts in redemptive history. They worshiped the Lord, the God of heaven and earth, and they showed concern for human life and fulfilled the vow they had made to Yahweh (1:16). In contrast, Jonah's prayer was self-centered (2:1–9).

The irony of Jonah's theology lies in his limiting God to his narrow perception of redemption. The prophet believed that God is the Creator of everything but that he redeems only the elect of Israel. Jonah believed that since God had chosen Israel from among the wicked nations, he had to show mercy to Israel, even if they were rebellious.

Herein is one of the book's canonical functions.[41] The prophecy contains a strong warning to all the godly. The elect may miss the blessing of seeing God's grace extended outside the immediate covenant community because they impose limits on God. While Jonah was praying anxiously for his deliverance, the sailors had been tasting the love of God for three days![42] Likewise, the people of Nineveh, who repented of their sin, rejoiced that the impending judgment had not come; at the same time Jonah was a miserable man.

The book of Jonah affirms God's freedom, sovereignty, and power.[43] He is the Creator of *everything* (1:9), and as the Creator he is free in his rule. His power extends over creation (storm, fish, vine, worm) and redemption.[44] God can never be bound, whether by a confessional understanding, a theological definition, or religious practices. Jonah rejoiced in his deliverance (2:9) and in the protection of the vine (4:6). But he missed out on God's delight in saving the sailors and the city of Nineveh, including the infants and the animals (v. 11).

The Lord's proclamation to Jonah sums up the prophetic message (4:10–11). According to these concluding verses, Yahweh's interest and mercy extend to all creation. This perspective may serve as a catalyst to fulfill the mission to the nations. When the righteous let God be God and open their eyes to his grace and his love for creation, they are free to do God's will. To the contrary, when they bind God to themselves, they bind themselves.[45]

MICAH: HOPE IN THE KINGDOM OF GOD AND OF HIS MESSIAH

Micah and His Time

Micah hailed from Moresheth-gath, a village in the low-lying hill country of Judah under the watchful eye of the military fortress at Lachish. He ministered the word of God in both Israel and Judah from 733 to 701 B.C.[46] By virtue of his being raised in the country, he was familiar with the poor of Judah (2:4, 8–9; 3:3, 5; see Isa. 3:14–15; 10:2; 11:4; 14:30, 32; 29:19). But he was also at home among the sages of Judah as he discerned the folly of Israel and Judah.[47] As God's prophet he dissociated the vision of the kingdom to come from the reality of Jerusalem, the seedbed of corruption. With the fall of Samaria the Israelites fled for asylum to Judah, and we may deduce from the archaeological record of Jerusalem that the city increased rapidly up to four times its previous size.[48] Her leaders grew more corrupt (3:9–12), and the moral fiber further disintegrated (7:1–6).[49]

Micah, a contemporary of Isaiah, spoke the word of Yahweh in the days of Jotham (750–731, coregent with Uzziah from 750 to 740 B.C.), Ahaz (735–715 B.C.), and Hezekiah (729–686, coregent with Ahaz from 729 to 715 B.C.), who were kings of Judah, and of Zechariah (753 B.C.), Shallum (752 B.C.), Menahem (752–742 B.C.), Pekahiah (742–740 B.C.), Pekah (740–732 B.C.), and Hoshea (732–722 B.C.), kings of Israel.

Both Micah and Isaiah spoke of the fall of Samaria and the end of the northern kingdom (Mic. 1:6), as Hosea and Amos had, but unlike them, Micah and Isaiah lived to witness the fall of the Aramean state under Rezin (740–732 B.C.) in 732 B.C. and of the northern kingdom in 722 B.C. They also witnessed the rise of Assyria, whose empire grew under the aggressive leadership of Tiglath-pileser III (745–727 B.C.), Shalmaneser V (727–722 B.C.), Sargon II (722–705 B.C.), and Sennacherib (705–681 B.C.). Assyria would dominate the ancient Near East for more than a century before being eclipsed by Babylon.[50]

Micah's ministry supported the significant reform programs of King Hezekiah. By the Spirit this godly king accepted prophetic critique and was greatly used by the Lord (2 Chron. 29:1–31:20).[51] A century later Micah's ministry was still remembered by some of the elders of Judah. They reminded King Jehoiakim that King Hezekiah had left Micah unharmed, even though he, like Jeremiah, had proclaimed the destruction of Jerusalem. Because of this remembrance of Micah, Jeremiah escaped death (Jer. 26:17–24).

Literary Form and Structure

Literary Form

Micah is largely poetic with prose sections.[52] The poetic features include parallelism, wordplay, use of catchwords,[53] and prophetic forms of speech (oracles of judgment, woe, and deliverance and a prophetic liturgy).

The oracles reflect the style of an orator. He made a dramatic appeal to God's people, using an extensive stock of rhetorical devices. The oracles resound with elements of both judgment and hope. Because the intermixture seems like a jumble, critics have carried out detailed analyses of authenticity.[54] But the repetitions are effective if understood from the vantage point of the audience. Micah's oracles are best understood as a polemic or *disputation*[55] against the leaders (administrators and royal officials) of Israel and Judah.[56]

Structure[57]

Superscription, 1:1
I. Oracles of judgment, 1:2–3:12
  A. Case against Samaria and Jerusalem, 1:2–7
  A'. Lament on the fall of Judah's cities, 1:8–16
    B. Judgment on the people, 2:1–11
      C. Words of comfort, 2:12–13
    B'. Judgment on the leaders, 3:1–12
II. Oracles of comfort, 4:1–5:15
  A. The exaltation of Zion, 4:1–5
    B. Restoration of God's kingdom, 4:6–5:1
  A'. The exaltation of Bethlehem, 5:2–5a
    B'. Restoration of the kingdom of David, 5:5b–15
III. Oracles of judgment and comfort, 6:1–7:20
  A. Prophetic case against Israel, 6:1–5
    B. Question and answer, 6:6–8
  A'. Case against Israel, 6:9–16
    B'. Prophetic lament and hope, 7:1–7
      C'. Prophetic liturgy, 7:8–20.
        1. The glory of Zion, 7:8–13
        2. Kingdom prayer, 7:14–17
        3. Prayer for forgiveness, 7:18–20

The Message of Micah

The name Micah (*mîkâ*) is an abbreviation of Micaiah ("who is like Yahweh," Jer. 26:18). The rhetorical question has the effect of an affirmative: "There is no other God like Yahweh!" The name of the prophet serves as a sign of the incomparability of Yahweh.[58]

The prophet proclaimed Yahweh's sovereignty, incomparability, and royalty. He condemned the leaders, the rich, and the false prophets for rebelling against God (3:9–12); they were complacent with their "little" kingdoms but apathetic to God's kingdom. Many suffered and longed for love, justice, and righteousness. In his disputes with the false shepherds of Israel and Judah, Micah led the poor and humble to trust in Yahweh and to seek the righteous order of his kingdom.

The major themes of Micah fall into three categories: (1) judgment, (2) purification and hope, and (3) the establishment of the kingdom of God and of his Messiah.

Judgment

The book opens with a magnificent vision of the great King entering history. When Yahweh enters into the arena of man, man's environment is destabilized. The phenomena associated with his coming are overwhelming as mountains melt and valleys split apart (1:4). The theophanic description evokes a sense of awe and wonder, as von Rad puts it: "Even when Jahweh appears . . . for judgment, to cast all human vainglory down into the dust, even there the prophets' eye gazes with delight on his self-manifestation and the phenomena which accompany it."[59] (See figure 35.)

Micah announced that their God, who loved them in the past (6:4–5; 7:14–15), was coming to establish his kingdom by expelling his covenant people.[60] This announcement undoubtedly shocked his audience who had expected God's blessing. They had violated God's trust by their idolatrous ways; they could not enter his kingdom because they had been loyal to the cultural practices of the nations (sacrifices, cultic prostitution, divination, and magic).[61] Instead of setting an example of being a counterculture, they became acculturated to the practices of the nations (1:7; 5:12–14). Instead of relying on the Lord, they depended on military advances, alliances, and fortifications for their security (5:11).

Their society as a whole was ruled by pragmatism. The prophet also condemned their lack of concern for one another (2:1–2, 8; 3:1–4, 9–11; 6:10–12; 7:2–4). Their insensitivity to justice had resulted in anarchy and had even created serious disillusionment with the institution of the family (7:5–6). The leadership scorned the covenant and the promises, disregarding God's blessing on their children (2:9). The religious leadership was no different because even the priests and prophets ministered in the name of Yahweh for personal gain (v. 11; 3:6–7, 11).[62]

Micah proclaimed that Israel (Samaria) and Judah (Jerusalem) would be exiled. *Samaria* represented the policies of Omri and Ahab: political, economic, and religious dependency of the northern kingdom on the nations (6:16). The structures of Israel would collapse on the Day of the Lord for Samaria (722 B.C.). Everything for which the people had worked so hard had to come to an end (1:6–7; 6:13–15). (See figure 35.)

Theophany
Yahweh's coming in judgment
Nature stirs at the coming of the great King
Yahweh comes against Samaria, Jerusalem, and all nations

Figure 35. Micah's Opening Theophany

Jerusalem was no exception; she, too, had adopted paganism and acculturation as the way of life.[63] Her social, religious, and political life was very sick (1:9). The people had given themselves to a self-centered way of life without any consideration of the Lord or their fellowman. This was true of the nation as a whole (2:1–4). Zion, the city of God, had to fall (3:12), even though it was inconceivable to Micah's contemporaries that Zion with her sacred symbols could fall. Zion stood for God's kingdom, the Davidic dynasty, and the blessed relationship of God with his people. The leadership felt itself secure and thought only of peace and prosperity (v. 5). Had not God promised to be with them? How could Yahweh turn against his own (v. 11)?

Micah experienced the anguish of these questions. He identified himself with the terror of exile as he mourned and went about barefoot like an exile (1:8). The prophet also gave himself to hope and prayer. He had hope because he trusted in his God.

> But as for me, I watch in hope for the LORD,
> I wait for God my Savior;
> my God will hear me.
>
> (7:7)

Unlike his contemporaries, he did not wait for political, economical, or social solutions. He felt alone and cried out in despair,

> What misery is mine!
> I am like one who gathers summer fruit
>   at the gleaning of the vineyard;
> there is no cluster of grapes to eat,
>   none of the early figs that I crave.
> The godly have been swept from the land;
>   not one upright man remains.

All men lie in wait to shed blood;
each hunts his brother with a net.
(7:1–2)

God's condemnation of Israel and Judah extends to all areas of life (1:16; 2:3; 6:13). His coming (1:3–5) marked the fuller inauguration of his kingdom in the judgment of Samaria and Jerusalem (1:6; 3:12; 4:10–11; 6:16).[64] This is a prophetic paradox! But Micah's vision goes beyond the judgments of Samaria and Jerusalem to all the kingdoms of the world (7:13, 16–17). The Day of Judgment is God's expression of wrath against all nations when he will appear in judgment to establish his kingdom on the earth.

Purification and Hope

Micah also held out the sure hope of redemption from exile (4:10).[65] The prophet called out a remnant from Israel and Judah[66] to prepare themselves for Yahweh's coming judgment. Yet beyond the immediate historical context the prophetic witness calls on the godly in every age to prepare for the kingdom of God and his Messiah.[67] (See figure 36.)

Micah affirmed that he and his followers would continue to walk in the way of the Lord (4:5), contrary to the false way of the nations (v. 5). He further elaborated that this way is the old way. The Lord had revealed to Moses that he expected a loyal commitment to him, as expressed in justice and love (6:6–8).[68] Justice (*mišpāṭ*), as it pertains to human beings, is that quality of integrity by which one deals with people in accordance with God's standard. Justice is not determined by social status, prior relationship, hearsay, appearances, or likes or dislikes. Justice is an expression of love (*ḥesed*), which is characterized by constancy, consideration, absence of discrimination or recrimination, and a readiness to cover a multitude of sins and wrongs.[69] As the Lord deals justly and lovingly with creation and with his children, he expects nothing less from them than a spirit that reveals a readiness to forgive, to be fair, and to give people the benefit of the doubt. The law of God's kingdom, to which all its citizens must conform (4:2), involves justice, love, and humility. God's way is always opposed to *Realpolitik*. (See figure 36.)

Micah's prayer (7:14–20) functions as a model for each generation of the remnant to look for the righteous establishment of God's kingship. Those who hope, pray for, and work for this new order will not be disappointed. They may pray with Micah,

Who is a God like you,
who pardons sin and forgives the transgression
of the remnant of his inheritance?
You do not stay angry forever

154

but delight to show mercy.
You will again have compassion on us;
    you will tread our sins underfoot
    and hurl all our iniquities into the depths of the sea.
You will be true to Jacob,
    and show mercy to Abraham,
as you pledged on oath to our fathers
    in days long ago.

(7:18–20)

Mourning in face of God's judgment
Submission to the Lord (humility)
Faithful living: justice, love
Waiting for the kingdom deliverance
Prayer for forgiveness
Prayer for God's mercy

Figure 36. Micah's Modeling of a Godly Response

Restoration

When Micah spoke of the future, he witnessed to a new era of God's involvement (4:1, 6–7; 5:10; 7:7–15). The new era will be a greater manifestation of the kingdom of God and his Messiah. The prophecy encourages hope in the kingdom of God and in the rule of his Messiah over all creation. Micah, *the* prophet of a new age,[70] also bore witness to the organic relation of a restoration from exile to the transformation of all things. Restoration begins with the renewal of God's favor to the remnant from exile (2:12–13; 4:6–7). Moreover, the restoration of the Jews is related to that of the Gentiles (7:12–13), and redemption is related to creation (v. 14).[71]

The Kingdom of God

The rule of God brings blessing and protection to the children of God. The great King promises to take the "outcasts" and make them citizens of his kingdom (4:7–8). As citizens they will receive his blessings, live securely, and enjoy the fullness of his promises, expressed in the imagery of rural life.

Every man will sit under his own vine
    and under his own fig tree,
and no one will make them afraid,
    for the LORD Almighty has spoken.

(v. 4)[72]

The Lord also promises to intervene on their behalf: "Their king will pass through before them, the LORD at their head" (2:13). Unlike the leaders of Judah (3:9–11), the great King will establish his rule justly and righteously.

> The law will go out from Zion,
>> the word of the LORD from Jerusalem.
> He will judge between many peoples
>> and will settle disputes for strong nations far and wide.
>
> (4:2b–3)

The result will be nothing less than peace as the Lord rules in the midst of his people, protecting them and guiding them like a shepherd. God's kingship will be celebrated throughout the earth, and his people will experience his blessing and his protection. (See figure 37.)

The kingdom will extend to the remnant of all twelve tribes (2:12; 4:6–7; 5:7–8; 7:18) *and* all Gentiles who will submit themselves to the Lord (4:1–4). Though the progress of the kingdom may be slow, the people of God need not be afraid (v. 13).

The Messianic Kingdom

Restoration also consists of the reestablishment of the kingdom under the Davidic Messiah, God's instrument for establishing his kingdom on earth. Micah confirmed God's promise to David but not without transforming the human conception or expectations. He dissociated the messianic reign from Jerusalem because Jerusalem had been tainted by the corruption of power, immorality, foreign influences, and idolatry. He purposefully associated the Davidic Messiah with Bethlehem.

> But you, Bethlehem Ephrathah,
>> though you are small among the clans of Judah,
> out of you will come for me
>> one who will be ruler over Israel,
> whose origins are from of old,
>> from ancient times.
>
> (5:2)[73]

The Davidic Messiah will truly accomplish the will of God on earth. He will establish the kingdom of God; deliver the children of the kingdom; restore the full enjoyment of the promises, blessings, and covenants to them; vindicate their rights; and avenge the oppressors. He is the Warrior sent by the great King to fight their battles. (See figure 37.)

The remnant have an important place in advancing the messianic rule as they, too, establish the kingdom of God on earth.[74]

KINGDOM OF GOD

Established by his Messiah of David

MESSIANIC KINGDOM

Objects: Outcasts, humble, Jews and Gentiles
Goal: Peace, blessing, protection
Means: God's righteous rule, deliverance, vindication
Messiah's righteous rule, deliverance, vindication
Messianic community as instruments of blessing and
curse ("dew" and "lion")

**Figure 37. The Messiah Is the Means of
Establishing God's Kingdom**

The *remnant of Jacob* will be
in the midst of many peoples
like dew from the LORD,
like showers on the grass,
which do not wait for man
or linger for mankind.
The remnant of Jacob will be among the nations,
in the midst of many peoples,
like a lion among the beasts of the forest,
like a young lion among flocks of sheep,
which mauls and mangles as it goes,
and no one can rescue.

(5:7−8, emphasis mine)

Since Micah also includes the Gentiles who submit themselves to the messianic rule, he announces that both Jews and Gentiles will share in the glorious messianic age.[75] The messianic community will be the means of blessing ("the dew") to those who submit themselves to the messianic claims. But they will bring a curse ("like a lion") to all who resist God's kingdom. The imagery of "dew" and "lion" may be explained from the proverb where the king's favor is likened to the life-giving quality of "dew" and his wrath is likened to the roar of a "lion" (Prov. 19:12).

The vision of the messianic kingdom is expressed in the language of the eighth century B.C. when Assyria was the power to be reckoned with. Thus the promise of the Messiah's victory over Assyria (5:5−6) signifies his subjugation of all resistance to the rule of God on earth (similarly "Babylon" in Rev. 18:1−24; see Dan. 2:44; 7:26−27; 1 Cor. 15:25−26). His kingdom will be a universal rule of peace.

He will stand and shepherd his flock
   in the strength of the LORD,
   in the majesty of the name of the LORD his God.
And they will live securely, for then his greatness
   will reach to the ends of the earth.

(5:4)

The messianic kingdom will be an everlasting kingdom in which the Lord will cleanse the earth of all immorality, idolatry, power play, and corruption (5:10–15). The kingdom will be the Lord's, his Messiah's,[76] and that of the people of God. They will forever enjoy the presence of God in protection and blessing, being fully satiated with the goodness of the Divine Warrior who cares for the remnant and for his creation. Redemption and creation are the objects of his love!

REVIEW

Obadiah's oracle of judgment on Edom calls for a panoramic interpretation. Edom represents the nations that oppose the kingship of God and persecute the people of God. The Lord has in store a day of reckoning when he will hold all nations accountable for their acts. On that day no nation, kingdom, or empire on earth will have the power to resist God's vengeance and wrath. Then he will sovereignly establish his kingdom.

The Lord will intervene on behalf of his people. He is the Divine Warrior, who rules in vengeance and in deliverance. Deliverance is empty unless he also avenges himself of all resistance on earth. The message of the Day of the Lord is relevant throughout the progression of redemptive history. Walter Kaiser observes, "Hence the day of the Lord ran throughout the history of the kingdom of God so that it occurred in each particular judgment as evidence of its complete fulfillment which was near and approaching."[77]

In its canonical function Obadiah still comforts the suffering people of God. But the children of the kingdom may never violate God's law of love! Wolff reminds us of how the nature of the Christian-Jewish relationship over the centuries is a strong condemnation of how Christians have reacted without love and compassion to the suffering of the Jews.[78] The church of Jesus Christ must bear witness to God's love, especially to the Jewish people.[79]

Jonah's message is universal and transcultural. The Lord shows that his people can never box him in. They cannot define or predict what he will do. He is free in showing compassion to his creation: the covenant people, pagans, infants, and even animals. The prophetic significance of Jonah lies in its message that Yahweh is gracious and compassionate, free in judgment and in mercy. He is free to deliver the nonelect and to

158

afflict the elect when they have lost sight of their mission and vision of God.

Micah opposed the established structures of Samaria and Judah. He lamented their leadership's lack of concern: immorality; acculturation; idolatry; indifference to the welfare of the people; and apathy to the theocratic ideal, the kingship of God, and the Zion theology. Micah protested in his quiet way that Yahweh is King and that the economic, cultural, and political structures of Samaria and Jerusalem ran counter to the structure of God's kingdom.

Micah's canonical function is associated with his witness to the kingdom of God and his criticism of human leadership as self-serving and corrupt. His prophetic witness affirms with hope that God will reinstate his rule and that his rule is continuous with what he has begun in Abraham, Moses, and David. The newness of the new era lies in the greater manifestation of his presence in blessing, protection, the transformation of all creation, and the everlasting dominion of the Messiah.

Who may belong to this new world order? Those who adopt God's way (love, justice, and humility, 6:8) and pray for the coming of God's kingdom and of the Messiah. In the restoration from exile Yahweh renewed covenant, forgave sin, showed compassion to his people, reestablished his presence with them in the temple, and restored his kingdom among them. However, the remnant was frustrated that the kingdom was not as powerful at that moment as Micah had announced. Later we shall see that the messianic kingdom was restored in "seed form" in Zerubbabel, but it was weak and unable to bring the victory over the nations and the prosperity and peace to the people of God.

Through the witness of the godly (Zechariah, Simeon, and Anna), of the Father and the Spirit, of Jesus himself (his teaching and works) and his apostles, the Gospels present us with the presence of the kingdom in Jesus as the Messiah (*autobasileia*). Yet the Gospels also present us with the hope that the prophetic word bears a greater fulfillment (see chap. 12: "Living the Prophetic Word"). Jesus is the Alpha and the Omega and has the key to Zion, the New Jerusalem (Rev. 1:17; 22:13). His kingdom has been established and will flourish into an everlasting kingdom that cannot be shaken. Micah helps us to live, hope, and pray for the era of transformation, renewal, and restoration of the fully realized kingdom of God and his Messiah!

QUESTIONS AND ISSUES

1. What is the historical context of Obadiah, Jonah, and Micah? What are some of the problems associated with the dating of Obadiah?

2. In terms of the possible historical background and in relation to the typological significance of Edom, explain why Obadiah singled out Edom. Does Scripture warrant the representative interpretation? Explain the significance of Babylon in the Apocalypse of John in this light.
3. What is the significance of Zion in the hope that Obadiah holds out for the remnant?
4. How is the book of Jonah unlike other prophetic books? What kind of literary genre may Jonah represent?
5. Explain how a canonical setting of Jonah in the exilic situation might change the meaning from that of a postexilic setting.
6. How is Jonah the message? How is God the message? Explain the parabolic force of Jonah's experience.
7. How does the book of Jonah contribute to our perspective on God, creation, and redemption?
8. What was Micah's perspective on his social-political milieu?
9. Explain how the theophanic opening sets the framework for interpreting the prophetic oracles of judgment in Micah.
10. How does Micah personally lead the reader to godly living?
11. What is the nature of the kingdom of God? Who may enter into his kingdom?
12. What are the qualities of the messianic kingdom? What are the benefits of his rule?
13. Explain how Micah exemplifies the compenetration of several motifs: Messiah, remnant, victory over Assyria, subjugation of the nations, the Divine Warrior, the blessing to the nations, and an era of peace, blessing, and rest.
14. How do these three prophetic works contribute to a richer view of God, the world of creation, the plan of redemption, and godly living?

CHAPTER 6

Nahum, Habakkuk, and Zephaniah

NAHUM: YAHWEH IS THE DIVINE WARRIOR

Nahum and His Time

The prophecy of Nahum is God's word against the kingdoms of this world symbolized by Nineveh. The prophecy begins with an unusually brief introduction to the prophet and his message: "An oracle concerning Nineveh. The book of the vision of Nahum the Elkoshite" (1:1).[1] The name *Nahum,* a verbal form from *n-ḥ-m* ("comfort"), means "comforted" (by Yahweh); this root is fairly common in proper names, as in Nehemiah ("Yahweh comforts"). The prophet is further identified as "the Elkoshite." The location of Nahum's village of Elkosh is more problematic. According to a sixteenth-century tradition, the birthplace and tomb of Nahum is at Al-Qush, located fifty miles north of Mosul on the Tigris River near the mound of Nineveh.[2] Jerome identified Elkosh with Hilkesi in Galilee. This location seems unlikely since the northern kingdom had fallen in 722 B.C. by the time of the earliest possible date for the book (662 B.C.). Pseudo-Epiphanius located Elkosh in Judah near what is now called Beth Gubrin, a village north of Lachish in the Shephelah and a short distance from Moresheth-gath, the birthplace of Micah. This is in accord with the meager internal evidence (v. 15).

Nahum ministered God's word during the decline of the Assyrian Empire under Ashurbanipal (668–627 B.C.). He knew of the defeat of Thebes, a city in Upper Egypt, which fell to the Assyrians in 663 B.C. (3:8–10),[3] but he did not yet know of the fall of Nineveh (612 B.C.), the subject of his prophecy.

If Nahum ministered God's word during the reign of Manasseh, king of Judah, his prophecy may be dated to ca. 650.[4] Manasseh (696–642 B.C.)[5] was a vassal of Assyria and had introduced the official Assyrian cult along with other heathen practices. The Assyrian presence during the period of Nahum's ministry raises the question of how the prophet could speak so openly against Assyria without losing his life. Possibly he did suffer persecution, or he could have just written his message on a "scroll" rather than make a public proclamation.[6] Van der Woude's proposal that Nahum was exiled to Assyria, as Manasseh had been, assumes that the prophecy was a letter written from exile to anti-Assyrian leaders in Judah.[7]

Assyria dominated the political scene throughout the seventh century B.C. In the first half of the seventh century B.C., Ashurbanipal, the son of Esarhaddon (681–669 B.C.), played an important role in international affairs. Some internal evidence suggests that Assyria was still a dominant power (1:12–13, 15; 2:1). During the last years of Ashurbanipal (632–627 B.C.), Assyria showed signs of weakening. The international changes could explain the context of Nahum's open critique of Assyria.[8]

A more popular view posits the context of Nahum's ministry shortly before the fall of Nineveh and still during the reform era of Josiah.[9] This explanation accounts for Nahum's encouraging words to the people of Judah, assuming that they had resumed the celebrations of the feasts and festivals (1:15; 2:2). However, this view does not help in understanding Nahum's portrayal of the ferocity of Assyria and her threat to Judah.

TABLE 7. THE HISTORICAL CONTEXT OF NAHUM

686	650	630	612
Judah: **Manasseh** (686–642)	**Amon** (642–640)	**Josiah** (640–609)	
Proposed dates for Nahum:	**650**	**630**	**615** B.C.
Assyrian kings:			
Esarhaddon (681–669)	Ashurbanipal (668–627)		
Assyrian power:			
Strong	Problems in Egypt, Babylonia, and Elam	Weak	Fall of Nineveh (612)

I conclude that Nahum spoke shortly before the death of Ashurbanipal (ca. 630 B.C.),[10] that he encouraged the reforms under Josiah, and that the generation of Josiah witnessed the vindication of God's word in the fall of Nineveh (612 B.C.).[11] By 605 the Assyrian Empire was thoroughly defeated, and Babylon had risen as a giant. As the dust settled, God's word through the prophet Nahum had vindicated Yahweh's sovereignty over the kingdoms of this world. (See table 7.)

Literary Form and Structure

Literary Form

Nahum is one of the great poetic works in the Old Testament.[12] The prophet's vivid imagery reflects a creative genius who was schooled in the prophetic tradition but moved independently, being led by the Spirit of God.[13] His work reveals many parallels with Isaiah, which leads Armerding to conclude that "in Nahum we have an outstanding example of OT prophetic interpretation and application within the OT itself."[14] The alphabetic acrostic (1:2–8 or 1:1–10),[15] metaphors,[16] parallelism, judgment oracle, irony and sarcasm, assonance, alliteration, symmetry, staccato phrases, and the rapid movement contribute to a varied and rich literary portrayal of God's just judgment on Assyria and compassion for his people. G. A. Smith's observation holds true: "His language is strong and brilliant; his rhythm rumbles and rolls, leaps and flashes, like the horsemen and chariots he describes."[17]

Structure

Superscription, 1:1
  I. God's determined judgment, 1:2–2:2
    A. In praise of Yahweh, 1:2–8
      1. His zeal, 1:2–3a
      2. His anger, 1:3b–6
      3. His care, 1:7–8
        B. Judgment oracle against Assyria and salvation oracle for Judah, 1:9–2:2
  II. Announcement of Nineveh's fall, 2:3–13
    A. Conquest of Nineveh, 2:3–6
    B. Mourning and confusion in the city, 2:7–10
      C. Desolation of Nineveh as a lion's lair, 2:11–13
  III. Announcement of Nineveh's fall, 3:1–7
    A. The city full of blood, 3:1–3
    B. The filthy harlot, 3:4–7
      C. Nineveh's fall likened to that of Thebes, 3:8–11
  IV. Announcement of Nineveh's fall, 3:12–19
    A. Nineveh's fall likened to figs, 3:12–13

B. Satirical description, 3:14–17
C. Joy of the world, 3:18–19

The Message of Nahum

The historical context of Nahum is still unclear, but the message of this servant of God is unambiguous! Nahum stands at the end of the epoch in which Assyria had dominated the ancient Near East for 150 years. He spoke of the Assyrian Empire, but more than that he pointed beyond the historical scene to the Lord who rules the nations (1:2–3). As great as the Lord's judgment is on his enemies (vv. 2–3), greater is his refuge and love for all who find their escape in him (vv. 2–8).

The introductory poem (1:2–8) elevates the diatribe against Nineveh to the level of typology. Assyria becomes a type of the nations and power structures over which the Divine Warrior-King exercises daily dominion in freedom and power. It is a mystery to the godly that he permits evil to exist on earth, but Nahum encouraged them to trust in the sovereign lordship over all creation and to submit themselves to his administration. He will judge Assyria and all expressions of human autonomy.[18]

The opening hymn (1:2–8) dramatically presents the warrior God who is determined to establish his kingdom on earth in Israel.[19] The Divine Warrior cares for his people by saving,[20] ruling, and judging. At the Red Sea, Israel praised him for the marvelous evidences of his kingship, deliverance, and vengeance (Ex. 15:2–18). Nahum called on the people of God to fix their hope on God who is always able to deliver from whatever power might threaten his kingdom on earth.

Nahum's vivid description of the rise of Assyrian sovereignty (her fortifications and military stratagems) and subsequent fall strengthened their hope in God's intervention. The theological perspective inspired the godly with the hope that Assyria, too, could fall. Their God is Yahweh, the great King, the Creator, who alone can unmask the great enemy as a powerless troublemaker.[21]

The book of Nahum functions as a "dramatic illustration of the final, eschatological triumph of God over all his adversaries."[22] The message is to be understood both in terms of *history* and in terms of *eschatology*. The kingdom of evil is being destroyed in every divine judgment and will come to a climactic end with the establishment of the sovereign and righteous kingdom of Yahweh. Thus Nahum consoled all who persevered in waiting for his coming.

The nature of the divine judgment against evil is illumined by the intertwining of oracles of judgment and promise (1:2–2:2). Yahweh abases and helps, puts down and protects, curses, and blesses. He is true to his covenant promise to curse all who threaten his people (Gen. 12:3).[23] Every judgment on the wicked confirms his promise of protection given to all who suffer, trusting and awaiting the justice of God.

Phenomena:	Occasion:
Earthquake	Coming of Yahweh
Smoke	In judgment (wrath) or
Clouds/winds	In deliverance (favor)
Trembling of earth	
Opening up of depths of sea	

Figure 38. Theophany

The Jealousy of the Lord

The Lord's anger has two aspects: *jealousy* and *zeal*. (See figure 39.) In his jealousy for his people, he is angry with Nineveh, and in his zeal, Yahweh protects and defends those who look to him for refuge. Since he is jealous of his name and of his kingdom on earth, he will not tolerate any opposition to his kingship. At the coming of the Lord in glory and power (theophany, see figure 38), all the powers of creation stand at his service.

> The LORD is a jealous and avenging God;
> > the LORD takes vengeance and is filled with wrath.
> The LORD takes vengeance on his foes
> > and maintains his wrath against his enemies.
> The LORD is slow to anger and great in power;
> > the LORD will not leave the guilty unpunished.
> His way is in the whirlwind and the storm,
> > and clouds are the dust of his feet.
> > > (1:2–3; see Ex. 34:6–7)[24]

When the Lord comes to establish his rule, nature trembles;[25] through judgment, he creates a cosmic upheaval.

> He rebukes the sea and dries it up;
> > he makes all the rivers run dry.
> Bashan and Carmel wither
> > and the blossoms of Lebanon fade.
> The mountains quake before him
> > and the hills melt away.
> The earth trembles at his presence,
> > the world and all who live in it.
> Who can withstand his indignation?
> > Who can endure his fierce anger?
> His wrath is poured out like fire;

166

the rocks are shattered before him.
(1:4–6)

If creation dries up, withers, quakes, melts, and trembles, how can humans prepare for his coming (v. 6; see Rev. 6:17)? On the Day of the Lord's wrath (1:6–8),[26] humans must submit to Yahweh's lordship and confess that their powers, kingdoms, and military stratagems were nothing but games. No evil will escape the terror of his majesty when he will subjugate all resistance: "No more will the wicked invade you; they will be completely destroyed" (v. 15). Then he will give his children rest (v. 15; Joel 2:19, 26–27; 3:17; Rev. 7:16; 21:4).[27]

The Zeal of the Lord

The people of God are in the eye of the hurricane. They find protection in the God who loves them and comforts them with a message of peace (1:15–2:2). In his wrath he is zealous for his own, promising to protect them and to share the glory of his victory with them.[28] Nahum presents two facets of God's zeal: defeat and deliverance; wrath and mercy; vengeance and goodness.[29] (See figure 39.) He will defeat, express his wrath on, and avenge himself on all his enemies, but he will deliver, have mercy on, and show his goodness to all who await him (1:15). As great as the Lord's wrath is, more tender is his mercy (v. 7). He protects (7–8) those who await the fullness of his goodness.

> The Lord is good,
>   a refuge in times of trouble.
> He cares for those who trust in him
>   (v. 7).[30]

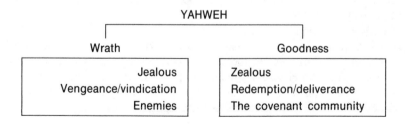

Figure 39. Yahweh—the Divine Warrior

The prophet Nahum was seriously concerned with the power and justice of God *in history.* God is the sovereign King who controls human destiny. Even the greatest world power—Assyria in Nahum's context—

must submit to him. Therefore, the godly must always pray for his kingdom to come, as Achtemeier encourages, "We are to pray that God's Kingdom will come and God's enemies will be defeated; and we are to walk and work as those who already live in the power of that coming Kingdom."[31]

HABAKKUK: DIVINE RIGHTEOUSNESS AND THE TRIUMPH OF FAITH

Habakkuk and His Time

Habakkuk served Judah as God's prophet (1:1). The designation "the prophet" indicates that he was officially recognized as the prophet of the Lord. The name *Habakkuk* (from Heb. "embrace") occurs twice (v. 1; 3:1), but its meaning is uncertain.[32] Little else is known about him, though speculations abound. Rabbinic explanations are not uniform. Some relate him to the son of the Shunammite woman in 2 Kings 4:16; others identify him with the watchman of Isaiah (Isa. 21:6; see Hab. 2:1). According to one of the apocryphal texts of Bel and the Dragon, Habakkuk was the "son of Jesus of the tribe of Levi." It is likely that Habakkuk was a Levite, associated with the temple singers (3:1, 19; 1 Chron. 25:1–8), who lived in Judah during the last days of Josiah (640–609 B.C.) and in the earlier part of the regime of Jehoiakim (608–598 B.C.).

Habakkuk's message fits historically in the context of the fall of Nineveh (612 B.C.) and the emergence of Babylon as the Neo-Babylonian kingdom (605 B.C.) mentioned in 1:6.[33] Habakkuk witnessed significant shifts as the death of Josiah brought an end to the era of reform and Judah rapidly lost her independence. She could only dance to the piping of the international powers around her. Jehoiakim, a selfish, tyrannical, and godless king, took over following the brief reign of Jehoahaz (609 B.C.).

Habakkuk cried out against the violence he witnessed (1:2). He spoke God's word in a crisis situation arising from an increased lawlessness and injustice in Judah (vv. 2–5), after Josiah's sudden death (609 B.C.) and the rise of Babylon. By 605 B.C. Assyria and Egypt had been defeated by Babylon at Carchemish, and Judah's days were numbered.

Literary Form and Structure

Literary Form

The book has two prophetic laments (1:2–4, 12–17) in which the prophet questions Yahweh's righteousness.[34] The Lord responds with oracles of judgment (vv. 5–11; 2:1–4). The dialogue between God and his prophet ends (2:5) only to be followed by a taunt, comprising five "woes" (vv. 6–20).[35] The connection between the dialogues (1:2–2:5) and the taunt is left for the reader to apprehend, but this ambiguity and the terse poetic style encourage the reader to listen closely to his speech to God, to God's speech to the prophet, and to the prophet's speech against Babylon.[36]

The third chapter is set apart with its own introduction, "A prayer of Habakkuk the prophet" (3:1), and with its musical notation ("On shigionoth," v. 1; "For the director of music. On my stringed instruments," v. 19). This chapter consists of several genres (hymn, lament, and thanksgiving).

Structure

Superscription, 1:1
  I. The first dialogue, 1:2–11
      A. Complaint, 1:2–4
      B. Yahweh's response, 1:5–11
  II. The second dialogue, 1:12–2:5
      A. Complaint, 1:12–17
      B. Yahweh's response, 2:1–5
  III. The taunt, 2:6–20
  IV. Habakkuk's prayer, 3:1–19
      A. Superscription, 3:1
      B. Prayer for Yahweh's intervention, 3:2–15
        C. Hope, 3:16–19

The Message of Habakkuk

Habakkuk deals with the moral question of God's raising up the Babylonians. The Assyrians had been cruel, Nineveh had been destroyed (612 B.C.), just as Nahum had prophesied, and the last vestiges of Assyrian power were to come to an end at Carchemish (605 B.C.). Assyria, "the rod of God's anger," had fallen prey to its own pride. God's people rejoiced in God's judgment on Assyria, but they wondered why he would afflict Judah by another foreign power. How could God use Babylon to inflict judgment on Judah when their cruelty and pagan ways further destroyed God's kingdom? The questions of Habakkuk encouraged the godly to develop an experiential faith ("the righteous will live by his faith," Hab. 2:4) and to submit to God's rule, who freely uses crooked instruments in the establishment of his kingdom.[37]

God's Freedom and Righteousness in Judgment

Habakkuk charged the Lord with being unfair, using the form of a prophetic *complaint* (1:2–4). How could the Lord permit the country of

Judah to continue breaking his covenant? Idolatry, immorality, and corruption were so prevalent that God's kingdom was "paralyzed" (v. 4). The wicked had overtaken the righteous in number. The days were so harsh that the godly were considered accursed, whereas the wicked prospered. The Lord's response (vv. 5–11) was not completely to Habakkuk's liking. Out of concern for the growing profligacy of his people, the Lord revealed that he would raise up the Babylonians as the instrument of his righteousness. Violence in Judah would meet the greater violence of the Babylonians. "Like" would be overcome by "like." (See figure 40.)

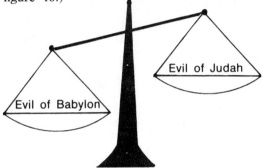

Figure 40. Scale of Divine Righteousness

But Habakkuk was far from satisfied with that response. How could the Lord permit a wicked nation to destroy a more righteous one? Babylon might accomplish God's purpose, but how could she, since she was the cause of anarchy and chaos in God's righteous kingdom? This frightened the prophet, who spoke out of concern for the righteous who remained.[38] What would happen to them? Can God be so unfeeling as to devastate his inheritance by the ruthless Babylonians?

Habakkuk's second complaint (1:12–17) was twofold. First, he charged Judah with destroying the foundations of God's kingdom by perverting justice and righteousness. Second, he lamented God's response, fearing that in his freedom, all righteousness might be uprooted from the land and result in absolute anarchy (v. 17). Habakkuk's problem posed a dilemma, and since he did not know the way out of his predicament, he stood watch like a guard. He watched for the Babylonians while looking for a new word from the Lord (2:1).

Living by Faith

The Lord revealed to Habakkuk that his righteous kingdom will be established in the end. This revelation was to be written down as a witness to successive generations (2:2).[39] These words were for their comfort so that they may know that he will reward them, even though his judgment may linger. They must persevere in faith! These familiar words encourage God's children to hold on regardless of how bad the times: "The righteous will live by his faith" (2:4; Rom. 1:17; 3:21–29; Gal. 3:11).[40] This is essentially the message of John's Apocalypse as well (Rev. 2:10; 19, 26; 22:7, 12–14).

The hope of the godly lies in the full establishment of God's righteous and glorious kingdom.[41] Hope is confirmed by the promises of God. The Lord has promised the full redemption of his people from aggressors, oppressors, the wicked, the bellicose, and idolaters (2:6–20; see Isa. 5:8–23; Matt. 23:13–32; Luke 6:24–26; Rev. 9:12; 11:14; 18:10, 16, 19).[42] He has promised to inaugurate his glorious kingdom.

> The earth will be filled with the
> knowledge of the glory of the LORD,
> as the waters cover the sea.
>
> (2:14)

He has also promised to judge the wicked. He is the great Judge who is "seated in his holy temple" and will hold all the earth accountable to him (v. 20). These promises may be delayed, but

> the revelation awaits an appointed time;
> it speaks of the end and will not prove false.
> Though it linger, wait for it;
> it will certainly come and will not delay.
>
> (v. 3)[43]

The Christian community should at the same time reflect on Paul's application of God's judgment to scoffers (1:5; see Acts 13:41). The author of Hebrews, too, encourages us to persevere in the spirit of Habakkuk 2:3–4.

> For in just a very little while,
> "He who is coming will come and will not delay.
> But my righteous one will live by faith.
> And if he shrinks back,
> I will not be pleased with him."
>
> (Heb. 10:37–38)

The Final Triumph of God's Righteousness[44]

The book of Habakkuk challenges the righteous to discern God's will in adverse times and calls for perseverance while awaiting the establishment of God's righteous kingdom. Habakkuk is a sage who—through dialogue, taunt song, and praise—has instructed the godly over the ages to develop a deeper living faith in the Redeemer. By his own example, he encouraged the godly to dialogue with God, to test their loyalty to him in harsh times, to develop hope in the Lord, and to praise him.

171

The last chapter is in the form of a liturgy with a prophetic prayer (3:1–19) to be sung (vv. 1, 19). By means of a regular liturgical use, the people of God encourage one another (see Eph. 5:19–20; Col. 3:16) to meditate on God's past acts and to hope for the glorious and victorious era to which Habakkuk has borne witness. Habakkuk's contribution to the development of prophetic wisdom lies in his inspired counsel on how to persevere by living with a vision. (See figure 41.)

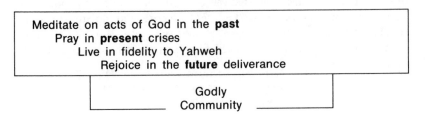

Figure 41. Perspective for Living With a Vision

The focus of the prayer is the revelation of God's being the Divine Warrior (3:2–12).[45] Habakkuk encouraged the godly to reflect on God's past acts as they await the Day of Judgment. What has happened at the time of the Exodus is a foreshadowing of that great and terrible day.[46] The godly should not be anxious about that day, but they must wait, persevere, and rejoice in the hope that is theirs.[47]

> I heard and my heart pounded,
>   my lips quivered at the sound;
> decay crept into my bones,
>   and my legs trembled.
> Yet I will wait patiently for the day of calamity
>   to come on the nation invading us.
> Though the fig tree does not bud
>   and there are no grapes on the vines,
> though the olive crop fails
>   and the fields produce no food,
> though there are no sheep in the pen
>   and no cattle in the stalls,
> yet I will rejoice in the LORD,
>   I will be joyful in God my Savior.
> The Sovereign LORD is my strength;
>   he makes my feet like the feet of a deer,
>   he enables me to go on the heights.
>   (3:16–19)

The hymn of Habakkuk is a celebration of the power, glory, and victorious nature of our God. His are the "victorious chariots" (3:8; lit.

"chariots of salvation," $y^e\check{s}\hat{u}\,{}^\cdot\hat{a}$), and his is the deliverance ($y\bar{e}\check{s}a\,{}^\cdot$, v.13, 2x; NIV "deliver . . . save") of his "messianic" community (NIV "anointed one," v. 13; Ps. 28:8). He is their Savior (3:18; lit. "the God of my salvation," $yi\check{s}\,{}^\cdot\hat{i}$). Habakkuk calls us to look expectantly for the Lord's salvation when Yahweh will establish his righteousness. Then the whole of the earth will be filled with his glory!

ZEPHANIAH: THE DAY OF THE LORD AND THE DAY OF SALVATION

Zephaniah and His Time

Zephaniah,[48] born during the oppressive regime of King Manasseh, probably ministered God's word during the early reign of Josiah.[49] Though a precise dating is difficult, there are several reasons for dating Zephaniah's ministry to shortly before the great reforms of Josiah (622 B.C.). First, the royal princes still practiced the excesses (Zeph. 1:8–9). Second, the idolatrous practices of 1:3–5 were already being abolished ("every remnant of Baal," v. 4).[50] Zephaniah's preaching may well have encouraged young King Josiah to develop a reform program and to align himself with God's program.[51] If this dating is correct,[52] Zephaniah and Jeremiah began their ministries at about the same time.[53]

When Josiah assumed kingship at an early age, the country was still persisting in the idolatrous, unjust, and corrupt practices that characterized the reigns of his predecessors (Manasseh and Amon). A halfhearted worship of Yahweh was intermingled with pagan worship, which in reality was idolatry.[54] The people were demoralized because of the atrocities committed during Manasseh's era and because of Judah's weak political position as an Assyrian satellite state.[55] The rich oppressed the poor in order to build up fortunes for themselves (Zeph. 1:8–9). Prophets and priests were arrogant, and people profaned the sanctuary of the Lord. Yet a remnant remained who were called to

> seek the LORD, all you humble of the land,
>   you who do what he commands.
> Seek righteousness, seek humility.
>
> (2:3)

Literary Form[56] and Structure

Literary Form

Zephaniah contributes to Israel's rich literary heritage. The book, mainly poetic,[57] opens with a dramatic judgment oracle on all creation (1:2–3) and on Judah (vv. 4–9). Zephaniah graphically develops the Day of the Lord in the imagery of war,[58] theophany, and judgment (vv. 14–18). He combines a universal message (vv. 2–3; 2:4–15; 3:6–8) and a particularistic judgment on Judah (1:4–6; 3:1–4). The prophet's direct style employs poetic devices: parallelism, wordplay, repetition, assonance, and metaphor. The prophetic speech forms reflect a paucity of extended descriptions or a creative use of the prophetic heritage. Zephaniah communicates his message in a straightforward manner.

Structure

Superscription, 1:1
   I. The Day of the Lord, 1:2–2:3
      A. Judgment on creation, 1:2–3
        B. Judgment on Judah, 1:4–9
          C. Lament in Jerusalem, 1:10–13
            D. The Day of the Lord, 1:14–18
            E. Call to repent, 2:1–3
   II. Oracles against the nations and Judah, 2:4–3:8
      A. Philistia, 2:4–7
        B. Moab and Ammon, 2:8–11
          C. Cush, 2:12
            D. Assyria, 2:13–15
            E. Judah, 3:1–8
  III. Oracle of salvation, 3:9–20
      A. Purification of Judah and the nations, 3:9–10
        B. Yahweh's love for the humble, 3:11–13
          C. Yahweh is King over his people, 3:14–20

The Message of Zephaniah

Zephaniah, like his contemporaries Habakkuk and Jeremiah, warned the southern kingdom of the terrible judgment to come, called them to repent, and encouraged the remnant (3:11–13). The canonical function of Zephaniah extends the message of the Day of the Lord, the proper response, and the blessedness of God's kingdom to all nations. The focus is on Judah, but the canonical import fans out far beyond the original audience to this very day.

The Day of the Lord

Zephaniah most extensively and dramatically developed the prophetic concept of the Day of the Lord.[59] His contribution became the source of the medieval hymn *Dies Irae* ("the day of wrath").[60] The Day of the Lord (*yôm Yahweh*) signifies first and foremost Yahweh's intrusion into human affairs. His coming (theophany) is portrayed in the conceptual imagery of Warrior, Judge, and the great King. (See figure 42.)

Second, the Day of the Lord brings God's judgment on all creation (1:2–3).[61] It is compared to the judgment of the Flood in Noah's day, but it is more extensive. Nothing will escape the purifying judgment of the Lord as it affects human beings, animals, the birds of the sky, and the fish of the sea. But it is unlike the Flood since it will be as by fire: "The whole world will be consumed by the fire of my jealous anger" (3:8; see 2 Peter 3:10). The wrath and jealousy of the Lord will come to expression against everything, and thus he establishes his everlasting kingdom.

COMING OF THE LORD

Judgment on all creation	Blessing and protection
Historical and eschatological	Historical and eschatological
Subjugation to his lordship	Awaiting his lordship
Vindication	Deliverance of godly
Restoration of order	Peace

Judgment / Eschatological perspective / Restoration

Figure 42. The Day of the Lord

That day will be a day of wrath,
a day of distress and anguish,
a day of trouble and ruin,
a day of darkness and gloom,
a day of clouds and blackness.
(1:15; see v. 18; Rev. 16:1)

Third, the Day of the Lord is historical and eschatological.[62] Though the Lord's acts of judgment take place throughout the history of redemption, each act foreshadows the final judgment when all the doers of evil, corruption, and sin will be absolutely and radically judged and removed from the earth (1:3). Each judgment in history is an intrusion of the eschatological judgment, whether on Israel, Judah, or the nations.

Fourth, on the Day of the Lord all creation must submit to his sovereignty, willingly or not. The call to be "silent" is a prophetic exhortation to recognize that Yahweh is Judge and to live in such a way as to prepare for his judgment: "Be silent before the Sovereign LORD, for the day of the LORD is near" (1:7; see Hab. 2:20). The Day of the Lord in history points to the final judgment; hence, it is always near: "The great day of the LORD is near—near and coming quickly" (v. 14).

Fifth, the Day of the Lord does not discriminate in favor of the rich and powerful. Nor does it discriminate in favor of religious people. However, the Lord does make a distinction between the wicked and the humble. On the one hand, nothing avails; man is completely abandoned by every structure that holds society together and makes human life meaningful (1:18). On the other hand, the humble are those who have abandoned themselves to God alone in this life, seeking him and his kingdom. They consist of all people, Jews and Gentiles, who have placed their hope in the Lord.

> Seek the LORD, all you humble of the land,
> you who do what he commands.
> Seek righteousness, seek humility;
> perhaps you will be sheltered
> on the day of the LORD's anger.
>
> (2:3; see v. 11; 3:9)

The Day of the Lord brings about a formal distinction between the righteous and the wicked; namely, those who will possess his kingdom and those who will not. It is a purification process (catharsis) for which the godly prepare themselves by purifying their way of life.

> But I will leave within you
> the meek and humble,
> who trust in the name of the LORD.
> The remnant of Israel will do no wrong;
> they will speak no lies,
> nor will deceit be found in their mouths.
>
> (3:12–13)

Sixth, the Day of the Lord signifies the day of vindication, glorification, and full redemption of the godly (3:14–20). Theirs is the kingdom and theirs is the enjoyment of God's presence in kingship.

> The LORD, the King of Israel, is with you;
> never again will you fear any harm. . . .
> The LORD your God is with you,
> he is mighty to save.
>
> (vv. 15, 17)

They need not fear any more and will be fully satisfied with the fulfillment of the promises: "They will eat and lie down and no one will make them afraid" (3:13; see vv. 14–17).[63]

The Day of Deliverance

Zephaniah's critique against the leaders (1:8–13; 3:1–4) could have led to a confrontation with the establishment. But he also opened the way of communication with the populace as a whole.[64] He called the people to reflect on the absolute justice of God, whose judgments are not arbitrary, contradictory, or brute expressions of power. His judgments reveal both his determination to rid the earth of evil and his will to establish a new world.

176

The LORD within her is righteous;
    he does no wrong.
Morning by morning he dispenses his justice,
    and every new day he does not fail,
    yet the unrighteous know no shame.

(3:5)

Zephaniah encouraged the remnant to look at God's constancy and to rejoice in his acts of vindication. Who makes up the remnant?[65] Who are the people of the future? Zephaniah explained how people may have hope that the future kingdom is theirs. The prophet called on the nation in his time to repent, and his call for repentance continues to this very day. He said,

Seek [*baqqᵉšû*] the LORD, all you humble of the land,
    you who do what he commands.
Seek [*baqqᵉšû*] righteousness, seek [*baqqᵉšû*] humility;
    perhaps you will be sheltered
    on the day of the LORD's anger.

(2:3; see 1:6; 2:1–2)

The remnant are true worshipers of the Lord. The imitators of godliness will have to stand trial and will never share in the privileges of the new community of God's people.[66] The remnant are the humble whose acts of "humility"[67] consist of nothing more, and nothing less, than an imitation of God (Matt. 5:3–10; 6:33). The Lord has promised to shelter all who trust in him (Joel 3:16; Nah. 1:7); and trust in the Lord casts out self-reliance, guile, and deception. The godly live by faith as they continually examine themselves and their motivations.[68] (See figure 43.)

THE REMNANT

Abandonment of human structures	Submission to God (= humility)
God's presence	Seeking God's kingdom
Renewal of covenants	= God's righteousness
	= God's complete deliverance
	Jews and Gentiles
	Purified for true worship

Figure 43. The Remnant in Zephaniah

Zephaniah also projects the universality of the new community. Jews and Gentiles will worship the Lord: "The nations on every shore will worship him, every one in its own land" (2:11). Zephaniah gives us a vision of the universal worship of God, similar to what Jesus said to the woman of Samaria, "The true worshipers will worship the Father in spirit and truth, for they are the kind of worshipers the Father seeks" (John 4:21, 23).

The new community will experience a cleansing and a transformation of the heart.

> Then will I purify the lips of the peoples,
>> that all of them may call on the name of the LORD
>> and serve him shoulder to shoulder.
>
> (3:9)

The spirit of paganism will be wholly removed (v. 11). The community of the humble will serve the Lord in devotion to him and in opposition to the way of the world. Theirs will be the joys of the new establishment of the kingdom of God among man (vv. 12–13).

The Lord reassures the remnant of any age that his kingdom will extend to this earth. Zephaniah did not know how the Lord would work out his plan of salvation, but he believed firmly that judgment and salvation are in the Lord's hands.[69] In the very establishment of his kingdom, the Lord will fulfill his promises made in the covenants. Only in the realization of the covenants of creation and redemption lies assurance of the final establishment of God's kingdom. The prophet became lyrical as he envisioned the blessedness of the kingdom to come.[70]

The vision focused on the presence of the great King, the Divine Warrior. He protects, vindicates his remnant,[71] and grants them the benefits of his victory. They need not fear because the great King is with and for his people. He will turn disgrace, suffering, and alienation into an experience of honor, blessing, and presence of God (3:13–20).

As a further expression of covenant renewal, Zephaniah encouraged the godly to contemplate the Lord's love, his willingness to be reconciled, and his power to deliver. This God sings to his people.

> He will take great delight in you,
>> he will quiet you with his love,[72]
>> he will rejoice over you with singing.
>
> (3:17)

In response, the prophet encourages the new community to sing songs of victory in praise of the Divine Warrior.

> Sing, O Daughter of Zion;
>> shout aloud, O Israel!
> Be glad and rejoice with all your heart,
>> O Daughter of Jerusalem!
>
> (v. 14).[73]

178

The heirs of the new covenant (i.e., the renewal of the covenants with creation, Abraham, and Moses) will live at peace and in harmony in the new world order. The world of creation is the sphere of redemption (2:7; 3:13, 19–20). The glory promised under the Mosaic covenant will be theirs (3:20; Deut. 26:19; see Rev. 21:24–26)!

REVIEW

Nahum's dramatic portrayal of Nineveh's fall is more than a prediction come true. He presents Yahweh as the Creator-Redeemer-King who alone can marshal all powers in heaven and on earth to accomplish his purpose. An integral part of that purpose is the removal of evil. To this end Yahweh gives himself to battle against wicked kingdoms, expressing his concern for his people even in the midst of the greatest upheavals. He is the Divine Warrior who rules in *judgment* (vindication/vengeance) and in *deliverance.*

The people of God are the blessed heirs of the salvation provided by the Lord. They are presently the heirs of the promise, but are encouraged to hope for the day of full redemption when all kingdoms of this world will come to an end. The New Testament portrayal of Jesus as the Divine Warrior is a necessary corrective to a fixation on Jesus' love. According to the book of Revelation, Jesus is the Warrior on the white horse who makes war on Satan and his kingdom, on all unbelief and oppression, and even on ungodliness in his church (Rev. 19:11–16, 19; 20:7–10; 21:8, 27).

Habakkuk complements the message of Nahum. Yes, Yahweh is just, though he may use the nations of this world to accomplish his purposes and though he may delay bringing the fullness of redemption to the righteous. The righteous will live! The righteous are characterized by "a childlike, humble, and sincere trust in the credibility of the divine message of salvation."[74] They will have a future, as theirs is the promise that the earth is the Lord's and that his kingdom will be gloriously established here on earth. The message of Habakkuk is a magnificent reminder that the Lord is actively establishing his universal kingdom.[75] Those who believe in him, persevere in their fidelity to the Lord, and await his kingdom will not be disappointed. Whatever their lot on earth, Habakkuk calls on them to wait expectantly and joyfully for the kingdom to come!

The fall of Babylon brought about a manifestation of the kingdom of God, as did the return of the Jews from exile. Moreover, the knowledge of God among the growing community of Jews and God-fearing Gentiles in the Diaspora evidenced the glory of God before the coming of Jesus Christ. Calvin shows an appreciation for the progressive dimension of Habakkuk's prophecy: "We know that the grace of

179

redemption flowed in a perpetual stream until Christ appeared in the world. . . . The Prophet, I have no doubt, sets forth here the greatness of God's power in the destruction of Babylon."[76]

Zephaniah speaks of Yahweh's universal claim on all creation (human beings and animals) in his judgment and in his transformation. He will transform all of his creation through judgment (the Day of the Lord). On the one hand, the wicked will be found guilty and will be judged. On the other, the Lord assures the humble that theirs is the kingdom, the glory, and the victory. The Lord will be present among his people in Zion, the City of God. He will rule in blessing and protection over his people with no one to intimidate, oppress, or persecute them any more.

QUESTIONS AND ISSUES

1. Define:
   Divine Warrior
   intrusion
   new community
   righteousness and faith (in Habakkuk)
   theophany
   vengeance
   vindication
   Yahweh's zeal/jealousy
2. What is the historical context of the ministry of Nahum, Habakkuk, and Zephaniah? What international changes took place during the seventh century B.C., and how did each prophet respond to the changes?
3. What is the biblical teaching on Yahweh as the Divine Warrior? What is his goal? How does this teaching threaten and encourage?
4. How does the prophecy of Nahum illustrate the compenetration of the historical and the eschatological?
5. What is a theophany, what phenomena attend a theophany, and what are the purposes of God's coming? How do Nahum, Habakkuk, and Zephaniah employ the motif of theophany?
6. What is Habakkuk's understanding of righteousness, and how does the Lord help him gain a deeper understanding of righteousness?
7. How does righteousness relate to faith in Habakkuk and in Paul?
8. What is the crisis of faith in Habakkuk? Does the prophet pave the way for living by faith?
9. What perspectives for living does Habakkuk give to the community of faith?
10. How does Zephaniah develop the teaching on the Day of the Lord? How should the remnant respond to this teaching?

11. What does Habakkuk's dialogue with the Lord teach concerning our relationship with him and his accommodation to our needs?
12. What is meant by seeking the kingdom of God and his righteousness?
13. What is the vision of God's kingdom in each of these three prophets?
14. Why do you think that they do not contribute *directly* to the teaching on the messianic reign of Jesus? How do they *indirectly* contribute to the messianic concept?

CHAPTER 7

Haggai, Zechariah, and Malachi

Introduction to the postexilic era
  Hope of restoration
  Hopes dashed and revived
  The ministry of Haggai, Zechariah, Malachi, Nehemiah, and
    Ezra
Haggai: Now is the day of fulfillment
  Haggai and his time
  Literary form and structure
    Literary form
    Structure
  The message of Haggai
    The temple
    The Spirit of God
    Token and reality
    The Davidic dynasty
    Conclusion
Zechariah: A vision of Zion's glory
  Zechariah and his time
  Literary form and structure
    Literary form
    Structure
  The message of Zechariah
    The age of responsibility
    The present reality of restoration
    The era of restoration: fulfillment of the promises
    The humble and glorious Messiah
Malachi: The victory belongs to the *s^egullâ*
  Malachi and his time
  Literary form and structure
    Literary form
    Structure
  The message of Malachi
    Yahweh is Father and King

Yahweh is righteous in his love
Yahweh loves the *sᵉgullâ*
Yahweh is the Divine Warrior in blessing and in judgment
Review

INTRODUCTION TO THE POSTEXILIC ERA

The postexilic prophets Haggai, Zechariah, and Malachi (and possibly Joel) ministered in the shadow of the exilic experience and in the light of the postexilic restoration.[1] The period after the Exile inaugurated a new era of fulfillment of the preexilic prophets (or "former prophets").[2] As God's covenant prosecutors they had forewarned the people of their imminent fall, disgrace, and exile while encouraging them to find refuge in the Lord (see Zech. 1:4).

The Exile as an intrusion of the eschatological judgment became a reality. Jerusalem and her temple were destroyed, the Davidic king was removed from office, and the people were exiled or disfranchised, experiencing a deep sense of alienation from God. A remnant of God's people, waiting seemingly forever, looked for signs of fulfillment of the prophetic word.[3]

But the exilic experience also had its beneficial side effects.[4] The Exile was a purification process, during which the Lord constituted a new community, made up of all who diligently sought him, trusted in him, and responded to him in the pursuit of righteousness, justice, and love, thus establishing his kingdom in their hearts.[5] During this period the remnant came together and began constructing forms of devotion that would in time become institutionalized in the *synagogue,* in *Torah* education, and in *orthopraxis* (doing the Law).[6] The remnant's emphasis on the place of the temple and on the Law would shape not only postexilic Judaism, but Judaism of the twentieth century![7]

Hope of Restoration

During the Exile the godly lived in the hope of the prophetic promises of the dawning of a new era.[8] The "former" or preexilic prophets had proclaimed the gospel of hope: the realization of the Lord's presence to bring blessing and protection in greater fullness and glory among his people. The oracles of deliverance held out the hope that the people of God would again enjoy the promises, the covenants, a transformation of nature, and a state of *shalom* under the protection of the Lord and of his messianic king.

The era of restoration, like the era of judgment, gradually came into focus in the progress of fulfillment.[9] The decree of Cyrus (538 B.C.), permitting the return of the Jews (Ezra 1:1–4; 6:3–5), was an answer to the prayers of the faithful (Lam. 5:1–22; Dan. 9:4–19).[10] When the

TABLE 8. CHRONOLOGY OF THE POSTEXILIC ERA

538	536	520	515	c. 480	458	445
Decree of Cyrus	Return to land under Sheshbazzar	Zerubbabel Jeshua	Temple dedicated	Esther	Return under Ezra	Nehemiah
Prophets:	*Haggai Zechariah*			*Malachi*		*Joel*
Persian kings: Cyrus II 559–530		**Cambyses II** 530–522	**Darius Hystaspes** 522–486	**Xerxes** 486–465	**Artaxerxes I** 464–424	

Jews finally returned, they came back in small numbers (fifty thousand; Ezra 2:64–65; Neh. 7:66–67). Great was the joy of the new generation when they reinstituted the temple services, but great, too, was the weeping of the older people when they remembered the former glory of the temple (Ezra 3:12–13). And great was the hope that with the restoration of the temple, the messianic age might more fully dawn.[11] (See table 8.)

Hopes Dashed and Revived

The mixture of joy and sorrow soon grew into despair when the Jews experienced opposition to the rebuilding of the temple (Ezra 4:1–24). Their dreams were dashed and their questions were many: Where was the vindication of the Lord? Where was his deliverance? Was this the new era of which the prophets had spoken?

The people responded in various ways to the disappointment of the new era.[12] Some interpreted the prophetic promises in the light of their present circumstances and then pragmatically and creatively found methods of adapting God's promises to the new situation.[13] Others began what later developed into a full-fledged apocalypticism. Most were more concerned with making a living. Their hope gone, they spent their days building houses and carving out a meager existence for themselves from the overgrown land. The postexilic community and prophets reveal a tension between the "present realization" and the eschatological hope.[14] This tension is quite evident in the message of Haggai and Zechariah as they addressed the issues of disillusionment, responsibility, and God's fidelity.

> The presence of this tension in the postexilic era has led some to advance the notion that prophecy was a dying phenomenon. Petersen connects the prophetic tradition with the monarchy and concludes that with the fall of the monarchy, prophetism had to cease.[15] But his thesis cannot satisfactorily deal with the postexilic prophets, as he readily admits.[16] Carroll, on the other hand, explains it from the dissonance theory, which holds that a gap formed between expectation and reality and that a hermeneutic framework developed to explain the lack of fulfillment.[17] In contrast to the pessimistic interpretation of the postexilic era, I agree with Mason that the changes must be explained from the "success" of prophecy because the Exile had come to pass and the people had begun to enjoy the beginnings of prophetic fulfillment.[18]

The Ministry of Haggai, Zechariah, Malachi, Nehemiah, and Ezra

Haggai, Zechariah, and Malachi emphasized that God was fulfilling his promises in the new era. They tried to explain what God was doing by speaking about the *discontinuity* between the present era and the preexilic era and about the *continuity* of the purposes of God in the new community.[19] Raitt observes, "God's nature does not change, and his overarching intention and purpose do not change. . . . While the Exile seems like a defeat to Israel, it liberates God from some religious baggage which was actually hindering his redemptive purpose. . . . *Exile is the time of victory for God.*"[20]

The preaching of Haggai and Zechariah helped the postexilic community to interpret their present situation in between the horizons of prophetic *proclamation* and the *anticipation* of fulfillment.[21] On the one hand, they confirmed that the temple, the priesthood, Zerubbabel, and the renewal of covenant were realizations of the prophetic proclamation. The new era of which the preexilic and exilic prophets had spoken was *here*. Bruce K. Waltke states, "For the preexilic and exilic prophets the new age began with the restoration of the exile."[22] This new era was nothing less than the intrusion of eschatology.

> *The time of judgment calls forth an eschatology, is necessary to set apart the beginning of the era of salvation.* . . . Therefore in this context *both* the era in which God gives up on *Heilsgeschichte* and the era which inaugurates the Kingdom of Heaven are eschatological. . . . As I perceive the eschatological dimension of these prophets' deliverance message, it accents and defines the change in eras, but without either moving away from the essential foundation of the prophets' faith or changing their understanding of God's basic goals.[23]

On the other hand, they confirmed that all the promises will be fulfilled. They encouraged the godly to resist complacency, to persevere in the practice of godliness, and to live in the present with the anticipation of fulfillment.

By the time Malachi, Ezra, and Nehemiah came on the scene, the fires of revival had died down.[24] The preaching of Haggai and Zechariah may not have been forgotten, but several generations separated the people of Malachi's time from these postexilic prophets. Some continued to live in this tension, hoping in the fulfillment of God's promises and interpreting the prophetic word allowing God to freely work out his plans. Malachi's call for radical loyalty to the Lord may well have prepared the people for a positive response to the reforms under Ezra and Nehemiah. These two leaders were realists who systematically set out to involve God's people in realizing the promises by social, religious, and political reforms.[25]

Ezra was a link between the initial stages of fulfillment, dating back to the generation of Haggai and Zechariah, and the eschatological fulfillment. He saw himself and his age as inaugurating the eschatological era: "His actions are . . . only a pre-eschatological step towards a future eschatological fulfillment."[26] (See table 8.)

Nehemiah was zealous for the temple, the Law, the Sabbath, and the theocracy. He believed that he was preparing the people and the city for the fullness of God's kingdom. His theocentric focus was on Zion, the city of God, which is in Wilhelm Vischer's words "a focus of the kingdom of God on earth."[27]

HAGGAI: NOW IS THE DAY OF FULFILLMENT

Haggai[28] and His Time

Haggai bridged the old and the new eras. He was born in the old Jerusalem, witnessed her desecration and destruction, and lived as an exile in Babylon.[29] He was also a man of the new era; he had joined the first wave of returnees under Sheshbazzar and had participated in the first stage of the rebuilding of the temple (Ezra 3:1–13). By the time he spoke these oracles, Haggai was an old man.

The date of the prophecy can be set by the references to King Darius I (Hystaspes, 522–486 B.C.), whose support of religious activities spurred a renewed interest in the Jewish community. The first address was given in the sixth month (August 29, 520) of the second year of Darius (1:1). Three more addresses followed within a four-month period (1:15–2:1; 2:10, 20), the last being given in December 520 B.C.[30]

Haggai and Zechariah (see Ezra 5:1; 6:14) ministered God's word to people who knew the harshness of life and the disappointment of unfulfilled hope. They were members of the new community in the Land of Promise, but the slowness of the restoration frustrated them. They were disappointed with the new era that had promised God's presence, kingship, blessing, and protection. They had come to think that their hopes were mistaken and that they had to bide their time in the land waiting for God to inaugurate the era of prophetic fulfillment.

The Jews had returned from Babylon sixteen years earlier. They had enthusiastically started a program of restoration (536 B.C.) but had been stopped by the Samaritans' opposition (Ezra 4:5). The project was suspended from 536 to 520 B.C., and by 520 B.C. much had changed. Darius had affirmed the original decree of Cyrus allowing the Jews to rebuild the temple (6:3–12), but the Jews had become apathetic about the temple and had suffered many adversities (Hag. 1:9–11). Moreover, they went through a vicious cycle believing that economic hardship signified God's absence and that God's absence meant that he did not want the temple rebuilt. They concluded that the prophetic fulfillment pertained to another generation. They were not atheistic or idolatrous, but they became complacent as they set aside hope of a speedy restoration.

In 520 B.C. Haggai spoke out. He criticized the people for not completing the temple and motivated them to begin work. Haggai knew that the people were disheartened, having left the security of Babylon to live in Judea as pioneers, that they had faced opposition, and that they had suffered. It is no wonder that each man had begun to think about his own needs.

Literary Form and Structure

Literary Form

The book consists of four oracles, dated between August 29 and December 18, 520 B.C.[31] The style is poetic prose.[32] The message is one of straightforward exhortation, teaching, and encouragement; and it is full of hope in God's future acts. The prophetic style involves (1) repetition of phrases ("give careful thought [to your ways]," 1:5, 7; 2:15, 18; "I will shake," 2:6, 21) and of addressees (1:12, 14; 2:2–4), and (2) rhetorical devices (1:4–5, 9; 2:11–13), chiasmus (1:4, 9–10; 2:23), and wordplay (*ḥārēḇ*, "ruin," 1:4, 9; *ḥōreḇ*, "drought," 1:11). The prophetic self-references in the third person may be a rhetorical device or an indicator of editorial activity by one of his disciples.[33] Haggai creatively employed the messenger formula ("declares [says] the LORD," 2:4, 7, 9, 14, 23).

The opening words set the framework for interpreting the oracles, "The word of the LORD came through the prophet Haggai to Zerubbabel . . . and to Joshua" (1:1; see 2:20). This framework emphasizes the continuity of the prophetic institution (Haggai), the Davidic dynasty (Zerubbabel), and the temple and the priesthood (Joshua).[34]

Structure

    A. Crisis, challenge, and response, 1:1–15a
      B. The presence of the Spirit of restoration and the renewal of promise, 1:15b–2:9
    A'. Crisis, challenge, and promise, 2:10–19
      B'. The presence of the messianic heir and the renewal of promise, 2:20–23

The Message of Haggai

The imperative for action is the central thrust of Haggai's message. A significant amount of time had elapsed since the people had returned to the land, and for various reasons they had become complacent. In fact, this attitude had become a lifestyle, which the people justified with a slogan, "The time has not yet come for the LORD's house to be built" (1:2).

And yet they were not happy, because they barely eked out an existence (1:6). They probably questioned God's fidelity and wondered how the prophetic words of salvation were to be applied to their time. But Haggai blamed them for being responsible for adversity (vv. 4–11). He aroused them from their apathy and self-sufficiency by asking them to assess their situation from God's point of view (vv. 5, 7; 2:15, 18). Had they not been unfaithful by responding negatively to adversity? Had they not become lukewarm in their devotion to the Lord? Had they not in their suffering found fault with God? Haggai reversed their charges by asking them to search their own hearts. He further called for loyalty to the Lord, the rebuilding of the temple, and the continued expectation of the new era of Yahweh's blessings.

The Temple

The temple and all it represented (the presence of Yahweh and the messianic hope, see Ps. 132) was the bridge between the past and the future. In short, the building of the temple was a necessary step of faith for the postexilic community in anticipation of a greater evidence of God's presence and kingdom.

The prophet introduced *the correlation of fulfillment and responsibility.* God's people can hasten the prophetic fulfillment of the promises![35] Haggai blamed the people for the present failure by asking them to judge themselves responsible for causing the failure in the continuation of the progress of redemption, "Give careful thought to your ways" (1:5, 7). Their way would lead them back to the very reason for the Exile. They were preoccupied with making a living, improving their standard of life, rationalizing their adversities, and accusing the Lord of being untrue to his promises. Haggai made it plain that their adversities were nothing less than a form of divine chastisement. These were harsh words to people who had left all they had in Babylon for a frontierlike existence in the desolate conditions of Judah.[36]

Haggai's proof lay in the material state of the people. They were busy in building and expanding their houses, but the temple was still in ruins. He asked them, "Is it a time for you yourselves to be living in your paneled houses, while this house remains a ruin?" (1:4). He called them away from their malaise to a life of devotion to the Lord, arguing that a divided loyalty defiles everything (2:14).

Haggai exhorted the new community to be bold in faith and trust that the Lord would be with them as he had been with the generation of the conquest (2:4; see Josh. 1:6–7, 9, 18; 23:6; 24:14). Thus far they had failed to enter this promised rest (Hag. 1:6; see Deut. 28:38–39; Hag. 2:17; see Deut. 28:22), but the promises remain as well as the responsibilities!

The Spirit of God

The manner in which the community responded to the prophetic challenge is refreshing. Gone were the rationalizations, the self-justifications, and the insistence on their own way. Instead, they acknowledged their guilt by action. It is apparent that the Spirit of God was working in the hearts of the leaders and of the remnant.

> So the LORD stirred up the spirit of Zerubbabel son of Shealtiel, governor of Judah, and the spirit of Joshua son of Jehozadak, the high priest, and the spirit of the whole remnant of the people. They came and began to work on the house of the LORD Almighty, their God (1:14).

The presence of the Spirit confirmed the continuity of God's kingdom in Israel. The Spirit of God, who had guided Moses and the elders and who had sent forth the prophets with the message of God, was in the midst of "the whole remnant" (1:14; see Num. 11:16–17, 25).[37] The godly response of the leaders and of the remnant bears witness to the spiritual transformation of the people (1:14) and to the working of the Holy Spirit. The Spirit was evidently present in renewing them, in reconciling them to their God, in guaranteeing the blessings, and above all in creating within them a yearning for the fullness of creation in restoration.[38] The eschatological era of the Spirit of God and of democratization had become a reality (v. 13; 2:4–5; see Zech. 4:6). (See figure 44.)

The prophet confirmed to the postexilic generation that the promises of God pertaining to the new era would be fulfilled:[39] the renewal of the covenants with creation, Abraham, Moses, and David. Theirs was the hope of the age of the Spirit of God and of the messianic era. Theirs was also the responsibility. Haggai clarified *the correlation between covenantal obedience and the fulfillment of the promises* as he called on the new community to take upon themselves the yoke of the kingdom with the hope that they might experience a measure of fulfillment and the presence of God's kingdom.

So while enjoying the benefits of God's presence in blessing and protection, that generation was responsible for hastening the final, climactic inauguration of its fullness: the new heaven and new earth, the New Jerusalem, the messianic era, and the kingdom of God. In this tension between the presence of the "new era" and the future (the "not-yet") fulfillment of God's promises,[40] the people of God would experience God's blessings while awaiting and hastening its fullness.[41]

Therefore, the prophet encouraged them to work out the promise to its fulfillment, "Be strong. . . . Be strong. . . . Be strong, . . . and work. For I am with you. . . . Do not fear" (2:4–5). Haggai called on the postexilic community to see things from God's perspective as the restoration was already present in token.

Token and Reality

Haggai further argued that the postexilic temple points forward rather than backward. He first asked the older generation to remember the former glory of Solomon's temple: "Who of you is left who saw this house in its former glory? How does it look to you now? Does it not seem to you like nothing?" (2:3). Then he called on his contemporaries to look beyond the present symbol and beyond their adversities (enemies, poverty, etc.) to the future glory of the kingdom of God, to which the temple witnessed. Haggai prophesied that "the desired"—the material bounty of the nations—will contribute to the glorious kingdom (v. 7).[42]

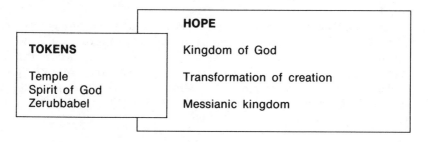

Figure 44. Tokens and Hope

The Lord confirmed his promise to establish his sovereignty over all creation. Haggai spoke of it as a divine shaking of heaven and earth (2:6–7, 21–22) in language reminiscent of the Lord's victory over Pharaoh's forces ("I will overthrow chariots and their drivers; horses and their riders will fall," 2:22; see Ex. 15:1, 4, 19, 21; Rev. 15:3–4), of Israel's despoiling the treasures of Egypt ("the desire of the nations" [NIV "the desired of all nations"], 2:7; see Ex. 12:35–36), and of his kingdom among his people (2:22; see Ex. 15:18; Rev. 15:3). The shaking of the nations suggests the imagery of the Day of the Lord when the Divine Warrior will establish his sovereignty over all his creation.[43] As the generation of the Exodus had witnessed God's mighty acts in Egypt, left with the spoils of Egypt, and experienced God's victory over Pharaoh (2:22; Ex. 15:1, 4, 19, 21), so the Lord spoke of another Exodus with the promises of deliverance, victory, and glory. The Lord had already used the treasures of the Persians in the building of his temple (Ezra 6:8), as promised by Isaiah (Isa. 60:5–13). But in time all nations will serve his purposes (see Rev. 21:24–26).

The Davidic Dynasty

The Lord confirmed his commitment to David. He will remove all opposition (2:22), end the era of warfare (see Isa. 14:16–17; Joel 3:1–16; Zech. 14:1–15; Rev. 19:11–16), renew the promises to David, and establish his kingdom.[44] He had cursed Zerubbabel's ancestry through Jeremiah, "As surely as I live ... even if you, Jehoiachin, son of Jehoiakim king of Judah, were a signet ring on my right hand, I would still pull you off. . . . for none of his offspring will prosper, none will sit on the throne of David or rule anymore in Judah" (Jer. 22:24, 30). Nevertheless, the Lord revoked the curse and renewed his covenant to David in Zerubbabel[45] as a token of the future of the Davidic dynasty. (See figure 44.) The Lord, who is free in cursing and in transforming a curse into a blessing, thus assured the continuity of David's dynasty through Jehoiachin and Zerubbabel to Jesus our Lord (Matt. 1:11–12).[46]

For Haggai's generation, Zerubbabel became God's signature guaranteeing the full redemption of his people, the messianic kingdom, and the new heaven and new earth (2:23; see Zech. 4:6–10).[47] The goal of the kingdom of God and the messianic rule is the same: the presence of God as evidenced in peace and in the blessedness of God's people (2:9, 19; see Num. 6:26; Ps. 72; Isa. 2:2–4; 11:1–9; 32:1–8, 15–20).[48]

Conclusion

The canonical function of Haggai clearly points the way in which God's people must participate to bring in the kingdom of God. Haggai was "both a visionary and activist,"[49] who led the postexilic community to realize that promises of *internalization* and the *democratization* by the Spirit were theirs. This explains why he roused the godly to seek the glory and interest of the kingdom of God while holding out the promise of greater glory.[50] In the progress and participation of the story of redemption, the godly remnant must ever realize that even a little defilement affects that progress (2:10–14). The promises are God's, but his people are responsible for hastening the realization of fulfillment.

Haggai was a reformer who called out a "remnant" from the remnant. He taught that the true people of God serve their great King with undivided loyalty (1:5, 7; 2:15, 18), have a zeal for holiness (2:10–14), and seek his kingdom (vv. 4–5; see v. 22). The Lord promised them the reality of his presence in glory, victory, blessings, and peace, while fulfilling his promises in token (v. 19). The tokens of the eschaton were already evident in the presence of the Spirit, the temple, the material blessings, and Zerubbabel.[51] (See figure 44.) Each token confirmed the renewal of the covenants: Creation, Abraham, Moses, and David. God is faithful, but he counts on the new community to be responsible citizens of his kingdom, persevering in doing good, and to await a greater fulfillment in continuity with the message of the prophets.[52]

ZECHARIAH: A VISION OF ZION'S GLORY

Zechariah and His Time

The genealogy (1:1) identifies Zechariah,[53] the grandson of Iddo,[54] as the author of these oracles (see v. 7; 7:1, 8). A common Hebrew name, Zechariah designates over thirty individuals in the Old Testament. His grandfather, Iddo, may be identified with the head of a priestly family who returned to Judah from the Exile (Neh. 12:4, 16). Zechariah may have served as priest upon his father's death, for he was the head of his family during Jehoiakim's high-priestly service (v. 16).

Several months after Haggai had begun preaching (August 29, 520 B.C.; Hag 1:1), the Lord also spoke to Zechariah (1:1). From October–November 520 to December 518 B.C. he proclaimed God's word. The oracles and visions in chapters 1–8 are dated by the year, month, and day (1:1, 7; 7:1), but chapters 9–14 contain no such dating formula.

The historical situation is the same as that of Haggai. The people of Judah had returned from exile in 536 B.C., but the joy and enthusiasm (see Ps. 126) that had characterized their return were gone. Almost twenty years had elapsed, and the temple had not yet been rebuilt. When Haggai and Zechariah began to prophesy in 520 B.C., the Jewish people were disheartened, apathetic, and generally depressed. Their failure to complete the temple had brought judgment from God in the forms of drought and poor harvests (Hag. 1:11). In response to Haggai's preaching, the Jews renewed their efforts at rebuilding the temple (v. 14). Two months later the Spirit of God spoke through Zechariah to the same people (1:1), encouraging them with a vision of God's kingdom and with the reality of prophetic fulfillment. They responded positively to the ministry of Haggai and Zechariah; the temple was dedicated on March 12, 515 B.C. (Ezra 6:15–18).

Literary Form and Structure

Literary Form

The book of Zechariah is "the obscurest and longest of the twelve prophets,"[55] but its complexity is in proportion to the significance of the message. Baldwin comments that it is a mosaic written by an "artist, adding colorful windows with their symbolism, gaiety and light."[56] The book is largely prosaic with poetic sections (chaps. 9–10). It contains a mosaic of hortatory oracles (1:2–6; 10:1–2), visions (1:7–6:8), symbolism (6:9–15), prophetic judgment oracles (9:1–8; 12:2–8), liturgy (9:9–10), salvation oracles (vv. 11–13; 13:1–6, 7–9), taunt song (11:1–3), narrative (vv. 4–17), and apocalyptic. The presence of visions, symbolism, and eschatological imagery classify Zechariah as a prophetic-apocalyptic writing.[57]

The first eight chapters are united by a dating formula (1:1, 7; 7:1), common theme (rebuilding of the temple and city),[58] and the messenger formula. The lack of dating, the variety of thematic content in chapters 9–14, and the absence of the messenger formula have led scholars to posit that another prophet (Deutero-Zechariah), whose concern was more with the restoration of the Davidic dynasty and the kingdom of God than the temple, may have written this section.[59] But it seems that statistics, rather than structure, have been used to bolster the division of Zechariah into two or even three parts.[60] A new approach to understanding chapters 9–14 has been presented by Baldwin, based on the work of P. Lamarche,[61] who attempts to explain the apparent variety and abrupt changes as resulting from a literary unity built on a chiastic pattern. Creative as the structural understanding is, Lamarche's argument has not been convincing to scholars.[62]

Accepting the division between chapters 1–8 and 9–14, Childs argues in favor of a relationship between the two sections. According to him the second section expands, develops, and sharpens the theological pattern of the "end time," which emerges from chapters 1–8. The book thus seeks to explain that notwithstanding the return from exile, the full experience of redemption still lies in the future.[63]

Zechariah is a theological reflection on the prophecies of restoration in Isaiah, Jeremiah, and Ezekiel, expanding and applying God's plan for his people who wait for the coming of the kingdom. It is not surprising that the book of Zechariah (esp. chaps. 9–14) is one of the most cited sections in explaining the passion narratives in the Gospels and has provided a rich imagery for John in the Apocalypse.[64]

Zechariah in all its diversity contributes to a vision of (1) the New Jerusalem (2:5; 9:8; 14:11); (2) the grandeur of fulfillment (1:17; 4:10; 8:6–15; 9:12); (3) the removal of evil and God's judgment on the nations (1:15, 21; 6:1–8; 9:1–8; 12:1–9; 14:1–5); (4) the participation of Jews and Gentiles in the mercies of God (2:11; 8:7–8, 22; 10:9–10; 14:16); (5) the cleansing, consecration, and empowering by the Spirit of restoration (4:6; 5:4; 12:10; 13:3); and (6) the humble and glorious messianic figure (3:8; 4:6; 9:9).

Structure

Introduction, 1:1–6
   I. Eight night visions, 1:7–6:8

194

A. Vision of the nations at rest, 1:7–17
   B. Vision of the judgment on the nations, 1:18–21
      C. Vision of the New Jerusalem, 2:1–13
         D. Vision of the new age: forgiveness and peace, 3:1–10
         D'. Vision of the new age: messianic ministry, 4:1–14
      C'. Vision of the removal of evil, 5:1–4
   B'. Vision of judgment on Babylon, 5:5–11
A'. Vision of the Spirit at rest, 6:1–8
II. Oracles of responsibility and promise, 6:9–8:23
   A. Promise of the new age, 6:9–15
      B. Question of fasting, 7:1–6
         C. Lesson from the past, 7:7–14
   A'. Promise of the new age, 8:1–8
      B'. Exhortation to fidelity, 8:9–17
         C'. Hope for the future, 8:18–23
III. Israel and the nations, 9:1–11:17
   A. Judgment on the oppressive nations, 9:1–8
      B. The coming universal rule, 9:9–13
         C. Judgment and deliverance, 9:14–17
      B'. The coming universal rule of God, 10:1–11:3
   A'. Judgment on the oppressive shepherd, 11:4–17
IV. The establishment of God's kingdom on earth, 12:1–14:21
   A. Jerusalem and the nations, 12:1–9
      B. Mourning for the pierced one, 12:10–14
         C. Promise of cleansing and forgiveness, 13:1–5
      B'. The shepherd struck, 13:6–9
   A'. Jerusalem and the nations, 14:1–21
      1. Troubles of Jerusalem, 14:1–2
         2. The coming of the King, 14:3–9
            3. Exaltation of Jerusalem, 14:10–11
            3'. Desolation of the nations, 14:12–15
         2'. Universal worship of the King, 14:16–19
      1'. Holiness and peace of Jerusalem, 14:20–21

The Message of Zechariah

The Age of Responsibility

Zechariah's prophecy complements that of Haggai.[65] He, too, was concerned with the completion of the temple and with the renewal of spiritual life. Haggai emphasized the *responsibility of the people* in view of the dawning of the new age. Zechariah urged the postexilic community not to repeat the mistakes of their ancestors, but instead to devote themselves to God (1:1–6) and to trust him in working out his promised deliverance.[66] Like Haggai, he attached great importance to the future of the temple and of the Davidic dynasty. But he focused on the *presence of God* with his people, and in this regard his concern comes closer to that of Ezekiel. So Hanson writes, "Zechariah sees his nation at the point in history prophesied by Ezekiel when Yahweh would return to Zion to dwell in the midst of his people."[67]

Zechariah provided a theological perspective on covenant life with its blessings and threats.[68] He exhorted the people to remember that the prophecies of exile had become a reality (1:6; 7:7–14). Fearing the recurrence of God's judgment, Zechariah encouraged the new generation to reflect on the past. They must not repeat the mistakes of their forerunners who had been led into exile and alienation and had received the curse of God (1:5–6; 7:14). The lessons from the past explain that the "former" (preexilic) prophets had called in vain for repentance (1:4; 7:6–7), that their ancestors had failed to respond (1:4; 7:11–12), that they had angered the Lord (1:2; 7:12), that he had stopped listening to their prayers and appeals to his covenant love (7:13), and that he had unleashed his curse on them.

The Present Reality of Restoration

Zechariah went beyond the past to a reflection on the situation and opportunity at hand. He inspired the people of God to see how the prophetic word regarding restoration was being fulfilled in their generation. Though the fulfillment seemed distant, God encouraged the new community with visions (1:7–6:8) that gave them a perspective on the progressive fulfillment of the prophetic oracles.[69]

The eight visions may be organized structurally as four parallel visions:

A. Vision of the nations at rest, 1:7–17
  B. Vision of the judgment on the nations, 1:18–21
    C. Vision of Zion, 2:1–13
      D. Vision of the new age: forgiveness and peace, 3:1–10
      D'. Vision of the new age: messianic ministry, 4:1–14
    C'. Vision of the removal of evil, 5:1–4
  B'. Vision of judgment on Babylon, 5:5–11
A'. Vision of the Spirit at rest, 6:1–8

These eight night visions portray what God was doing for his people. Through the interpretation of the angelic intermediary, the prophet explains what he sees. The visions, like John's in the Apocalypse, were given for the purpose of comfort that the godly might know that the Lord was zealously working out all aspects of redemption. This redemption consists of the vengeance on God's enemies, the vindication and glorification of his cleansed and holy people, and the consequent glorious establishment of his holy rule (1:13–15).

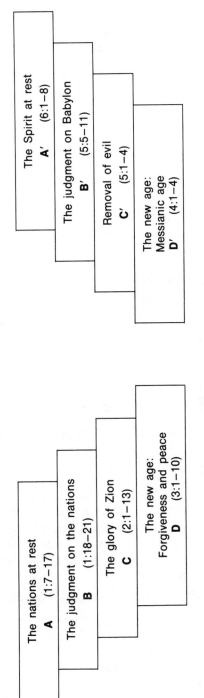

Figure 45. Zechariah's Night Visions

The Spirit at rest
A' (6:1–8)

The judgment on Babylon
B' (5:5–11)

Removal of evil
C' (5:1–4)

The new age:
Messianic age
D' (4:1–4)

The nations at rest
A (1:7–17)

The judgment on the nations
B (1:18–21)

The glory of Zion
C (2:1–13)

The new age:
Forgiveness and peace
D (3:1–10)

The night visions may be viewed as a set of stained glass windows placed opposite each other: the first and the last, the second and the seventh, the third and the sixth, and finally the fourth and the fifth. The central visions (four and five) form the acme and the focus of the symmetry. All aspects of restoration are rooted in the hope of God's presence, and the presence of God is at the same time the goal of restoration. (See figure 45.)

On the periphery are the visions with the contrasting view of the nations at rest and the people of God filled with anxiety. The godly receive the encouragement that his Spirit remains involved in the process of restoration (visions A–A'). The Lord will bring his judgment on the nations so they will no longer oppress, harass, or intimidate the remnant (visions B–B'). He will restore Zion so magnificently and her population will be so extensive that no walls will suffice (visions C–C'). Moreover, the New Jerusalem, Zion, will not need any walls, because the great King is in her midst to bless and protect his people.

The visions of the reassurance of the renewal of covenant are climactic (D–D'). Though the word *covenant* does not occur, the symbolic cleansing of Joshua, the high priest, signifies the renewal of the Mosaic covenant. Further, the correlation of the high priest with Zerubbabel reveals the Old Testament ideal of cooperation between the priesthood and the Davidic monarch.[70] Both are called the "anointed" (messiahs) of the Lord (4:14). The oracle explaining the fourth vision amplifies the place of the priesthood, the temple, and the messianic monarch in bringing in the era of restoration, " 'Listen, O high priest Joshua and your associates seated before you, who are men symbolic of things to come: I am going to bring my servant, the Branch. . . . In that day each of you will invite his neighbor to sit under his vine and fig tree,' declares the LORD Almighty" (3:8, 10).

The vision of the *mᵉnôrâ* ("lampstand")[71] gives insight into the special place of the priest and the Davidic Messiah as representatives of the people in the presence of God.[72] Joshua, the high priest, symbolizes the efficacy of his covenant, atonement, forgiveness, and the restoration. He is God's token of the new age, even as Zerubbabel is his token of the continuity of the Davidic dynasty and of the messianic age. Thus God assures the godly remnant of the continuity and effectiveness of the covenant and of his theocratic officers, whose ministry is empowered by the Spirit of God (see 4:6).

These visions offer a framework for interpreting the postexilic era in the light of the prophetic word. On the one hand, the people had been defiled by sin and alienated from God; on the other hand, with their restoration to the land, the Lord inaugurates an era of covenant renewal and blessing. The postexilic era marked the presence ("now") of the restoration.[73]

> "But now I will not deal with the remnant of this people as I did in the past," declares the LORD Almighty. . . . "So *now* I have determined to do good again to Jerusalem and Judah. Do not be afraid" (8:11, 15, emphasis mine).

> Never again will an oppressor overrun my people, for *now* I am keeping watch (9:8, emphasis mine).

The rebuilding of the temple, the priesthood of Joshua, and the leadership of Zerubbabel foreshadow greater developments. As tokens of restoration, they may be small but should not be despised: "Who despises the day of small things?" (4:10). To this end the prophet also encouraged them not to be afraid but to take heart (8:15), as blessing will overtake the people of God.

> Return to your fortress, O prisoners of hope; even *now* I announce that I will restore twice as much to you (9:12, emphasis mine; see 8:11).

The Era of Restoration: Fulfillment of the Promises

Zechariah confirmed the promises concerning the people, the land, and the presence of the Lord in blessing, protection, peace, the spiritual metamorphosis (forgiveness, cleansing, and holiness), the inclusion of the nations, and the renewal of creation.

The presence of Yahweh in blessing and protection is the present guarantee of the restoration as well as the hope of the transformation to come. We have already seen how the postexilic prophets emphasized that the fulfillment was already theirs in token. The focus of the promises is the return of God's presence symbolized by the temple people (1:16). His presence will assure the covenant relationship, symbolized in the names associated with the city of God: "Then Jerusalem will be called the City of Truth, and the mountain of the LORD Almighty will be called the Holy Mountain" (8:3). Yahweh's presence was experienced in the postexilic community, as God affirmed: "Now I have determined to do good again to Jerusalem and Judah. Do not be afraid" (8:15). The Lord promised to remove their fear and to give them reasons to rejoice in his goodness.

> "Shout and be glad, O Daughter of Zion. For I am coming, and I will live among you," declares the LORD. "Many nations will be joined with the Lord in that day and will become my people. I will live among you and you will know that the LORD Almighty has sent me to you" (2:10–11).

The Lord was present in blessing (8:12–14), in protection, and in keeping watch over his people (vv. 12–14; 9:8). Though they might suffer adversity, he is with them as their God, for they are his precious people (9:8–16; 14:3–7, 9).[74]

The Lord is King, and the people make up his kingdom on earth. He gives them the peace that the preexilic prophets had proclaimed: "In that day each of you will invite his neighbor to sit under his vine and fig tree," declares the LORD Almighty" (3:10). His peace will extend to all the nations, as envisioned in God's covenant with David.

> He will proclaim peace to the nations.
> His rule will extend from sea to sea
> and from the River to the ends of the earth.
> (9:10; see Ps. 72:8–11)

He is God's instrument of righteousness, who establishes order in God's world and avenges the enemy. When his kingdom is fully established, his people will be secure forevermore; "It will be inhabited; never again will it be destroyed. Jerusalem will be secure" (14:11).[75]

The people of the Lord will increase in number as Jews and Gentiles together will seek shelter in Zion (3:10; 8:20–23). Zion, the city of God, denotes here, as elsewhere in the Old Testament, God's blessing and protection that come from God's presence with his people (see Ps. 46). Yahweh declares that he is zealous for his people, and his zeal comes to concrete expression in the restoration of the people to the land and cities (1:17), in the joy and prosperity of his people (8:4–6), and in the honor his children will enjoy instead of shame (9:16–17). No one will be permitted to hurt his people without hurting himself (10:4–12). Hence, the vision of Zion without walls portrays both the great number of the redeemed and the protection of the Lord (2:1–13).

Yahweh reassures his people and the godly from the nations that he will be zealous in working out the restoration of his children (1:14; 8:2). They constitute the new community, composed of people who have been cleansed and forgiven by "the blood of my covenant" (9:11; see Matt. 26:28; Zech. 13:1). The benefits come through God's grace, but the Lord delights in children who are zealous for the Lord, his kingdom, and his worship. They will enter into the fullness of the covenant privileges (8:20–23; 14:20–21).

The land is intimately connected with the restoration of the people of God. He will grant his blessing on the land by giving rain and increasing the crops (10:1). In the vision of the new creation the prophet affirms the hope of the cooperation of creation with the redeemed because of God's kingship, symbolized by light and water (14:6–11). He will establish his kingship "over the whole earth" (14:9).

The benefits of God's rule confirm the promises of all the covenants. Zechariah used promise and covenant language to assure them that the Lord is faithful in the progress of fulfillment. However, God also expects his people to be involved. Involvement in Zechariah's time pertained to the temple of God, which was still not complete (8:9–10).

This involvement also pertains to God's concern for justice on earth.[76] Wicked and selfish people (i.e., covenant breakers) have no place in the eschatological kingdom (13:2). Covenant keepers establish the kingdom of God by living in accordance with the principles of God's rule of justice, righteousness, and love (8:16–22; see 7:9). The Lord promises to bless his people in proportion to their commitment to his kingdom.

As slow as the process of restoration may be, it will come to pass. The guarantee of the new age lies in the present tokens of the eschaton: removal of sin, Zerubbabel, Joshua, and the temple.[77] The certainty of restoration is ensured by the very nature of God's fidelity and righteousness (8:7–8). The Spirit of God will not rest until the whole plan of God is executed (6:8; see 4:6–7).

The Humble and Glorious Messiah[78]

In the visions Zechariah portrayed the harmonious relationship between the high priest and the Branch, the Davidic descendant. The Branch will foster the worship of God and bring in an era of peace and prosperity. He appears both humble and glorious. He is humble in his entrance. The prophet spoke of the mystery of the Incarnation as he announced the coming of the great King.

> Rejoice greatly, O Daughter of Zion!
> Shout, Daughter of Jerusalem!
> See, your king comes to you,
>   righteous and having salvation,
>   gentle and riding on a donkey,
>   on a colt, the foal of a donkey.
>   (9:9)[79]

The prophet also intimates that this Messiah is to suffer as the smitten shepherd (11:7–14; 13:7–9).[80] But this humble Messiah is powerful enough to bring to his people full deliverance from suffering, to be God's means of grace and purification, and to bring the gift of the Spirit of restoration to all who mourn over his being pierced (12:10–13:1; see Rev. 1:7).

He is the Priest-King who serves "the LORD of all the earth" (4:14) and rules over all who believe on him, Jews and Gentiles (8:20–23). The presence of God will be evident: "The house of David will be like God, like the Angel of the LORD going before them" (12:8). In the end, the Messiah will establish the kingdom of God on earth. He will vindicate the saints and judge the unbelieving nations: "On that day his feet will stand on the Mount of Olives, . . . Then the LORD my God will come, and all the holy ones with him" (14:4–5).[81] On that glorious day the Lord and Creator of humankind will transform everything (14:6–8) and grant his blessing on the new community, which may share in this transformed and holy world (14:20–21).

MALACHI: THE VICTORY BELONGS TO THE SᴱGULLÂ

Malachi and His Time

According to the superscription (1:1) the prophecy is accredited to Malachi ("my messenger").[82] Although there is some question about the authorship of this prophecy, I attribute it to a prophet named Malachi, of whom little else is known.[83] Malachi prophesied during the Persian period, after the reconstruction and dedication of the temple in 515 B.C. His interaction with the priests at the temple suggests that he lived in or around Jerusalem.

The book of Malachi reflects a period of tension. God had not brought in the greatness of his kingdom after the construction and dedication of the temple (see Hag. 2:6–9). He had not magnificently demonstrated his presence by the rich blessings of which Haggai (2:19) and Zechariah (8:9–11) had spoken. But neither had his people conformed to God's expectations. True, the new community had not practiced outright idolatry, but they were not zealous for the Lord either. They failed to pay the tithe (3:8–10; see Neh. 10:32–39; 13:10–13), divorced their wives (Hag. 2:14), married non-Jewish women (Mal. 2:10–12; see Ezra 9:1–2; Neh. 5:1–5), and brought maimed and diseased animals to God's altar, which the priests accepted as fit for sacrifice to Yahweh.

The people of God were in dire straits. They had suffered from drought and famine. The poor were forced to sell their sons and daughters into slavery if they could not pay their debts. Since financial gain was hard, many divorced their wives in order to marry pagan women for financial profit. In contrast to God's people who struggled, the wicked prospered. God seemed to overlook their evil and to be apathetic to the condition of his own people. Malachi entered into this historical context to explain the delay in fulfillment and to set before his hearers the unpopular message of "human failure and divine promise."[84]

The date of Malachi's ministry may be set in the postexilic period after the completion of the temple (515 B.C.) and before or during the ministry of Ezra and Nehemiah (ca. 458 B.C.). With the support of King Artaxerxes a second wave of returnees joined Ezra (458 B.C.) in an effort to establish a theocratic community held together by the observance of God's Law and the temple (Ezra 7:6–7, 17–26; Neh. 8:1–14). The royal encouragement and the inspiration of Ezra's teaching ministry strengthened the godly community of Judea, who then gave themselves more to the Torah and the temple (Neh. 7:73–10:39).

Ezra's reform efforts (Ezra 9–10) were bolstered by the courageous leadership of Nehemiah, who arrived in 445 B.C.[85] Together they encouraged a theocratic development of the community, submissive to Yahweh's Law (Neh. 5; 13:1–3, 15–28), zealous for the development of the temple worship (12:1–47; 13:4–14, 30–31), and concerned with Jerusalem (Zion) as the theocratic center. Jerusalem's walls were restored (3; 4; 6; 7:1–3) and the city was repopulated (chap. 11). If Malachi spoke after Nehemiah's reforms, it would appear that the people had reverted to the problems that Ezra and Nehemiah had dealt with.

It is also possible that Malachi's preaching prepared the hearts of the people for the reforms under Ezra and Nehemiah.[86] If so, Malachi's ministry antedated 458 B.C., the year of Ezra's return.[87] It is equally possible that Malachi prophesied prior to the reforms of Nehemiah in 445 B.C. since Nehemiah's work is not mentioned and the abuses that Malachi spoke against are the same as those Nehemiah condemned. Either way, serious abuses had entered Jewish life: mixed marriage and divorce (2:10–12), little concern for social justice (3:5), and ritualism (1:7–8). They were cheap with the Lord as they tried to get by with offering blemished animals (1:7–12, 14). The priests had become lax and degenerate (2:1–9), even to the point of being indifferent to the Lord's command (1:12–13). In not paying their tithes, the people failed to support the temple officers (3:8). The priests and Levites were unexacting in their teaching because they felt dependent on the goodwill of the people. Since they were all caught in a spiral of spiritual decline, Malachi preached a message to restore the people to a right relationship with God.

Literary Form and Structure

Literary Form

The discussion speech is the characteristic form of prophetic speech in Malachi.[88] He chose not to address actual questions but anticipated or verbalized the questions of the people as a rhetorical device (1:2, 6–7; 2:17; 3:7–8, 13). He addressed a mixture of God-fearing, religious, and apostate Jews. The God-fearing Jews made up a remnant concerned with Yahweh's honor more than with personal advantage and committed to the belief in God's freedom to reward and punish. The religious ones were traditionalists for whom God had to live up to their expectations. The wicked were those Jews who abandoned principle for the sake of personal advantage. These distinctions are made clearer toward the end of the prophecy: "'But now we [i.e., religious Jews] call the arrogant [i.e., wicked Jews] blessed. Certainly the evildoers prosper, and even those who challenge God escape.' Then those who feared the LORD talked with each other, . . . those who feared the Lord and honored his name" (3:15–16).

Structure

The major themes of the book are developed in a structured pattern of six discussions.[89]

Introduction: God's word through Malachi, 1:1
    A. The deep love of God for his people, 1:2–5
       B. Appeal to love God as Father and King, 1:6–14
          C. Judgment on the unfaithful priests, 2:1–9
          C'. Judgment on unfaithfulness in marriage, 2:10–16
             D. The Day of Judgment, 2:17–3:5
          C". Judgment on unfaithfulness to God, 3:6–12
       B'. Appeal to serve the Lord, 3:13–16
    A'. The deep love of God for his loyal remnant, 3:17–4:3
Conclusion: Moses and Elijah, 4:4–6

The Message of Malachi

The people in the postexilic era suffered from theological myopia. They, like their predecessors, wanted a comfortable religion. Good religion for them was a form of worship and a set of expectations that did not interfere with everyday life; in effect they limited their concept of God. Malachi, like the prophets before him, criticized their complacency with God. He presented a theology of Yahweh, so great and magnificent, so wise and glorious, showing that humankind cannot restrict him to time and space. He is the King over the world and the Father of the *sᵉgullâ* ("the treasured possession"). As King he will extend his kingdom (1:5), and as Father he will give the benefits of his fatherhood only to those who fully submit to his rule.

Yahweh Is Father and King

God's people contentedly thought of God as their Father, but their theology of God encouraged them to seek their own ease and not appropriately worship him as his children. They argued with the prophet, saying, "Have we not all one Father? Did not one God create us?" (2:10). Malachi answered that Yahweh is also the great King: " 'A son honors his father, and a servant his master. If I am a father, where is the honor due me? If I am a master, where is the respect due me?' says the Lord Almighty" (1:6). Malachi referred to him as "the Lord [Yahweh] of Hosts" (NIV "the Lord Almighty");[90] that is, Yahweh is the Divine Warrior-King who controls all armies in heaven and on earth. The prophet further concluded that since Yahweh's kingdom extends beyond Jerusalem, her temple, and her priesthood to the whole earth, the worship of Yahweh may never be restricted to the temple. Indeed, the Lord would rather receive true worship from his children living anywhere in his kingdom than suffer through the rituals in the temple.

"My name is [NIV "will be"] great among the nations, from the rising to the setting of the sun. In every place incense and pure offerings are brought (NIV "will be brought") to my name, because my name is (NIV "will be") great among the nations," says the LORD Almighty (1:11; see v. 10).[91]

Malachi's words point to the fulfillment of the prophetic word. Gentile proselytes, together with Jews in the Diaspora, were already worshiping the Lord. Yet this prophecy also reveals a dynamic progression of fulfillment from the postexilic era till the glorious coming of Jesus Christ. I agree with Kaiser: "If the Jewish diaspora and Gentile proselytism already signaled the firstfruits, the full harvest anticipated in these verses was yet to come. . . . This text then carries us from what was begun in Malachi's day, as a sort of harbinger of things to come, to the messianic age."[92] No matter how his people may respond to this prophetic word, they must know that he is and always will be the great King: "I am a great king . . . my name is and will be feared among the nations" (1:14, translation mine).

Yahweh Is Righteous in His Love

Malachi sought to change the community's misunderstanding of God's righteousness and love. They expected God's blessings as promised by the prophets. When the fullness of restoration did not come with the building of the temple, and when Zerubbabel, the Davidic descendant, died, the fire of anticipation died down. The new community did not persevere in doing good or in waiting for the restoration. They were satisfied with carving out their own little kingdom. More than that, they challenged God's love and righteousness. In their complacency, they felt that they deserved the victory, glory, and prosperity associated with the kingdom of God. Since they were not victorious, glorious, and prosperous, they wondered why they were still governed by the Persians and why the Edomites were still in existence (see chap. 5: "Obadiah"). Malachi answered their questions by identifying their root problem: The people had limited their conception of Yahweh and were content with a human perception of justice.

Yahweh Loves the S^egullâ

By means of discussion speech[93] the prophet openly expressed the questions that he knew were in the hearts of his community, and then he answered them. The first and last questions challenged God's love for his people. In the first question, the people asked how God has demonstrated his love for them (1:2). Malachi asked them to reflect on

Yahweh's love[94] of Jacob. The historic bond between the Lord and Jacob forms the basis for hope. All descendants of Jacob must define hope by God's fidelity to his promises in the past and in the future. The prophet explained that God had shown his love for their ancestor Jacob in the past and that in the future Edom (the nations) will be broken beyond recovery: "You will see it with your own eyes and say, 'Great is the LORD—even beyond the borders of Israel!'" (1:5; see Amos 9:12; Obad. 19).

But Malachi qualified the general love of the Lord. The present covenant privileges may belong to the descendants of Jacob; yet individuals are at risk if they do not respond to God's grace but choose to live to themselves and complain. Instead, the fulfillment of the promises belongs to the *sᵉgullâ*. The *sᵉgullâ* ("treasured possession," 3:17; see Ex. 19:5; Deut. 7:6; 14:2; 26:18; Ps. 135:4) are the children of God who serve God for his sake, persevere, and form a counterculture (Mal. 3:16; see 1 Peter 2:4–12). God's love is restricted to those who persevere in loving him: "But for you who revere my name, the sun of righteousness will rise with healing in its wings. And you will go out and leap like calves released from the stall" (Mal. 4:2)

What does the Lord require of his faithful servants? He expects nothing less than to receive the honor due him. The priests should have remained faithful to their charge given to them centuries ago when the Lord granted them the privilege of serving him (Num. 25:10–13). He made a covenant[95] with them, expecting them to be faithful in honoring his name by giving the reverence due the Lord, by walking with him, and by teaching God's people to follow the Lord (2:5–7). Instead, they showed lack of discernment, an utter disregard for God's glory, and a preoccupation with material concerns. Thus they led God's people astray by carelessness and selfishness. This perversion of godliness received God's strongest judgment (2:8–9).

The prophet appealed to the people to be loyal and devoted to the great King. Fidelity takes concrete forms: (1) honoring God by giving of one's substance (1:6–14; 3:6–8); (2) being faithful in marriage (2:10–16); (3) assuming social responsibility (3:5); and (4) showing devotion to Yahweh (3:16). God takes note of the remnant, writing down their names and deeds in a "scroll of remembrance" (3:16; see Ex. 32:32; Ps. 69:28; Ezek. 13:9). They may be forgotten by their generation, but the Lord will not forget!

Malachi further urged the faithful to guard themselves against temptation and against infidelity: "So guard yourself in your spirit, and do not break faith with the wife of your youth. . . . So guard yourself in your spirit, and do not break faith" (2:15–16). They must live in marital fidelity, not only because God expects it, but because in this way his kingdom is built up with God-fearing children (2:15).[96]

He also expected his faithful servants to provide regularly for the needs of the priests and Levites (Neh. 13:10–12). This provision was called for in the Law in the form of the *tithe* (Lev. 27:30; Num. 18:21). Because the people had shown a disregard for God's law, they had come under a curse (Mal. 3:9) that the Lord alone can transform into blessing (vv. 10–12). He expects his loyal servants to trust him and to be generous, regardless of the cost of discipleship.[97]

The *s*ᵉ*gullâ* are to be seen in contrast to the arrogant and the religious. The arrogant pride themselves in their power and luxurious way of life, and they challenge God's justice. The religious bless the wicked (3:15), looking with envy on their prosperity and questioning whether godliness has its rewards. They divorce and marry for financial and social advantages, with little regard for God, his word, or even their children. They lay claim to their heritage in Jacob, but as far as God is concerned, they are *cast out;* all who fear him, even if they are Gentile believers (1:11), belong to the new community![98]

Yahweh Is the Divine Warrior in Blessing and in Judgment

Malachi also confirmed Yahweh's fidelity to the prophetic oracles of judgment. Since the Lord had not brought to fruition the promises and the blessings and had not yet brought the rule of evil to an end, the community had begun to question the validity of the promises and hence the fidelity and justice of the Lord. They asked how God had shown his distinctive love for them by vindicating them from the enemies. They were waiting for a new demonstration of the vengeance of their Divine Warrior-King, as they asked, "Where is the God of justice?" (2:17). Had not Yahweh promised to bless all who persevere in their loyalty to him and to curse the wicked?

Malachi responded to their cynicism by upholding the principle of retribution. In confirming this principle, he turned it against many who wanted to enter the kingdom but had no right to it. In other words, Malachi's response excluded many from the era of blessing because they had come under Yahweh's curse. The judgment of the Lord rests on all who disregard his commandments and do not live in the light and hope of the kingdom to come (3:5, 18; 4:1, 3, 6). That Day of Judgment will be preceded by the coming of God's servant Elijah (John the Baptist, Mal. 3:1; Matt. 11:10; Mark 1:2; Luke 1:76; see Mal. 4:5)[99] and the messenger of the covenant (the Messiah, 3:1). Their purpose in coming was to purify the people of God and confirm the covenant with them (3:2–4). Only those who have been cleansed can stand the coming judgment and are marked for the day of redemption (3:16; 4:2). But all who do not persevere in fidelity will be cast out (3:5; see Ps. 1:5–6; Rev. 21:8; 22:15).

The book of "remembrance" contains the names of the *s*ᵉ*gullâ*.[100] The *s^egullâ* constitute the remnant or what Augustine called "the invisible Church." The *s^egullâ* are those who respond to the Lord with a humble and submissive spirit and are prepared to do whatever he expects from them. In Malachi's day this meant submitting oneself to God's revelation to Moses (4:4). For the Christian it means submitting oneself first to the Messiah of God, of whom the Father said, "This is my Son, whom I love . . . . Listen to him!" (Matt. 17:5; see 3:17; Ps. 2:7; Isa. 42:1).[101]

Underlying Malachi's message of God's love is an eschatological perspective on the kingdom,[102] where ethics and eschatology are thus woven together.[103] The vision of the kingdom properly belongs to those who persevere in living in fidelity to God. They may have to wait for the process of purification and salvation (i.e., redemptive history) to reach the fullness, but at God's time the righteous will prevail, receive their reward, enjoy glory ("the sun of righteousness," 4:2; see Luke 1:78–79), healing (4:2; see Isa. 45:8; 46:13; 53:5; Jer. 30:17; Hos. 14:4), and freedom (Mal. 4:3). However, sinners will perish (3:18; 4:1, 3; see Ps. 1:6). Malachi teaches that there is no hope (eschatology) without fidelity (ethics) and that there is no fidelity where there is no zeal for God. The theocentric and eschatological ethics of the prophet finds its confirmation in the teaching of our Lord and the apostles, who also hold out hope but restrict the entrance to the kingdom to those who do the will of God for the sake of God and of his Messiah and seek his righteous kingdom (Matt. 5:3–12, 17–20; 6:18; Luke 18:29–30; Gal. 5:16–26; Rev. 21:7–8; 22:14–15).

REVIEW

The postexilic era witnesses to a significant shift in the prophetic message.[104] The prophets explained both the presence of the new era and the future of God's promises. Their explanations form the basis for interpreting the preexilic and exilic prophets.[105] The postexilic prophets, like the apostles after the Ascension, were God's inspired interpreters of the progressive fulfillment of God's promises.

The postexilic era witnesses a beginning of the restoration: the new era. This had been the concern of the preexilic and exilic prophets as they comforted the godly with the hope of return to the land, of the restoration of the temple, of God's presence and kingship in their midst with the resultant blessing and protection. It is evident that the Spirit of restoration was working in their hearts.

The postexilic prophets also stressed the role of God's people in participating in the new era and hastening its fulfillment. The correlation between God's plan and man's responsibility was ever so important if the remnant were to enjoy the fulfillment of the promises and the full inauguration of the kingdom of God.[106] The postexilic prophets emphasized the present fulfillment and the more glorious fulfillment in the future.[107]

The remnant stood on the portal of the new age as they enjoyed a foretaste of the restoration and as they looked forward to the greater fulfillment of the prophetic word. Baldwin observes, "Thus present obedience sets God's people in line with fulfillment of His ultimate purpose, and His Spirit fills them with the conviction that they are experiencing in a small measure 'realized eschatology.'"[108] Fulfillment was real, but the kingdom was not realized in the postexilic community.[109] Hanson puts it well: "The message of Haggai and Zechariah . . . offered the wonders of the eschaton now, if only the people rallied behind the hierocratic program."[110] Mason sums up the "now" and "not yet" in the postexilic era.

> Since the tensions involved in keeping the relationship between "spirit" and "institutions," and between the "now" and the "not yet" of the Biblical promises, remain lively ones for the community of faith in every generation, perhaps these prophets deserve even closer attention than they have sometimes been accorded.[111]

Haggai's emphasis on the temple has its place in God's plan of restoration. The restored community could not be apathetic about the temple because it represented the presence, the blessings, and the protection of God. The restored community had to learn that devotion to the Lord involved being zealous for his honor and glory. Though the temple was a symbol and though it was less glorious than the former (Solomonic) temple, it signified the presence of God's kingship among his people.

The apathy of the remnant was due to political opposition and a mistaken theology. They believed that they had to wait for the fulfillment. Haggai set the record straight. The godly had to act in faith and live in the hope that the Lord would extend his kingship over all creation and inaugurate the glory of his kingdom! Since the temple also signified the kingdom of God, the people were expected to respond to the great King as if his kingdom was already fully established. Did he not teach them that a little defilement defiles everything (Hag. 2:14)?

The Spirit of God among the remnant signified that in time the Lord would bring in the fullness of restoration. This restoration would involve all the earth. The Lord had promised his covenant people peace, tranquillity, freedom from curse and enemies, and the spiritual and material enjoyment of his kingship. The presence of the Spirit of restoration among the new community gave a certain reality to his kingdom as the Lord renewed his promise that he would bless his people. Ackroyd observes that in Haggai, we have a picture of a restored community, centred on the Temple and needing to know itself as the people of God. It is a people which needs to be purified if it is to appropriate the divine blessings which its position entails, and this position is no narrow or provincial one, for at its centre is the Temple which is where God reveals himself, a centre therefore both to the life of the world and to the total action of God.[112]

Haggai assured the new community that they were heirs of the "new covenant," centered in David. Though Zerubbabel was only a "signet ring," he was "God's *sign* to the world that he intended to continue to fulfill his ancient promise."[113]

Zechariah combined these same motifs in his own artistic manner. He pointed to the present reality and to the more glorious fulfillment of the promises. On the one hand, he pointed to the temple, Joshua (the high priest), and Zerubbabel (the governor) as signs of the presence of the new age. On the other hand, he challenged the people to prepare themselves for the new age in the power of the Spirit of restoration.[114] The prophet forewarned them about the danger of apostasy and of the reality of adversity, but he proclaimed the reality of God's presence as the Divine Warrior-King and the magnificent vision of the fulfillment of God's promises in the kingdom age.

Malachi looked back at God's continual mercy on the remnant from the Exile, while at the same time he looked forward to the greater demonstrations of Yahweh's love for the *segullâ*, who make up God's remnant. Between the two horizons, the book of Malachi challenges each generation to prepare for the Lord and seek his kingdom. The eschatologically oriented ethical emphasis of Malachi is rooted in the conception of Yahweh's kingship, which reflects justice, righteousness, fidelity, and love. He has revealed his way to Moses (Mal. 4:4) and has challenged his people to listen to the prophets, represented by Elijah (v. 5). Yahweh expects his people to respond to his revelation, to submit to his kingship, and to order their lives and community in preparation for the Kingdom-to-come.

QUESTIONS AND ISSUES

1. What did the exilic people hope for, and how was their hope realized? How did reality fail to meet their expectations of the fulfillment of the prophetic word?
2. Show how the postexilic prophets ministered from the conviction that the restoration was already present, even when in embryonic form. What were the signs?

3. What was the historical context of the ministry of Haggai, Zechariah, and Malachi? What distinct issues concerned these prophets?
4. Compare the emphasis in the message of the preexilic and the postexilic prophets. Compare the response of the postexilic community with that of the preexilic people. Explain the differences in the message and in the response.
5. What was Haggai's contribution to the prophetic teaching on the temple?
6. How do the postexilic prophets relate fulfillment of the prophetic word and individual responsibility?
7. How was the Spirit of God already present in Haggai's day? In what way is Zerubbabel a token of fulfillment?
8. How did Haggai contribute to the motif of internalization and democratization of the covenant community?
9. How did Zechariah visualize the glory of Zion in his eight visions? What was God's work in fulfilling his word, and how were his people responsible for bringing in the kingdom?
10. How was the new age already present, according to Zechariah, and how was it still eschatological? What are the tokens of the new age?
11. How did Zechariah visualize the kingdom of God and the kingdom of the Messiah of David?
12. How did Malachi restrict the fatherhood of God and why? How did he also expand the teaching on the fatherhood of God?
13. What are the qualities of the *segullâ*?
14. How do Haggai, Zechariah, and Malachi contribute to the vision of transformation?

CHAPTER 8

Summary of Prophetic Motifs

Introduction
The Day of the Lord
   Introduction
   The Day of the Lord in the Minor Prophets
   Aspects of the Day of the Lord
      Accountability
      Imminence of the theophany
      Imagery of court and war
      Transformation and preparation
   The Day of the Lord and the progress of redemption
The kingdom of God in creation
   Introduction
   Joel
   The preexilic prophets on the kingdom of God
   The postexilic prophets on the kingdom of God
   Conclusion
The Messiah and the messianic kingdom
   Hosea and Amos
   Micah
   The exilic era
   The postexilic era
   Conclusion
The Spirit of restoration
The new people of God
   Introduction
   The preexilic prophets
   The postexilic prophets
Israel and the nations
   Introduction
   The preexilic prophets
   The postexilic prophets
Review

INTRODUCTION

The study of the Minor Prophets has unveiled a variety of motifs, forms of speech, and imagery. These prophets spoke a relevant message to their contemporaries as they explained the ways of God *in time* and *out of time*. They were not ascetics or revolutionaries, but served the great King in the role of *covenant prosecutors*[1] and called for absolute submission to the revelation of Yahweh and for a complete abandonment of the manipulative ways of humans in any form (paganism, divination, magic, syncretism, *Realpolitik,* or *vox populi*).[2]

Though their images, expressions, and oracles reflect the historical context, the prophets are eschatological bearers of the good news of a new era. They helped humans to see that God's way in the past is a dim reflection of the future acts of God, that living in the present is significant in view of God's coming, and that the glorious future is already present in the hearts of the faithful. The prophetic contribution to eschatology lies in its importance as a frame of reference by which present decisions and actions can be seen in the light of the new age that God opens for all who submit to him.[3] In other words, the prophetic word gives new perspectives only to those who receive the sight to see, but it closes the vision of God to all who focus on this world of manipulation, power, and peer pressure.

The prophetic message speaks of salvation in the widest sense. Regardless of when and where the prophets ministered God's word, they bore faithful witness to God's promise that he will inaugurate a new era characterized by the fullness of blessing, goodness, joy, and his presence with his people (see Ps. 46). Salvation or deliverance comprehends all God's promises, the center of which is his promise to be with his people and all the benefits associated with his presence (see Rev. 21:22).

The prophetic message changed over time, most noticeably after the Exile. The preexilic prophets had spoken of the rebelliousness of Israel and Judah and God's judgment in the Day of the Lord. They had also proclaimed a new era of transformation, encouraging the godly remnant to persevere in fidelity and to prepare for a fuller manifestation of God's kingdom on earth. The godly were receptive to this revelation, entrusting it to their children and transmitting it within the community of the faithful. By and large, the tribes of Israel and Judah were unresponsive and hostile and often persecuted the prophets of God.

With the postexilic era the Lord bestowed his favor again by covenant renewal, forgiveness, and his blessings (see Ps. 126). Thus the remnant experienced a foretaste of the prophetic vision of the kingdom of God, of the messianic era, and of the world of transformation. But vision remained vision. To keep the vision before God's people, the postexilic

213

prophets stressed individual and corporate responsibility in preparing for the full establishment of God's kingdom. They encouraged them to interpret the prophetic word in the light of the reality of the present and to look at the present evidences of God's goodness as tokens of the eschatological reality.

The prophetic eschatology falls into six related topics: (1) the Day of the Lord; (2) the kingdom of God; (3) the messianic kingdom; (4) the Spirit of restoration; (5) the new people of God; and (6) Israel and the nations.

THE DAY OF THE LORD

Introduction

The Day of the Lord (*yôm Yahweh*) is the era in which the Lord judges, purifies a remnant for himself, avenges his name, vindicates his people, renews his creation, brings in the full deliverance, and establishes his rule on earth.[4] It is a highly useful, but complex, motif.

Mowinckel associated the Day of the Lord with Israel's cult where the people celebrated the coming of the Lord during the enthronement festival.[5] He held that Israel's celebration was intended to ensure Yahweh's presence in giving victory and prosperity. Three significant and widely different approaches were published by von Rad, F. Charles Fensham, and Meir Weiss. Von Rad expanded Mowinckel's conclusions by connecting the Day of the Lord with Israel's traditions of holy war.[6] He contends that Israel celebrated Yahweh's involvement in her wars and that his involvement in war assured them of victory. Hence, the Day of the Lord was originally not an eschatological concept, but was transformed by the prophets to this end: "Thus, under the influence of this traditional element, the prophetic concept of the *eschaton* was also to some extent systematized; that is to say, predictions connected with the Day of Yahweh which began from different traditions were to some extent blended."[7] Fensham looked at the Day of the Lord from the *covenantal* perspective of treaty curses.[8] He understands Yahweh's coming as an invocation of the treaty curses on account of Israel's breach of covenant. Weiss approached the Day of the Lord against the background of divine *theophany*.[9] According to Weiss, Amos coined the phrase and related it to the "ancient motif-complex of the theophany-descriptions."[10] Recently Yair Hoffmann has accentuated the eschatological function of this complex motif.[11] He argues that the phrase "Day of the Lord" has undergone a metamorphosis from an uncrystallized, noneschatological usage to a defined, eschatological meaning.

The Day of the Lord in the Minor Prophets

The definition of the Day of the Lord must begin with Amos (760 B.C.),[12] who transformed a popular, but mistaken, point of view. For his contemporaries the Day of the Lord was to be a more glorious era than the golden age under Jeroboam II. They mistakenly believed that God had promised to be their God and to bless them because they were the elect and blessed people. They were blind to their selective interpretation of revelation; they did not apply the razor edge of revelation to their pagan lifestyle. Amos sarcastically criticized their bigotry and declared that God can and will turn against the children of the covenant! He will turn the light of revelation into darkness. Then they will grope anxiously, looking for deliverance. For them the Day of the Lord will signify only divine abandonment, dread, judgment, and alienation.

> Woe to you who long
> for the day of the LORD!
> Why do you long for the day of the LORD?
> That day will be darkness, not light.
> It will be as though a man fled from a lion
> only to meet a bear,
> as though he entered his house
> and rested his hand on the wall
> only to have a snake bite him.
> Will not the day of the LORD be darkness, not light—
> pitch-dark, without a ray of brightness?
> (Amos 5:18–20)

The Day of the Lord in Hosea (750 B.C.) indicates a period of human accountability to God, of divine punishment (9:7), resulting in devastation of the land and the exile of Israel (1:4; 5:9; 10:10).[13] Human structures and institutions are powerless against his coming in judgment (9:5–9). (See figure 46.)

The prophet Micah (725 B.C.) relates the Day of the Lord to the language of *theophany*. A theophany (from *theos* ["God"] and *phanein* ["to appear"]) is an overwhelming manifestation of God's splendor and holiness.

A century after Micah and about 150 years after Amos, Zephaniah (630 B.C.) reflects the end of the long development of prophetic usage and makes creative contribution to the image of the Day of the Lord.

> The great day of the LORD is near—
> near and coming quickly.
> Listen! The cry on the day of the LORD will be bitter,

215

the shouting of the warrior there.
That day will be a day of wrath,
    a day of distress and anguish,
a day of trouble and ruin,
    a day of darkness and gloom,
    a day of clouds and blackness,
a day of trumpet and battle cry
    against the fortified cities
    and against the corner towers.
I will bring distress on the people
    and they will walk like blind men,
    because they have sinned against the LORD.
Their blood will be poured out like dust
    and their entrails like filth.
Neither their silver nor their gold
    will be able to save them
    on the day of the LORD's wrath.
In the fire of his jealousy
    the whole world will be consumed,
for he will make a sudden end
    of all who live in the earth.
                    (1:14–18)[14]

Here the Day of the Lord is associated with Yahweh's coming in judgment, resulting in death, slaughter, and bloodshed.[15] In Zephaniah the Day of the Lord clearly has a universal and eschatological dimension.[16]

THE COMING OF THE LORD

Era of accountability
Imminence of the theophany
Metaphors: Court and war
Ultimate goal: Transformation
Present goal: Godly living
Means: Judgment and deliverance

Figure 46. The Day of the Lord

Aspects of the Day of the Lord

Accountability

The word *day* refers to a period of time in redemptive history (an epoch) or an epochal event[17] when the Lord makes humans accountable for their actions. It is "the day of reckoning" (*peqûdâ*, Isa. 10:3).[18] The

216

prophets taught that God is just and patient in his sovereign rule over the nations and that everyone will suffer the consequences of their acts. The apostle Paul confirmed that human accountability has not changed with the coming of our Lord: "Do not be deceived: God cannot be mocked. A man reaps what he sows. The one who sows to please his sinful nature, from that nature will reap destruction" (Gal. 6:7–8). The Lord still has a day in store in which he holds humans accountable.

The Lord may judge people at any time. When he judges in history, his expression of displeasure and wrath is a foreboding token of the final and climactic judgment. In other words, any judgment of God is an intrusion of the eschatological judgment. This explains the relevance of the prophets for millennia as they still speak of accountability to God and his hatred of human arrogance. Isaiah puts it poetically,

> The Lord Almighty has *a day in store*
>   for all the proud and lofty,
>   for all that is exalted
>   (and they will be humbled),
> for all the cedars of Lebanon, tall and lofty,
>   and all the oaks of Bashan,
> for all the towering mountains
>   and all the high hills,
>   for every lofty tower
>   and every fortified wall,
> for every trading ship
>   and every stately vessel.
> *The arrogance of man will be brought low*
>   and the pride of men humbled;
> the Lord alone will be exalted in that day,
>   and the idols will totally disappear.
>   (Isa. 2:12–18, emphasis mine)

Nothing can deliver humans from God's judgment. Human structures will fail him, the earth itself will be unstable, and the sky will be dark when the creature renders account to his Creator.[19] Again we turn to Isaiah for a moving portrayal of that day.

> Wail, for the day of the Lord is near;
>   it will come like destruction from the Almighty.
> Because of this, all hands will go limp,
>   every man's heart will melt.
> Terror will seize them,
>   pain and anguish will grip them;
>   they will writhe like a woman in labor.
> They will look aghast at each other,
>   their faces aflame.
>   (Isa. 13:6–8, see 22:5; 26:21; 30:30; 63:1; 66:15)

Imminence of the Theophany

The Day of the Lord overshadows all human history and hence is always near. It has a sobering effect on the godly but will bring sudden calamity and weeping on all who have not prepared to meet their God.

> See, the day of the LORD is coming
> —a cruel day, with wrath and fierce anger—
> to make the land desolate
> and destroy the sinners within it.
>
> (Isa. 13:9)

On this day the Lord reveals his incomprehensible glory, justice, and power to his creation. When he comes into his created order, nothing stands in his way; the mountains melt, the hills become plains, and the valleys open up. These images explain Israel's concept of God's sovereignty over creation (see Pss. 18:9; 96:11–13; 144:5; Isa. 26:21; 31:4; 64:1–3; Mic. 1:2–4; Nah. 1:3–6). Yahweh's coming in judgment is an overwhelming experience. Creation cowers, quakes, and trembles as he approaches, as it did when God led his people out of Egypt.

> The waters saw you, O God,
>   the waters saw you and writhed;
>   the very depths were convulsed.
> The clouds poured down water,
>   the skies resounded with thunder;
>   your arrows flashed back and forth.
> Your thunder was heard in the whirlwind,
>   your lightning lit up the world;
>   the earth trembled and quaked.
> Your path led through the sea,
>   your way through the mighty waters,
>   though your footprints were not seen.
>
> (Ps. 77:16–19)

The psalmist evokes a picture of Yahweh's absolute authority and the readiness of nature to do his bidding. In the presence of the great King, creation bows humbly, and human kingdoms will be reduced to nothingness.

The word *theophany* means "the appearance of God," but in biblical usage his appearances are always attended by natural phenomena.[20] The language of the Lord's coming also goes back to Mount Sinai where the Lord revealed his glory to Israel (Ex. 24:15–18; see 19:18–19). The "coming" of the great King into the midst of his people required extensive preparations (construction of the ark and tabernacle; consecration of the priests, Levites, and people). At Mount Sinai Israel had been terrified of the coming of God, evident in the phenomena of thunder, lightning, darkness ("thick cloud"), smoke, fire, earthquake, and a loud noise (Ex. 19:16, 18–19; see Heb. 12:18–21). The prophets employed the imagery of theophany, associated with the historic deliverance from Egypt and the revelation at Mount Sinai, to communicate how awesome God's coming in judgment will be.

Further, they shattered human ideologies, structures, and popular misconceptions by challenging people to discern whether this God will come *for* or *against* them. The prophets asked rhetorically, "Who can withstand his indignation? Who can endure his fierce anger?" (Nah. 1:6; Zeph. 1:14–18; see Pss. 76:7; 147:17; Rev. 6:17). The prophets sounded a discordant note whenever they spoke of God's being a consuming fire (see Heb. 12:29; Deut. 4:24). For example, Micah said:

> Look! The LORD is coming from his dwelling place;
> > he comes down and treads the high places of the earth.
> The mountains melt beneath him
> > and the valleys split apart,
> like wax before the fire,
> > like water rushing down a slope.
> All this is because of Jacob's transgression.
>
> (Mic. 1:3–5)

In this way Micah heralded the coming of God against "Jacob" (Israel and Judah).

The God who has inspired the nations with awe of his mighty acts in nature and history (Ex. 15:11; Josh. 2:11) will act anew. But this time he will also hold his people accountable. They will not escape because everybody is accountable to him. By and large, Israel and Judah rejected this revolutionary teaching. They could not conceive how the God of the covenants could turn against his people.

Imagery of Court and War

The Lord's coming may be compared to a court scene. In his court Yahweh is the *prosecutor, witness,* and *judge.*[21] He is the sovereign judge seated above his creation: "But the LORD is in his holy temple; let all the earth be silent before him" (Hab. 2:20; see Zeph. 1:7). When he comes, he will assemble all nations and "enter into judgment against them" (Joel 3:2). He brings the charges (Hos. 4:1–3), serves as witness for the prosecution (Jer. 29:23; 42:5; Mic. 1:2), condemns, and executes the verdict. The bases of the accusation and condemnation are human arrogance, the rejection of his kingdom, and a selfish and greedy lifestyle: "So I will come near to you for judgment. I will be quick to testify against sorcerers, adulterers and perjurers, against those who defraud laborers of their wages, who oppress the widows and the fatherless, and deprive aliens of justice, but do not fear me" (Mal. 3:5; see Matt. 25:31–46).

In the second image, Yahweh is the *Divine Warrior,* who comes to establish order out of the chaos, anarchy, and autonomy of the kingdoms of humankind.[22] The Warrior vents his wrath against all opposition in his realm.

> Therefore I will make the heavens tremble;
>   and the earth will shake from its place
>   at the wrath of the LORD Almighty,
>   in the day of his burning anger.
>
>   (Isa. 13:13)[23]

In his wrath he comes with vengeance, likened to war and a bloodbath.

> But that day belongs to the Lord, the LORD Almighty—
>   a day of vengeance, for vengeance on his foes.
> The sword will devour till it is satisfied,
>   till it has quenched its thirst with blood.
> For the Lord, the LORD Almighty, will offer sacrifice
>   in the land of the north by the River Euphrates.
>
>   (Jer. 46:10)

The imagery of trial and war is a metaphorical expression of God's rule. He rules in his judgments and in his battles. In his wrath, he vindicates his name, but he also vindicates all who belong to him and who trust in him for protection and deliverance. The verb "deliver" (*y-š-ʿ*) and its cognate forms signify the Lord's commitment to identify with his people, defend them, give them relief, encourage them with his judgments in history, vindicate them in the presence of their enemies, and in the end usher in an era of peace, blessing, and glory in which the Lord will be present with his people (see Hab. 2:4, 14; 3:2–19; Zeph. 3:14–20).[24]

Transformation and Preparation

The goal of the Day of the Lord is the total transformation of all creation. Transformation has two aspects: *desolation* as a form of judgment, and *renewal* as a form of free grace (2 Peter 3:11–13). First, transformation is the time of "desolation" (*šôd*) brought about by the "Almighty" (*šaddai,* Isa. 13:6; Joel 1:15). Creation will travail, the mountains and fertile valleys will mourn, animals will make loud noises, and the land will become desolate (Isa. 13:9, 13; Amos 1:2; Zeph. 1:2–3; see 2 Peter 3:10).

Second, transformation denotes the renewal of creation, when the Lord will open up all the benefits of God's goodness to his children (Hos. 2:21–23; Joel 2:19–26; 3:18; Amos 9:13–15). His Spirit will also renew humans with physical and spiritual strength, consecrate them, and endow them with grace so that they may live in harmony with the kingdom of God (Jer. 24:7; 29:12–13; 31:31–34; 32:39; Ezek. 11:19–21; 36:22–32; 37:14, 21–28).[25]

Over the centuries the Lord has raised up a remnant of loyal devotees who respond to the proclamation of the Day of the Lord with prayer, confession of sin, and absolute abandonment to the Lord.[26] The prophets repeatedly called on the people to respond to God's gracious offer of a new future, to seek his protection, and to live righteously.

> Before the appointed time arrives
> and that day sweeps on like chaff,
> before the fierce anger of the LORD comes upon you,
> before the day of the LORD's wrath comes upon you.
> Seek the LORD, all you humble of the land,
> you who do what he commands.
> Seek righteousness, seek humility;
> perhaps you will be sheltered
> on the day of the LORD's anger.
>
> (Zeph. 2:2–3)

The godly responded in faith, preparing themselves for the day of deliverance. They lived in the hope of redemption and with the assurance that the Lord is good to those who wait for him and do his will on earth.

The Day of the Lord and the Progress of Redemption

The composite and complex presentation of the Day of the Lord provides an inspired framework for interpreting the events in redemptive history. The expulsion from the Garden of Eden, the distribution of languages and nations at Babel, the overthrow of Sodom and Gomorrah, the plagues in and victory over Egypt, the conquest, God's judgments in the history of Israel and Judah, the fall of Samaria (722 B.C.), the siege of Jerusalem by Sennacherib (701 B.C.), the fall of Nineveh (612 B.C.), the defeat of Egypt and the ascendancy of Babylon (605 B.C.), the fall of Jerusalem (586), the end of Babylon (538 B.C.)—all have a place in the larger eschatological framework of the Day of the Lord.[27] Each judgment confirms the sovereign rule of our God. He is Lord, and as King over creation, he rules by judgment. Each judgment is an intrusion and inauguration of the Day of the Lord. Each judgment must be interpreted as a theophany, and each theophany points to the final Day of the Lord. Then all opposition will cease, and the Lord will dwell among his loyal subjects! (See figure 47).

How did this framework help the postexilic community understand their place in redemptive history? They were struck both by the realization and by the lack of realization of the prophetic word. On the one hand, they saw a fulfillment of the prophetic word in the fall of

221

Aram, Israel, Assyria, Judah, and Babylon. On the other hand, the prophetic word was being fulfilled differently and less gloriously than they had expected. The fall of Assyria and Babylon had not brought about the radical transformation of creation, the cessation of enmity, and the full and beneficent presence of the kingdom of God. The dissonance[28] created between the expectations raised by the prophets and the reality of their situation helped the godly live in the hope of an eschatological dimension of the Day of the Lord.[29] God still had another day, or better other days, in which he holds his own people and the nations accountable for their acts. Thus, the Day of the Lord was a framework for interpreting history, for understanding the present under divine control, and also for projecting a final day of reckoning (the eschatological Day of the Lord). They were given to understand that the Day of the Lord is past, present, and future. The compenetration of history and eschatology helped them live with an edge as they looked in faith to the Lord of creation and the King of the nations.

Judgments in History

Eschatological Day of the Lord

throughout the progress of redemption

					722	586
Garden of Eden	Babel	Sodom and Gomorrah	Egypt	Canaan	Samaria	Jerusalem

Figure 47. Intrusion of the Day of the Lord

For example, Joel relates the historical event of the locust plague to the eschatological judgment of the nations under the Day of the Lord. He called on the people who had just suffered a severe agricultural and economic crisis to prepare themselves for an even greater manifestation of the Day of the Lord.

> Blow the trumpet in Zion;
>   sound the alarm on my holy hill.
> Let all who live in the land tremble,
>   for the day of the LORD is coming.
> It is close at hand—
>   a day of darkness and gloom,
>   a day of clouds and blackness.
> Like dawn spreading across the mountains
>   a large and mighty army comes,
> such as never was of old
>   nor ever will be in ages to come. . . .

> Before them the earth shakes,
> > the sky trembles,
> the sun and moon are darkened,
> > and the stars no longer shine.
> The LORD thunders
> > at the head of his army;
> his forces are beyond number,
> > and mighty are those who obey his command.
> The day of the Lord is great;
> > it is dreadful.
> Who can endure it?
>
> > (Joel 2:1–2, 10–11)

The historical and eschatological compenetration in Joel's description of the Day of the Lord finds expression in the language of the cosmic phenomena associated with *theophany* ("the earth shakes, the sky trembles, the sun and moon are darkened, and the stars no longer shine," 2:10; see vv. 30–31; 3:15), in the images of *war* (2:2–11; 3:9–13), and in the images of *judicial proceedings*.

> I will gather all nations
> > and bring them down to the Valley of Jehoshaphat.
> There I will enter into judgment against them
> > concerning my inheritance, my people Israel,
> for they scattered my people among the nations
> > and divided up my land.
>
> > (3:2)

The verdict will be quickly rendered on the basis of the principle of retribution, "I will swiftly and speedily return on your own heads what you have done" (3:4; see vv. 5–8).

What is the meaning of *eschatology*? Buss defines it as the idealized and distant order.[30] Kapelrud objects to this and argues in favor of a realized eschatology, which is a fulfillment of judgment and salvation within the life experience of the prophet's audience.[31] Raitt argues similarly that the oracles of judgment and salvation form a synthesis: "Salvation eschatology was an extremely creative answer to the problem of theodicy. . . . It was the real beginning of a 'theology of hope.'"[32] He defines the new eschatology as "the search for and discovery of a frame of reference to explain events which are not understandable in terms of any previous tradition."[33] (For my agreement with Raitt's definition of eschatology, see chap. 3: "Prophecy and Eschatology.")

The apostle Paul develops the doctrine of the Day of the Lord in 1 Thessalonians 5:1–15. His teaching reveals a clear continuity with the prophetic teaching, but discontinuity occurs in three aspects. First, Christ has undergone the wrath of God, suffering the full extent of God's judgment for sinners (Rom. 5:6–11; Gal. 3:13). This means that all who are in Christ need not fear the Day of the Lord, but may wait for it with longing, "to wait for his Son from heaven, whom he raised from the dead—Jesus, who rescues us from the coming wrath" (1 Thess. 1:10; 5:9–10). (See figure 48.)

The death of Christ is God's ultimate sacrifice. Throughout the Old Testament the Lord has cared for his people in concrete acts of deliverance, victory, and vindication so they could say with Nahum,

> The LORD is good,
>   a refuge in times of trouble.
> He cares for those who trust in him.
>   (Nah. 1:7)

But the greatest expression of his love is found in the greatest act of condescension, the death of our Lord (Rom. 5:8). In other words, since the death, resurrection, and exaltation of the Lord Jesus Christ, the Christian has even more reason to wait with joy and anticipation of the Day of the Lord, having experienced the depth of God's love in Christ!

THE COMING OF JESUS CHRIST

Era of accountability
Imminence ("like thief at night")
Metaphors: Court and war
Ultimate goal: Transformation
Present goal: Godly living
Means: Judgment and deliverance

Figure 48. The Day of Jesus Christ

Second, the remnant consists of Jews and Gentiles who confess that Jesus is the Messiah and Lord (Rom. 1:1–6; 10:9). They belong to the new people of God, the church of Jesus Christ, and constitute a new humanity whose future lies in a restoration of creation over which Jesus is Lord (Col. 1:15–23).

Third, Jesus Christ is the Lord of glory who will bring all things under his control. He is the Divine Warrior, appointed by the Father to rule over his kingdom till all opposition is removed (1 Cor. 15:23–28; Rev. 6:16–17; 16:15; 19:11–21). He has said, "The Son of Man will send out his angels, and they will weed out of his kingdom everything that

224

causes sin and all who do evil" (Matt. 13:41). This explains the New Testament usage of the phrase "the day of the Lord [Jesus]" (2 Cor. 1:14; 2 Thess. 2:2) or "the day of Christ" (Phil. 1:10; 2:16).

In Jesus' coming and in the mission of the Holy Spirit, the eschatological moment is more clearly present. The Spirit is with the saints (2 Cor. 5:5–7) in that he takes away their fear, reconciles them continually to the Father, endows them with spiritual gifts, and prepares them for their eternal heritage. Paul writes, "Therefore you do not lack any spiritual gift as you eagerly wait for our Lord Jesus Christ to be revealed. He will keep you strong to the end, so that you will be blameless on *the day of our Lord Jesus Christ.* God, who has called you into fellowship with his Son Jesus Christ our Lord, is faithful" (1 Cor. 1:7–9, emphasis mine).

Still, the continuity is also clear. Jesus is the Divine Warrior who will deliver the saints and who will avenge the enemies of God. The teaching of the Day of the Lord in the New Testament, like that in the Prophets, is in the context of ethics. The purpose of the apostolic teaching on the future, like that of the Prophets, is to activate Christians to godly living. Paul, for example, calls for consecration, purification, and anticipation. Christians demonstrate their godliness by being "sons of the light" (1 Thess. 5:5), that is, "alert and self-controlled" (v. 6), having put on "faith and love as a breastplate, and the hope of salvation as a helmet" (v. 8). They are full of mutual encouragement (v. 11) and are respectful of the teachers of the Word (vv. 12–13). They live in peace with one another (v. 13), being diligent, compassionate, patient, and kind (vv. 14–15).

Moreover, living in the anticipation of the Day of the Lord, the godly in Christ have no reason to dread the sudden coming of our Lord "like a thief in the night" (1 Thess. 5:2; see 2 Peter 3:10), for it is against all the ungodly that "destruction will come . . . suddenly, as labor pains on a pregnant woman, and they will not escape" (1 Thess. 5:3).

THE KINGDOM OF GOD IN CREATION

Introduction

The kingdom of God is *the rule of God over all creation.*[34] God established his rule at creation, and he has maintained it by caring for his creation. Yahweh rules with the purpose of establishing his sovereignty over this world and of transforming creation into a holy and blessed place for a holy people. He blesses it with food, with the enjoyment of offspring and relationships, and with a meaningful existence (Ps. 104). He is patient with human sin and transgression, leading some to mistake his patience and forbearance for his absence (2 Peter 3:8–9).

The kingdom of God is further extended in his rule over the community of God's people who submit to his authority, trust in his care, exist by his blessings, and live to his glory. He, in turn, has promised to care for their needs, protect them, and keep adversity from them. These people bring into concrete existence the kingdom of God by their witness as a counterculture, transformed by God's revelation, bound together by the Holy Spirit, and committed to promote righteousness, justice, love, fidelity, and peace.

The kingdom of God—in creation and in redemption—is both present (inaugurated) and eschatological. It is *inaugurated* as evidenced in the order of nature, the joys of life, God's sovereignty over creation, the existence of the new community, and the involvement of the triune God in this world and in the community of the redeemed. Only faith in a good, compassionate, righteous, and patient King explains the meaning and the possibility of life on earth. (See figure 49.)

THE KINGDOM OF GOD

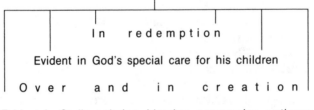

Figure 49. The Kingdom of God in Creation and in Redemption

The kingdom of God, as an *eschatological* concept, is the era of peace prepared for the children of God who persevere in loving him, seeking his kingdom, and consecrating themselves away from the defilements of human structures and kingdoms. They form a counterculture by being faithful, loving, compassionate, just, and peaceful people who live in the anticipation of the eschatological era of righteousness, justice, peace, harmony, and love. This is what Calvin meant by the spirituality of the kingdom:

> As, then, the kingdom of Christ is spiritual and celestial, it cannot be comprehended by human minds, except he raises up our thoughts, as he does, by degrees. This, then, is the reason why the Prophets have set forth the kingdom of Christ by comparing it to earthly kingdoms. We also know that there was a peculiarity in the Old Testament, when

God covered with shadows what was afterwards clearly revealed in the Gospel; in Christ the heavens are opened to us.[35]

The prophets knew all too well that kingship corrupts. Even the Davidic dynasty was not devoid of injustice, dictatorship, and oppression, which explains the prophetic emphasis on Yahweh's rule over his people. God alone can and will establish peace for his people.[36] (See figure 50.) The kingdom of God embraces the promises and covenants of God pertaining to creation and redemption. Since God's children enjoy the firstfruits of covenant renewal, we who are in Christ live in between the enjoyment of the promises (tokens) of the covenant and the fulfillment (reality) of the covenant.[37]

Joel

Joel likens the kingdom to the full beneficence of God's presence in subduing evil, protecting his people, and blessing them. His people rejoice when they receive the benefits of his kingdom. The kingdom embraces all his creation: his people, the earth, and even wild animals (Joel 2:21–23). The hope in the kingdom to come is rooted in God's promise: "The LORD will be jealous for his land and take pity on his people" (v. 18). The goal of the kingdom is the uninterrupted enjoyment of God's beneficent presence with his people (vv. 20–27). The token of the restoration of God's kingdom is the Spirit; he recreates, renews, and motivates the godly as they yearn for the day of restoration (vv. 28, 32). The Lord establishes his kingdom by his acts of *inclusion* and *exclusion*. He *includes* the new community of the Spirit. They need not be afraid, because they have been sealed with the Spirit of restoration (v. 29) and have received the promise of his protection (3:8, 16) and of a transformed creation (v. 18).

The Lord has assured his children throughout the progressive unfolding of his kingdom that he will establish his kingdom for them alone. This is the *inclusive* aspect of the kingdom.

> Then you will *know* that I, the LORD your God,
>   dwell in Zion, my holy hill.
> Jerusalem will be holy;
>   never again will foreigners invade her.
> (Joel 3:17, emphasis mine; see 2:27; Mal. 3:16)

The kingdom of God *excludes* all forms of evil and sinners. The reality of evil in this world takes many forms (drought, famine, hunger, war, murder, oppression, persecution, injustice), and each evil challenges the godly to long for his kingdom to come. His kingdom will be evident when evil is no more. The Lord will also exclude all proud, arrogant, and rebellious people. Everything that frustrates the full experience of God's blessing will be totally removed, and all who have oppressed, persecuted, and harassed God's people and have not repented will likewise be excluded. When he has expelled the clouds of sin and human anarchy from his creation, God's people will be fully at rest, enjoying the radiance of God's goodness (Joel 3:18; see Rev. 21:2–7). The remnant, having been cleansed, forgiven, and consecrated, will enjoy God's goodness forever. Theirs is the fullness of the presence of God (*visio dei*):

> "Their bloodguilt, which I have not pardoned,
>   I will pardon."
> The LORD dwells in Zion!
>
> (Joel 3:21)

The Preexilic Prophets on the Kingdom of God

Hosea spoke of God's dynamic relation to creation and redemption. Yahweh desired his people to know him (2:20; 4:1),[38] that is, to seek him and to submit to his anointed Messiah (3:5). He has prepared a kingdom of love, righteousness, and blessing for his beloved bride (2:16–23; 14:4–8). But he gives the benefits of his kingdom only to those who find in him alone deliverance, meaning, and the joy of life (12:6). As recipients of his goodness (2:21–23), they will establish his kingdom by doing his will on earth.

> Sow for yourselves righteousness,
>   reap the fruit of unfailing love,
> and break up your unplowed ground;
>   for it is time to seek the LORD,
> until he comes
>   and showers righteousness on you.
>
> (10:12)

Amos condemned the anarchy of autonomy. The leaders had undermined God's kingdom by having no regard for God's order and by despising justice and compassion (5:7; see 5:24; 6:12). They will be excluded from his kingdom when the Lord will transform this earth into a veritable Garden of Eden (9:13–15) in which even righteous Gentiles may share with the remnant of Israel (9:9, 12). His kingdom includes all who cooperate with his rule: "But let justice roll on like a river, righteousness like a never-failing stream!" (5:24).

Jonah, Obadiah, and Nahum related God's present and future kingdom to the establishment of his sovereignty over all the nations. The book of Jonah portrays God's freedom in his patience with and compassion toward the nations. Obadiah (585 B.C.) singled out Edom as representative of the nations, which will be judged on the day of the Lord's establishment of his kingdom (vv. 15–16, 21). Similarly, Nahum (630 B.C.) focused on Nineveh, the capital of the Assyrian kingdom, as a sign of what the Lord will do to all the kingdoms of the world (1:2–6) and of God's power when he comes to establish his sovereignty over all creation. Nothing can stand in the way of his accomplishing his purpose. The humiliation of human kingdoms and pride is directly related to the exaltation of God's kingdom (see Obad. 17, 21; Mic. 4:1–4).

"THY KINGDOM COME . . ."

Inaugurated	Eschatological
Creation order	Peace
New community	Holy and royal people
Redemptive history:	Consecration of creation:
Acts of judgment	Final judgment
Acts of redemption	Eternity of fulfillment
Protection	Presence of God
Blessings	Blessings

Figure 50. The Kingdom: Present and Future

The prophet Micah (725 B.C.) developed the imagery of the great King as the Good Shepherd. The Shepherd-King will bring in a universal kingdom of peace (4:1–4). This kingdom is redemptive in the fullest sense of the word: forgiveness, the fulfillment of all the covenantal promises, and vengeance on the nations (Mic. 2:12–13; 4:6–7; 5:15; 7:9–17). All this is not because of the righteousness of his people, but because the Lord is a forgiving God who keeps covenant forever (7:18–20).

Habakkuk (605 B.C.) asked when the Lord would establish his righteous rule. The Lord assured him that while the whole earth will be full of his glory (2:14), the righteous will have to wait for it (vv. 3–4). The prophet called the faithful to reflect on how the Lord had established his victorious kingship over the Egyptians and thus encouraged them to await with endurance, hope, and joy the full manifestation of God's kingdom (3:2–19), when "the earth will be filled with the knowledge of the glory of the LORD, as the waters cover the sea" (2:14).

Zephaniah (ca. 630 B.C.) stressed the universality of God's judgment and the necessity of transformation. All creation is affected by sin (1:2–3:8) and is therefore reserved for judgment, as by fire (1:2–3; 3:8; see 2 Peter 3:10). However, he also proclaimed the universal kingdom of God in which Israel and the nations may rejoice in the presence of the great King. He will purify a people to himself, who may worship him wherever they live (2:11; 3:9–11).

The remnant (the humble) are those who submit themselves to his rule (Zeph. 2:3; 3:12–13). Their future lies secure in God's hands because their King (3:14, 16) will be for them and with them (vv. 15, 17). Therefore, they have hope that God will deliver them from disgrace, enmity, and troubles (v. 18) and exalt all who belong to him (vv. 19–20).

The Postexilic Prophets on the Kingdom of God

The postexilic prophets (Haggai, Zechariah, Malachi, and Joel) witnessed to the *presence and future continuity of God's kingdom.* They proclaimed that the kingdom was a present reality because the Lord was again present with his people (Hag. 2:4–5, 19; Zech. 1:16–17; 3:9–10; 8:3, 11–15; 9:8) and because the restored temple was a token of his glorious kingdom. The restoration of the kingdom began when the Jews returned to the land and rebuilt their homes and the temple. They also proclaimed that the Lord loves his people and the land. Consequently he is zealous to subjugate and reduce the opposition to his covenant people. (See figure 50.)

Yet the fullness of the glorious kingdom is not here. The postexilic prophets encouraged God's people to keep hope alive for the establishment of God's kingdom, the subjugation of evil, the consecration of his people, and the full enjoyment of the blessings that flow from his universal kingship and presence. The Lord is faithful to his promises, even though he may delay the establishment of his kingdom.

Haggai (520 B.C.) spoke of another "shaking." The Lord, who had shaken Samaria, Jerusalem, and Babylon in judgment, will again shake heaven and earth for the full redemption of the new community. On the Day of the Lord he will establish his kingdom (Hag. 2:6–9, 21–22; see Heb. 12:26–27).

Zechariah (520 B.C.) developed the twofold aspects of God's kingdom. First, the Lord's kingdom was inaugurated to the extent that God was present with his people and to the extent that they would bring in God's kingdom by living righteously and justly, in love and in peace (see Rom. 14:17). Yahweh promised to be in their midst and to bless them, "Even now I announce that I will restore twice as much to you" (Zech. 9:12). This kingdom will be established by the Spirit and not by human ingenuity or power: "Not by might nor by power, but by my Spirit" (4:6). Yet he also looked for a response because the building and progression of the kingdom is in direct proportion to the responsiveness of God's people (6:15; 7:9–10; 8:16–19; see Rom. 14:7).

Second, the kingdom is also future. The visions and oracles visualize and explain God's plan of redemption. It involves rest from the enemies (Zech. 6:8), the inclusion of righteous Jews and Gentiles (8:20–23), and a radical transformation of creation. Zechariah portrayed the transformation in the phenomenal language of light, the change in seasons, the living water (14:6–8; see Rev. 22:1–5), the removal of evil, and the consecration of all creation (14:20).

Zechariah realistically portrayed the tensions of living between the present age of darkness and the future age of glory. He encouraged the godly to endure suffering, to do good, and to persevere with the hope that the Lord will protect his people, cleanse them, subjugate their enemies (2:10–12; 12:4, 8–9; 14:9, 11, 16, 20–21), and establish his kingdom.

The prophet Malachi (460 B.C.) also affirmed God's covenant love as an expression of his kingdom. Those whom he loves respond to his love in expressions of loyalty by which they honor him as the great King. He is the Master of the universe, but he is also the Father of all who are devoted to him (Mal. 1:6; 2:10–16; 3:17) and worship him in fidelity and in the Spirit, whether they be Jews in Judah or in the Diaspora or God-fearing Gentiles (1:11, 14; see John 4:23–24).

Those who make up this remnant are the "treasured possession" (s^egullâ, Mal. 3:17). They will witness the enlargement of God's kingdom and the greatness of their great King: "You will see it with your own eyes and say, 'Great is the LORD—even beyond the borders of Israel!'" (1:5; 3:18; 4:1–3).

Conclusion

The kingdom of God is inaugurated in God's creative activities. He sustains, governs, and rules over this world in wisdom, love, compassion, patience, and righteousness in spite of human opposition to his kingdom. His kingdom also comes to expression in his judgments and in his acts of deliverance. His judgments in history point to the final climactic judgment when he will establish his rule in sovereignty and glory. His acts of deliverance in history point to the era of transformation and blessing when he delivers his children from the present bondage, from suffering, and from the powers of this age.

The kingdom of God is a metaphor derived from human kingdoms and is in contrast to the best of human systems of government.[39] The prophets adumbrate Yahweh as the only King who truly delivers his people, blesses them, and sustains them as part of his creation. He is righteous, just, compassionate, full of love, and wise, and so is his kingdom rule.

The great King has also ordained that humans rule for him and with him (Gen. 1:26–27; 9:1, 7). This explains why the prophets often relate the kingdom of God to the people of God directly or indirectly. They relate it *directly* through the fulfillment of God's promises made to Israel, according to which the people of God make up his "holy nation," that is, "a kingdom of priests" (Ex. 15:6; see 1 Peter 2:9). They are the objects of his grace and are appointed to rule (Isa. 55:3–5) as the blessed servants of the Lord (Isa. 65:8–9, 13–15). The prophets also apply the kingdom *indirectly* by relating the kingdom of God to the people by means of an appointed ruler, the Messiah of David. The Messiah ("anointed one") of David is the servant of the Lord charged with executing God's will on earth, providing the benefits of his kingdom to his people, and establishing his kingdom on earth (see Pss. 2; 72; 132). (See figure 51.)

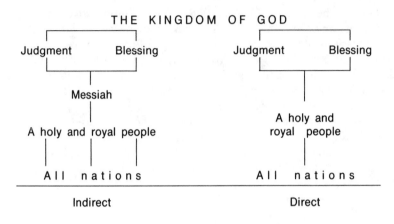

Figure 51. The Extension of God's Kingdom

THE MESSIAH AND THE MESSIANIC KINGDOM

The Lord has decreed that he will establish his kingdom on earth *through* a descendant of David.[40] He has confirmed by covenant[41] to bestow his grace on David and his children, to relate to them as his sons (2 Sam. 7:14; Ps. 2:7), and to administer his protection and blessings. The Lord is the Shepherd of his flock (Ps. 23:1), and the Davidic king was to be a "good" shepherd, that is, a mediator of the benefits of God's kingdom to his subjects (1 Chron. 11:2; see 2 Sam. 23:2–7).

The symbol of God's presence was the ark of the covenant in the temple. It was his "footstool" (Ps. 132:7–8, 13–14) by which he assured his kingdom, his care for the Davidic monarch, and the resultant blessings of his kingdom (peace, prosperity, and the worship of God without fear, see vv. 13–18). The Davidic monarch was responsible for cultivating the worship of the Lord and for representing the great King by a just and righteous rule (Deut. 17:14–20; Ps. 72:1–7, 12–14).[42] Thus the promises to David assured the continuity of Yahweh's protection and blessing.

The promises to David also assured the universal extent of God's kingdom. The kingdoms of the world shall recognize God's kingship in the Davidic king (Ps. 2) to whom he has given all authority "from sea to sea" (Ps. 72:8; see also vv. 9–11, 15–16). The Davidic monarch serves as a covenant mediator between Yahweh and the nations and will bring God's blessing to the nations (Ps. 72:17), thereby fulfilling all promises of the Abrahamic covenant in a grandiose manner.

The prophets may not explicitly develop the messianic age or the messianic person, but they witness in one form or another to the coming of the Christ, the agent of redemption (1 Peter 1:10–12).[43] As a general rule, the prophetic teaching on the kingdom of God forms a larger framework than the messianic kingdom. Hence, even when the prophets did not speak regarding the Messiah directly, they proclaimed the excellencies of the kingdom of Jesus Christ by their annunciation of the new age. They spoke from within the larger framework in which creation, redemption, the kingdom of God, the loyal community, the Day of the Lord, the Spirit of God, and the messianic kingdom are interrelated.

The prophets are God's eschatological messengers of salvation and of the establishment of the messianic kingdom. Even when they relate salvation directly to the kingdom of God, they do not deny the significant place of the Messiah. Since salvation and the kingdom are interrelated concepts, all the prophets adumbrate the kingdom of God and his salvation through the Messiah.[44]

Hosea and Amos

Hosea and Amos envision a time of universal reign of the Davidic Messiah in harmony with the kingdom of God. They announced that after the Exile a remnant of the Ten Tribes would return to the worship of Yahweh in his temple *and* serve Yahweh's anointed king. Hosea wrote: "Afterward the Israelites will return and seek the LORD their God and David their king. They will come trembling to the LORD and to his blessings in the last days" (3:5; see 1:11). God will renew the covenant sovereignly and graciously so as to usher in a grand era of peace, blessing, and his presence. That is to say, God will establish his kingdom in restoration, forgiveness, love, and peace (14:2–8).

Amos concludes his prophecy of restoration with an allusion to the reestablishment of the Davidic dynasty. This era of renewal reveals the qualities of universal restoration, blessing, and God's compassion (Amos 9:11–15).

Micah

Micah relates the restoration of the Davidic era to the renewal of God's kingdom. The messianic era inaugurates the restoration by a renewal of covenants, promises, and the full, unhindered enjoyment of the covenant benefits. The Messiah's coming from Bethlehem Ephrathah (5:2) signifies *continuity* with David, who hailed from Bethlehem, but also a *discontinuity* from the establishment in Jerusalem. The prophet projects the realization of the messianic kingdom as an era of peace, universal dominion, prosperity, and victory (vv. 4–15).

The Exilic Era

The exilic period saw the fall of Jerusalem and the end of the Davidic dynasty. Jeremiah had declared God's curse on the dynasty of David.

> None of his offspring will prosper,
> none will sit on the throne of David
> or rule anymore in Judah.
>
> (22:30)

Jehoiachin went into exile some ten years before Jerusalem's fall (2 Kings 24:12–16), fulfilling God's word through Jeremiah (Jer. 22:25–27). The Exile vindicated the word of God's prophets. However, Yahweh was free to deal graciously with Jehoiachin who, when treated royally by King Evil-Merodach in Babylon (561 B.C.), became an object of hope for those who remained in exile (2 Kings 25:27–30).

The Postexilic Era

In the postexilic period Jehoiachin's descendant, Zerubbabel, was a leader of the returnees and responded to the challenge of rebuilding the temple. Haggai and Zechariah affirmed God's blessing on Zerubbabel and God's freedom in restoring the promises of the Davidic covenant to Zerubbabel, who like David is called the "servant" of the Lord. He received the "signet ring," symbolic of his God-given authority and of God's promise to David that he will establish the messianic kingdom to be an everlasting kingdom (Hag. 2:21–23).

Zechariah spoke of the responsibility of the Davidic monarch, who, like David, builds God's temple and brings in an era of peace and blessing (3:9–10) in which Gentiles share (8:20–23). He saw in the administration under Joshua (the high priest) and Zerubbabel (the Persian governor) a renewal of the Davidic era, although it was in embryonic form. Thus he encouraged the people with the message of continuity of the Sinaitic and Davidic covenants, as both Joshua (the priest) and Zerubbabel (the governor) were designated as God's "anointed ones" (Messiahs, 6:12–13).

Zechariah also introduced the discordant element of the humble Messiah. The King comes riding on a donkey (Zech. 9:9–13; Matt. 21:5; John 12:15). God's Servant-Shepherd submits himself to God, who delivers him into the hands of men to be smitten for the purpose of bringing in a greater era of covenant renewal (Zech. 12:10; 13:7–9; see Rev. 1:7–8). Although the inauguration of the messianic era will be unpretentious, the Messiah will be crowned with success and victory; he will subdue the nations and redeem his people. This messianic king brings in an era of righteousness and full deliverance!

Conclusion

The Messiah is God's instrument to bring in the fullness of redemption and to assure God's blessings, presence, victory, and peace. He is in the service of God; rules with loyalty, justice, righteousness, and wisdom; and extends his kingdom to all creation. Even the nations may come under his protection and blessing, but he is also God's instrument of subjugation, vindication, and execration!

The prophetic and apostolic words confirm the reality of the kingdom in Jesus Christ, who is the glory of God in the flesh.[45] All nations will submit to him. He will bring in the kingdom of God in glory and power; he will rule from shore to shore. His is the dominion and the power and the glory.

THE SPIRIT OF RESTORATION

The progress of restoration is the work of the Spirit of God.[46] He brings about the new heart, enables individuals to seek God, and consecrates them for holy service. He also works powerfully in bringing about the messianic age, the kingdom of God, and the transformation of this creation.[47] (See figure 52.)

It is a serious error to restrict the operation of the Spirit to the church age, because he, too, is God. He has fully involved himself with creation and with redemption from the very beginning of time. He was active at creation (Gen. 1:2; Job 33:4; Ps. 104:30) and sustains it (Ps. 104:30). He was also involved in the redemption of Israel from Egypt and in the conquest (Ex. 31:3; 35:31; Num. 11:17, 25–26, 29; 24:2; Deut. 34:9). He worked powerfully through humans to deliver God's people from adversity (Judg. 3:10; 6:34; 9:23; 11:29; 13:25; 14:6, 19; 15:14). The power of God in creation, redemption, and governance witnesses to the direct involvement of his Spirit in the history of redemption.

> Then his people recalled the days of old,
>   the days of Moses and his people—
> where is he who brought them through the sea,
>   with the shepherd of his flock?
> Where is he who set
>   his Holy Spirit among them . . . ?
>   They were given rest by the Spirit of the Lord.
> This is how you guided your people

> to make for yourself a glorious name.
>
>   (Isa. 63:11, 14)

The Spirit of God strives to bring about the fullness of God's kingdom on earth by restructuring human values and structures to correspond with God's values and structures. He is independent from human organizations and systems, but also freely uses them to accomplish God's purposes. From the prophetic perspective, Israel could not function within God's purposes unless the Spirit of the living God was in them. The purpose of God's revelation through Moses was to continuously involve the Spirit of God in renewing the hearts of human beings (Deut. 10:16; 30:6).

Father	Son	Holy Spirit
Kingdom of God	Messianic kingdom	Restoration
Involvement in creation, redemption, and history		

Figure 52. A Trinitarian View of the Plan of Redemption

But human autonomy challenges the operation of the Spirit and evokes God's judgment (Isa. 30:1; 63:10; Zech. 7:12). Unbelief in God's ability to deliver or to fulfill his promises to his people is nothing but rebellion against the Spirit of God (Ps. 106:33). So also is dependence on political, military, economic, and social systems (*Realpolitik*). This explains the prophetic emphasis on judgment as a catharsis (cleansing) and the beginning of a new era. In other words, the Spirit's operation can never be restricted by a rebellious and unresponsive people. He removes the obstacles, changes structures, and renews a people as he executes the grand plan of bringing in the era of restoration.

After the Exile the prophets saw in the new acts of God the evidences of the new age of the Spirit. They spoke of God's acts of judgment by the Spirit and also of his deliverance and restoration by the Spirit.

> Till the Spirit is poured upon us from on high,
>   and the desert becomes a fertile field,
>   and the fertile field seems like a forest.
>
>   (Isa. 32:15)

> For I will pour water on the thirsty land,
>   and streams on the dry ground;
> I will pour out my Spirit on your offspring,

and my blessing on your descendants.
(44:3; see 11:2; 42:1; 48:10; 61:1; Mic. 2:7; 3:8)

From Joel we have learned that the Lord will send his Spirit ("I will pour out," 2:28–32), that the Spirit of God is associated with the days of deliverance and judgment (vv. 18–27; 3:1–17), and that the children of God at large receive the Spirit as an assurance of God's care, protection, and blessing. The Spirit comes to the aid of all who call on him as he seals the covenant, brings in the restoration, and draws the godly into closer communion with their covenant God. The promise of the Spirit is the Father's assurance to his people that regardless of what may happen on earth or in heaven (wonders, blood, and fire, Joel 2:30–31; see 2:11; 3:16), they are protected by the covenant (Joel 2:27).

THE NEW PEOPLE OF GOD

Introduction

The Lord extended to Adam's descendants the privileges of enjoyment, procreation, and rule over his earth (Gen. 1:26–27). He renewed these to all humankind in Noah (9:1, 7) and incorporated them as promises to Abraham and his descendants (Gen. 12:2–3). The covenant with Abraham contains the fourfold promise: (1) God's blessing of Abraham's descendants,[48] comprised of peoples and kingdoms (12:2–3; 17:2, 5–6, 16; 22:17; 26:4; 28:14; 35:11); (2) God's blessing on the earth (12:7; 13:17; 15:18–20); (3) God's presence in protection and blessing, resulting in glory, exaltation, and praise (Gen. 12:2–3; 15:1; 17:7); and (4) the blessing of Israel to the nations (12:3; 26:4; see Acts 3:25). These promises are nothing less than kingdom promises in that the Lord commits himself to be present, to bless, to protect, and to vindicate his people on earth.

That the people of God are a royal nation is ever so clear in the Mosaic covenant. The Lord graciously consecrated Israel, established his kingship in Israel (symbolized by the ark of the covenant), instituted ways of reconciliation and forgiveness in the tabernacle cult (priesthood and offerings), and gave Israel specific and concrete instruction (Torah) as to how they could live as God's holy people on earth.

The Mosaic covenant is by definition *a sovereign administration of grace and promise by which the Lord consecrates a people to himself under the sanctions of his Torah.* This covenant confirms the gracious promises of the Abrahamic covenant and assures the enduring privileges in the symbolic institutions of God's kingdom in Israel (tabernacle/temple, the sacrifices, and priestly/Levitical system). At the core of the Mosaic covenant is God's commitment to all who respond to him from the heart (Deut. 4:29; 6:4–5; 10:12; 11:13; 13:3; 30:6).[49] Hence circumcision of the heart was an important requisite for covenant inclusion (Deut. 30:6).[50]

Spirit + Law	Flesh + Law
New community:	Old community:
Circumcision of heart	Hard of heart
Love for God	Love for self
Perseverance	No loyalty
Acts of righteousness, justice, love	Acts of greed, injustice
Heir of promises	Heir of curses

Figure 53. The Contrast Between the Spirit and the Flesh

The Law as revelation has an inherent tension. As revelation from God, the Law is good and holy, but it is given to humans who are neither good nor holy. Although the Mosaic era offered "life to a people under judgment,"[51] the prophets looked to a new community of the Spirit.[52] (See figure 53.)

The Preexilic Prophets

Hosea foresaw that a remnant will return to the Lord, confess their sins, diligently seek Yahweh for deliverance (5:15), and demonstrate that they "know" him by their concern for justice, love, and compassion (6:6). The wise will walk in the ways of the Lord (14:9). In turn, Yahweh promises to "heal" all who trust in him alone for full deliverance (14:1–4).[53] Amos, too, called on the remnant to declare their loyalty to Yahweh alone (Amos 5:6). Seeking the Lord signifies a living faith, that is, a concern with justice and righteousness (vv. 14–15).

A generation or so after the ministry of Hosea and Amos, Micah spoke God's word to both kingdoms. He followed his magnificent vision of the New Jerusalem (Mic. 4:1–4) with a call for a response.

> All the nations may walk
>   in the name of their gods;
> we will walk in the name of the LORD
>   our God for ever and ever.
>   (v. 5).

Only those who walk with Yahweh will have a share in the New Jerusalem! The remnant are those who know Yahweh and glorify him in their lives (6:6–8). Though the full deliverance may be delayed, the remnant wait patiently and hopefully for the era of salvation, of covenant renewal, of forgiveness, of removal of evil, and of the full establishment of his kingdom.

> But as for me, I watch in hope for the LORD,
>   I wait for God my Savior;
>   my God will hear me.
>
> (7:7, see vv. 8–20)

Nahum ministered God's word to Judah during the fall of Assyria's power. Assyria had exiled the northern kingdom and had reduced Judah to a satellite kingdom. Though Judah was still threatened by the Assyrian presence, God's word comforted the remnant.

> The LORD is good,
>   a refuge in times of trouble.
> He cares for those who trust in him.
>
> (1:7)

Zephaniah clearly developed the Day of the Lord motif and also gave hope to all who humble themselves before the Lord, separating themselves from arrogant and rebellious people. The future belongs to the humble, who do the Lord's will and look forward to his deliverance (3:12–13).

Habakkuk encouraged the godly to persevere in fidelity to God, regardless of how long it took before they enjoyed God's full deliverance and saw his judgment on the wicked (2:3–4). In his prayer Habakkuk reflects on God's deliverance of his people in Egypt and at the Red Sea. The remembrance of those events has a sacramental significance; they are tokens of God's final deliverance. With this in mind, God's people must wait in faith and hope, rejoicing in their faithful covenant God (3:16–19).

The Postexilic Prophets

The experience of the postexilic community was like that of the post-Resurrection community. The postexilic community lived in the *presence* of God's goodness, forgiveness, renewal, and yes, even the eschatological age.[54] The post-Resurrection community lives in the power of the Spirit, in the present rule of Christ over the church, and in the enjoyment of all the benefits that come from adoption into the family of the Father. As such, Christians live in an advanced stage of eschatological fulfillment, but are still exiles who wait for the Lord's coming in glory to rid the earth of the squatters and to give his people the promised rest.

The postexilic prophets called for greater loyalty. No longer did they address Judah and Israel separately, because the godly remnant of Israel was joined with the godly remnant of Judah into one people: Israel. "Israel" denotes the new people of God. Haggai called them "the [whole] remnant of the people" (*šeʾērît hāʿām,* 1:12; 2:3); "the people" (*hāʿām,* 1:12–13); "these people" (*hāʿām hazzeh,* 1:2; 2:14; "this people and this nation," *hāʿām hazzeh . . . wehaggôy hazzeh*). Zechariah

239

addressed God's word to "all the people of the land" (*kol 'am hā'āreṣ,* 7:5); "the remnant of this people" (*šᵉ'ērît̠ hā'ām, hazzeh,* 8:6, 11, 12); Israel (12:1; see "all the tribes of Israel," 9:1); and the eschatologically flavored language "Jerusalem" and "Zion" (1:14, 16–17; 2:2, 4, 12; 8:2–3; 9:9).[55]

Those who returned from the Exile and the believing Jews in the Dispersion made up the remnant of 536 B.C., and yet the remnant needed continual internal renewal.[56] The external call for devotion, loyalty, and zeal for God evoked an inner response by the Spirit of God. Haggai (520 B.C.) asked them to search their hearts (1:5, 7; 2:15, 18) and thus provoked God's people to a greater allegiance by the Spirit (1:13–14; see 2:4–5). Furthermore, he encouraged the remnant to trust and obey God, assuring them that there was a direct correlation between their obedience and the manifestation of Yahweh's kingdom among them. The Lord will shake heaven and earth to establish his kingdom for the sake of his children, but he expects them to live in anticipation of his glorious kingdom!

The certainty of fulfillment lies in God's promise (Zech 1:13–14, 16; 8:2–3, 8) and in his zeal to dwell among his faithful people, to bless and protect them, and to transform this earth, but he also expects his new people to fully trust him and to be loyal to him in practicing justice, righteousness, compassion, and love (8:13–17, 19).

Similarly Zechariah, a contemporary of Haggai, correlated Yahweh's zeal in fulfilling the prophetic word to the responsiveness of his people to his kingship. Yahweh promised to "return" to them in glory, blessing, and protection, but he also expected his people to "return" to him with full devotion (Zech. 1:3).

Shortly before the ministry of Ezra and Nehemiah, Malachi exhorted priests and people alike to honor Yahweh as their Father and as the great King of the universe by living in accordance with his covenants. The priests were to walk with the Lord and to show concern for the people of God (Mal. 2:5–7). The people were to return to him (3:7), care for others (v. 5), and protect the family institution (2:10–16). For this reason Malachi challenged them, "So guard yourself in your spirit, and do not break faith with the wife of your youth. . . . So guard yourself in your spirit, and do not break faith" (2:15–16).

The Lord rewards those who serve him quietly and diligently, persevering in their faith and commitment to him. Yahweh promises to single them out for the future. They alone are his *sᵉgullâ* ("treasured possession," Mal. 3:17), whom he marks for glory and full deliverance.

ISRAEL AND THE NATIONS

Introduction

The prophets spoke God's word to Israel and Judah before the Exile and to the remnant of the twelve tribes after the Exile. They also extended the oracles of salvation and judgment to the nations. It is not surprising that judgment is emphasized, because the nations had harassed, troubled, seduced, and oppressed the people of God. Nevertheless, the prophets also spoke of the inclusion of the Gentiles within God's redemptive purposes.

The Preexilic Prophets

Amos alluded to the inclusion of the Gentiles: "the remnant of Edom and all the nations that bear my name" (9:12). The phraseology is terse, and the meaning is complicated by an alternate reading in the LXX (see Acts 15:17). G. F. Hasel has made a convincing case for understanding "the remnant of Edom" as objects of God's promise to David.[57] Walter Kaiser has further developed this line of thought in line with the Davidic covenant, according to which David was charged with a "charter for humanity."[58] He concludes that the Lord promised to include the nations that call on his name, even a remnant from Edom.[59] They, too, may be known as the people of God if they "bear the name of Yahweh together with Israel."[60] I wholeheartedly agree with Kaiser's conclusion: "It definitely meant to teach that Gentiles will be included in some future reign of God."[61]

Micah's vision of Zion included the nations if they, too, learned to walk in accordance with God's law (4:1–5). The prophet did not develop the inclusion of the Gentiles any further, except for the metaphor of "dew."

> The remnant of Jacob will be
> in the midst of many peoples
> like dew from the LORD,
> like showers on the grass,
> which do not wait for man
> or linger for mankind.
> (5:7)

In some special way the new community will be God's means of blessing the nations (see Gen. 12:3; 26:4; Acts 3:25).

Zephaniah's oracle pertaining to the inclusion of the Gentiles is one of the most revolutionary among the preexilic prophets. He proclaimed that Gentiles may worship the Lord wherever they live: "The nations on every shore will worship him, every one in its own land" (2:11). Their

241

worship will be acceptable, even though they call on the name of the Lord, each in their own land and in their own language (3:9).

The Postexilic Prophets

The postexilic prophets further developed the internationalism of the preexilic prophets. Zechariah (520 B.C.) encouraged the postexilic remnant by assuring them of the inclusion of Gentiles in the messianic era (8:20–23). The Messiah will extend his kingdom to the ends of the earth and bring *shalom* to the nations.

> He will proclaim peace to the nations.
> His rule will extend from sea to sea
> and from the River to the ends of the earth.
>
> (9:10; see Ps. 72:8–17)

Malachi (460 B.C.) puts the national and cultic concerns of the Jews over against the vision of God's kingdom. Yahweh is the Master of the universe whose kingdom extends to all creation (1:14; see v. 6, 11). Throughout the prophecy Malachi used the language of *exclusion* and *inclusion*. Yahweh excludes from the covenant, promises, and future blessing all who despise him, break covenant with him, and fail to honor him as Father and King. On the other hand, the Lord includes all who worship him with fidelity and in the spirit of humility. They are the heirs of the promise. Yahweh is the Father of the "treasured possession," made up of all who fear him and do his will (3:17).

Joel used the phrase "call on the name of the LORD" (2:32) as a way of defining the new people of God. The prophet envisions Zion as a new community, a "new world-order" under the protection and rule of God,[62] whose citizenry consists of all persons the Lord has called, Spirit-filled people, and those who call on his "name" for salvation. The apostle Paul reads God's new act of grace in Jesus toward the Gentiles in Joel 2:32 as *all* who call on the name of the Lord Jesus—regardless of age, sex, social standing, or race (Rom. 10:12–13; Gal. 3:28; Eph. 2:13)—may share in the age of the Spirit.

REVIEW

Yahweh will gloriously establish his kingdom through his Messiah, whose rule will be from shore to shore. The people of the Messiah, both Jews and Gentiles, will be characterized by holiness and righteousness and by the renewal of the Spirit. The fullness of the glory of God's kingdom will not be entered into until Yahweh brings about the transformation of all things. At the coming of his kingdom in its fullness, creation, including the new community, will undergo a complete transformation.

What is so marvelous is that each person of the Trinity (Father-Son-Spirit) is involved in the process of redemption from the beginning to the end. The teaching of the prophets may be conveniently summarized by the acronym *TRUMPET*.

1. Transformation of all things.
2. Rule of God: *the great King.*
3. Unbroken covenants: creation and redemption.
4. Messianic kingdom: *Messiah.*
5. Purification and glorification of the remnant.
6. Enemy avenged: judgment, vindication, vengeance.
7. Torah of God internalized: *Spirit of restoration.*

I trust that we are now in a better position to study the Major Prophets (Isaiah, Jeremiah, Ezekiel, and Daniel). My hope is that the motifs we have discovered in the Minor Prophets may help unfold the message of the Major Prophets and the Word of God, including the New Testament. In reading the next several chapters, please bear in mind that God has not given us the prophetic literature to develop a systematic treatment on eschatology. In fact, the major reason for the Prophets is to give us a present framework for living in the light of who the triune God is and of what he has prepared for his children who remain faithful to him, that is, theocentric and eschatological ethics. (See chap. 12: "Living the Prophetic Word.")

QUESTIONS AND ISSUES

1. Define:

accountability	autonomy	compenetration
covenant	epiphany	eschatological
exclusion	favor	freedom of God
humility	inclusion	intrusion
justice	kingdom of God	perseverance
promise and	prosecutor	*Realpolitik*
fulfillment	remnant	retribution
righteousness	salvation	*s^{e}gullâ*
Spirit of	theophany	token and reality
restoration	transformation	vengeance
vindication	*visio Dei*	*vox populi*
		yôm Yahweh

2. Which metaphors contribute to the understanding of the Day of the Lord? How does this motif develop over the centuries, and how does it remain the same?

3. What components contribute to a clear understanding of the Day of the Lord? How can it be both historical and eschatological? How does the New Testament teaching transform the prophetic teaching?

4. How does the doctrine of God's kingship give us hope for a new creation?

5. How was the kingdom of God inaugurated and eschatological in the Old Testament? Contrast human forms of government with God's kingship. How do the preexilic prophets contrast the kingdom of God with the corruption of human kingship?

6. Explain the nature, role, and purpose of the Messiah of David according to the prophets. How is he like and unlike the rulers of David's dynasty?

7. What is the preexilic and postexilic teaching on the messianic kingdom?

8. How are the kingdom of God and the kingdom of the Messiah parallel, and how do they differ?

9. Make an attempt to synthesize the many facets of the prophetic teaching on the kingdom of God.

10. How has the Spirit been involved throughout the progress of redemption?

11. Based on your reading of this chapter, demonstrate how God is faithful to all covenants: creation, Abraham, Moses, and David. Further, defend or reject the thesis that each covenant finds its renewal in the new covenant.

12. What was God's purpose for Israel as a counterculture?

13. What is the relation of Israel to the nations, and what should the relation of the church be toward Israel?

14. Explain from the Old Testament and the New Testament how each person of the Trinity is fully involved with creation and with redemption. Define *redemption* as an eschatological term. Will creation be redeemed?

Part 3

The Message of the Major Prophets

Introduction to Part 3

The reasons for considering the Major Prophets (Isaiah, Jeremiah, Ezekiel, and Daniel) last are pedagogical. Because of their size and variety of motifs, these prophetic books often discourage one from reading the Prophets. Yet they constitute a crucial part of God's Word and contribute significantly to the framework for interpreting the Minor Prophets, God's working in the Old Testament, and the ministry of our Lord and his apostles.

In the previous chapter we looked at the variety of motifs in the Prophets. These motifs will also occur in chapters 9–12, but instead of structuring the contents of these books around the motifs, I shall develop the message of each prophet with its variety of emphases. It is my hope that the reader may grow in the ability to interpret the prophetic word by the illumination of the Spirit; to relate the various motifs to each other, to our Lord Jesus Christ, and to the whole of Scripture (*tota Scriptura*); to discern the progress of redemption; to fix hope in Christ, the hope of glory; and to apply God's Word to life.

The prophets witness in their diversity to the involvement of the triune God in creation and redemption. Their teaching on the kingdom of God, the messianic kingdom, and the Spirit of restoration is sublime, transcending our ability to comprehend. But the vision of the triune God leads the righteous to awe, worship, and godly living, "Therefore, since we are receiving a kingdom that cannot be shaken, let us be thankful, and so worship God acceptably with reverence and awe, for our 'God is a consuming fire'" (Heb. 12:28).

CHAPTER 9

The Message of Isaiah

247

ISAIAH AND HIS TIME

Isaiah loved the old Jerusalem[1] but at the same time looked forward to a New Jerusalem.[2] He was probably born and educated in Jerusalem. He was married (8:3), had at least two sons, Shear-Jashub and Maher-Shalal-Hash-Baz, and ministered to God's people during an era of great political turmoil (740–700 B.C.).[3] Isaiah's ministry falls into four periods: (1) the period of social criticism (chaps. 2–5), ca. 740–734 B.C.; (2) the Syro-Ephraimite war (chaps. 7–9), 734–732 B.C.; (3) the anti-Assyrian rebellion (chaps. 10–23), 713–711 B.C.; and (4) the anti-Assyrian rebellion and Jerusalem's siege (chaps. 28–32; 36–39), 705–701 B.C.

These periods correspond to the kings mentioned in the superscription: "The vision concerning Judah and Jerusalem that Isaiah son of Amoz saw during the reigns of Uzziah [d. 740 B.C.], Jotham [750–731 B.C.], Ahaz [735–715 B.C.] and Hezekiah [729–686 B.C.], kings of Judah" (1:1). (See table 9.)

TABLE 9. CHRONOLOGY OF ISAIAH'S MINISTRY

740	732	722	715	713	701	686

Fall of Damascus   Fall of Samaria

Jotham (750–731)

Death of Uzziah

Ahaz (735–715)

Hezekiah (729–686)

PERIODS OF ISAIAH'S MINISTRY

740–734   734–732   713–711   705–701

Assyrian kings:
Tiglath-pileser III (745–727)
Shalmaneser V (727–722)
Sargon II (722–705)
Sennacherib (705–681)

Uzziah

The beginning of Isaiah's ministry can be dated by the reference to Uzziah's death (6:1), approximately 740 B.C.[4] Under Uzziah, Judah gained remarkable economic achievements (2 Chron. 26:6–15) and attempted to reassert herself as a political power.

Jotham

Jotham ruled over Judah from 750 to 731 B.C., first as co-ruler with Uzziah and then with his son, Ahaz. He inherited a Judah that was materially strong, but corrupt in her values and apostate. Isaiah spoke against power, greed, and injustice in Israel and Judah prior to a rapid shift in the political makeup of the ancient Near East. Assyria, under Tiglath-pileser III (745–727 B.C.; "Pul" in 2 Kings 15:19), subjugated the cities along the route from Nineveh to Damascus, including Damascus (732 B.C.). When Jotham died, the storm clouds were also forming on Judah's horizon, and soon she would be thrown into the midst of a tempest of international developments that would reduce her to a vassal state of the Assyrian Empire.

Ahaz (Jehoahaz I)

From 735 to 715 B.C. the iniquitous King Ahaz ruled (2 Kings 16:3). The Chronicler lists the objectionable practices instituted by Ahaz and explains that these idolatrous observances were the reason for his international troubles (2 Chron. 28:2–4).[5] Ahaz was an impudent man who relied on political solutions rather than God's promises. When he faced the alliance of King Rezin of Aram with Pekah of Israel and the expansionist drive of Assyria, he wanted to be his own man, independent of Yahweh, uninvolved with the Aramean-Israelite alliance and autonomous from Assyria. But he responded with great fear when Aram and Israel came against him for the purpose of dethroning him and setting up another king who would be sympathetic to their political scheming (2 Kings 16:5; Isa. 7:5–6). Isaiah challenged him not to fear their power (v. 4) but instead to look for God's presence in Jerusalem as the strength of Judah (v. 7; 8:10). Ahaz went around the prophet by asking Tiglath-pileser, the Assyrian, to help him (2 Kings 16:7). Tiglath-pileser, reacting swiftly to the threat of the Syro-Ephraimite alliance on the western front, marched through Phoenicia as far as Philistia (734 B.C.), destroyed Damascus (732 B.C.), and subjugated Israel. He also reduced Judah to a vassal state (2 Kings 15:29; 16:7–9; 2 Chron. 28:19; Isa. 8:7–8).

When King Hoshea of Israel refused to pay tribute to Assyria, Shalmaneser (727–722 B.C.) campaigned against Samaria, brought her down, and exiled her population in 722 B.C.[6] Ahaz did not turn to the

Lord, because his eyes were fixed on his own kingdom and its place in the changing political configurations under Shalmaneser V and Sargon II.

Hezekiah

Hezekiah (729–686 B.C.) was a godly king who sought counsel from the prophet Isaiah in times of national and personal tragedy. He ruled independently from 715 B.C. till his death in 686 B.C.[7] While leading Judah into an era of reforms (2 Kings 18:4, 22), a process that climaxed in the celebration of the Passover Feast (2 Chron. 30), he had the difficult task of adjusting to the Assyrian presence. Hezekiah had to cope with the expansionist policy of Sargon II (722–705 B.C.), who was active in military campaigns, subjugating nations in the east (Elam, Babylon), west (Syria-Ephraim region), and south as far as the Wadi-el-Arish on the southwestern border of Judah (715 B.C.).

In the providence of God, Hezekiah was able to do just that! He set out to develop Judah's interests apart from Assyria by inviting the remnant from the north to the Passover Feast and by leading the nation into true reform. Sargon's reaction came in 712 B.C. when he returned to subdue Philistia and to demand tribute from Hezekiah.[8]

At Sargon's death (705 B.C.), his successor Sennacherib (705–681 B.C.) faced a coalition of Egypt, Philistia, and Judah (2 Kings 18:7).[9] His forces moved through Judah (701 B.C.) and may have taken as many as forty-six cities (some of which may have been listed in Isa. 10:28–32 and Mic. 1:10–16). Sennacherib recounts this victory in his *Annals,*

> But as for Hezekiah, the Jew, who did not bow in submission to my yoke, forty-six of his strong walled towns and innumerable smaller villages in their neighbourhood I besieged and conquered by stamping down earth-ramps and then by bringing up battering rams, by the assault of foot-soldiers, by breaches, tunnelling and sapper operations. I made to come out from them 200,150 people, young and old, male and female, innumerable horses, mules, donkeys, camels, large and small cattle, and counted them as the spoils of war.[10]

Finally, Sennacherib besieged Jerusalem, and Hezekiah was among those trapped. Despite Jerusalem's being well prepared for the aggressors, the Assyrians had the fortitude to wait for her surrender (701 B.C.).[11] Sennacherib described the situation in the following manner: "He himself I shut up like a caged bird within Jerusalem, his royal city. I put watch-posts strictly around it and turned back to his disaster any who went out of its city gate."[12]

The Lord, true to his promise of being present to deliver, sent the angel of the Lord. Sennacherib retreated with an empty victory while the people of Judah celebrated the miraculous deliverance from a cruel tyrant who had already destroyed Judah (2 Kings 19:35–36). This desperate situation may well be the background of the first chapter of Isaiah (see vv. 5–9).

About that same time Hezekiah became sick but miraculously recovered and received another fifteen years of life (2 Kings 20:1–19; 2 Chron. 32:24–26; Isa. 38:1–22). During these years the Lord prospered Hezekiah, who strengthened Jerusalem and Judah against a future Assyrian attack (2 Chron. 32:27–29). But these years turned out to be a mixed blessing. The king pridefully showed his treasures and fortifications to the envoys of the Babylonian king, Merodach-Baladan (Babylonian Marduk-Apla-Iddina). God's condemnation would haunt Judah for another hundred years: "The time will surely come when everything in your palace, and all that your fathers have stored up until this day, will be carried off to Babylon. Nothing will be left" (Isa. 39:6). These words set the background for interpreting Isaiah's oracles of deliverance from Babylon (chaps. 40–48).

LITERARY FORMS AND STRUCTURE

Literary Forms

The prophet Isaiah was a master of the Hebrew language. His style reflects a rich vocabulary and imagery with many words and expressions unique to him. Much of the book's brilliance derives from imagery: war (63:1–6), social life (3:1–17), and rural life (5:1–7). He also personifies creation: the sun and the moon (24:23), the desert (35:1), the mountains and the trees (44:23; 55:12). He employs taunt (14:4–23), apocalyptic imagery (chaps. 24–27), sarcasm (44:9–20), personification, metaphors, wordplay, alliteration, and assonance.

Isaiah was an extremely gifted preacher who fully mined the riches of the Hebrew language. R. B. Y. Scott expressed it well, "Isaiah indeed was an aristocrat of the spirit. He moved like a prince among men. He spoke with a dignity and moral authority which he knew befitted an ambassador of the Most High and it is evident he was a product of the finest culture of Judah."[13] Isaiah's poetic imagination and message evoke a reaction. His prophecy was written down, not to be agreed with, but to generate a response.[14] The godly have responded in awe and worship; the ungodly have hardened themselves against the Lord.[15]

The conservative position holds to the single authorship of Isaiah (of Jerusalem) and to the unity of Isaiah (1–66), based on similarity and repetition of themes and vocabulary throughout the book.[16] Critics have come to recognize that the older arguments for isolating passages and dividing the book by different motifs are no longer tenable. This does not mean that they accept the unity of the book; rather, they now acknowledge the similarity of motifs. For example, Peter R. Ackroyd explains that the significance of Isaiah is in the import of the motifs, the names, the oracles of deliverance, and the allusive wording to which other oracles were readily appended.[17] John Eaton, likewise, sees a cohesiveness in what he calls the Isaiah "tradition," chief of which are the motifs of Zion, the advent of God, the Davidic representative, and the outworking of Yahweh's sovereign plan.[18] Joseph Jensen's evidence of the use of the theme of the Lord's plan as an overarching motif opens up the unifying message of judgment and salvation.[19]

Structure

    I. Yahweh is the Holy One of Israel, 1:1–12:6
       A. Oracles of judgment and hope, 1:1–5:30
       B. The prophetic call, 6:1–13
       C. Oracles of judgment and hope, 7:1–11:16
       D. The hymn of the redeemed, 12:1–6
   II. The Day of the Lord for all creation, 13:1–23:18
       A. Babylon, 13:1–14:23
       B. Assyria, 14:24–32
       C. Moab, 15:1–16:14
       D. Damascus, 17:1–14
       E. Cush/Egypt, 18:1–20:6
       F. Babylon, 21:1–10
       G. Edom, 21:11–12
       H. Arabia, 21:13–17
       I. Jerusalem, 22:1–25
       J. Tyre, 23:1–18
  III. The little apocalypse, 24:1–27:13
       A. The Day of the Lord, 24:1–23
       B. Restoration, 25:1–12
       C. Praise and waiting, 26:1–27:1
       D. Restoration, 27:2–13
  IV. Judgment and salvation, 28:1–35:10
       A. The kingdoms of this world, 28:1–33:24
       B. Vengeance and favor, 34:1–35:10
          1. The day of vengeance, 34:1–17
          2. The year of favor and restoration, 35:1–10
   V. Isaiah and Hezekiah, 36:1–39:8
       A. Sennacherib and Jerusalem, 36:1–37:38
       B. Hezekiah's illness, 38:1–22
       C. Hezekiah and the exile of Judah, 39:1–8
  VI. The glorious kingdom of God, 40:1–48:22
       A. The proclamation of restoration, 40:1–31
       B. Israel as Yahweh's servant, 41:1–29

THE MESSAGE OF ISAIAH

Yahweh is the Holy One of Israel, 1:1–12:6

Isaiah presents Yahweh as "the Holy One of Israel." In the "call vision" he received a vision of the holiness of God and his glorious kingdom. This vision was to be a guiding force throughout his ministry. The prophetic call (chap. 6) is not placed first in the book as in Jeremiah and Ezekiel (see Jer. 1:4–19; Ezek. 2:1–3:15) but is wedged between oracles of judgment and deliverance (chaps. 1–5; 7–12). These twelve chapters may be likened to a triptych, a painting with three panels.[20] (See figure 54.) Each panel is related to the other, but the central panel (chap. 6) helps us understand the other two (chaps. 1–5; 7–12). The first panel introduces Yahweh's holiness, kingdom, and judgment. The central panel explains why Isaiah is consumed with Yahweh's holiness and kingdom. The third panel applies the holiness of the great King to the context of the kingdoms of Judah, Israel, Aram, and Assyria.

Oracles of judgment and hope Chaps. 1–5	Vision of the Holy One of Israel Chap. 6	Oracles of judgment and hope Chaps. 7–12

Figure 54. Isaiah 1–12: The Triptych

The Prophetic Call, 6:1–13

The call narrative with its vision of God's holiness, the establishment of his kingdom, and his judgment on humans is singularly important in giving the reader a focus on the book as a whole and on chapters 1–12 in particular. Isaiah had a vision of the great King, the Lord (*Adonai,* 6:1; see 1:24; 3:1; 10:33), the Master of the universe. The great King is "seated on a throne, high and exalted" (6:1; see Pss. 99:5; 132:7), surrounded by seraphs.[21] The phenomena attending God's presence are like those of his theophany[22] at Mount Sinai and at the dedication of the tabernacle/temple (Ex. 19:16; 40:34–35; 1 Kings 8:10–11): the effulgence of the divine glory, the shaking of the earth, and the smoke.

The prophet was overcome with awe at God's coming. Like Moses, he received a vision of the glory of the Lord (Ex. 34:29–35), and he, like Israel at Mount Sinai, was ready to receive God's call and serve the great King. Israel heard a great noise (Ex. 20:18) when God came to them, but Isaiah heard the seraphic choir announcing the coming of the great and glorious King: "Holy, holy, holy is the LORD Almighty; the whole earth is full of his glory" (6:3). Unlike Israel's earlier readiness to receive God's kingdom among them (Ex. 24:3), Isaiah confessed Israel's guilt, including his own. The people of his generation were not prepared for the coming of God's kingdom in holiness and glory! This background explains his dismay: "'Woe to me!' I cried. 'I am ruined! For I am a man of unclean lips, and I live among a people of unclean lips, and my eyes have seen the King, the LORD Almighty'" (Isa. 6:5).

The call narrative introduces Isaiah's Lord. He is the great King, the Master, the Lord of the heavenly armies,[23] who alone is holy and who comes to extend his glorious kingdom to his creation.[24] The Holy One of Israel (1:4; 5:19, 24; 10:17, 20, 33) is King (6:5)![25] Isaiah is the court prophet of the Lord who stood within the divine counsel and was called to be the herald of the coming of God's kingdom.[26]

In the context of the revelation of Yahweh's glory and holiness, the prophet was given the mission of preparing the holy remnant for the Lord's glorious establishment of his kingdom. His teaching and preaching must be of such a quality that the people at large would condemn themselves by unbelief (6:9–10; Matt. 13:14–15; Mark 4:12; Luke 8:10)[27] while a remnant (6:13) would prepare itself for God's holy and glorious kingdom.[28] As Vriezen puts it, "Isaiah saw the new world of godly people *sub specie sanctitatis Dei,* i.e., in terms of God's holiness."[29]

Oracles of Judgment and Hope, 1:1–5:30[30]

As a minister of royal anointing, Isaiah proclaimed a new age of transformation and invited a remnant from the old era to prepare for the coming of the great King. He called for the "old" community to turn away from the old, perishable structures and to await the new, imperishable structures of God's kingdom. The new community constitutes all who are set apart by God's cleansing, forgiveness, and consecration and by their qualities of humility, love of justice, righteousness, peace, and fidelity. They are the "stumps" (6:13), that is, "the holy seed" of the new era of salvation. In contrast, Isaiah spoke of the old community as (1) foolish children, (2) a rebellious city, and (3) an unproductive vineyard. (For contrast, see a discussion of chaps. 25–27: "Metaphors for Deliverance," below; also see figure 57.)

FOOLISH CHILDREN

Though Yahweh has done everything to train up his children, they have acted foolishly (1:2–4) and have no sense of how to live in the presence of the Holy One.

> Ah, sinful nation,
> a people loaded with guilt,
> a brood of evildoers,
> children given to corruption!
> They have forsaken the LORD;
> they have spurned the Holy One of Israel
> and turned their backs on him.
>
> (v. 4)

Yahweh had disciplined them in many ways, but they had not responded to his fatherly correction (vv. 5–6). Instead, they placated their seared conscience with pious acts and multiplied their offerings and prayers (vv. 11–15), but did not have the sense to know that Yahweh desires nothing less than to have devoted children who acknowledge him by establishing justice and righteousness in their everyday affairs (vv. 16–17).[31]

A REBELLIOUS CITY

God's people had forsaken their reason for existence as well as their mission. They were to be God's kingdom on earth, characterized by righteousness, justice, and fidelity.

> See how the faithful [ne'emānâ] city
>   has become a harlot!
> She once was full of justice [mišpāṭ];
>   righteousness [ṣedeq] used to dwell in her—
>   but now murderers!
>
> (1:21)

The leaders of God's people had led them astray (1:23; 3:14) into a lifestyle of narcissism, exploitation, ruthless capitalism, and opportunism (2:6–22; 3:1–15; 5:11–25). The leaders and the people had become like the wicked cities of Sodom and Gomorrah, which the Lord had overturned on the day of his wrath (1:10; Gen. 19:24–25).

AN UNPRODUCTIVE VINEYARD

Isaiah also likened God's people to an unproductive vineyard,[32] whose owner and caretaker is none other than Yahweh. He expected much from them, but they produced poor fruit (5:1–7). Yahweh called on the people to respond to his dilemma of keeping the vineyard or abandoning it. Thus he made it plain that his abandonment of Judah was only reasonable. They had received his glorious kingdom but had opposed it in every conceivable way.

GOD'S JUDGMENT AND HIS HOPE FOR THE REMNANT

Isaiah most strongly condemned man's cultural, military, religious, economic, and political achievements as being motivated and characterized by the exaltation of man. He likewise condemned the calumny of the wicked, who were not afraid of Yahweh's judgment, saying,

> Let God hurry,
>   let him hasten his work
>   so we may see it.
> Let it approach,
>   let the plan of the Holy One of Israel come,
>   so we may know it.
>
> (5:19)

The abasement of man is in stark contrast to the exaltation of Yahweh, who alone is King.

YAHWEH'S KINGDOM	
	HUMAN KINGDOMS AND STRUCTURES
Holy	Autonomous
Glorious	Proud
Blessing	Concerned for self-preservation
King of kings	Self-exalting

Figure 55. The Contrast Between the Two Kingdoms

> The eyes of the arrogant man will be humbled
> and the pride of men brought low;
> the LORD alone will be exalted in that day.
>
> (2:11; see v. 17)

This is the great Day of Judgment when there is no forgiveness, favor, or possibility of repentance for the hard-hearted: "But the LORD Almighty will be exalted by his justice, and the holy God will show himself holy by his righteousness" (5:16; see 1:24–25; 3:13). In regard to the Day of the Lord Isaiah spoke of an earthquake (2:21; 5:25), a period of national anarchy (3:1–9, 11–12), a cosmic upheaval (5:30), and wartime and exile (5:13–14; 25–29).

God's judgments in history are tokens of the eschatological judgment (the Day of the Lord). On this day the Lord will appear (theophany)[33] as the great King[34] to show man up. Man apart from God is nothing but a creature filled with pride who boasts of his accomplishments. Man as a social being relates with other beings, but always so as to live independently of God (autonomy). As a political being, he makes alliances with others so as to secure his economic, cultural, and political ends and to establish human kingdoms in defiance of God's kingship. (See figure 55.) The religiosity of humans is a smoke screen (2:6–8). Men and women equally share in their collusion against the Creator (3:16–4:1).[35]

Yet the prophetic proclamation of judgment was an occasion for repentance. The Lord desires repentance, godliness, and true devotion to his kingdom (1:16–19) rather than acts of piety, such as offerings and prayers (vv. 11–16). Hence, Isaiah called on the people to follow the way of the Lord in wisdom, loyalty, and productiveness.

> Come, O house of Jacob,
> let us walk in the light of the LORD. . . .

> Stop trusting in man,
>> who has but a breath in his nostrils.
> Of what account is he?
>
> (2:5, 22)

Those who respond will make up the new, holy, and glorious community.

His righteous children need not be afraid of this terrifying Day of Judgment: "Tell the righteous it will be well with them, for they will enjoy the fruit of their deeds" (3:10). They will make up the new city.

> "I will restore your judges as in days of old,
>> your counselors as at the beginning.
> Afterward you will be called
>> the City of Righteousness,
>> the Faithful City."
> Zion will be redeemed with justice,
>> her penitent ones with righteousness.
>
> (1:26–27)

They will also constitute the new branch (*ṣemaḥ*, 4:2),[36] that is, the new "shoot" that comes out of the old (see 6:13). The new community consists of all who have been forgiven, cleansed, and made holy by the great King (4:3–4). They will be the objects of his glory, blessing, and protection, for he will be present with them as he was with Israel in the wilderness.

> In that day the Branch [*ṣemaḥ*] of the LORD will be beautiful and glorious, and the fruit of the land will be the pride and glory of the survivors in Israel. . . . Then the LORD will create over all of Mount Zion and over those who assemble there a cloud of smoke by day and a glow of flaming fire by night; over all the glory will be a canopy. It will be a shelter and shade from the heat of the day, and a refuge and hiding place from the storm and rain (vv. 2, 5–6).

The renewal of God's presence among the godly manifests his commitment to establish his glorious kingdom on earth (6:3, 13; see 4:2)! He will establish his universal kingdom of peace, justice, righteousness, and holiness (2:2–4; see vv. 5–6) for the sake of his holy people.[37]

Oracles of Judgment and Hope, 7:1–11:16

These oracles, unlike those of chapters 1–5, are set within a historical context.[38] Aram and Israel had allied themselves against the Assyrian threat and had prepared for war against Judah (see the section "Isaiah and His Time: Ahaz"). Ahaz had thought of every conceivable means of *Realpolitik* to avert the threat of Israel and Aram, but had not looked to the Lord. Yet Yahweh intervened and declared that the northern nations would fall to Assyria and that Judah would escape, though narrowly (7:3–8:10). The Lord sovereignly and graciously promised to be present with his people and to protect them.

The sign of God's presence is the Immanuel prophecy (7:14).[39] The name *Immanuel* ("God is with us") is a part of the name theology found in the prophecy of Isaiah: "Here am I, and the children the LORD has given me. *We are signs and symbols* in Israel from the LORD Almighty, who dwells on Mount Zion" (8:18, emphasis mine). The names of Isaiah ("Yahweh is salvation") and his sons (Shear-Jashub ["a remnant will return"] and Maher-Shalal-Hash-Baz ["booty will very quickly be taken"]; see 7:3; 8:3) convey the essence of the book: (1) Yahweh is the source of salvation; (2) Yahweh will spare a remnant for himself; and (3) Yahweh's judgment is coming.

Of particular interest are the names of his sons in the context of the Syro-Ephraimite crisis. Isaiah took his son Shear-Jashub with him to meet Ahaz, as God had commanded. Why did the Lord ask him to take his young son on this mission? It appears that the name of the son was significant in this historic moment. Shear-Jashub signifies that only a remnant will survive, namely, a remnant that will respond in faith.[40] The speedy dissolution of the crisis is represented by Isaiah's other son, born during this crisis, Maher-Shalal-Hash-Baz.[41] Thus the names point to God's sovereignty over the nations, his protection of the people, and hope for the godly.

In its immediate context the name *Immanuel* signifies God's protection of Judah (8:8, 10) and his rejection of Ahaz in favor of another son of David.[42] God promised to be gracious to Judah, though she had been unresponsive. His judgment would begin with Damascus and Samaria, but God's patience allowed an opportunity for repentance. If Judah did not repent, she, too, would experience his judgment, leaving a small remnant (Shear-Jashub) for the future. Thus Immanuel indicates judgment upon the rebels but favor toward the faithful. The Immanuel prophecy comes to a greater fulfillment in the birth of the God-man, who is both the Protector-Deliverer and the Divine Warrior. Matthew properly applied this prophecy to Jesus the Messiah (Matt. 1:23).

International crises are under God's sovereign control (8:6–10). He appointed "the mighty floodwaters of the River" (8:7, a metaphor for Assyria) to destroy the nations and used Assyria as his means ("rod of [his] anger," 10:5) to establish some order in the chaos and anarchy of the nations. They had been preoccupied with their petty interests and were oblivious to Yahweh's love of justice, righteousness, and peace. By

God's will, Assyria brought down the Arameans, Israel, and other nations (Amos, Hosea, Micah, and Isaiah). These kingdoms had to fall because they had exalted themselves and were full of pride (9:8–10:4). Of course, the spirit of Assyria was no different, even while it served God's purposes, and he would bring about its downfall for the same reason (10:5–19).

Why then did he spare Judah in Ahaz's time? He spared her simply because he desired to do so (10:24–34). The respite provided another opportunity for Ahaz and Judah to be awed by the holy King.

> The LORD Almighty is the one you are to regard as holy,
> he is the one you are to fear,
> he is the one you are to dread,
> and he will be a sanctuary.
>
> (8:13–14)

He is the sovereign and holy King. He is *sovereign* over the power systems of this world, and he is *holy* in his separation from human structures, means, and goals.

To this end, Isaiah's mission was to call Judah to repent from her identification with the nations. They were secure with their structures and religious symbols, even magic and mantic (8:19). However, if they would not respond to the Holy One in their midst (v. 13), he would become "a stone that causes men to stumble and a rock that makes them fall . . . a trap and a snare" (v. 14). When they fall, they will grope in darkness, curse their king, and be "thrust into utter darkness" (v. 22; see v. 21).

By contrast, the godly seek the Lord. The prophet called for disciples who would follow him in seeking the Lord and in awaiting his kingdom (8:16–17). His followers distinguish themselves by separating themselves from human structures (see 2:22), by consecrating themselves to the Lord (8:13), by trusting in his salvation (v. 14), by submitting themselves to his revelation (vv. 16, 20), and by waiting for the new age (v. 17).

YAHWEH, THE MESSIAH, AND THE REMNANT

Yahweh will bring about the new age of transformation in creation and in a redeemed community through his Messiah.[43] The descendants of David had fallen far short of his expectations, as is implied by Isaiah's magnificent adumbration of the Messiah. According to him, the Messiah (1) descends from David, (2) has the Spirit of God, (3) enjoys a Father-Son relationship, (4) brings in a new era of unparalleled peace, prosperity, and righteousness, and (5) establishes a new community (9:2–7; 11:1–9).[44] Clearly, the prophetic portrayal of the Messiah was a

261

criticism of the age in which Isaiah lived; it was what Koch calls "a massive *criticism of the king*—even of court ideology as such."[45]

Both the certainty and the fulfillment of God's promises are in the divine guarantee and in the names and perfections of the Messiah. First, the Lord guarantees the new age and the new leadership, "The zeal of the LORD Almighty will accomplish this" (9:7). No king in Judah or power coalition could bring about the era of fulfillment. Restoration is the work of God alone, and he shall accomplish it in accordance with his word. Therefore man's hope lies in God: the Beginning and the End, the First and the Last. Yahweh alone will bring about the complete fulfillment of the promises made to David.

Second, the names of the Messiah signify the power, presence, protection, and blessing of God.

> For to us a child is born,
>   to us a son is given,
>   and the government will be on his shoulders.
> And he will be called
>   Wonderful Counselor, Mighty God,
>   Everlasting Father, Prince of Peace.
>
> (9:6)[46]

He is the Servant of God, the Son of David (11:1; Luke 1:32–33; Rev. 22:16), and he is empowered by the Spirit of restoration (11:1–4; Luke 3:22). The Immanuel of God (7:14; see Matt. 1:22–23) will bring in a universal rule of peace to humankind and creation. However, the wicked will not escape his wrath (11:4–8; Luke 2:14; Rev. 19:11–16).[47] The Messiah is faithful and will establish the kingdom of God in justice, righteousness, peace, and fidelity. Further, the Messiah will inaugurate an era of happiness. His kingdom will bring a new age of glory and holiness on earth. The blessedness of the new age is the "light" (9:2; Luke 1:78–79; 2 Cor. 4:6) against the "darkness" of divine abandonment (8:22). The Messiah is God's instrument of bringing the light of deliverance, glory, holiness, and rest.

> They will neither harm nor destroy
>   on all *my holy mountain*,
> *for the earth will be full of the knowledge of the* LORD
>   as the waters cover the sea.
>
> In that day the Root of Jesse will stand as a banner for the peoples;
> the nations will rally to him, and his place of rest will be *glorious* (11:9–
> 10, emphasis mine; see 2:2–4; 6:3; Rom. 15:7–13).

The future belongs to the remnant, who follow Isaiah's example of hoping in the Lord (8:17; 10:20–21). They constitute a purified and renewed community.[48] The hope of the godly will be rewarded by the messianic King, whose rule will bring a renewal of God's blessing to his people (9:2–7; 11:11–12).[49]

The Hymn of the Redeemed, 12:1–6

The various descriptions of the messianic King, the messianic era, and the establishment of God's kingdom in judgment and in deliverance evoke a response in the form of a hymn. In this hymn Isaiah called on the godly remnant to rejoice in Yahweh, the Divine Warrior, the Holy One of Israel, who alone will work out full and final deliverance for his people. He forgives sinners, comforts them, and gives them the fullness of deliverance (12:2). He is the joy of his waiting people as they receive the tokens of his salvation in anticipation of the full deliverance (v. 3) and as they witness his mighty acts of judgment and deliverance. The God of the Exodus and the Red Sea is still with his people, bringing them deliverance and rendering judgment upon their enemies.[50] Moreover, this great King, the holy and glorious Yahweh, will reside among his people and will be the object of their praise: "Shout aloud and sing for joy, people of Zion, for great is *the Holy One of Israel among you*" (v. 6, emphasis mine).[51]

With this hymn the first part of the book closes on a climactic note. Isaiah had seen God's coming to establish his holy and glorious kingdom (6:3), he had witnessed the evil of his generation (v. 5), and he longed for God's kingdom among the godly. The vision of God's kingdom burned within the prophet as he spoke with the hope that even a few might return to the way of the Lord.

The Day of the Lord for All Creation, 13:1–23:18

These oracles against the nations apply God's judgment to Babylon (13:1–14:23; 21:1–10), Assyria (14:24–32), Moab (15:1–16:14), Damascus (17:1–14), Cush/Egypt (18:1–20:6), Edom (21:11–12), Arabia (21:13–17), Jerusalem (22:1–25), and Tyre (23:1–18) as representative of all the kingdoms of the world.[52]

The nations that the prophet addressed formed a web of international relations within which each had its place. Jerusalem, lying at the very center of the web, determined her international diplomacy based on the needs of the day (*Realpolitik*). With the growth of Assyria and the threat of the northern alliance of Israel and Damascus, King Ahaz looked to Assyria for help. Once Assyria had established its border a few miles to the north of Jerusalem and exacted tribute from Judah, Jerusalem also cooperated with the nations to overthrow the Assyrian yoke.[53]

Isaiah declared that all political, military, and economic aspirations would fail as long as people were more concerned with protecting their own interests and with keeping their petty kingdoms alive, without

depending on the Lord and seeking his kingdom. He even charged
Hezekiah and the leadership with duplicity.

> You built a reservoir between the two walls
> > for the water of the Old Pool,
> but you did not look to the One who made it,
> > or have regard for the One who planned it long ago.
>
> > > > (22:11)

The oracles against the nations are encouragements to exchange
Realpolitik for a vision of Zion (the kingdom of God). Zion—by its very
nature as a counterculture—invites opposition, negative reactions, and
persecution. The many enemies of God's kingdom may be categorized
by three types: (1) the oppressors; (2) the troublers; and (3) the
seducers. God's judgment rests on all the ungodly who have responded
negatively to his kingdom in Israel and in Judah. The prayer of the godly
for the establishment of God's kingdom entails the end of evil, that is, of
the evil kingdoms of this world (Ps. 83). This is also the message of
Isaiah. (See figure 56.)

THE DAY OF THE LORD

VENGEANCE	DELIVERANCE
Oppressors:	Remnant from
Babylon, Assyria	Israel
Troublers:	Judah
Moab, Philistia, Aram, Edom	Nations
Seducers:	
Cush/Egypt, Tyre	

Figure 56. The Day of the Lord

The Oppressors

Babylon, as well as Assyria, exemplified the spirit of independence,
pride, and self-glory: "Babylon, the jewel of kingdoms, the glory of the
Babylonians' pride" (13:19). She showed no compassion to her victims
because the state, the empire, and the king were the instruments of the
gods to bring prosperity to Babylon. The subjected nations were mere
vehicles toward their success. Isaiah elsewhere likens Babylon to a
princess endowed with beauty and grace, whose favor the nations sought
(47:1). But Babylon, too, shall fall! Her end will be that of Sodom and
Gomorrah (13:19), and her advanced culture will be reduced to rubble,

a habitat for wild animals (13:20–22). Yahweh will break the power of her ruthless rule (14:4–6; see 44:24–48:22 [below]).

In the Day of the Lord, the great King will hold her accountable to himself (13:11–12).[54] The terror of that day may be compared to that brought about by earthquake (13:9, 13), war (v. 4), and cosmic upheaval (vv. 10, 13). Though it seems far off, it is always imminent: "Wail, for the day of the LORD is near; it will come like destruction from the Almighty" (v. 6). No human power or ingenuity will be able to withstand God's judgment (vv. 7–8) when he comes to establish his kingdom on earth (v. 9). None will escape his fury (vv. 14–16)! Great was the rejoicing of the nations when Babylon fell (539 B.C.), but greater will be the rejoicing of the godly when all ruthless oppressors receive God's righteous judgment (21:9–10; Rev. 18:2–24).

The Troublers

The troublers are nations and people who scorn, harass, and persecute the people of God. The Lord declares that he holds accountable all who have made the existence of his countercommunity difficult. In this light we may understand his judgment on the nations that have troubled Israel and Judah in the past: Moab, Philistia, Edom, and Aram. These nations together with other kingdoms had taken it upon themselves to antagonize the people of God. Throughout the history of Israel from the wilderness to the Exile, their peace was interrupted by hostile raids, incursions, and acts of war. The troublers are well described by Joshua as "whips on your backs and thorns in your eyes" (Josh. 23:13). The Philistines had tormented Israel from the period of the judges till the time of David. Moab, too, is representative of the troublers (1 Kings 3:1–27). Damascus, the capital of the Aramean kingdom, was the source of many wars with Israel and to a lesser extent with Judah. At times it allied itself with the one nation or the other. The nations may rage like a sea, but Yahweh will still the troubled waters (17:12–13; see Ps. 46:6).

The Seducers

The seducers offered material gain, economic development, military aid, and political advantages to entice Israel further into *Realpolitik.* They tempted Israel and Judah to rely on human ingenuity and power rather than on the Lord. Israel and Judah, each in its own unwise, ambitious way, aspired to be important by developing connections with the nations that brought prosperity, prestige, advanced culture, and military support.

Isaiah condemned most strongly any alliance, affinity, or dependency on human structures. Yahweh's judgment will come on all flesh, on all human cultural achievements, and on all the structures of society (2:6–

22). How foolish Ahaz was to rely on Assyria to help him in his trouble with Aram and Israel! How foolish were Hezekiah's advisers to hope for Egyptian military and political aid against Assyria! The nations may be busy with political alignments and realignments, their military and economic negotiations, and their concern with the balance of power and with preservation, but Yahweh has determined the day when he will act (18:4–5). He will confound the counsel of the wise, take away the resources of the richest, and cause the honored to be despised (19:2–15).

Tyre is representative of the Phoenician capitalistic system and culture. The ships of Phoenician merchants plied the seas, established colonies, traded, and controlled the international markets. The captains were like princes as they enticed the nations with greed, prosperity, and cultural advances (23:8). The revelry of Tyre will cease and nations will ask,

> Is this your city of revelry,
>   the old, old city,
> whose feet have taken her
>   to settle in far-off lands?
>   (23:7)

As far as God is concerned, the shipping and trade of Tyre and Sidon, and the Phoenician culture as a whole, are worthless and deserve his judgment. Yahweh, the God of Israel, is sovereign over all human aspirations, including the seas and distant lands that had given Phoenicia her security and power (23:9).

Hope for a Remnant

Yahweh's sovereignty is both inclusive and exclusive. He will exclude all who will not submit to him, but include the remnant of the nations that will recognize his uniqueness and sovereignty. The oracles against the nations contain a sufficient number of allusions to a new future beyond the judgment and to the inclusion of the Gentiles to permit the hope of a new era (14:1–3, 32; 16:5; 18:7; 19:18–25; 23:18).[55]

The Little Apocalypse, 24:1–27:13

The Day of the Lord

Isaiah 24–27 proclaims judgment and deliverance.[56] God's judgment rests on all creation (24:1). His judgment is likened to a massive holocaust, a war, and an earthquake (vv. 3–4, 10–12, 19–21). In contrast, Yahweh will shine forth gloriously and victoriously in the establishment of his kingdom and in his subjugation of the regime of evil, autonomy, and rebellion.

> The LORD Almighty will reign
> on Mount Zion and in Jerusalem,
> and before its elders, gloriously.
>> (v. 23)

Only the remnant, compared to the gleanings of olives and grapes, will remain (v. 13), and wherever they may be found, they will praise the Lord as they await his deliverance on that day (vv. 14–16). The godly rejoice at the dissolution of the systems of this world (25:5).[57]

Metaphors for Deliverance

BANQUET

The prophet compared the era of restoration/deliverance to a banquet to which the Lord invites only his children, whether Jews or Gentiles.[58] He fulfills all their needs, symbolized by the phrase "the best of meats and the finest of wines" (25:6). Further, he will remove all causes of suffering,[59] "the shroud that enfolds all peoples, the sheet that covers all nations" (v. 7). The new era knows no disgrace, sickness, or death because the Lord "will swallow up death forever" (v. 8).[60] Then all the godly will have occasion for uninterrupted rejoicing.

> The Sovereign LORD will wipe away the tears
> from all faces;
> he will remove the disgrace of his people
> from all the earth.
>> (v. 8; see 35:10; 51:11; 65:19; Jer. 31:16; Rev. 7:17; 21:4)

THE CITY

Another metaphor for this era of salvation is the city. The city of God is an all-inclusive concept in that all the godly are its citizens. They share in the common experience that "God makes salvation its walls and ramparts" (26:1). They share in a common commitment to the Lord; all are righteous and persevere in fidelity to the Lord (v. 2, see v. 4). They do not fear, because Yahweh grants peace to his subjects.

> You will keep in perfect peace
> him whose mind is steadfast,
> because he trusts in you.
>> (v. 3)

He is their "Rock" (v. 4), their Redeemer who will most certainly judge the exalted and exalt the oppressed (vv. 5–6, 10–11). They do not take justice into their own hands but wait quietly for their Divine Warrior to act on their behalf (v. 9). Isaiah intimates that the restoration process may be gradual; he encourages the godly to quietly wait for the Divine Warrior to act in vengeance. He will punish all ungodliness, especially

Satan and his host (Leviathan, vv. 20–21; 27:1; see Rev. 12:9; 19:19–21; 20:10).[61]

The members of the new community are, not only protected, but also blessed by the King. He blesses them with an increase in population, extension of the boundaries (26:15), and peace (v. 12). Their prayers are richly answered (vv. 16–18), and all who suffer will receive the fullness of the goodness of their great King. This extends even to the dead.

> Your dead will live;
>   their bodies will rise.
> You who dwell in the dust,
>   wake up and shout for joy.
> Your dew is like the dew of the morning;
>   the earth will give birth to her dead.
>   (v. 19)

A FRUITFUL VINE

The era of restoration is also discussed in terms of a fruitful vine. The lament on the vineyard of chapter 5 changes into a song of a productive vineyard (27:2). Its productivity is due to the Lord's watchfulness. Yahweh is the vintner who cares for his vineyard ("I water it continually") and protects it ("I guard it day and night so that no one may harm it," v. 3). All who come to destroy will be destroyed, but all who seek shelter and peace with God will find it (v. 5).

The new era of transformation requires a spiritual change of heart and commitment. The sin of Jacob must be first atoned for (27:9). They must suffer the shame and deprivation of exile (vv. 7–11) as expressions of divine abandonment (v. 11). But the Lord will call out the penitent and restore them to himself from wherever they may have been scattered, whether from the Euphrates or Egypt (vv. 12–13). A "great trumpet will sound," calling the remnant to gather together to worship "the LORD on the holy mountain in Jerusalem" (v. 13; see Num. 10:1–10). The transformation of Israel and Judah will be so dramatic that it is likened to a single vine that spreads and fills the whole earth "with fruit" (v. 6).[62]

How different are the metaphors of chapters 1–5 from the ones we have just encountered! (See figure 57.)

Judgment and Salvation, 28:1–35:10

The Kingdoms of This World, 28:1–33:24

This collection contains six oracles of woe detailing the arrogance of Israel and Judah. Both kingdoms were filled with pride and looked for cultural, economic, and political security rather than to the Lord.

The first oracle portrays Ephraim's geographical location and the fertility as the reason for haughtiness. Its roads led to the great cities of the ancient Near East. Its valleys were lush and productive. But on the Day of the Lord Ephraim's beauty will be trampled down. Isaiah exhorted the godly to be wise in observing the ways of God in nature and in history (28:23–29) and to cling to Yahweh who alone is "wonderful in counsel and magnificent in wisdom" (v. 29).[63]

Chapters 1–5	Chapters 25–27
Foolish children	Guests at God's banquet
A rebellious city	Citizens of the City of God
An unproductive vineyard	A fruitful vine

Figure 57. Comparison of the Old and the New

In the second oracle, Judah is the Ariel ("lion of God"), where the Lord has established the footstool of his kingdom and where the Davidic king ruled (29:1).[64] The Day of the Lord will also fall on her and her enemies (vv. 2–8) when suddenly

> the LORD Almighty will come
> with thunder and earthquake and great noise,
> with windstorm and tempest and flames of a devouring fire.
>
> (v. 6)

The third oracle displays Judah as busy in making political and military plans with Egypt (29:15–18), believing that the Lord did not see. They, too, will receive their just judgment (vv. 20–21). His kingdom belongs to all who humbly rely on "the Holy One of Israel" (v. 19). They and their descendants will make up the true Israel (v. 22; see v. 24) because they will

> keep my name holy;
> they will acknowledge the holiness of
> the Holy One of Jacob,
> and will stand in awe of the God of Israel.
>
> (v. 23)

The prophet, in the fourth oracle, charged Judah with rebelliousness and political subterfuge (30:1–31:9). They depended on Egypt for military aid (30:1–7) and resisted God's rebuke through his prophets (vv. 10–11). The Holy One of Israel warns of devastation and desolation (vv. 12–14, 17) because they had persistently rejected the way of entering into his rest (vv. 15–16). But he will grant grace and compassion to those who wait for his redemption (v. 18). He will answer their prayers and supply all their material (vv. 23–24) and spiritual (vv. 19–21) needs.

The fifth oracle portrays the prophet again condemning Judah's reliance on Egypt for military supplies (horses and chariots) to be used against the Assyrian threat (chap. 31). They did not seek the Lord (v. 1), who truly is their shield, the *Immanuel* ("God with us," see vv. 4–5). The might of the nations is nothing compared to him (vv. 6–9).

Isaiah invited all who resisted the *Realpolitik* of human systems (political, military, economic, or cultural) to look with hope to God's kingdom of righteousness and justice (32:1). Great and terrible is God's judgment on evil (vv. 9–14), but wonderful will be the transformation and restoration resulting from the new age of the Spirit of God. The Spirit, the agent of transformation for all creation and humankind (v. 15), will not rest until

> justice will dwell in the desert
>> and righteousness live in the fertile field.
> The fruit of righteousness will be peace;
>> the effect of righteousness will be
> quietness and confidence forever
>> (vv. 16–17)

He will bring in the kingdom of righteousness, justice, peace, security, and prosperity in which the people of God will fully share (vv. 18–20).

Finally, God's vengeance rests on all the enemies of his kingdom and people. The nations will not share in this era of restoration. Instead, God's judgment will wipe them out as an expression of his wrath (33:1). Great and awe-inspiring will be his vengeance (v. 3), but gracious is he to all who long for him (v. 2). He is their "strength every morning, [their] salvation in time of distress" (v. 2). He is the Divine Warrior who is exalted in heaven and who will establish his kingdom among his people on earth (vv. 5–6). To accomplish this, he will bring great devastation to the earth (vv. 7–13) so that sinners will marvel at his power (v. 14) and ask, Who may then enter into his kingdom? Who can enjoy fellowship with a God who is like a consuming fire?

Isaiah's response is in the form of a liturgical invitation to join the righteous remnant.

> He who walks righteously
>> and speaks what is right,
> who rejects gain from extortion
>> and keeps his hand from accepting bribes,
> who stops his ears against plots of murder
>> and shuts his eyes against contemplating evil—
> this is the man who will dwell on the heights,
>> whose refuge will be the mountain fortress.

His bread will be supplied,
and water will not fail him.
(33:15–16; Ps. 15)

The righteous will witness the glorious kingdom (33:17) whose very source of everlasting blessedness lies in the presence of God.

There the LORD will be our Mighty One.
It will be like a place of broad rivers and streams.
No galley with oars will ride them,
no mighty ship will sail them.
For the LORD is our judge,
the LORD is our lawgiver,
the LORD is our king;
it is he who will save us.
(vv. 21–22).

The Lord is the King, Judge, and Protector who blesses his people.[65] They will no longer need to depend on Egypt and Phoenicia for trade, cultural exchanges, and political interplay. They will be richly blessed, forgiven of all their sins (v. 24), and without fear (vv. 17–19).

Vengeance and Favor, 34:1–35:10

THE DAY OF VENGEANCE, 34:1–17

Isaiah returns to the theme of the Day of the Lord for all nations by reference to Edom (see chap. 5: "Obadiah"). Clearly the introductory words (v. 1) have a cosmic scope because God is angry with "all nations" and their "armies" (v. 2). He will eradicate all evil and opposition in his cosmos (vv. 2–7). On this day the Lord shatters the force of the nations and brings desolation to their cities and fortifications so as to make them inhabitable (34:9–15). It is the "day of vengeance, a year of retribution" (v. 8).

THE YEAR OF FAVOR AND RESTORATION, 35:1–10

Though his people may experience desolation, ruination, and abandonment like "a desert," the Lord will restore everything to them (see Luke 18:29–30). Creation will welcome and cooperate with the great King in bringing about the fullness of that restoration (vv. 1–2), so "they will see the glory of the LORD, the splendor of our God" (v. 2). The prophetic encouragement anticipates the fuller development of this motif in chapters 40–66.

Strengthen the feeble hands,
steady the knees that give way;
say to those with fearful hearts,
"Be strong, do not fear;

271

> your God will come,
>> he will come with vengeance;
> with divine retribution
>> he will come to save you.
>>
>> (35:3–4)

The redeemed of the Lord will see the wonders of God and "shout for joy" (35:6). The transformation will be great; all things will work out for the good of those whom the Lord loves. The images of streams in the desert (vv. 6–7), vegetation (v. 7), and a highway (v. 8) are metaphors for the certainty, the grace, and the fullness of redemption. The redeemed are protected by the Lord (v. 9) and holy to the Lord (v. 8). They will never again be disgraced or suffer the limitations imposed on them by their sin, judgment, alienation, or the enmity of man against God.

> But only the redeemed will walk there,
>> and the ransomed of the LORD will return.
> They will enter Zion with singing;
>> everlasting joy will crown their heads.
> Gladness and joy will overtake them,
>> and sorrow and sighing will flee away.
>>
>> (35:9–10)

Isaiah and Hezekiah, 36:1–39:8.

See "Isaiah and His Time."[66]

The Glorious Kingdom of God, 40:1–48:22[67]

The Proclamation of Restoration, 40:1–31

The good news is that God cares for an uncared-for people. He has sent his messengers with the command to "comfort" his people (40:1)![68] The basis for that comfort is God's commitment to reveal his glorious kingdom on earth (v. 5). The prophets of the postexilic era, John the Baptist (Luke 3:4–6), and the apostles were faithful in calling on God's people to prepare for God's kingdom. Individually and in harmony they make up the "voice"[69] in the wilderness, preparing for the glorious theophany.

> The glory of the LORD will be revealed,
>> and all mankind together will see it.
> For the mouth of the LORD
>> has spoken.
>>
>> (40:5; see 6:3)

The epiphany of our Lord has two aspects: *judgment* on all humankind (40:6–8) and the *restoration* of the people of God (vv. 9–11). (See figure 58.) The "good tidings" to Zion (v. 9) pertain to the proclamation

272

of forgiveness, God's presence, the promise of full redemption, and the transformation of creation.[70] Isaiah stood at the beginning of a long stream of prophets, proclaiming the new age of divine forgiveness, compassion, transformation, and covenant renewal.[71] The essence of the gospel of the new age is "Here is your God!" (v. 9). This began with the restoration after the Babylonian exile and will continue as long as the gospel is proclaimed.

EPIPHANY OF GOD'S GLORY

Judgment	Restoration
All mankind is like grass	The remnant are like sheep

Figure 58. The Kingdom of God

Who is this God? He is no other than the Divine Warrior-King who delivers his people and bears them gently like a Shepherd (40:10–11). He is the Creator-Redeemer (vv. 12–31),[72] the Incomparable (vv. 18, 25), "the Holy One" (v. 25), Yahweh (the LORD), the Restorer (vv. 28–29, 30–31).[73] The focus of the gospel since the first coming of our Lord is on Jesus, the Messiah of God, whom the Father has appointed to be the Judge, Warrior, and Deliverer (1 Cor. 15:20–28; see Rom. 10:9–13).

Israel as Yahweh's Servant, 41:1–44:23

Yahweh renews his covenant of love with Israel, and in so doing, he calls the individual as well as the renewed community to be his "servant" (41:8–9).[74] This title signifies honor, closeness, and a special place in the progress of redemptive history. For example, Moses (Num. 12:7), David (2 Sam. 7:5, 8), and the prophets (Jer. 7:25) are among his servants. Isaiah applied this exalted title to all God's children. The servants of the Lord share in the new era of the democratization of the covenant community in which each individual moved by the Spirit of God lives to the glory of the Lord and bears witness to God's acts of redemption (see 43:10, 12; 44:8).[75] Yahweh encourages them, as he did Joshua upon entering the land of Canaan, "Do not fear, but go out in the strength of God's presence" (41:10, vv. 13–14). After all he is "the LORD, your Redeemer, the Holy One of Israel" (vv. 14, 16) and they are his people (vv. 17–20).

Nothing can obstruct the execution of his plan of redemption, because he is Yahweh: "I, the LORD—with the first of them and with the last—I am he" (41:4; see Heb. 13:8; Rev. 1:8, 17; 2:8; 21:6; 22:13)!

273

Further, he renews the covenant with the new community and endows them with his Spirit so they may be his witness to the nations. This covenant is also known as the "covenant for the people" (42:6)[76] and is the concern of the first Servant Song (vv. 1–9).[77] The covenant assures that each member of the new community is the object of his love, is commissioned to establish God's kingdom among the nations (vv. 3–4),[78] and is endowed with his Spirit (v. 1)[79] to bear the light of his kingdom to the nations ("a light for the Gentiles," see Luke 2:32; Acts 13:47).[80] (See figure 60.)

The new people of God sing a new song celebrating the acts of God (42:10–13). The Divine Warrior will bring desolation on all who trust in their idols (vv. 14–17), but the redeemed of the Lord need not fear, because he, like a woman ready to give birth, will deliver his people (vv. 14, 16)![81] Though they had been exiled because of their sin (vv. 23–25), Yahweh freely renews his call (43:1), encourages them with his presence and purpose (vv. 1–7), and calls on Israel to be his witnesses (v. 10) to the era of restoration (vv. 19–21).[82]

The renewal of covenant and the democratization of Israel as servants of the Lord are expressions of the new era (44:1–4) when each member of the covenant community will know the Lord (v. 5). The ground for hope in restoration lies in Yahweh, the Incomparable One (vv. 6–7). There is no other God (vv. 8–20)![83] He alone renews covenant and forgives sinners (v. 22).

Yahweh's Use of Cyrus as an Instrument of Restoration, 44:24–48:22

Yahweh has planned the era of restoration, which has been the object of his revelation and plan of redemption. Restoration, creation, redemption, and election in time reveal the outworking of his plan, and the prophets are the spokesmen who witness to his eternal purposes in time (44:24–28; 45:19–21). The object of restoration is the creation of a habitat in which his people may enjoy the fullness of blessing (45:4–5) in the kingdom of God (vv. 6–7, 18–19). His people are the objects of his righteousness, salvation, and the new era of a redeemed creation.[84] For Isaiah, "righteousness" (*ṣᵉdāqā, ṣedeq*) denotes that state of restoration in which the redeemed enjoy the fullness of God's kingdom in salvation, victory, and glory.[85] (See figure 59.)

The rise of Persian King Cyrus and the fall of Babylon were expressions of Yahweh's gracious plan of restoration. Cyrus is God's instrument in Israel's restoration to the land (44:28–45:3; see 44:1–4, 25)[86] because "the Holy One of Israel" (45:11; see vv. 9–10) has "anointed" (*m-š-ḥ*) him to inaugurate his kingdom (v. 13). The nations of the earth will contribute to the restoration grandeur, desiring to participate in the covenant relationship (v. 14).[87]

The fall of Babylon is also a sign of the inauguration of the new era.

When the restoration from exile took place, the Lord restored "salvation to Zion, my splendor to Israel" (46:13), but the "Virgin Daughter of Babylon" was disgraced (47:1–3). She had thought of herself as eternal and invulnerable, and as already having established the kingdom of the gods on earth (vv. 5–11). She had not recognized that she was nothing but God's instrument for judging his people. She had exalted herself and had become independent from the great King. The gods of Babylon (Bel = Marduk; Nebo/Nabu) could not deliver her from the power of Yahweh (46:9–11), nor could her wisdom, strategy, or her forms of magic and mantic (47:12–15). She could not escape the vengeance of Yahweh when he came to redeem his people (vv. 4–5)[88] because he is the Lord Almighty ("the Lord of Hosts"), the Divine Warrior, the Creator, the Judge of all humankind.

YAHWEH			
CREATOR	REDEEMER	KING	WARRIOR
Establishment of his order in creation and redemption			

Means: Vengeance, vindication	Deliverance, favor
Objects: Enemies Nature: Proud	The new community Nature: Humble
Result: Judgment on the king- doms of this world	Full deliverance: Synonyms: City, Zion, right- eousness, justice, salvation, peace, splendor, glory, light

Figure 59. God's Plan of Redemption

Thus the prophet encouraged the faithful with a vision of the restoration of God's presence, his blessing, his protection, and the work of the Spirit of restoration (48:16). He also exhorted them to be ready to leave Babylon whenever God opened the way.

> Leave Babylon,
>> flee from the Babylonians!
> Announce this with shouts of joy
>> and proclaim it.
> Send it out to the ends of the earth;
>> say, "The LORD has redeemed his servant Jacob."
>
> (v. 20)

The restoration from exile is comparable in significance to God's deliverance of Israel from Egypt (v. 21).[89] The godly will share in it, but

275

sinners continued in their unbelief to their own destruction: " 'There is no peace,' says the LORD, 'for the wicked' " (v. 22).

Reflections: Isaiah 40–48

In Isaiah 40–48 we have seen the development of a number of motifs: the good news of the kingdom, God's sovereignty over the nations (Cyrus, the fall of Babylon), redemption from the misery of exile, restoration to service, and the promise of participation in a new and glorious era. The prophet encourages the people of God with the good news that the Creator-Redeemer-King cares for sinners and that their future is completely in his hands. His favor is free, and his redemption is complete. This redemption extends the benefits of God himself to the people by promising them his *shalom*.

In the postexilic era the remnant from the twelve tribes experienced some of these benefits, yet they, too, longed for a greater revelation of God's salvation. Before the birth of our Lord, Mary and Zechariah gave beautiful expression to the hope of the godly, as did Simeon and Anna after his birth (Luke 1:46–55, 67–79; 2:29–32, 36–38). Their witness confirmed that the hope of Israel and of the Gentiles lies in Jesus the Messiah. Even the angels sang his praises, "Glory to God in the highest, and on earth peace to men on whom his favor rests" (Luke 2:14). Our Lord proclaimed the good news that all who believe in him for salvation will find rest, salvation, God's favor, and *shalom* in him. Just as the restoration from exile was like a second Exodus, so the coming of Christ is like a third Exodus because he has come to lead sinners—Jews and Gentiles—into the full experience of salvation.

We, too, still await the greater fulfillment of what the prophet has declared. We, too, still live in exile, watch for the fall of Babylon (see Rev. 17:1–19:8), and long for the full restoration. The prophecy of Isaiah remains highly relevant; it testifies that God is sovereign over the nations, that he is faithful in delivering his people from exile and in renewing covenant with them, that all the promises of God are confirmed in Jesus Christ, that the Spirit is working out the restoration in individuals and in the world, and that it challenges the church of Jesus Christ to be prepared for our being called out from exile for the judgment of God upon the structures of this world and for the full revelation of his glorious kingdom on earth.

The Ministry of Restoration, 49:1–55:13

Servants of the Lord, 49:1–50:11

There can be no doubt that Yahweh's commitment to Israel continued after the Exile. Isaiah encouraged the remnant of godly Israelites and Judeans to be bound together in fidelity to Yahweh. They

SERVANT THEOLOGY IN ISAIAH

Four Servant Songs

First Song 42:1–9	Second Song 49:1–13	Third Song 50:4–11	Fourth Song 52:13–53:12
Nature: Spirit Humility Strong in Spirit Called	Word Weak Strengthened by promise Called	Instructed Submissive Strong in hope Suffers	Wise Submissive Despised Vicarious in suffering
Purpose: Kingdom of God Covenant for people Light for Gentiles	Exalted above kings Mission to Israel and light for Gentiles	Hope in God's vindication Proclamation of comfort	Rewards Victorious Justifies many Source of light Intercession

Figure 60. The Servant of the Lord in Isaiah

may not escape the ravages of war, the disgrace of exile, and the bitterness of starvation, famine, sickness, and death, because of their rebellion (50:1–3; 51:17–20). But they may look forward in faith and hope to God's renewal of his relationship with the new community. The Lord promises to renew his love and call them to the exalted status as "servants" of God (49:1, 3; chaps. 40–48).[90]

The mission of the remnant is twofold. First, they are commissioned to call ethnic Israel to participate in the new grace of God, the restoration, and the new community (49:5–6).[91] Second, they are commissioned to carry the light of God's revelation and redemption to the nations: "I will also make you a light for the Gentiles, that you may bring my salvation to the ends of the earth" (v. 6). (See figure 60.)

The success of the mission lies in Yahweh who has promised to bring in the era of restoration. To this end the prophet reminds the godly that these words of encouragement originate with God, their Creator-Redeemer (49:7; 51:13, 15). Yahweh is the covenant God of all who await his salvation (v. 23). He will risk his reputation as the Divine Warrior[92] in fulfilling his promises. So they need not fear nations or kingdoms. Yahweh will protect them as he did by the Red Sea (v. 25). The nations will again hear about his mighty acts and shudder in awe (v. 26).

Renewal of covenants   ⟶   Democratization
Greater benefits   ⟶   Greater responsibilities
Servants of God   ⟶   Mission: Witness to Israel
                                              Light to nations

Figure 61. The Era of Restoration

The era of restoration is a complete reversal from disgrace to royal splendor (49:7), from alienation to answered prayer (v. 8), from exile to restoration of the people to the land (vv. 8–9, 17–20), from being accursed to renewal of God's blessing (vv. 9–10), from divine abandonment to renewal of God's grace and compassion (v. 10). The new era consists of all acts that extend God's favor; it is "the time of my favor," "the day of salvation" (v. 8). (See figure 61.)

So miraculous will be the progress of restoration that those who have felt forsaken by Yahweh will suddenly recognize his hand in the providential ordering of their restoration to the land (49:14–21). Isaiah speaks of the Lord's compassion as being like that of a mother who may for a while leave her child, but willingly and lovingly returns to take care of her baby.

278

Can a mother forget the baby at her breast
and have no compassion on the child she has borne?
Though she may forget,
I will not forget you!

(v. 15; see vv. 13, 16)

(For the third Servant Song [50:4−11], see chap. 2: "True and False Prophets: The Prophetic Mission and Vision." Also see figure 60.)

The Good News of God's Presence, 51:1−52:12

Isaiah encouraged the small godly remnant by reminding them of their beginnings. Had not God been faithful to Abraham and Sarah (51:1−2), by the fulfillment of his promise to make a mighty nation out of them (Gen. 17:6, 16)? Small as the remnant may have been at times, such as during and after the Exile, Yahweh renews the promise to be faithful to all who "pursue righteousness and who seek the LORD" (51:1). He will renew his blessing, allowing his people to have occasion for rejoicing and song (v. 3). The Exodus from Egypt was a small occasion in comparison with the full restoration of all things. However, both the desolation upon the Egyptians and the salvation for Israel point to the power of the Divine Warrior (vv. 9−10). The godly must hope and pray that Yahweh will bring about his full salvation, his kingdom, the messianic age, and the era of restoration.

The return from exile was a token of the restoration, as Yahweh graciously delivered his people from foreign oppressors (51:1−6). Even as he announced their affliction through Isaiah and the prophets, so he also foretold the gospel,[93] the "good news" of their release from captivity, the renewal of covenant, and the greater inauguration of God's kingdom on earth.

How beautiful on the mountains
are the feet of those who bring good news,
who proclaim peace,
who bring good tidings,
who proclaim salvation,
who say to Zion,
"Your God reigns!"

(52:7)[94]

The Lord did return to his people after the Exile[95] and extend his mercy to them. His people responded with joy as they witnessed with their own eyes the inauguration of restoration (vv. 8−10).[96] Those who believed waited for the Lord, lived in hope of his salvation, and prepared themselves by not being too deeply rooted in the economic, social, and political soil of Babylon. The life of faith continually responds to the prophetic-apostolic call not to become entangled in the structures of this world but to cling to the Lord our Redeemer (vv. 11–12).[97]

The Servant of the Lord, 52:13–53:12[98]

The paradigm of the ministry of reconciliation lies in the work of the Suffering Servant. Everything the servants of the Lord receive by grace is theirs by virtue of the vicarious work of the Servant. Who is the Servant? (See figure 60.) From the revelation of God in the incarnate Son, it is apparent that the Servant is none other than Jesus the Messiah.[99] This portion of the prophetic word points beyond Israel as the servant of the Lord to the Messiah. The Messiah is the wisdom (52:13; 53:9; Jer. 23:5), the glory (52:13), and the kingdom of God (v. 15).[100]

The kingdom of Jesus Christ is not of this world. The kings and nations were astonished at his kingship (53:1–2). He was exalted only after he had been rejected by this world (vv. 3,4) and had suffered for the sake of others (vv. 4–6). His vicarious suffering was in total obedience to the Father (v. 7). More than that, he died because the Father willed it (v. 10). Through his obedience to the Father, even to death, the Servant obtained power, glory, and dominion. All the blessings of the covenant promises are secure in him (vv. 10–12). Through him, the new community—the "many"—will be justified and glorified (v. 11).[101]

The Covenant of Peace, 54:1–55:13

The new covenant is known as "my covenant of peace," as it confirms the promise of full restoration (*shalom*) of all things (54:10). This covenant incorporates all the promises of God: *Creation* covenant—care and blessing (vv. 9–10);[102] *Abrahamic* covenant—numerical explosion of the covenant community (vv. 1–3), the inclusion of children; *Mosaic* covenant—consecration to the Lord (vv. 5–7), compassion and everlasting kindness (vv. 7–8), the democratization of the new community ("taught by the LORD," v. 13); and *Davidic* covenant—the enjoyment of a state of glory, blessing, and divine presence (vv. 11–12), the establishment of a state of peace and righteousness (vv. 13–17), and the vindication of enemies (v. 17). The renewal of covenant, grace, and restoration itself is anchored in the work of the Suffering Servant. Because of his obedience and because of the Father's reward, there is hope for the new community (chap. 54).

The prophet invited the people to freely receive the fullness of God's goodness, referred to in terms of a banquet (55:1–2; see 25:6).[103] The repetition of the invitation in so many forms impresses the urgency of response (55:1–3). The prophetic call resembles that of the teacher of wisdom who invites, beckons, and encourages the pursuit of divine wisdom as more desirable than gold, silver, and health (Prov. 9:1–12;

see 2:4–8). It offers fellowship with the Lord as the basis for responsible service.

Invitation to the royal banquet also entails an invitation to high office. Everyone is invited to be a leader of the nations, even as David had been. The Lord had promised his love to David (*ḥaṣᵉdē david,* 55:3; see 2 Sam. 7:8–16), and by elevating each member of the new community to the glorious status of being a Davidite, he democratizes his love and the privileges associated with the Davidic covenant (55:3–5).[104] Participation is not based on requirements that only a few may achieve, but involves all who respond to the Lord's gracious invitation (vv. 6–7).[105] The lofty invitation to participate in God's kingdom may seem unwarranted because of man's sinful condition. How can God trust disgraced, hardened, and rebellious sinners in high office? God gives no answer to this question; instead he declares that his wisdom is beyond man's comprehension (vv. 8–9; see Rom. 11:33–36). God's promises are true, and he will accomplish the fullness of redemption as a part of the new creation (vv. 10–13).[106]

Responsibility Toward and Certainty of the Glorious Kingdom, 56:1–66:24[107]

The New Community, 56:1–58:14

The new community consists of the descendants of Abraham and Jacob who seek the Lord, the kingdom of God, and the full deliverance ("righteousness") that he alone provides. The Lord challenges them to practice their faith and bring in God's kingdom by responsible and royal leadership.

> Maintain justice
>> and do what is right,
> for my salvation is close at hand
>> and my righteousness will soon be revealed.
>> (56:1)[108]

Faith in action also relates to Sabbath observance. The Sabbath was the sign of the Mosaic covenant (Ex. 31:13–17) and expressed submission to the will of God. The Sabbath is emphasized, therefore, not for its own sake but as an expression of loyalty. God will reward those who are loyal to him,

> who *bind themselves* to the LORD
>> to *serve* him,
> to *love* the name of the LORD,
>> and to *worship* him,
> all who *keep the Sabbath* without desecrating it
>> and who *hold fast to my covenant.*
>> (56:6–8, emphasis mine)[109]

281

All who submit to God's rule are blessed (56:2−7) and constitute the new community (v. 8), "a house of prayer for all nations" (56:7).[110] God's blessing extends to Gentiles, too, as they submit themselves to his radical demands (vv. 6−7).[111]

But God will judge all who destroy or corrupt his kingdom. Israel's watchmen had been blind (56:10), had obstructed God's kingdom (57:1), and were bound by religious forms. Their practices were lewd, idolatrous, and filled with magic and mantic (vv. 3−11). Therefore, the Lord was angry with them and declared that in his judgment, he would not hear their cries for mercy. The wicked will never enter into God's "peace" (vv. 20−21).

God has compassion on the remnant (57:13). They will share in his redemption, restoration, and the establishment of his kingdom (v. 14). Even more than that, they will live in the presence of the great King.

> For this is what the high and lofty One says—
>   he who lives forever, whose name is holy:
> "I live in a high and holy place,
>   but also with him who is contrite and lowly in spirit,
> to revive the spirit of the lowly
>   and to revive the heart of the contrite."
>
> (v. 15)

He promises to heal (vv. 18−19), that is, to extend to them his presence, guidance, comfort, joy, and the promise, "Peace, peace, to those far and near" (v. 19). *Peace* denotes the full restoration and enjoyment of the covenant privileges, as defined in the covenant of peace (54:10).

True godliness is expressed in *orthopraxis* ("right practices," or true religion, as defined in James 1:27). Theocentric ethics includes a concern for God's creatures, for justice, and for compassion. This kind of orthopraxis receives God's blessing (56:2) and communion (58:9), whereas anyone who observes pious practices (prayer and fasting) for their own sake will never enter into God's kingdom (1:10−17; 58:1−6).[112] Isaiah's teaching is identical to that of our Lord in the Sermon on the Mount. He blessed the meek, those who seek the kingdom of righteousness, justice, and peace (Matt. 5:3−10), but rejected sacrifices, prayer, and fasting done for the sake of human beings (vv. 23−26; 6:5−24).

The presence of the kingdom (and in fact the closeness of the reality of God's kingdom) is contingent on the response of individuals (58:10−13). How great will be the joy of God's people and how great will be their light, glory, and fullness of redemption if only the righteous remnant will respond in fidelity (v. 14)!

Sin, Confession, and Redemption, 59:1–60:22

The Lord is able and can respond to our prayers at any time (59:1), but the sins and rebellious ways of his children interfere with his redemption (vv. 2–8; see 58:10–14). Sin in the community of believers has a darkening effect because the reality and blessedness of the covenant are hidden as if by a cloud (v. 9). The search for deliverance, answered prayer, fullness of blessing, and the reality of the kingdom will not come unless God's people practice justice and righteousness (vv. 11–15).

Human beings could not and did not produce this kind of kingdom life, but thanks be to the Lord, who has stepped in again and again when his people have failed (59:16–17).[113] The Divine Warrior, who rules in judgment and in deliverance (vv. 18–21), will establish his kingdom (vv. 20–21). Truly, God will be with his people as he renews covenant with them and gives his Spirit to them and to their children (vv. 20–21). The prophet compares the fullness of salvation and the presence of God to "light" and the revelation of "the glory of the LORD" to his people (60:1–2). So evident will be his magnificent kingdom that the nations will seek its blessings (v. 3) and join in advancing it (vv. 5–10).

> This promise led Paul to reflect on the mystery of the Gentile inclusion and the Jewish rejection of the Messiah (Rom. 9–11). He agonized over the tension of God's promises to Israel, his fidelity, the Gentile inclusion, and the hardening of Israel. Had not Isaiah proclaimed, "He shall come as a redeemer to Zion, to those in Jacob who turn back from their sin" (Isa. 59:20 JPS)? God's people had prayed, "Oh, that salvation for Israel would come out of Zion! When the LORD restores the fortunes of his people" (Ps. 14:7). His hope is rooted in the prophetic message of the inclusion of Israel and Gentiles, but this cannot mean the exclusion of the Jews, as he reflects on a conflation of Isaiah 59:20 and Psalm 14:7: "The deliverer will come from Zion; he will turn godlessness away from Jacob." Paul faced the tension of the reality of the gospel of the kingdom in Christ and the dissonance of fulfillment. The apostle did not resolve the tension, nor did he explain the manner of fulfillment. In the end he, too, submits himself to the wisdom of God, "Oh, the depth of the riches of the wisdom and knowledge of God! . . . For from him and through him and to him are all things. To him be the glory forever! Amen" (Rom. 11:33, 36).[114]

The state of transformation creates an era of peace and prosperity (60:11–14). Zion will be known as "the City of the LORD, Zion of the Holy One of Israel" (v. 14) and will be full of joy, peace, and righteousness (vv. 15–17; see Rev. 21:1–5, 21–27). Gone will be the days of disgrace and alienation. Instead, the walls of the city will be known as "Salvation," its gates as "Praise" (v. 18), and the Lord himself will be present (vv. 19–20).

Redemption focuses on Zion, or as Buber observed, it is Zion-centric: "The renewal of the world and the renewal of Zion are one and the same thing, for Zion is the heart of the renewed world."[115] All the citizens of this city, the New Jerusalem, share in a common salvation and in God's rich blessings (60:21). Each will share in the joy of the Lord and in his spiritual and material existence (vv. 21–22). Further, the Lord promises to bring in the reality of his kingdom "swiftly" (v. 22).

Hope in the Reality of the Kingdom, 61:1–63:6

Isaiah and the prophets have prepared the way for our Lord by speaking in the power of the Spirit of the Sovereign Lord (61:1; see also 50:4).[116] They have spoken regarding judgment and deliverance: "the year of the LORD's favor and the day of vengeance of our God" (v. 2).[117] The good news of God is always good news to those who have not found deliverance and meaning in the structures of human society. They are the mourners, the poor, the oppressed in spirit who hunger and thirst for divine deliverance. The gospel is the good news that God knows their affliction and that he will make right whatever is wrong. The good news also consists of the message that God renews his love in a grander fashion than ever before (vv. 2–5), even permitting their service as "priests of the LORD" (v. 6).

The outcasts of human kingdoms receive citizenship in the kingdom of God! Great is the Lord's love, and great will be the transformation from disgrace to glory and from sorrow to joy. He will renew his covenant with the godly and with their descendants (61:8–9) so that all will be blessed, rejoicing in his provision of "garments of salvation" and "a robe of righteousness" that will be the full establishment of his kingdom in blessing, glory, and protection (vv. 9–11).[118]

The prophet vowed not to keep silent until the fullness of redemption is here. He prayed for the *shalom* of God's people, the coming of God's kingdom in righteousness, salvation, and the evidence of God's delight ("Hephzibah" and "Beulah," 62:1–4).

Further, he even posted watchmen to wait for signs of the new age. Thus he called on the godly to join in prayer, anticipate the day of redemption, and not find peace in the structures of political reality.

> You who call on the LORD,
>   give yourselves no rest,
> and give him no rest till he establishes Jerusalem

> and makes her the praise of the earth.
> (62:6–7)

The certainty of the full establishment of his kingdom lies in the divine promise. The Lord has sworn to redeem and to reward his people when he comes to establish his kingdom on earth.

> See, your Savior comes!
> See, his reward is with him,
>   and his recompense accompanies him.
> (62:11; see 40:10)

The citizens of his kingdom are members of Zion.

> They will be called the Holy People,
>   the Redeemed of the LORD;
> and you will be called Sought After,
>   the City No Longer Deserted.
> (62:12)

With all the emphasis on the glorious hope of God's people, one may tend to forget that the other side of the year of favor is the day of vindication. There can be no lasting favor unless the Lord rid the earth of evil and opposition to his kingdom. To this end, these verses assure the godly that Yahweh is the Divine Warrior who will come "in splendor" and "in the greatness of his strength" (63:1) against the nations on "the day of vengeance" (v. 4).[119] He will accomplish this. The Apocalypse clarifies that the Divine Warrior is none other than the Lamb, who will come on a white horse to subjugate all enemies, including Satan (Rev. 19:11–20; 20:11–15).

The Prayer of the Godly and God's Response, 63:7–66:24

The godly remnant praise the Lord for his "kindnesses" (63:7). He has established a Father-son relationship, identifying with their distresses, loving them, having compassion on them, carrying them through crises, being present in his Holy Spirit, and manifesting his glorious and royal power on their behalf as in Egypt (vv. 8–14). In the reality and anguish of exile the numbers of the godly community also confess their sin. They share in a history of grieving the Spirit of God (v. 10) and praying that their Father in heaven will again show mercy on his children (vv. 15–16) and restore them speedily and fully in spite of their history of sin (63:17–19). They look with great anticipation to another theophany: the appearance of God's kingdom in glory (64:1–2). They wait for him to act (v. 4), confessing their unworthiness (vv. 5–7), while believing that he is still their heavenly Father (v. 8). They wonder whether the Lord will continue the exile and devastation of Jerusalem (vv. 9–12), but in the final question there is a quiet confidence that

285

Yahweh will act: "Will you keep silent and punish us beyond measure?" (v. 12).

Yahweh's response is fourfold. First, he has revealed himself in the past, and he has presented himself repeatedly to his people, saying, "Here am I, here am I," like a Father expecting his children to return to his arms (65:1). Instead, the Lord's children did as they wished and got their just deserts (vv. 3–7).

Second, the Lord still has a plan for the godly. The prophet likens the godly to the good grapes that are saved for the purpose of blessing (65:8). The Lord promises to restore "his servants" (i.e., his loyal remnant). Exile and judgment must separate the righteous from the wicked because the future bliss of God's people is reserved for his children alone. His children consist only of "my people who seek me" (v. 10). They will live, enjoy the Lord's good earth, eat, drink, receive a blessing and a new name, and be filled with joy (vv. 9–10, 13–16). The disgrace of exile ("the past troubles" or "the former things")[120] will be forgotten (vv. 16–17), and instead, they will share in the era of newness, the "new heavens and a new earth" and a New Jerusalem (vv. 17–18).[121] The main element of newness lies in the Lord's renewed joy in his people so that he, their Father, will respond to their prayer (v. 24) and bless their lives, livelihood, and families with peace and prosperity (vv. 20–25). These promises are not to be viewed as eschatological in the narrow sense, that is, as belonging to the era of consummation. Calvin rightly applies them in the broad sense as intrusions of the new era from the postexilic era of restoration to the present. He writes,

> Yet the Prophet speaks of the restoration . . . after the return from Babylon. This is undoubtedly true; but that restoration is imperfect, if it be not extended as far as to Christ; and even now we are in the progress and accomplishment of it, and those things will not be fulfilled till the last resurrection.[122]

Third, the Lord blesses those who yearn for his kingdom, who seek him as the ultimate good. Though his kingdom extends to all creation (66:1–2),[123] he promises to be present with the humble.

> This is the one I esteem:
> he who is humble and contrite in spirit,
> and trembles at my word.
> (v. 2, see v. 5)

The humble are those who listen to him by doing his will and by hoping in the full establishment of his kingdom. They "fear" him and his word.

The Lord will see to it that his kingdom will come into being and that Zion will be established even amidst toil, like a woman who gives birth to a child (66:7–8).[124] Yahweh encourages his people to hope and long for joy because he has brought Zion to the moment of birth, and *he* will deliver (vv. 9–10). The godly prayed to the Lord as their Father, and he responds with the compassion of a mother.[125] Therefore, they have reason for joy.

> Rejoice with Jerusalem and be glad for her,
>   all you who love her;
> rejoice greatly with her,
>   all you who mourn over her.
> For you will nurse and be satisfied
>   at her comforting breasts;
> you will drink deeply
>   and delight in her overflowing abundance."
> For this is what the LORD says:
> "I will extend peace to her like a river,
>   and the wealth of nations like a flooding stream;
> you will nurse and be carried on her arm
>   and dandled on her knees.
> As a mother comforts her child,
>   so will I comfort you;
> and you will be comforted over Jerusalem.
>   (vv. 10–13)

Fourth, the Day of the Lord is an ever-present reality. His people need not be afraid (66:14), for he will avenge himself of his enemies on the day of his coming (vv. 15–16). Isaiah clarifies that Gentiles, too, may participate in the covenant fellowship. They, too, may serve the Lord and enter into his glorious kingdom (vv. 18–21, 23). Jews and Gentiles may enjoy forever the bliss of "the new heavens and the new earth" (v. 22). But the wicked will be slain on the day of battle, and their corpses will be rotting with maggots eating away without ceasing. What a picture of hell (v. 24)!

REFLECTIONS ON ISAIAH, THE EVANGELICAL PROPHET

The prophecy of Isaiah played a major role in the postexilic era.[126] The remnant of Israel and Judah had longed for the glory, the freedom, the prosperity, and the peace that Isaiah associated with the new era of restoration. These prophecies inspired them to establish a new theocracy under the dynamic leadership of Zerubbabel and Joshua, under Haggai and Zechariah, under Malachi, Ezra, and Nehemiah. Though they were the objects of covenant renewal, of God's grace, and of the working of the Spirit of God in their midst, the full glory of Zion remained distant.

The scope of the book takes us beyond Isaiah's days and beyond the days of the postexilic reconstruction to the new heaven and the new earth. The prophecy spans the era from Isaiah till the final consummation as it unfolds God's plan for the redemption of his people. The meaning of the name *Isaiah* ("salvation is of the Lord" or "Yahweh is salvation") sums up the prophecy: Yahweh delivers! The godly may experience God's peace, righteousness, love, justice, and fidelity here and now, yet they await a greater fulfillment in the full establishment of God's kingdom at his appointed time.

It is small wonder that our Lord explains his ministry in terms of the prophecy of Isaiah. In his ministry he brings in more fully the restoration, and his gospel is the good news that Jesus is the fulfiller of the promises (Luke 4:16–21). His ministry of suffering is a vicarious identification with the remnant in fulfillment of the servant passages, especially that of the Suffering Servant (Isa. 52:13–53:12; see Luke 24:44–47). In his present and future ministry, our Lord is working out God's plan of extending his kingdom to the earth, of caring for his children, of inaugurating the full deliverance from the bondage of this world, of renewing all things (creation and a redeemed community), and of subjugating rebels to himself. Every aspect of this prophecy relates to the ministry of our Lord in the past, present, and future. This also means that the prophecy of Isaiah is most relevant for the Christian, as Oswalt writes, "If the book is read in its wholeness today it will continue to unite the two Testaments as no other book can."[127]

Truly salvation is of the Lord. This is the essence of the gospel found throughout the prophecy. Salvation in Isaiah has two aspects: (1) victorious vindication of the righteous remnant, and (2) disgrace of and vengeance on the ungodly. The prophecy inspires the righteous with a vision of the new creation and the New Jerusalem while motivating them to greater loyalty and acts of righteousness, love, and justice.[128] They cannot bring in the fullness of God's kingdom, but they can prepare themselves for the holy and glorious era of transformation.[129]

Salvation is not limited to the Jewish people. Isaiah, as the "evangelical" prophet, speaks also to the Gentiles. As we read the book of Isaiah, we must keep in mind that we, too, are the beneficiaries of the salvation of which the prophet speaks. However, the inclusion of the Gentiles in God's plan of salvation does not exclude the Jews from redemption or from a special place in God's kingdom program (see Rom. 9–11).[130] Regardless of our background or ethnic origin, the new community in Christ is included in the promises of Yahweh's salvation.

QUESTIONS AND ISSUES

1. What is the historical context of Isaiah's ministry? What major crises in the history of Israel and Judah did he witness?

2. How did the vision of Yahweh's holiness and glory (chap. 6) transform Isaiah and affect his ministry? How does theophany function in the prophecy?

3. Explain how chapters 1–12 are held together by the common motifs of the Day of the Lord, judgment, hope, holiness, glory, and the kingdom of God. How do these motifs relate to each other?

4. Compare and contrast Isaiah's perspective on Judah's apostasy and on her restoration (chaps. 1–5; 24–27).

5. How do the meanings of the names (Isaiah, Shear-Jashub, Immanuel, and Maher-Shalal-Hash-Baz) function as "signs and wonders" to Israel?

6. What was Isaiah's vision of the kingdom of God in contrast to human kingdoms as to its nature and purpose? How do the Messiah and the messianic kingdom fulfill all the qualities of the kingdom of God?

7. What is Isaiah's vision of the new community as developed throughout the prophecy?

8. What are the two aspects of the Day of the Lord? Explain the nature of vengeance and the objects of God's wrath (see chaps. 2; 13–24). What is the nature of his "favor," and who are the objects of his favor?

9. In the light of the above question, how are we to interpret the specific references to the nations mentioned in chapters 13–23?

10. What is God's purpose for and what are his expectations of his transformed people? How is God's purpose for the new Israel more exalted after the Exile? How do the servant passages relate to the messianic community and to the Messiah?

11. How did Cyrus fulfill God's expectations, and how is he an encouragement to the postexilic community?

12. What is Isaiah's concept of the new covenant as to the relations, subjects, benefits, and expectations? How does this renewal relate to the previous covenants?

13. Explain the paradox of divine sovereignty (freedom) and human responsibility in bringing about the era of restoration.

14. What is the nature of Zion (the New Jerusalem) in Isaiah? For this answer you have to extrapolate from discussions and allusions found throughout Isaiah. How is Zion a present and yet a future reality?

CHAPTER 10

The Message of Jeremiah

INTRODUCTION

The book of Jeremiah is most rewarding and at the same time most puzzling. It is rewarding proportionately to the effort expended on the study of the prophetic person, the literary form, and the historical context of the prophet's ministry. Each aspect of this study gives an insight into the prophecy, but when taken together, they draw the reader into an empathetic understanding of the prophetic person and his message.

The experiences of Jeremiah and the composition of his book speak of the trauma resulting from the dissolution of one era and of the hope in a new era. Jeremiah is a prophet of destruction and construction, of analysis and synthesis, of old and new. The tensions inherent in the book are those of the prophet and of his time.

The book of Jeremiah opens itself up through an attentive study of (1) the literary form and structure, (2) Jeremiah's suffering, (3) the crises in redemptive history, and (4) his vision of the new era.

LITERARY FORM AND STRUCTURE

The prophecy of Jeremiah with its inner tensions has the watermark of its author. The reader is immediately impressed by the literary magnificence and poetic passion of the prophet.[1] But interest cannot be easily maintained, due to sheer frustration with the material itself. The book has no apparent chronological or topical organization.[2] It is full of movement, yet it lacks direction. Getting swept away by the emotional and literary tidal waves, the reader can eventually be left feeling cast adrift.

Form and Structure

Jeremiah contains a complex and puzzling web of judgment speech, oracles against the nations, salvation oracles, hymns, (auto)biographical materials, symbolic acts,[3] object lessons,[4] and historical narratives. The prophecy has many linking devices, parallelism, repetition,[5] alliteration, assonance,[6] and metaphors.

Jeremiah employs such a unique combination of prose and poetry[7] that critics in the past resolved the differences in favor of two separate traditions. Yet the book of Jeremiah does not lend itself easily to formal literary classifications. Jeremiah reflects a deep love for the theological and literary heritage of Israel and Judah but remains free in the manner of communication. His literary artistry evokes an emotive reaction in the reader[8] because of the prophet's creative use of the literary heritage.[9] Jeremiah freely related to the theological emphasis of Deuteronomy, to the approach that Hebraic wisdom offers, and to the literary forms of his day (i.e., lament genre). All in all he shows himself a creative and literate poet.[10]

Collection of Collections

Jeremiah is a collection of anthologies. Several are clearly defined, but others overlap, remaining puzzling and somewhat elusive. There is

TABLE 10. CHRONOLOGY OF JEREMIAH

PERIODS OF PROPHETIC MINISTRY

627–622		608–605			593–586		586–585
627	609		603	597		586	

Major events:

Call	Josiah's death	Babylonian invasion	Babylonian deportation	Babylonian exile

Kings of Judah:

Josiah (640–609)	Jehoahaz (609)	Jehoiakim (608–598)	Jehoiachin (598–597)	Zedekiah (597–586)

little consensus on the formation of the collection of the Jeremiah material. It appears that the prophetic book is composed of "collections of prophetic sayings and other material which have a long and complex history of transmission behind them. The more carefully one studies them, the more apparent this becomes."[11] The differences between the Hebrew and the Greek text are significant and further aggravate the difficulty of ascertaining the literary form and composition of Jeremiah.[12]

The variety in the literary units and in themes has led many to distinguish three distinct stages in the formation of the present work: the words of Jeremiah, the post-Jeremiah traditions, and a Deuteronomic redaction.[13] Rhetorical analysis,[14] with its goal of understanding the literary units from within,[15] has replaced form-critical analysis with its exclusive attention to units and external criteria. On the basis of rhetorical analysis Jeremiah appears to be shaped chronologically and thematically:[16]

I. Prophecies and poems of Jeremiah, chaps. 1–20
II. Historical narratives from the time of Jehoiakim and Zedekiah, chaps. 21–36
III. Events immediately prior to and following the fall of Jerusalem, chaps. 37–45
IV. Oracles against the nations, chaps. 46–51
V. Historical appendix, chap. 52

The literary blocks were collected during the life of the prophet and after his death. It is possible to fix as many as four distinct periods of ministry in relation to the collections: (1) the early years under Josiah (627–622 B.C.); (2) the early years under Jehoiakim (608–605 B.C.); (3) from the fourth year of Zedekiah till the fall of Jerusalem (593–586 B.C.); and (4) from Jerusalem's fall till Jeremiah's stay in Egypt (586–585 B.C.). (See table 10.)

By 605 B.C. (36:1) Jeremiah began to fix the oral message in writing (chaps. 1–20 or chaps. 1–25). What the original scroll looked like we may never know, but we do know that Jeremiah wrote two editions at God's command. The first edition was written on the scroll that Jehoiakim had cut up and burned. The second scroll (chaps. 1–25) developed more extensively the judgment oracles as a result of Jehoiakim's brazen act of destroying the first collection (chap. 36).[17]

The second major division (chaps. 26–52) is also an anthology of anthologies. It contains collections of material written in the third person, autobiographical materials, the book of consolation (chaps. 30–33), and the oracles against the nations (chaps. 46–51). The last chapter may be an addition. Chapter 51 ends with a concluding statement, "Jeremiah had written on a scroll about all the disasters that would come upon Babylon—all that had been recorded concerning Babylon"

(v. 60). Moreover, verse 64 reads, "The words of Jeremiah end here." The "appendix" (chap. 52) closely resembles 2 Kings 24:18–25:30 and may have been added to serve as a canonical witness that Jeremiah's message of judgment and exile had come true and to foster the hope that his oracles of salvation and restoration would equally come true.[18]

The present canonical shaping reflects an affinity with the exilic setting, a time of upheaval. The Exile had a dramatic effect on Israel and Judah, and the book of Jeremiah reflects the chaotic times in which the prophecy received its final, canonical shape. Whoever gave the final shape to the book was inspired by the Spirit to give the generation of the Exile an anthology of Jeremiah's preaching and life.[19] It also provided the new generation a record of the reasons for the Exile and a glimpse of Yahweh's plan of restoration.[20]

JEREMIAH AS THE SUFFERING SERVANT OF GOD

We know virtually nothing about Jeremiah's life before his call. He was of priestly lineage and hailed from Anathoth in Benjamin (1:1; see 11:21, 23; 29:27; 32:7–9), a Levitical city a few miles north of Jerusalem. The Lord called him to be his prophet, and his ministry extended from the early years of King Josiah (627 B.C.)[21] till well after the fall of Jerusalem (586 B.C.). For a period of more than forty years Jeremiah was severely tested, but he remained faithful to the Lord.[22]

The very nature of Jeremiah, the man of God, is stamped on the book. He is a man of paradox, and his life testifies to the paradox of faith. He lived in the constant tension between God's judgment in alienation and the promise of the new era of transformation.

Jeremiah: The New Moses

In a period of international and national crises, Jeremiah was called to be God's ambassador "to the nations" (1:5)[23] with a twofold commission: to proclaim the end of the old era and to announce the beginning of a new era. The Lord said to him, "See, today I appoint you over nations and kingdoms to uproot and tear down, to destroy and overthrow, to build and to plant" (v. 10).[24] Jeremiah's preaching applied the curses of the Mosaic covenant, and by that he closed one stage of the Mosaic era. (See figure 62.)

Jeremiah was a "new" Moses in that he announced the end of the Mosaic era and the beginning of a new era. Jeremiah, like Moses, questioned his being chosen to be God's servant, readily dialogued with the Lord, interceded for God's people, and fulfilled his mission.[25] He fully stood in the covenant tradition while affirming God's freedom in fulfilling his promises and in applying the curses of the covenant. Unlike Moses, Jeremiah had a ministry characterized more by condemnation

(11:1–14) than by mediation. He declared that God's patience had come to an end and that the Lord would appear (theophany) to his people in judgment. Unlike Moses, he was God's spokesman against the people, proclaiming God's wrath on the people of the covenant. His words were Yahweh's arrows of fire that set the people ablaze like dry wood (5:14).

| Moses: | Curses of the covenant |
| | Renewal of the covenant |

| | Jeremiah, the new Moses: | Reality of the curses |
| | | Annunciation of a new age |

Figure 62. Moses and Jeremiah

Jeremiah loved God's people and wanted to intercede for them (14:7, 20), but his was a mission of death. He had to speak of starvation, death, exile, and alienation. The prophet could not escape experiencing the pangs of exile before it happened. The Lord even prohibited him from praying for Judah (15:1). Instead, he called on Jeremiah to repent.

> If you repent, I will restore you
>   that you may serve me;
> if you utter worthy, not worthless, words,
>   you will be my spokesman.
> Let this people turn to you,
>   but you must not turn to them.
>   (15:19)

Jeremiah's loneliness was heightened by the prohibition against marriage (16:2–4). The only encouragement in his lonely mission was the Lord's reassurance of his presence.

> I will make you a wall to this people,
>   a fortified wall of bronze;
> they will fight against you
>   but will not overcome you,
> for I am with you
>   to rescue and save you. . . .
> I will save you from the hands of the wicked
>   and redeem you from the grasp of the cruel.
>   (15:20–21; see 1:18–19)

The prophet stood between God and the people. Judgment was inevitable, and his prayers for his people would go unanswered (7:16;

11:14; 14:11) because of the greatness of Judah's sin (9:2). In spite of all his suffering, Jeremiah loved the rebellious nation of Judah. He was called to be God's strong man, even though he was like wax within. He consoled himself in his personal lament, praying silently for God's people,

> Oh, that my head were a spring of water
>> and my eyes a fountain of tears!
> I would weep day and night
>> for the slain of my people. . . .
> I will weep in secret
>> because of your pride;
> my eyes will weep bitterly,
>> overflowing with tears,
> because the LORD's flock will be taken captive.
>> (9:1; 13:17)

Jeremiah, the new Moses, is a dramatic figure. Like Moses, he could not lead the remnant into the era of restoration. Like Moses, he left a literary composition as a testimony to the new era that he could not enter.[26] Like Moses, he was an eschatological prophet.

Jeremiah's Confessions

Jeremiah, forsaken and rejected by people, experienced many setbacks during his lengthy ministry, but he gradually adjusted to being a loner. Kings, leaders, priests, and false prophets opposed him. His "confessions" draw us into the personality of the prophet and into his dialogical communion with his God.[27] In these confessions, unlike the confessions of Saint Augustine, Jeremiah did not confess his life of sin, conversion, and growth in grace.[28] They are in the form of lament (soliloquies) by which he—like the psalmists and our Lord Jesus in the Garden—struggled with God's will.[29] The laments draw attention to a deeply felt sense of alienation.[30] Jeremiah contended with himself, with his God, and with the perfidy of humans.

What is the function of these soliloquies? Many different answers have been given to this question.[31] It appears that the prophet's suffering is a means of identifying himself with the suffering,[32] disgrace, and alienation of the godly in exile. In Jeremiah, the suffering servant of God and the spokesman of God are one.[33] His distress is vicarious in the sense that he bridges the gap between the old era and the new era, between curse and blessing, between despair and hope, between abandonment and promise. Jeremiah had to cope with the necessity of the end of the old era (the temple, monarchy, and covenant), the intensity of God's wrath, and his longing for the new era. He is a pilgrim in his own land, awaiting God's desolation and the renewal of his kingdom on earth. Accordingly, Jeremiah became a paradigm for all who suffer and await the fullness of restoration.[34]

Jeremiah's confessions lead to a realistic view of this world and to a transforming vision of the kingdom of God. On the one hand, he agonized over the desolation, disgrace, humiliation, suffering, and exile before the new era could be ushered in.[35] On the other hand, the prophet rejoiced in the prospect of God's righteousness and justice and in his plan for purification, renewal, and restoration. His anguish has helped God's people to develop hope amidst struggle, resulting from the tension of the ending of the old age and the beginning of the new age. In this regard, Jeremiah experienced the agony of longing for the new age, as did Paul (Rom. 8:18–21). Similarly, the confessions of Jeremiah and Paul's magnificent insights into his personal struggles (7:14–25)[36] and his prophetic anguish for Israel (chaps. 9–11) have emboldened the people of God to endure persecution and hardship. Jeremiah remains an encouragement[37] to the godly remnant in any age that the only way "to withstand the erosive effects of timidity, anguish, helplessness, hostility, loneliness, despair, misunderstanding, and failure"[38] is in communion with God and in hope of the coming restoration. The soliloquies have helped the godly through the ages to join with the prophet in his lament, in his experience of alienation and anguish, and in his renewed sense of mission and vision.

Yet the confessions should not be construed so as to lead one to believe that Jeremiah was timid about his mission. As God's prophet he boldly proclaimed the word of God. But this word was not easy, nor did he take his task lightly. He experienced God's word as a fire (5:14; 20:9; 23:29), a "hammer that breaks a rock in pieces" (23:29), and an overpowering force (20:7, 9).[39] He struggled with the God he served, and God prevailed.[40]

The soliloquies witness to God's freedom in fulfilling his word and in vindicating the prophet and his message. With this background we may now consider the five soliloquies of Jeremiah (11:18–12:6; 15:10–21; 17:12–18; 18:18–23; 20:7–18).[41]

11:18–12:6

Jeremiah lamented over the betrayal of his friends and family in Anathoth. They considered him an embarrassment to the community and intimidated him by saying, "Do not prophesy in the name of the LORD or you will die by our hands" (11:21). Jeremiah felt like a sheep being led to the slaughter (v. 19).

He asked how a righteous Yahweh could put up with an unrighteous nation and why the wicked prospered. The prosperity of the wicked was an impediment to Jeremiah because their well-being frustrated his message. For about twenty-five years he had been God's faithful prophet of judgment. But nothing had happened to Judah. Instead tragedy had come to God's prophet. The Lord assured Jeremiah of judgment on *his* day, "the year of their punishment" (11:23). He called on Jeremiah not to be so easily intimidated and challenged him not to worry about former friends and family members. He must be prepared to live a lonely life (12:5–6), awaiting God's righteous judgment, even when it involves suffering and persecution.

15:10–21[42]

Jeremiah asked the Lord why he should continue his mission since Yahweh had already determined to destroy his people.[43] He affirmed his loyalty to Yahweh and his delight in proclaiming his word (vv. 16–17) but lamented his pain, alienation, and persecution (vv. 17–18). It seemed to him that Yahweh was unpredictable (v. 18).

Yahweh called on Jeremiah to repent from his charge of perfidy (v. 19). Without explaining the delay of fulfillment, he encouraged Jeremiah to submit to his freedom. In his submission to the Lord,[44] Jeremiah would become strong like "a fortified wall of bronze" because of God's presence (v. 20).[45]

17:12–18

Suffering the agony of being faithful to the Lord and being abandoned by his people, Jeremiah turned again to his God. He could see nothing but the "terror" of those who persecuted him (vv. 17–18). The conflict arising from his doctrine of his God and his experience occupied his thoughts. He believed that Yahweh is King and rightfully can judge his rebellious people: "A glorious throne, exalted from the beginning, is the place of our sanctuary" (v. 12; see v. 13). He also believed that Yahweh is "the hope of Israel" (v. 13). With him alone is life ("the spring of living water," v. 13) and healing from affliction (v. 14).

Caught between the tension of the delay of judgment and the hope in Yahweh's deliverance, Jeremiah felt that his words lacked power. He was bothered because fulfillment had not been accomplished, and the people taunted him by saying, "Where is the word of the LORD? Let it now be fulfilled!" (v. 15).

Jeremiah lamented God's freedom, praying for immediate vindication and justification,

> Let my persecutors be put to shame,
>   but keep me from shame;
> let them be terrified,
>   but keep me from terror.
> Bring on them the day of disaster;

destroy them with double destruction.
(v. 18).

But Yahweh was silent.

18:18–23

The attacks on Jeremiah were unrelenting. The people challenged his prophetic calling and his message. They fiercely upheld the structures of their society and the continuity of their ways (v. 18). All that Jeremiah could do was to pray for Yahweh's vindication (vv. 19–23).

20:7–18

The final complaint is the most vehement. Yahweh has not responded to his prayers for vindication. Jeremiah felt himself betrayed ("you deceived me"),[46] exploited, and persecuted (v. 7). He felt that the Lord had coerced him into service but had left his prophet to fend for himself. Jeremiah saw nothing but darkness, doom, and oppression.

> I hear many whispering,
>   "Terror on every side!
>   Report him! Let's report him!"
> All my friends
>   are waiting for me to slip, saying,
>   "Perhaps he will be deceived;
> then we will prevail over him
>   and take our revenge on him."
>   (v. 10)

The word in which Jeremiah had greatly delighted had brought him nothing but grief and caused disparagement (v. 8). Yet he confessed that God's word was like a fire burning within him.

> But if I say, "I will not mention him
>   or speak any more in his name,"
> his word is in my heart like a fire,
>   a fire shut up in my bones.
> I am weary of holding it in;
>   indeed, I cannot.
>   (v. 9).

He struggled with his God, with his mission, and with God's message.

The prophet was alone, but he had hope in Yahweh's coming as the Divine Warrior. This hope sustained him, even though it seemed an eternity for the judgment to be realized. In hope Jeremiah rejoiced in the fidelity of Yahweh and his word.[47]

> But the LORD is with me like a mighty warrior;
>   so my persecutors will stumble and not prevail.

They will fail and be thoroughly disgraced;
  their dishonor will never be forgotten.
O Lord Almighty, you who examine the righteous
  and probe the heart and mind,
let me see your vengeance upon them,
  for to you I have committed my cause.
Sing to the Lord!
  Give praise to the Lord!
He rescues the life of the needy
  from the hands of the wicked.
  (vv. 11–13)

In the midst of this magnificent high point, he renewed his lament, cursing the day of his birth (20:14–18; see Job 3:1–21). He asked why he was born for that particular time and why he had to be the bearer of bad tidings. In this soliloquy he identified himself with the suffering, reproach, trouble, and sorrow of God's people.[48]

Several other passages have a bearing on the personal grief of Jeremiah.[49] In 4:19–26 he agonized over the Lord's judgment on the land and the people.

Oh, my anguish, my anguish!
  I writhe in pain.
Oh, the agony of my heart!
  My heart pounds within me,
  I cannot keep silent.
For I have heard the sound of the trumpet;
  I have heard the battle cry.
Disaster follows disaster;
  the whole land lies in ruins.
In an instant my tents are destroyed,
  my shelter in a moment.
How long must I see the battle standard
  and hear the sound of the trumpet?
  (vv. 19–21)

Jeremiah also lamented over God's judgment (8:18–9:1). He identified with the exilic community, as they would be abandoned without comfort, healing, or God.

O my Comforter in sorrow,
  my heart is faint within me. . . .
Is there no balm in Gilead?
Is there no physician there?
Why then is there no healing
  for the wound of my people?
  (8:18, 22)

Jeremiah is moved to agony, to tears, and to soul-searching.

Since my people are crushed, I am crushed;
  I mourn, and horror grips me. . . .
Oh, that my head were a spring of water
  and my eyes a fountain of tears!
I would weep day and night
  for the slain of my people.

(v. 21; 9:1)

Conclusions

Gerhard von Rad observes that "the confessions are central for the interpretation of Jeremiah."[50] But how? First, the prophet is more than a tragic figure. He is a mediator, even when he can no longer pray for his people.[51] He is empathetic, full of love, and desires nothing but the fulfillment of God's promises for his people. In this regard, his place in redemptive history is unique. Though he served as another Moses, he is different from Moses in that he was called to be God's warrior against his children. W. L. Holladay states, "In his life and ministry Jeremiah symbolically represents that holy war which Yahweh will wage against Judah."[52]

Second, the prophet suffered, lamenting his inability to comprehend God's freedom or understand his ways.[53] He proclaimed Yahweh's freedom in abandoning the covenant, in destroying Jerusalem with its temple, and in exiling his people, but his psychology bears out his difficulty in apprehending the ways of God. Jeremiah's agony has helped God's people to find comfort in the prophet's suffering and encouragement in his hope for restoration. Living in the tension between God's judgment and promise, the prophet experienced a renewal of the vision of God. Tension can have a positive place in the lives of the godly when they submit to God, develop a living faith in the Savior, and go from faith to faith. In the tension of suffering and submission to God's freedom, the godly focus their hope in God alone. Hope focuses on the freedom of God to act anew in his time, as Crenshaw writes, "The logic of faith suggests that God has sent all the trouble that has overtaken them; therefore only one question remains. Do we dare place our hope in such a one?"

Third, Jeremiah's confessions have helped the community of faith struggle with Yahweh's promises, with the anguish of suffering, and with their need for security.[54] The godly remnant in exile lived in the conflicting experience of memories of God's loving acts in the past, the harshness of his judgment in the present, and the hope of a new future. In identifying themselves with Jeremiah's struggles, they, too, learned to rest in the righteousness and freedom of Yahweh. They had witnessed the demonstration of his righteousness in the desolation of Jerusalem and in the abandonment of his people. But they persevered in the faith

301

that their God is also free to transform judgment and curse into restoration and blessing. As long as the fullness of this new era is not realized, all God's children, like Jeremiah, remain pilgrims, awaiting the new era.

THE CRISES IN REDEMPTIVE HISTORY

The People of Judah and Israel

Jeremiah faced a hardened populace that had received God's grace over the centuries. Like Hosea, Jeremiah spoke of the redemptive acts of Yahweh's grace and love in the Exodus, wilderness, and conquest (2:1–7; 32:16–23), of God's covenant as a marriage relationship, and of Israel's idolatry as whoring after other gods (2:2–3; 3:1–3, 6–7, 9, 20). Yahweh had demonstrated his acts of fidelity (*hesed,* "love"),[55] but the people had responded with treachery, infidelity, and idolatry.

> "Be appalled at this, O heavens,
>   and shudder with great horror,"
> declares the LORD.
> "My people have committed two sins:
> They have forsaken me,
>   the spring of living water,
> and have dug their own cisterns,
>   broken cisterns that cannot hold water."
>   (2:12–13; see vv. 4–13, 20–28; 3:1–5;
>   16:10–13, 20; 22:9; 32:29; 44:2–3, 8,
>   17–19, 25)[56]

The Lord had treated his people graciously as his child (3:19), his wife (2:2; 3:14, 20; 31:32), and a "choice vine" (2:21), but they had become wild like a she-camel, a donkey (vv. 23–24), an adulterous wife (3:20).

Like Hosea 150 years earlier, Jeremiah criticized the people of God for having abandoned the covenant ideal of being a holy people, consecrated by the sanctions of divine law, called to reflect the kingdom of God in the rule of love, justice, and righteousness on earth. Jeremiah charged them with having broken faith with God. In this sense he was a critic of society,[57] but his critique was not moralistic. It arose from a deep conviction that love, justice, and righteousness are correlative with the knowledge of God and the kingdom of God on earth. Israel and Judah had failed to mirror the covenant ideal (i.e., the kingdom of God).

Jeremiah is a "testimony to the kingdom of God."[58] He complained that the whole of society was corrupt. The people of God had become like the nations around them, a community of infidels. Even worse, they did not know Yahweh (9:2–8). The leaders ("shepherds": kings, priests, false prophets, and elders) were largely to blame for this corruption;

they had become self-centered and had corrupted God's righteous and just kingdom ideals by their own ideals, by corruption of justice, and by oppression (23:1–2, 9–11; see 2:8; 10:17–22; 13:18–20).[59]

Jeremiah saw the hearts of men as he observed the atrophy of justice in society at all levels (5:1–5). The Lord had expected from his people fidelity (honesty/truth), wisdom, and the practice of godliness (vv. 1–5). Instead, graft, power, cheating, greed, and perfidy were the order of the day. The people were very religious. They believed in Yahweh, the covenants, the prerogatives of the Davidic dynasty, the manifest destiny of Judah, and the inviolability of Zion. But Jeremiah declared that their security was "false" (*šeqer*).[60] He deplored their insensitivity to justice because it revealed the lack of a real, heartfelt commitment (11:3–4; see Deut. 27:15–26). This is what Jeremiah meant by adultery (23:10–11).

Jeremiah was more than a commentator on Judean society. He was God's man who used social criticism as a means of determining how the people had failed to live up to the covenantal ideal.[61] The emphasis on injustice in a variety of forms in chapters 1–25 bears out the importance of this criticism.[62] But Judah had not learned anything from God's patience and from her history because she had not responded to the Lord's forms of discipline (drought, famine, and the sword, see 14:1–15:9).

Why did Judah resist Yahweh's revelation? Jeremiah explained that Judah did not suffer from lack of religious devotion or symbols. Indeed, they had reserved a prominent place for religion. They did not lack belief; they lacked a living *faith,* that is, a radical loyalty to Yahweh and his revelation. They were all too comfortable with their doctrine of God. They believed that Yahweh was nearby in the temple, that he was theirs and would only deal kindly with them. Their failure was not only in breaching the covenant, but in limiting God to a house (23:23), to their interpretation of his promises, to their traditions, and to their popular theology.[63] They held onto the promises given at Sinai (Sinai theology) and to David (Zion theology), but failed to see the living God who is free to cast off a rebellious people and to destroy their false hopes.[64] (See figure 63.)

In reviewing the history of the nation after the Exodus, Jeremiah concluded that the people had resisted the way of Yahweh (5:20–27), that they had no distinct reason for existence (7:28), and that Yahweh's wrath rested on the nation (5:29). Like Isaiah and Micah, Jeremiah declared Judah's inner decay and Yahweh's imminent judgment on Jerusalem. However, unlike his predecessors, he would witness the end of the belief in the inviolability of Jerusalem/Zion.[65]

303

SINAI THEOLOGY	ZION THEOLOGY	YAHWEH'S JUDGMENT
Covenant	Covenant	Covenant broken
Presence of God	Presence	Abandonment
Tabernacle/temple	Glory of temple	Temple destroyed
Forgiveness	Protection	End of Davidic monarchy
Blessings	Blessings	Curse

Figure 63. Jeremiah and Orthodoxy

Jeremiah, the Kings of Judah, and the International Scene[66]

Jeremiah was born during the regime of King Manasseh (696–642 B.C.). Manasseh had opened the doors to a pro-Assyrian policy and had instituted all kinds of pagan cults and practices in Judah.[67] He was like Ahab of Israel in his openness to foreign cultures, but worse (2 Kings 21:11)! Following the death of Manasseh, his son Amon reigned for a couple of years, died, and was succeeded by his infant son, Josiah.

Josiah

Josiah's reign (640–609 B.C.) coincided with the collapse of Assyrian power. Nationalism, combined with a zeal for Yahweh, encouraged Josiah to institute significant reforms involving the cleansing of the temple, the destruction of pagan cultic sites, and instruction in the Torah-revelation of God. Jeremiah had paved the way for these reforms by declaring the guilt of both Israel and Judah and by calling all twelve tribes to repentance.[68] His mission to the twelve tribes found some reality in Josiah's vision of a united kingdom under one God and under the Davidic monarch. Josiah's efforts at bringing together the remnant of Israel with the people of Judah in a Passover celebration is one illustrious example reminiscent of the days of Samuel (2 Chron. 35:18). Further, the "reunited" tribes expedited the destruction of pagan sites, altars, and temples in the north and in Judah. Thus Josiah extended his power base to the territory over which his forefathers David and Solomon had ruled (34:6–8).

The prophet probably continued his ministry after the reforms were instituted under Josiah's leadership (2 Kings 22–23; 2 Chron. 34–35). Immediately upon the death of Josiah (609 B.C.), the reforms ceased. This sudden collapse was indicative of the people's spiritual condition. The death of the king meant liberty to return to the old ways of *vox populi* and a definitive break with the requirements of revelation. This crisis propelled the prophet to oppose the political and religious "new deal" of Josiah's successors. He lamented the death of the godly king

304

TABLE 11. THE LAST DAYS OF JUDAH

B.C.	
609	Battle at Megiddo, death of Josiah
	Jehoahaz enthroned as king over Judah, deposed and exiled to Egypt (Jer. 22:11–12; see Ezek. 19:1–4)
	Jehoiakim enthroned with Egyptian approval; Judah under Egyptian control
609–605	Egyptian extension of power over all territory from Egypt to Euphrates
605	Battle at Carchemish. Defeat of Egypt and subjugation of Judah to Babylon: temple vessels taken and elite exiled (Dan. 1:1–2). Pro-Egyptian sentiment in Judah
604	Destruction of Ashkelon; fasting in Judah (Jer. 36:9)
603	Subjugation of Judah to Babylon (Jer. 26:1)
601–600	Heavy casualties in Babylonian war against Hatti, encouraging subjugated nations to plot rebellion against Babylon
600	Revolt of Jehoiakim (2 Kings 24:1)
599–598	Babylonia regains territories (Jer. 49:28–33)
598–597	Babylonia determined to regain control over Judah (2 Kings 24:10–11)
	Death of Jehoiakim, enthronement of **Jehoiachin**, siege and conquest of Judah (2 Kings 24), limited deportation (Jer. 13:18–19; 52:28) followed by major deportation (2 Kings 24:12, 14; Jer. 24:1; 29:2): exile of Jehoiachin and elite. **Zedekiah** enthroned as king over Judah (2 Chron. 36:10)
596–594	Rebellion in and subjugation of Elam and Babylon (Jer. 49:34–38)
593	Ezekiel's call (Ezek. 1:1–2); anti-Babylonian conference (Jer. 27) and encouragement by the false prophets; renewed preaching of hope by Hananiah and other false prophets (Jer. 28:1; see 27:9–15; 29:8–9; Ezek. 14:1–9)
591	Fulfillment date of Hananiah's prophecy, elders' consultation with Ezekiel (Jer. 28:17; Ezek. 20:1)
589	Accession of Hophra to throne in Egypt. Open rebellion by Judah against Babylon
588	Beginning of siege of Jerusalem (2 Kings 25:1; Jer. 52:4; Ezek. 24:1–2)
587	Egyptian relief; Jeremiah's purchase of field at Anathoth; exile of 832 deserters (Jer. 52:29)
586	Fall of Jerusalem (2 Kings 25:8–9; Jer. 39:2; 52:6–7, 12); report received in exile (Ezek. 33:21)

(2 Chron. 35:25), calling on his contemporaries not to weep for Josiah, but for themselves (Jer. 22:10). Shortly after the death of Josiah,[69] Jeremiah wrote down the oracles he had delivered over a twenty-three-year period. It had become all too apparent that Josiah's reforms, though well intended, had not been internalized by the people. They conformed externally, but as soon as Josiah died, their loyalty to Yahweh died.[70] From this point onward Jeremiah was even more critical of Judah's hardness.

Assyria, Egypt, and Babylon

On the international scene Jeremiah witnessed the decline of Assyria and Egypt.[71] Under Josiah, Judah extended her boundaries northward, as Assyria was unable to control Judah's ambitions. Nabopolassar freed Babylon in 626 B.C. and increased pressure on the crumbling Assyrian kingdom. The Medes took the ancient Assyrian capital Asshur (614 B.C.). By 612 B.C. Nineveh fell to the Babylonians and Medes. Though Egypt, under Pharaoh Necho, came to the rescue of Assyria in 609 B.C., she was unable to halt the growth of Babylon's power. After Josiah unsuccessfully tried to stop Necho at Megiddo and lost his life in battle (609 B.C.), Egypt extended her influence over Judah. (See table 11.)[72]

Jehoahaz

Jehoahaz (or Shallum in 22:11) followed Josiah in becoming king, but he departed from his father's reforms. Shortly after Jehoahaz's coronation, Pharaoh Necho demanded a heavy tribute from Judah (2 Kings 23:31–33), exiled Jehoahaz, and installed Jehoiakim[73] as vassal-king (v. 34; 2 Chron. 36:2, 5). Within three months Judah had lost her great king, Josiah, his son, and her independence (Jer. 22:10–12)!

Jehoiakim and Jehoiachin

The years of Jehoiakim (609–598 B.C.) vindicated the prophetic witness of Judah's imminent exile to Babylon. Jeremiah had proclaimed the victory of Babylon over Egypt, Judah, and the kingdoms of his time (25:1, 8–11, 15–25). Egypt could not maintain her position in Canaan after Nebuchadnezzar's victory over the joint armies of Assyria and Egypt at Carchemish in 605 B.C. (46:2; see 2 Chron. 35:20). This signified the end of Assyria, the retreat of Egypt, and the ascendancy of Babylon. Nebuchadnezzar's troops continued their advance, taking Philistia (47:5–7), and then forced Jehoiakim to become a vassal of Babylon (603 B.C.; 2 Kings 24:1).

Jehoiakim's rule was marked by a determination to throw off the Babylonian yoke by placing faith in *Realpolitik* and by keeping popular hope (*vox populi*) alive. Jeremiah faced a leadership and a population that rejected his message of God's coming judgment. They were so confident of their rights as the elect people of God and as heirs of the promises that the prophet could not shake their confidence in their societal structures or in their religious convictions. Jeremiah's insistence that the covenant, the temple, and the kingship would provide no guarantee for Judah (7:1–8:3; 26:1–24) struck at the heart of Judah's confidence. He addressed the people with the greatest urgency, calling them to repent and to fast rather than use the temple as a fetish, claiming, "This is the temple of the LORD, the temple of the LORD, temple of the LORD!" (7:4).

Jeremiah also had Baruch read the prophetic words that he had spoken during the previous twenty-three years and had written down (36:2). He exhorted the people to believe in Yahweh and to repent from their wicked practices (v. 3). When the officials heard about this event, they took Baruch aside, had him read the prophetic message to them, and then took him to read it to the king. As the scroll was read aloud to him, Jehoiakim defied the pessimistic and critical message of the prophet and had it burned section by section (vv. 11–24). God's response was immediate. He commanded Jeremiah to write another scroll in which the judgment on Judah and Jehoiakim was more severe than before (vv. 29–31).[74]

Jehoiakim was intent on ridding the land of this messenger of doom (36:26), but a small circle of powerful friends protected Jeremiah (26:24). These years were hard on the prophet because he was persecuted (12:6; 15:15–18), he was the object of plots (11:18–23; 18:18), he was beaten and imprisoned (20:2), and he faced popular hostility (26:10–11). These events form the background of Jeremiah's confessions.

Jehoiakim rebelled (598 B.C.) against Babylon, contrary to Jeremiah's warnings (27:2–11).[75] By the time the Babylonians came to subdue the troublemakers, Jehoiakim either had died naturally or had been assassinated[76] (22:18–19; 36:30), and his son, Jehoiachin, had been crowned (2 Kings 24:8) in 597 B.C. During his three months' reign, the Babylonians advanced, set up siege works against Jerusalem, despoiled the temple, and exiled Jehoiachin and leading citizens[77] to Babylon (vv. 8–17)—all in fulfillment of Jeremiah's words (Jer. 22:22–30).[78]

This event was interpreted differently by the population of Judah and by Jeremiah. The people of Judah believed that only the wicked were exiled and that Yahweh had left them as the righteous remnant. Jeremiah opposed this false view in the vision of the two baskets (24:1–10).[79] He declared that what was left in Judah and Jerusalem was corrupt and that the future was with the people in exile![80] Jeremiah also sent a letter (chap. 29) to the newly exiled community in which he encouraged them to make their living in Babylon and await the restoration there.

Zedekiah

Zedekiah, the uncle of Jehoiachin and son of Josiah, was installed as vassal-king by Babylon (597 B.C.; see 2 Kings 24:17–18). Zedekiah (597–586 B.C.) was a puppet king[81] who was easily controlled by the pro-Egypt party and by the prophets of hope in Jerusalem, like Hananiah (28:1–4) and Shemaiah (29:24–28). Hananiah predicted the speedy return of the exiles and the temple treasures, but Jeremiah advised the king to submit to Babylon (21:1–7; 37:17–21; 38:7–28).[82]

Jeremiah consistently spoke of Jerusalem's impending doom (21:1–10; 34:1–22; 37:3–10; 38:14–23) and was consequently treated as a pro-Babylonian traitor (37:13; 51:59–64).[83] He was thrown into a dungeon (37:16) and a cistern (38:1–13), and he was put in the guardhouse (37:21).[84] Zedekiah rejected Jeremiah's counsel but did listen to his own officials and was responsive to the rebellious plots of Pharaoh Hophra (589–570 B.C.). Zedekiah rebelled against Babylon in 589 B.C.

The End of Judah

When Jerusalem was besieged by Babylon, the people still hoped for a military solution. It came in the form of Egyptian support (37:5–8), forcing the Babylonians temporarily to halt their siege. During this time Jeremiah may have gone out to Anathoth to purchase a tract of land as a token of his belief in the restoration of the people to the land (32:6–15).[85] Soon the Babylonians returned with greater determination and breached the walls of Jerusalem. In the end, Jerusalem, the city of God, lay in ruins (586 B.C.). The temple, the palaces, and the buildings were looted and burned. King Zedekiah went into exile, having witnessed the execution of his sons just before he was blinded (39:1–7). A part of the population was also exiled, but Jeremiah was permitted to stay with a remnant in Judah.

Nebuchadnezzar appointed Gedaliah as the governor of the province of Judah (40:1–6), but he could not satisfy the unruly elements and was assassinated (chap. 41). In fear of Babylonian reprisal the rebels left Judah for Egypt, taking Jeremiah as hostage (chap. 42). They consulted Jeremiah for a word from the Lord (v. 3), and he exhorted them to remain in Judah, to repent, and to share in the promise of restoration (vv. 10, 12). But they resisted God's word and settled in Tahpanhes in Egypt.

Jeremiah stands as God's witness to the *old age* and to the continuity with Moses and the prophets.[86] His prophetic ministry was partly vindicated in the Exile when God annulled his promises confirmed to Israel through Moses and abandoned his people. Even in Egypt,

Jeremiah kept explaining God's freedom in judging the people in Babylon (44:4–6) and in Egypt (v. 30).

Jeremiah also bore witness to the *new age*. The purchase of the tract of land in Anathoth symbolizes his hope in the new age of restoration that would open up after the seventy years—a period of time decreed for Babylon's rule.[87] At Babylon's fall (539 B.C.), God planned to give a new future to his people.

> This is what the LORD says: "When seventy years are completed for Babylon, I will come to you and fulfill my *gracious promise* to bring you back to this place. For I know the plans I have for you," declares the LORD, "plans to prosper you and not to harm you, plans to give you *hope and a future.* Then you will call upon me and come and pray to me, and I will listen to you. You will seek me and find me when you seek me with all your heart. I will be found by you," declares the LORD, "and will bring you back from captivity. I will gather you from all the nations and places where I have banished you," declares the LORD, "and will bring you back to the place from which I carried you into exile" (29:10–14, emphasis mine; see Zech. 1:12; 7:5).

Jeremiah proclaimed that God is free, sovereign, and faithful in inaugurating a new era in which the Lord will renew his covenants with a new community that will live in submission to him and that will be richly blessed by the ministry of a righteous Davidic Messiah.[88] We shall now consider his vision of the new era.

VISION OF THE NEW ERA

Jeremiah was a minister of God's word in a crisis situation. The prophetic revelation shattered the ideology of his contemporaries who relied on the institutions rooted in the Mosaic and Davidic covenants. They had held onto traditions shaped by a selective interpretation of revelation (*vox populi*) and had adapted to the crises caused by a policy of *Realpolitik*. But Jeremiah denounced the institutions (temple, priesthood, and kingship) and spoke of the need of a radical transformation. To his contemporaries, Jeremiah was a traitor, a skeptic, a proclaimer of doom, even a revolutionary. Jeremiah is God's prophet of destruction and of transformation, as Brueggemann writes, "Informed by a tradition of the freedom and sovereignty of God, who could create and destroy, who could begin things and end things, he took as his program that Yahweh will 'build/plant, tear down/pluck up.'"[89]

Jeremiah, the new Moses, is the messenger of the "new era."[90] Jeremiah functioned in his historical context as Jesus did in his. Both were sent by the Lord, lived in absolute devotion to God, spoke out against human institutions, and announced the fall of Jerusalem, including her temple. Both were misunderstood, reviled, and disgraced. Both were empathetic with the people, mediated on their behalf, and encouraged the godly remnant to look with hope beyond the fall of Jerusalem.

Jeremiah, however, failed to bring in the new era. He witnessed the fall of Jerusalem and spoke of the fuller inauguration of the kingdom of God, the messianic age, and the renewal of God's people. Jesus, in giving his life as an atonement for sin, brought in the messianic era and a fuller inauguration of the kingdom of God to all who believe on him! Jesus, too, points beyond the experiences of his life and death to the greater glory awaiting all who believe on him, to which his resurrection, his glorification, and the gift of the Spirit witness.

Transformation of All Things

The teaching on the radical transformation of all things runs throughout Jeremiah's ministry. He stands between the old and the new, proclaiming Yahweh's judgments and his restoration.[91] The old era came to an end in the fall of the temple, the dissolution of the structures and institutions of Judah, and the exile of her people. The Exile was an era of spiritual renewal; the godly abandoned themselves completely to the Lord and looked for his monergistic and gracious inauguration of the new era. They raised their eyes in hope of the new era Jeremiah announced.

The prophet himself longed for this new age of restoration, purification, transformation, and rest. The certainty of the new age lies in God's *monergistic* (from *monos* ["alone"] and *ergon* ["work"]) involvement with his people and the free fulfillment of his promises. He promises to deal graciously with all who "know" him (9:24) and with his creation. Mourning will change to laughter, want to plentitude, curse to blessing, and enmity to peace. The groaning of creation will be transformed, and creation itself will be fully liberated to serve the Creator-Redeemer. In this new state God will rule supreme in wisdom and grace. His righteous order will ensure the bliss of his covenant children and the complete removal of evil, sin, and whatever wreaks havoc in God's world.

The Rule of God

The prophet's struggle with Yahweh and his submission to the freedom of the Creator-Redeemer gave him a new insight into God's rule over creation. Yahweh, the Sovereign King is free, unrestricted by human expectations or reasoning, but he is not fickle like the gods of the nations.

He who is the Portion of Jacob is not like these,
    for he is the Maker of all things,
including Israel, the tribe of his inheritance—
    the LORD Almighty is his name.
                                        (10:16)

He, the Sovereign Ruler over creation and the nations, has the power to uproot and destroy as well as to build and plant.

Jeremiah impressed on faithless Judah that creation is submissive to Yahweh, whereas his own covenant people have rebelled (10:11, 14–15). Yahweh's kingdom does not depend on the recognition of his people. Yahweh "is the true God; he is the living God, the eternal King" (v. 10). He is King over the earth and over the nations: "When he is angry, the earth trembles; the nations cannot endure his wrath" (10:10; see vv. 12–13; 51:15–19).[92]

His kingdom extends beyond Judah and Jerusalem: "Do not I fill heaven and earth?" (23:24).[93] Jeremiah likened the Lord to a potter, who freely and sovereignly molds the clay, using some parts and rejecting others in accordance with his purpose (18:6–10; see Isa. 29:16; 45:9; 64:8; Rom. 9:21). Yahweh is the Creator-Redeemer-King, who is not subject to human rules of logic or expectations.[94] He is free to change his love into judgment (5:22–25),[95] and he is also free to turn judgment into blessing. God is free to use Babylon as his instrument of judgment,[96] and he freely sets Babylon aside (29:10). Though the purposes of God are hidden, the progress of redemption reveals his plan (32:17–23, 25).

Nothing is too difficult for Yahweh: "I am the LORD, the God of all mankind. Is anything too hard for me?" (32:27).

The future lies with those who would surrender all for the sake of God and submit to his kingdom of kindness, justice, and righteousness (9:23–25; see Heb. 13:13).[97] Jeremiah's preaching encouraged God's people (17:12–14) to long for God's kingdom, regardless of what might happen to Jerusalem and in Israel and Judah. He looked beyond the ruins of Jerusalem to a new land with a new people, blessed by God.[98] But Jeremiah's vision of the kingdom of God always included judgment. Prescott H. Williams appropriately writes, "Are we allowed to hope for salvation apart from our judgment, and that of others? I believe Jeremiah would utter a resounding 'NO!' "[99]

Jeremiah helped the covenant community focus their hope on Yahweh. Hope begins with submission to the establishment of his kingdom, even in judgment. This seems paradoxical, but true! Jeremiah urged the godly not to become entangled with the structures and institutions of Jerusalem, but to pray for God's mercy.

> For the sake of your name do not despise us;
> do not dishonor your glorious throne.
> Remember your covenant with us
> and do not break it. . . .
> No, it is you, O LORD our God.
> Therefore our hope is in you,
> for you are the one who does all this.
>   (14:21–22)

The Messianic Reign

Jeremiah was critical of the institutions (the temple, the covenant) because they had become little more than human structures maintained by human effort and protected by human ingenuity.[100]

He was also critical of the ruling Davidic monarchs. The prophet clashed repeatedly with kings Jehoiakim, Jehoiachin, and Zedekiah. None lived up to his name. *Jehoiakim* and *Jehoiachin* signify "Yahweh will establish his kingdom in the Davidic king," and *Zedekiah* means "Yahweh is righteous." These three kings had, in fact, demonstrated little interest in the establishment of God's righteous kingdom; each one perpetuated the policy of *Realpolitik* and opposed Jeremiah's prophetic message.

Jeremiah directed the eyes of faith to a new era after God's purifying judgment. He looked beyond the structures of Judean society to the new era of righteousness that the Lord would monergistically inaugurate: a reign of righteousness under a Davidic monarch who would faithfully serve him as a theocratic and priestly leader and be a blessing to the new community (33:21; see 23:5–6; 33:15–20; Ps. 110:1).[101]

People of God

Jeremiah is first and foremost the preacher of "the new covenant."[102] We have already seen how the canonical shape of the material presents him as the new Moses. As the second Moses he spoke of (1) the reunification of Israel and Judah and of (2) the renewal of the covenants.

The Reunification of Israel and Judah

Jeremiah addressed the word of God primarily to Israel and Judah. He announced that the Lord would renew his covenant with the remnant of all twelve tribes and would constitute them into *one* people. Jeremiah repeatedly included the remnant of Israel with the remnant of Judah in the renewal of covenant privileges: " 'The days are coming,' declares the LORD, 'when I will bring *my people Israel and Judah* back from captivity and restore them to the land I gave their forefathers to possess,' says the LORD. These are the words the LORD spoke concerning

Israel and Judah" (30:3–4, emphasis mine). In spite of a history of sin and judgment, Yahweh spoke tenderly of the godly remnant of the twelve tribes as "my people." The descendants of Jacob are his house, his inheritance, his children, his wife, his vineyard, the sheep of his pasture, and the people he loves (3:19–20; 12:7–10; 23:1).

The process of reunification took place before, during, and after Jeremiah's time. Hezekiah had already sent an invitation to the remnant of the northern tribes to submit to the Lord and to the Davidic king by celebrating the Passover *together* in Jerusalem. Though few heeded the royal invitation, it signified an early fulfillment of God's word through his prophets (Hosea, Amos, Micah, and Isaiah).[103] Jeremiah had witnessed the renewal of God's favor to Israel when Josiah called on the remnant again—one hundred years after Hezekiah—to join in the celebration of the Passover in Judah (2 Kings 23:21–23; 2 Chron. 35:17).

The people of Judah may have felt offended or betrayed because they had thought that they were so much more righteous than their northern neighbors. However, Jeremiah severely denounced any attempt at self-justification and called for nothing less than a full commitment to God: "Circumcise yourselves to the LORD, circumcise your hearts" (4:4). He declared that since all tribes share in the guilt, anyone from *any* of the tribes may repent and freely receive Yahweh's mercy (3:6–4:4).

The Renewal of the Covenants

The new era will be far better than the old! The renewal of the covenants and of the promises is the focus of the book of consolation (chaps. 30–33). These chapters confirm the continuity of the previous covenants: with creation, with Abraham, with Moses, with the priesthood, and with David. Yet, the "new covenant" will radically differ from the old covenant.[104] In what ways is the new covenant "new?"

First, let us consider the elements of continuity. Yahweh addressed the remnant as his servant.

> "So do not fear, O *Jacob my servant;*
>   do not be dismayed, O Israel," declares the LORD.
> "I will surely *save* you out of a distant place,
>   your descendants from the land of their exile.
> Jacob will again have *peace and security,*
>   *and no one will make him afraid.*
> *I am with you and will save you,"*
>   declares the LORD.
> "Though I completely destroy all the nations
>   among which I scatter you,
>   I will not completely destroy you.
> I will *discipline* you but only with justice;

I will not let you go entirely unpunished."

(30:10–11, emphasis mine)

This text teaches us that the Exile was a form of "discipline" and that after the Exile Yahweh would renew his presence ("I am with you") in blessing and protection. Further, Israel will again "serve" Yahweh (v. 9), being endowed with the privileges inherent in the covenant.

The hope of the new community remains the same covenantal promise: "So you will be my people, and I will be your God" (30:22; see 31:1). Though the promise is conditioned on responsiveness (7:23), Jeremiah is here more concerned with God's love than with the response of the people of God. Yahweh will care for, have compassion for, restore, heal, and forgive (30:17–18) those who are uncared for.[105] Walter Brueggemann calls attention to this free act of Yahweh's grace: "God cares precisely for the uncared-for, and out of that caring in the face of rejection comes new life for Israel. But the new move . . . is wrought utterly and completely in God's heart and nowhere else. . . . The newness comes solely from God."[106] The new initiative on God's part evokes the praise of the godly and their children (vv. 19–20).

The new community is thus envisioned in continuity with the Abrahamic and Mosaic covenants as its members enjoy the realization of the promises: (1) God's love, compassion, and forgiveness (31:3, 34); (2) rest, security, and peace (v. 2); (3) restoration of the people to the land (vv. 4–5; see vv. 18–19, 24, 26–28, 35–40); (4) fulfillment, joy, and removal of sorrow (vv. 4, 6, 12–14; see vv. 15–17, 25); (5) witness to the nations (v. 7; see vv. 10, 12); (6) God's fatherhood and ability to redeem (vv. 7–9; see vv. 11, 20); and (7) divine blessing and consecration of the people (v. 23).

The distinctive difference between the old covenant and the new covenant lies in the heartfelt responsiveness of the new community.[107] The old community was characterized by "wrongdoings" and "sins," but the new community will be completely forgiven from these.[108] The old community focused their hopes on institutions: the ark of the covenant, the tablets of the covenant, the traditions of Exodus and conquest, the promises to David, the Zion theology, and the temple. Jeremiah projected a complete change from the physical to the spiritual reality of the covenant.[109] He sadly commented on the old community,

> The heart is deceitful above all things
> and beyond cure.
> Who can understand it?
>
> (17:9)

A new heart signifies a spiritual change, expressed in a responsive, flexible, affectionate, and receptive relationship with Yahweh. Instead of sin being engraved on the tablets of their hearts (v. 1), Yahweh's law will be written on their hearts (31:33). In its deepest and grandest sense the internalized "law" of God will motivate God's people to establish the will of God on earth by practicing love, righteousness, justice, and peace for the sake of God and in the imitation of God (9:24).

The promise of internalization assures the success of the new community. The Spirit of God will effect a change in their hearts so that more than ever before and in greater number the godly will persevere in doing God's will by the power of the Spirit. Internalization does not remove the legitimate place of intermediaries (priest, king, prophet), but puts a greater responsibility on individuals, as we read,

> They will be my people, and I will be their God. I will give them singleness of heart and action, so that they will always fear me for their own good and the good of their children after them. I will make an everlasting covenant with them: I will never stop doing good to them, and I will inspire them to fear me, so that they will never turn away from me. I will rejoice in doing them good and will assuredly plant them in this land with all my heart and soul (32:38–41; see 31:22).

The hope of democratization of the covenant community goes back to God's promise to Israel at Sinai where he promised to make Israel a holy and royal nation, distinct from and favored above all nations (Ex. 19:5–6). As God's *segullâ* ("treasured possession," v. 5), they were to be the servants of the living God, that is, called and commissioned by the Lord to establish his kingdom on earth (Deut. 26:18–19, Ps. 114:2).

Jeremiah spoke of a new era that Yahweh sovereignly, monergistically, freely, and graciously opens up. In spite of Israel's history, Yahweh will renew the covenant administration and offer the members of the new community even greater privileges. He will stand by them and sustain them, as he has done with his servants of old—Moses, Joshua, Phinehas the priest, and David the king. The new royal and priestly community will be servants of the Most High. While not denying the place of king and of priest, Jeremiah concentrates on a new community of servants of God. H. D. Potter observes,

> Jeremiah predicts that elitism will now cease. God will give direct, intuitive knowledge of his law. . . . No one will teach it, no one will be able, by his superior expertise, to use it to his own advantage, no one will be able to claim mitigation through ignorance.[110]

Jeremiah looked forward to a new community inaugurated by Yahweh's sovereign renewal of covenant, sustained by God's involvement in his people, and enlarged by a greater number of people submissive to God.[111] The goal of the new covenant is rest, a goal that is ever so much more possible because of Yahweh's greater commitment (31:2; see 6:16).

From my perspective, the new covenant is an eschatological reality whose fulfillment takes place in the progression of redemption, including the postexilic era, the renewal of covenant in Jesus Christ, and the present church age.[112] I am greatly indebted to Calvin, who wrote,

> Hence the Prophet here intimates that God's favour would be certain, because he would not only give leisure to the Jews, when they returned, to plant vines, but would also cause them to enjoy the fruit in peace and quietness. . . . He extends God's favour to the country and the villages, as though he had said, that the land would be filled with inhabitants, not only as to the fortified towns, but as to the fields. . . . Now, were one to ask, when was this fulfilled? We must bear in mind what has been said elsewhere,—that the Prophets, . . . included the whole Kingdom of Christ from the beginning to the end. And in this our divines go astray, so that by confining these promises to some particular time, they are compelled to fly to allegories; and thus they wrest, and even pervert all the prophecies. But the Prophets, as it has been said, include the whole progress of Christ's Kingdom when they speak of the future redemption of the people. The people began to do well when they returned to their own country; . . . It was, therefore, necessary for them to look for the coming of Christ. We now taste of these benefits of God. . . . *We hence see that these prophecies are not accomplished in one day, or in one year, no, not even in one age, but ought to be understood as referring to the beginning and the end of Christ's Kingdom.*[113]

I conclude that the new covenant extends the benefits of the Father through Christ from creation to the new creation and that the kingdom of Jesus Christ unfolds throughout the progress of redemption. Each renewal is continuous and discontinuous with the older forms of the covenants. The elements of *continuity* include the following:

1. The covenant is between *Yahweh and his people.*
2. The covenant is an administration of *grace and promise,* including all the promises of the previous covenants (forgiveness of sin, reconciliation, and covenant restoration).
3. The people of God receive and cultivate the *kingdom* of God in godly living.
4. The priests and the Davidic king have a *mediatorial* role in the covenant administration (Jer. 33:15–26).

The elements of *discontinuity* in this renewal include the following:

1. The Spirit of God *internalizes* God's will, and the godly are more involved in establishing God's kingdom.
2. The people of God, who are endowed with greater splendor and joy, are *democratized.* They are the servants of the Lord who do God's will on earth and work to enhance God's glory. In seeking

his kingdom, they establish God's kingdom of righteousness and peace.

3. The *monergistic* emphasis assures the new era of righteousness, peace, and rest. Nothing will separate his children from the realization of his goals (Rom. 8:31–39).

4. The *messianic* kingdom would extend the benefits of God uninterruptedly because of God's promise, righteousness, and the harmonious relation of king and priest.

Enemies Avenged and God's People Vindicated

The judgment of God is against all the "uncircumcised" of heart, whether they belong to Israel, Judah, or any of the nations (9:25–26; see Rom. 2:25–29). Jeremiah proclaimed God's judgment on all humanity in a separate corpus "the oracles of the nations" (chaps. 46–51; see Isa. 13–23; Ezek. 25–32; Amos 1–2; Zeph. 2:4–15).[114] These oracles, too, reflect Jeremiah's concern with his historical context. Judah had relied on the nations, which were also under God's judgment: Egypt (46), Philistia (47), Moab (48), Ammon (49:1–6), Edom (vv. 7–22), Damascus (vv. 23–27), Kedar and Hazor (vv. 28–33), and Elam (vv. 34–39). But most extensive is the prophecy of Babylon's fall (chaps. 50–51).

These prophecies reiterate that Yahweh is King over the nations and that the people of God should never align themselves with the structures (economic, cultural, political, military) of this world: "I will bring upon that land all the things I have spoken against it, all that are written in this book and prophesied by Jeremiah against all the nations" (25:13).[115] All who depend on the nations will fall with them!

These chapters also portray Yahweh's *international concern*. He is King over the nations and is free to invite the nations to submit to his kingship and thus to share in his blessings. Jeremiah has a word of encouragement to several nations.

"Later, however, Egypt will be inhabited as in times past," declares the LORD. (46:26)

"Yet *I will restore the fortunes* of Moab
in days to come,"
declares the LORD.

Here ends the judgment on Moab.
(48:47, emphasis mine)

"Yet afterward, *I will restore the
fortunes of the Ammonites,*"
declares the LORD.
(49:6, 39, emphasis mine)

317

The promise—"I will restore the fortunes of"[116]—was also given to Israel and Judah in the book of consolation (see 30:18; 32:44; 33:11, 26). The Lord promised to deal kindly with the nations with the remnant of his people. Jeremiah, unlike Isaiah, Amos, and Zephaniah, said little on the inclusion of the nations together with Israel and Judah. His emphasis is on what Orlinsky calls the dual motifs of nationalism and internationalism.[117]

Though Jeremiah's *national* concerns were closely intertwined with the nations, his historical context may explain the hope in a national restoration. For example, an oracle of salvation of Jacob (46:27–28) concludes the oracle against Egypt (chap. 46), even though it is a virtual repetition of 30:10–11. Jeremiah spoke of the fulfillment of Yahweh's promise regarding the remnant of the twelve tribes of Jacob, their return from wherever they have been scattered, and their exalted status as the "servant" of the Lord.[118] This privileged position involves communion, purpose, and, above all, the protection and blessing of the great Yahweh who has chosen them to be his people.

> Do not fear, O Jacob my servant;
>   do not be dismayed, O Israel. . . .
> Do not fear, O Jacob my servant,
> for I am with you.
>
> (46:27–28)

The promise also involves his presence, protection, and blessing. He will deliver them from their enemies so they may enjoy security and prosperity: "Jacob will again have peace and security, and no one will make him afraid" (46:27).

The redeemed from Babylon will experience a second Exodus, as Yahweh delivers his people in a powerful demonstration of his strength. Though the judgment was deserved, Yahweh had not completely forsaken[119] his people (51:5). The prophet exhorted the remnant in exile not to associate themselves with the structures of Babylon in order to avoid bringing the same judgment that Yahweh will visit on Babylon upon themselves.

> Flee from Babylon!
>   Run for your lives!
>   Do not be destroyed because of her sins.
> It is time for the LORD's vengeance;
>   he will pay her what she deserves.
>
> (51:6)

In response to their salvation, the restored community will sing in praise of the Divine Warrior (50:28, 34). Jeremiah called on the remnant to hope in the Lord, who is sovereign over the nations.

> The Lord has vindicated us;
>> come, let us tell in Zion
> what the LORD our God has done.
>>>> (51:10)[120]

Theology of hope is a theology of God, the Creator-Redeemer-King. This is the theme of another hymn (51:15–16, 19; see also 50:28, 34).[121] The redemption of the Lord will be holistic as Yahweh takes upon himself the cause (*rîb*) of his people.

> See, I will defend your cause
>> and avenge you;
> I will dry up her sea
>> and make her springs dry.
>>>> (51:36; see vv. 34–40)

Yahweh will not rest until the kingdoms of this world topple (30:23–24), including "Babylon" (51:49–55). Yahweh assures thereby that Babylon, too, is subject to the Lord Almighty.[122]

REVIEW

Jeremiah stood between the old and the new. He was filled with tensions, experiencing within himself the alienation and anguish of exile. His confessions and autobiographical narratives reveal a human being, God's spokesperson, a mediator of the people, an instrument of war, and a consoler of Israel. He spoke critically of the decay, injustice, and bankruptcy of the covenantal institutions of his day. He argued and disputed with his contemporaries to convince them that their concerns were petty in view of the greatness and freedom of Yahweh.[123] He encouraged the godly to commit themselves wholly to Yahweh and to seek his kingdom and his righteousness. He spoke of a new era when Yahweh would unilaterally renew the covenant, transform the people, bring in the messianic era, and fulfill all the promises in a grandiose manner.

At the heart of Jeremiah's message is Yahweh's freedom. Yahweh is free in wrath, judgment, vengeance, vindication, and restoration.[124] Therefore there is hope for the godly. But Jeremiah also warns us not to take Yahweh for granted, to attempt to institutionalize him or to limit him. In his acts God reveals the mystery of his purpose, grace, and freedom. Great is Yahweh and wonderful is his plan for his people. Jeremiah creates within the godly a yearning for the fullness of redemption.

QUESTIONS AND ISSUES

1. Explain the seeming lack of order and the repetitions in Jeremiah on the assumption that the book of Jeremiah is a collection of collections.
2. What were the periods of his most active ministry, and what was his distinctive message in each period?
3. In what aspects was Jeremiah like and unlike Moses and our Lord?
4. What are the purposes of the confessions of Jeremiah? Relate the confessions to Paul's suffering.
5. Explain the affirmation of Yahweh's freedom, so important to understanding the person and message of Jeremiah.
6. For what reasons will God judge Judah? What was the nature of their popular belief, based on their theology of Sinai and of Zion? What was Jeremiah's response to their false confidence?
7. Explain the nature of Jeremiah's criticism of the people and of her leaders. What is the basis of his criticism?
8. Evaluate the last kings of Judah in relation to their names. How did they "destroy" rather than "establish" the kingdom of God?
9. What is the kingdom of God, according to Jeremiah?
10. How is the messianic kingdom contrastive to that of the last kings of Judah?
11. Explain why Jeremiah is the preacher of "the new covenant."
12. Relate Jeremiah as the new Moses to his concern for the twelve tribes.
13. How is the new covenant like and unlike the previous covenant administration? How is the new covenant realized and eschatological? Relate the new covenant to the postexilic community, to our Lord's coming, to the church, and to the coming of God's kingdom.
14. Explain what may account for Jeremiah's emphasis on the national and international rather than the universal dimension of the new age.

CHAPTER 11

The Message of Ezekiel and Daniel

THE MESSAGE OF EZEKIEL: ALIENATION AND RECONCILIATION

Ezekiel and His Time

The ministry of the prophet Ezekiel can be best understood against the background of the last days of Judah.[1] If we assume with Origen that the vague reference to "the thirtieth year" (1:1) marks the age of the prophet, he may have been born around 623 B.C., during the reforms of King Josiah of Judah (640–609 B.C.).[2] As a youth, Ezekiel saw the decline and fall of Assyria, the growing power of Babylon, the foreign control of Jerusalem (Egypt in 609 B.C.), and the defeat of Egypt and Assyria by Nebuchadnezzar at Carchemish (605 B.C.). In 603 B.C. Nebuchadnezzar deported many of Judah's leading men, including Daniel (Dan. 1:1).

After this deportation Jehoiakim was allowed to continue as king on the condition that he remain loyal to Babylon. However, after three years, Jehoiakim rebelled against his overlord, repeating the mistake of Hoshea of Israel and of Hezekiah by relying on Egypt for support. As a result Judah incurred the wrath of Nebuchadnezzar and on March 16, 597 B.C., witnessed the looting of the city and the temple (2 Kings 24:13), and experienced a second deportation. Jehoiakim's son, Jehoiachin, and ten thousand leading citizens were taken into captivity (v. 14).[3] (See figure 64.)

Among these deportees was twenty-five-year-old Ezekiel, the son of Buzi (1:3) and a member of a priestly family. Although it is not known whether he had actually served in the temple as a priest, in exile Ezekiel was God's spokesman announcing the end of the old temple and the beginning of a more glorious temple, a symbol of the transformed world. Ezekiel stood between the old age and the new age at a critical point in redemptive history.

Ezekiel's ministry was a prophetic critique of popular ideology[4] that hoped for a speedy restoration. From 593 to 571 B.C. Ezekiel spoke God's word in Tel Abib, located by the canal of Kebar. There thousands of deportees eked out a meager existence, hoping for a swift return to Judah. Their hope was inflamed by the spirited preaching of the prophets of positive thinking, who deceived the people with their message of peace at a time when God's judgment was about to be poured out more fully on Jerusalem (13:10). These "jackals among ruins" (v. 4) encouraged the people with words of peace, but Ezekiel sharply retorted, " 'Peace,' when there is no peace" (v. 10). He exposed their lies for what they were because these men had not been sent by the Lord (vv. 1–16). The prophetic conflict resulted in distrust, even cynicism, of Ezekiel's message.[5] The people put off the prophet's exhortation with a proverb of their own, "The days go by and every vision comes to nothing" (12:22). Ezekiel explained through symbolic actions, parables, and prophetic teaching that the exile of Judah was inevitable.

605	603	597	593	586
Carchemish	First deportation: Daniel	Second deportation: Jehoiachin Ezekiel	Ezekiel's call	Fall of Jerusalem Third deportation: Exile

Figure 64. The Three Deportations

Moreover, Ezekiel exposed their essentially religious frame of reference by pointing out their faith in magical charms by which the women thought they could secure peace: "Woe to the women who sew magic charms on all their wrists and make veils of various lengths for their heads in order to ensnare people. Will you ensnare the lives of my people but preserve your own?" (13:18).

Ezekiel: The Priest-Prophet-Watchman

Ezekiel's ministry lasted from 593 to 571 B.C. He, like Jeremiah, was born into a priestly family (1:3).[6] He was married (24:15–18) and had his own home (3:24; 8:1) in a colony of transplanted Judeans in Tel Abib by the river Kebar, a canal of the Euphrates, south of Babylon and north of Nippur (1:1, 3; 3:15).[7] As a member of the priestly family, Ezekiel was trained in the laws pertaining to the temple and to sacrifice. This background may explain his concern with the future of the temple: the sacred symbol of God's presence, covenant, and rule (1 Kings 8:10–11; see Ps. 132). However, it also appears from his unique literary skills and knowledge of his world that Ezekiel, like Jeremiah, had received an internationally oriented education.

In 593 B.C. Ezekiel received a call to serve Yahweh as a prophet.[8] In that year he turned thirty, and if he had been in Jerusalem, he would have joined his father (Buzi) in serving the Lord at the temple. Instead, he was in exile and received a call to serve the Lord as the prophet-watchman.[9] (See figure 65.)

Ezekiel, *the priest,* had a vision of God's glory in exile.[10] He had witnessed the glory of the Lord, even as Moses (Ex. 33:18; 34:29–35) and Isaiah (Isa. 6:1–5). But how different was this revelation of God's glory from that at Mount Sinai! There Israel could look forward to the future, but in exile they were cast away from his presence. It is no wonder that Ezekiel was overcome by the splendor of God's majesty, but at the same time by the deep sense of guilt that he shared with his contemporaries. He fell down in his human weakness, but the Spirit of God raised him and empowered him (2:1–2). The Spirit commissioned him to minister to the exilic community (vv. 3–4), a community that differed very little in their response from the community left in Judah (v. 5; 3:4–7, 11). God's priest, Ezekiel, was responsible for teaching and applying the message of guilt and condemnation through word and symbolic acts. He also spoke of the glorious transformation of the new era, represented by the return of God's glory to his temple.

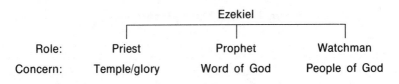

	Ezekiel		
Role:	Priest	Prophet	Watchman
Concern:	Temple/glory	Word of God	People of God

Figure 65. Ezekiel, the Priest-Prophet-Watchman

Ezekiel, *the prophet,* was God's spokesman in exile. Like Jeremiah in Jerusalem, Ezekiel served the Lord as his instrument of warfare: "I will make you as unyielding and hardened as they are. I will make your forehead like the hardest stone, harder than flint. Do not be afraid of them or terrified by them" (3:8–9). Thus the Lord promised to strengthen his prophet and to protect him (2:6–7).[11]

Ezekiel received the word of God on a scroll that contained nothing but oracles of woe, judgment, and laments (2:8–10). This was the message on which he had to meditate. Though it was a bitter message, Ezekiel's submission to the Lord and trust in his Sovereign made it sweet (3:1–3).[12]

Ezekiel served as Yahweh's *watchman* over Israel (3:17–21). He had to forewarn the people of what Yahweh was about to do in Jerusalem, explain their responsibility for God's abandonment, and call them to repent. In the oracles of judgment (5:5–7:27) he declared that Judah's suffering was because of her long-standing apostasy. However, lest the generation of Ezekiel become indignant, believing that their suffering was on account of their fathers, he explained that each man was responsible for himself. In fact, individual responsibility is one of the distinct emphases of the prophet-watchman (14:12–23; 18:2; 33:1–20; see Jer. 31:29). (See figure 65.)

Ezekiel was responsible to the people as God's priest-prophet-watchman. But once he had forewarned them, they became individually responsible for their actions. Brownlee has observed the great responsibility placed on the prophet: "The conception of the prophet in the sense of watchman is not new (cf. Hos. 9:8), but the deep sense of responsibility involved, so that the prophet forfeits his own right to life if he does not carry it [his mission] out, is new."[13]

Ezekiel: The Suffering Servant

Ezekiel lived an extraordinary life during a puzzling period of Israel's history. He, like Jeremiah, suffered vicariously and empathetically for his people.[14] Even though Ezekiel was already in exile, he had to undergo the siege, deportation, and exile of Judah (3:22–5:17). Through dramatic acts of self-inflicted but divinely mandated suffering, Ezekiel was fully involved in the suffering of his people back in Judah. His acts were no less revelatory than his words to the community in exile.[15]

Of great significance was Ezekiel's use of dramatic symbolism.[16] He had to lie on his side in his house for 390 days,[17] be bound with ropes, and eat defiled food (chap. 4). After this ordeal Ezekiel shaved off his hair with a sword, weighed it, and then divided it into three piles (5:1–4). Through these symbolic acts he explained to the exiles that the fall of Jerusalem was inevitable and that one-third of the population was to be burned, a third to be killed by the sword, and another third to be exiled.[18] Moreover, the symbolic affliction dramatized to the exilic community the tension that the people in Jerusalem experienced during the Babylonian siege, or what Ellison calls "the inner meaning of the agony that was going on in their father-land."[19]

Further, he was strictly prohibited from speaking about anything except what the Lord revealed to him (3:26; 24:27). He was mute only to the extent that he could not associate with his fellowman in an ordinary way. The Lord also instructed Ezekiel not to mourn publicly over the death of his wife (24:15–18). Between the time of his wife's death and the fall of Jerusalem, Ezekiel had to be silent, groaning only within himself, until the exiles would hear of the fall of Jerusalem and mourn over the death of their relatives in Judah. He was God's sign in exile of what Yahweh was already doing.[20]

The symbolic acts must not have had a dramatic effect on his fellow exiles. Even if they refused to listen to his words, they could not but wonder why Ezekiel was willing to suffer personally for the word of God. The oracles of Yahweh's warfare against Judah made a deep impression on the prophet. No one could accuse Ezekiel of rejoicing in the fate of Judah and Jerusalem, because the prophet identified with the adversity of his people.[21] He, too, experienced God's abandonment of Judah and Jerusalem (5:8).[22]

Literary Form and Structure

Literary Form

The book of Ezekiel has its own literary style and may best be appreciated by creative and artistically oriented people. Gottwald describes it as "woefully dull and repetitive,"[23] but to the contrary, the repetitions ("son of man";[24] "and you may know";[25] "I am the LORD"[26]), the dating formula,[27] rhetorical questions, and images convey a message organically held together.[28] The book, as a whole or in part, encourages visualization of life in exile, of God's judgment on Jerusalem, and of the promised restoration. Ezekiel paints pictures with words, and their interpretation can never match the richness of expression of the original work.[29]

Symmetry in the prophecy opens up the relations of the various sections and chapters.[30] The vision of the departure of God's glory from the temple (chaps. 1–11) has its counterpart in the return of the glory of the Lord, the vision of the new temple, and the presence of the Lord among his people (chaps. 40–48). Ezekiel's call to be God's watchman in 3:16–21 finds its complement in 33:1–20. The oracles, allegories, and laments pertaining to Jerusalem's fall (chaps. 12–24) find their parallel in the vision of the restoration of the people to the land (chaps. 34–39). The oracles against the nations (chaps. 25–32) separate the oracles of judgment and salvation. The symmetry may be outlined as follows:

A. Vision of Yahweh's glory and Ezekiel's call, 1:2–3:15
  B. Departure of Yahweh's glory and Israel's guilt, chaps. 1–11
    C. Reasons for God's judgment, chaps. 12–24
      D. Oracles against the nations, chaps. 25–32
A'. Ezekiel's call as watchman, chap. 33
    C'. Vision of the restoration, chaps. 34–39
  B'. Return of Yahweh's glory, the new temple, transformation, chaps. 40–48

Symbolism figures prominently in Ezekiel's writing. It is possible that his priestly background had prepared him for communicating God's word in symbolic acts and representations. More likely, he chose this vehicle as the most effective means of communicating God's word to those who, hardened in their sin, waited optimistically for their release from exile and their return to Judah. Ezekiel enacts Jerusalem's siege on a clay tablet (4:1–3). He represents the iniquity of the people by lying first on his left side and then on his right (vv. 4–8). The anguish of Jerusalem's siege is shown by his partaking of rationed food and drink (vv. 9–17); and her destruction by the symbolic act of cutting off his hair (5:1–4).

Ezekiel set forth Israel's apostasy and divine judgment in many forms of prophetic speech: oracles of judgment (6:1–7:27); the vision of the temple (chaps. 8–11); the parable of the worthless vine (15:1–8); the allegory of Jerusalem (16:1–63); the riddle of the eagles, the cedar, and the vine (17:1–24); the proverb of the sour grapes (18:1); an allegorical lament (19:1–14), the allegory of the two sisters (23:1–49); and the parable of the cooking pot (24:1–14).[31]

The visions (1:3–3:15; chaps. 8–11; 37:1–14; chaps. 40–48) form an integral part of Ezekiel's prophecy. The prophet was personally involved in what he saw, much like the apostle John in the Apocalypse.[32] Zimmerli designates this dimension as "autodramatic," that is, the involvement of the prophet in the vision and in the message.[33]

Powerful as the variety of prophetic imagery is, Ezekiel's contemporaries dismissed his message as fabrications, "Isn't he just telling parables?" (20:49), and responded, as we saw earlier, with a proverb of their own, "The days go by and every vision comes to nothing" (12:22). Many loved to listen to the magnificence of Ezekiel's expressions and imaginations. He was a sweet singer in a foreign land, but his prophetic speech had little impact on his hearers (33:32).[34]

The book's chronological arrangement provides a framework for interpreting the prophecy in relation to the exile of Jehoiachin (1:1–3).[35] Chapters 1–24 may be dated to the period between Ezekiel's call and the beginning of the siege of Jerusalem (593–588 B.C.). The oracles against the nations (chaps. 25–32) are not in chronological sequence; several are dated in respect to the years of Jerusalem's siege and destruction (24:1; 26:1; 29:1; 30:20; 31:1); some from shortly after the fall of Judah (32:1, 17; 33:21; 40:1); and the latest oracle is dated 571 B.C. (29:17). Apparently factors other than chronology were operative in the selection and collection process of these oracles. The third collection (oracles of salvation, chaps. 33–48) is associated with the post-586 events. When the exiles received word of Jerusalem's fall (33:21), all hope in a speedy return was dashed. God's word in exile had been confirmed. But this occasion was also the moment to comfort the godly with the hope of restoration and transformation. Thus the news of Jerusalem's fall provides a transition from the message of judgment (1:1–24:27) to the proclamation of hope and the glorious future for the remnant (chaps. 33–48).

Structure

    I. Yahweh's judgment on Judah, 1:1–24:27
      A. Ezekiel's call, 1:1–3:21
      B. Ezekiel's vicarious suffering, 3:22–5:4
      C. Oracles of judgment, 5:5–7:27
      D. Vision of the temple, 8:1–11:25

E. The Exile, 12:1–20
F. True and false prophecy, 12:21–13:23
G. Oracles of judgment, 14:1–23
H. Extended metaphors, 15:1–17:24
 I. Individual responsibility, 18:1–32
J. Lament, 19:1–14
K. Oracles of judgment, 20:1–23:49
L. Parable of the cooking pot, 24:1–14
M. The death of Ezekiel's wife, 24:15–27
II. Oracles against the nations, 25:1–32:32
  A. Ammon, 25:1–7
  B. Moab, 25:8–11
  C. Edom, 25:12–14
  D. Philistia, 25:15–17
  E. Tyre, 26:1–28:19
  F. Sidon, 28:20–26
  G. Egypt, 29:1–32:32
III. Oracles of salvation, restoration, and transformation, 33:1–48:35
  A. Ezekiel's call as watchman, 33:1–33
  B. Oracles of restoration and desolation, 34:1–39:29
  C. Vision of the glorious and holy temple, 40:1–43:12
  D. Regulations of access, 44:1–46:24
  E. Vision of transformation, 47:1–48:35

The Message of Ezekiel

The Vision of Yahweh's Glory

The book of Ezekiel opens with a magnificent and awe-inspiring vision of the glory (*kābôd*) of God. Ezekiel saw a windstorm, an immense cloud, flashing lightning, and brilliant light (1:4). As he watched the cloud coming from the north, he saw more clearly the strange phenomena associated with it: fire, like glowing metal, and an appearance of four living creatures, which he identified as cherubim (v. 5; 10:20). The four cherubim could move like lightning in any direction the Lord wanted them to move (1:5–12). The fact that there were four and that they were different in appearance may denote the sovereignty of God over "the four corners" of the earth, that is, his whole creation.

Ezekiel also saw wheels, which were parts of a chariot. It was his prophetic manner of portraying the coming of the Divine Warrior. Yahweh was approaching on his chariot of war to bring judgment on his people (1:15–18). As he observed the cherubim and the wheels move harmoniously (vv. 19–21), Ezekiel slowly began to focus on the *visio Dei*. He saw God from afar. There was a separation between God and the prophet (vv. 22–23), but he heard "a voice" from above "the expanse." Then he saw the throne of God.

> A throne of sapphire, and high above on the throne was a figure like that of a man. I saw that from what appeared to be his waist up he looked like glowing metal, as if full of fire, and that from there down he looked like fire; and brilliant light surrounded him. Like the appearance of a rainbow in the clouds on a rainy day, so was the radiance around him. This was the appearance of the likeness of the glory of the LORD (1:26–28).

This vision of God's glory was to remain with the prophet throughout his ministry. The glorious Yahweh appeared to Ezekiel in exile.[36] Yahweh's presence in a foreign land confirms his sovereignty and his freedom; that is, he cannot be restricted to any one place, including the temple.[37] On subsequent occasions Ezekiel saw the glory of the Lord.[38] The wonder of God's glory bespoke the uniqueness of God's revelation[39] as he revealed to Ezekiel what he was about to do in Jerusalem. The prophet received a vision of the horrendously pagan practices of the old Jerusalem so that he could explain to the exiles why the Lord would abandon his people and his temple (chaps. 8–10; 11:22–25).

Yahweh also revealed to Ezekiel that he would return. Ezekiel asked, "Will you completely destroy the remnant of Israel?" (11:13). The Lord assured him that he had marked all the godly for himself. Even though they would suffer with the wicked, they were "marked" as his remnant (9:3–4, 11). The glory of the Lord departed from Jerusalem (11:22–24), leaving the people unprotected and vulnerable to the judgment.[40]

Yahweh is free in judgment and in restoration, in leaving Jerusalem and in being with the exiles in Babylon. Klein sees in the opening vision "a cascade of images" that "declares Yahweh's mobility and his ability to be present in Babylon."[41] This God is free in promising his presence to all who wait for him, wherever they may be found. There is hope, even in the midst of judgment.[42] Ezekiel speaks and acts because of Yahweh's antecedent speech and actions.[43] Yahweh promises to renew his involvement in the *regathering* of the remnant (11:17), to bring about a spiritual *transformation* (vv. 19–20; 18:31), and to effect covenant *renewal* (11:20). Yahweh, therefore, is the hope of Israel.

I Am Yahweh

The focus of this hope lies in his name, "I am Yahweh." In Ezekiel the distinctive phrase "I am the LORD" is generally associated with the recognition formula "you will know"[44] (*y-d-ʿ*, "know") as a demonstration of Yahweh's covenant lordship.[45] The self-disclosure formula[46] is rooted in the tradition of the Exodus and conquest,[47] according to which Yahweh had promised to fulfill all his promises (see Ezek. 20)[48] with the guarantee of his name, "I am Yahweh." By it Yahweh had encouraged an exasperated Moses that he was true to his promises of deliverance and had guaranteed it with his own signature: "I am Yahweh" (Ex. 6:2). He had commanded Moses to proclaim to the Israelites that deliverance, covenant, and their future bliss are *guaranteed* by the threefold self-disclosure of his name, "I am Yahweh. . . . I am Yahweh. . . . I am Yahweh" (vv. 6–8).

Ezekiel reflected on this stage in redemptive history, namely, on the marvel of Yahweh's self-disclosure to Israel and on his fidelity. Yahweh is the God of the fathers, the God of Israel, the God of the past, present, and future. He chose Israel and guaranteed the fulfillment of the promises by means of his very name, Yahweh (Ezek. 20:5). Further, he stipulated that he expected absolute loyalty from his covenant people (vv. 7, 19), especially the keeping of the Sabbath as the sign of the covenant relationship (v. 20; see Ex. 31:12–17). Though Israel had severely strained this relationship by her frequent rebellions (vv. 8–31), Yahweh graciously planned to purify a remnant to himself in his name: "I will purge you of those who revolt and rebel against me. Although I will bring them out of the land where they are living, yet they will not enter the land of Israel. Then you will know that I am Yahweh" (v. 38).

Ezekiel affirmed that Yahweh is faithful and that the name of the Lord is his guarantee of hope to those who look to him, even when they witness his judgments. This explains the frequent use of the phrase "I am Yahweh" in the context of judgment on Judah (6:7, 10, 13; 7:4, 27; 11:10, 12; 12:15, 20; 13:14, 21, 23; 14:8; 15:7; 22:16) and in the oracles against the nations (25:5, 7, 11, 17; 26:6; 28:22–23; 30:8, 19, 25–26; 32:15). (See figure 66.)

The basis for covenant renewal lies in God's signature: "You will know that *I am the LORD,* when I deal with you for my name's sake" (20:44, emphasis mine). The token of the promised restoration is the return of the Jews to the land: "Then you will know that I am the LORD, when I bring you into the land of Israel, the land I had sworn with uplifted hand to give to your fathers" (v. 42).

The prophetic use of the name of the Lord has elements of continuity and discontinuity. The Lord will be true to his promises, but not apart from judgment. The Lord freely opens up a new era in the progress of fulfillment, but in an unexpected, magnificent way! He will gather his people into the land (39:28), renew his covenant with the remnant (34:25), transform his creation (vv. 27, 30), bless his people (36:11, 38), and transform them by his Spirit (37:6, 14).[49]

Yahweh's fidelity to his very name is also related to his glory and holiness as the great King over all the earth, who delivers his people, provides for them, blesses them, and protects them. The name Yahweh is the testimony of God to the nations.[50]

I will show the holiness of my great name, which has been profaned among the nations, the name you have profaned among them. Then the nations will know that I am the LORD, declares the Sovereign LORD, when I show myself holy through you before their eyes (36:23).

And so I will show my greatness and my holiness, and I will make myself known in the sight of many nations. Then they will know that I am the LORD (38:23).

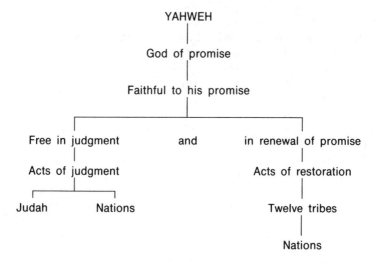

"THEN YOU WILL KNOW THAT I AM YAHWEH"

Figure 66. The Self-Disclosure Formula in Ezekiel

The nations will live to witness God's fidelity in judgment, but also in restoration, or in the words of Gottwald, "The restored Israel will exist as a constant demonstration to the nations that Yahweh is Lord. Precisely for this reason the nations are not to be destroyed, for dead men cannot acknowledge the honor of Yahweh."[51]

Restoration and Transformation

Ezekiel's ministry was not crowned with success. The exiles preferred to listen to the blind optimism of the false prophets (chap. 13)—the "shepherds" who fattened themselves at the expense of the flock (34:2–3). The prophet declared God's judgment on these shepherds (vv. 2–10), but he also announced a new future when the Lord will be the faithful Shepherd of the remnant. He will gather the flock and care for them himself (vv. 11–22).[52] (See figure 67.)

PROMISE AND FULFILLMENT

Hope in the new age lies in the acts of Yahweh, who promises to restore a new people to himself. The acts of God include (1) the renewal of the covenant relationship (36:20–36; 37:23, 26; 39:25); (2) Israel's restoration to the land (36:1–15, 24; 37:14–23; 39:27); (3) the spiritual transformation of the people (36:25–27; 37:14; 39:29); (4) blessing (36:8–12, 29–30, 33–35; 37:26), including victory over enemies (35:1–15; 36:36; 37:28; 38:1–39:24); (5) the restoration of a Davidic king, the Messiah (37:24–25); and (6) his presence in the temple (37:26–27). (See figure 67.)

The new acts are in grand fulfillment of the creation, Abrahamic, Mosaic, and Davidic covenants—in the new context of transformation. Transformation involves both the redeemed community and creation. Transformation of creation opens up the fullness of the enjoyment of God's blessings.

In a vision, Ezekiel saw the blessing of God on the restored land (chaps. 47–48) and the presence of God with his people (43:6–11). He portrayed the transformation of heaven and earth by the presence of God. In metaphors and in the language of accommodation, Ezekiel spoke of God's plan to restore a people who in the end would enjoy eternal bliss.[53] He saw in a vision the New Jerusalem as the symbol of restoration; because of that city it may be said, "The LORD is there" (48:35).

Yahweh the Great Shepherd

David, the Messianic Shepherd-Prince

One   flock

Spiritual transformation
Messianic community
Presence of the Lord
Blessings
Protection

Figure 67. The Transformation

RENEWAL OF THE COVENANTS

The rejection of God's people in exile did not last forever. The Lord promised to take a faithful remnant to himself and to raise out of them a new people. Ezekiel proclaimed the good news to the exiles that the Lord would again renew, restore, and relate to them as his "people" (37:12–13) so that all the nations might recognize his holy name (39:7, 25, 27). The new community would consist of the remnant who are purified by the Spirit of God[54] and who serve God as living witnesses to the nations.[55]

The promise also extends to the land, which was originally given to Abraham and his descendants. Ellison restores the place of the land to the people.

> For the average modern man a juxtaposition of land and people in a spiritual setting is meaningless. . . . So a man and the land on which he lives and from which he draws his nourishment are linked. . . . The New Testament neither denies nor abrogates this basic truth of man's being.[56]

The token of God's presence is the Spirit of God. He is the Spirit of transformation, assuring God's people of the victorious outcome of his intervention on their behalf. The Spirit renews human beings and internalizes God's law so that they will experience a new freedom (36:26–27). The presence of the Spirit signifies a renewal of relationship, the benefits of the restoration (37:14; see John 16:15; Acts 2:38; 3:19; Rom. 8:2, 4, 15), and peace (34:25). His presence among them is for blessing and protection.

God's restless people in exile were also promised rest from their searching, from their enemies, and from their toil. This explains the emphasis on God's judgment on the nations before (chaps. 25–32)[57] and in the middle of (35:1–15; 36:36; 37:28; 38:1–39:24) the oracles of salvation (34:1–48:35). Throughout these magnificent chapters of restoration, the Lord reminds his people that restoration is always in relation to the nations.[58]

This may account for the oracle against Gog and Magog (38:1–39:20) being set in the context of oracles of salvation (37:15–28; 39:21–29). The seemingly discordant element of trouble amidst the promises of restoration has a sobering effect on how we read the oracles of deliverance. Why did Ezekiel introduce this dissonance? First, restoration is God's act of self-disclosure to the nations. The transition from the oracle of salvation to the oracle against Gog and Magog significantly prepares the reader for understanding God's acts in restoration and in judgment: "Then the nations will know that I the LORD make Israel holy, when my sanctuary is among them forever" (37:28). Restoration is God's work of consecrating a people to himself, and each aspect of restoration witnesses to God's fidelity in the context of his creation: "The nations will know that I am the LORD" (or "I am Yahweh," v. 28).

Second, restoration elicits a negative response from the nations *on earth* as they anxiously protect their interests and war against the coming of God's kingdom on earth. The vision of the glorious transformation is set in the framework of reality. Restoration, fulfillment, and transformation provoke opposition to the rule of God and evoke a response of perseverance.[59] The godly receive the glorious assurance that the Sovereign Lord is already present in his kingdom.[60] Yet Yahweh will manifest his glory to all the nations that he is Lord and that no power can resist him, not even Gog and Magog: "I will display my glory among the nations, and all the nations will see the punishment I inflict and the hand I lay upon them" (39:21). (See figure 68.)

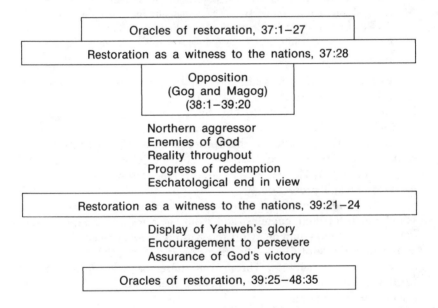

Figure 68. The Oracles of Deliverance and of Judgment

Third, the Gog-Magog motif cannot be restricted to an exclusive historical[61] or eschatological[62] relevance. The language of chapters 38–39 contains both historical and eschatological motifs. The kingdom of God evokes acts of hostility and persecution from human kingdoms. Be that as it may, God's people are forewarned to prepare for the reality of opposition throughout the progress of redemption. The prophecy may also be understood in the light of Israel's subsequent history. The kingdoms of the north are symbolic of any opposition. Indeed, aggressors came from the north: the Greeks, the Seleucids, and the Romans. This leads me to agree with Aalders, who views this prophecy as a progressive fulfillment from the days of Israel's restoration to the

334

land to the Day of the Lord when all opposition will be put down. He writes,

> Ezekiel's prophecy has already received its incipient and direct fulfillment in the historical events associated with the Seleucid aggression against Israel, in the name of Antiochus Epiphanes and his successors, but it will be completely and finally fulfilled in the eschatological opposition of a world power, opposed to God and to the Christian church.[63]

I would go one step further by emphasizing the continual opposition of the kingdoms of this world to the kingdom of Christ. As long as this opposition lasts, the power of Gog and Magog is real,[64] but so is the assurance that our Lord will overcome (Rev. 20:1–10)![65]

Fourth, the conclusion of the oracles against the nations (39:21) leads into a summary of God's acts of deliverance (vv. 25–29). The Lord promises to reveal his glory in his judgment on the rebels *and* in his establishment of his kingdom among his people (v. 21; see Isa. 40:5). The vision of opposition, of God's victory over the enemies, and of his involvement with his people is an encouragement to all the godly to persevere and to await the redemption by the Lord of glory. (See figure 68.)

Renewal of the Mosaic Covenant

The Lord also confirmed the Mosaic covenant in the revelation concerning the temple, the priesthood, the sacrificial regulations, and the festivals. A large section of the last division is devoted to the description of the restored temple (40:1–46:24) and the return of the glory of God. The vision of the presence of God, who had departed in judgment from Jerusalem (10:18–19; 11:22–24), reassures the remnant that God will renew grace and forgiveness to his people (43:2–5). He will again dwell among them, and the temple will be the symbol of his presence: "My dwelling place will be with them" (37:27).[66]

The new community (11:19; 18:31; 36:26; 39:29) is discontinuous with the previous era. The old community consisted of a rebellious majority and a godly minority. The new community has the Spirit of God and is united by having undergone a spiritual transformation, cleansing, and consecration (36:25) and by having a desire to do the will of God (vv. 26–27). The Spirit is the token of restoration, of communion with God, and of the covenant: "I will put my Spirit in you and you will live, and I will settle you in your own land. Then you will know that I the LORD have spoken, and I have done it" (37:14; see 39:29).

Renewal of the Davidic Covenant

The Lord also assured the renewal of the Davidic covenant,[67] transformed by a harmonious relationship[68] between Yahweh and his Messiah (34:24).[69] The Messiah is the Royal Shepherd who will walk in fellowship with Yahweh and establish Yahweh's kingdom in righteousness and justice.[70] He will rule forever over all God's people (37:15–25), and they will establish God's kingdom: "My servant David will be king over them, . . . and they will follow my laws. . . . and David my servant will be their prince forever" (vv. 24–25).

The messianic Shepherd-Prince leads the flock in the way of righteousness. His kingdom advances and establishes the kingdom of God by encouraging the flock to follow his example: "They will follow my laws and be careful to keep my decrees" (37:24). He truly is God's servant. He promotes God's interests on earth (v. 25) and fosters the relationship between the people; the closeness of fellowship is set forth in his relation to the priests and in his kingship (44:3). He, too, will receive tribute from the people (45:16) as he exalts the worship of Yahweh in the temple (v. 17; see v. 22; 46:2–18).

Ezekiel did not fully comprehend the significance of these prophecies as he spoke of the kingdom of God, the Davidic Messiah, obedient service, atonement, and the worship of Yahweh. From the New Testament revelation we conclude that the Shepherd-King-Prince-Servant is none other than Jesus the Messiah, who is both the Suffering Servant and the Lord of Glory. He was an obedient Servant even unto death, whom the Father has glorified (Acts 3:13). He is the Good Shepherd (John 10:1–2). He is the Prince-King-Messiah, by whom the Lord grants forgiveness of sin (Acts 5:31), who will bring the "times of refreshing" (3:19), and by whom the Father will "restore everything" (v. 21). (See figure 67.)

The new covenant of peace (34:25) includes all essential elements of the previous covenants, but is even more glorious and permanent. First, it is more glorious because the Lord repeatedly affirms his involvement. The monergistic emphasis of the renewal of the covenant does not keep individuals from seeking to implement the kingdom of God, but it makes the promises and the fulfillment firmer. God has guaranteed to supervise, execute, and finish his plan. Second, it is more glorious because all tribes share in the kingdom of God on an equal basis (47:13–48:29).[71] All subjects of the kingdom enjoy the benefits of the one Shepherd-King and the one Shepherd-Prince. Clearly, Ezekiel is striving to level all distinctions between the tribes and to advance the new notion of the democratization of the people of God.[72] Even Gentiles have a place in Israel (47:22–23)! Third, the glorious theocracy is more permanent because of the transformation of the people, the land, and the institutions. The focal point of all the promises is the one promise of the presence of the glorious and holy Shepherd-King among his people in blessing and protection (34:25–31).

Yahweh (the Shepherd-King), the Davidic descendant (the Shepherd-Prince), and the Spirit will inaugurate a grand era of transformation involving Israel, the nations, and creation. A significant metaphor of transformation is the river that flows from the presence of God and changes death to life, sickness to healing, and adversity to prosperity (47:1–12). It is no wonder that John borrows this ancient imagery when he describes the New Jerusalem with the River of Life flowing from it (Rev. 21:1–22:6).[73] I appreciate Levenson's concluding words of his intriguing work.

> Two and a half millennia after the composition of the program of restoration of Ezek. 40–48, it still stands as a judgment upon all human history and as a beacon to all who, even in the bleakest days, continue to hope for what it promises and to labor for what it mandates, humbly, in expectation on that "very high mountain" (40:2) and catching a glimpse of the city whose name is "The Lord is there" (48:35).[74]

Review

The book of Ezekiel reveals a symmetrical balance. It begins with exile and the departure of Yahweh's glory from Jerusalem (chaps. 1–24). It concludes with a vision of the restoration from exile and the return of God's glorious presence among his people (chaps. 33–48). The former era is characterized by disgrace, defilement, and the opposition of the kingdom of man against the kingdom of God. The latter chapters emphasize the glory, consecration, and harmonious coexistence between Yahweh and his people, between Yahweh and the Prince-Messiah, and between the kingdom of God universal and his kingdom among his people. The prophet also proclaimed God's judgment on the nations, typical of everything that is human: pride, autonomy, and disregard of Yahweh (chaps. 25–32).

The tension between old and new remains even in the era of restoration. Nevertheless, the light of the eschaton shines throughout the progress of redemption in the return from exile, the renewal of covenant, the restoration of the kingdom, the times of refreshing, the ministry of the Messiah-Shepherd-Servant-Prince, and the presence of God (chaps. 33–48). Yahweh guarantees the fulfillment of his promises of a transformed people and of a transformed world. The river flowing from the throne of God (see Ps. 46:4–6) symbolizes life, blessing, and the restoration of God's people. Transformation is present in the people who have undergone a spiritual metamorphosis. Central to the harmonious relationship between God and his people (Shepherd and sheep) is the place of the Davidic king. Through the submission of the Davidic king to the suzerainty of the great King, creation is renewed.[75]

The focus of the era of transformation is the temple.[76] This vision encouraged the postexilic community to consider the temple as the symbol of God's presence.[77] Yet the prophetic vision goes beyond the temple institution to a state of transformation by the very presence of Yahweh. As Levenson expressed it, "The Temple is the epitome of the world, a concentrated form of its essence, a miniature of the world . . . a microcosm of which the world itself is a macrocosm . . . The real Temple is the one to which it points, the one in 'heaven.'"[78]

THE MESSAGE OF DANIEL: THE KINGDOM IS THE LORD'S AND OF THE SAINTS

Daniel and His Time

Daniel[79] was exiled in "the third year of the reign of Jehoiakim"[80] along with a cross section of prominent citizenry and craftsmen (1:1; see Jer. 25:1; 46:2). In that tragic hour "the Lord [*Adonai*] delivered" (v. 2) precious articles from his temple and prominent young men of Jerusalem to Babylon. This was the beginning of the devastation of Judah, announced by Isaiah, Micah, Zephaniah, and Habakkuk. It was by the will of Adonai that they went into exile and that the temple vessels were placed in the treasury of "the temple of his [Nebuchadnezzar's] god in Babylonia" (v. 2)

Daniel was selected to become the king's courtier in a foreign land. He received special training in Babylon and distinguished himself by a God-given ability to interpret dreams. As he had done with Joseph in Egypt, God raised up Daniel to be his spokesman in a foreign court. He served under Nebuchadnezzar, Belshazzar,[81] and Darius the Mede[82] from about 600 to 536 B.C.

Daniel and his friends (Hananiah, Mishael, Azariah) were placed in a pagan environment where they received a pagan education. As part of their cultural integration, they received new names (Belleshazzar, Shadrach, Meshach, Abednego, respectively). (See figure 69.)

Nebuchadnezzar entrusted Ashpenaz, principal of the royal academy, with teaching the Jewish lads the history, structures, and superiority of Babylonian culture. All students at the royal academy were required to be without physical handicap, to be attractive in appearance, to show "aptitude for every kind of learning, [to be] well informed, quick to understand, and qualified to serve in the king's palace" (1:4). Ashpenaz was expected to transform the Judean youths into cultured Babylonian princes, well read in Babylonian language and literature, including Aramaic, the official language of the empire. The curriculum lasted some three years, during which time the young men were to develop into competent and cultured statesmen who would be expected to perpetuate the political, social, judicial, and economic structures of the Babylonian kingdom.

Name	Meaning	New Name	Meaning[83]
Daniel	"My judge is God"	Belteshazzar	"May he [a god] protect his life"
Hananiah	"Yahweh has been gracious"	Shadrach	"I am fearful [of god]"
Mishael	"Who is what God is"	Meshach	"I am of little account"
Azariah	"Yahweh has helped"	Abednego	"Servant of the shining one"

Figure 69. Daniel and His Friends

The Lord gives wisdom to those who seek him diligently. In exile Daniel did not raise issues about nonissues. He wisely chose to deal with those matters that were of concern to his faith. In a foreign court and in a pagan environment he could have tried to bear witness, to criticize, or to reconstruct the Babylonian system; instead, devotion, service, discretion, and diligence characterized Daniel's life. He did not seek rewards, power, or prestige for his own sake. This servant of the great King feared the Lord of creation while he served a human king.

Daniel and his friends lived as a counterculture in Babylon. They set themselves apart as servants of the Most High God in their use of food, their absolute refusal of idolatry, and their devotion to prayer. It is not entirely clear why they abstained from all meat and the use of wine, because not all meat was unclean and wine was never prohibited in the Law, except in the case of a Nazirite vow (Num. 6:1–4). It may well have been that they had taken a vow to consecrate themselves to the Lord for the sake of the kingdom of God in a foreign land. Since food and drink were offered to idols, the association with idolatry may have made the food unclean. Though we do not know why these youths chose not to eat certain foods, they witness to the development of a counterculture even in exile. Amidst all the pagan entrapments, these godly men lived by the Word of God and knew how to wisely distinguish between *revelation* and *tradition*. Their integrity was to be a living witness to the Lord, and in every word spoken, "Dan[iel] displays no fanaticism or rudeness."[84]

Faith has its own rewards. The Lord was with Daniel in that Ashpenaz showed "favor and sympathy to Daniel" (1:9), even though he greatly feared the wrath of the king. He gave them a ten-day trial period (v. 14), found them to be in excellent health (v. 15), and permitted them to continue their way of life (vv. 15–16). When they were presented to Nebuchadnezzar, he found the lads to be superior to his courtiers in "every matter of wisdom and understanding" (v. 20).

Daniel distinguished himself in serving the Lord and his king (2:48; 5:29; 6:3). He did not elbow his way in to become the leader but considered his friends as well (2:49). Nobody could find fault with him (6:5). Daniel's friends resisted opportunism by refusing to submit themselves to Nebuchadnezzar's decree to worship his image, symbolic of the Babylonian system. When the king challenged their faith in the face of a fiery death (3:15), they firmly held to their faith that God was able to deliver them (vv. 16–17). Their faith was so strong that they were determined to submit to the Lord, even if he would not miraculously deliver them (v. 18). The narrative portrays the transformation of a powerful and rational emperor into an irrational and overzealous monomaniac. But when he saw four men walking in the fire, Nebuchadnezzar had to recognize that the men were "servants of the Most High God" (v. 26).

Throughout his lengthy service to the kings of Babylon and Persia, Daniel wisely adapted to the political changes (see 10:1). The Lord was with his Judean prince. He gave Daniel wisdom and prominence in Babylon's court for sixty-five years (ca. 601–536 B.C.).

Literary Form and Structure

Literary Form

The book of Daniel has come to us written in Hebrew (1:1–2:4a; 8:1–12:13) and Aramaic (2:4b–7:28). The work reflects the historical situation in Babylon; Imperial Aramaic had become the official language of the Near East.[85]

The book's position in the English Bible is different from that in the Hebrew Bible (Masoretic text). In the Hebrew Bible Daniel is placed in the third division (the Writings), after Esther and before Ezra-Nehemiah. The reason is not entirely clear. Critics have argued that the book was not written until after the prophetic era—after the second section (the Prophets) was already closed—and therefore it could be included only in the last section of the Hebrew Bible.[86]

Beckwith has argued convincingly that the present Hebrew canonical order is relatively late.[87] Koch confirms this thesis with particular reference to Daniel. He demonstrates that a shift took place in Judaism from eschatology to law, and with that change in emphasis Daniel was relocated from the Prophets to the Writings, the third division of the

Hebrew canon.[88] According to the claims of the book (9:2; 10:2), the New Testament (Matt. 24:15), and Jewish and Christian tradition, the "prophet" Daniel is its author.[89]

The book of Daniel consists of two major sections. Chapters 1–6, presenting Daniel as God's spokesman in Babylon, are written largely in a third person narrative style and relate the experiences of Daniel and his friends in the foreign court. They depict the challenge of a pagan culture to a living faith. These stories are intertwined with dreams and interpretations of the dreams.

Chapters 7–12, written in the first person, are comprised of visions and their interpretations. Characteristic is the apocalyptic genre.[90] Hanson has argued in favor of the continuity of the prophetic and apocalyptic eschatology.[91] Collins has demonstrated that Daniel does not offer an escape type of apocalyptic eschatology.[92] The visions of Daniel are symbolic but relate to time and space. They encourage human beings to live wisely in anticipation of God's kingdom, as human action is important in God's grand plan.[93]

The critics now attempt to escape the trap that they themselves have set up. Scholars have advanced learned arguments for the unity of Daniel,[94] demonstrating convincingly that the work was composed in the second century B.C. But recently many have argued in favor of a sixth-century date of the narratives (chaps. 1–6) and a later literary development (chaps. 7–11).[95] For example, Childs explains the book of Daniel as a composite of a sixth-century work consisting of the stories of Daniel (chaps. 1–6) and a midrashic reinterpretation of Daniel and other prophecies (chaps. 7–12).[96] Joyce Baldwin rightly concludes, "Prove that part of the book comes from an earlier period, and the Maccabean dating becomes untenable unless its unity is abandoned."[97] Undaunted by the evangelical arguments in favor of the unity of a sixth-century book of Daniel,[98] John G. Gammie proposes that there were three steps in the literary development of Daniel;[99] he indicates that the sixth-century original was modified in view of changing historical circumstances.[100]

The book must have been completed shortly after the capture of Babylon. It records the transfer of authority from Babylon to Persia, but is completely silent on the decree of Cyrus permitting the return of the Jews (538 B.C.).

Structure

In her commentary Joyce Baldwin argues persuasively for the unity and literary integrity of Daniel: "The skilful use of literary pattern and progression reaffirms the unity of the book, with its one main theme: the cost but final vindication of witness in a hostile society."[101] The structure of the book of Daniel displays a progressive parallelism;

chapters 2, 7–9, and 11 unfold from different angles the motif of God's kingdom in confrontation with human kingdoms.[102]

Section 1: Daniel, his friends, and royalty, 1:1–6:28

  Introduction: The preparation of Daniel and his friends, 1:1–21
    I. The kingdoms of this world face the kingdom of God, 2:1–6:28
      A. Dream of the image of the four kingdoms, 2:1–49
        B. The rescue of Daniel's friends from the fiery furnace, 3:1–30
          C. Nebuchadnezzar's dream of the tree, Daniel's interpretation, and Nebuchadnezzar's humiliation, 4:1–37
          C'. Belshazzar's feast, the writing on the wall, and God's judgment 5:1–31
        B'. The rescue of Daniel from the lions' den, 6:1–28
  Section 2: Visions and interpretations, 7:1–12:13
      A. Vision of the four beasts, 7:1–28
    II. Vision of the kingdoms, 8:1–27
    III. Daniel's prayer and vision of the seventy weeks, 9:1–27
    IV. Vision of the coming troubles and victory, 10:1–12:13

The Message of Daniel

The message focuses on the sovereignty of the Creator-Redeemer over the kingdoms of this world, on the suffering and perseverance of the saints during the wars among the kingdoms of this earth, and on their final reward. Difficult as it may be to fit all the pieces together, the general scope of Daniel, like that of Revelation, gives a kingdom perspective. It presents a realized eschatology, giving the saints a vision of the Lord's working out his plan of redemption in history. This revelation is not intended to further speculation but to encourage perseverance in faith, hope, and love. It is to inspire confident hope in the final establishment of the everlasting kingdom of God.[103]

The complexity of Daniel reflects the wisdom of God's plan of redemption. God holds the key to understanding the prophecy of Daniel and has given it to his Messiah to establish his kingdom. We do well to take our cue from Jesus, who saw in the prophecies of Daniel an interaction between the acts of God and of man, as well as an encouragement to persevere (see Matt. 24; Luke 21).[104] At the intersection of the divine and the human, God is victorious in establishing his kingdom, judging the proud, and redeeming his own. The redeemed are the saints who have persevered in their lives and will receive the privilege of royalty from their Redeemer.

Yahweh Is the Sovereign King

The royal confessions and the living faith of Daniel and his friends stir the godly to ponder the grandeur and sovereignty of the Lord. After the first revelation, Daniel praised the God of his fathers,

> Praise be to the name of God for ever and ever;
>   wisdom and power are his.
> He changes times and seasons;
>   he sets up kings and deposes them.
> He gives wisdom to the wise
>   and knowledge to the discerning.
> He reveals deep and hidden things;
>   he knows what lies in darkness,
>   and light dwells with him.
> I thank and praise you, O God of my fathers:
>   You have given me wisdom and power,
> you have made known to me what we asked of you,
>   you have made known to us the dream of the king.
>   (2:20–23)

He alone is "God in heaven who reveals mysteries" and announces beforehand what will happen (2:28). To him alone belongs all sovereignty, which he gives freely and may freely take away: "The God of heaven has given you dominion and power and might and glory; in your hands he has placed mankind and the beasts of the field and the birds of the air. Wherever they live, he has made you ruler over them all" (vv. 37–38).

Pagan kings, such as Nebuchadnezzar and Darius, confessed the power and wisdom of the Lord. Nebuchadnezzar, the great king of Babylon, had to admit that the religious and intellectual system of Babylon was inferior: "Surely your God is the God of gods and the Lord of kings and a revealer of mysteries, for you were able to reveal this mystery" (2:47). Further, he was forced to confess that the Lord alone can deliver from danger.

> Praise be to the God of Shadrach, Meshach and Abednego, who has sent his angel and rescued his servants! They trusted in him and defied the king's command and were willing to give up their lives rather than serve or worship any god except their own God. . . . for no other god can save in this way (3:28–29).

Nebuchadnezzar also had to confess privately and publicly that the Lord alone is king and that he is free in humbling the proud and in exalting the humble (4:1–3, 34–35, 37; see v. 32; 5:21).

The lessons of the past were not remembered. Several decades later, Daniel rebuked Belshazzar for not having learned from what happened to Nebuchadnezzar, who "acknowledged that the Most High God is sovereign over the kingdoms of men and sets over them anyone he wishes. But you his son, O Belshazzar, have not humbled yourself, though you knew all this. . . . But you did not honor the God who holds in his hand your life and all your ways" (5:21–23).

Darius's decree in the last narrative sums up what the Lord has taught through his faithful servant (6:26–27). Darius affirms that the Lord (1) is the living God, (2) is the everlasting King ("he endures forever; his kingdom will not be destroyed, his dominion will never end"), (3) is able to save, (4) shows his power by "signs and wonders," and (5) extends his sovereignty to all creation ("in the heavens and on the earth").

The righteous rejoice in the present rule of God. Though the Babylonian Empire was powerful and extended over the civilized world of that time, God's kingdom is so much greater! The contrast is continually drawn between the kingdoms of man and the kingdom of God. The kingdoms of man rise and fall according to the will of God, but God's kingdom endures forever. It is *present* as well as *future*. The present aspect of the kingdom extends to God's sovereignty over human kingdoms, to his judgments, to his acts of redemption, and to his providence and governance. If the Babylonian Empire could be likened to a tree, which "grew large and strong and its top touched the sky; it was visible to the ends of the earth. Its leaves were beautiful, its fruit abundant, and on it was food for all. Under it the beasts of the field found shelter, and the birds of the air lived in its branches; from it every creature was fed" (4:11–12)—how much more so God's kingdom!

Thy Kingdom Come

God's children long for the establishment of the kingdom of God in power, glory, and victory. The canonical message of Daniel encourages a hope in the establishment of his kingdom while living in a real world ruled by power politics, egomaniacs, jealousy, and greed.

THE KINGDOMS OF MAN

In chapters 2, 7, 8–9, and 11 the Lord reveals the rise and fall of the kingdoms of man. Through the dream of the image of gold, silver, bronze, iron, and feet mingled with iron and clay, the Lord revealed how one empire would succeed another (chap. 2). The Lord gave Nebuchadnezzar "dominion and power and might and glory" (v. 37) over man and animals (v. 38), but other kingdoms would arise. No matter how powerful the kingdoms of man may appear, all their authority is derived from "the God of heaven." In the end, Yahweh will establish his kingdom, "a kingdom that will never be destroyed, nor will it be left to another people. It will crush all those kingdoms and bring them to an end, but itself will endure forever" (v. 44).

In the first year of Belshazzar (ca. 552/551 B.C.), Daniel had a vision (chap. 7) whose message parallels the first dream of Nebuchadnezzar (chap. 2). Four beasts symbolic of the nations (see Ps. 65:7; Rev. 13:1; 21:1) came out of "the great sea." The appearance of the beasts in each vision had familiar as well as unusual features so that the impact was disturbing (7:15). The prophet used mythopoetic imagery to dramatize the chaotic forces of the kingdoms of this world and Yahweh's sovereignty over them. John Day explains that the animals were derived from Hosea 13:7−8.

> So I will come upon them like a lion,
>   like a leopard I will lurk by the path.
> Like a bear robbed of her cubs,
>   I will attack them and rip them open.
> Like a lion I will devour them;
>   a wild animal will tear them apart.[105]

It is as if Daniel is saying that even if the kingdoms would prove to be like a lion, leopard, bear, or any other "beast," Yahweh is much more powerful! The imagery underwent an eschatologization in Daniel in order to represent the nations as hostile to the kingdom of God.[106] The symbol of human kingship is the "little horn" (7:8) that came out of the horrendous beast (vv. 7−8), opposed God, and was thrown into "the blazing fire" (v. 11). It represents the antichrist, that is, the embodiment of human pride, autonomy, and opposition against the kingdom of God.

The identification of these kingdoms occupies a large place in the interpretation of Daniel. Figure 70 presents the traditional interpretation of the elements in chapters 2 and 7.

Chap. 2	Chap. 7	Traditional Identification
Head of gold	Lion with wings of an eagle	Babylon
Chest and arms of silver	Bear with 3 ribs	Persia
Belly and thighs of bronze	Leopard with 4 wings and 4 heads	Greece
Legs of iron Feet and 10 toes of iron and clay	Beast with iron teeth, 10 horns, and little horn with eyes and mouth	Rome

Figure 70. Daniel 2 and 7

Recently, several evangelical writers have identified the kingdoms with Babylon, Media, Persia, and Greece.[107] This conclusion has come merit in view of the development of the kingdoms in chapters 8, 9, and 11. These three chapters progressively develop a focus on the third kingdom (Greece) with its climactic acts of atrocity during the Seleucid period under Antiochus IV (Epiphanes).

In 550/549 B.C. Daniel saw the vision of the ram (Persia) and the goat (Greece/Macedonia). The two-horned ram was strong and charged to the north, west, and south with amazing strength (8:3–4). Suddenly he faced an even greater power from a goat that charged with lightning speed into the ram and overcame him (vv. 5–7). When a large horn (Alexander the Great) had broken off, it was replaced by four horns (representative of the fourfold division of the Macedonian kingdom). A little horn developed out of one of the four horns and set himself up against God and his people (vv. 9–12). The subsequent interpretation (vv. 19–26) concludes with the assurance that his kingdom, too, will come to an end, "but not by human power" (v. 25).

In 539 B.C. Daniel received the vision of the seventy weeks (chap. 9), in which Gabriel reveals that God's purposes for his people will be accomplished but not without suffering. Suffering comes through "the people of the ruler" who will "destroy the city and the sanctuary" (v. 26). It is a time of "abomination" and "desolation" (v. 27).

In 539 B.C. Daniel received another revelation concerning a human kingdom (chap. 11). It was revealed to him that Persia would fall to Greece (v. 2) and that Greece would be broken up into four kingdoms (vv. 3–4). The focus falls on two of these kingdoms: the North and the South, that is, the Seleucid versus the Ptolemaic (vv. 5–20). Then the spotlight comes on "a contemptible person" (v. 21) who opposes God and persecutes the saints. No doubt this ruler is to be identified with Antiochus Epiphanes (175–164 B.C.), whose atrocities are well known from secular history. The subsequent Jewish revolt under the Maccabees brought an end to the abominations, but not to the Hellenizing process or to the kingdoms of this world.

The further elaboration on the king who "will do as he pleases" (11:36), the ensuing battle, and the encouragement to persevere (11:40–12:4) provide an eschatological framework for interpreting human history. This vision, like previous ones, encourages the godly to look at human events as an unfolding scenario of the continual hostility of human powers against the kingdom of God and his saints. However we may designate the power, it is the antichrist, that is, human power against the Christ of God. This means that the visions of the human kingdoms—with their gradually narrowing focus on Persian rulers, Alexander the Great, and Antiochus Epiphanes—are to be understood in a prophetic framework: humanity versus God. The preexilic prophets similarly had spoken of Edom, Assyria, Babylon, and Tyre as symbolic of the spirit of pride that exalts itself against God. Daniel develops this same characteristic in apocalyptic language, as we also find in the Apocalypse. Here, I agree with Baldwin, who states,

> Consequently the chapter (11) speaks to generations of believers and is not confined in its scope to the second century BC. Rulers will commit themselves wholly to fulfil their ambitions, regardless of what is right. Antiochus is the prototype of many who will come after him, hence the interest shown here in his methods and progress.[108]

Since prophetic usage permits us to look at the four kingdoms as real and yet as representative of the kingdoms of man, I do not think that the historical identification is as important as the kingdom-perspective that these visions give. The rise and fall of human kingdoms and the subsequent rise of the kingdom of God in its fullness did not take place in the Hasmonean victory. Even the coming of Jesus Christ did not fully establish the kingdom of God, though he did inaugurate it more fully. Jesus, too, spoke of the continuing conflict between his kingdom and the kingdoms of this world. He further developed the imagery, derived from Daniel, of the "abomination" and "desolation" (Matt. 24:15–29). According to Luke, our Lord's words found some fulfillment in the desolation of Jerusalem by the Roman armies (Luke 21:20–24). Yet the words of our Lord, like those of the prophets, reveal an eschatological compenetration of the near and the distant. Indeed, the kingdom was in him (Mark 1:1, 11), but the King of glory himself spoke of the continuing battle between the saints and the kingdoms of this world, and of his second coming to establish his kingdom (see Matt. 24).

The graphic description of the battles between the kings of the North and the South (11:2–35), the rise of the wicked king (vv. 36–45), and the promises of protection and the reward of life (12:1–4) encourage the righteous to persevere amidst their trials. It is tempting to restrict the significance of the battles to the events surrounding the rise and fall of Antiochus Epiphanes (169–165 B.C.). But the prophetic-apocalyptic language mixes historical details with a grand picture of opposition by the kingdoms of this world lasting until the final, climactic victory and the full establishment of God's kingdom. This compenetration is not unique to Daniel but is characteristic of prophetic-apocalyptic language. In spite of the disagreements in interpretation, the outcome is sure. The conflicts between the kingdom of God and the kingdoms of this world will continue, but in the end the Lord will establish his glorious kingdom (vv. 40–45).[109]

THE KINGDOM OF GOD

The vision of the human kingdoms gives way to a vision of God ("the Ancient of Days") enthroned on high as the great King (7:9). Daniel described God in more detail than any of the prophets before or after him (see Ezek. 1:15–21, 26–27); his clothing is as white as snow, and his hair is white like wool (v. 9). The throne of God is flaming with fire and is mobile like a chariot, with wheels ablaze (v. 9). The Lord is the great Judge who is seated to judge the kingdoms of this world. There is no escape from his judgment, as a river of fire flows forth from before him. He is the Lord of Hosts with thousands upon thousands awaiting his command (v. 10). The acts of men are recorded in his books, and he is the Judge of all flesh (v. 10).

The Ancient of Days gave authority over the remaining kingdoms to "one like a son of man" (*kebar 'enās,* 7:13). The Son of Man was permitted to approach the throne of the Ancient of Days without experiencing personal hurt and without being judged (v. 13). Instead, he received "authority, glory and sovereign power" and the worship of "all peoples, nations and men of every language" (v. 14; see Rev. 5:9). His kingdom is not temporary or subject to God's judgment; rather, it is "an everlasting dominion that will not pass away, and his kingdom is one that will never be destroyed" (v. 14). Who is the Son of Man?[110] He is the Messiah, whose kingdom will last forever (vv. 14, 27) and who will rule with his saints (v. 27; see Rev. 5:10).[111] He will finally and victoriously crush (see 1 Cor. 15:24–25) the power of the fourth empire and all the kingdoms arising from the fourth empire, including the king who will "speak against the Most High" and who will persecute the saints (7:25).

The four kingdoms symbolize human kingdoms (7:17), which are transitory and in the service of God. But the everlasting kingdom belongs to the Father ("the Ancient of Days"), the Son of Man, and "the saints of the Most High"[112] (*qaddîsê 'elyonîm,* v. 18; see Matt. 19:28–29; Luke 22:29–30; Rev. 5:10).[113] The kingdoms of this world may appear to be victorious over the saints,[114] but the Ancient of Days will intervene on their behalf and judge the horn "in favor of the saints of the Most High" (v. 22). Then the righteous will receive the kingdom as their reward. They will rule with "sovereignty, power and greatness" and enjoy the everlasting kingdom (v. 27).

I conclude that (1) the kingdom has always been God's (Ps. 145:13), (2) the Father has granted sovereignty to the Messiah, our Lord Jesus, (3) the Father, the Son, and the Spirit rule in and over the world, especially the church over which Christ is the head, and (4) we await the full establishment of the kingdom at the glorious return of our Lord. Then Daniel 2:44 will be fulfilled: "In the time of those kings, the God of heaven will set up a kingdom that will never be destroyed, nor will it be left to another people. It will crush all those kingdoms and bring them to an end, but it will itself endure forever."

THE SEVENTY "SEVENS"

For Daniel, the end of Babylon signified the beginning of the establishment of God's kingdom. He was familiar with the prophecy of Jeremiah, according to which the Lord had decreed Babylon's sovereignty to last seventy years (Jer. 25:11–12). Because Babylon had come to an end by 539 B.C., Daniel was expecting the restoration of God's people of which Jeremiah had also spoken. Therefore he prayed for the restoration of the people, the city, Jerusalem, and the temple (9:17–19). He acknowledged the sin of Israel, but trusted in the Lord's mercy and righteousness to be faithful to his promises. Suddenly, the angel Gabriel appeared to him in a vision (vv. 20–21) and explained God's plan. The speedy response was an expression of God's special love for Daniel, "for you are highly esteemed" (v. 23).

Building on the motif of seventy, the angel revealed that the Lord had decreed "seventy 'sevens'" (9:24). The purpose of the "seventy 'sevens'" is to finalize judgment on sin, to atone for sin and transgression, to bring in everlasting righteousness, to fulfill all the prophetic word, and to anoint the most holy (v. 24). The exact identification of the "sevens" is open to interpretation.[115] The emphasis is on the events and the certainty of the progression of redemption[116] rather than on the length of time.[117] The first period of seven "sevens" pertains to the return of the people from exile, the rebuilding of the temple and Jerusalem (from ca. 536 to 445 B.C.).[118] This period begins with "the issuing of the decree to restore and rebuild Jerusalem," but opinions differ whether this took place with Jeremiah's prophecy,[119] with Cyrus's decree to restore the temple in Jerusalem (538 B.C.), or with Nehemiah's permission to restore the walls of Jerusalem (445 B.C.). A longer period of sixty-two "sevens" brings us to the crucifixion of the Messiah (A.D. 27).[120] The last "seven" will witness the death of the Messiah (v. 26a) and the desecration of the temple (vv. 26b–27). Yet human power rises and topples by divine decree (9:27).[121] The book of Daniel, like the book of Revelation, encourages and comforts God's people by its universal message of hope in God's involvement in human affairs. (See figure 71.)

7 "Sevens"	62 "Sevens"	1 "Seven"
Restoration of Jerusalem	Coming of the "Anointed One"	Covenant, desolation, end

Figure 71. Daniel's Seventy "Sevens"

YAHWEH CARES FOR HIS PEOPLE

The godly find comfort in the Lord's caring for his own. The story of Daniel and his friends reflects the correlation of human responsibility and divine sovereignty. On the one hand, "Daniel resolved not to defile himself with the royal food and wine" (1:8). On the other hand, "God had caused the official to show favor and sympathy to Daniel" (v. 9) and gave Daniel "knowledge and understanding of all kinds of literature and learning" (v. 17).

Daniel's prayer (chap. 9)—many years later—also reflects faith and hope in Yahweh's fidelity to his promises. In the first year of Persian rule (539/538 B.C.) Daniel meditated on the prophecy of Jeremiah, who had announced that the Babylonian kingdom was to last seventy years (Jer. 25:11–12) and that subsequently Jerusalem would be restored (chaps. 30–33). Daniel longed for the fulfillment of God's promises as he gave himself to fasting and to prayer (9:3). Daniel's prayer of confession consists of four elements: (1) Israel's rebellious attitude to the Law and the Prophets, (2) Yahweh's righteousness in judgment, (3) the fulfillment of the curses, and (4) the hope in renewal of divine mercy and grace. Throughout the prayer Daniel confessed his faith in Yahweh's fidelity: "LORD, the great and awesome God, who keeps his covenant of love with all who love him and obey his commands" (v. 4). Daniel also affirmed the righteousness of Yahweh in all his acts, including the discipline of his people (v. 14). In this petition Daniel threw himself on the mercy of God; he prayed for the restoration of Jerusalem, the temple, and his presence among his people.

> For your sake, O Lord, look with favor on your desolate sanctuary. . . .
> We do not make requests of you because we are righteous, but because of your great mercy. O Lord, listen! O Lord, forgive! O Lord, hear and act! For your sake, O my God, do not delay, because your city and your people bear your Name (9:17–19)

The Rewards of Perseverance

Victory will not come without persecution and perseverance. These words encourage the godly in any age to await the kingdom of God and to willingly endure suffering. The saints are promised life everlasting and joy, whereas the ungodly will experience everlasting disgrace. The saints who die will be raised to life and will enjoy everlasting bliss, as their names are recorded in the Book of Life (12:1; see Mal. 3:16–18). The saints consist of all who respond wisely to God and who lead others to life, wisdom, and righteous living (Prov. 10:11; 11:30; 13:14; James 5:20). Their future will be glorious; they will share in the victory of the Lord: "Those who are wise will shine like the brightness of the heavens, and those who lead many to righteousness, like the stars for ever and ever" (12:3). The visions were to be sealed so that the wise might read them and gain understanding.

Revelation of the future is for the encouragement and development of hope, faith, and love rather than for speculation. The godly will always find comfort in the revelation of God. Since the coming of our Lord, the Christian community has gained greater insights. The revelation of the Father in Jesus' incarnate ministry and the revelation of Jesus in the Apocalypse assure us that our Lord will be victorious throughout the history of his church till his triumph over "Babylon the Great" and the defeat of Satan. He is the First and the Last (Rev. 1:17), who has revealed to his churches the things that will take place (v. 11).

Daniel received further assurance that these visions are true and will come to pass. He saw two witnesses, one on one bank of the river and the other on the opposite bank. Between the two was the angelic messenger, "the man clothed in linen," who was *above* the river. The fulfillment will take place "for a time, times and half a time" (12:7; see 7:25). Concerned about what he heard, Daniel asked about the outcome. He did not receive much of an answer, but the angelic messenger assured him that the Lord will always have a faithful remnant. This remnant will endure the process during which they "will be purified, made spotless and refined" (v. 10). But the wicked will persevere in their evil and will be cast out of the kingdom to come (v. 10; see v. 2; Rev. 22:11). Blessed are all who wait for the end (12:12; see Rev. 22:10).

The saints may suffer humiliation and disgrace (7:21, 25; see 8:12) while awaiting the kingdom of heaven, but the righteous know that they are citizens of the eternal kingdom of our God and of his Messiah. They also believe that the Lord is the Divine Warrior, and on the day of his vengeance, he will avenge himself on his enemies, establish his kingdom, and grant his saints the privileges of entering that everlasting kingdom and of ruling: "Then the sovereignty, power and greatness of the kingdoms under the whole heaven will be handed over to the saints, the people of the Most High. His kingdom will be an everlasting kingdom, and all rulers will worship and obey him" (v. 27).

The timing of the end is enigmatic. The Lord revealed to Daniel the visions of the progression of redemption up to the final and victorious establishment of his kingdom. These words are to encourage godliness in the face of evil (12:9–10). John Goldingay has put this perspective well.

> We would do well to look at what happens to us as individuals and as the church as part of the struggle between chaos and cosmos which is the world's story from its beginning to its end, and to see these things as the dealings of the eschatological God. In all the power, holiness,

and love that belong to creation and to the end, he is with us in each crisis, and we can experience another foretaste of the final victory.[122]

Though the oppression and persecution may be longer (1,335 days) than the seven years of Antiochus Epiphanes (1,290 days), blessed is everyone who perseveres to the end (v. 12). Jesus said, "But he who stands firm to the end will be saved" (Matt. 24:13).

QUESTIONS AND ISSUES

1. What is the context of Ezekiel's ministry? How does his priestly heritage have a bearing on his message?
2. In what sense was Ezekiel a prophet-watchman? Was the reception of Ezekiel's message better than that of Jeremiah's in Jerusalem? Compare the agony of Ezekiel with that of Jeremiah.
3. What are the literary qualities that explain the popular interest in Ezekiel's message and the problem of understanding what Ezekiel was saying?
4. How does the vision of God relate to the message of Ezekiel? What is the background of the phrase "I am Yahweh"? How does Ezekiel creatively employ it in his prophecy?
5. Explain the prophetic critique implied in the prophet's message that Yahweh will be the Shepherd of the new community. What is the role and function of the Messiah of David?
6. How does the presence of the Spirit secure the transformation and restoration program of Ezekiel? Explain Ezekiel's vision of the renewal of the covenants.
7. Why are several oracles against the nations (Gog and Magog) set within the context of God's promises of restoration? What is the significance of this?
8. What was the historical context of Daniel's ministry? How did Daniel demonstrate that he lived by revelation and wisdom rather than by religious forms?
9. What are some literary characteristics of Daniel? What is apocalyptic? (See also the appendix: "Forms of Prophetic Speech.")
10. How does Daniel live with a kingdom perspective? How does he model this perspective in his own life? Distinguish between the kingdoms of man and the kingdom of God.
11. Discuss the content, progress, and purpose of the confessions of the Babylonian kings in the book of Daniel.
12. Explain how the dream of chapter 2 and the vision of chapter 7 are parallel. What are some of the explanations? What do you think? How does the hermeneutic of progressive fulfillment attempt to

understand these chapters? What is the meaning of "the little horn"?

13. Of what elements does Daniel's prayer (chap. 9) consist? How does the Lord respond to Daniel's prayer? Explain the purpose of the "seventy sevens."

14. What forms of encouragement does the book of Daniel give toward godly living? What is meant by the correlation of human responsibility and divine sovereignty?

CHAPTER 12

Living the Prophetic Word

INTRODUCTION

Thus far an approach to the Prophets has been developed that is open to the interpretation of the prophetic word. This approach flows from a

threefold concern with the future of the Christian faith: the power of
the Spirit in working out God's purposes; *Tota Scriptura;* and the
progress of redemption. I believe that a renewed interest in these three
concerns will go far in inaugurating a Spirit-filled renewal of the church
of Jesus Christ and that this renewal from within may be greatly used by
the Spirit to extend the gospel of the kingdom to the ends of the earth.

This threefold concern is a double-edged sword—it cuts both ways.
The prophets, our Lord, and the apostles warned the community of faith
never to assume privilege: "Therefore, since we are receiving a kingdom
that cannot be shaken, let us be thankful, and so worship God
acceptably with reverence and awe, for our "God is a consuming fire"
(Heb. 12:28–29). The Spirit, however, being God, is free, and in his
freedom he works through the word of revelation (*tota Scriptura*) and
involves individuals and institutions in the progress of redemption. He
may also abandon them (John 15:6; 1 Cor. 3:17; 10:1–13; Heb.
12:16–17; Rev. 2:5; 3:16) if they do not live by the Word, if they
develop their own structures apart from the Spirit, or if they are secure
in their own systems of belief.[1]

I am concerned that the *Spirit*, who carries out the work of the Father
and of our Lord Jesus Christ, would involve the Christian community in
the progress of transformation. I am also concerned that the *whole of
Scripture* be heard and that the individual parts be related to each other.
Further, I am concerned that the people of God be rooted in the *progress
of redemption*—a redemption that involves all God's people from
creation to the new creation—and that they, too, involve themselves in
advancing redemption to the ends of the earth.

The prophets, our Lord, and the apostles urgently set before us the
way of the Spirit, of the whole counsel of God (*tota Scriptura* or "total
interpretation"), and of involvement in the progress of redemption.
There is no higher calling than to seek the kingdom of God and his
righteousness (Matt. 6:33)! This is the way of Christian discipleship
(Luke 18:17, 29–30)—the cutting edge of the razor. All who live on
the razor's edge find that it cuts and keeps on cutting either to our
blessing or to our condemnation (Heb. 4:12–13). (See figure 72.)

SPIRIT: ESCHATOLOGICAL ETHICS

The prophetic books witness to the Spirit's work in creation,
redemption, revelation, and history. The presence of the Spirit is most
evident in human weakness (see 2 Cor. 12:10), as is the absence of the
Spirit in human pride. God's involvement with Israel bears out this
paradox.

The Lord planned to establish his royal kingdom order on earth through Israel and consecrated them to be a holy nation and a royal priesthood (Ex. 19:5–6; Deut 26:18–19; Pss. 114:1–2; 135:4). He also promised to provide rest for his "treasured possession" (*sᵉgullâ,* Ex. 19:5; see Mal. 3:17) from trouble, turmoil, adversity, disgrace, and alienation (Deut. 26:18–19; see Isa. 48:17–19). But he expected his children to conform to his will on earth and to establish a counterculture.

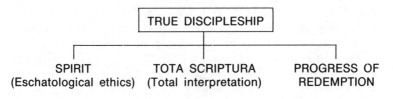

Figure 72. True Discipleship

Israel did not respond; hence they did not enter into his rest (Ps. 95:11). Apart from individuals in whom the Holy Spirit worked, the masses of people remained hardened in their hearts (Deut. 5:29; see 1 Cor. 10:1–13; Heb. 4:6–11). They did not worship the Lord in the Spirit and did not rejoice in doing God's will, but were thoroughly entrenched in the way of religion and thus in the way of the nations.

The prophets charged Israel and Judah with having forsaken their purpose of being God's kingdom on earth. They had exalted themselves like the nations and had little concern with the essential qualities of God's kingdom: righteousness, justice, peace, and fidelity (Rom. 14:17). Isaiah said,

> See how the faithful city
>   has become a harlot!
> She once was full of justice;
>   righteousness used to dwell in her—
>   but now murderers! . . .
> The vineyard of the LORD Almighty
>   is the house of Israel,
> and the men of Judah
>   are the garden of his delight.
> And he looked for justice, but saw bloodshed;
>   for righteousness, but heard cries of distress.
>   (Isa. 1:21; 5:7)

In his freedom God broke covenant, because the nation of Israel did not have the heart to live by divine revelation. The "heart" signifies ultimate love. It is an expression used to denote devotion and loyalty, regardless of the self-sacrifice (see Prov. 2:1–4). Moses had already stressed the vital importance of renewal of the heart: "Oh, that their hearts would be inclined to fear me and keep all my commands always, so that it might go well with them and their children forever! . . . Circumcise your hearts, therefore, and do not be stiff-necked any longer" (Deut. 5:29; 10:16; see Jer. 4:4; 9:25). But Moses had also anticipated a renewal of the covenant (see Deut. 4:30–31; 30:2–10; 32:43) with a greater involvement of the Holy Spirit in transforming the covenant community (Num. 11:29). On the basis of the Mosaic revelation, the prophet Ezekiel challenged the people to return to the Lord for renewal.

> Therefore, O-house of Israel, I will judge you, each one according to his ways, declares the Sovereign LORD. Repent! Turn away from all your offenses; then sin will not be your downfall. Rid yourselves of all the offenses you have committed, and get a new heart and a new spirit. Why will you die, O house of Israel? For I take no pleasure in the death of anyone, declares the Sovereign LORD. Repent and live! (Ezek. 18:30–32)

Thus if Israel would turn from her stiff-necked religious arrogance and in humility look to the Lord, he would relent from his divine abandonment and once again dwell with his people.

Internalization and Democratization

The Lord promised to confirm all his promises and covenants and to involve his people and their offspring more fully by the work of his Spirit. The work of his Spirit was to affect two vital aspects of community life: *internalization* of the revelation of God and *democratization* of the people of God. (See figure 73.)

Internalization

Moses had spoken of internalization in terms of a greater number of people who with changed hearts would live in submission to God's revelation: "The LORD your God will circumcise your hearts and the hearts of your descendants, so that you may love him with all your heart and with all your soul, and live" (Deut. 30:6; Rom. 3:30; Col. 2:11). (See figure 73.)

The prophets developed the Mosaic eschatology by speaking of a new era in which the remnant from Israel and Judah will constitute the new community, bound together by a common loyalty to Yahweh, endowed with the Spirit of God, and blessed with a great increase in number. They make up the new community of the Spirit whose circumcision is that of the heart. This spiritual community will share in the benefits of God's new work, as Isaiah said,

> till the Spirit is poured upon us from on high,
>   and the desert becomes a fertile field,

WORK OF THE SPIRIT IN SCRIPTURE		
C R E A T I O N	**INTERNALIZATION** DEMOCRATIZATION	**R E D E M P T I O N**

WORK OF THE SPIRIT IN SCRIPTURE

C R E A T I O N

INTERNALIZATION   DEMOCRATIZATION

R E D E M P T I O N

Submission to will of God   Servant of God
Individuals   Priest
Children   Prophet
New community   King

Qualities: Righteousness
Justice
Love
Peace

Figure 73. The Work of the Spirit

and the fertile field seems like a forest.
Justice will dwell in the desert
and righteousness live in the fertile field.
The fruit of righteousness will be peace;
the effect of righteousness will be quietness and confidence forever.
My people will live in peaceful dwelling places,
in secure homes,
in undisturbed places of rest.
(Isa. 32:15–18)

Jeremiah encouraged the godly with these words of comfort:

"This is the covenant I will make with the house of Israel
after that time," declares the LORD.
"I will put my law in their minds
and write it on their hearts.
I will be their God,
and they will be my people.
No longer will a man teach his neighbor,
or a man his brother, saying, 'Know the LORD,'
because they will all know me,
from the least of them to the greatest,"
declares the LORD.
"For I will forgive their wickedness
and will remember their sins no more."
(Jer. 31:33–34)

Ezekiel spoke of the Holy Spirit as the agent of transformation and restoration.

> I will sprinkle clean water on you, and you will be clean; I will cleanse you from all your impurities and from all your idols. I will give you a new heart and put a new spirit in you; I will remove from you your heart of stone and give you a heart of flesh. And I will put my Spirit in you and move you to follow my decrees and be careful to keep my laws. You will live in the land I gave your forefathers; you will be my people, and I will be your God (Ezek. 36:25–28).

The Holy Spirit applies the benefits of the new age by assuring the remnant of forgiveness, by drawing them closer to God, and by empowering them with the grace of the new age. The work of the Holy Spirit internalizes the covenant by transforming the covenant community and by adding to their number. Haggai witnessed this glorious reality in the generation after the Exile.

> So the LORD stirred up the Spirit of Zerubbabel son of Shealtiel, governor of Judah, and the Spirit of Joshua son of Jehozadak, the high priest, and the Spirit of the whole remnant of the people. . . . "But now be strong, O Zerubbabel," declares the LORD. "Be strong, O Joshua son of Jehozadak, the high priest. Be strong, all you people of the land," declares the LORD, "and work. For I am with you," declares the LORD Almighty. "This is what I covenanted with you when you came out of Egypt. And my Spirit remains among you. Do not fear" (Hag. 1:14; 2:4–5; capitalization of Spirit in 1:14 is mine).

The Spirit also transforms the offspring, assuring the continuity of the new community from generation to generation. Isaiah declared, " 'As for me, this is my covenant with them,' says the LORD. My Spirit, who is on you, and my words that I have put in your mouth will not depart from your mouth, or from the mouths of your children, or from the mouths of their descendants from this time on and forever' " (Isa. 59:21; see 61:9; 65:23; Acts 2:39). Joel's proclamation extends the promise to all, regardless of sex, age, and social status. These words were more fully realized in the coming of the Spirit at Pentecost (Joel 2:28–32; see Acts 2:17–21, 38–39; Rom. 10:11–13; Gal. 5:16–26).

The goal of the internalization is the full involvement of God's children in his kingdom purposes. God wants them to know him (Ezek. 39:28–29; Hos. 2:20; Joel 2:27; 3:17)! Knowledge of God is the relationship between God and his people that secures their happiness and *shalom* by his very presence, by his blessings, and by his protection. They know that he is Yahweh by his dynamic presence (Ezek. 39:27–28) and that they are the royal children of God and heirs of the covenants and the promises. In this privileged relationship they also know to do the will of God on earth without instruction, additional motivation, or clarification. By the Spirit they live in harmony with God's will with enthusiasm and joy. Those who serve God in the Spirit, having been renewed, are truly free: "Therefore, if anyone is in Christ, he is a new creation; the old has gone, the new has come!" (2 Cor. 5:17; see Gal. 5:1, 16).

Clearly the reality of this new and transformed relationship is still future. The fulfillment lies beyond this present age, but the tokens of the eschaton are given to the children of God by the Spirit. He has begun a good work in us: transformation (renewal, regeneration), the fruit of the Spirit, the knowledge of God, and individual motivation. Left to ourselves, our lights burn out fast. When we depart from the path of the Spirit, our lamps flicker, but in the power of the Spirit our lights are bright as we enjoy victory upon victory and go from joy to joy (Rom. 8:26–39).[2]

Democratization

The democratization of the covenant advances the kingdom of God by the operation of the Holy Spirit. The Father renews the covenant, mediates the benefits, and applies them through the Spirit. The prophetic vision of covenant renewal does not signify the end of the previous covenants or the cessation of the mediatorial role of the covenant officers (priest, prophet, king). But the renewal of the covenant does confirm the benefits and promises of the covenants because of the sovereign administration (monergism) of God, the mediation of the messianic King, and the regenerating, reconciling, and sanctifying work of the Spirit. (See figure 73.)

The Spirit draws individuals, regardless of race, sex, social status, or age, to God. He consecrates them as servants of the living God. The Spirit consecrates them and their children to exalted service: royal priests (Ex. 19:5; Isa. 61:6; 66:21; see 1 Peter 2:9), prophets (Joel 2:28–29), and king (Isa. 55:3–5; see Rev. 5:10). The Father's goal of establishing a holy and royal priesthood on earth (Ex. 19:5; see 1 Peter 2:9) is possible only by the work of the Spirit.

The coming of the Holy Spirit at Pentecost signified a most important event. It marked the coronation of our Lord Jesus Christ, at which time he shared gifts with his church through the Spirit (Rom. 12:4–8; 1 Cor. 12:12–31; Eph. 4:7–13) and gave increase to the church. The democratization promise holds before us the vision of the empowering presence of the Holy Spirit in a greater number of people, permitting them to rise to new heights in the kingdom of God. Democratization of the Spirit liberates human beings for the highest service of God!

360

Theocentric Living/Eschatological Ethics

The godly long for God's presence and seek his kingdom by putting into practice the vision of the transformed world they have received by the Holy Spirit. By the Spirit they draw near to God, live for the sake of God (Pss. 15:1–4; 24:3–6), and seek his kingdom by *imitating God*, that is, theocentric ethics.[3]

Theocentric living begins with a fear of God as expressed in Malachi's question: "But who can endure the day of his coming? Who can stand when he appears? For he will be like a refiner's fire or a launderer's soap" (Mal. 3:2). The question evokes a response in the heart of the godly, and the Spirit comes to their aid and motivates them to practice righteousness, to speak with fidelity, and to seek God's honor, even to their own hurt (Pss. 15:1–5; 24:1–6; Isa. 33:14–16; Mic. 6:8; Luke 3:8–9; John 15:1–8; Rom. 13:11–14; 1 Thess. 5:5–8; Rev. 22:15). The revelation of God receives a new dimension through the Spirit who gives insight, a framework for interpreting God's Word in the light of the divine perfections, and wisdom. The imitation of God (*imitatio Dei*) goes beyond traditional morality in that it begins with the revelation of God, submits to the triune God, reflects on the character of God, consciously applies the revelation of God in the light of Jesus' teaching and ministry, and produces the fruit of the Holy Spirit. (See figure 74.)

Theocentric ethics: For the sake of the **Father**
Framework of God's perfections
Framework of **Jesus'** teaching and life
Fruits of the **Spirit**

Eschatological ethics: Framework of biblical teaching on the **Kingdom:**

Righteousness
Justice
Love and fidelity
Peace

Revelation of God

Wisdom of God, internalized by the Spirit of God

Figure 74. Royal Ethics

Eschatological ethics is a direct outgrowth of theocentric ethics. The vision of the world of transformation, the New Jerusalem, and the new heaven and new earth so influence one's perspective on this world that

361

eschatology (the reflection of the new age) affects every area of life. Hoekema incisively writes,

> Being a citizen of the kingdom, therefore, means that we should see all of life and all of reality in the light of the goal of the redemption of the cosmos. This implies, as Abraham Kuyper once said, that there is not a thumb-breadth of the universe about which Christ does not say, "It is mine." This implies a Christian philosophy of history . . . of culture . . . of vocation: all callings are from God, and all we do in everyday life is to be done to God's praise, whether this be study, teaching, preaching, business, industry, or housework.[4]

Jesus taught that righteousness and justice are pleasing to God when done for the sake of God (theocentric ethics) and for the sake of establishing his kingdom (eschatological ethics). The ethics of Jesus are not revolutionary or novel. They are the ethics of the kingdom, and the ethics of the kingdom are eschatological ethics,[5] to which Moses, the prophets, and the apostles bear harmonious witness.

Jesus did not abrogate the prophetic word but focused it on himself. He taught that he is the focus of the Law and the Prophets (Matt. 5:17–20). Against the Pharisees, Jesus set ethics again in its proper perspective; all ethical decisions, grounded in the Word of God, motivated by the Spirit of God, done out of love for God, inaugurate the eschatological kingdom in space and time. Jesus taught that human beings may carry the yoke of the kingdom by following him and thus be instrumental in bringing the kingdom of God to earth (Matt. 11:28–30). (See figure 74.)

Eschatological ethics—by its very nature—provides a framework for interpreting and applying the words of Moses and the prophets and the teaching of our Lord and his apostles. Eschatological ethics after all is the putting into practice of the rule of God in one's life with one's hope fixed on the final establishment of his kingdom of righteousness, justice, and peace.[6]

Eschatological ethics is *royal ethics*, that is, ethics of the kingdom. (See figure 74.) The prophets looked for the democratization of the royal privileges, permitting the splendor, special relationship, communion, royal authority, presence of the Spirit of God, and royal responsibilities to be democratized (Isa. 4:2; 55:3–5; Mic. 5:7–8; Hag. 2:5; Mal. 4:1–3).[7]

Christian ethics is the harmonious correlation of *the way of man* with *the way of God in Christ,* having a purpose, a movement, and a point of consummation: the New Jerusalem. To this end the Holy Spirit prepares the new community of the Spirit for the age of restoration by renewing the hearts of individuals with a concern for the kingdom of the Son in this present age. He also internalizes the concern for God (theocentric ethics) and the concern for his kingdom (eschatological ethics). The internalization by the Spirit brings about a harmony between the Father, the Son, and the community of the Holy Spirit. Where the Spirit is operative, the qualities of the Spirit—righteousness, justice, love, fidelity, and peace—are present.[8]

Righteousness

Righteousness is an expression of God's rule.[9] *Righteousness* denotes that perfect quality whereby God relates to his creation and brings about a wise, harmonious, and blessed order. It is a dynamic and relational term for the kingdom that embraces the beginning, process, and goal of redemptive history. God rules over his creation, sustains it, and transforms it to bring everything into conformity to his will. In his righteous rule he reestablishes peace, harmony, and goodness. (See figure 75.)

The goal of God's condescension in human history is the transformation of creation into a world of peace, harmony, order, beauty, and perfection. In the righteous establishment of his kingdom, the Lord judges the nations, avenges his enemies, and delivers his children. The gospel is the good news that the great King involves himself in the restoration of his fallen creation (Rom. 1:17) and plans to elevate it from its being originally good to its being consecrated as holy! To this end the Father has involved the Son by granting him the rule over creation (1 Cor. 15:25–28; Col. 1:15–20).

God's righteousness is dynamic. He acts righteously by defending the needy, fighting for the oppressed, and victoriously suppressing evil. All his acts work together harmoniously in creating a better world, a world of *shalom!* The psalmists and the prophets have a vision of God's righteous rule.

> In your majesty ride forth victoriously
> in behalf of truth, humility and righteousness;
> let your right hand display awesome deeds.
> (Ps. 45:4; see Pss. 2; 72; Isa. 46:12–13; 51:5–8; 59:17; Jer.
> 23:6; 33:16; Matt. 6:33; John 17:25; Rom. 5:17–21).[10]

The godly respond by doing righteous acts. They, too, cultivate relations that reflect God's righteousness by dispensing mercy, giving to the needy, caring for the poor, and advancing God's righteous rule.[11]

Olley's study on the use of "righteousness" in the Septuagint version of Isaiah helps us to see the dynamic connection between the Hebrew context, the Jewish community in the Diaspora, the Jewish hope, and the New Testament application of "righteousness" to Jesus Christ.[12] The translator of the Hebrew into Greek adapted the message of Isaiah to his theological context, reflecting

363

the needs of the Jews in the Diaspora.[13] Plato, Aristotle, and the Greek authors defined *dikaiosunē* ("righteousness") as doing "what is necessary to correct an act or state of injustice."[14] Against the secular use and background of *dikaiosunē* ("righteousness") as a corrective punishment, the Greek translation of Isaiah places the stress on "vindication and also upon the possibility of forgiveness."[15] The Septuagintal usage shows the closeness to the Greek concept of righteousness as justice, except for the additional element of love. God is just, but also "shows mercy to the genuinely repentant."[16]

The translator comforted the Jewish community in the Diaspora by sympathizing with their unfair treatment and by encouraging them to look for "God's acting to right this as an act of 'justice.' "[17] Thus the Septuagint provides the link between the Old Testament and the hope of the Jews at the time of Jesus' coming. The Greek-speaking Jews believed that "salvation is an act of justice, correcting injustices, bringing about a just situation in regard to the life of the Jews amongst their neighbours and in their relationship with God himself."[18]

Further, Olley states that the Septuagint translation bears out the hope of Gentile inclusion in the age of restoration. Where the Hebrew text was ambiguous or unclear, the translator clarified the text—in my opinion correctly—in favor of the union of Jews and Gentiles as members of the covenant of grace. So Olley concludes that the Jews were called to bear the light of God's revelation, his law, and forgiveness to the nations: "When compared with MT, LXX has a stronger emphasis upon the going forth from the restored Zion of 'law' and 'judging' as a 'light' for kings and nations."[19]

Justice

God is a just King. He acts *without* discrimination or recrimination and *with* wisdom and equity. His just rule brings favor and joy to all who seek him because the ruthless, legalist, opportunist, and oppressor will be removed from his presence. (See figure 75.)

God justifies those who come to him in faith by bestowing his grace, favor, and blessing on them. He continues to deal justly in his world. He looks for the qualities of innocence, concern, love, gentleness, wisdom, and concern for others, but he hates greed, avarice, discord, opportunism, egoism, and selfishness. The prophets condemned the commercialization of justice, such as bribes and social discrimination. They uniformly condemned greedy opportunists who manipulated the law to obtain their selfish ends at the expense of a fellow human.[20] The prophetic vision opens a window to what true justice is.[21] Justice establishes God's order (i.e., righteousness) when God's children deal fairly with all parties.[22]

THE RULE OF GOD OVER CREATION

Qualities:	**Righteous**	**Just**	**Love**	**Faithful**	**Peaceful**
Evident in:	Order	Judgments	Abundance	Constancy	Harmony

Figure 75. The Qualities of the Spirit

Love and Fidelity

The way of covenant is the way of love, and the way of love is expressed in the constancy of commitment.[23] This commitment entails a radical obedience to the Lord of the covenant and to his Messiah. It also requires a new way of relating to the people of God and to the world. The whole of the Law may be summarized as Micah did:

> He has showed you, O man, what is good.
> And what does the LORD require of you?
> To act justly and to love mercy [*ḥesed*]
> and to walk humbly with your God.
>
> (Mic. 6:8)

The pursuit of "love" (NIV "mercy") is nothing less than living in accordance with the nature of God, whose royal way has been revealed to God's people at Sinai and confirmed in our Lord's teaching. God is "the compassionate and gracious God, slow to anger, abounding in love and faithfulness, maintaining love to thousands, and forgiving wickedness, rebellion and sin" (Ex. 34:6–7). The phrase "abounding in love and faithfulness" combines two dimensions of God's love: commitment and fidelity (*ḥesed* wᵉ *ᵉmet*, lit. "love and truth," see Pss. 25:10; 57:10; 86:15).[24]

The way of love is an imitation of God. (See figure 75.) He rules over his creation and lovingly bestows his favor on all creation. His commitment to creation is so strong that he deals with it patiently, gently, and graciously while holding all humans accountable to himself. God expects from his children nothing less than their mirroring his perfections in their lives by being patient, gentle, and self-controlled.

> Let love and faithfulness never leave you;
> bind them around your neck,
> write them on the tablet of your heart.
>
> (Prov. 3:3; see Gal. 5:22–24)

365

God's standard of love is not impossible or unrealistic. It is one of the pillars of his kingdom and hence also of the counterculture. The royal law is the same for both Israel and the church. Compare these passages in Leviticus and James:

> Do not go about spreading slander among your people. Do not do anything that endangers your neighbor's life. I am the LORD. Do not hate your brother in your heart. Rebuke your neighbor frankly so you will not share in his guilt. Do not seek revenge or bear a grudge against one of your people, but love your neighbor as yourself. I am the LORD (Lev. 19:16–18).

> Who is wise and understanding among you? Let him show it by his good life, by deeds done in the humility that comes from wisdom. But if you harbor bitter envy and selfish ambition in your hearts, do not boast about it or deny the truth. Such "wisdom" does not come down from heaven but is earthly, unspiritual, of the devil. For where you have envy and selfish ambition, there you find disorder and every evil practice. But the wisdom that comes from heaven is first of all pure; then peace-loving, considerate, submissive, full of mercy and good fruit, impartial and sincere. Peacemakers who sow in peace raise a harvest of righteousness (James 3:13–18).

This lifestyle reflects the wisdom from above, the fruit of the Spirit of God (Gal. 5:22–25), and a life of "integrity" (*tāmîm,* Gen. 6:9; 17:1; Ps. 15:2). The way of integrity is not to be equated with morality, legalism, or pharisaism. The person of integrity lives in the presence of the Lord, serves him out of love, and lives out the way of God's kingdom in space and time. The way of love is the way of freedom for the child of God.[25] It is "the royal law" (James 2:8), the law of love (John 15:9–12), the law of the kingdom of Jesus Christ (1 Cor. 13). This way can only lead to peace (*shalom*).

Peace

The apostle Paul defined the law of the kingdom by its resultant expression, promotion, and experience of peace: "The kingdom of God is . . . a matter of . . . righteousness, peace and joy in the Holy Spirit, because anyone who serves Christ in this way is pleasing to God and approved by men. Let us therefore make every effort to do what leads to peace and to mutual edification" (Rom. 14:17–19). (See figure 75.) Zechariah gave an excellent summary of the Prophets.

> These are the things you are to do: Speak the truth to each other, and render true and sound judgment in your courts; do not plot evil against your neighbor, and do not love to swear falsely. I hate all this. . . . Therefore love truth and peace (Zech. 8:16–19).

The biblical perspective on *shalom* extends to all aspects of human existence on earth: individual, society, ecumenical relations, churches, ecology, and the world.[26]

Peace is the mark of Christian maturity. Such people have peace with God (Rom. 5:1) and show great concern for harmony, reconciliation, and mutual relations. Peace does not provoke, irritate, or frustrate. For the sake of peace Christians may and must deprive themselves of rights and privileges. The Holy Spirit creates peace within the children of God, and he uses them in extending the peace of God on earth: "Peacemakers who sow in peace raise a harvest of righteousness" (James 3:18).

Conclusion

The prophetic ethics cannot be divorced from the perfections of God, from his plan of salvation, from the Father's revelation in Jesus Christ, and from the work of the Holy Spirit. Ethics, therefore, is not society ethics, but kingdom ethics.[27] Ethics, therefore, is not intended to establish the human community separate from the kingdom of God.[28] Ethics fosters relations between the triune God, the members of the new community of faith (the church of Jesus Christ), the old community of faith (the Jews), and the world. This is what Jesus meant by "the children of light" shining like lights in the world or by our being "the salt" to season the world in which we live. Sanders has aptly expressed the prophetic perspective.

> Prophetic hermeneutics means not so much comforting the afflicted as afflicting the comfortable. It means applying the text sociologically and politically to a situation today in which we are involved, just as the prophets in like manner applied the traditions they inherited to ancient Israel . . . and as Jesus in large measure did in his day.[29]

The prophetic oracles challenge the community of the Spirit to serve as witnesses and lightbearers to the coming kingdom of God, the new creation.

The Spirit of Christ transforms the vision of all who keep in step with the Spirit. They gain a vision of God's plan through the revelation of God by the illumination of the Spirit. Nevertheless, he cannot be bound by humans because he is always working in submission to the Father and to the Son. (see figure 76)

The message of the prophets keeps God's people (B.C. and A.D.) living in anticipation of the greater expectation of the fulfillment: the new creation. God's people are members of the Dispersion as the apostle Peter defines it, "God's elect, strangers in the world, scattered . . . , who have been chosen according to the foreknowledge of God the Father, through the sanctifying work of the Spirit, for obedience to Jesus Christ and sprinkling by his blood" (1 Peter 1:1–2). They are members of the new people of God, characterized by transformation, the internalization of the law, and the working of the Spirit of God. Their hope is in God's ability to deliver and in his freedom to work out his plan. Their joy lies in the certainty of redemption as guaranteed by the blood of Jesus Christ, by the indwelling of the Spirit of God, and by the Scriptures.

**MOVEMENT OF THE SPIRIT
FROM CREATION TO THE NEW CREATION**

Creation   New Creation

Involvement through and outside of humans, institutions, and structures

Involvement through and outside the people of God

Involvement in nature, nations, and human history

Figure 76. Work of the Spirit in Creation and in Redemption

TOTA SCRIPTURA: THE PROPHETS IN THE LIGHT OF JESUS' COMING

Old and New Testaments harmoniously witness to the direct involvement of the triune God in the redemption of creation, "a new heaven and a new earth, the home of righteousness" (2 Peter 3:13). The prophetic word is God's word to his church (2 Tim. 3:16–17; see Luke 24:44–47; Rom. 1:2–4; Heb. 1:1–3; 2 Peter 1:19–21; 3:2). It is God's witness to his involvement with creation and to his condescension to work in history. God has repeatedly vindicated the prophetic word in the events of history: the fall of Samaria, of Jerusalem, and of great kingdoms; the coming of Jesus Christ; the apostolic mission; and the progress of restoration.

God's revelation through the prophets also has power to transform life (2 Tim. 3:17). God's Word is relevant for growing in Christian maturity in righteousness and for opening vistas on the world of transformation: the kingdom, the messianic age, the New Jerusalem, and the age of the Spirit. The revelation of God in the Old and the New opens up the Word when the Old is read in the context of the New and when the words of our Lord and his apostles are read in the dual context of the Old Testament revelation and the anticipation of fulfillment.[30]

368

Interpretation of God's Word

The danger inherent in the study of inscribed revelation lies in the fixation of interpretation. Interpretation is necessary because the written Word requires interpretation and application by the illumination of the Spirit of God. Fixation sets in when a particular interpretation becomes a hallmark of a theological system or a thesis to support other theses. Brevard S. Childs' warning is most relevant.

> The role of the Holy Spirit in biblical interpretation is not to add a new dimension to the literal sense, but to effect the proper actualization of the biblical text in terms of its subject matter for every succeeding generation of the church. The critical role of the Spirit is to resist all human efforts to undercut the force of the Gospel.[31]

The prophets are constant reminders of the dangers of the fixation of interpretation. They were the objects of ridicule and harsh treatment by religious people who had fixed their interpretation of Moses but did not understand that the Lord is free. He is sovereign over human affairs, and he is sovereign over his Word. He does not contradict his own Word but is free in the working out of his Word, even if it means going against human expectations.

The prophetic contribution lies in the doctrine of the freedom of God. The preexilic prophets bore witness that the Lord could come against his people, being free in his judgment of Israel. The Exile marked a historical era of judgment. The Lord purified a people through the process of judgment, but he also inflamed the godly remnant with the hope of a new era of salvation, characterized by forgiveness, covenant renewal, and an "open-ended future."[32] So the prophets also proclaimed his freedom in bringing about a new era of covenant renewal, as Zimmerli puts it,

> It is their secret that, in spite of their close relationship to contemporary history, they were conscious of being the ambassadors of the God who stood above this history and who controlled it. He was the God who foretold the events of history, but who also retained the freedom to change a given announcement, and to make another. Behind the word of the prophet was not the river of history, rushing with invincible force, and by its rigid laws forcing its way on and breaking down all opposition. Behind their preaching stood the Lord of freedom, in whose hands all history remains a tool which can be wielded freely by him.[33]

Every stage subsequent to the restoration from exile turned out to be a further denouement in the progress of eschatological fulfillment: the postexilic era,[34] the period of the Maccabees (Dan. 11:2–12:12), the coming of the Christ, the outpouring of the Holy Spirit, the Gentile mission, the persecutions in the church of Jesus Christ, the growth of Christianity, the Reformation, the age of missions, and the present age.

Old and New

Throughout the book the essential bond of the two Testaments[35] has been assumed, and there is no better place to see how Old and New relate than in the Gospels, particularly in the birth narrative in the gospel of Luke.[36] The birth narrative in Luke (1:5–2:40) gives a clear theological perspective on the relation of Old to New and of Christ to the prophets.[37]

Mary's Magnificat

In the Magnificat (Luke 1:46–55), Mary praised the great King for having regard for the lowly and the hungry. Israel had, again, come to a low point in her history under Roman rule. Under the leadership of the Sadducees, Pharisees, priests, and Levites, the common people were forgotten, and the kingdom of God was dwarfed by the power of the Roman Empire. Mary magnified the Lord who, by sending Jesus as the Messiah, showed his royal regard for the humble among his people. In the coming of the Messiah, God entered into the human arena, being faithful to his promises made to Abraham and to his seed. (See table 12.)

Zechariah's Prayer

Zechariah, the father of John the Baptist, also longed for the fulfillment of God's promises to Abraham and David in the advent of Jesus the Messiah and in John's role as forerunner of the Messiah. He hoped for victory over the enemies (Luke 1:69; see Ps. 132:17–18), the establishment of the messianic kingship in conformity to the "loyalty" sworn to David, the fulfillment of the promises guaranteed to the prophets and to Abraham (vv. 70, 72–73), and the uninterrupted bliss of the Jews (vv. 78–79; see Isa. 60; Mal. 4:2). (See table 12.)

The Hope of Simeon and Anna

Simeon gave thanks that, in Jesus, the Lord had prepared his salvation in the sight of all peoples. He considered Jesus to be the focus of the prophetic hope regarding Gentiles and Jews (Luke 2:32). Jesus alone will lead people into the kingdom of God, messianic bliss, and the New Jerusalem! He is the expression of God's glory to Israel, which will be revealed even to the Gentiles (vv. 30–32). At the same time, Simeon warned Mary that Jesus would become a cause of contention (v. 34). Anna, too, recognized Jesus as the One sent by the Lord to bring redemption to Jerusalem (v. 38). She shared the good news with others who had joined her in "looking forward to the redemption of Jerusalem" (v. 38). (See table 12.)

370

Old and New in Luke's Birth Narrative

Luke carefully connects the Old Testament prophets and Jesus' ministry by describing the messianic era as a progression in God's plan: forgiveness (Isa. 40:1–2; 43:25; 44:22; Jer. 31:34), universal "light," and the full enjoyment of peace and redemption (Isa. 60:1–22; 62:1–12).

The inclusion of two witnesses (Mary and Zechariah) before Jesus' birth and two (Simeon and Anna) after his birth is itself a magnificent statement of the continuity of the new age. The new age connects with the old, as witnessed to by two women and two men, by a young woman and an old one, by a priest (Zechariah), and by Spirit-filled laypersons (Simeon and Anna). These men and women stood on the threshold of the new age and saw in Jesus the focus of the prophetic hope,[38] the covenants, the promises, and the prophetic oracles of salvation. In like manner, Paul declared that in Jesus all the promises of God are assured: "For no matter how many promises God has made, they are 'Yes' in Christ. And so through him the 'Amen'" (2 Cor. 1:20). (See table 12.)

Hope in Messianic Era

Excitement for the new era lies in the coming of the Christ, the center of redemptive history. Saints from the "old" era join with the saints of the "new" era in the worship of the Christ. Attention shifts *from* hope in comfort, reconciliation, consolation, redemption, and the kingdom *to* Jesus. He is the focus of the fulfillment of the prophetic word, and in this way the glorious future is present in Jesus.[39]

The Witness of Luke Concerning the Messiah

Jesus Christ is the ultimate realization of the Old Testament. Luke, the theologian, works from the schema of progressive fulfillment; all aspects of Jesus' life—from the birth narratives to his post-Resurrection appearances—relate to the Old Testament: "Everything must be fulfilled that is written about me in the Law of Moses, the Prophets and the Psalms" (Luke 24:44).

Jesus is the glorious Lord, who will establish the kingdom at God's time.[40] Luke presents us with Jesus as the Messiah,[41] the Son of God,[42] the Son of Man,[43] the Lord,[44] Savior (Luke 2:11), "the author of life" (Acts 3:15), the Prince (Acts 5:31), the suffering "servant of God,"[45] and the glorious King,[46] whose authority extends over all creation.[47] He will bring in the anticipated times of restoration (3:19) as well as the judgment (10:42; 17:31).

Luke shows Jesus to be the connection between Old and New. Jesus was not a radical teacher who broke away from the revelation of the Old Testament. Instead, Jesus truly understood the Scriptures by the Spirit

TABLE 12. THE ELEMENTS OF HOPE BASED ON GOD'S WORD TO THE PROPHETS

HOPE IN THE MESSIANIC ERA

Mary: (1) Justice and righteousness with regard to evil: "He has scattered those who are proud in their inmost thoughts. He has brought down rulers from their thrones. . . . [He] has sent the rich away empty."

(2) Justice and righteousness with regard to the humble: "[He] has lifted up the humble. He has filled the hungry with good things. . . . He has helped his servant Israel, remembering to be merciful to Abraham and his descendants forever, even as he said to our fathers."

(3) Hope based on God's promises to Abraham and his descendants

Zechariah: (1) Full freedom from enemies: "To rescue us from the hand of our enemies, and to enable us to serve him without fear in holiness and righteousness before him all our days."

(2) Forgiveness of sin

(3) Full experience of deliverance: "The tender mercy of our God, by which the rising sun will come to us from heaven to shine on those living in darkness and in the shadow of death, to guide our feet into the path of peace."

(4) Hope based on God's promises to Abraham, David, and the prophets

Simeon: "Salvation, . . . in the sight of all people, a light for revelation to the Gentiles and for glory to your people Israel."

Anna: The redemption of Jerusalem

of wisdom and authoritatively taught from them (Luke 2:47, 52; 4:36–37). His teaching was not novel, but his interpretation and application shattered the traditions of his contemporaries. For example, Jesus contrasted the Old Testament era—the period of "the Law and the Prophets"—with his presence, "the good news of the kingdom of God" (16:16). But the context of this passage helps us gain a better perspective on what Jesus meant. Jesus had just put before the Pharisees an ultimatum: either God or money (v. 13); that is, either the kingdom of God or the kingdom of man. Jesus called people *away from* their self-sufficiency *to* a renewed devotion to and understanding of the Law and the Prophets. The Pharisees were complacent with their interpretation of the Law and their understanding of God's kingdom. They thought that they understood the Old Testament because they had stabilized the tensions into a system. Jesus shattered the system and destabilized it while confirming the revelation of God: "It is easier for heaven and earth to disappear than for the least stroke of a pen to drop out of the Law" (v. 17). By way of emphasis, Luke records Jesus' story of the rich man and Lazarus immediately after this incident to teach that "Moses and the Prophets" have abiding value (v. 31). Jesus' teaching was a corrective of *vox populi*. (See figure 77.)

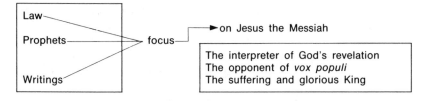

Figure 77. Jesus and the Old Testament

Jesus' teaching on the messianic kingdom was also in continuity with the kingdom of God. Indeed, he taught that Abraham, Isaac, and Jacob as well as the prophets shared in the kingdom of God (Luke 13:28). What the Gospels reveal, however, is that a new stage of restoration and fulfillment takes place in his advent.[48] The coming of Jesus allows the meek, sinners, and even Gentiles to enter the kingdom and permits them full privileges as its citizens. The Pharisees had taught that all the children of Abraham who assume the yoke of the Law, as interpreted by them, may enter into the kingdom of God. But Jesus proclaimed that the righteous kingdom of God is open to those who follow Jesus, as they receive the privilege of adoption by his Father, are heirs together with Christ, and live righteously by the power of his Spirit (18:14, 29; 21:34–36). Thus Jesus is the *fulfiller* of the Old Testament prophets. Ridderbos writes,

> It is *the* great kingdom, *the* coming of God into the world for redemption and judgment. The future, as it were, penetrates into the present. The world of God's redemption, the great whole of his concluding and consummative works pushes its way into the present time of the world. This means the entirely new fact, in many respects incomprehensible and unacceptable to Jesus' contemporaries, that Jesus is to call "the mystery of the kingdom." The kingdom will start

before the time of the great judgment, the time is fulfilled before "the end of the world."[49]

Jesus is present in his Spirit, who operates freely in Jews and Gentiles, sowing the incorruptible seed of the kingdom of God.[50] The Spirit is the sign of the presence of the eschaton, guaranteeing restoration, working transformation, and purifying the children of God for the day of their redemption.[51] This means that Luke presents Jesus as the One who alone will bring to consummation the promises of God and guarantees them by his Spirit.

The resurrection of our Lord is also the token of the age of restoration. This is the *kerygma,* the proclamation of the early church,[52] or what E. Earle Ellis calls "the vertical dimension"; that is, the Lord in heaven brings down to earth the consummation of the progress of salvation history.[53] The token of his present glory is the Holy Spirit.[54] The token of his kingdom is nothing less than the "power from on high," the Holy Spirit (Luke 11:13). In the Spirit, Jesus continues to be present as the glorified Christ who has promised to fulfill all things at his Parousia ("coming").[55]

The Spirit of Christ is here and at work in a powerful way! He is free in bringing about the fullness of this age and in preparing the church for the coming of Christ (Acts 1:8). But the church has to be careful not to bypass the work of the Spirit in favor of programs, institutions, or even charismatic leadership. In the early church this temptation was represented by Simon the Sorcerer, who asked for the ability to produce the Holy Spirit at will (8:19).

Dissonance in Fulfillment

Luke began his two-volume work with the account of believing Jews (Luke 1:46–2:38) who awaited "the redemption of Jerusalem" (2:38)— that is, the "times of refreshing" (Acts 3:19)—and ended it with Paul's witness to unbelieving Jews (28:17–29). Zechariah confirmed that the promises belong to Israel, "The Lord God will give him the throne of his father David, and he will reign over the house of Jacob forever; his kingdom will never end" (Luke 1:32–33). Mary believed that "his mercy extends to those who fear him, from generation to generation" (v. 50). Simeon's waiting for "the consolation of Israel" (2:25) leaves the issue of God's plan for Israel an open possibility; his hope included the inauguration of an era of "glory to your people Israel" (v. 32). Anna, too, awaited the new era of transformation and the inclusion of the Jews in this era as she bore witness "to all who were looking forward to the redemption of Jerusalem" (v. 38).

Jesus proclaimed that the gospel is in himself. At Nazareth he related his ministry to the fulfillment of the prophetic word of Isaiah 61 by saying, "Today this scripture is fulfilled in your hearing" (Luke 4:21). The gospel is the good news of restoration, spiritual as well as material. The miracles and the declaration of divine forgiveness witness to his authority and role as the Bringer of the restoration as proclaimed by the prophets.[56]

On Palm Sunday the crowd excitedly welcomed Jesus as the Bringer of peace: "Blessed is the king who comes in the name of the Lord!" and "Peace in heaven and glory in the highest!" (Luke 19:38). The connection between their joyful praise and that of the angels has been carefully observed by exegetes of Luke 2:14: "Glory to God in the highest, and on the earth peace to men on whom his favor rests." Why, we may ask, is there a shift from "earth" to "heaven"?

First, something shocking had happened between the prophetic hope expressed by Jews at Jesus' advent (Zechariah, Simeon, and Anna) and the generation after his advent. The Jews had largely rejected the Messiah, and instead, by the power of the Spirit, Gentile churches were coming into being. The rejection of the Jews created a period of tension in redemptive history that led to the fall of Jerusalem in A.D. 70. Jesus declared, "For this is the time of punishment in fulfillment of all that has been written" (Luke 21:22).[57]

Second, Acts maintains the dynamic tension of rejection and hope. Jerusalem is the object of both judgment and mercy. Thus Luke maintains the connection of the prophetic message and the Jews in the book of Acts (10:36, 42; 13:26). According to Baarlink, these texts "leave no doubt regarding the continuity of 'the proclamation of peace by Jesus Christ' to them [the Jews] after Easter."[58] The Jews have received the message of "peace" in Christ, and the proclamation continues to the very end of Acts (28:17–29), where it is recorded that the apostle Paul disputed with the Jews.[59]

Third, judgment need not be interpreted as God's permanent abandonment of his people. Luke's inclusion of Paul's challenge to the Jewish leaders (Acts 28:17–29) keeps the doors open. The Jews are still the object of grace, though they have hardened themselves against the present stage of fulfillment of the prophetic word.[60] The birth narrative stands as a continual invitation to the Jews to return to the study of the prophetic word in the light of Jesus' ministry and of the coming of the Spirit. All who believe with Zechariah, Simeon, and Anna that this Jesus is the Messiah may enter into the kingdom of Christ.[61]

Conclusions

The work of Luke-Acts brings out the close connection between Old and New. The hope of God's people lies in Jesus Christ. He is the focus of the fulfillment of God's promises. The content of the promises is found in the Old Testament Scriptures. These Scriptures were the Bible for our Lord and the apostles. Their preaching did not bring the previous revelation to an end but confirmed that revelation (2 Cor. 1:20; 2 Tim. 3:16–17). They opened the canon with the revelation of God in Christ reconciling the world.

Our Lord and the apostles were steeped in God's revelation in the Old Testament as the basis for their arguments, teaching, and application. On this major premise they developed the premise that the revelation of God in his Son is continuous with the previous revelation. They spoke in the power of the Spirit, who alone can open the eyes of the blind and renew the hearts of the hardened (1 Cor. 2:6–15). They lived with the conviction that openness to all of the Scriptures (*tota Scriptura*) proved that Jesus is the Messiah by whom the Father administers the promises. Beecher summarized the apostolic view in these words,

> But the apostolic world-view . . . is certainly Christocentric. It is Christ to whom the promise points forward. It is on account of its containing Christ that the promise is cited with so much reiteration, and not for anything it contains apart from Christ. The promise passages connect themselves with everything that is essential in Christian doctrine. They outline the nature and the person of Christ. The theology of the Holy Spirit is in them, he being the divine Agent in carrying out the promise. They are a study in the doctrine of the divine decree, that decree having Christ as its determinative point.[62]

The Spirit works in and through *tota Scriptura,* purifying the children of God, enlarging their vision, and equipping them for service. In other words, the mission of the church will fail unless the Spirit of Christ is permitted to work in and through the Scriptures. The modern revival of Marcionism (practical denial of the Old Testament as Scripture), the lack of concern for the Jews, and the emphasis on programs affect our view of Christ, the ministry of the Spirit of God, and the mission of the church. Berkhof observes:

> Separated from this movement [i.e., of the Spirit], either the institutional church or the religious life of the individual easily becomes a goal in itself. The Spirit . . . touches us, transforms us, and enlists us for service in his ongoing work, . . . Whatever he does is a guarantee but at the same time a postponement of the consummation. It is under the guidance of the Spirit that we remain on the way.[63]

PROGRESS OF REDEMPTION: LIVING BETWEEN THE TIMES

The study of and meditation on the prophetic writings is a must for our age. The perennial danger lies in our hearing our Master's voice through our cultural milieu and traditions. Christianity cannot accomplish her mission unless Christians continually hear the Master's voice against the background of the prophets. Since the prophetic words have their focus in Jesus the Messiah, in whom all the promises of God hold validity (2 Cor. 1:20), the prophets help us in hearing afresh the words of our Lord.

In the good pleasure of the *Father,* he has sent his Son to hasten the progress of redemption of which the prophets have spoken. In fidelity to the Father, the *Son* came, gave himself for the redemption of creation, and sent the Spirit of restoration to prepare all things for the glorious transformation. In submission to the Father and the Son, the *Spirit* works out the plan of God *and* involves transformed human beings as agents of transformation. So the story of redemption is also ours to write! (See figure 78.)

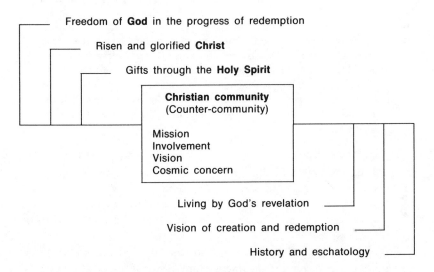

Freedom of **God** in the progress of redemption

Risen and glorified **Christ**

Gifts through the **Holy Spirit**

Christian community
(Counter-community)

Mission
Involvement
Vision
Cosmic concern

Living by God's revelation

Vision of creation and redemption

History and eschatology

**Figure 78. The Trinity and the Community in the Progress
of Redemption**

In Christ, creation, redemption, and eschatology hold together.[64] History and eschatology are in a paradoxical relationship.[65] The people of God are called to participate in the progress of redemption, and it is our failure that we see so little of the working of the Spirit.[66] Those who live by the Spirit are God's agents in history, working out and bringing about the consummation. Yet the consummation does not depend on the people of God. The Father is free in working out his plan of redemption through the Son and the Spirit,[67] but invites his redeemed community to share in the progress of redemption by their individual[68] and corporate witness.

Faith Implies Hope in the Risen and Glorified Lord

Old and New witness together that God is in control and that he progressively unfolds his plan of redemption. Green says that God is "ever revealing his eschatological purpose for all the world."[69] The Christian community lives and works in this hope of the vision of a redeemed community and of a redeemed creation. The focus of this hope is the glorified Christ.[70]

With the ascension of our Lord, he is, not less than what he was on earth, but more! He is the Lord of Lords and King of Kings to whom all nations shall offer homage. This means that the Father rules in Jesus as his anointed (messianic) vassal-king (Ps. 2), as Paul explicates in 1 Corinthians 15:

> For he must reign until he has put all his enemies under his feet. The last enemy to be destroyed is death. For he "has put everything under his feet." Now when it says that "everything" has been put under him, it is clear that this does not include God himself, who put everything under Christ. When he has done this, then the Son himself will be made subject to him who put everything under him, so that God may be all in all (vv. 25–28).

Hope is Christian hope as long as a dynamic tension exists between the present enjoyment of the benefits of God and the yearning for the fullness of our redemption. Stephen Travis has put it well, "Only where these two aspects of hope are held in tension can genuine Christian hope be said to exist, and only then can the future of man be said to be rightly understood."[71]

Hope is Christian hope as long as hope is in the Lord of glory; eschatology can never be separated from Jesus or Jesus disconnected from eschatology. The focus on his birth, ministry, suffering and resurrection, separated from his present glory and the hope of his coming in glory, detracts from hope. In the present age the Christian may enjoy union with the risen Christ and at the same time long for union with Christ. Lindars expressed this hope in terms of Pauline eschatology.

> Nearness to Christ in this life paves the way for nearness to Christ in the life to come. That is all we need to know in order to reaffirm the Christian hope. The sound of the trumpet, with the subsequent completion of the process of transformation, can await its proper time in the secret counsels of God.[72]

We do well to learn from Calvin, "the theologian of hope,"[73] who brings together the doctrine of Christ, eschatology, and Christian living, says T. F. Torrance.

> Perhaps at no point do we need to listen to the teaching of Calvin today more than in our understanding of "the last things." We need Calvin's Biblical sanity and his doctrinal consistency to deliver us from the one-sidedness of so much modern literature. Calvin's main teaching about eschatology can be formulated by saying that eschatology is the application of Christology to the work of the church in history. It is the understanding of the church and all creation—in terms of the *Regnum Christi.* Calvin's teaching here pivots upon the doctrine of union with Christ. Because we are united to Christ and participate in His risen humanity, eschatology is essential to our faith.[74]

Faith Implies Love of a Cosmic Dimension

Eschatological concern is meaningless unless it is in relation to God and to God's world. To this end, Verweij, a Dutch theologian, relates salvation to Christ's *cosmic concern.*[75] He contends that since the days of Augustine Western Christianity has de-emphasized eschatology and has secularized the gospel by making Christ acceptable and adaptable to the world.[76] Similarly, Oliver O'Donovan comments,

> Within modern Christian political thought the Augustinian secularist stream has yielded a policy of involvement in social and political tasks, which presumes upon the opacity of secular history to ultimate values and hence upon the neutrality, in moral and spiritual terms, of the political realm.[77]

The process has been gradual, but de-eschatologization, demythologization,[78] and the present secularization have greatly affected Christianity, resulting in an "immanentistic Christianity."[79] (See figure 79.) With the increasing secularization of the church and a nonloving spirit toward all who did not "adopt" Christianity as the system, the power of the Spirit was supplanted by the institution of the church, by the powers of bishops and archbishops, by creeds and confessions, and by pious expressions of devotion and morality. I agree with Ellul's observation: "The church never reforms itself. Experience shows a hundred times that the honest and scrupulous search for better institutions, reform by the legal route of regimentation, and the serious search for more authentic means of inner and outer evangelization are all futile and will inevitably fail."[80]

In response to de-eschatologization, Verweij encourages Christians to wake up. Now is the time for preparation, for sanctification, for the full use of the gifts of the Spirit, for the proclamation of the gospel of Christ, and for the expression of a cosmic dimension by deeds of love and the practice of justice and righteousness.[81] Verweij's approach goes beyond the radical antithesis of Abraham Kuyper.[82] He holds to Christian separatism while encouraging a Christian outreach into the world, cooperative programs, and joint ventures between Christians and non-Christians.[83]

Christianity without a living hope: **De-eschatologization**
Practical denial of Jesus' promises and of the
prophetic and apostolic hope
Emphasis on here-and-now

Christianity without a living faith: **De-mythologization**
Practical denial of a spiritual reality
Emphasis on rationalism

Christianity without a kingdom vision: **Secularization**
Practical denial of the kingdom of God
Emphasis on human institutions

Figure 79. Threats to the Gospel

But Christian involvement in this world does not carry with it just one program for Christianizing society. Christian involvement and separation are grounded in the hope of the "new world of the Kingdom of God on earth."[84] The difference lies in orientation. The Christian looks at this world, at creation, and at history from the perspective of our Lord, the King of Kings.[85] Acts that are motivated for the betterment of humankind as an end in itself (that is, with a de-eschatological or a secular orientation) are not Christian. The absolute submission to the Messiah requires of all Christians a global concern, a denial of self,[86] a concern for proclamation and missions,[87] and a vision of the eschatological structures of the messianic kingdom. The visions in the book of Revelation bear out this kind of involvement over against the modern activity of political action. Accordingly, Oliver O'Donovan writes that a true witness includes confrontation and prophetic criticism: "We must claim John for the point of view which sees criticism, when founded in truth, as genuine political engagement. A right ordering of society is realised [*sic*] when mankind in Christ *participates* in the exercise of the Messiah's authority."[88]

Faith Implies Love for Israel

The New Testament has a paradoxical approach to the future of the Jews.[89] They are the beloved of God and yet are hardened in their rejection of the Messiah. Still the New Testament leaves the matter of Israel's future an open possibility.[90] Paul, like Luke, is the theologian of

380

the Spirit of Christ,[91] and he, too, holds out a future for the Jews.[92] On the one hand, he presents Jesus as the Messiah in accordance with the prophetic word at the beginning and end of his epistle to the Romans.

> The gospel he promised beforehand *through his prophets* in the Holy Scriptures regarding his Son, who as to his human nature was a descendant of David . . . Now to him who is able to establish you by my gospel and the proclamation of Jesus Christ, according to the revelation of the mystery hidden for long ages past, but now revealed and made known *through the prophetic* writings by the command of the eternal God, so that all nations might believe and obey him—to the only wise God be glory forever through Jesus Christ! Amen (1:2–3; 16:25–27, emphasis mine).

On the other hand, he explains Israel's present condition as an irresponsible and sinful response to the presence of the Lord of glory.[93] Nevertheless, he affirms that they are still "holy" (Rom. 11:16) and "loved" (v. 28). Though the apostle does not develop the precise nature of Israel's future, he peers into the future of regenerate Israel with the Gentiles as members of the church of Christ.[94] The doxological focus sets forth the mystery of God's future with regard to the Jews.

> Oh, the depth of the riches of the wisdom and knowledge of God!
>   How unsearchable his judgments,
>   and his paths beyond tracing out! . . .
> To him be the glory forever! Amen.
>
> (vv. 33, 36).[95]

I agree with Ladd that somehow the inclusion of the Jews with the Gentiles into one church may still be the object of God's design: "Israel's future salvation will issue in a new order of blessedness and happiness for the Gentile world that is likened to the emergence of life from the dead . . . . Paul does not tell us when or how this era of blessing will occur."[96]

The history of the church sadly reveals how quickly her gold lost its luster as Christianity became identified with temporal and spatial concerns. Christianity was first persecuted by the Roman authorities, but identified itself with the power structures after Constantine had made Christianity the religion of the state (A.D. 313). Christians who had first proclaimed the gospel of Jesus to the Jews became hostile toward the very people from whom our Lord had come. The separation of Jews and Christians in the second century came only after bitter arguments.[97] Instead of speaking of the Messiah in love and from a thorough knowledge of the prophetic word to all who longed for the consolation of Israel, Christians even forgot their mission to the Jews.[98] Hendrikus Berkhof sadly remarks, "The community began to write off 'the Jews'.

She saw herself as the terminal point of God's ways. The pain of incompleteness was felt less and less."[99]

Since God is free, who are we not to engage continually in dialogue with Israel?[100] True, Christians share in the new covenant in Christ. But the new covenant is both present and future.[101] We have not yet arrived, and while we await the fullness of promise, the Christian community has a responsibility of speaking to the older community, the Jews. The new community cannot afford to lock horns with the older community on what divides us. Both communities do well in studying together the prophetic word. For Christians, this means living in the power of forgiveness, not of pride.[102]

Faith Implies Living with a Prophetic Vision

We have seen how the prophets repeatedly and insistently held before God's people the way of Yahweh in opposition to the way of man. On the one hand, the prophets opposed human structures, ideologies, expressions of power, and attempts at maintaining little kingdoms on earth as idolatrous. They charged people with idolatry in their endeavors to maintain institutions, social order, and the organization of life in such a way that it excluded the freedom of God and the work of the Spirit. On the other hand, the prophets adumbrated the glory of *Zion as a symbol of Yahweh's cosmic and majestic kingship*. They envisioned God's establishment of order over all creation, his provision for the needs of the people, and the kingdom of his Messiah-King. The prophetic teaching concerning Zion as the city of God goes far beyond institutions and structures. Zion is rooted in the creation order of God and symbolizes God's new world-order. The Zion theology of the prophets and the Psalms bring together the teaching of God's role as Creator, his universal rule, his monopoly of power, his care for his people, the new community of people who trust in the Lord and share in the royal splendor of their King.[103]

A prophetic view of this world as the sphere of the Spirit's operation rejects Christian isolation from creation. By spiritual renewal in the image of God, Christian men and women must realize their God-given endowments in subduing this world, raising Christian families, establishing Christian community, and creating a holistic witness to their being a spiritual countercommunity (eschatological ethics, Spirit-filled living, excellence in work and play).[104] McKane's conclusion is still relevant: "But the prophet believes that faith or confidence has a creative potential and can transform a situation. If we had faith in God and loved our neighbour and were prepared to take the absolute risk for the sake of Christ, the world would cease to be an armed camp. So speaks the contemporary Christian prophet."[105]

The Lord calls on his people to serve him alone, to free themselves

from the structures of society, to look with suspicion at the institutionalization of religion, and to pray for the continual operation of the Spirit
of God in establishing the kingdom of God. Raitt's application of the
exilic experience is appropriate for twentieth-century Christianity:
"Persons who take their Christianity with consistent seriousness will
soon be cultural exiles within American society. . . . When God comes
to these exiles, he is perceived in his Godness. With them he has an
open-ended future."[106] There is the only alternative for Christians, as
Brueggemann writes, "Prophetic criticism aims to create an alternative
consciousness with its own rhetoric and field of perception. That
alternative consciousness . . . has to do with the cross. . . . This kind of
prophetic criticism does not lightly offer alternatives, does not mouth
assurances, and does not provide redemptive social policy."[107]

> Living together with both futurology and eschatology may lead
> to nothing less than Christian schizophrenia.[108] Berkhof argues in
> favor of a convergence of the two; the Christian must live in the
> anticipation of the transformation of creation and involve himself
> in the rule over God's world into a new creation.[109] A fellow
> Dutch theologian, van Genderen, levels a criticism against Berk-
> hof's thesis. He rejects the element of apparent continuity
> between futurology and eschatology.[110] For him, eschatology and
> faith are twin categories as the Christian walks in faith awaiting the
> re-creation of everything.[111] However, van Genderen misses
> Berkhof's central argument. The latter operates from a historical
> perspective; he confesses that "the God of redemption is the God
> of the whole history and also the God of nature"[112] who is
> redemptively present and involved in the Christ and in the Spirit.

CONCLUSIONS

We have come to the end of our exploration of the prophets.
Without reviewing or bringing all motifs together, I shall conclude this
work with seven observations regarding our place in redemptive history.

First, the events in redemptive history fit within a grand design
planned by the Triune God and harmoniously executed by the Father,
our Lord Jesus, and the Holy Spirit. All events in redemptive history
reveal aspects of the grand mosaic, such as the Garden of Eden, the
Flood, the call of Abraham, the Exodus, the revelation at Sinai, the
conquest, the promises to David, the Exile, the restoration from exile,
the advent of our Lord, his death, resurrection, and ascension,
Pentecost, and the Gentile mission. Redemptive history is the unfolding
of the plan of God in stages that are organically related to each other,
each stage being a step closer to the kingdom to come.

The history of the Christian church ties in with the progress of redemption. Because we have no further revelation from God, we do not know where we stand in relation to the progress of redemption. Is twentieth-century Christianity with her lack of unity, her divisiveness, and tendencies toward secularization to be likened to Israel during the time of the judges? Is it like the days of the secession, and if so, how far are we from God's purposes? Are we like Samaria with her *Realpolitik* and religious forms? In this case the words of our Lord to the church at Thyatira apply to us: "You tolerate that woman Jezebel, who calls herself a prophetess. By her teaching she misleads my servants into sexual immorality and the eating of food sacrificed to idols" (Rev. 2:20). Or are we like Jerusalem with her *Realpolitik* and traditions (*vox populi*)? Possibly, the words of our Lord to the church at Ephesus apply to us:

> You have persevered and have endured hardships for my name, and have not grown weary. Yet I hold this against you: You have forsaken your first love. Remember the height from which you have fallen! Repent and do the things you did at first. If you do not repent, I will come to you and remove your lampstand from its place (vv. 3–5).

Is the Spirit of God ready to abandon us? Has he abandoned us? Or are we so full of the Spirit that our lampstand is burning brightly?

The prophetic voice challenges all forms of religiosity as deviations from revelation. It encourages the community of God's people to live in the tension of form and reform, of vision and revision.[113] When this dynamic tension is resolved in favor of one or the other, Christians are in danger of formalism, iconoclasm, or secularization. Paul D. Hanson observes,

> As *form* was transformed by *reform* in Israel's earlier history, in the era of late prophecy *vision* was subjected to *revision* in the process of prophetic translation. God's people would continue to be drawn forward by vision of the kingdom of God, but the interpretation of contemporary events as stages on the way toward that kingdom led in turn to an ongoing revision of eschatological hope.[114]

Second, both preoccupation with eschatology and a practical lack of concern with eschatology deny a real place of hope in the Christian community. We have seen that eschatology provides a frame of reference for living.[115] We do not know the future because our God is free in the outworking of his plan, and the study of the prophetic word must recognize the Creator-creature distinction. He is God and we are his creatures. He works out his plan and involves the Christian in the progress of redemption. For this purpose our Father has given us his Word so we may know that everything leads to a grand consummation. Likewise, we may know that our knowledge and interpretation are imperfect: "For we know in part and we prophesy in part, but when perfection comes, the imperfect disappears. . . . Now we see but a poor reflection as in a mirror; then we shall see face to face. Now I know in part; then I shall know fully, even as I am fully known" (1 Cor. 13:9–10, 12).

Faith, hope, and love are eschatological by their very nature. A neglect of relating the doctrine of God, the work of Christ, the work of the Spirit, and the nature and ministry of the church to eschatology nullifies our hope.[116] The prophetic oracles of salvation encourage the people of God by visions of God to prepare themselves for the future acts of God in redemption, transformation, and the inauguration of the new heaven and new earth.[117]

The prophetic word and the teaching of our Lord and the apostles encourage an eschatological frame of reference. The words of John in the Apocalypse apply equally well to all prophetic revelation: "Blessed is the one who reads the words of this prophecy, and blessed are those who hear it and take to heart what is written in it, because the time is near" (Rev. 1:3).

Third, the crisis of true and false prophets is still ours. The people of God were expected to test the prophetic word by the Mosaic revelation, by the signs given by the prophets, and by the vindication of their message.

But the New Testament also warns the new community of God's people to be cautious in testing the spirits and the words of all who speak. Our Lord forewarned us of false prophets who speak in the name of our Lord, preach his word, and give marvelous signs (Matt. 7:15–23; see 24:29). But they will not enter into his kingdom (Matt. 7:23). The New Testament apostles also warn against false teachers; that is, people who selectively interpret God's Word and thus twist the message of God to the liking of people. The danger of *vox populi* is as grave as that of heretical teachers (2 Peter 2:1–22)!

The lesson from the Old Testament prophets is that with the changing social and political conditions, the community of faith must constantly adapt herself to the new challenges of her time. She may have warded off the great heresies that plagued her in the past, but she must constantly test the spirits and be vigilant for the truth while renewing herself in the study of God's Word.[118] We live in the tension of fending off the "false prophets" and of being invited to an ever-new understanding of the Word of God. God's people test, reflect, approve, and reject with the assurance that the Spirit of God guides them in all truth (John 16:13).[119]

Our Lord's warning to the church of Laodicea not to be complacent with their understanding of revelation or with their wealth is highly applicable to us. He shows us the other way of discipleship and its inherent rewards.

> These are the words of the Amen, the faithful and true witness, the ruler of God's creation. . . . So, because you are lukewarm—neither hot nor cold—I am about to spit you out of my mouth. You say, "I am rich; I have acquired wealth and do not need a thing." But you do not realize that you are wretched, pitiful, poor, blind and naked. I counsel you to buy from me gold refined in the fire, so you can become rich; and white clothes to wear, so you can cover your shameful nakedness; and salve to put on your eyes, so you can see. Those whom I love I rebuke and discipline. So be earnest, and repent. Here I am! I stand at the door and knock. If anyone hears my voice and opens the door, I will come in and eat with him, and he with me. To him who overcomes, I will give the right to sit with me on my throne, just as I overcame and sat down with my Father on his throne. He who has an ear, let him hear what the Spirit says to the churches (Rev. 3:14, 16–22).

Fourth, the greatest danger facing the modern church is the separation of Christ from the Old Testament, from creation, and from the new creation. The Old Testament will contribute significantly to a greater understanding of the Messiah and of his mission, as Walther Zimmerli puts it,

> The Church is always in danger of fashioning for herself a Christ who rules in a spiritual remoteness, and who experiences his true veneration in the church building or in theological discussions. But when the gospel of Christ is explained in terms of the Old Testament, then we see clearly that it is sent into the world, to the humble and to the suffering, as also to those in power and responsible for the laws of the state and of society; and so it becomes clear that God, the Lord and the creator of the whole world, will not be venerated in the world as the one who is beyond at an awesome distance, but will be loved again as the one who has come to the world in love.[120]

John presents us with our Lord Jesus Christ as the Creator-Ruler: "These are the words of the Amen, the faithful and true witness, the ruler of God's creation. . . . You are worthy, our Lord and God, to receive glory and honor and power, for you created all things, and by your will they were created and have their being" (Rev. 3:14; 4:11). He is the Lord of history and of all the people of God, whose names are written in the Book of Life "from the world" (13:8; 17:8). This includes the Old Testament saints. Further, his ministry is in accord with the announcement of the Old Testament prophets and remains so because he brings in the redemption of which the prophets have spoken. This redemption involves nothing less than the full deliverance of all the children of God, their resurrection, and the everlasting blessedness of God's presence. The Old Testament saints have enjoyed certain benefits, as we do, but all saints (B.C. and A.D.) have one common confession, "Salvation belongs to our God, who sits on the throne, and to the Lamb" (Rev. 7:10). This salvation is holistic in that it includes the promises of God given to his saints under the Mosaic covenant and the new covenant in Jesus Christ.

> Never again will they hunger;
>> never again will they thirst.
> The sun will not beat upon them,
>> nor any scorching heat.
> For the Lamb at the center of the throne will be their shepherd;
>> he will lead them to springs of living water.
> And God will wipe away every tear from their eyes.
>> (Rev. 7:16–17; see Ps. 23:1–2; Isa. 25:8; 49:10;
>> Jer. 2:13; Ezek. 34:23)

> "Now the dwelling of God is with men, and he will live with them. They will be his people, and God himself will be with them and be their God. He will wipe every tear from their eyes. There will be no more death or mourning or crying or pain, for the old order of things has passed away." He who was seated on the throne said, "I am making everything new!" (Rev. 21:3–5; see Lev. 26:11–12; 2 Chron. 6:18; Isa. 25:8; 35:10; 65:19; Ezek. 37:27).

Fifth, the prophetic perspective challenges us to pray for God's kingdom,[121] to experience renewal by the Spirit, and to live righteously in God's world. Israel's problem is still the church's today. Instead of living, working, and ministering in the power of the Spirit, Christians, too, have developed a sophisticated machinery of keeping Christian institutions operative. They do so by institutionalization, programs, and establishment of structures by which they set up little kingdoms in the name of God. The original intent may have been to advance the kingdom of our Lord, but the danger lies in the human heart with its desire to rule, to monopolize, and to manage.

The perennial danger is in substituting programs, principles, and new institutions. Activism and pragmatism are not solutions to the modern dilemma.[122] Any attempt to equate the kingdom of our Lord with temporal and/or spatial categories results in autonomy, desacralization, despiritualization, and politicization.

The prophets spoke about the kingdom that is to come. Our Lord also spoke about that kingdom and taught us to pray, "Thy kingdom come," even though the kingdom was already present in himself (*autobasileia*). The paradox of the present and future of the kingdom escaped his listeners. They expected nothing less than the full intrusion of the eschaton in the establishment of God's kingdom of righteousness, peace, and divine beneficence.[123] Our Lord and his apostles had love for

Jerusalem and her institutions, but they criticized the despiritualization of the temple and the leader. Shortly before the siege and fall of Jerusalem, the author to the Hebrews had to remind the Jewish Christian community that they had to be ready to leave Jerusalem, keeping in mind that they were citizens of a city "whose architect and builder is God" (Heb. 11:10) and that they had to be willing to suffer loss because Jesus had also suffered outside the city (Heb. 13:12–13). Philip E. Hughes comments,

> In any case, the security of earthly cities, establishments, and institutions, however religious they may be, is illusory. The history of Judaism had already shown that even Jerusalem, the city of God, and its magnificent temple . . . were destructible; and soon would prove again, with the approach of A.D. 70, the transitoriness of the restored city and temple.[124]

Sixth, Moses, the prophets, our Lord, and the apostles insistently challenged the children of God to establish a countercommunity grounded on the revelation of God. But as Jacques Ellul has incisively observed, Christians have too often chosen a "contrary" course.

> They have freely chosen this course. They have voluntarily forsaken revelation and the Lord. They have opted for a new bondage. They have not aspired to the full gift of the Holy Spirit that would have enabled them to take the new way that he opened up. They have made a different choice and left the Holy Spirit unemployed, idle, present only on sufferance. . . . Why have Christians taken a contrary course? . . . For human aggrandizement and nothing else.[125]

What we need to do most urgently is to reevaluate the place of the Christian community in the world. This we may do best by discerning Satan's entrapments in the structures and patterns of "civil religion." The people of God before Christ and the history of the church warn us not to be entrapped by a syncretistic way of life: religion and revelation, civil religion and Christianity. A recent study reveals the contemporary tension in present-day America between private and public life. The private life longs for finding oneself, for love and marriage, for social contact, and for individualism. The public life calls for involvement, citizenship, civil religion, and a national society in America.[126] How can Christ compete with Washington, D.C., Wall Street, Fifth Avenue, and Hollywood? He will not! But he wills his followers to walk in his footsteps by rejecting civil religion and by standing critically opposed to the "public life." The Christian community can bear witness as agents of "transformation"[127] when they sense again they are like exiles in this world. Klein declares,

We need to follow Jeremiah's advice and make ourselves at home in this exile. . . . Exile is a time for maintaining identity. . . . Exile is a time for hope, not triumphantalism. . . . Exile is a time for new obedience. . . . Exile was and is a catalyst for translating the faith. . . . Exile for Christians is a time for viewing the world through the eyes of the cross. . . . Exile is a time for praying to Yahweh. . . . Exile is a time for examination of ourselves, our community, our country and our church.[128]

Seventh, the prophets and the apostles witness to the rule of God over all creation, the present ministry of the Messiah, the work of the Spirit of restoration in creating a new humanity, and the transformation and glorification of the creation and of the redeemed. The Father looks for those who have ultimate faith, that is, a faith that Jesus alone can lead us to the Father and that looks at everything else as loss. Radical discipleship is nothing less than a commitment to follow Moses, the prophets, our Lord, and his apostles in seeking the kingdom of God, to form a counterculture, and to bear witness to our faith in the deliverance offered by the triune God. Living in the presence of God opens up a new dimension to life: *a passionate hope* in the transformation of this world, the establishment of the kingdom of God and of our Messiah. Maranatha! Come, Lord Jesus!

QUESTIONS AND ISSUES

1. Define:

autonomy	eschatological ethics	secularization
contrary course	internalization	*segullâ*
cosmic concern	justice	servant of God
counterculture	love/fidelity	submission
de-eschatologization	peace	theocentric ethics
democratization	politicization	token
demythologization	reality	*tota Scriptura*
desacralization	righteousness	transformation
despiritualization	royal ethics	

2. What is the prophetic vision regarding the involvement of the Spirit in creation? What is the prophetic vision regarding the involvement of the Spirit in redemption?
3. What are God's purposes in the processes of internalization and democratization? How are they still eschatological?
4. Explain ethics in relation to each person of the Trinity. Explain why God's revelation apart from the Spirit was never intended to be a sufficient guide for living.

389

5. Explain how the nature of God, the example of our Lord, and the nature of the kingdom of God (eschatology) provide a framework for ethics. What happens when Christian living is separated from eschatology?

6. Relate righteousness, justice, love, fidelity, and peace to the nature of God, to the nature of God's kingdom, and to Christian living. How can a Christian or a Christian institution be set aside by the Spirit of God?

7. What hope did God's people express at the coming of Jesus? How did Jesus fulfill these hopes, and how is their hope still our hope?

8. Defend or reject this thesis: The New Testament is the fulfillment of the Old Testament.

9. What are the dangers inherent in separating Jesus from the prophets and from his present and eschatological mission?

10. What dangers are inherent in the interpretation of God's Word? How does fixation set in? Is it possible that fixation has also affected the various views of eschatology? What does it mean to have an "open" system of eschatology? How does this openness help in Christian-Jewish relations?

11. How are the persons of the Trinity involved in the progress of redemption?

12. What are the dimensions of hope? How do we cultivate and focus our hope?

13. What are the implications of a cosmic concern? What dangers are inherent in asceticism, isolationism, and Christian involvement?

14. How can Christians involve themselves in the progress of redemption? What are the dangers inherent in this involvement? How can we maintain a focus on the Christian mission and vision?

Abbreviations

AB	Anchor Bible Commentary. Garden City: Doubleday.
ANET	*Ancient Near Eastern Texts.*
ASTI	*Annual of the Swedish Theological Institute.*
AUSS	*Andrews University Seminary Studies.*
AUSSDS	Andrews University Seminary Studies: Dissertation Series.
Bib	*Biblica.*
BibetOr	Biblica et Orientalia. Rome: Biblical Institute Press.
BibSac	*Bibliotheca Sacra.*
BJRL	*Bulletin of the John Rylands Library.*
BKAT	Biblischer Kommentar Altes Testament. Neukirchen-Vluyn: Neukirchener.
BN	*Biblische Notizen.*
BSC	Bible Student's Commentary.
BTB	*Biblical Theology Bulletin.*
BZ	*Biblische Zeitschrift.*
BZAW	Beihefte Zeitschrift für die alttestamentliche Wissenschaft. Berlin: Walter de Gruyter.
CBC	Cambridge Bible Commentary on the New English Bible. Cambridge: Cambridge University Press.
CBQ	*Catholic Biblical Quarterly.*
CCOTT	W. J. Dumbrell. *Covenant & Creation: An Old Testament Covenantal Theology.* Exeter: Paternoster, 1984.
COT	Commentaar op het Oude Testament. Kampen: Kok.
CTJ	*Calvin Theological Journal.*
CTM	*Concordia Theological Monthly.*
CurTM	*Currents in Theology and Mission.*

DOTT	*Documents from Old Testament Times.* Ed. D. Winton Thomas. New York: Harper & Row, 1958.
DSB	Daily Study Bible. Philadelphia: Westminster.
EBC	*Expositor's Bible Commentary.*
ECB	*Evangelical Commentary on the Bible.* Ed. Walter A. Elwell. Grand Rapids: Baker, 1989.
EDB	*Evangelical Dictionary of Theology.* Ed. Walter A. Elwell. Grand Rapids: Baker, 1984.
EDT	*Evangelical Dictionary of Theology.*
EJ	*Encyclopaedia Judaica.*
EQ	*Evangelical Quarterly.*
ETL	*Ephemerides Theologicae Lovanienses.*
EvT	*Evangelische Theologie.*
ExpT	*Expository Times.*
FOTL	Forms of Old Testament Literature. Grand Rapids: Eerdmans.
FRLANT	Forschungen zur Religion und Literatur des Alten und Neuen Testaments.
GTJ	*Grace Theological Journal.*
HAR	*Hebrew Annual Review.*
Herm	*Hermathena.*
Hermeneia	Hermeneia. Philadelphia: Fortress.
History	*History.*
HS	*Hebrew Studies.*
HSM	Harvard Semitic Monographs. Atlanta: Scholars Press.
HTR	*Harvard Theological Review.*
HUCA	*Hebrew Union College Annual.*
IB	*The Interpreter's Bible.*
IBD	*Illustrated Bible Dictionary.*
ICC	The International Critical Commentary.
IDB	*Interpreter's Dictionary of the Bible.*
IDBS	*IDB Supplementary Volume.*
IEJ	*Israel Exploration Journal.*
IHCIP	Willem A. VanGemeren. "Israel as the Hermeneutical Crux in the Interpretation of Prophecy," pt. 1, *WTJ* 45 (1983): 132–44; pt. 2, ibid., 46 (1984): 254–97.
IJH	*Israelite and Judaean History.* Ed. John H. Hayes and J. Maxwell Miller. Philadelphia: Westminster, 1977.
Int	*Interpretation.*
Interpretation	Interpretation. Atlanta: John Knox.

IOT	R. K. Harrison, *Introduction to the Old Testament*. Grand Rapids: Eerdmans, 1969.
IOTS	Brevard S. Childs, *Introduction to the Old Testament as Scripture*. Philadelphia: Fortress, 1979.
ISBE	*International Standard Bible Encyclopedia*. Ed., G. W. Bromiley. 4 vols. Grand Rapids: Eerdmans, 1979–88.
JAAR	*Journal of the American Academy of Religion.*
JAOS	*Journal of the American Oriental Society.*
JBL	*Journal of Biblical Literature.*
JBR	*The Journal of Bible and Religion.*
JETS	*Journal of the Evangelical Theological Society.*
JNES	*Journal of Near Eastern Studies.*
JNSL	*Journal of Northwest Semitic Languages.*
JPS	*The Jewish Publication Society.*
JQR	*The Jewish Quarterly Review.*
JR	*Journal of Religion.*
JSOT	*Journal for the Study of Old Testament.*
JSOTSS	JSOT Supplement Series. Sheffield: JSOT.
JSS	*Journal of Semitic Studies.*
JTS	*Journal of Theological Studies.*
LaSor, *OTS*	William Sanford LaSor, David Allan Hubbard, and Frederic William Bush, *Old Testament Survey*. Grand Rapids: Eerdmans, 1982.
LXX	Septuagint.
MT	Masoretic Text.
NBD	*The New Bible Dictionary*. Ed., J. D. Douglas, London: InterVarsity, 1962.
NCB	New Century Bible. London: Oliphants.
NEB	New English Bible.
NGTT	*Nederduits Gereformeerde Teologiese Tydskrif.*
NICNT	New International Commentary on the New Testament.
NICOT	New International Commentary on the Old Testament.
NIV	New International Version.
NKJV	New King James Version.
NTT	*Nederlands Theologisch Tijdschrift.*
OBT	Overtures in Biblical Theology.
OTCT	Brevard S. Childs. *Old Testament Theology in a Canonical Context*. Philadelphia: Fortress, 1985.
OTG	Old Testament Guides. Sheffield: JSOT.

OTL	Old Testament Library. Philadelphia: Westminster.
OTS	*Oudtestamentische Studien.*
OTT	G. von Rad. *Old Testament Theology.* Trans. D. M. G. Stalker. 2 vols. New York: Harper & Row, 1962, 1965.
OTTO	Walther Zimmerli. *Old Testament Theology in Outline.* Trans. David E. Green. Atlanta: John Knox, 1978.
Progress	Willem A. VanGemeren. *The Progress of Redemption: The Story of Salvation from Creation to the New Jerusalem.* Grand Rapids: Zondervan, 1988.
Prophets	Klaus Koch. *The Prophets.* 2 vols. Vol. 1, *The Assyrian Period;* vol. 2, *The Babylonian and Persian Periods.* Trans. Margaret Kohl. Philadelphia: Fortress, 1982.
RB	*Revue Biblique.*
ResQ	*Restoration Quarterly.*
RevExp	*Review and Expositor.*
RevScRel	*Revue des sciences religieuses.*
RTR	*Reformed Theological Review.*
SBLDS	Society of Biblical Literature: Dissertation Series. Atlanta: Scholars Press.
SBT	Studies in Biblical Theology. Naperville: Allenson.
SEÅ	*Svensk Exegetisk Årshok.*
SH	*Scripta Hierosolymitana.*
SJOT	*Scandinavian Journal of the Old Testament.*
SJT	*Scottish Journal of Theology.*
SR	*Studies in Religion/Sciences Religieuses.*
ST	*Studia Theologica.*
StudBT	*Studia Biblica et Theologica.*
SVT	Supplements to Vetus Testamentum.
TB	*Tyndale Bulletin.*
TBT	*The Bible Today.*
TDNT	*Theological Dictionary of the New Testament.*
TDOT	*Theological Dictionary of the Old Testament.*
THAT	*Theologisches Handbuch zum Alten Testament.*
TNT	G. E. Ladd. *A Theology of the New Testament.* Grand Rapids: Eerdmans, 1974.
TOT	W. Eichrodt. *Theology of the Old Testament.* Trans. J. A. Baker. 2 vols. Philadelphia: Westminster, 1961, 1967.

TOTC	Tyndale Old Testament Commentaries. Downers Grove, Ill.: InterVarsity Press.
TOTT	Walter C. Kaiser, Jr. *Toward an Old Testament Theology.* Grand Rapids: Zondervan, 1978.
TrinJ	*Trinity Journal.*
TWOT	*Theological Wordbook of the Old Testament.*
VT	*Vetus Testamentum.*
WBC	Word Biblical Commentary. Waco, Tex.: Word.
WTJ	*Westminster Theological Journal.*
ZAW	*Zeitschrift für die alttestamentliche Wissenschaft.*
ZPEB	*The Zondervan Pictorial Encyclopedia of the Bible.*
ZTK	*Zeitschrift für Theologie und Kirche.*

ABBREVIATIONS FOR FESTSCHRIFTEN (FS/FSS)

Ackroyd	*Israel's Prophetic Tradition: Essays in Honour of Peter R. Ackroyd.* Ed. Richard J. Coggins, Anthony Phillips, and Michael Knibb. Cambridge: Cambridge University Press, 1982.
Ahlström	*In the Shelter of Elyon: Essays on Ancient Palestinian Life and Literature in Honor of G. W. Ahlström.* Ed. W. Boyd Barrick and John R. Spencer. Sheffield: JSOT Press, 1984.
Albright	*Near Eastern Studies in Honor of William Foxwell Albright.* Ed. Hans Goedicke. Baltimore: Johns Hopkins Press, 1971.
Allis	*The Law and the Prophets: Old Testament Studies Prepared in Honor of Oswald Thompson Allis.* Ed. John H. Skilton. Nutley, N.J.: Presbyterian & Reformed, 1974.
Bertholet	*Festschrift für Alfred Bertholet zum 80. Geburtstag.* Ed. Walter Baumgartner, Otto Eissfeldt, Karl Elliger, and Leonhard Rost. Tübingen: Mohr, 1950.
Botterweck	*Bausteine biblischer Theologie. Festgabe für G. Johannes Botterweck zum 60. Geburtstag dargebracht von seinen Schülern.* Ed. Heinz-Josef Fabry. Cologne: Peter Hanstein, 1977.
Cameron	*Michigan Oriental Studies in Honor of Georg Cameron.* Ed. L. L. Orlin et al. Ann Arbor: University of Michigan Press, 1976.
Casey	*Biblical and Patristic Studies: In Memory of Robert Pierce Casey.* Ed. J. Neville Birdsall and Robert W. Thomson. Freiburg: Herder, 1963.

Coppens	*De Mari à Qumrân: L'Ancien Testament: Son Milieu. Ses Écrits. Ses relectures juives. Hommage à Mgr. J. Coppens.* Ed. H. Cazelles. Paris: P. Lethielleux, 1969.
Cross	*Ancient Israelite Religion. Essays in Honor of Frank Moore Cross.* Ed. Patrick D. Miller, Jr., Paul D. Hanson, and S. Dean McBride. Philadelphia: Fortress, 1987.
Davies	*Proclamation and Presence: Old Testament Essays in Honour of Gwynne Henton Davies.* Ed. John I. Durham and J. R. Porter. Richmond: John Knox, 1970.
Dodd	*The Background of the New Testament and Its Eschatology. In Honour of Charles Harold Dodd.* Ed. W. D. Davies and D. Daube. Cambridge: Cambridge University Press, 1964.
Fohrer	*Prophecy: Essays Presented to Georg Fohrer on His Sixty-fifth Birthday.* Ed. J. A. Emerton. Berlin: Walter de Gruyter, 1980.
Freedman	*The Word of the Lord Shall Go Forth: Essays in Honor of David Noel Freedman.* Ed. Carol F. Meyers and M. O'Connor. Winona Lake, Ind.: Eisenbrauns, 1983.
Gross	*Freude an der Weisung des Herrn, Beiträge zur Theologie der Psalmen, Festgabe zum 70. Geburtstag von Heinrich Gross.* Ed. Ernst Haag and Frank-Lothar Hossfeld. Stuttgart: Katholisches Bibelwerk, 1986.
Hughes	*Through Christ's Word: A Festschrift for Dr. Philip E. Hughes.* Ed. W. Robert Godfrey and Jesse L. Boyd III. Phillipsburg, N. J.: Presbyterian & Reformed, 1985.
Iwry	*Biblical and Related Studies Presented to Samuel Iwry.* Ed. Ann Kort and Scott Morschauser. Winona Lake, Ind.: Eisenbrauns, 1985.
Jepsen	*Schalom: Studien zu Glaube und Geschichte Israels. Alfred Jepsen zum 70. Geburtstag.* Ed. Karl-Heinz Bernhardt. Stuttgart: Calwer Verlag, 1971.
Johnson	*Continuity and Discontinuity: Perspectives on the Relationship between the Old and New Testaments in Honor of S. Lewis Johnson, Jr.* Ed. John S. Feinberg. Westchester: Crossway, 1988.

Koole	*De Knecht: Studies rondom Deutero-Jesaja door collega's en oud-leerlingen aangeboden aan Prof. Dr. J. L. Koole.* Kampen: Kok, 1978.
Landsberger	*Studies in Honor of Benno Landsberger on His Seventy-fifth Birthday April 21, 1965,* by The Oriental Institute of the University of Chicago in *Assyriological Studies* 16. Chicago: University of Chicago Press, 1965.
LaSor	*Biblical and Near Eastern Studies: Essays in Honor of William Sanford LaSor.* Ed. Gary A. Tuttle. Grand Rapids: Eerdmans, 1978.
May	*Translating and Understanding the Old Testament: Essays in Honor of Herbert Gordon May.* Ed. Henry Thomas Frank and William L. Reed. Nashville: Abingdon, 1970.
McKane	*A Word in Season: Essays in Honour of William McKane.* JSOTSS 42. 1986.
Mendenhall	*The Quest for the Kingdom of God: Studies in Honor of George E. Mendenhall.* Ed. H. B. Huffmon, F. A. Spina, and A. R. W. Green. Winona Lake, Ind.: Eisenbrauns, 1983.
Morris	*Reconciliation and Hope: New Testament Essays on Atonement and Eschatology Presented to L. L. Morris on His 60th Birthday.* Ed. Robert Banks. Grand Rapids: Eerdmans, 1974.
Muilenburg	*Israel's Prophetic Heritage: Essays in Honor of James Muilenburg.* Ed. Bernard W. Anderson and Walter Harrelson. New York: Harper & Row, 1962.
Muilenburg (FSS)	*Rhetorical Criticism: Essays in Honor of James Muilenburg.* Ed. Jared J. Jackson and Martin Kessler. Pittsburgh: Pickwick, 1974.
Myers	*A Light Unto My Path: Old Testament Studies in Honor of Jacob M. Myers.* Ed. Howard N. Bream, Ralph D. Heim, and Carey A. Moore. Philadelphia: Temple University Press, 1974.
Nötscher	*Alttestamentliche Studien: Friedrich Nötscher zum 60. Geburtstag gewidmet.* Bonn: Peter Hanstein, 1950.
van der Ploeg	*Von Kanaan bis Kerala: Festschrift für Prof. Mag. Dr. J. P. M. van der Ploeg O.P. zur Vollendung des siebzigsten Lebensjahres am 4. Juli 1979.* Ed. W. C. Delsman, J. T. Nelis, J. R. T. M. Peters,

	W. H. Ph. Römer, and A. S. van der Woude. Neukirchen-Vluyn: Neukirchener, 1982.
von Rad	*Probleme biblischer Theologie: Gerhard von Rad zum 70. Geburtstag.* Ed. Hans Walter Wolff. Munich: Kaiser, 1971.
Ridderbos	*Loven en Geloven: Opstellen van Collega's en Medewerkers aangeboden aan Prof. Dr. Nic. H. Ridderbos.* Ed. M. H. van Es, et al. Amsterdam: Ton Bolland, 1975.
Robinson	*Studies in Old Testament Prophecy: Presented to Professor Theodore H. Robinson.* Ed. H. H. Rowley. Edinburgh: T. & T. Clark, 1957.
Rost	*Das Ferne und Nahe Wort: Festschrift Leonhard Rost zur Vollendung seines 70. Lebensjahres am 30. November 1966 gewidmet.* Ed. Fritz Maass. Berlin: Töpelmann, 1967.
Rowley	*Wisdom in Israel and in the Ancient Near East: Essays Presented to Professor Harold Henry Rowley.* Ed. M. Noth and D. Winton Thomas. SVT 3. Leiden: Brill, 1969.
Silberman	*The Divine Helmsman: Studies on God's Control of Human Events, Presented to Lou H. Silberman.* Ed. James L. Crenshaw and Samuel Sandmel. New York: Ktav, 1980.
Stinespring	*The Use of The Old Testament in the New and Other Essays: Studies in Honor of William Franklin Stinespring.* Ed. James M. Efird. Durham, N.C.: Duke University Press, 1972.
Terrien	*Israelite Wisdom: Theological and Literary Essays in Honor of Samuel Terrien.* Ed. J. G. Gammie, et al. Missoula, Mont.: Scholars Press, 1978.
Thomas	*Words and Meanings: Essays Presented to David Winton Thomas on His Retirement from the Regius Professorship of Hebrew in the University of Cambridge, 1968.* Ed. Peter R. Ackroyd and Barnabas Lindars. Cambridge: Cambridge University Press, 1968.
Torrance	*Creation, Christ, and Culture: Studies in Honour of T. F. Torrance.* Ed. Richard W. A. McKinney. Edinburgh: T. & T. Clark, 1976.
Vischer	*Maqqēl shâqēdh: La Branche d'amandier. Hommage à Wilhelm Vischer.* Montpellier: Causse, Graille, Casteneau, 1960.

Vriezen	*Studia Biblica et Semitica: Theodoro Christiano Vriezen qui munere Professoris Theologiae per XXV Annos functus est, ab Amicis, Collegis, Discipulis dedicata.* Wageningen: Veenman, 1966.
Wehr	*Ekklesia Festschrift für Bischof Dr. Matthias Wehr.* Paulinus-Verlag Trier, 1962.
Weiser	*Tradition und Situation. Studien zur alttestamentlichen Prophetie: Artur Weiser zum 70. Geburtstag am 18.11.1963 dargebracht von Kollegen, Freunden, und Schülern.* Ed. Ernst Würthwein and Otto Kaiser. Göttingen: Vandenhoeck & Ruprecht, 1963.
Westermann	*Werden und Wirken des Alten Testaments: Festschrift für Claus Westermann zum 70. Geburtstag.* Ed. Rainer Albertz, Hans-Peter Müller, Hans Walter Wolff, and Walther Zimmerli. Göttingen: Vandenhoeck & Ruprecht, 1980.
Wolff	*Die Botschaft und die Boten: Festschrift für Hans Walter Wolff zum 70. Geburtstag.* Ed. Jörg Jeremias and Lothar Perlitt. Neukirchen-Vluyn: Neukirchener, 1981.
Wright	*Magnalia Dei. The Mighty Acts of God: Essays on the Bible and Archaeology in Memory of G. Ernest Wright.* Ed. Frank Moore Cross, Werner E. Lemke, and Patrick D. Miller, Jr. Garden City: Doubleday, 1973.
Zimmerli	*Beiträge Alttestamentlichen Theologie: Festschrift für Walther Zimmerli zum 70. Geburtstag.* Ed. Herbert Donner, Robert Hanhart, and Rudolf Smend. Göttingen: Vandenhoeck & Ruprecht, 1977.

Appendix
Forms of Prophetic Speech

1. The prophetic lawsuit (RÎB), oracle of judgment, and related forms
2. Prophecy/oracle/proclamation of salvation
3. Visions
4. Apocalyptic

1. THE PROPHETIC LAWSUIT (RîB), ORACLE OF JUDGMENT, AND RELATED FORMS

The prophetic lawsuit correlates covenant, law, and the prophetic tradition.[1] The prophets spoke from within the covenant tradition, remaining loyal to the Mosaic revelation. This revelation contained stipulations and sanctions, promises and blessing. The sanctions of the covenant were applied depending on covenant loyalty or disobedience.[2] D. R. Hillers speaks of the treaty curses as "maledictions,"[3] which the prophets employed as the basis for their oracles of doom. It appears that the prophets employed a covenant lawsuit form (genre) by which they appealed to the people to repent and by which they held out the judgment to come. This lawsuit is known by the Hebrew word *rîb* (pronounced "reev").[4] The prophet gave a *trial speech* or *judicial speech* in which he was God's prosecutor.[5] The *rîb* pattern may be explained on the basis of judicial procedure or against the background of the ancient Near Eastern treaty form. The latter may well be the preferable *Sitz-im-Leben,* as argued by Huffmon.[6] G. E. Wright carefully examined the elements of the lawsuit in his study on Deuteronomy 32. The elements include a call on (1) witnesses, (2) the case itself, (3) a statement of the Lord's acts of loyalty, (4) the indictment, and (5) the sentence.[7] Further, Wright drew a parallel between the prophetic lawsuit and the heavenly council in which Yahweh is the judge, plaintiff, witness, and jury. He witnessed against his people, based on their breach of covenant, stated his case through his *prosecutor,* the prophet, and rendered his sentence. The *rîb* has occasioned further discussion as to its association with the cult or juridical practice. The pervasiveness of the covenantal structure of thought affected all Israelite traditions: prophetic, wisdom, and law. Hence, as Clements has shown, it is impossible to identify the lawsuit as a distinctively prophetic contribution.[8]

For example, Isaiah presents God as prosecuting his people[9] from the very opening of his prophecy (Isa. 1:2–31).

a. Witnesses

> Hear, O heavens! Listen, O earth!
> For the LORD has spoken:

b. The Case and God's Past Acts of Loyalty

> "I reared children and brought them up,
> but they have rebelled against me.
> The ox knows his master,
> the donkey his owner's manger,
> but Israel does not know,
> my people do not understand."
> Ah, sinful nation,
> a people loaded with guilt,
> a brood of evildoers,
> children given to corruption!
> They have forsaken the LORD;
> they have spurned the Holy One of Israel
> and turned their backs on him.
>
> (vv. 2b–4)

c. The Indictment

> When you spread out your hands in prayer,
> I will hide my eyes from you;
> even if you offer many prayers,
> I will not listen.
> Your hands are full of blood;
> wash and make yourselves clean.
> Take your evil deeds
> out of my sight!
> Stop doing wrong,
> learn to do right!
> Seek justice,
> encourage the oppressed.
> Defend the cause of the fatherless,
> plead the case of the widow.
> "Come now, let us reason together,"
> says the LORD.
> "Though your sins are like scarlet,
> they shall be as white as snow;
> though they are red as crimson,
> they shall be like wool.

> If you are willing and obedient,
>   you will eat the best from the land;"
>   (vv. 15–19)

d. The Sentence

> "but if you resist and rebel,
>   you will be devoured by the sword."
>   For the mouth of the LORD
>   has spoken. . . .
> Therefore the Lord, the LORD Almighty,
>   the Mighty One of Israel, declares:
> "Ah, I will get relief from my foes
>   and avenge myself on my enemies.
> I will turn my hand against you;
>   I will thoroughly purge away your dross
>   and remove all your impurities. . . .
> But rebels and sinners will both be broken,
>   and those who forsake the LORD will perish.
> "You will be ashamed because of the sacred oaks
>   in which you have delighted;
> you will be disgraced because of the gardens
>   that you have chosen.
> You will be like an oak with fading leaves,
>   like a garden without water.
> The mighty man will become tinder
>   and his work a spark;
> both will burn together,
>   with no one to quench the fire."
>   (vv. 20, 24–25, 28–31)

A related form is the *disputation speech* in which the prophet plays the devil's advocate. He "prosecutes" the guilty by interrogating them. He challenges the arrogant, whether political, false righteousness, or apostasy. He also encourages the "humble" to look to the Lord alone for hope of salvation.[10] Graffy includes the following parts of the disputation speech proper, as illustrated in Ezekiel 33:10–20:

Introduction

> This is what you are saying:

Quotation

> "Our offenses and sins weigh us down, and we are wasting away because of them. How then can we live?" (v. 10)

Explanatory or Preparatory Remark

> Say to them, "As surely as I live, declares the Sovereign LORD, I take no pleasure in the death of the wicked, but rather that they turn from their

ways and live. Turn! Turn from your evil ways! Why will you die, O house of Israel?" (v. 11)

Refutation

Therefore, son of man, say to your countrymen, "The righteousness of the righteous man will not save him when he disobeys, and the wickedness of the wicked man will not cause him to fall when he turns from it. The righteous man, if he sins, will not be allowed to live because of his former righteousness." If I tell the righteous man that he will surely live, but then he trusts in his righteousness and does evil, none of the righteous things he has done will be remembered; he will die for the evil he has done. And if I say to the wicked man, "You will surely die," but he then turns away from his sin and does what is just and right—if he gives back what he took in pledge for a loan, returns what he has stolen, follows the decrees that give life, and does no evil, he will surely live; he will not die. None of the sins he has committed will be remembered against him. He has done what is just and right; he will surely live. (vv. 12–16)

Programmatic and Concluding Refutation

Yet your countrymen say, "The way of the Lord is not just." (v. 17a)

Rejoinder

But it is their way that is not just. If a righteous man turns from his righteousness and does evil, he will die for it. And if a wicked man turns away from his wickedness and does what is just and right, he will live by doing so. Yet, O house of Israel, you say, "The way of the Lord is not just." But I will judge each of you according to his own ways." (vv. 17b–20)

Malachi reveals the further development of the disputation into a *discussion speech*. The discussion speech differs in that usually the prophet does not quote the people or enter into an argument. Instead, the discussion speech is a form of prophetic speech that derives from the disputation speech.[11] For example:

a. Declaration

"I have loved you," says the LORD. (Mal. 1:2a)

b. Discussion

But you ask, "How have you loved us?" (v. 2b)

c. Response

"Was not Esau Jacob's brother?" the LORD says. "Yet I have loved Jacob, but Esau I have hated, and I have turned his mountains into a wasteland and left his inheritance to the desert jackals."

Edom may say, "Though we have been crushed, we will rebuild the ruins."

But this is what the LORD Almighty says: "They may build, but I will demolish. They will be called the Wicked Land, a people always under the wrath of the LORD." (vv. 2c–4)

d. Declaration of Assurance

You will see it with your own eyes and say, "Great is the Lord—even beyond the borders of Israel!" (v. 5)

Another related form is the *Woe Oracle.* The woe oracle begins with the cry "woe" (HÔY), followed by a participial clause describing the offense and an announcement of judgment.[12] For example, in Isaiah 31:1–4 the prophet proclaims God's judgment on all who rely on political and military alliances. Hezekiah's emissaries had gone down to Egypt seeking political and military assistance against the Assyrian threat. In this woe oracle Isaiah announces God's judgment:

a. Opening

Woe to those who go down to Egypt for help,
    who rely on horses,
who trust in the multitude of their chariots
    and in the great strength of their horsemen,
                   (31:1a)

b. Accusation

but do not look to the Holy One of Israel,
    or seek help from the LORD.
                   (v. 1b)

c. Judgment

Yet he too is wise and can bring disaster;
    he does not take back his words.
He will rise up against the house of the wicked,
    against those who help evildoers.
But the Egyptians are men and not God;
    their horses are flesh and not spirit.
When the LORD stretches out his hand,
    he who helps will stumble,
    he who is helped will fall;
        both will perish together.
This is what the LORD says to me:

> "As a lion growls,
> a great lion over his prey—
> and though a whole band of shepherds
> is called together against him,
> he is not frightened by their shouts
> or disturbed by their clamor—
> so the LORD Almighty will come down
> to do battle on Mount Zion and on its heights."
>
> (vv. 2–4)

In a *prophecy of disaster* the prophet is called upon to speak to the people, give a reason for the impending disaster, and declare that the disaster comes from the Lord.[13] The latter part, known as the "prediction of the disaster," begins with "therefore" (*lākēn*) and/or "thus declares the LORD" (*kōh 'āmar YHWH*). The speech concludes with a "motive clause" (*kî*, "because").[14] The structure of the unit was not fixed; it changed depending on whether it was addressed to an individual or to a group. It changed also due to what Westermann explains as a loosening of the structure.[15] For example, in Jeremiah 28:13–17, the Lord's word comes to Hananiah, a false prophet:

a. The Word of the Lord

Go and tell Hananiah, "This is what the LORD says. . ." (28:13a)

b. The Reason for the Disaster

"You have broken a wooden yoke. . . ."
Then the prophet Jeremiah said to Hananiah the prophet, "Listen, Hananiah! The LORD has not sent you, yet you have persuaded this nation to trust in lies." (vv. 13b, 15)

c. The Disaster

". . .but in its place you will get a yoke of iron. This is what the LORD Almighty, the God of Israel, says: I will put an iron yoke on the necks of all these nations to make them serve Nebuchadnezzar king of Babylon, and they will serve him. I will even give him control over the wild animals."
. . . "Therefore, this is what the LORD says: 'I am about to remove you from the face of the earth. This very year you are going to die, because you have preached rebellion against the LORD.'"
. . . In the seventh month of that same year, Hananiah the prophet died. (vv. 13c, 14, 16–17)

The judgment speech was also directed against foreign nations in *oracles against the nations*. Gottwald has argued, possibly with just-ification, that this form was one of the oldest prophetic forms.[16] It occurs at Mari and was used by Balak, the Moabite king, to have Israel

405

cursed by Balaam (Num. 22–24). Though several original life situations have been proposed,[17] Lutz is correct in saying that the oracles against the nations originated out of the Zion theology, according to which the Lord protected his people against enemies and foreign invaders.[18] The Major Prophets contain a collection of oracles against the nations (Isa. 13–23; Jer. 46–51; Ezek. 25–32), and several of the Minor Prophets, notably Amos (1:3–2:6) and Zephaniah (2:4–15), employ this form as well. The oracles affirm the sovereignty of Yahweh over the nations, encourage God's people with the hope of absolute deliverance from oppression or seduction by the nations, and the establishment of God's kingdom on earth. At times a specific enemy was the focus of the oracles (as in Isa. 7–23),[19] and at other times the enemy lacked precise definition.[20] Duane L. Christensen has connected the oracles against the nations with the war oracles.[21]

A related form is the *summons to repentance*. The prophet, having spoken of the disaster to come, appeals to the people to make an appropriate response. The origin of this form lies in the covenant renewal ceremony. The prophets call on the loyal remnant to renew their loyalty to the Lord. The formal features of this genre are not consistent, but according to Raitt, they include admonition, accusation, threat.[22] For example, in Amos 5:4–7, 14–15, the prophet gives summons after summons:

Summons 1

> This is what the Lᴏʀᴅ says to the house of Israel:
>
> "Seek me and live;
>> do not seek Bethel,
> do not go to Gilgal,
>> do not journey to Beersheba.
> For Gilgal will surely go into exile,
>> and Bethel will be reduced to nothing."
>>> (vv. 4–5)

Summons 2

> Seek the Lᴏʀᴅ and live,
>> or he will sweep through the house of Joseph like a fire;
> it will devour,
>> and Bethel will have no one to quench it.
> You who turn justice into bitterness
>> and cast righteousness to the ground.
>>> (vv. 6–7)

Summons 3

> Seek good, not evil,
>> that you may live.
> Then the LORD God Almighty will be with you,
>> just as you say he is.
> Hate evil, love good;
>> maintain justice in the courts.
> Perhaps the LORD God Almighty will have mercy
>> on the remnant of Joseph.

(vv. 14–15)

2. PROPHECY / ORACLE / PROCLAMATION OF SALVATION

The *prophecy of salvation* is the counterpart of the prophecy of judgment.[23] In the prophecy of salvation the prophet briefly states the situation in which the people find themselves, predicts their deliverance, and concludes with an affirmation of the Lord's ability to accomplish his promise. For example, in Jeremiah 32:36–41[24] the prophet introduces the prophecy with a description of the situation: "You are saying about this city, 'By the sword, famine and plague it will be handed over to the king of Babylon'" (v. 36). The prediction of salvation commences with "this is what the LORD, the God of Israel, says" (v. 36). The salvation message consists of a prediction of restoration from exile, forgiveness, covenant renewal, and a promise of a changed heart and of perpetual rest and peace. The final "characterization" is the assurance that the Lord rejoices to do good to his people and will "assuredly" accomplish his promises (v. 41). The structure of this genre is as follows:

a. *Indication of the Situation*

You are saying about this city, "By the sword, famine and plague it will be handed over to the king of Babylon;" (Jer. 32:36a)

b. *Prediction of Salvation*

but this is what the LORD, the God of Israel, says: "I will surely gather them from all the lands where I banish them in my furious anger and great wrath; I will bring them back to this place and let them live in safety. They will be my people, and I will be their God. I will give them singleness of heart and action, so that they will always fear me for their own good and the good of their children after them. I will make an everlasting covenant with them: I will never stop doing good to them, and I will inspire them to fear me, so that they will never turn away from me." (vv. 36b–40)

c. Concluding Characterization

"I will rejoice in doing them good and will assuredly plant them in this land with all my heart and soul." (v. 41)

In Isaiah 40–48 we find the *oracle of salvation* with a promise of divine deliverance, an encouragement not to be afraid, and a declaration that the Lord will deliver.[25] For example, in Isaiah 44:1–5 the prophet gives a divine oracle, predicting God's fulfillment of his promise-word:

a. Declaration of God's Fidelity

"But now listen, O Jacob, my servant,
Israel, whom I have chosen.
This is what the LORD says—
he who made you, who formed you in the womb,
and who will help you:
Do not be afraid, O Jacob, my servant,
Jeshurun, whom I have chosen."

(Isa. 44:1–2)

b. Oracle of Salvation

"For I will pour water on the thirsty land,
and streams on the dry ground;
I will pour out my Spirit on your offspring,
and my blessing on your descendants."

(v. 3)

c. Purpose of Salvation

"They will spring up like grass in a meadow,
like poplar trees by flowing streams.
One will say, 'I belong to the LORD';
another will call himself by the name of Jacob;
still another will write on his hand, 'The LORD's,'
and will take the name Israel."

(vv. 4–5)

Sometimes a distinction is further made between the prophecy, the oracle, and the proclamation of salvation, depending on the specificity of the announcement of God's future acts. Westermann defines the oracle of salvation as addressing present needs and the *proclamation of salvation* as being a more general announcement.[26] For example, in Isaiah 41:17–20 the prophet predicts salvation, but the salvation is not set in a particular context:

a. A General Need

"The poor and needy search for water,
but there is none;

their tongues are parched with thirst.

(Isa. 41:17a)

b. Prediction of Salvation

"But I the LORD will answer them;
I, the God of Israel, will not forsake them.
I will make rivers flow on barren heights,
and springs within the valleys.
I will turn the desert into pools of water,
and the parched ground into springs.
I will put in the desert
the cedar and the acacia, the myrtle and the olive.
I will set pines in the wasteland,
the fir and the cypress together,"

(vv. 17b–19)

c. Purpose (Recognition Formula)

"so that people may see and know,
may consider and understand,
that the hand of the LORD has done this,
that the Holy One of Israel has created it."

(v. 20)

3. VISIONS

The visions constitute a separate form. Susan Niditch has made a careful diachronic study of this genre, and she concludes that the "symbolic vision" of the preexilic prophets (Jer. 1:11–12, 13–14; 24; Amos 7:7–9; 8:1–3) developed into a literary narrative (Zechariah) and that the visions reveal continuity.[27] She discovered that the prophets adapted this form "in exciting, flexible, and creative ways to suit the changing needs of Israelite history and to continue the process of divine revelation."[28] The use of symbolic visions in the preexilic prophets lies in the revelation of what is about to happen through an everyday object.[29] They predict the judgment through the symbolic visions, but also open up the possibility of a new era of forgiveness and restoration (Jer. 24). In contrast, Zechariah employs "conceptual" imagery that requires interpretation and hence narration.[30] His symbolic visions point to deliverance and restoration. Daniel's visions further develop the conceptual imagery in which symbols receive interpretation, but the interpretation is cloaked in a veil of mystery.[31] She designates this as "the baroque stage."

409

4. APOCALYPTIC

The basic issue in the study of apocalyptic is its relation to the prophetic.[32] In a seminal study Otto Plöger distinguished between two developments in the postexilic era: theocratic and apocalyptic.[33] The former concerned itself with the temple, the Torah, and the priesthood (cf. Chronicles, Ezra-Nehemiah), and the latter developed in reaction to the Zadokite priesthood, being a movement of disillusionment. He posits that the apocalyptic arose as an ideology or hermeneutic in the context of pessimism.[34] Klaus Koch distinguishes between apocalyptic as a form of literature and as an ideological movement.[35] Paul Hanson further refines the definition by restricting the term *apocalypse* to a literary genre, *apocalypticism* to a socioreligious movement, and *apocalyptic eschatology* to a religious perspective, "which views divine plans in relation to historical realities in a particular way."[36] He operates from the basic position that the prophets functioned as "translators" of the divine vision into a sociopolitical milieu and contrasts their contribution with the apocalyptic eschatologists, being preoccupied with vision and having no or little interest in translating it into political, historical, and social realities.[37] Because both prophets and visionaries share in the vision of restoration, Hanson concludes that there is "one unbroken strand extending throughout the history of prophetic and apocalyptic eschatology."[38] Hanson's distinctions between prophetic hope (eschatology) and eschatological visions, and between hierocratic and visionary/eschatological have raised new issues with few definitive answers.[39]

The relationships between prophetic and apocalyptic are far from clear, and it appears that apocalyptic should not carry such negative associations, as Koch rightly concludes,

> In the sphere of the biblical writings, accordingly, there is little which is so significant as apocalyptic. True, the apocalyptists do not know anything about the social activity of believers, but they apparently proclaim that the world is constantly being shaped and reshaped by God; they announce a mighty and ultimate divine revolution, and hold up to the eyes of the reader the goal of a renewed human society which has become one with its God and thus with the enduring ground of all reality. Do they not even paint the picture of a society in which the rule of man over man has hence been set aside forever? The apocalyptists demand that believers, on their own historical plane, "project" themselves in the direction of this hope. Is this of no importance for our present time?[40]

Apocalyptic eschatology may express itself in dualism, pessimism, and futurism. It is *dualistic* in its sharp division of right and wrong; the evil of this age is devoid of common grace and the goodness of God's reign over his creation. It is *pessimistic* in its rejection of human involvement with the plan of God of bringing in a new era of salvation and restoration. It is *futuristic* in its living for and with the vision of the splendor of the new age with little regard to the impact of the vision on present realities. However, all apocalyptic elements do not fall into this categorization. The Prophets anticipate a radical transformation, have a clearly developed eschatology, and even incorporate apocalyptic forms. The process of interpretation, of relating prophetic and apocalyptic, promise and fulfillment, and reality and eschatology, is a complex hermeneutic task.[41] The study of the Prophets separately and in conjunction with the New Testament writings will help us see the living Christ.

Hanson's study on the rise of apocalyptic and the distinction between the *prophetic* vision in concrete historical, sociopolitical realities and the *apocalyptic* eschatology with its pre-occupation with the heavenly visions is a sober warning for the twentieth-century Christian. Too much discussion of the prophets has bordered on the apocalyptic as the prophetic teachings have been charted out into systems of eschatology and as prophetic conferences have encouraged Christians to live "in heaven" while earning a living on this earth. The prophets maintain the dialectic tension between hope and reality, whereas successive generations after the prophets, as we are prone to do, departed from what Hanson calls "the firm mooring of the prophetic message in history."[42]

Apocalypse has a canonical place. The prophets and the apostle John employ apocalyptic imagery.[43] The apocalyptic genre, much like the prophetic, presents the truth of God not consecutively or logically, but multidimensionally. The eschatology of the prophetic word and the apocalyptic visions have one common origin: the Spirit of prophecy. On a historical plane, the community of God's people have to adjust continually to the resultant tensions between prophecy and vision, vision and reality, present and future, and between creation and redemption must remain. As long as this tension is real in our lives, the prophetic word propels us toward action in evangelism, church work, and involvement in society as light bearers. The light dims when Christians work out the details of the heavenly vision while awaiting redemption from this world. The development of schisms and ideologies preceding the incarnation of our Lord with the consequent rejection of the Messiah of Israel is a vivid reminder of the traps— systematization, rigidity in interpretation, and failure of correlation— that are still with us.[44]

Selected Bibliography

Ackroyd, Peter R. "Historians and Prophets." *SEÅ* 33 (1968): 18–54.
————. "The History of Israel in the Exilic and Post-Exilic Periods." In *Tradition and Interpretation: Essays by Members of the Society for Old Testament Study,* edited by G. W. Anderson, Oxford: Clarendon, 1979, 320–50.
Albright, William F. "Samuel and the Beginnings of the Prophetic Movement." In *Interpreting the Prophetic Tradition,* edited by Harry M. Orlinsky, New York: Ktav, 1969, 151–76.
Alden, Robert L. "Study of the Prophets Since World War II." In *New Perspectives on the Old Testament,* edited by J. B. Payne, Waco, Tex.: Word, 1970, 131–45.
Alter, Robert. *The Art of Biblical Poetry.* New York: Basic Books, 1985.
Armerding, Carl Edwin, and W. Ward Gasque, eds. *Dreams, Visions and Oracles: The Layman's Guide to Biblical Prophecy.* Grand Rapids: Baker, 1977.
Baarlink, H. *Vrede op Aarde: de Messiaanse Vrede in bijbels Perspectief.* Kampen: Kok, 1985.
Baltzer, Klaus. "Considerations Regarding the Office and Calling of the Prophet." *HTR* 61 (1968): 567–81.
Barr, James. "Jewish Apocalyptic in Recent Scholarly Study." *BJRL* 58 (1975–76): 9–35.
Becker, Joachim. *Messianic Expectation in the Old Testament.* Translated by David E. Green. Philadelphia: Fortress, 1980.
Becker, Robert. "The Redemptive Focus of the Kingdom of God." *CTJ* 14 (1979): 154–86.
Beecher, Willis Judson. *The Prophets and the Promise.* 1905. Reprint. Grand Rapids: Baker, 1963.
Bergren, Richard Victor. *The Prophets and the Law.* Cincinnati: Hebrew Union College, 1974.
Blenkinsopp, Joseph. *A History of Prophecy in Israel.* Philadelphia: Westminster, 1983.
————. *Prophecy and Canon: A Contribution to the Study of Jewish Origins.* Notre Dame, Ind.: University of Notre Dame Press, 1977.
Bright, John. *Covenant and Promise: The Prophetic Understanding of the Future in Preexilic Israel.* Philadelphia: Westminster, 1976.
Brueggemann, Walter. *The Prophetic Imagination.* Philadelphia: Fortress, 1978.
————. *Tradition for Crisis: A Study in Hosea.* Richmond: John Knox, 1968.
Buber, Martin. *The Prophetic Faith.* New York: Harper & Brothers, 1949.

Selected Bibliography

Caird, G. B. *The Language and Imagery of the Bible.* Philadelphia: Westminster, 1980.

Carroll, Robert P. "Ancient Israelite Prophecy and Dissonance Theory." *Numen* 24 (1977–78): 135–51.

―――――. "Eschatological Delay in the Prophetic Tradition." *ZAW* 94 (1982): 47–58.

―――――. "Prophecy and Dissonance: A Theoretical Approach to the Prophetic Tradition." *ZAW* 92 (1980): 108–19.

―――――. "Rebellion and Dissent in Ancient Israelite Society." *ZAW* 89 (1977): 176–204.

―――――. "Twilight of Prophecy or Dawn of Apocalyptic." *JSOT* 14 (1979): 3–35.

―――――. *When Prophecy Failed: Cognitive Dissonance in the Prophetic Traditions of the Old Testament.* New York: Seabury, 1979.

Childs, Brevard S. "The Canonical Shape of the Prophetic Literature." *Int* 32 (1978): 46–55.

―――――. "The Old Testament as Scripture of the Church." *CTM* 43 (1972): 709–22.

―――――. *Old Testament Theology in a Canonical Context.* Philadelphia: Fortress, 1985.

―――――. "The Sensus Literalis of Scripture: An Ancient and Modern Problem." *FS Zimmerli*, 80–93.

Christensen, Duane L. *Transformations of the War Oracle in Old Testament Prophecy: Studies in the Oracles Against the Nations.* Missoula, Mont.: Scholars Press, 1975.

Clements, Ronald E. "Covenant and Canon in the Old Testament." *FS Torrance*, 1–12.

―――――. *God and Temple.* Philadelphia: Fortress, 1965.

―――――. "Interpreting the Prophets." In *One Hundred Years of Old Testament Interpretation*, Philadelphia: Westminster, 1976, 51–75.

―――――. *Isaiah and the Deliverance of Jerusalem.* JSOTSS 13. 1980.

―――――. *Old Testament Theology: A Fresh Approach.* London: Marshall, Morgan & Scott, 1978.

―――――. "Patterns in the Prophetic Canon." In *Canon and Authority: Essays in Old Testament Religion and Theology*, edited by George W. Coats and Burke O. Long, Philadelphia: Fortress, 1977, 42–55.

―――――. *Prophecy and Covenant.* London: SCM, 1965.

―――――. *Prophecy and Tradition.* Atlanta: John Knox, 1975.

Cogan, Morton. *Imperialism and Religion: Assyria, Judah and Israel in the Eighth and Seventh Centuries B.C.E.* Missoula, Mont.: Scholars Press, 1974.

Coggins, Richard A. "An Alternative Prophetic Tradition?" *FS Ackroyd*, 77–94.

Collins, John J. "The Place of Apocalypticism in the Religion of Israel." *FS Cross*, 539–58.

Crenshaw, James L. "Prophecy, False." *IDBS*, 67–69, 701–2.

―――――. *Prophetic Conflict: Its Effect upon Israelite Religion.* Berlin: Walter de Gruyter, 1971.

―――――. *A Whirlpool of Torment: Israelite Traditions on God as an Oppressive Presence.* Philadelphia: Fortress, 1984.

413

_____, ed. *Theodicy in the Old Testament*. Philadelphia: Fortress, 1983.

Cross, F. M. *Canaanite Myth and Hebrew Epic*. Cambridge: Harvard University Press, 1973.

Davidson, A. B. *Old Testament Prophecy,* edited by J. A. Patterson. Edinburgh: T. & T. Clark, 1905.

Davies, G. I. "Apocalyptic and Historiography." *JSOT* 5 (1978): 15–28.

De Vries, Simon J. *Prophet Against Prophet: The Role of the Micaiah Narrative (1 Kings 22) in the Development of Early Prophetic Tradition*. Grand Rapids: Eerdmans, 1978.

Dumbrell, William J. *Covenant & Creation: An Old Testament Covenantal Theology*. Exeter: Paternoster, 1984.

_____. *The End of the Beginning: Revelation 21–22 and the Old Testament*. Grand Rapids: Baker, 1985.

Eichrodt, W. *Theology of the Old Testament*. Translated by J. A. Baker. 2 vols. Philadelphia: Westminster, 1961, 1967.

Everson, A. Joseph. "The Days of Yahweh." *JBL* 93 (1974): 329–37.

Fairbairn, Patrick. *The Interpretation of Prophecy*. 1865. Reprint. London: Banner of Truth, 1964.

Fensham, F. Charles. "A Possible Origin of the Concept of the Day of the Lord." In *Biblical Essays,* Bepeck: Potschefstroom Herald, 1966, 90–97.

Freedman, David Noel. "The Flowering of Apocalyptic." *Journal for Theology and the Church* 6 (1969): 166–74.

_____. "Pottery, Poetry, and Prophecy: An Essay on Biblical Poetry." *JBL* 96 (1977): 5–26.

Fuhs, Hans F. *Sehen und Schauen: Die Wurzel ḥzh im Alten Orient und im Alten Testament: Ein Beitrag zum prophetischen Offenbarungsempfang*. Würzburg: Echter Verlag, 1978.

Girdlestone, R. B. *The Grammar of Prophecy*. Grand Rapids: Kregel, 1955.

Goldingay, John. *God's Prophet, God's Servant: A Study in Jeremiah and Isaiah 40–55*. Exeter: Paternoster, 1984.

Gottwald, Norman K. *All the Kingdoms of the Earth: Israelite Prophecy and International Relations in the Ancient Near East*. New York: Harper & Row, 1964.

Gowan, Donald E. *Eschatology in the Old Testament*. Philadelphia: Fortress, 1986.

Graffy, Adrian. *A Prophet Confronts His People: The Disputation Speech in the Prophets*. Analecta Biblica 104. Rome: Biblical Institute Press, 1984.

Gray, John. "The Day of the Lord in Cultic Experience and Eschatological Prospect." *SEÅ* 39 (1974): 5–37.

_____. "The Kingship of God in the Prophets and Psalms." *VT* 11 (1961): 1–29.

Green, Joel B. *How to Read Prophecy*. Downers Grove, Ill.: InterVarsity Press, 1984.

Greenberg, Moshe. *Biblical Prose Prayer: As a Window to the Popular Religion of Ancient Israel*. Berkeley: University of California Press, 1983.

Hammershaimb, E. *Some Aspects of Old Testament Prophecy from Isaiah to Malachi*. Copenhagen: Rosenkilde Og Bagger, 1966.

Hanson, Paul D. *The Dawn of the Apocalyptic*. Rev. ed. Philadelphia: Fortress, 1979.

————. *The Diversity of Scripture*. Philadelphia: Fortress, 1982.

————. "From Prophecy to Apocalyptic: Unresolved Issues." *JSOT* 15 (1980): 3–6.

————. "Israelite Religion in the Early Postexilic Period." *FS Cross*, 485–508.

————. "Jewish Apocalyptic Against Its Near Eastern Environment." *RB* 78 (1971): 32–58.

————. "Old Testament Apocalyptic Reexamined." *Int* 25 (1971): 454–79.

————. "Prophets and Kings." *Humanitas* 15 (1979): 287–303.

Haran, Menahem. "From Early to Classical Prophecy: Continuity and Change." *VT* 27 (1977): 385–97.

Harrelson, Walter. "Prophetic Eschatological Visions and the Kingdom of God." *FS Mendenhall*, 117–26.

Harris, R. Laird. "Prophecy, Illustration and Typology." In *Interpretation & History. Essays in Honour of Alan A. MacRae*, edited by R. Laird Harris, Swee-Hwa Quek, and J. Robert Vannoy, Singapore: Christian Life Publishers, 1986, 57–66.

Harvey, Julien. *Le Plaidoyer prophétique contre Israël après la rupture de l'alliance*. Paris: Desclée de Brouwer, 1967.

Hasel, Gerhard F. *The Remnant: The History and Theology of the Remnant Idea from Genesis to Isaiah*. Berrien Springs, Mich.: Andrews University Press, 1972.

Hillers, D. R. *Treaty-Curses and the Old Testament Prophets*. Biblica et Orientalia 21A. Rome: Pontifical Biblical Institute, 1978.

Hölscher, G. *Die Propheten: Untersuchungen zur Religionsgeschichte Israels*. Leipzig: J. Hinrichs, 1914.

Hoekema, Anthony A. *The Bible and the Future*. Grand Rapids: Eerdmans, 1979.

Hoffmann, Yair. "The Day of the Lord as a Concept and a Term in the Prophetic Literature." *ZAW* 93 (1981): 37–50.

Hossfeld, Frank Lothar, and Ivo Meyer. *Prophet gegen Prophet. Eine Analyse der alttestamentlichen Texte zum Thema: wahre und falsche Propheten*. Fribourg: Schweizerisches Katholisches Bibelwerk, 1973.

Hubbard, David A. "Hope in the Old Testament." *TB* 34 (1983): 33–59.

Huffmon, Herbert B. "The Origins of Prophecy." *FS Wright*, 171–86.

Inch, Morris A. *Understanding Bible Prophecy*. New York: Harper & Row, 1977.

Jeremias, Jörg. *Kultprophetie und Geschichtsverkundigung in der späten Königszeit Israels*. Neukirchen: Neukirchener, 1970.

————. *Theophanie: Die Geschichte einer alttestamentlichen Gattung*. Neukirchen-Vluyn: Neukirchener, 1972.

Johnson, A. R. *The Cultic Prophet and Israel's Psalmody*. Cardiff: University of Wales, 1979.

Kaiser, Walter C., Jr. "The Blessing of David: The Charter for Humanity." *FS Allis*, 298–318.

————. "The Davidic Promise and the Inclusion of the Gentiles (Amos 9:9–15 and Acts 15:13–18): A Test Passage for Theological Systems." *JETS* 20 (1977): 97–111.

415

————. "Messianic Prophecies in the Old Testament." In *Dreams, Visions and Oracles: The Layman's Guide to Biblical Prophecy,* edited by Carl Edwin Armerding and W. Ward Gasque, Grand Rapids: Baker, 1977, 75–88.

————. *Toward an Old Testament Theology.* Grand Rapids: Zondervan, 1978.

————. *Toward Rediscovering the Old Testament.* Grand Rapids: Zondervan, 1987.

Kaufmann, Yehezkel. *The Religion of Israel: From Its Beginnings to the Babylonian Exile.* Translated and abridged by Moshe Greenberg. New York: Schocken, 1960.

Kirkpatrick, A. F. *The Doctrine of the Prophets.* London: Macmillan, 1917³.

Klein, Ralph W. *Israel in Exile: A Theological Interpretation.* Philadelphia: Fortress, 1979.

Knibb, Michael A. "Prophecy and the Emergence of Jewish Apocalypses." *FS Ackroyd,* 155–80.

Knight, Douglas A., ed. *Tradition and Theology in the Old Testament.* Philadelphia: Fortress, 1977.

Koch, K. "Das Profetenschweigen des deuteronomistischen Geschichtswerks." *FS Wolff,* 115–28.

————. "Die Entstehung der sozialen Kritik bei den Profeten." *FS von Rad,* 236–57.

————. *The Growth of the Biblical Tradition: The Form-Critical Method.* Translated by S. Cupitt. New York: Scribner, 1969.

————. *The Prophets.* Vol. 1, *The Assyrian Period.* Translated by Margaret Kohl. Philadelphia: Fortress, 1982.

————. *The Prophets.* Vol. 2, *The Babylonian and Persian Periods.* Translated by Margaret Kohl. Philadelphia: Fortress, 1984.

————. *The Rediscovery of Apocalyptic: A Polemical Work on a Neglected Area of Biblical Studies and Its Damaging Effects on Theology and Philosophy.* SBT 2/22. London: SCM, 1972.

————, ed. *Um das Prinzip der Vergeltung in Religion und Recht des Alten Testaments.* Darmstadt: Wissenschaftliche Buchgesellschaft, 1972.

Labuschagne, C. J. *The Incomparability of Yahweh in the Old Testament.* Leiden: Brill, 1966.

Lang, Bernhard. "Prophetie, prophetische Zeichenhandlung und Politik in Israel." *Theologische Quartalschrift* 161 (1981): 275–80.

————. *Wie wird man Prophet in Israel? Aufsätze zum Alten Testament.* Düsseldorf: Patmos, 1980.

Laurin, Robert B. "Tradition and Canon." In *Tradition and Theology in the Old Testament,* edited by Douglas A. Knight, Philadelphia: Fortress Press, 1977, 261–74.

Levenson, Jon D. *Sinai and Zion: An Entry into the Jewish Bible.* Minneapolis: Winston Press, 1985.

Levin, Christoph. *Die Verheissung des neuen Bundes in ihrem theologiegeschichtlichen Zusammenhang ausgelegt.* FRLANT 137. Göttingen: Vandenhoeck & Ruprecht, 1985.

Long, Burke O. "Reports of Visions Among the Prophets." *JBL* 95 (1976): 353–65.

Malamat, Abraham. "A Forerunner of Biblical Prophecy: The Mari Documents." *FS Cross,* 33–52.

March, W. Eugene. "Prophecy." *Old Testament Form Criticism.* Ed. John H. Hayes, San Antonio: Trinity University Press, 1974, 141–77.

Mason, Rex. "The Prophets of Restoration." *FS Ackroyd,* 137–54.

McCarthy, Dennis J. "Prophets and Covenant Community." *Jeevadhara* 11 (1981): 105–12.

McComiskey, Thomas E. *The Covenants of Promise: A Theology of the Old Testament Covenants.* Grand Rapids: Baker, 1985.

McKane, William. "Prophecy and the Prophetic Literature." In *Tradition and Interpretation: Essays by Members of the Society for Old Testament Study,* edited by G. W. Anderson, Oxford: Clarendon Press, 1979, 163–88.

_____. "Prophet and Institution." *ZAW* 94 (1982): 251–66.

_____. *Prophets and Wise Men.* SBT 44. London: SCM, 1965.

Mickelsen, A. Berkeley. *Interpreting the Bible.* Grand Rapids: Eerdmans, 1963.

Miller, Patrick D., Jr. *Sin and Judgment in the Prophets: A Stylistic and Theological Analysis.* Chico: Scholars Press, 1982.

Muilenburg, J. "The 'Office' of the Prophet in Ancient Israel." *The Bible in Modern Scholarship,* edited by J. Hyatt, 74–97. Nashville: Abingdon, 1967.

Newsome, James D., Jr., *The Hebrew Prophets.* Atlanta: John Knox, 1984.

Nicholson, Ernest W. "Apocalyptic." In *Tradition and Interpretation: Essays by Members of the Society for Old Testament Study,* edited by G. W. Anderson, Oxford: Clarendon, 1979, 189–213.

_____. *God and His People: Covenant and Theology in the Old Testament.* Oxford: Clarendon, 1986.

Niditch, Susan. *The Symbolic Vision in Biblical Tradition.* Chico: Scholars Press, 1980.

Ollenburger, Bennie Charles. "Zion, the City of the Great King: A Theological Investigation of Zion Symbolism in the Tradition of the Jerusalem Cult." Ph.D. diss., Princeton Theological Seminary, 1982.

Oppenheim, A. L. *Ancient Mesopotamia: Portrait of a Dead Civilization.* Chicago: University of Chicago Press, 1964.

_____. *The Interpretation of Dreams in the Ancient Near East.* Philadelphia: American Philosophical Society, 1956.

_____. "Perspectives on Mesopotamian Divination." In *La Divination en Mésopotamie ancienne et dans les régions voisines,* XIVᵉ Rencontre Assyriologique Internationale. Paris: Presses Universitaires de France, 1966, 35–43.

Oxtoby, Gurdon C. *Prediction and Fulfillment in the Bible.* Philadelphia: Westminster, 1966.

Perdue, Leo G., and Brian W. Kovacs, eds. *A Prophet to the Nations: Essays on Jeremiah Studies.* Winona Lake, Ind.: Eisenbrauns, 1984.

Petersen, David L. *Late Israelite Prophecy: Studies in Deutero-Prophetic Literature and in Chronicles.* Missoula, Mont.: Scholars Press, 1977.

_____. "The Prophecy of the New Covenant in the Argument of Hebrews." *RTR* 38 (1979): 74–81.

_____. *The Roles of Israel's Prophets.* JSOTSS 17. 1981.

————, ed. *Prophecy in Israel: Search for an Identity*. Philadelphia: Fortress, 1987.

Phillips, Anthony. "Prophecy and Law." *FS Ackroyd*, 217–32.

————. Plöger, Otto. *Theocracy and Eschatology*. Translated by S. Rudman. Richmond: John Knox, 1968.

Ploeg, J. P. M. van der. "Eschatology in the Old Testament." In *The Witness of Tradition*, Leiden: Brill, 1972, 89–99.

Porter, J. R. "The Origins of Prophecy in Israel." *FS Ackroyd*, 12–31.

Quistorp, Heinrich. *Calvin's Doctrine of the Last Things*. Translated by Harold Knight. Richmond: John Knox, 1955.

Rad, Gerhard von. "Die falschen Propheten." *ZAW* 51 (1933): 109–20.

————. *God at Work in Israel*. Translated by John H. Marks. Nashville: Abingdon, 1980.

————. "Les Idées sur le temps et l'histoire en Israël et l'eschatologie des prophètes." *FS Vischer*, 198–209.

————. *The Message of the Prophets*. Translated by D. M. G. Stalker. New York: Harper & Row, 1965.

————. *Old Testament Theology*. Translated by D. M. G. Stalker. 2 vols. New York: Harper & Row, 1962, 1965.

————. "The Origin of the Concept of the Day of Yahweh." *JSS* 4 (1959): 97–108.

Raitt, Thomas M. "The Prophetic Summons to Repentance." *ZAW* 83 (1971): 30–49.

————. *A Theology of Exile: Judgment/Deliverance in Jeremiah and Ezekiel*. Philadelphia: Fortress, 1977.

Ramlot, L. "Prophétisme. II. La prophétie biblique." *Dictionaire Biblique Supplement* 8:909–1222.

Ramm, Bernard. *Protestant Biblical Interpretation*. Boston: Wilde, 1956.

Robertson, O. Palmer. *The Christ of the Covenants*. Grand Rapids: Baker, 1980.

Ross, James F. "Prophecy in Hamath, Israel, and Mari." *HTR* 63 (1970): 1–28.

————. "The Prophets as Yahweh's Messenger." *FS Muilenburg*, 98–107.

Sanders, James A. "Hermeneutics in True and False Prophecy." In *Canon and Authority: Essays in Old Testament Religion and Theology,* edited by Burke O. Long and George W. Coats, Philadelphia: Fortress, 1977, 21–41.

Sawyer, John F. A. "A Change of Emphasis in the Study of the Prophets." *FS Ackroyd*, 233–49.

Scharbert, J. "Die Prophetische Literatur: Der Stand der Forschung." In *De Mari à Qumrân: L'Ancien Testament: Son Milieu. Ses Écrits. Ses relectures juives. Hommage à Mgr. J. Coppens,* edited by H. Cazelles, Gembloux, J. Duculot, 1969, 58–118.

Schmid, Hans Heinrich. *Gerechtigkeit als Weltordnung. Hintergrund und Geschichte des alttestamentlichen Gerechtigkeitsbegriffes*. Tübingen: Mohr, 1968.

————. "Schöpfung, Gerechtigkeit und Heil 'Schöpfungstheologie' als Gesamthorizont biblisher Theologie." *ZTK* 70 (1973): 1–19; "Creation, Righteousness, and Salvation: 'Creation Theology' as a Broad Horizon of Biblical Theology." In *Creation in the Old Testament,* edited by Bernard W. Anderson, Philadelphia: Fortress, 1984, 102–17.

Schmidt, Werner H. "Die Prophetische 'Grundgewissheit': Erwägungen zur Einheit prophetischer Verkündigung." *Wege der Forschung* 307 (1979): 537–64.

Schultz, Samuel J. *The Prophets Speak: Law of Love—the Essence of Israel's Religion.* New York: Harper & Row, 1968.

Scott, R. B. Y. *The Relevance of the Prophets.* New York: Macmillan, 1944.

Smith, George A. *The Book of the Twelve Prophets.* 2 vols. London: Hodder & Stoughton, 1898.

Steck, Odil Hannes. "Theological Streams of Tradition." In *Tradition and Theology in the Old Testament,* edited by Douglas A. Knight, Philadelphia: Fortress, 1977, 183–214.

Teeple, Howard M. *The Mosaic Eschatological Prophet.* Philadelphia: Society of Biblical Literature, 1957.

Torrance, Thomas F. *Kingdom and Church: A Study in the Theology of the Reformation.* Edinburgh: Oliver & Boyd, 1956.

————. *Reality and Evangelical Theology.* Philadelphia: Westminster, 1982.

————. *The School of Faith; the Catechisms of the Reformed Church.* London: James Clarke & Co., 1959.

Towner, W. Sibley "On Calling People 'Prophets' in 1970." *Int* 24 (1970): 492–509.

Travis, Stephen H. *Christian Hope & the Future.* Downers Grove, Ill.: InterVarsity Press, 1980.

————. "The Value of Apocalyptic." *TB* 30 (1979): 53–76.

Tucker, Gene M. "Prophecy and Prophetic Literature." In *The Hebrew Bible and Its Modern Interpreters,* edited by Douglas A. Knight and Gene M. Tucker, Philadelphia: Fortress, 1985, 325–68.

————. "Prophetic Speech." *Int* 32 (1978): 31–45.

————. "The Role of the Prophets and the Role of the Church." *Prophecy in Israel: Search for an Identity,* edited by David L. Petersen, 159–74. Philadelphia: Fortress, 1987.

VanGemeren, Willem A. "Israel as the Hermeneutical Crux in the Interpretation of Prophecy." pt. 1, *WTJ* 45 (1983): 132–44; pt. 2, ibid., 46 (1984): 254–97.

————. "Perspectives on Continuity." In *Continuity and Discontinuity: Perspectives on the Relationship between the Old and New Testaments in Honor of S. Lewis Johnson, Jr.,* edited by John S. Feinberg, Westchester: Crossway, 1988. 37–62.

————. *The Progress of Redemption: The Story of Salvation from Creation to the New Jerusalem.* Grand Rapids: Zondervan, 1988.

————. "The Spirit of Restoration." *WTJ* 50 (1988): 81–102.

VanLier, Hunter A. *Seek the Lord! A Study of the Meaning and Function of the Exhortations in Amos, Hosea, Isaiah, Micah, and Zephaniah.* Diss., University of Basel. St. Mary's Seminary & University: Baltimore, 1982.

Vawter, Bruce. "Were the Prophets *nāḇîʾs*" *Bib* 66 (1985): 206–20.

Verweij, H. *De Komende Messias: Wereld en Welzijn in profetisch Perspectief.* Kampen: Kok, 1971.

Vos, Geerhardus. *Biblical Theology: Old and New Testament.* Grand Rapids: Eerdmans, 1948.

_____. "The Kingdom of God." In *Redemptive History and Biblical Interpretation: The Shorter Writings of Geerhardus Vos,* edited by Richard B. Gaffin, Jr., Phillipsburg: Presbyterian & Reformed, 1980, 304–16.

Vriezen, Th. C. "Prophecy and Eschatology." SVT 1 (1953): 199–229.

Waldow, E. von. *Der traditionsgeschichtliche Hintergrund der prophetlichen Gerichtsreden.* BZAW 85. Berlin: Töpelmann, 1963.

Warmuth, Georg. *Das Mahnwort: Seine Bedeutung für die Verkündigung der vorexilischen Propheten Amos, Hosea, Micha, Jesaja und Jeremia.* Bern: Peter Lang, 1976.

Weiss, Meir. "The Origin of the 'Day of the Lord'—Reconsidered." *HUCA* 37 (1966): 29–60.

Westermann, Claus. *Basic Forms of Prophetic Speech.* Translated by Hugh Clayton White. Philadelphia: Westminster, 1967.

_____. "Boten des Zorns: Die Begriffe des Zornes Gottes in der Prophetie." *FS Wolff,* 147–56.

_____. "Das Hoffen im Alten Testament." In *Forschung am Alten Testament; Gesammelte Studien,* München: Kaiser, 1964, 219–65.

_____. "Die Mari-Briefe und die Prophetie in Israel." In *Forschung am Alten Testament: Gesammelte Studien,* München: Kaiser, 1964, 171–88.

_____. "Das Verhältnis des Jahweglaubens zu den Ausserisraelitischen Religionen." In *Forschung am Alten Testament: Gesammelte Studien.* München: Kaiser, 1964, 189–218.

_____. "Zur Erforschung und zum Verständnis der prophetischen Heilsworte." *ZAW* 98 (1986): 1–13.

Whitelam, Keith K. *The Just King: Monarchical Judicial Authority.* JSOTSS 12. 1979.

Whitley, C. F. *The Prophetic Achievement.* Leiden: Brill, 1963.

Whybray, R. N. "Prophecy and Wisdom." *FS Ackroyd,* 181–99.

Williams, James G. "The Prophetic 'Father': A Brief Explanation of the Term 'Sons of the Prophets.'" *JBL* 85 (1966): 344–48.

_____. "The Social Location of Israelite Prophecy." *JAAR* 37 (1969): 153–65.

Wilson, Robert R. "Prophecy and Ecstasy: A Reexamination." *JBL* 98 (1979): 321–37.

_____. *Prophecy and Society in Ancient Israel.* Philadelphia: Fortress, 1980.

_____. *Sociological Approaches to the Old Testament.* Philadelphia: Fortress, 1984.

Wolff, Hans Walter. "Die eigentliche Botschaft der klassische Propheten." *FS Zimmerli,* 547–57.

_____. "Prophecy from the Eighth through the Fifth Century." *Interpreting the Prophets,* edited by James Luther Mays and Paul J. Achtemeier, Philadelphia: Fortress, 1987, 14–26.

_____. *Prophetische Alternativen: Entdeckungen des Neuen im Alten Testament.* München: Kaiser, 1982.

_____. "Was ist das Neue im neuen Bund?" *Prophetische Alternativen: Entdeckungen des Neuen im Alten Testament,* München: Kaiser, 1982, 55–69.

Wright, G. Ernest. "The Lawsuit of God: A Form-Critical Study of Deuteronomy 32." *FS Muilenburg,* 26–67.

Young, Edward J. *My Servants the Prophets*. Grand Rapids: Eerdmans, 1952.

Zimmerli, Walther. "Frucht der Anfechtung des Propheten." *FS Wolff*, 131–46.

—————. "Das Gottesrecht bei den Propheten Amos, Hosea, Jesaja." *FS Westermann*, 216–35.

—————. "The Hope of Israel and the Hope of the World." In *The Old Testament and the World*, translated by John J. Scullion, 122–36. Atlanta: John Knox, 1976.

—————. *The Law and the Prophets: A Study of the Meaning of the Old Testament*. Translated by R. E. Clements. New York: Harper & Row, 1965.

—————. *Gottes Offenbarung*. Münich: Kaiser, 1969.

—————. *Old Testament Theology in Outline*. Translated by David E. Green. Atlanta: John Knox, 1978.

—————. "Prophetic Proclamation and Reinterpretation." In *Tradition and Theology in the Old Testament*, edited by Douglas A. Knight, 69–100. Philadelphia: Fortress, 1977.

—————. "Der Wahrheitserweis Jahwes nach der Botschaft der beiden Exilspropheten." *FS Weiser*, 133–51.

Zimmerli, W., and J. Jeremias. *The Servant of God*. London: SCM, 1965.

ISAIAH

Commentaries

Clements, R. E. *Isaiah 1–39*. NCBC. 1980.

Elliger, Karl. *Deuterojesaja 40:1–45:7*. BKAT. 1978.

Gray, G. Buchanan. *Isaiah. Vol. 1, Chapters 1–27*. ICC. 1912.

Grogen, Jeoffrey W. "Isaiah." *EBC*. 6:3–354.

Herbert, A. S. *The Book of the Prophet Isaiah*. 2 vols. CBC. 1973, 1975.

Holladay, William L. *Isaiah: Scroll of a Prophetic Heritage*. Grand Rapids: Eerdmans, 1978.

Kaiser, Otto. *Isaiah, 1–12*. OTL. 1983.

—————. *Isaiah, 13–39*. OTL. 1974.

Knight, George F. *Isaiah 40–55: Servant Theology*. ITC. 1984.

—————. *Isaiah 56–66: The New Israel*. ITC. 1985.

Oswalt, John N. *The Book of Isaiah: Chapters 1–39*. NICOT. 1986.

Ridderbos, J. *Het Godswoord der Propheten*. 2 vols. Kampen: Kok, 1932.

—————. *Isaiah*. Translated by John Vriend. Grand Rapids: Eerdmans, 1985.

Sawyer, John F. A. *Isaiah. Vol. 1*. DSB. 1984.

Watts, John D. W. *Isaiah 1–33*. WBC. 1985.

—————. *Isaiah 34–66*. WBC. 1987.

Westerman, Claus. *Isaiah 40–66*. OTL. 1969.

Whybray, R. N. *Isaiah 40–66*. NCBC. 1981.

Wildberger, Hans. *Jesaja 1–12*. BKAT. 1980.

—————. *Jesaja 13–27*. BKAT. 1978.

—————. *Jesaja 28–39*. BKAT. 1982.

Young, E. J. *The Book of Isaiah*. 3 vols. NICOT. 1969–72.

Articles and Monographs

Ackroyd, Peter R. "Isaiah I–XII: Presentation of a Prophet." SVT 29 (1978): 16–48.

————. "Isaiah 36–39: Structure and Function." FS van der Ploeg, 3–21.

Albertz, Rainer. Weltschöpfung und Menschenschöpfung: Untersucht bei Deuterojesaja, Hiob und in den Psalmen. Stuttgart: Calwer Verlag, 1974.

Anderson, Bernard W. "Exodus and Covenant in Second Isaiah and Prophetic Tradition." FS Wright, 339–60.

————. "Exodus Typology in Second Isaiah." FS Muilenburg, 177–207.

Auld, A. Graeme. "Poetry, Prophecy, Hermeneutic: Recent Studies in Isaiah." SJT 33 (1980): 567–81.

Barton, John. "Ethics in Isaiah of Jerusalem." JTS 32 (1981): 1–18.

Beecher, Willis J. "The Servant." In Classical Evangelical Essays in Old Testament Interpretation, edited by Walter C. Kaiser, Jr., Grand Rapids: Baker, 1972, 187–204.

Carroll, Robert P. "Inner Tradition Shifts in Meaning in Isaiah 1–11." ExpT 89 (1978): 301–4.

————. "Second Isaiah and the Failure of Prophecy." ST 32 (1978): 119–31.

Clements, R. E. Isaiah and the Deliverance of Jerusalem: A Study in the Interpretation of Prophecy in the Old Testament. JSOTSS 13. 1980.

Clifford, Richard J. "The Function of Idol Passages in Second Isaiah." CBQ 42 (1980): 450–64.

Clines, David J. A. I, He, We, and They: A Literary Approach to Isaiah 53. JSOTSS 1. 1976.

Coggins, R. J. "The Problem of Isaiah 24–27." ExpT 90 (1978–79): 328–33.

Dumbrell, William J. "The Purpose of the Book of Isaiah." TB 36 (1985): 111–28.

Eaton, John H. Festal Drama in Deutero-Isaiah. London: SPCK, 1979.

————. "The Isaiah Tradition." FS Ackroyd, 58–76.

Eichrodt, Walther. "Prophet and Covenant: Observations on the Exegesis of Isaiah." FS Davies, 167–88.

Erlandsson, Seth. The Burden of Babylon: A Study of Isaiah 13:2–14:23. Lund: Gleerup, 1970.

Fensham, F. C. "Die Siro-Efraimitiese Oorlog en Jesaja-'n historiese Perspektief." NGTT 24 (1983): 236–46.

Gitay, Jehoshua. "The Effectiveness of Isaiah's Speech." JQR 75 (1984): 162–72.

————. Prophecy and Persuasion: A Study of Isaiah 40–48. Bonn: Linguistica Biblica, 1981.

Hamborg, G. R. "Reasons for Judgement in the Oracles Against the Nations of the Prophet Isaiah." VT 31 (1981): 145–59.

Hardmeier, Christoff. "Jesajaforschung im Umbruch." Verkündigung und Forschung 31 (1986): 3–31.

Huber, Friedrich. Jahwe, Juda und die anderen Völker beim Propheten Jesaja. BZAW 137. 1976.

Jensen, Joseph. "The Age of Immanuel." CBQ 41 (1979): 220–39.

_____. *The Use of* tôrâ *by Isaiah: His Debate with the Wisdom Tradition.* Washington: Catholic Biblical Association, 1973.

_____. "Yahweh's Plan in Isaiah and in the Rest of the Old Testament." *CBQ* 48 (1986): 443–55.

Kaiser, Otto. *Der Königliche Knecht.* Göttingen: Vandenhoeck & Ruprecht, 1959.

Klein, Hans. "Der Beweis der Einzigkeit Jahwes bei Deuterojesaja." *VT* 35 (1985): 267–73.

Kraus, Hans-Joachim. "Die ausgebliebene Endtheophanie: Eine Studie zu Jes. 56–66." In *Biblisch-theologische Aufsätze.* 134–50. Neukirchen: Neukirchener, 1972.

Lindars, Barnabas. "Good Tidings to Zion: Interpreting Deutero-Isaiah Today." *BJRL* 68 (1986): 473–97.

Lindblom, Johannes. *A Study on the Immanuel Section in Isaiah: Isa. vii.1–ix.6.* Lund: Gleerup, 1958.

Martin-Achard, Robert. "Sagesse de Dieu et Sagesse humaine chez Isaï'e." *FS Vischer,* 136–44.

Melugin, Roy F. *The Formation of Isaiah 40–55.* BZAW 141. 1976.

Mettinger, Tryggve N. D. "In Search of the Hidden Structure: JHWH as King in Isaiah 40–55." *SEÅ* 51–52 (1986–87): 148–57.

Millar, William R. *Isaiah 24–27 and the Origin of Apocalyptic.* HSMS 11, Missoula, Mont.: Scholars Press, 1976.

Odendaal, Dirk H. *The Eschatological Expectations of Isaiah 40–66 with Special Reference to Israel and the Nations.* Phillipsburg: Presbyterian & Reformed, 1970.

Olley, John W. *"Righteousness" in the Septuagint of Isaiah: A Contextual Study.* Missoula, Mont.: Scholars Press, 1979.

Payne, D. F. "The Servant of the Lord: Language and Interpretation." *EQ* 43 (1971): 131–43.

Roberts, J. J. M. "Isaiah 2 and the Prophet's Message to the North." *JQR* 75 (1985): 290–308.

_____. "Isaiah and his Children." *FS Iwry,* 193–203.

Schoors, A. *I Am God Your Saviour: A Form-Critical Study of the Main Genres in Is. XL–LV.* SVT 24. Leiden: Brill, 1973.

_____. "Isaiah, The Minister of Royal Anointment?" *OTS* 20 (1977): 85–107.

Steck, Odil Hannes. "Aspekte des Gottesknechts in Deuterojesajas 'Ebed-Jahwe Liedern.'" *ZAW* 96 (1984): 372–90.

_____. *Friedensvorstellungen im alten Jerusalem: Psalmen, Jesaja, Deuterojesaja.* Zürich: Theologischer Verlag, 1972.

VanGemeren, Willem A. "Isaiah." *ECB.* Forthcoming.

Vermeylen, J. *Du Prophète Isaïe à l'Apocalyptique: Isaïe, I–XXXV, miroir d'un demi-millénaire d'expérience religieuse en Israël.* 2 vols. Paris: Librairie Lecoffre, 1978.

Vriezen, Th. C. "Essentials of the Theology of Isaiah." *FS Muilenburg,* 128–46.

Ward, James M. "The Servant's Knowledge in Isaiah 40–55." *FS Terrien,* 121–36.

Watts, John D. W. "The Characterization of Yahweh in the Vision of Isaiah." *RevExp* 83 (1986): 439–50.

Westermann, Claus. *Sprache und Struktur der Prophetie Deuterojesajas.* Stuttgart: Calwer, 1981.

Whedbee, J. William. *Isaiah and Wisdom.* Nashville: Abingdon, 1971.

Whybray, R. N. *Thanksgiving for a Liberated Prophet: An Interpretation of Isaiah Chapter 53.* JSOTSS 4. 1978.

————. *The Message of Isaiah.* OTG. 1983.

Zimmerli, Walther. "Verkündigung und Sprache der Botschaft Jesajas." In *Studien zur Alttestamentlichen Theologie und Prophetie,* 73–87. Münich: Kaiser, 1974.

JEREMIAH

Commentaries

Bright, John. *Jeremiah.* AB. 1965.

Brueggemann, Walter. *Jeremiah 1–25. To Pluck Up, To Tear Down.* ITC. 1988.

Carroll, Robert P. *Jeremiah, A Commentary.* OTL. 1986.

Cunliffe-Jones, H. *The Book of Jeremiah.* London: SCM, 1960.

Davidson, Robert. *Jeremiah.* Vol. 1. DSB. 1983.

Feinberg, Charles L. "Jeremiah." *EBC* 6:357–691.

Harrison, R. K. *Jeremiah and Lamentations.* TOTC. 1973.

Hermann, Siegfried. *Jeremia.* BKAT. Forthcoming.

Holladay, William L. *Jeremiah 1: A Commentary on the Prophet Jeremiah Chapters 1–25.* Hermeneia. 1986.

McKane, W. *Jeremiah Vol. 1, 1–25.* ICC. 1986.

Nicholson, E. W. *Jeremiah: 1–25.* CBC. 1973.

Thompson, J. A. *The Book of Jeremiah.* NICOT. 1980.

Articles and Monographs

Ackroyd, Peter R. "The Book of Jeremiah—Some Recent Studies." *JSOT* 28 (1984): 47–59.

Ahuis, Ferdinand. *Der Klagende Gerichtsprophet.* Stuttgart: Calwer, 1982.

Anderson, Bernhard W. " 'The Lord Has Created Something New': A Stylistic Study of Jer. 31:15–22." *CBQ* 40 (1978): 463–78.

————. "The New Covenant and the Old." In *The Old Testament and Christian Faith: A Theological Discussion,* edited by Bernhard W. Anderson, New York: Harper & Row, 1963, 225–42.

Berridge, John Maclennan. *Prophet, People, and the Word of Yahweh: An Examination of Form and Content in the Proclamation of the Prophet Jeremiah.* Zürich: EVZ-Verlag, 1970.

Bogaert, P. M., ed. *Le Livre de Jérémie: le prophète et son milieu, les oracles et leur transmission.* Leuven: Leuven University Press, 1981.

Bright, John. "The Book of Jeremiah: Its Structure, Its Problems, and Their Significance for the Interpreter." *Int* 9 (1955): 259–78.

Brueggemann, Walter. "The Book of Jeremiah: Portrait of the Prophet." *Int* 37 (1983): 130–45.

_____. "Israel's Sense of Place in Jeremiah." *FSS Muilenburg,* 149–65.

Carroll, Robert P. "A Non-Cogent Argument in Jeremiah's Oracles Against the Prophets." *ST* 30 (1976): 43–51.

_____. "Prophecy, Dissonance, and Jeremiah xxvi." In *A Prophet to the Nations: Essays in Jeremiah Studies,* edited by Leo G. Perdue and Brian W. Kovacs, Winona Lake, Ind.: Eisenbrauns, 1984, 381–91.

Clements, R. E. *Isaiah and the Deliverance of Jerusalem.* JSOTSS 13. 1980.

Clendenen, E. Ray. "Discourse Strategies in Jeremiah 10:1–16." *JBL* 106 (1987): 401–8.

Crenshaw, James L. "A Living Tradition: The Book of Jeremiah in Current Research." *Int* 37 (1983): 117–29.

Hobbs, T. R. "Some Proverbial Reflections in the Book of Jeremiah." *ZAW* 91 (1979): 62–72.

_____. "Some Remarks on the Composition and Structure of the Book of Jeremiah." *CBQ* 34 (1972): 257–75.

Holladay, William L. *The Architecture of Jeremiah 1–20.* Lewisburg: Bucknell University Press, 1976.

Ittmann, Norbert. *Die Konfessionen Jeremias: Ihre Bedeutung für die Verkündigung des Propheten.* Neukirchen-Vluyn: Neukirchener, 1981.

Kaiser, Walter C., Jr. "The Old Promise and the New Covenant: Jeremiah 31:31–34." *JETS* 15 (1972): 11–23.

Lundbom, Jack R. *Jeremiah: A Study in Ancient Hebrew Rhetoric.* Missoula, Mont.: Scholars Press, 1975.

Nicholson, E. W. *Preaching to the Exiles: A Study of the Prose Tradition in the Book of Jeremiah.* New York: Schocken, 1970.

Overholt, Thomas W. "Jeremiah 27–29: The Question of False Prophecy." *JAAR* 35 (1967): 241–49.

_____ *The Threat of Falsehood: A Study in the Theology of the Book of Jeremiah.* SBT 2/16. 1970.

Perdue, Leo G. "Jeremiah in Modern Research: Approaches and Issues." In *A Prophet to the Nations: Essays in Jeremiah Studies,* edited by Leo G. Perdue and Brian W. Kovacs, 1–32. Winona Lake, Ind.: Eisenbrauns, 1984.

Polk, Timothy. *The Prophetic Persona: Jeremiah and the Language of the Self.* JSOTSS 32. 1984.

Raitt, Thomas M. *A Theology of Exile: Judgment/Deliverance in Jeremiah and Ezekiel.* Philadelphia: Fortress, 1977.

Ridouard, André. *Jérémie, l'épreuve de la foi.* Paris: Cerf, 1983.

Sanders, James A. "Jeremiah and the Future of Theological Scholarship." *Andover Newton Quarterly* 13 (1972): 133–45.

Sisson, Jonathan Paige. "Jeremiah and the Jerusalem Conception of Peace." *JBL* 105 (1986): 429–42.

Stulman, Louis. *The Prose Sermons of the Book of Jeremiah: A Description of the Correspondence with the Deuteronomistic Literature in the Light of Recent Text-Critical Research.* SBLDS 83. 1986.

Weinfeld, M. "Jeremiah and the Spiritual Metamorphosis of Israel." *ZAW* 88 (1976): 17–56.

Weippert, Helga. *Die Prosareden des Jeremiabuches.* BZAW 132, 1973.

Wisser, Laurent. *Jérémie, critique de la vie sociale: Justice sociale et connaisance de Dieu dans le Livre de Jérémie.* Geneva: Labor et Fides, 1982.

EZEKIEL

Commentaries

Aalders, G. Ch. *Ezechiel, 1–24.* COT. 1955.
_____. *Ezechiel, 25–48.* COT. 1957.
Alexander, Ralph H. "Ezekiel." *EBC* 6:737–996.
Brownlee, William H. *Ezekiel 1–19.* WBC. 1986.
Carley, Keith W. *The Book of the Prophet Ezekiel.* CBC. 1974.
Cooke, G. A. *Ezekiel.* ICC. 1936.
Craigie, Peter C. *Ezekiel.* DSB. 1983.
Eichrodt, Walther. *Ezekiel: A Commentary.* OTL. 1970.
Ellison, H. L. *Ezekiel: The Man and His Message.* Grand Rapids: Eerdmans, 1956.
Hals, Ronald M. *Ezekiel.* FOTL. 1988.
Taylor, John B. *Ezekiel: An Introduction and Commentary.* TOTC. 1969.
Wevers, John W. *Ezekiel.* NCBC. 1969.
Zimmerli, Walther. *Ezekiel: A Commentary on the Book of the Prophet Ezekiel.* 2 vols. Hermeneia. 1979, 1983.

Articles and Monographs

Aalders, G. Ch. *Het Herstel van Israël volgens het Oude Testament.* Kampen: Kok, 1934.
Aalders, Jan Gerrit. *Gog and Magog in Ezechiel.* Kampen: Kok, 1951.
Boadt, Lawrence. *Ezekiel's Oracles Against Egypt: A Literary and Philological Study of Ezekiel 29–32.* BibetOr 37. 1980.
Block, Daniel I. "Gog and the Pouring Out of the Spirit: Reflections on Ezekiel xxxix 21–29." *VT* 37 (1987): 257–70.
Carley, Keith W. *Ezekiel Among the Prophets.* SBT 2/31. n.d.
Van Dijk, H. J. *Ezekiel's Prophecy on Tyre (Ez. 26,1–28,19): A New Approach.* BibetOr, 1968.
Ellison, H. L. *Ezekiel: The Man and His Message.* Grand Rapids: Eerdmans, 1956.
Greenberg, Moshe. "The Design and Themes of Ezekiel's Program of Restoration." In *Interpreting the Prophets,* edited by James Luther Mays and Paul J. Achtemeier, Philadelphia: Fortress, 1987, 215–36.
_____. "Ezekiel's Vision: Literary and Iconographic Aspects." In *History, Historiography and Interpretation: Studies in Biblical and Cuneiform Literatures,* edited by H. Tadmor and M. Weinfeld, Jerusalem: Magnes, 1984, 159–68.
_____. "The Vision of Jerusalem in Ezekiel 8–11: A Holistic Interpretation." *FS Silberman,* 143–64.
Hossfeld, Frank. *Untersuchungen zu Komposition und Theologie des Ezechielbuches.* Forschung zur Bibel 20. Wurzburg: Echter Verlag, 1977.
Lang, Bernhard. *Kein Aufstand in Jerusalem: Die Politik des Propheten Ezechiel.* Stuttgart: Katholisches Bibelwerk, 1978.

Levenson, Jon D. *Theology of the Program of Restoration of Ezekiel 40–48.* Missoula, Mont.: Scholars Press, 1976.

Newsom, Carol A. "A Maker of Metaphors—Ezekiel's Oracles Against Tyre." *Int* 38 (1984): 151–64.

Wilson, Robert R. "Prophecy in Crisis: The Call of Ezekiel." *Int* 38 (1984): 117–30.

Woudstra, Marten H. "Edom and Israel in Ezekiel." *CTJ* 3 (1968): 21–35.

―――――. "The Everlasting Covenant in Ezekiel 16:59–63." *CTJ* 6 (1971): 22–48.

York, Anthony D. "Ezekiel 1: Inaugural and Restoration Visions?" *VT* 27 (1977): 82–98.

Zimmerli, Walther. "Die Eigenart Der Prophetischen Rede Des Ezechiel: Ein Beitrag zum Problem an Hand von Ez.14,1–11." In *Gottes Offenbarung,* 148–77. Münich: Kaiser, 1969.

―――――. "Erkenntnis Gottes Nach Dem Buche Ezechiel." In *Gottes Offenbarung,* 41–119. Münich: Kaiser, 1969.

―――――. *"Das Gotteswort des Ezechiel." Gottes Offenbarung,* 133–47. Münich: Kaiser, 1969.

―――――. *I Am Yahweh.* Translated by Douglas W. Stott. Atlanta: John Knox, 1982.

―――――. "Ich Bin Yahwe." In *Geschichte und Altes Testament,* 179–209. Tübingen: 1953. = *Gottes Offenbarung,* 11–40. Münich: Kaiser, 1969.

―――――. " 'Leben' und 'Tod' im Buche des Propheten Ezechiel." In *Gottes Offenbarung,* 178–91. Münich: Kaiser, 1969.

―――――. "Le nouvel 'Exode' dans le message des deux grands prophètes de l'Exil." *FS Vischer,* 216–27.

DANIEL

Commentaries

Aalders, G. Ch. *Daniel.* Korte Verklaring, Kampen: Kok, 1962.

Anderson, Robert A. *Daniel: Signs and Wonders.* ITC. 1984.

Archer, Gleason L. "Daniel." *EBC* 7:3–157.

Baldwin, Joyce. *Daniel: An Introduction and Commentary.* TOTC. 1978.

Collins, John J. *The Apocalyptic Vision of the Book of Daniel.* HSM 16. 1977.

―――――. *Daniel, with an Introduction to Apocalyptic Literature.* FOTL. 1984.

Ford, Desmond. *Daniel.* Nashville: Southern Publishing Association, 1978.

Goldingay, John E. *Daniel.* WBC. 1988.

Hartman, Louis F., and Alexander A. Di Lella. *The Book of Daniel.* AB. 1978.

Heaton, E. W. *The Book of Daniel: Introduction and Commentary.* London: SCM, 1964.

Montgomery, James A. *Daniel.* ICC. 1927.

Porteous, N. W. *Daniel: A Commentary.* OTL. 1965.

Pusey, E. B. *Daniel the Prophet.* New York: Funk & Wagnalls, 1885.

Russell, D. S. *Daniel.* DSB. 1981.

Towner, W. Sibley. *Daniel.* Interpretation. 1984.

VanGemeren, Willem A. "Daniel." *ECB.* forthcoming.

Veldkamp, Herman. *Dreams and Dictators: On the Book of Daniel.* St. Catharines: Paideia, 1978.

Wallace, Ronald S. *The Lord Is King: The Message of Daniel.* Downers Grove, Ill.: InterVarsity Press, 1979.

Young, E. J. *The Prophecy of Daniel.* Grand Rapids: Eerdmans, 1949.

Articles and Monographs

Bauckham, Richard J. "The Rise of Apocalyptic." *Themelios* 3 (1978): 10–23.

Beale, G. K. "The Influence of Daniel upon the Structure and Theology of John's Apocalypse." *JETS* 27 (1984): 413–23.

Collins, John J. "Daniel and His Social World." *Int* 39 (1985): 131–43.

Ferch, Arthur J. *The Son of Man in Daniel 7.* AUSSDSS 6, Berrien Springs, Mich.: Andrews University Press, 1979.

Gammie, J. G. "The Classification, Stages of Growth, and Changing Intentions in the Book of Daniel." *JBL* 95 (1976): 194–204.

Gurney, Robert J. M. "The Four Kingdoms of Daniel 2 and 7." *Themelios* 2 (1977): 39–45.

Goldingay, John E. "The Book of Daniel: Three Issues." *Themelios* 2 (1977): 45–49.

Kline, Meredith G. "The Covenant of the Seventieth Week." *FS Allis,* 452–69.

Koch, Klaus. "Is Daniel Also Among the Prophets?" *Int* 39 (1985): 117–30.

McComiskey, Thomas Edward. "The Seventy 'Weeks' of Daniel Against the Background of Ancient Near Eastern Literature." *WTJ* 47 (1985): 18–45.

Millard, A. R. "Daniel 1–6 and History." *EQ* 49 (1977): 67–73.

Poythress, Vern Sheridan. "Hermeneutical Factors in Determining the Beginning of the Seventy Weeks (Daniel 9:25)." *TrinJ* 6 (1985): 131–49.

————. "The Holy Ones of the Most High in Daniel vii." *VT* 26 (1976): 208–13.

Shea, William H. "Further Literary Structures in Daniel 2–7: An Analysis of Daniel 4." *AUSS* 23 (1985): 193–202.

————. "The Neo-Babylonian Historical Setting for Daniel 7." *AUSS* 24 (1986): 31–36.

Wilson, Robert Dick. *Studies in the Book of Daniel.* 2 vols. 1917–18. Reprint. Grand Rapids: Baker, 1972.

THE MINOR PROPHETS

Commentaries

Achtemeier, Elizabeth. *Nahum–Malachi.* Interpretation. 1986.

Allen, Leslie C. *The Books of Joel, Obadiah, Jonah and Micah.* NICOT. 1976.

Boice, James Montgomery. *The Minor Prophets: An Expositional Commentary.* 2 vols. Grand Rapids: Zondervan, 1983, 1986.

Calvin, John. *Commentaries on the Twelve Minor Prophets.* 5 vols. Translated by John Owen. Grand Rapids: Baker, 1979.

Craigie, Peter C. *Twelve Prophets.* 2 vols. DSB. 1984–85.

Selected Bibliography

Driver, S. R. *The Minor Prophets: Nahum, Habakkuk, Zephaniah, Haggai, Zechariah, Malachi.* The Century Bible. Edinburgh: T. C. & E. C. Jack, 1906.

Horton, R. F. *The Minor Prophets: Hosea, Joel, Amos, Obadiah, Jonah, Micah.* The Century Bible. Edinburgh: T. C. & E. C. Jack, n.d.

McKeating, Henry. *The Books of Amos, Hosea, Micah.* CBC. 1971.

Mitchell, H. G., J. M. P. Smith, and J. A. Brewer. *Haggai, Zachariah, Malachi and Jonah.* ICC. 1912.

Smith, George A. *The Book of the Twelve Prophets.* 2 vols. London: Hodder & Stoughton, 1898.

Smith, J. M. P., W. H. Ward, and J. A. Brewer. *Micah, Zephaniah, Nahum, Habakkuk, Obadiah and Joel.* ICC. 1911.

Smith, Ralph. *Micah–Malachi.* WBC. 1984.

Stuart, Douglas. *Hosea–Jonah.* WBC. 1987.

Watts, John D. W. *The Books of Joel, Obadiah, Jonah, Nahum, Habakkuk, and Zephaniah.* CBC. 1975.

HOSEA

Commentaries

Andersen, Francis I. and David Noel Freedman. *Hosea.* AB. 1980.

Gelderen, Cornelis van, and W. H. Gispen. *Het Boek Hosea.* COT. 1953.

Harper, W. R. *Amos and Hosea.* ICC. 1905.

Mays, James L. *Hosea.* OTL. 1969.

Wolff, Hans Walter. *Hosea.* Hermeneia. 1974.

Wood, Leon J. "Hosea." *EBC* 7:161–225.

Articles and Monographs

Bitter, Stephan. *Die Ehe des Propheten Hosea: Eine auslegungsgeschichtliche Untersuchung.* Göttingen: Vandenhoeck & Ruprecht, 1975.

Brueggemann, Walter. *Tradition for Crisis: A Study in Hosea.* Richmond: John Knox, 1968.

Buss, Martin J. *The Prophetic Word of Hosea: A Morphological Study.* BZAW, 111. Berlin: Töpelmann, 1969.

Eichrodt, Walther. "The Holy One in Your Midst: The Theology of Hosea." Translated by Lloyd Gaston. *Int* 15 (1961): 259–73.

Emmerson, Grace I. *Hosea: An Israelite Prophet in Judean Perspective.* JSOTSS 28. 1984.

Gelston, A. "Kingship in the Book of Hoseä." *OTS* 19 (1974): 71–85.

Jeremias, Jörg. "Zur Eschatologie des Hoseabuches." *FS Wolff,* 217–34.

McKenzie, Steve. "Exodus Typology in Hosea." *ResQ* 22 (1979): 100–108.

_____. "The Jacob Tradition in Hosea xii 4–5." *VT* 36 (1986): 311–22.

Swaim, Gerald D. "Hosea the Statesman." *FS LaSor,* 177–83.

Utzschneider, Helmut. *Hosea: Prophet vor dem ende.* Orbis Biblicus et Orientalis 31. Göttingen: Vandenhoeck & Ruprecht, 1980.

van der Woude, A. S. "Three Classical Prophets: Amos, Hosea, and Micah." *FS Ackroyd,* 32–57.

Weinfeld, Moshe. "Hosea and Deuteronomy." In *Deuteronomy and the Deutero-nomic School,* 366–70. Oxford: Clarendon, 1972.

Zimmerli, W. "Das Gottesrecht bei den Propheten Amos, Hosea, Jesaja." *FS Westermann,* 216–35.

JOEL

Commentaries

Allen, Leslie C. *The Books of Joel, Obadiah, Jonah and Micah.* NICOT. 1976.

Ogden, Graham S., and Richard R. Deutsch. *A Promise of Hope—A Call to Obedience: Joel and Malachi.* ITC. 1987.

Patterson, Richard D. "Joel." *EBC* 7:229–66.

Wolff, Hans Walter. *Joel and Amos.* Translated by Waldemar Janzen, S. Dean McBride, Jr., and Charles A. Muenchow. Hermeneia. 1977.

————. *Joel und Amos.* BKAT. 1975.

Articles and Monographs

Mallon, Elias D. "A Stylistic Analysis of Joel 1:10–12." *CBQ* 45 (1983): 537–48.

Ogden, Graham S. "Joel 4 and Prophetic Responses to National Laments." *JSOT* 26 (1983): 97–106.

Prinsloo, Willem S. *The Theology of the Book of Joel.* BZAW, 163.

Thompson, John Alexander. "The Date of Joel." *FS Myers,* 453–64.

VanGemeren, W. A. "The Spirit of Restoration." *WTJ* 50 (1988): 81–102.

AMOS

Commentaries

Harper, W. R. *Amos and Hosea.* ICC. 1905.

Martin-Achard, Robert, and S. Paul Réemi. *Amos and Lamentations: God's People in Crisis.* ITC. 1984.

Mays, James L. *Amos.* OTL. 1969.

McComiskey, T. E. "Amos." *EBC* 7:269–331.

Smith, Gary V. *Amos: A Commentary.* LBI. 1988.

Soggin, J. Alberto. *The Prophet Amos.* Translated by John Bowden. London: SCM, 1987.

Wolff, Hans Walter. *Amos the Prophet: The Man and His Background.* Translated by Foster R. McCurley. Philadelphia: Fortress, 1973.

————. *Joel and Amos.* Hermeneia. 1977.

Articles and Monographs

Barstad, Hans M. *The Religious Polemics of Amos: Studies in the Preaching of Am 2, 7 B–8; 4, 1–13; 5, 1–27; 6, 4–7; 8, 14,* SVT 34. Leiden: Brill, 1984.

Berg, Werner. *Die sogenannten Hymnenfragmente im Amosbuch.* Bern: Herbert Lang, 1974.

Brueggemann, Walter. "Amos' Intercessory Formula." *VT* 19 (1969): 385–99.

Coote, Robert B. *Amos Among the Prophets: Composition and Theology*. Philadelphia: Fortress, 1981.

Crenshaw, James L. *Hymnic Affirmation of Divine Justice: The Doxologies of Amos and Related Texts in the Old Testament*. SBLDS 24. Missoula, Mont.: Scholars Press, 1975.

————. "The Influence of the Wise upon Amos: the 'Doxologies of Amos' and Job 5:9–16 and 9:5–10." *ZAW* 79 (1967): 42–52.

————. "*YHWH S⁀bä'ot Semô:* A Form-Critical Analysis." *ZAW* 81 (1969): 156–75.

Davies, G. Henton. "Amos—The Prophet of Re-Union." *ExpT* 92 (1980–81): 196–200.

Garrett, Duane A. "The Structure of Amos as a Testimony to Its Integrity." *JETS* 27 (1984): 275–76.

Gitay, Yehoshua. "A Study of Amos's Art of Speech: A Rhetorical Analysis of Amos 3:1–15." *CBQ* 42 (1980): 293–309.

Kaiser, Walter C. "The Davidic Promise and the Inclusion of the Gentiles (Amos 9:9–15 and Acts 15:13–18): A Test Passage for Theological Systems." *JETS* 20 (1977): 97–111.

Limburg, James. "Sevenfold Structures in the Book of Amos." *JBL* 106 (1987): 217–22.

Martin-Achard, Robert. *Amos: l'homme, le message, l'influence*, 13–45. Geneva: Labor et Fides, 1984.

McComiskey, Thomas. "The Hymnic Elements of the Prophecy of Amos: A Study of Form-Critical Methodology." *JETS* 30 (1987): 139–57.

Sailhamer, Frank H. "The Role of Covenant in the Mission and Message of Amos." *FS Myers*, 435–51.

Terrien, Samuel. "Amos and Wisdom." *FS Muilenburg*, 106–15.

van Leeuwen, C. "The Prophecy of the *Yôm YHWH* in Amos V 18–20." *OTS* 19 (1974): 113–34.

Van der Wal, Adri. "The Structure of Amos." *JSOT* 26 (1983): 107–13.

Watts, John D. W. *Visions and Prophecy in Amos*. Grand Rapids: Eerdmans, 1958.

Wolff, Hans Walter. *Die Stunde des Amos: Prophetie und Protest*. Münich: Kaiser, 1969.

OBADIAH

Commentaries

Aalders, G. Ch. *Obadja en Jonah*. COT. 1958.

Armerding, Carl E. "Obadiah." *EBC* 7:335–57.

Coggins, R. J., and S. Paul Réemi. *Nahum, Obadiah, Esther*. ITC. 1985.

Watts, John D. W. *Obadiah: A Critical Exegetical Commentary*. Grand Rapids: Eerdmans, 1969.

Wolff, Hans Walter. *Obadiah und Jonah*. BKAT. 1977.

Articles and Monographs

Bartlett, J. R. "From Edomites to Nabataeans: A Study in Continuity." *PEQ* 111 (1979): 53–66.

Cresson, Bruce C. "The Condemnation of Edom in Postexilic Judaism." *FS Stinespring,* 125–48.

Fohrer, George. "Die Sprüche Obadjas." *FS Vriezen,* 81–93.

Gordis, Robert. "Edom, Israel and Amos—An Unrecognized Source for Edomite History." In *Essays on the Occasion of the Seventieth Anniversary of the Dropsie University (1909–1979),* edited by Abraham I. Katsh and Leon Nemoy, Philadelphia: Dropsie, 1979, 109–32.

Lillie, J. R. "Obadiah—A Celebration of God's Kingdom." *CurTM* 6 (1979): 18–22.

Myers, J. M. "Edom and Judah in the Sixth–Fifth Centuries B.C." *FS Albright,* 377–92.

JONAH

Commentaries

Aalders, G. Ch. *Obadja en Jonah.* COT. 1958.

Ellison, H. L. "Jonah." *EBC* 7:361–91.

Hasel, Gerhard F. *Jonah: Messenger of the Eleventh Hour.* Mountain View, California: Pacific Press, 1976.

Knight, George A. F., and Friedemann W. Golka. *The Song of Songs and Jonah: Revelation of God.* ITC. 1988.

van der Woude, A. S. *Jona/Nahum.* Nijkerk: Callenbach.

Wolff, Hans Walter. *Obadiah und Jonah.* BKAT. 1977.

Articles and Monographs

Childs, Brevard S. "The Canonical Shape of the Book of Jonah." *FS LaSor,* 122–28.

Clements, R. E. "The Purpose of the Book of Jonah." SVT 28 (1975): 16–28.

Ellul, Jacques. *The Judgment of Jonah.* Translated by Geoffrey W. Bromiley. Grand Rapids: Eerdmans, 1971.

Landes, George M. "Jonah: A Māšāl?" *FS Terrien,* 137–58.

———. "The Kerygma of the Book of Jonah." *Int* 21 (1967): 3–31.

Merrill, Eugene H. "The Sign of Jonah." *JETS* 23 (1980): 23–30.

Payne, David F. "Jonah from the Perspective of Its Audience." *JSOT* 13 (1979): 3–12.

Stek, J. H. "The Message of the Book of Jonah." *CTJ* 4 (1969): 23–50.

Wiseman, Donald J. "Jonah's Nineveh." *TB* 30 (1979): 29–51.

MICAH

Commentaries

Hillers, Delbert R. *Micah: A Commentary on the Book of Micah.* Hermeneia. 1984.

Mays, James L. *Micah.* OTL. 1976.

McComiskey, T. E. "Micah." *EBC* 7:395–445.

Rudolf, B. *Kommentar zum Alten Testament.* 13, 3. Gütersloh: Gütersloher Verlag, 1975.

Wolff, Hans Walter. *Micah the Prophet.* Translated by Ralph D. Gehrke. Philadelphia: Fortress, 1981.

Articles and Monographs

Beyerlin, Walter. *Die Kulttraditonen Israels in der Verkündigung des Propheten Micha.* Göttingen: Vandenhoeck & Ruprecht, 1959.

Hammershaimb, E. "Some Leading Ideas in the Book of Micah." In *Some Aspects of Old Testament Prophecy from Isaiah to Malachi,* Copenhagen: Rosenkilde Og Bagger, 1966, 29–50.

Jeppesen, Knud. "New Aspects of Micah Research." *JSOT* 8 (1978): 3–32.

Renaud, B. *Structure et attaches Littéraires de Michee IV–V.* Paris: J. Gabalda, 1964.

Schulz, Hermann. *Das Buch Nahum: Eine redaktionskritische Untersuchung.* BZAW, 1973.

van der Woude, A. S. "Deutero-Micha: ein Prophet aus Nord-Israel?" *NTT* 25 (1971): 365–78.

_____. "Micah in Dispute with the Pseudo-Prophets." *VT* 19 (1969): 244–60.

_____. *Micha.* Nijkerk: Callenbach, 1977.

_____. *Profeet en Establishment.* Kampen: Kok, 1985.

Vincent, Jean M. "Michas Gerichtswort gegen Zion (3,12) in seinem Kontext." *ZTK* 83 (1986): 167–87.

Willis, John T. "Micah 2:6–8 and the 'People of God' in Micah." *BZ* 14 (1970): 72–87.

_____. "The Structure of the Book of Micah." *SEÅ* 34 (1969): 5–42.

Wolff, H. W. "Micah the Moreshite—The Prophet and His Background." *FS Terrien,* 77–84.

_____. "Wie verstand Micha von Moreschet sein prophetisches Amt?" SVT 29 (1978): 403–17.

NAHUM

Commentaries

Armerding, Carl E. "Nahum." *EBC* 7:449–89.

Coggins, R. J., and S. Paul Réemi. *Nahum, Obadiah, Esther.* ITC. 1985.

Kapelrud, A. S. *The Message of the Prophet Zephaniah.* Oslo: Universitets Forlaget, 1975.

Maier, Walter. *The Book of Nahum.* St. Louis: Concordia, 1959.

Articles and Monographs

Allis, O. T. "Nahum, Nineveh, Elkosh." *EQ* 27 (1955): 67–80.

Cathcart, Kevin. "Treaty Curses and the Book of Nahum." *CBQ* 35 (1973): 179–87.

De Vries, S. J. "The Acrostic of Nahum in the Jerusalem Liturgy." *VT* 16 (1966): 476–81.

Fensham, F. C. "Legal Activities of the Lord According to Nahum." In *Biblical Essays: Proceedings of the Twelfth Meeting of Die Ou-Testamentiese Werkgemeenskap in Suid-Africa,* edited by A. H. van Zijl, 13–20. Potchefstroom: Pro Rege-Pers, 1969.

Renaud, Bernard. "La Composition du Livre de Nahum." *ZAW* 99 (1987): 198–219.

Schulz, Hermann. *Das Buch Nahum: Eine redaktionskritische Untersuchung.* BZAW, 1973.

van der Woude, A. S. "The Book of Nahum: A Letter Written in Exile." *OTS* 20 (1977): 108–26.

HABAKKUK

Commentaries

Armerding, Carl E. "Habakkuk." *EBC* 7:493–534.

Eszenyei, Scéles Maria. *Wrath and Mercy: Habakkuk and Zephaniah.* ITC. 1987.

Gowan, Donald E. *The Triumph of Faith in Habakkuk.* Atlanta: John Knox, 1976.

van der Woude, A. S. *Habakkuk/Zefanja.* Nijkerk: Callenbach.

Articles and Monographs

Hiebert, Thedore. *God of My Victory: The Ancient Hymn in Habakkuk 3.* HSM 38. 1986.

Janzen, J. Gerald. "Eschatological Symbol and Existence in Habakkuk." *CBQ* 44 (1982): 394–414.

Prinsloo, W. S. "Die boodskap van die Boek Habakuk." *NGTT* 20 (1979): 146–51.

Robertson, O. Palmer. " 'The Justified (By Faith) Shall Live by His Steadfast Trust'—Habakkuk 2:4." *Presb* 9 (1983): 52–71.

van der Woude, A. S. "Der Gerechte wird durch seine Treue Leben: Erwägungen zu Habakuk 2:4f." *FS Vriezen,* 367–75.

ZEPHANIAH

Commentaries

Kapelrud, A. S. *The Message of the Prophet Zephaniah: Morphology and Ideas.* Oslo: Universitetsforlaget, 1975.

VanGemeren, Willem A. "Zephaniah." *ECB.* forthcoming.

Walker, Larry Lee. "Zephaniah." *EBC* 7:537–65.

Articles and Monographs

Anderson, George W. "The Idea of the Remnant in the Book of Zephaniah." *ASTI* 11 (1977–78): 11–14.

Christensen, Duane L. "Zephaniah 2:4–15: A Theological Basis for Josiah's Program of Political Expansion." *CBQ* 46 (1984): 669–82.

de Roche, Michael. "Zephaniah i 2–3: The 'Sweeping' of Creation." *VT* 30 (1980): 104–9.

Irsigler, Hubert. *Gottesgericht und Jahwetag: Die Komposition Zef 1,1–2,3 untersucht auf der Grundlage der Literarkritik des Zefanjabuches.* St. Ottilien: EOS Verlag, 1977.

HAGGAI, ZECHARIAH, MALACHI

Commentaries

Alden, Robert L. "Haggai." *EBC* 7:569–91.

————. "Malachi." *EBC* 7:701–25.

Baldwin, Joyce. *Haggai, Zechariah, Malachi.* TOTC. 1972.

Barker, Kenneth L. "Zechariah." *EBC* 7:595–697.

Beuken, W. A. M. *Haggai-Sacharja 1–8.* Assen: Van Gorcum, 1967.

Kaiser, Walter C., Jr. *Malachi: God's Unchanging Love.* Grand Rapids: Baker, 1984.

Koole, J. L. *Haggai.* COT. 1967.

Mason, Rex. *The Books of Haggai, Zechariah and Malachi.* CBC. 1977.

Mitchell, Hinckley, Thomas Gilbert, J. M. Powis, and Julius A. Bewer. *A Critical and Exegetical Commentary on Haggai, Zechariah, Malachi, and Jonah.* ICC. 1912.

Petersen, David L. *Haggai and Zechariah 1–8, A Commentary.* OTL. 1984.

Stuhlmueller, Carroll C. P. *Haggai and Zechariah: Rebuilding With Hope.* ITC. 1988.

Wilhelm, Rudolph. *Haggai—Sacharja 1–8—Sacharja 9–14—Maleachi.* KAT 13/4. Gütersloh: Gerhard Mohn, 1976.

VanGemeren, Willem A. "Malachi." *ECB.* Forthcoming.

van der Woude, A. S. *Haggai/Malachi.* Nijkerk: Callenbach, 1982.

Verhoef, Pieter A. *The Books of Haggai and Malachi.* NICOT. 1976.

Articles and Monographs

Ackroyd, P. R. "Studies in the Book of Haggai." *JSS* 2 (1951): 163–76; JSS 3 (1952): 1–13.

Bloomhardt, P. F. "The Poems of Haggai." *HUCA* 5 (1928): 153–95.

Cunliffe-Jones, Hubert. *A Word for Our Time? Zechariah 9–14, the New Testament and Today.* London: Athlone, 1973.

Fischer, James A. "Notes on the Literary Form and Message of Malachi." *CBQ* 34 (1972): 315–20.

Glazier, McDonald Beth. *Malachi: The Divine Messenger.* SBLDS 98. 1983.

Kaiser, Walter C., Jr. "The Promise of the Arrival of Elijah in Malachi and the Gospels." *GTJ* 3 (1982): 221–33.

Kessler, John A. "The Shaking of the Nations: An Eschatological View." *JETS* 30 (1987): 159–66.

Lamarche, Paul. *Zacharie IX–XIV. Structure littéraire et messianisme.* Paris: J. Gabalda, 1961.

Lutz, Hans-Martin. *Jahwe, Jerusalem und die Völker: Zur Vorgeschichte von Sach 12, 1–8 und 14, 1–5.* Neukirchen-Vluyn: Neukirchener, 1968.

Mason, R. A. "The Purpose of the 'Editorial Framework' of the Book of Haggai." *VT* 27 (1977): 413–21.

McKenzie, Steven L., and Howard N. Wallace. "Covenant Themes in Malachi." *CBQ* 45 (1983): 549–63.

Miller, John H. "Haggai—Zechariah: Prophets of the Now and Future." *CurTM* 6 (1979): 99–104.

Petersen, David L. "Zechariah's Visions: A Theological Perspective." *VT* 34 (1984): 195–206.

Wallis, Gerhard. "Wesen und Struktur der Botschaft Maleachis." *FS Rost*, 229–37.

Wolf, Herbert. "'The Desire of all Nations' in Haggai 2:7: Messianic or Not?" *JETS* 19 (1976): 97–102.

Notes

Introduction to Part 1

[1] See the fine Jewish translation *Tanakh—The Holy Scriptures: The New JPS Translation According to the Traditional Hebrew Text* (Philadelphia: Jewish Publication Society, 1988).

[2] For a study on the Old Testament canon, see Roger Beckwith, *The Old Testament Canon of the New Testament Church and Its Background in Early Judaism* (Grand Rapids: Eerdmans, 1985).

Chapter 1

[1] For a further development, see VanGemeren, *The Progress of Redemption,* 155–68.

[2] Edward J. Young, "Appendix: Extra-Biblical 'Prophecy' in the Ancient World," in *My Servants the Prophets* (Grand Rapids: Eerdmans, 1952), 193–205. See the extensive study by Alfred Guillaume, *Prophecy and Divination Among the Hebrews and Other Semites* (London: Hodder & Stoughton, 1938). For a religio-historical survey of prophetism outside Israel, see Johannes Lindblom, *Prophecy in Ancient Israel* (Oxford: Blackwell, 1962), 1–46.

[3] Jacques Ellul defines *religion* as "a global interpretation of the world and of life" (*The New Demons,* trans. C. Edward Hopkin [New York: Seabury, 1975], 127).

[4] See the excellent discussion on mythology by Ellul. He writes, "Myth is always explanatory. It explains a situation and a purpose whenever reason is unable to do so, and that characteristic has scarcely changed from the archaic myth to the modern myth. The location and object of myth have changed, but not its function" (ibid., 93–94).

[5] Wilhelm Koppers, "Prophetism and Messianic Beliefs as a Problem of Ethnology and World History," in *Proceedings of the IXth International Congress for the History of Religions* (Tokyo & Kyoto, 1958), 39–50.

[6] For further background, see J. S. Wright, "Divination," *IBD* 1:391–92; J. S. Wright and K. A. Kitchen, "Magic and Sorcery," *IBD* 2:931–35; I. Mendelsohn, "Divination," *IDB* 1:856–58; idem, "Magic," *IDB* 3:223–25; D. E. Aune, "Divination," *ISBE* 1:971–74; idem, "Magic, Magician," *ISBE* 3:213–19; Thomas W. Overholt, *Prophecy in Cross-Cultural Perspective: A Sourcebook for Biblical Researchers* (Atlanta: Scholars Press, 1986).

[7] See K. Koch, *The Prophets,* trans. Margaret Kohl (Philadelphia: Fortress, 1982), 1:7.

[8] Erle Leichty reports on a list of omens derived from the birth abnormalities

in "Teratological Omens," in *La Divination en Mésopotamie ancienne et dans les régions voisines,* XIVᵉ Rencontre Assyriologique Internationale (Paris: Presses Universitaires de France, 1966), 131–39.

[9]C. J. Gadd, "Some Babylonian Divinatory Methods, and Their Interrelations," in ibid., 21–34; A. L. Oppenheim, "Perspectives on Mesopotamian Divination," in ibid., 35–43; A. K. Grayson, "Divination and the Babylonian Chronicles," in 69–76; Harry A. Hoffner, Jr., "Ancient Views of Prophecy and Fulfillment: Mesopotamia and Asia Minor," *JETS* 30 (1987): 257–65.

[10]J. Lindblom, *Prophecy in Ancient Israel,* 85–86.

[11]A specialized form of divination was the inspection of the liver (*hepatoscopy*). The popularity of hepatoscopy is well-attested to by the finds of clay liver models in archaeological digs. See H. Tadmor and B. Landsberger, "Fragments of Clay Liver Models at Hazor," IEJ 14 (1964): 201–18.

[12]Ivan Starr, "The *Bārû* Rituals" (Ph.D. diss., Yale University, 1974; Ann Arbor: University Microfilms, 1981). The general practice of inspection of the entrails of animals is known as *extispicy.*

[13]"Given: a liver part, a two-fold path, the left path lying upon the right path. The enemy will furiously vent his weapons over the weapons of the princes. . . . Five unfavorable signs here. Favorable do not appear. It is unfavorable. . . . Will he go, will he with warriors, troops of Ashurbanipal, wage armed conflict . . . fight with them? Not good," cited by B. O. Long, "Divination," *IDBS,* 242. Jussi Aro, "Remarks on the Practice of Extispicy in the Time of Esarhadon and Assurbanipal," in *La Divination en Mésopotamie ancienne,* 109–17.

[14]Or *oneiromancy.* See Gen. 37:5–11; 41:1–36; Num. 12:6; Deut. 13:1, 3, 5; 1 Sam. 28:6; Isa. 29:7; Jer. 23:25–32. See A. L. Oppenheim, *The Interpretation of Dreams in the Ancient Near East* (Philadelphia: American Philosophical Society, 1956); Hoffner, "Ancient Views of Prophecy and Fulfillment," 261–62.

[15]Or *leconomancy.* This may have been the purpose of Joseph's cup (Gen. 44:5). A related form is *hydromancy,* divination through water. Giovanni Pettinato, "Zur Überlieferungsgeschichte der aB-Ölomentexte," in *La Divination en Mésopotamie ancienne,* 95–107.

[16]Or *pyromancy.*

[17]Or *kleromancy.* See Hoffner, "Ancient Views of Prophecy and Fulfillment," 260–61.

[18]Or *belomancy.* See J. Iwry, "New Evidence for Belomancy in Ancient Palestine and Phoenicia," JAOS 81 (1961): 26–34; Yigael Yadin, "New Gleanings on Resheph from Ugarit," in *FS Iwry,* 259–74.

[19]Or *rhabdomancy;* see Ezek. 21:21.

[20]The Old Testament strictly prohibits *necromancy,* though it was practiced in Israel (Lev. 19:31; 20:6, 27; Deut. 18:11; 2 Kings 21:6; 1 Chron. 10:13; 2 Chron. 33:6); also see Mark 1:23–38; Acts 16:16–18. In necromancy the "medium" owned a divining "pit" through which she would call up the spirit of the departed (1 Sam. 28).

[21]Teraphim were associated with forms of divination and are related to the worship of ancestors (1 Sam. 15:23; Ezek. 21:21; Zech. 10:2).

[22]See 1 Sam. 6:7–12. Hoffner details the augury of bird-watching and its

importance among the Hittites, "Ancient Views of Prophecy and Fulfillment," 260.

[23]This art of divination was particularly developed in Assyria and Babylon (Dan. 1:20; 2:27; 4:7; 5:7, 11). The Assyrians venerated Sakkuth and Kaiwan (Saturn [Amos 5:26, NIV margin note]), and the Babylonians idolized Ishtar, the Queen of Heaven (Venus [Jer. 7:18; 44:17–19; see 8:2; 19:13]). The Old Testament denounced astrology as pagan (Deut. 4:19; 17:3; 2 Kings 17:16; 21:3; 2 Chron. 33:5; Zeph. 1:5) and supported this by the contention that the Lord has made the heavenly bodies (Isa. 40:26; 47:13; Jer. 31:35). They were the first to develop horoscopes. For the practice in New Testament times, see the story of the Magi in Matt. 2:1–12. Paul taught that all things are under the sovereignty of Jesus Christ, including the planets (Col. 2:15, 20; see Rom. 8:39; Eph. 6:12). See A. L. Oppenheim, *Ancient Mesopotamia: Portrait of a Dead Civilization* (Chicago: University of Chicago Press, 1964), 224–25, 309–10; Eric Burrows, "Some Cosmological Patterns in Babylonian Religion," in *The Labyrinth: Further Studies in the Relation Between Myth and Ritual in the Ancient World,* ed. S. H. Hooke (London: SPCK, 1935), 43–70; Hoffner, "Ancient Views of Prophecy and Fulfillment," 259–60.

[24]G. Dossin, "Sur le Prophétisme a Mari," in *La Divination en Mésopotamie Ancienne,* 77–86. See Herbert B. Huffmon, "Prophecy in the Mari Letters," *The Biblical Archaeologist* 31 (1968): 101–24; Friedrich Ellermeier, *Prophetie in Mari und Israel* (Göttingen: Ellermeier, 1977).

[25]Abraham Malamat, "A Forerunner of Biblical Prophecy: The Mari Documents," in *FS Cross,* 33–52.

[26]See the biblical terms in Deut. 13:2; 18:15, 18; Jer. 1:17; Ezek. 2:2; 3:22–24; Dan. 8:17–18.

[27]Malamat, "A Forerunner of Biblical Prophecy," 44.

[28]Hoffner, "Ancient Views of Prophecy and Fulfillment," 265. For other connections, see James F. Ross, "Prophecy in Hamath, Israel, and Mari," *HTR* 63 (1970): 1–28.

[29]The close relationship between magic and religion has been observed by Helmer Ringgren, *Religions of the Ancient Near East* (Philadelphia: Westminster, 1973), 35–36, 89–99, 168–69. Edith K. Ritter, "Magical-Expert (= AŠIPU) and Physician (= ASÛ). Notes on Two Complementary Professions in Babylonian Medicine," in *FS Landsberger,* 299–321.

[30]Alexander Heidel, *The Babylonian Genesis* (Chicago: University of Chicago Press, 1951), 20.

[31]See "The Instruction for King Meri-ka-re" (ca. 2200 B.C.), in *ANET,* 414–18.

[32]Edwin M. Yamauchi, "Magic in the Biblical World," *TB* 34 (1983): 169–200.

[33]For example, in Egypt curses were called on all who would not submit themselves to her sovereignty. In a special ceremony the magicians shattered pottery shaped in the head of the enemy or destroyed lists with the names of the enemy with the intent to intimidate the enemy ("The Execration Texts," in *ANET,* 328–29).

[34]Harry A. Hoffner, Jr., "Symbols for Masculinity and Femininity: Their Use in Ancient Near Eastern Sympathetic Magic Rituals," *JBL* 85 (1966): 326–34.

See Lev. 19:26–29, 31; Deut. 22:5, 9–11; Isa. 3:18–23; Ezek. 13:18, 20; Nah. 3:4.

[35] For a fuller treatment, see VanGemeren, *Progress,* 40–97.

[36] Benjamin Warfield, "On the Antiquity and the Unity of the Human Race," in *Biblical and Theological Studies* (Philadelphia: Presbyterian & Reformed, 1952), 238–61.

[37] Paul Kennedy, *The Rise and Fall of the Great Powers* (New York: Random House, 1987).

[38] For the Canaanite religious background, see P. D. Miller, "Aspects of the Religion of Ugarit," in *FS Cross,* 53–66.

[39] Ezekiel spoke of the Babylonian king deciding at the intersection his next action by use of three rituals of divination (arrows, teraphim, and the liver): "For the king of Babylon will stop at the fork in the road, at the junction of the two roads, to seek an omen: He will cast lots with arrows, he will consult his idols, he will examine the liver" (Ezek. 21:21).

[40] Ernest W. Nicholson connects the covenant with the prophets but virtually denies the place of the covenant in Israel's early existence (*God and His People: Covenant and Theology in the Old Testament* [Oxford: Clarendon, 1986]).

[41] Walter Brueggemann, *The Prophetic Imagination* (Philadelphia: Westminster, 1978), 28–43.

[42] Burke O. Long, "2 Kings III and Genres of Prophetic Narrative," *VT* 23 (1973): 337–48; idem, "The Effect of Divination upon Israelite Literature," *JBL* 92 (1973): 489–97.

[43] See Ex. 22:18; Lev. 19:26, 31; 20:6, 27; Deut. 18:10–11; Isa. 44:25; Jer. 27:9–10; Ezek. 22:28; Mic. 5:12; Zech. 10:2. *Divination vocabulary:* forms from the roots *q-s-m* ("practice divination," "divination by casting lots"), see Deut. 18:10; 2 Kings 17:17; *n-ḥ-š* ("interpret omen," "give an omen," "practice divination"), see Gen. 44:5, 15; 1 Kings 20:33; 2 Kings 21:6; the nominal form occurs in Num. 24:1; one who consults an *'ôb* (lit. "spirit," hence "medium"), see Lev. 20:27; Deut. 18:11; 2 Kings 21:6; *y-d-'* (*yid'ōnî,* "spiritist," "one who possesses a spirit of the dead"), see Deut. 18:11; 2 Kings 21:6; and other technical phrases: "consult (the dead)" (*d-r-š,* Deut. 18:11; Isa. 8:19); "astrologers" (Isa. 47:13; Dan. 2:2, 10; 4:7; 5:7, 11). *Magic vocabulary:* forms from the roots *k-š-p* ("engage in witchcraft," "sorcerer"), see Ex. 7:11; 22:17; Deut. 18:10; 2 Kings 9:22; 2 Chron. 33:6; Jer. 27:9; Nah. 3:4; *ḥ-r-ṭ-m* ("magician," "soothsayer-priest"), see Gen. 41:8, 24; Dan. 1:20; *ḥ-b-r* ("charm," "conjure up," "cast spells"), see Deut. 18:11; *ḥeres* ("magician," "soothsayer"), see Isa. 3:3; *'-n-n* (*po'el* form, "conjure up spirits," NIV "sorcery"), see Lev. 19:26; Deut. 18:10, 14; 2 Kings 21:6; 2 Chron. 33:6; Isa. 2:6; 57:3; Jer. 27:9; Mic. 5:11. See O. Eissfeldt, "Wahrsagung im Alten Testament," in *La Divination en Mésopotamie ancienne,* 141–46.

[44] See VanGemeren, *Progress,* 182–208.

[45] R. B. Y. Scott, *The Relevance of the Prophets* (New York: Macmillan, 1944), 12.

[46] Young, *My Servants the Prophets,* 38–55.

[47] So also Joshua (Josh. 24:29), Samuel (1 Sam. 3:10), David (2 Sam. 3:18), and Elijah (2 Kings 9:36). "Servant" may be likened to a cabinet member or secretary of state.

⁴⁸For a study on the use of "servant," see W. Zimmerli and J. Jeremias, *The Servant of God* (London: SCM, 1965).

⁴⁹Childs concludes, "Thus laws attributed to Moses were deemed authoritative, and conversely authoritative laws were attributed to Moses. . . . When correctly interpreted, the Mosaic authorship of the Pentateuch is an important theological confirmation which is part of the canonical witness" (*IOTS,* 134–35).

⁵⁰Walter C. Kaiser, Jr., *Toward an Old Testament Ethics* (Grand Rapids: Zondervan, 1983); Chr. J. H. Wright, *An Eye for an Eye: The Place of Old Testament Ethics Today* (Downers Grove, Ill.: InterVarsity Press, 1983); VanGemeren, *Progress,* 146–68.

⁵¹Walter Brueggemann, "The Royal Consciousness: Countering the Counter-Culture," in *Prophetic Imagination,* 28–43.

⁵²See Lev. 19:26–29, 31; Deut. 22:5, 9–11.

⁵³VanGemeren, *Progress,* 158–60.

⁵⁴For an excellent treatment on the dynamics of law and grace, see Thomas E. McComiskey, *The Covenants of Promise: A Theology of the Old Testament Covenants* (Grand Rapids: Baker, 1985), 94–137.

⁵⁵VanGemeren, *Progress,* 146–48, 169–77.

⁵⁶Howard M. Teeple, *The Mosaic Eschatological Prophet* (Philadelphia: Society of Biblical Literature, 1957), 43–48.

⁵⁷John Bright, *Covenant and Promise: The Prophetic Understanding of the Future in Preexilic Israel* (Philadelphia: Westminster, 1976), 24–28.

⁵⁸VanGemeren, *Progress,* 161–62.

⁵⁹Gnana Robinson, "The Idea of Rest in the Old Testament and the Search for the Basic Character of Sabbath," *ZAW* 92 (1980): 32–42.

⁶⁰The MT differs from the LXX, Qumran, and Heb. 1:6 by the addition of "and let all the angels worship him" after "rejoice, O nations, with his people" (Deut. 32:43).

⁶¹Walter Brueggemann refers to this hope as "the alternative community of Moses" (*Prophetic Imagination,* 11–27).

⁶²Moshe Weinfeld, "The Day of the Lord: Aspirations for the Kingdom of God in the Bible and Jewish Liturgy," *SH* 31 (1986): 371–72.

⁶³Walter Harrelson defines the Mosaic heritage as "Yahweh's Promise on the Way to Consummation" in "Life, Faith, and the Emergence of Tradition," in *Tradition and Theology in the Old Testament,* ed. Douglas A. Knight (Philadelphia: Fortress, 1977), 30.

⁶⁴Henning Graf Reventlow relates the prophets to Moses' place as authoritative spokesmen and of intermediaries, but assumes that the prophets were also connected to Israel's cult ("Prophetenamt und Mittleramt," *ZTK* 58 [1961]: 269–84).

⁶⁵VanGemeren, *Progress,* 171–72.

⁶⁶Brueggemann also sees Moses "as the paradigmatic prophet" (*Prophetic Imagination,* 15).

⁶⁷Rolf Rendtorff admits that "the oldest elements of the history of Israelite prophecy" reveal the function of the prophets as that of being guardians of God's law ("Reflections on the Early History of Prophecy in Israel," *Journal for Theology and Church* 4 [1967]: 26).

⁶⁸The Lord made a covenant with Aaron and his descendants (Num. 25:12;

Mal. 2:4–5) and with David and his descendants (2 Sam. 7:5–16). For both, see Jer. 33:19–26; Zech. 4:1–14.

[69] As for the early association of the Spirit with the prophetic ministry, see Num. 11:29: "But Moses replied, 'Are you jealous for my sake? I wish that all the LORD's people were prophets and that the LORD would put his Spirit on them!'"

[70] See Teeple, *Mosaic Eschatological Prophet,* 49–68.

[71] William F. Albright, "Samuel and the Beginnings of the Prophetic Movement," in *Interpreting the Prophetic Tradition* (New York: Ktav, 1969), 151–76.

[72] Herbert B. Huffmon explains the rise of prophetism in relation to the crises in Israelite history ("The Origins of Prophecy," in *FS Wright,* 177).

[73] See VanGemeren, *Progress,* 189–90, 206, 208.

[74] Paul D. Hanson speaks of "the Samuel compromise" in *The Diversity of Scripture* (Philadelphia: Fortress, 1982), 28.

[75] Geerhardus Vos defined the prophets as "guardians of the unfolding theocracy, and the guardianship was exercised at its center, the kingdom" (*Biblical Theology: Old and New Testament* [Grand Rapids: Eerdmans, 1948], 204).

[76] See Merrill, *History,* 345–46; 380–81.

[77] See VanGemeren, *Progress,* 255–58.

[78] B. S. Childs, "On Reading the Elijah Narratives," *Int* 34 (1980): 128–37.

[79] Num. 11:10–15; see E. v. Nordheim, "Ein Prophet kündigt sein Amt auf (Elia am Horeb)," *Bib* 59 (1978): 153–73.

[80] See Ernst Würthwein, "Elijah at Horeb: Reflections on 1 Kings 19:9–18," in *FS Davies,* 152–65.

[81] Rudolf Smend concludes that it is possible to speak about Elijah and Moses in the same breath ("Der biblische und der historische Elia," SVT 28 [1975], 184).

[82] R. Davidson states that the new phenomenon in the theophany signifies that God will no longer be found in traditional categories of faith, but rather in an antithetical and new way ("Some Aspects of the Theological Significance of Doubt in the Old Testament," *ASTI* 7 [1970]: 41–52). Christian Macholz establishes that Yahweh is the *totaliter aliter* from Baal in "Psalm 29 und 1. Könige 19. Jahwes und Baals Theophanie," in *FS Westermann,* 325–33.

[83] R. A. Carlson, "Élisée—Le Successeur d'Élie," *VT* 20 (1970): 385–405.

[84] See Zimmerli, *OTTO,* 183.

[85] Gerhard F. Hasel designates this promise as the *locus classicus* of remnant theology in *The Remnant: The History and Theology of the Remnant Idea from Genesis to Isaiah,* 172; see 159–73. See J. J. Stamm, "Elia Am Horeb," in *FS Vriezen,* 327–34.

[86] R. A. Carlson, "Élie à l'Horeb," *VT* 19 (1969): 416–39; R. P. Carroll, "The Elijah-Elisha Sagas: Some Remarks on Prophetic Succession in Ancient Israel," *VT* 19 (1969): 400–415.

[87] VanGemeren, *Progress,* 337–39.

[88] Carroll comments, "Yet the model of Moses for the prophetic figure was a seminal idea in Israel" ("The Elijah-Elisha Sagas," 415).

[89] Scott, *Relevance of the Prophets,* 165–67.

[90] H. W. Hertzberg negates the place of the prophetic function as intercessors ("Sind die Propheten Furbitter?" in *FS Weiser,* 63–74). For a positive evaluation, see Walter Brueggemann, "Amos' Intercessory Formula," *VT* 19 (1969): 385–99.

Chapter 2

[1] Robert R. Wilson demonstrates the complexity of the prophetic phenomenon in "Early Israelite Prophecy," in *Interpreting the Prophets,* ed. James Luther Mays and Paul J. Achtemeier (Philadelphia: Fortress, 1987), 1–13. See also Georg Fohrer, "Bemerkungen zum Neueren Verständnis der Propheten," *Wege der Forschung* 307 (1979): 475–92; Werner H. Schmidt, "Die Prophetische 'Grundgewissheit': Erwägungen zur Einheit prophetischer Verkündigung," *Wege der Forschung* 307 (1979): 537–64.

[2] Robert L. Alden challenged the members of the Evangelical Society to return to a serious and honest interpretation of the prophetic word: "We must teach true interpretation with conviction, scholarship, and devotion; and with no less apology, documentation, and Christian grace, we must reveal and renounce the false. Let us be sure of our position. Let us love God, our friends, and our enemies. Let us be first class in our academic integrity" ("Study of the Prophets Since World War II" in *New Perspectives on the Old Testament,* ed. J. B. Payne [Waco, Tex.: Word, 1970], 145).

[3] J. R. Porter observes that "different forms of prophetic activity probably arose as a response to historical changes in Israel's life and religion" ("The Origins of Prophecy in Israel," in *FS Ackroyd,* 19).

[4] The etymology of *nāḇî'* has not yielded reliable results. In the past the word for "prophet" was associated with the meaning "gush forth" (of ecstatic utterances), whether the Lord poured forth his word or the prophet poured them out like a spring. The ecstatic dimension in the prophetic experience was assumed in either interpretation. The Akkadian *nabû* ("to call") has given rise to another form of explanation; the prophet has been *called* by deity (Ex. 3:1–4, 17; Isa. 6; Jer. 1:4–19; Ezek. 1–3; Hos. 1:2; Amos 7:14–15; Jonah 1:1). R. R. Wilson links *n-b-'* with stereotypical prophetic behavioristic patterns that might vary from group to group ("Prophecy and Ecstasy: A Reexamination," *JBL* 98 [1979]: 321–37). Simon B. Parker argues against the relation of the possession trance and Israelite prophecy in "Possession Trance and Prophecy in Preexilic Israel," *VT* 28 (1978): 271–85.

[5] Hermann Gunkel, "The Prophets as Writers and Poets," *Prophecy in Israel: Search for an Identity,* ed. David L. Petersen (Philadelphia: Fortress, 1987), 22–73.

[6] William McKane rightly rejects the treatment of the prophets as individuals ("Prophet and Institution," *ZAW* 94 [1982]: 251–66).

[7] Hermann Gunkel, "Die geheimen Erfahrungen der Propheten Israels: Eine religionspsychologische Studie," *Das Suchen der Zeit: Blätter Deutscher Zukunft* 1 (1903): 112–53; G. Hölscher, *Die Propheten: Untersuchungen zur Religionsgeschichte Israels* (Leipzig: J. Hinrichs, 1914); Johannes Lindblom, *Prophecy in Ancient Israel* (Oxford: Blackwell, 1962).

[8] Max Weber, "The Prophet," in *Prophecy in Israel: Search for an Identity,* 99–111.

[9] Sigmund Mowinckel, "Cult and Prophecy," in *Prophecy in Israel: Search for an Identity,* 74–98.

[10] Frank Moore Cross, Jr., *Canaanite Myth and Hebrew Epic* (Cambridge: Harvard University Press, 1973), 223–29. See the rejection of the cultic association by James G. Williams, "The Social Location of Israelite Prophecy," *JAAR* 37 (1969): 153–65.

[11] See Thomas W. Overholt, *Prophecy in Cross-Cultural Perspective: A Sourcebook for Biblical Researchers* (Atlanta: Scholars Press, 1986).

[12] David L. Petersen, *The Roles of Israel's Prophets,* JSOTSS 17 (Sheffield: JSOT, 1981): 30–34.

[13] Ibid., 38–40.

[14] Ibid., 40–50.

[15] Ibid., 51–69.

[16] James F. Ross, "The Prophet as Yahweh's Messenger," in *FS Muilenburg,* 112–21.

[17] J. Muilenburg, "The 'Office' of the Prophet in Ancient Israel," in *The Bible in Modern Scholarship,* ed. J. Hyatt (Nashville: Abingdon, 1967), 74–97.

[18] Petersen, *Roles of Israel's Prophets,* 70–88. For an alternate definition of the prophetic terms, see Porter, "The Origins of Prophecy in Israel," 18–20. See also R. R. Wilson, *Prophecy and Society in Ancient Israel* (Philadelphia: Fortress, 1980); idem., *Sociological Approaches to the Old Testament* (Philadelphia: Fortress, 1984).

[19] Gerhard von Rad, *The Message of the Prophets,* trans. D. M. G. Stalker (New York: Harper & Row, 1965).

[20] A. F. Kirkpatrick rightly observes that the prophets reinforce each other, albeit that their emphases and ways of speaking differ greatly (*The Doctrine of the Prophets* [London: Macmillan, 1917], 518).

[21] Ronald E. Clements, "Patterns in the Prophetic Canon," in *Canon and Authority: Essays in Old Testament Religion and Theology,* ed. George W. Coats and Burke O. Long (Philadelphia: Fortress, 1977), 42–55. See especially Hans Walter Wolff, "Die eigentliche Botschaft der klassischen Propheten," in *FS Zimmerli,* 547–57.

[22] Norman K. Gottwald, *All the Kingdoms of the Earth: Israelite Prophecy and International Relations in the Ancient Near East* (New York: Harper & Row, 1964), 364.

[23] Dirk H. Odendaal, *The Eschatological Expectations of Isaiah 40–66 with Special Reference to Israel and the Nations* (Phillipsburg: Presbyterian & Reformed, 1970), 32.

[24] See Geerhardus Vos, *Biblical Theology: Old and New Testament* (Grand Rapids: Eerdmans, 1948), 206–8.

[25] Herbert B. Huffmon, "The Origins of Prophecy," in *FS Wright,* 171–86.

[26] Ibid., 181. Though I agree with J. R. Porter's emphasis on diversity, I disagree with his statement that "it must remain very doubtful whether it is possible either to see so clearly unified a prophetic continuity in the Old Testament evidence" ("The Origins of Prophecy in Israel," 15).

[27] Koch introduces the term *metahistory* to explain the prophetic perspective.

Metahistory is "a theory of cohesion of all reality as a single, all-embracing though complex process, in which Israel and Yahweh form the two essential poles" (*Prophets* 1:73). The Lord connects the events of past, present, and future within himself and in his plan of redemption through Israel.

[28] Zimmerli correctly writes, "Here, too, however, it must be insisted that the prophet's message to his people is not Cassandra's announcement of a fate that is sealed, but encounter with the living God. That encounter is never fate" (*OTTO*, 192).

[29] Nathan is always referred to as "the prophet" (2 Sam. 7:2; 1 Kings 1:8, 10, 22, 32, 38, 44, 45; 1 Chron. 17:1; 29:29; 2 Chron. 9:29; 29:25) and never as "the seer." Ilse von Loewenclau ("Der Prophet Nathan im Zwielicht von theologischer Deutung und Historie," in *FS Westermann*, 202–15) concludes that the author of Samuel views Nathan's prophetic role as guardian of the kingdom of God as represented in the Davidic dynasty.

[30] See 2 Sam. 7:1–17; 1 Kings 1:32–34; 2 Chron. 29:25.

[31] See 2 Sam. 24:11; 1 Chron. 21:9; 2 Chron. 29:25.

[32] 1 Chron. 25:5.

[33] See 1 Chron. 29:9–10, 20, 22.

[34] Huffmon, "The Origins of Prophecy," 179–80; David L. Petersen, *Late Israelite Prophecy: Studies in Deutero-Prophetic Literature and in Chronicles* (Missoula, Mont.: Scholars Press, 1977), 55–87. Gary V. Smith postulates that the singing prophets Saul met "performed the duties of the Levitical singers before the time of David" ("Prophet; Prophecy," *ISBE* 3:993).

[35] Hermann Gunkel, "The Prophets as Writers and Poets," 22–73; D. N. Freedman, "Pottery, Poetry, and Prophecy: An Essay on Biblical Poetry," *JBL* 96 (1977): 5–26; J. H. Eaton, *Vision in Worship: The Relation of Prophecy and Liturgy in the Old Testament* (London: SPCK, 1981).

[36] Paul D. Hanson, "Prophets and Kings," *Humanitas* 15 (1979): 287–303; Gottwald, *Israelite Prophecy*, 53–57.

[37] Gottwald, *Israelite Prophecy*, 56.

[38] Nathan and Gad kept records for David (1 Chron. 29:29); Iddo recorded the events during the reigns of Solomon, Rehoboam, and Abijah (2 Chron. 9:29; 12:15; 13:22).

[39] H. B. Huffmon holds that with the monarchy a separation of power took place, whereby the charismatic and political leadership of the judges became separated into prophetic and royal powers ("The Origins of Prophecy," 177).

[40] Walter Gross, "Lying Prophet and Disobedient Man of God in 1 Kings 13: Role Analysis as an Instrument of Theological Interpretation in an OT Narrative Text," *Semeia* 15 (1979): 97–129.

[41] Ibid., 108–10, 121–22.

[42] Ibid., 124.

[43] Ibid., 125.

[44] Alfred Jepsen, "Gottesmann und Prophet: Anmerkungen zum Kapitel 1. Könige 13," in *FS von Rad*, 171–81.

[45] Klaus Koch, "Das Profetenschweigen des deuteronomistischen Geschichtswerks," in *FS Wolff*, 115–28.

[46] I disagree with the basic thesis of David L. Petersen that the vitality of the

prophetic movement depended on the co-existence with the monarchy in *Roles of Israel's Prophets;* idem, *Late Israelite Prophecy.*

[47] For the history of Israel, see Merrill, *History,* 315–402; see also VanGemeren, *Progress,* 242–60.

[48] For a definition of the term *classical,* see Hans Walter Wolff, "Prophecy from the Eighth Through the Fifth Century," in *Interpreting the Prophets,* ed. Mays and Achtemeier, 14–26. I disagree with the definition of the classical prophet given by Menahem Haran, who distinguishes between the ecstatic, irrational aspect of the prophets and the rational, literary expression ("From Early to Classical Prophecy: Continuity and Change," *VT* 27 [1977]: 385–97).

[49] See Morton Cogan, *Imperialism and Religion: Assyria, Judah and Israel in the Eighth and Seventh Centuries B.C.E.* (Missoula, Mont.: Scholars Press, 1974).

[50] See VanGemeren, *Progress,* 246, 268–79.

[51] For a fine summary of Zion theology, see Jon D. Levenson, *Sinai and Zion: An Entry into the Jewish Bible* (Minneapolis: Winston Press, 1985), 89–184.

[52] See Merrill, *History,* 433–36.

[53] For a survey of this era, see Merrill, *History,* 469–87; VanGemeren, *Progress,* 286–99.

[54] See esp. VanGemeren, *Progress,* 300–312.

[55] For the literature on prophetic dissonance, see Robert P. Carroll, "Ancient Israelite Prophecy and Dissonance Theory," *Numen* 24 (1977–78): 135–51; idem, "Second Isaiah and the Failure of Prophecy," *ST* 32 (1978): 119–31; idem, "Inner Tradition Shifts in Meaning in Isaiah 1–11," *ExpT* 89 (1978): 301–4; idem, "Twilight of Prophecy or Dawn of Apocalyptic," *JSOT* 14 (1979): 3–35; idem, *When Prophecy Failed: Cognitive Dissonance in the Prophetic Traditions of the Old Testament* (New York: Seabury, 1979); idem, "Prophecy and Dissonance: A Theoretical Approach to the Prophetic Tradition," *ZAW* 92 (1980): 108–19; idem, "Eschatological Delay in the Prophetic Tradition?" *ZAW* 94 (1982): 47–58; idem, "Prophecy, Dissonance, and Jeremiah xxvi," in *A Prophet to the Nations: Essays on Jeremiah Studies,* ed. Leo G. Perdue and Brian W. Kovacs (Winona Lake, Ind.: Eisenbrauns, 1984), 381–91; J. Collins, "The Place of Apocalypticism in the Religion of Israel," in *FS Cross,* 539–58; David L. Petersen, *Roles of Israel's Prophets;* idem, *Late Israelite Prophecy.*

[56] Carroll, *When Prophecy Failed,* 157–68.

[57] See VanGemeren, *Progress,* 313–24.

[58] There is an extensive literature on this phenomenon: Robert P. Carroll, "A Non-Cogent Argument in Jeremiah's Oracles Against the Prophets," *ST* 30 (1976): 43–51; James L. Crenshaw, *Prophetic Conflict: Its Effect upon Israelite Religion* (Berlin: Walter de Gruyter, 1971); idem, "Prophecy, False," *IDBS,* 701–2; idem, *A Whirlpool of Torment: Israelite Traditions on God as an Oppressive Force* (Philadelphia: Fortress, 1984); Simon J. De Vries, *Prophet Against Prophet: The Role of the Micaiah Narrative (1 Kings 22) in the Development of Early Prophetic Tradition* (Grand Rapids: Eerdmans, 1978); Frank Lothar Hossfeld and Ivo Meyer, *Prophet gegen Prophet. Eine Analyse der alttestamentlichen Texte zum Thema: wahre und falsche Propheten* (Fribourg: Schweizerisches Katholisches Bibelwerk, 1973); Ronald E. Manahan, "A Theology of Pseudoprophets: A Study of Jeremiah," *GTJ* 1 (1980): 77–96; Robert Martin-Achard, "Hanania contre Jérémie: Quelques Remarques sur Jérémie 28," *Bulletin du centre*

Protestant d'études 29 (1977): 51–57; Thomas W. Overholt, *The Threat of Falsehood: A Study in the Theology of the Book of Jeremiah* SBT 2/16 (Naperville: Allenson, 1970); idem, "Jeremiah 27–29: The Question of False Prophecy," *JAAR* 35 (1967): 241–49; James A. Sanders, "Jeremiah and the Future of Theological Scholarship," *Andover Newton Quarterly* 13 (1972): 133–45; idem, "Hermeneutics in True and False Prophecy," in *Canon and Authority,* ed. Coats and Long, 21–41; Gary V. Smith, "Prophecy, False," *ISBE* 3:984–86; A. S. van der Woude, "Micah in Dispute with the Pseudo-Prophets," *VT* 19 (1969): 244–60; W. A. VanGemeren, "Prophets, the Freedom of God, and Hermeneutics," *WTJ* 52 (1990): forthcoming. For earlier studies, see Martin Buber, "False Prophets [Jeremiah 28]" in *On the Bible: Eighteen Studies by Martin Buber,* ed. Nahum N. Glatzer (New York: Schocken, 1982), 166–71; Gerhard von Rad, "Die falschen Propheten," *ZAW* 51 (1933): 109–20.

[59] Goldingay asks, "The visible mark of prophecy is, does the prophet turn people away from their evil way? Does he follow them in sin or lead them from it? Does he encourage adultery and deceit or resist it? Does he offer vain hope or unpleasant truth?" (*God's Prophet, God's Servant: A Study in Jeremiah and Isaiah 4–55* [Exeter: Paternoster, 1984], 53).

[60] Zimmerli concludes, "The special task of the prophets was the historical declaration of what was about to happen" (*The Law and the Prophets: A Study of the Meaning of the Old Testament,* trans. R. E. Clements [New York: Harper & Row, 1967], 65–66).

[61] See Manahan, "A Theology of Pseudoprophets: A Study of Jeremiah," 77–96.

[62] See Martin-Achard, "Hanania contre Jérémie."

[63] Werner E. Lemke's rhetorical analysis of Jer. 23:23–24 supports this thesis ("The Near and the Distant God: A Study of Jer. 23:23–24 in Its Biblical Theological Context," *JBL* 100 [1981], 541–55).

[64] Koch writes, "Whereas the optimistic nabis insist on the nearness of God, the prophet boasts that the God he has experienced is a far-off God" (*Prophets* 2:59).

[65] See also the interaction between Jeremiah and Shemaiah, who publicly repudiated Jeremiah's ministry and denounced Jeremiah as an imposter, a madman who should be imprisoned (29:24–27).

[66] Overholt, *Threat of Falsehood,* 71, 85.

[67] De Vries, *Prophet Against Prophet,* 142–44. See Hossfeld and Meyer, *Prophet gegen Prophet. Eine Analyse der alttestamentlichen Texte zum Thema: wahre und falsche Propheten.* Burke O. Long argues in favor of social legitimacy of the prophetic words and traditions, but concludes that "the authority of a prophet was a vulnerable, shifting social reality—closely tied to acceptance and belief" ("Prophetic Authority and Social Reality," in *Canon and Authority,* ed. Long and Coats, 19; see 3–20.

[68] A. S. van der Woude, "Micah in Dispute with the Pseudo-Prophets," 258.

[69] Crenshaw, *Prophetic Conflict,* 23–38, 69–73; John Bright speaks of "collision in theology" in *Covenant and Promise: The Prophetic Understanding of the Future in Preexilic Israel* (Philadelphia: Westminster, 1976), 165.

[70] Crenshaw, *Prophetic Conflict,* 67–69.

[71]Thomas W. Overholt, "Jeremiah 27–29: The Question of False Prophecy," 241–49.

[72]G. von Rad, *OTT* 2:209–10, esp. n. 27.

[73]Carroll, *When Prophecy Failed,* 184–204.

[74]Crenshaw, *Prophetic Conflict,* 110–11; idem, "Prophecy, False," *IDBS,* 701–2.

[75]Joseph Blenkinsopp, *A History of Prophecy in Israel* (Philadelphia: Westminster, 1983), 186.

[76]Ibid., 188.

[77]R. P. Carroll well illustrates the tension between the true and the false in "A Non-Cogent Argument in Jeremiah's Oracles Against the Prophets."

[78]Wilson, *Sociological Approaches,* 70–71.

[79]They did not consider what Motyer calls the "Exodus Quadrilateral" of "Holiness (Obedience), Peace, Sin, and Judgment," *IBD* 3:1282.

[80]Paul D. Hanson distinguishes between a faith that erects a cult "dedicated to the preservation of eternal structures" and a faith that confesses deity "to be active, creatively and redemptively, in the movement of time" ("Prophets and Kings," *Humanitas* 15 [1979]: 289).

[81]Sanders, "Hermeneutics in True and False Prophecy," 31.

[82]Ibid., 41.

[83]Walther Zimmerli, "Prophetic Proclamation and Reinterpretation," in *Tradition and Theology in the Old Testament,* ed. Douglas A. Knight (Philadelphia: Fortress, 1977), 100.

[84]Buber, "False Prophets (Jeremiah 28)," 169–71.

[85]The prophetic ethics receives further development in chap. 12: "Living the Prophetic Word."

[86]Koch, *Prophets* 2:78–80.

[87]See chap. 10: "The Confessions of Jeremiah"; Walther Zimmerli, "Frucht der Anfechtungen des Propheten," in *FS Wolff,* 131–46.

[88]Childs, *OTCT,* 140–41.

[89]H. W. Wolff, *Prophetische Alternativen: Entdeckungen des Neuen im Alten Testament* (Munich: Kaiser, 1982): 77–79.

[90]Zimmerli, *The Law and the Prophets,* 66.

[91]Terence E. Fretheim, *The Suffering of God: An Old Testament Perspective,* OBT 14 (Philadelphia: Fortress, 1984), 159.

[92]Zimmerli, *OTTO,* 216.

[93]See Hans Jochen Boecker, "Überlegungen zur Kultpolemik der vorexilischen Propheten," in *FS Wolff,* 169–80.

[94]As emphasized by Porter ("The Origins of Prophecy in Israel," 28) and many contemporary Old Testament scholars.

[95]R. E. Clements, *Prophecy and Tradition* (Atlanta: John Knox, 1975).

[96]R. E. Clements, *Prophecy and Covenant* (London: SCM, 1965), 17.

[97]Ibid., 18.

[98]John Bright defines this new eschatology as "a vision of God's final provision for his people, the farthest future of his dealings with them within history, the definitive consummation of his purposes for them beyond which no further development was envisioned or expected" (*Covenant and Promise,* 111).

Chapter 3

[1] This issue was pointedly raised in a report of the Christianity Today Institute as reported in "Our Future Hope: Eschatology and its Role in the Church," in *Christianity Today*, February 6, 1987, 1–141. The moderator, Kenneth Kantzer, concludes that we must recognize "legitimate differences," continue our work as students of the Word, and remain in dialogue together.

[2] Bernard Ramm, *Protestant Biblical Interpretation* (Boston: Wilde, 1956), 225.

[3] R. B. Girdlestone, *The Grammar of Prophecy* (Grand Rapids: Kregel, 1955).

[4] A. B. Davidson, *Old Testament Prophecy*, ed. J. A. Patterson (Edinburgh: T. & T. Clark, 1905).

[5] Ramm, *Protestant Biblical Interpretation*, 234.

[6] Ibid., 242.

[7] A. Berkeley Mickelsen follows Ramm in his six procedures for interpreting the prophetic message: (1) general hermeneutics; (2) the nature of the message and the audience; (3) distinction between direct and typological fulfillment; (4) Christological orientation; (5) sensitivity to apocalyptic imagery; and (6) balanced interpretation of literal and figurative elements (*Interpreting the Bible* [Grand Rapids: Eerdmans, 1963], 299–305).

[8] Joel B. Green, *How to Read Prophecy* (Downers Grove, Ill.: InterVarsity Press, 1984), 23–32.

[9] Ibid., 28.

[10] C. F. Whitley concludes that the nature of prophetic inspiration "resists exact definition" (*The Prophetic Achievement* [Leiden: Brill, 1963], 23).

[11] Ford Lewis Battles, "God Was Accommodating Himself to Human Capacity," *Int* 31 (1977): 19–38.

[12] John Calvin, *Institutes of the Christian Religion*, trans. Ford Lewis Battles, 2 vols. (Philadelphia: Westminster, 1960), 1:8.2.

[13] Cited by von Rad, *OTT* 2:33, n. 1.

[14] See the helpful article by Tremper Longman III, "Form Criticism, Recent Developments in Genre Theory, and the Evangelical," *WTJ* 47 (1985): 46–67.

[15] G. B. Caird, *The Language and Imagery of the Bible* (Philadelphia: Westminster, 1980), 131–97, 243–70.

[16] David Tracy, "Metaphor and Religion: the Test Case of Christian Texts," in *On Metaphor*, ed. Sheldon Sacks (Chicago: University of Chicago Press, 1979), 89–104.

[17] Paul Ricoeur, *The Rule of Metaphor*, trans. Robert Caerny, Kathleen McLaughlin, and John Castello (Toronto: University of Toronto Press, 1979), 9–43.

[18] Paul Ricoeur, *Biblical Hermeneutics*, ed. John Dominic Crossan, *Semeia* 4 (1975): 99.

[19] Ibid., 115.

[20] Ronald E. Clements, "Patterns in the Prophetic Canon," in *Canon and Authority: Essays in Old Testament Religion and Theology*, ed. Burke O. Long and George W. Coats (Philadelphia: Fortress, 1977), 53.

[21] Davidson, *Old Testament Prophecy*, 184.

[22] Clements writes, "Not least the classical prophets appear to have been well

aware that they stood in a prophetic tradition and fulfilled a particular role in the divine ministry to Israel" (*Prophecy and Tradition* [Atlanta: John Knox, 1975], 39).

[23]W. R. Smith expresses the prophetic consciousness well: "[God] speaks to His prophets, not in magical processes or through the vision of poor phrenetics, but by a clear intelligible word addressed to the intellect and the heart. The character of the true prophet is that he retains his consciousness and self-control under revelation" (*The Old Testament in the Jewish Church,* cited by H. H. Rowley, *The Servant of the Lord* [Oxford: Blackwell, 1965], 100).

[24]Robert Alter, *The Art of Biblical Poetry* (New York: Basic Books, 1985), 138.

[25]Ibid., 162.

[26]See chap. 2: "True and False Prophets."

[27]The traditio-historical and redaction-critical approaches of Gerhard von Rad, H. W. Wolff, and Zimmerli isolated the original sayings, explaining the developments in the prophetic tradition. Too often this research was marred by the assumption that much of the material was not original with the prophet, but was a later addition. Further, it was assumed that the later additions come from the circle of prophetic disciples.

[28]I value greatly the work of R. E. Clements as he defines the prophetic movement in relation to covenant, the nations, wisdom, prophecy, and apocalyptic in *Prophecy and Tradition.* By his own admission he limited his previous study (*Prophecy and Covenant* [London: SCM, 1965]), not seeing the variegation of the prophetic tradition and not realizing the freedom of the prophetic speech forms (*Prophecy and Tradition,* 86–92).

[29]Jörg Jeremias, *Theophanie: Die Geschichte einer alttestamentlichen Gattung* (Neukirchen-Vluyn: Neukirchener, 1977).

[30]Duane L. Christensen, *Transformations of the War Oracle in Old Testament Prophecy: Studies in the Oracles Against the Nations* (Missoula, Mont.: Scholars Press, 1975).

[31]Von Rad made a distinction between the Law and the Prophets: "Confronted with the eschatological situation, the prophets were set the task of taking the old regulations and making them the basis of an entirely new interpretation of Yahweh's current demands on Israel" (*OTT* 2:400); see the discussion by Tucker in "Prophecy and Prophetic Literature," in *The Hebrew Bible and its Modern Interpreters,* ed. Douglas A. Knight and Gene M. Tucker (Philadelphia: Fortress, 1985), 326–29. Similarly, Zimmerli evaluates the prophetic contribution to the law as novel, a development in Israel's thinking (*The Law and the Prophets: A Study of the Meaning of the Old Testament,* trans. R. E. Clements [New York: Harper & Row, 1965]). R. E. Clements, *Prophecy and Covenant;* idem, *Prophecy and Tradition.* W. Brueggemann, *Tradition for Crisis: A Study in Hosea* (Richmond: John Knox, 1968). For a survey, see Anthony Phillips, "Prophecy and Law," in *FS Ackroyd,* 217–32 (with bibliography).

[32]J. Fichtner, "Isaiah Among the Wise," in *Studies in Ancient Israelite Wisdom,* ed. J. L. Crenshaw (New York: Ktav, 1976), 429–38; J. Lindblom, "Wisdom in the Old Testament Prophets," in *FS Rowley,* 192–204; R. Martin-Achard, "Sagesse de Dieu et sagesse humaine chez Isaïe," in *FS Vischer,* 136–44; Samuel Terrien, "Amos and Wisdom," in *FS Muilenburg,* 106–15; J. L. Crenshaw, "The

Influence of the Wise upon Amos," *ZAW* 79 (1967): 42–52; H. W. Wolff, *Amos the Prophet: The Man and His Background,* trans. Foster R. McCurley (Philadelphia: Fortress, 1973); idem, "Wie verstand Micha von Moreschet sein prophetisches Amt?" *SVT* 29 (1978): 403–17; William McKane, *Prophets and Wise Men,* SBT 44 (London: SCM, 1965); J. William Whedbee, *Isaiah and Wisdom* (Nashville: Abingdon, 1971); Joseph Jensen, *The Use of tôrâ by Isaiah: His Debate with the Wisdom Tradition* (Washington: Catholic Biblical Association, 1973); R. N. Whybray, "Prophecy and Wisdom," in *FS Ackroyd,* 181–99 (see bibliography).

[33] Franz Hesse, "Wurzelt die prophetische Gerichtsrede im israelitischen Kult?" *ZAW* 65 (1953): 45–53; Arvid S. Kapelrud, "Cult and Prophetic Words," *ST* 4 (1950): 5–12; Walter Beyerlin, *Die Kulttraditionen Israels in der Verkundigung des propheten Micha,* FRLANT 54 (Göttingen: Vandenhoeck & Ruprecht, 1959); Jorg Jeremias, *Kultprophetie und Geschichtsverkundigung in der späten Königszeit Israels* (Neukirchen: Neukirchener, 1970); A. R. Johnson, *The Cultic Prophet and Israel's Psalmody* (Cardiff: University of Wales, 1979); Robert Murray, "Prophecy and the Cult," in *FS Ackroyd,* 200–216 (with bibliography).

[34] Menahem Haran, "From Early to Classical Prophecy: Continuity and Change," *VT* 27 (1977): 385–97. See also J. Lindblom, *Prophecy in Ancient Israel* (Oxford: Blackwell, 1962), 148–65.

[35] Clements' conclusion is representative of critical scholars: "Since in no case has the extant book been given its final shape by the prophet himself whose preaching it records, a great importance attaches to an understanding of the processes by which the prophet's original spoken word was committed to a book, or collection of books" (*Prophecy and Tradition,* 45).

[36] For a critical attempt at explaining the process, see J. Lindblom, *Prophecy in Ancient Israel,* 239–79.

[37] Hermann Gunkel was one of the first to propose that the prophetic forms be studied separately as literary phenomena in an essay "Nahum 1," *ZAW* 13 (1893): 223–44; idem, "The Prophets as Writers and Poets," in *Prophecy in Israel: Search for an Identity,* ed. David L. Petersen (Philadelphia: Fortress, 1987), 22–73.

[38] Ronald E. Clements, "Interpreting the Prophets," in *One Hundred Years of Old Testament Interpretation* (Philadelphia: Westminster, 1976), 51–75. W. Eugene March, "Prophecy," in *Old Test Form Criticism,* ed. John H. Hayes (San Antonio: Trinity University Press, 1974), 141–77 (see esp. the valuable bibliographical notes on pp. 141–43; 157–58); Robert E. Alden, "Study of the Prophets since World War II," in *New Perspectives on the Old Testament,* ed. J. B. Payne (Waco, Tex.: Word, 1970), 131–45.

[39] Claus Westermann, *Basic Forms of Prophetic Speech,* trans. Hugh Clayton White (Philadelphia: Westminster, 1967), 98–128. The messenger formula is distinctive of the prophets, as they generally begin or end their speech with: "this is what the LORD says" (*kōh 'āmar YHWH*). On the other hand, the formulaic usage has been demonstrated not to be a reliable criterion; see Rolf Rendtorff, "Botenformel and Botenspruch," *ZAW* 74 (1962): 165–77.

[40] Westermann, *Basic Forms of Prophetic Speech,* 90–91. More recently, he has complemented his somewhat exclusive focus on the oracles of judgment in *Prophetische Heilsworte im Alten Testament,* FRLANT 145 (Göttingen: Vanden-

hoeck & Ruprecht, 1987). For a brief, though dated, treatment of the prophetic forms, see R. B. Y. Scott, *The Relevance of the Prophets* (New York: Macmillan, 1944), 100–102.

[41] Klaus Koch, *The Growth of the Biblical Tradition: The Form-Critical Method,* trans. S. Cupitt (New York: Scribner, 1969), and Gene M. Tucker, "Prophetic Speech," *Int* 32 (1978): 31–45.

[42] Martin J. Buss, *The Prophetic Word of Hosea: A Morphological Study,* BZAW 111 (Berlin: Töpelmann, 1969), 1; A. S. Kapelrud, *The Message of the Prophet Zephaniah: Morphology and Ideas* (Oslo: Universitets Forlaget, 1975), 27; Richard A. Coggins concludes that the inner-dependency within the prophetic tradition explains the borrowing of motifs and linguistic expressions and should not be considered inferior by the critical scholars "An Alternative Prophetic Tradition?" in *FS Ackroyd,* 92–93.

[43] Northrop Frye, *Anatomy of Criticism: Four Essays* (Princeton: Princeton University Press, 1957), 99.

[44] Kapelrud, *Zephaniah,* 25.

[45] Rhetorical criticism is more concerned with *how* a work is composed (the form) rather than the content (what the text says). See the classic studies by Jack R. Lundbom, *Jeremiah: A Study in Ancient Hebrew Rhetoric* (Missoula, Mont.: Scholars Press, 1975); Yehoshua Gitay, *Prophecy and Persuasion: A Study of Isaiah 40–48* (Bonn: Linguistica Biblica, 1981); Martin Kessler, "A Methodological Setting for Rhetorical Criticism," in *Art and Meaning: Rhetoric in Biblical Literature,* ed. David J. A. Clines, David M. Gunn, and Alan J. Hauser, JSOTSS 19 (Sheffield: JSOT, 1982): 1–19.

[46] Gitay, *Prophecy and Persuasion: A Study of Isaiah 40–48,* 235.

[47] Lundbom, *Ancient Hebrew Rhetoric,* 114–15.

[48] Ibid., 116.

[49] W. Eugene March observes that Gunkel's literary categories (*Gattung* or genre) are too readily defined by content ("Prophecy," in *Old Testament Form Criticism,* 147).

[50] Alter, *Art of Biblical Poetry,* 141. He divides the forms of prophetic speech into (1) direct accusation, (2) satire, and (3) monitory evocation of impending disaster (141). See his fine examples and analysis of prophetic poetry (142–62).

[51] Koch, *Prophets* 2:189.

[52] Whitley, *Prophetic Achievement,* 24–44.

[53] Thomas M. Raitt, *A Theology of Exile: Judgment/Deliverance in Jeremiah and Ezekiel* (Philadelphia: Fortress, 1977), 12.

[54] Ibid., 17–34; see also Patrick D. Miller, Jr., *Sin and Judgment in the Prophets: A Stylistic and Theological Analysis* (Chico: Scholars Press, 1982).

[55] Ibid., 35–82.

[56] See Raitt's diagram, ibid., 92.

[57] Ibid., 106–73.

[58] Ibid., 145–46. For a definition of the content of the deliverance message, see 174–222.

[59] Ibid., 215–17. Raitt observes, "As I perceive the eschatological dimension of these prophets' deliverance message, it accents and defines the changes in eras, but without either moving away from the essential foundation of the prophets' faith or changing their understanding of God's basic goals" (221).

[60] See Carl Edwin Armerding, "Prophecy in the Old Testament," in *Dreams, Visions and Oracles: The Layman's Guide to Biblical Prophecy,* ed. Carl Edwin Armerding and W. Ward Gasque (Grand Rapids: Baker, 1977), 61–73.

[61] I disagree with the emphasis of Georg Fohrer that the message of the prophets was "wholly and exclusively" relevant for the age of the prophet ("Remarks on Modern Interpretation of the Prophets," *JBL* 80 [1961]: 319).

[62] R. Laird Harris, "Prophecy, Illustration and Typology," in *Interpretation and History: Essays in Honour of Alan A. MacRae,* ed. R. Laird Harris, Swee-Hwa Quek, and J. Robert Vannoy (Singapore: Christian Life Publishers, 1986), 57–66; Walter C. Kaiser, Jr., *TOTT,* 182–269; idem, "The Davidic Promise and the Inclusion of the Gentiles (Amos 9:9–15 and Acts 15:13–18): A Test Passage for Theological Systems," *JETS* 20 (1977): 97–111; idem, "Messianic Prophecies in the Old Testament," in *Dreams, Visions and Oracles,* 75–88; idem, *Toward Rediscovering the Old Testament* (Grand Rapids: Zondervan, 1987), 101–20; Thomas E. McComiskey, *The Covenants of Promise: A Theology of the Old Testament Covenants* (Grand Rapids: Baker, 1985); Willem A. VanGemeren, IHCIP; idem, *Progress;* idem, "Systems of Continuity," in *FS Johnson,* 37–62.

[63] Bruce K. Waltke writes, "The recognition that the text's intention became deeper and clearer as the parameters of the canon were expanded. Just as redemption itself has a progressive history, so also older texts in the canon underwent a correlative progressive perception of meaning as they became part of a growing canonical literature" ("A Canonical Process Approach to the Psalms," in *Tradition and Testament: Essays in Honor of Charles Lee Feinberg,* ed. John S. and Paul D. Feinberg [Chicago: Moody, 1981], 7).

[64] Brevard S. Childs, "The Canonical Shape of the Prophetic Literature," *Int* 32 (1978): 50–51.

[65] Ronald E. Clements, "Patterns in the Prophetic Canon," in *Canon and Authority, 51.*

[66] Ibid., 25.

[67] Walter C. Kaiser, Jr., *Toward Rediscovering the Old Testament,* 101–20. Richard Longenecker, *Biblical Exegesis in the Apostolic Period* (Grand Rapids: Eerdmans, 1975); VanGemeren, "Systems of Continuity," in *FS Johnson,* 37–62; O. Palmer Robertson, "Hermeneutics of Continuity," in *FS Johnson,* 89–108; Paul D. Feinberg, "Hermeneutics of Discontinuity," in *FS Johnson,* 109–28.

[68] Willis Judson Beecher, *The Prophets and the Promise* (1905; reprint, Grand Rapids: Baker, 1963), 376.

[69] Robert B. Laurin, "Tradition and Canon," in *Tradition and Theology in the Old Testament,* ed. Douglas A. Knight (Philadelphia: Fortress, 1977), 261–74.

[70] See the challenging study by Peter R. Ackroyd, "Continuity and Discontinuity: Rehabilitation and Authentication," in ibid., 215–34.

[71] See James A. Sanders, "Hermeneutics in True and False Prophecy," in *Canon and Authority.* He defines *hermeneutics* as the "mid-term between canon's stability and adaptability" (29).

[72] Douglas A. Knight, "Revelation through Tradition," in *Tradition and Theology in the Old Testament,* 143–80.

[73] Knight writes, "An interpretation should not tend to petrify earlier revelation or its interpretation, absolutizing it into a convention that stifles rather than promotes life" (ibid., 175).

[74] T. F. Torrance observes, "Since biblical statements indicate more than they can signify at any time, and more than we can express in our interpretation of them, they manifest a *predictive quality,* for they point above and beyond themselves to the inexhaustible Truth of God" (*Reality and Evangelical Theology* [Philadelphia: Westminster, 1982], 144 [emphasis mine]).

[75] On the problem of Christian and Jewish resistance to revelation, see Paul M. van Buren, *Discerning the Way: A Theology of the Jewish Christian Reality* (New York: Seabury, 1980), 40–44.

[76] Von Rad incisively argues, "For its (that is, the Old Testament) testimony to Christ can only be divorced from its Old Testament background at the cost of a radical reinterpretation" (*OTT* 2:387).

[77] See the salutary warning by Richard N. Longenecker, " 'Who is the prophet talking about?' Some Reflections on the New Testament's Use of the Old," *Themelios* 13 (1987): 4–8.

[78] Kaiser, *Toward Rediscovering the Old Testament,* 35–58.

[79] James A. Sanders, "Habakkuk in Qumran, Paul, and the Old Testament," *JR* 39 (1959): 232–44.

[80] See VanGemeren, *Progress,* 81, 484, n. 3.

[81] Ibid., 104–8, 115–30.

[82] Ibid., 146–55; 172–77.

[83] Ibid., 230–37.

[84] Ibid., 282–324.

[85] Yehezkel Kaufmann, *The Religion of Israel: From Its Beginnings to the Babylonian Exile,* trans. and abr. Moshe Greenberg (New York: Schocken, 1960), 362.

[86] I. Howard Marshall, "Slippery Words. I: Eschatology," *ExpT* 89 (1977/78): 268.

[87] Goswin Habets points out that the prophetic teaching reveals a progressive unfolding of the distinctive elements of Old Testament eschatology ("Eschatologie—Eschatologisches," in *FS Botterweck,* 351–69). J. P. M. van der Ploeg concludes that "eschatology" always signifies "the knowledge of the end" ("Eschatology in the Old Testament," in *The Witness of Tradition* [Leiden: Brill, 1972], 89–99). R. E. Clements speaks of both an end and a beginning, "Eschatology is the study of ideas and beliefs concerning the end of the present world order, and the introduction of a new order" (*Prophecy and Covenant,* 105). Thomas M. Raitt sees eschatology as the opening up of a new perspective: "an open-ended future" (*Theology of Exile,* 217).

[88] See chap. 8: "The Day of the Lord."

[89] Simon J. De Vries speaks of the future as an extrapolation from the past and present: "Thus, in an ultimate meaning, both historiography and eschatology are forms of parenesis, holding the covenant people to an ever present choice between 'life and good, death and evil' (Deut. 30:15)" (*Yesterday, Today and Tomorrow: Time and History in the Old Testament* [Grand Rapids: Eerdmans, 1975], 282, see 281–331).

[90] Beecher, *Prophets and the Promise,* 377.

[91] See Donald E. Gowan's approach to Old Testament eschatology. He sees the center of Old Testament eschatology in "Zion" and develops it in three aspects: (1) peace in Zion—the transformation of human society; (2) the

people of Zion—the transformation of the human person; and (3) highest of the hills—the transformation of nature (*Eschatology in the Old Testament* [Philadelphia: Fortress, 1986]).

⁹²Kaiser, *Toward Rediscovering the Old Testament,* 35–46, 83–100.

⁹³See the challenging article by Ronald E. Clements, "Patterns in the Prophetic Canon," in *Canon and Authority,* 42–55. He views the events of 722, 587, and 538 B.C. as "the catalysts, relating prophecies firmly to political realities and giving them a basis of 'fulfillment' " (50).

⁹⁴W. A. VanGemeren, "The Spirit of Restoration," *WTJ* 50 (1988): 81–102.

⁹⁵I owe this phraseology to a discussion with John Gerstner (Spring 1987).

⁹⁶So B. S. Childs writes, "Keep a holistic interpretation of the Bible whenever you seek to interpret it. Read each individual story in the light of the whole history of God's activity with his people, but conversely, rethink one's overarching categories in the light of the detailed study of its parts" ("On Reading the Elijah Narratives," *Int* 34 [1980]: 137).

⁹⁷Richard N. Longenecker cautions against our deduction and imitation of principles of Old Testament interpretation, based on apostolic usage of the Old Testament (" 'Who is the prophet talking about?' " 8).

⁹⁸W. A. VanGemeren, IHCIP, 269–97; idem, "Perspectives on Continuity," in *FS Johnson,* 37–62; idem, *Progress,* 23–27.

⁹⁹Anthony A. Hoekema coins the term *inaugurated eschatology,* but limits his discussion to the realization of the eschatological benefits in the coming of Jesus Christ to the present church age (*The Bible and the Future* [Grand Rapids: Eerdmans, 1979], 1; see 1–75). Yet, he admits that "the faith of the Old Testament believer was eschatological through and through" (ibid., 12).

¹⁰⁰Ladd, *TNT,* 48.

¹⁰¹See Hoekema, *Bible and the Future,* 23–40.

¹⁰²John F. A. Sawyer, "A Change of Emphasis in the Study of the Prophets," in *FS Ackroyd,* 240–46.

¹⁰³Beecher, *Prophets and the Promise,* 376.

¹⁰⁴Gurdon C. Oxtoby, *Prediction and Fulfillment in the Bible* (Philadelphia: Westminster, 1966), 119.

¹⁰⁵James A. Sanders reminds us of the adage: "God's Word comforts the afflicted and afflicts the comfortable" (*God Has a Story Too* [Philadelphia: Fortress, 1979], 16–17).

¹⁰⁶John Bright, *Covenant and Promise: The Prophetic Understanding of the Future in Pre-exilic Israel* (Philadelphia: Westminster, 1976), 198.

¹⁰⁷H. Berkhof, *Christ the Meaning of History,* trans. L. Buurman (Grand Rapids: Baker, 1979). Von Rad writes, "No special hermeneutic method is necessary to see the whole diversified movement of the Old Testament saving events, . . . as pointing to their fulfillment in Jesus Christ" (*OTT* 2:374).

¹⁰⁸G. B. Caird, "The Language of Eschatology," in *The Language and Imagery of the Bible* (Philadelphia: Westminster, 1980), 242–71.

¹⁰⁹Frederick Ferre, "Metaphors, Models, and Religion," *Soundings* 51 (1968): 327–45. Sallie McFague, *Metaphorical Theology: Models of God in Religious Language* (Philadelphia: Fortress, 1982), 1–66.

¹¹⁰Moshe Weinfeld, "The Day of the Lord: Aspirations for the Kingdom of

God in the Bible and Jewish Liturgy," *SH* 31 (1986): 349–55. See chap. 8: "The Day of the Lord."

[111] Beecher, *Prophets and the Promise,* 377.

[112] Ibid., 130.

[113] Sanders, *God Has a Story Too,* 15.

[114] For the tension in Jesus' theology, see I. H. Marshall, *Eschatology and the Parables* (London: Tyndale, 1963); Raymond E. Brown, "The Pater Noster as an Eschatological Prayer," in *New Testament Essays* (Garden City: Doubleday, 1968), 275–320; in Pauline theology, see Geerhardus Vos, *Pauline Eschatology* (Grand Rapids: Eerdmans, 1961); Andrew T. Lincoln, *Paradise Now and Not Yet* (Cambridge: Cambridge University Press, 1981).

[115] Bruce K. Waltke, "Kingdom Promises as Spiritual," in *FS Johnson,* 263–87; see also Walter C. Kaiser, Jr., "Kingdom Promises as Spiritual and National," in *FS Johnson,* 289–307.

[116] Davidson, *Old Testament Prophecy,* 496.

[117] Kirkpatrick, *The Doctrine of the Prophets* (London: Macmillan, 1917), 528–29.

[118] Ibid., 529.

[119] C. K. Barrett, "New Testament Eschatology," *SJT* 6 (1953): 240 (emphasis mine).

[120] Torrance, *Reality and Evangelical Theology,* 144.

[121] See the emphases in the inaugural address at Calvin Theological Seminary by Robert Becker, "The Redemptive Focus of the Kingdom of God," *CTJ* 14 (1979): 154–86.

[122] H. H. Schmid, "Creation, Righteousness, and Salvation: 'Creation Theology' as a Broad Horizon of Biblical Theology," in *Creation in the Old Testament,* ed. Bernard W. Anderson (Philadelphia: Fortress, 1984), 115, see 102–17; see also the schematization by William J. Dumbrell, *The End of the Beginning: Revelation 21–22 and the Old Testament* (Grand Rapids: Baker, 1985), 196.

[123] Gerhard von Rad, *God at Work in Israel,* trans. John H. Marks (Nashville: Abingdon, 1980), 167.

[124] Beecher, *Prophets and the Promise,* 413.

[125] John Bright, *Covenant and Promise,* 47.

[126] See the penetrating analysis of hope in the Old Testament by David A. Hubbard, "Hope in the Old Testament," *TB* 34 (1983): 33–59.

Introduction to Part 2

[1] Samuel J. Schultz gives his work on the prophets a subtitle, reflecting on this unifying theme: *The Prophets Speak: Law of Love—the Essence of Israel's Religion* (New York: Harper & Row, 1968). Walter C. Kaiser, Jr., too, has worked out the integration of promise in the prophets in his epochal work *TOTT.*

Chapter 4

[1] The superscription gives significant background information on Hosea's time: "The word of the LORD that came to Hosea son of Beeri during the reigns of Uzziah [792–740 B.C.], Jotham [750–731 B.C.], Ahaz [735–715 B.C.] and

Hezekiah [729–686 B.C.], kings of Judah, and during the reign of Jeroboam son of Jehoash king of Israel [i.e. Jeroboam II, 793–753 B.C.]." Wilson concludes from the superscription that Hosea "is linked with the Ephraimite prophetic tradition" (*Prophecy and Society in Ancient Israel* [Philadelphia: Fortress, 1980], 226–27).

²Samaria (7:1; 8:5–6; 10:5, 7; 13:16), Shechem (6:9), Bethel (4:15; 5:8; 10:5; 12:4), Gilgal (4:15; 9:15; 12:11), Valley of Achor (2:15), Gilead (6:8; 12:11), Egypt (8:13; 9:3; 11:11), Assyria (5:13; 7:11; 8:9; 9:3; 10:6; 11:5, 11; 12:1; 14:3), and Tabor (5:1).

³Hans Walter Wolff, *Hosea*, Hermeneia (Philadelphia: Fortress, 1974), xxi.

⁴For an overview of this period, see Merrill, *History*, 373–77.

⁵Shalom M. Paul, "Amos iii 15—Winter and Summer Mansions," *VT* 28 (1978): 358–60.

⁶Morton Cogan, *Imperialism and Religion: Assyria, Judah and Israel in the Eighth and Seventh Centuries B.C.E.* (Missoula, Mont.: Scholars Press, 1974), 104.

⁷J. A. Soggin, "Hosea und die Aussenpolitik Israels," in *FS Fohrer*, 131–36.

⁸See Merrill, *History*, 391–401.

⁹Note Wolfgang Schütte supposes that 5:8–6:6 came from a Judean leader during the Syro-Ephraimite war ("Eine originale Stimme aus dem syrish-ephraimitischen Krieg: Zu Hos 5, 8–66," *ZAW* 99 [1987]: 406–8).

¹⁰See Cogan, *Imperialism and Religion*, 97–110.

¹¹The book has been the subject of intensive study and critical assessment. See Harrison, *IOT*, 861–68, 868–73; Childs, *IOTS*, 374–77.

¹²Buss concludes that prophetic speech and divine word are "not separable genres existing independently but that they are factors of style, perhaps even not necessarily rigid ones" (*The Prophetic Word of Hosea: A Morphological Study*, BZAW 11 [Berlin: Töpelmann, 1969], 65).

¹³Ibid., 79.

¹⁴Wolff, *Hosea*, xxiii.

¹⁵Ibid., xxiii–xxiv.

¹⁶For further analysis of the literary forms, see W. Brueggemann, *Tradition for Crisis* (Richmond: John Knox, 1968), 55–90; Buss, *Prophetic Word*.

¹⁷Wolff, *Hosea*, xxiv.

¹⁸See Buss, *Prophetic Word*, 38–50; Wolff, *Hosea*, xxiv. Karol Nandrasky has also made a significant contribution to the use of metaphor in Hosea, in "Die Anschauungsweise und die Logik in der metaphorischen Ausdrucksweise des Propheten Hosea," *LB* 54 (1983): 61–95.

¹⁹See esp. Grace I. Emmerson, *Hosea: An Israelite Prophet in Judean Perspective*, JSOTSS 28 (Sheffield: JSOT, 1984). Mays, *Hosea*, OTL (Philadelphia: Westminster, 1969), 5.

²⁰For a discussion on the threefold structure (1–3; 4–11; 12–14), see Buss, *Prophetic Word*, 31–37. For a different analysis but similar conclusions, see David B. Wyrtzen, "The Theological Center of the Book of Hosea," *BibSac* 141 (1984): 315–29. For Hosea's message of hope, see Philip J. King, "Hosea's Message of Hope," *BTB* 12 (1982): 91–95.

²¹For a discussion of the various views, see Leon J. Wood, "Hosea," *EBC* 7:164–66; LaSor, *OTS*, 335–36; A. S. van der Woude, "Three Classical

Prophets: Amos, Hosea, and Micah," in *FS Ackroyd*, 45–46. For a historical survey, see the excellent study of Stephan Bitter, *Die Ehe des Propheten Hosea: Eine auslegungsgeschichtliche Untersuchung* (Göttingen: Vandenhoeck & Ruprecht, 1975); see also E. Ball, "Hosea," *ISBE* 2:762–64.

[22]The religion of the Canaanites encouraged lewd and sensuous practices, against which the Lord had forewarned them (Lev. 18:27–29; Deut. 7:1–6). Baal and the hosts of other deities promised fertility, blessing, and prosperity in all areas of life. Yahweh had made a better offer to Israel. He promised to bless Israel in all areas of life if only she would worship him *alone* (Deut. 7:12–14; 8:6–9; 11:13–15).

[23]See P. A. Kruger, "Israel, the Harlot (Hos. 2:4–9)," *JNSL* 11 (1983): 107–16.

[24]For a study of the symbolism, see Dianne Bergant, "Symbolic Names in Hosea," *TBT* 20 (1982): 159–60.

[25]Jon D. Levenson observes that the prophetic emphasis on covenant implies "an unqualified rejection of *Realpolitik*" (*Sinai and Zion. An Entry into the Jewish Bible* [Minneapolis: Winston Press, 1985], 72).

[26]Else Kragelund Holt, "*d'̔t 'lhym* und *ḥsd* im Buche Hosea," *Scandinavian Journal of the Old Testament* 1 (1987): 87–103. Koch defines *da'at* as "an understanding with emotional and sympathetic connotations and practical consequences, which is possible only as a result of close personal community with what is known" (*Prophets* 1:91). See the significant works by Katherine D. Sakenfeld, *The Meaning of Hesed in the Hebrew Bible: A New Inquiry*, Harvard Semitic Monographs 17 (Missoula, Mont.: Scholars Press, 1978); idem, *Faithfulness in Action* (Philadelphia: Fortress, 1985).

[27]For a study on Hosea's language of threat and accusation, see Buss, *Prophetic Word*, 83–105.

[28]Wolff appropriately comments, "The punishment is executed with extreme sympathy because its goal is to return Israel both to a knowledge of God as Lord of her history and to a bond of loyalty with him" (*Hosea*, 129–30).

[29]See Cogan, *Imperialism and Religion*, 97–110.

[30]For a liturgical approach to Hosea 5:8–6:6 as a "liturgy of repentance," see Millard C. Lind, "Hosea 5:8–6:6," *Int* 38 (1984): 398–403.

[31]For the connection of wisdom and waiting, see Buss, *Prophetic Word*, 137–38.

[32]For the covenantal-conjugal significance of *ḥesed*, see Claude J. Peifer, "The Marriage Theme in Hosea," *TBT* 20 (1982): 139–44.

[33]Buss concludes, "Thus the negative structure of man's direction and the positive word of God's purpose are intimately connected with each other and are not to be considered as separate. The promises serve to underline the inescapability of the threats, while the threats lead on to a new situation" (*Prophetic Word*, 129).

[34]H. W. Wolff speaks of the depth of Yahweh's love in contrast to the philosophical conception that defines God as the "unmovable mover." His word is effective, not only in judgment, but also in healing (*Prophetische Alternativen: Entdeckungen des Neuen im Alten Testament* [Munich: Kaiser, 1982], 24–39). Von Rad insightfully comments, "Hosea's whole preaching is rooted in the saving history" (*OTT* 2:140).

[35] Helen Schüngel-Straumann, "Gott als Mutter in Hosea 11," *Theologische Quartalschrift* 166 (1986): 119–34.

[36] Steve McKenzie, "Exodus Typology in Hosea," *ResQ* 22 (1979): 100–108.

[37] For a perceptive study on God's identification with his people, see Reidar B. Bjornard, "Hosea 11:8–9, God's Word or Man's Insight?" *Biblical Research* 27 (1982): 16–25. See also Walther Eichrodt: "The holy God exalted in his majesty above all human thoughts, who nevertheless strives in judgment and grace for the turning of his people to his saving love: this is the real content of the theology of Hosea" ("The Holy One in Your Midst: The Theology of Hosea," trans. Lloyd Gaston, *Int* 15 [1961], 273).

[38] See the allusion to Jacob's wrestling with the Lord in 12:1–4. So Israel, too, must struggle and come to the realization that Yahweh is Victor. I owe this identification to Steve McKenzie, "The Jacob Tradition in Hosea xii 4–5," *VT* 36 (1986): 311–22.

[39] Hendrikus Berkhof, *Christian Faith: An Introduction to the Study of Faith,* trans. Sierd Woudstra, rev. ed. (Grand Rapids: Eerdmans, 1986), 131. G. von Rad writes similarly, "To be sure, the Old Testament does contain statements about holiness that are most lofty in their spirituality—Hos. XI.9 is one of the most sublime" (*OTT* 1:206).

[40] Koch expresses the imagery of Yahweh as lover as "a relationship with God which is determined by masculine love and expects feminine surrender and devotion" (*Prophets* 1:89).

[41] Von Rad concludes, "It is a remarkable fact that the same prophet who thinks so emphatically in terms of saving history can at the same time move Jahweh's relationship to Israel over into the horizons of an almost vegetable natural growth and blossoming, where all the drama of the saving history ebbs out as if in a profound quiet" (*OTT* 2:146).

[42] The prophetic imagery reflects the fertility religions of Canaan. Yahweh gives rain (10:12) and fertility to the soil. He prospers animal, vegetative, and human life (2:18, 21–23).

[43] On the use of Deuteronomic language and concepts, see Moshe Weinfeld, "Hosea and Deuteronomy," in *Deuteronomy and the Deuteronomic School* (Oxford: Clarendon, 1972), 366–70.

[44] Anne Marie Sweet, "A Theology of Healing," *TBT* 20 (1982): 145–49. Dennis J. McCarthy is right in insisting that though the word "covenant" (*bᵉrît*) is rarely used, Hosea's message reflects an intensely deep covenantal experience ("Prophets and Covenant Community," *Jeev* 11 (1981): 105–12.

[45] J. Gerald Janzen concludes that Hosea's use of questions in Hosea 11 opens up a negation of the past ways and a fresh start: "the possibility of an open future for the covenant relation, a future which imparts eschatological character both to human life and, it may be, to the life of God" ("Metaphor and Reality in Hosea 11," *Semeia* 24 [1982]: 7–44). Buss writes on the eschatology of Hosea: "The End, however, is approached with openness to the divine, in which there is eternal joy" (*Prophetic Word,* 138).

[46] We assume the essential continuity of God's commitment to creation in the Noahic covenant, see Dumbrell, *CCOTT.*

[47] The knowledge of God is an underlying motif in both judgment and salvation. Lack of "knowledge" is ground for lawsuit and judgment (4:1, 6). The

"knowledge" of God brings blessing (2:20). The root *y-d-'* ("know") and the noun *da'at* ("knowledge") have a relational, conjugal sense. Negatively, Israel did not respond to Yahweh's love. Positively, Israel will again respond to his love and do his will. See Buss, *Prophetic Word*, 106.

[48]Eichrodt, "The Holy One in Your Midst," 271.

[49]E. Hammershaimb connects the preexilic message of Hosea, Isaiah, and Micah with the hope of restoration in a union of the tribes under the headship of the messianic king ("Some Leading Ideas in the Book of Micah," in *Some Aspects of Old Testament Prophecy from Isaiah to Malachi* [Copenhagen: Rosenkilde Og Bagger, 1966], 29–50).

[50]For the marriage formula, see Mordechai A. Friedman, "Israel's Response in Hosea 2:17b: 'You Are My Husband,'" *JBL* 99 (1980): 199–204. Jon D. Levenson looks at Israel's relationship with Yahweh as a marriage contract, a *ketubbah* (*Sinai and Zion*, 75–80).

[51]Eichrodt contends, "Over this whole *renewal of creation* stands in powerful self-expression the divine Person, who is here at work in his creative deed and beside whom nothing else can become a subject" ("The Holy One in Your Midst," 272).

[52]O. Palmer Robertson writes, "Thus Hosea anticipates the continuing significance of God's broader covenant commitments squarely in the context of God's purposes to redeem a people to himself" (*The Christ of the Covenants* [Grand Rapids: Baker, 1980], 111).

[53]Buss speaks of "the Garden of Eden" in this context (*Prophetic Word*), 109.

[54]Gerald D. Swaim, "Hosea the Statesman," in *FS LaSor*, 177–83.

[55]For a critical analysis of the relevant texts in Hosea, see A. Gelston, "Kingship in the Book of Hosea," *OTS* 19 (1974): 71–85.

[56]Eichrodt, "The Holy One in Your Midst," 263. Wolff comments, "God does what is impossible according to the law" (*Hosea*, 63).

[57]*Joel* means "Yahweh is God." Joel was a common name in Israel.

[58]For a discussion of these issues, see Leslie C. Allen, *The Books of Joel, Obadiah, Jonah and Micah*, NICOT (Grand Rapids: Eerdmans, 1976): 19–25; Harrison, *IOT*, 876–79; LaSor, *OTS*, 438–39; Childs, *IOTS*, 386–89. An excellent survey of the options is found in "The Date of Joel," by John Alexander Thompson, in *FS Myers*, 453–64.

[59]See E. J. Young, *An Introduction to the Old Testament* (Grand Rapids: Eerdmans, 1964), 254–57; G. L. Archer, *A Survey of Old Testament Introduction* (Chicago: Moody Press, 1974), 303–7.

[60]For cautions against an exclusive use of Joel's language in dating, see Ahlstrom, *Joel and the Temple Cult of Jerusalem*, SVT 21 (Leiden: Brill, 1971): 1–22.

[61]H. C. M. Vogt, *Studie zur nachexilischen Gemeinde in Esra-Nehemia* (Werl: Dietrich-Coelde Verlag, 1966).

[62]Allen, *Joel, Obadiah, Jonah and Micah*, 23–24; G. W. Ahlstrom, *Joel and the Temple Cult*, 111–29.

[63]Dates range from ca. 445 to ca. 343 B.C.; see Hans Walter Wolff, *Joel and Amos*, trans. Waldemar Janzen, S. Dean McBride, Jr., and Charles A. Muenchow, Hermeneia (Philadelphia: Fortress, 1977), 4–5.

64 John Calvin, "Preface" to Joel, in *Joel, Amos & Obadiah: A Commentary on the Minor Prophets*, trans. John Owen (Edinburgh: Banner of Truth, 1986), 2:xv.

65 Hans Walter Wolff calls this a great "lamentation liturgy" (*Joel and Amos*, 9).

66 For citations of sentences, see 1:15 = Isa. 13:6; Ezek. 30:2–3; Zeph. 1:7; 2:1, 2 = Zeph. 1:14, 15; 2:32 = Obad. 17; 3:16 = Amos 1:2; Isa. 13:13. Several phrases closely parallel the usage by other prophets: "every face turns pale" (2:6b = Nah. 2:10b); "earth shakes, the sky trembles" (2:10a = Isa. 13:13); "the sun and moon . . . and the stars" (2:10b = Isa. 13:10); "I am the LORD your God and that there is no other" (2:27 = Isa. 45:5, 6, 18, 22; 46:9; Ezek. 36:11); "I will pour out my Spirit" (2:28 = Ezek. 39:29); "all nations" (3:2 = Isa. 66:18a); "mountains will drip new wine" (3:18a = Amos 9:13).

67 2:3b, see Isa. 51:3a; 3:10, see Isa. 2:4 (Mic. 4:3).

68 For other examples, see Richard A. Coggins, "An Alternative Prophetic Tradition?" in *FS Ackroyd*, 89–90; Wolff, *Joel and Amos*, 10–11. Allen is helpful in his extensive analysis of Joel's language. Though I follow Wolff's structure, Allen's careful analysis of Joel's phraseology demonstrates the highly structured order (*Joel, Obadiah, Jonah and Micah*, 39–42).

69 For a good example of and encouragement to stylistic analysis, see Elias D. Mallon, "A Stylistic Analysis of Joel 1:10–12," *CBQ* 45 (1983): 537–48; Wolff, *Joel and Amos*, 8–11.

70 See Wolff, *Joel and Amos*, 6–10.

71 For a more comprehensive treatment, see chap. 8: "Summary of Prophetic Motifs."

72 For a similar use, see Jer. 31:31, 33: " 'The time is coming,' declares the LORD, 'when I will make a new covenant with the house of Israel and with the house of Judah. . . . This is the covenant I will make with the house of Israel after that time,' declares the LORD." The phrases are clearly parallel (ABCDE–C'D'A'B'): " 'The time is coming,'(A) declares the LORD, (B) 'when I will make a new covenant (C) with the house of Israel (D) and with the house of Judah (E). . . .This is the covenant (C') I will make with the house of Israel (D') after that time,' (A') declares the LORD." (B')

73 W. A. VanGemeren, "The Spirit of Restoration," *WTJ* 50 (1988): 81–102.

74 Richard C. Oudersluys, "Eschatology and the Holy Spirit," *Reformed Review* 19, no. 2 (1965): 3–12.

75 Donald E. Gowan, *Eschatology in the Old Testament* (Philadelphia: Fortress, 1986), 75.

76 The apostle Paul extends this blessing to the inclusion of Gentiles together with Jews in his application of the promise of Joel 2:32 (Rom. 10:12–13).

77 Graham S. Ogden, "Joel 4 and Prophetic Responses to National Laments," *JSOT* 26 (1983): 97–106.

78 Wolff writes, "The text of Joel may be able to help modern Israel to recognize liberation from horrible calamities as a basis for the hope that God wants to be near . . . to make into a reality the prophetic promise of a new life in unreserved communion with him through the gift of his spirit" (*Joel and Amos*, 70).

79 Ibid., 86.

80 The theological contribution of each is distinctive. Hosea develops the "love" and "knowledge" of God as expressions of his rule, whereas Amos looks

at the aspects of justice and righteousness of divine rule. Both evaluate human action from their respective theological framework. For the historical context of Amos, see "Hosea: Hosea and His Time."

[81] See also Zech. 14:5. The earthquake may be dated to sometime between 765–760 B.C., see Y. Yadin et al., *Hazor II: An Account of the Second Season of Excavation, 1956* (Jerusalem: Magnes, 1960), 24–26, 36–37.

[82] Although some scholars dispute this because his ministry was in Israel rather than Judah, the statement in 7:12 shows that Amaziah, priest of Bethel, clearly regarded Judah as Amos's home.

[83] Robert Gordis, "Edom, Israel and Amos—An Unrecognized Source for Edomite History," in *Essays on the Occasion of the Seventieth Anniversary of the Dropsie University (1909–1979),* ed. Abraham I. Katsh and Leon Nemoy (Philadelphia: Dropsie, 1979), 109–32.

[84] Robert Martin-Achard, "L'Homme: son cadre de vew—ses activités," in *Amos: L'Homme, le message, l'influence* (Geneva: Labor et Fides, 1984), 13–45.

[85] See Frank H. Seilhamer for the covenantal framework and terminology in "The Role of Covenant in the Mission and Message of Amos," in *FS Myers,* 435–51.

[86] Wolff, *Joel and Amos,* 108–11; idem, *Amos the Prophet: The Man and His Background,* trans. Foster R. McCurley (Philadelphia: Fortress, 1973); see Charles D. Isbell, "A Note on Amos 1:1," *JNES* 36 (1977): 213–14. For a critical evaluation, see J. L. Crenshaw, "The Influence of the Wise upon Amos: The 'Doxologies of Amos' and Job 5:9–16 and 9:5–10," *ZAW* 79 (1967): 42–52; Hans M. Barstad, *The Religious Polemics of Amos: Studies in the Preaching of Am 2, 7 B–8; 4, 1–13; 5, 1–27; 6, 4–7; 8, 14* SVT 34 (Leiden: Brill, 1984): 9. So also A. S. van der Woude, "Three Classical Prophets," 34–43.

[87] For a study on the prophet's awareness of his call, see Gerhard Pfeifer, "Die Denkform des Propheten Amos (iii 9–11)," *VT* 34 (1984): 476–81; see also Hans Walter Wolff, "The Irresistible Word (Amos)," *CurTM* 10 (1983): 4–13.

[88] Wolff concludes that Amaziah was not hostile (7:13), but sought a pledge from Amos whereby he would agree not to prophesy at Bethel. Amaziah was afraid of political repercussions, as he said, "Don't prophesy anymore at Bethel, because this is the king's sanctuary and the temple of the kingdom" (*Joel and Amos,* 315).

[89] Joseph G. Bailey further speaks of Amos as an entrepreneur, well familiar with the business practices of his age in "Amos: Preacher of Social Reform," *TBT* 19 (1981): 306–13. See also P. C. Craigie, who observes that Amos was a "manager" who supplied meat and wool and who by necessity had to travel extensively ("Amos the *noqed* in the Light of Ugaritic," *SR* 11 (1982): 29–33). To the contrary, Y. Ziv ("*bôqēr ûbôlēš šiqmîm*—in Tekoa?" *Beth Mikra* 28 [1982–83], 49–53 [Hebrew]) concludes from the location of Tekoa that Amos could not have been a farmer and that 7:14 be understood as a figure for "a simple person."

[90] Wolff suggests from the boldness and sharpness of his speech (4:1; 5:5; 6:12) that Amos "appears youthful" (*Joel and Amos,* 90).

[91] Evidence from Hazor supports Amos' reference to this event (ibid., 89, 124).

[92] See Yehoshua Gitay, "A Study of Amos's Art of Speech: A Rhetorical Analysis of Amos 3:1–15," *CBQ* 42 (1980): 293–309; Hans M. Barstad, *Religious Polemics of Amos*. Wolff categorizes the rhetorical sections as "free witness-speech" (*Joel and Amos*, 93–94).

[93] See Gerhard Pfeifer, "Die Ausweisung eines lästigen Ausländers Amos 7 10–17," *ZAW* 96 (1984): 112–18.

[94] Susan Niditch, *The Symbolic Vision in Biblical Tradition* (Chico: Scholars Press, 1980); Martin-Achard, *Amos: L'Homme, le Message, l'Influence*, 107–19.

[95] Wolff, *Joel and Amos*, 91–98. See the numerical-structural analysis of James Linburg, "Sevenfold Structures in the Book of Amos," *JBL* 106 (1987), 217–22.

[96] Ibid., 100; idem, *Amos the Prophet*, 6–53.

[97] Harrison, *IOT*, 890–94; Childs, *IOTS*, 397–409. For a careful, but critical study of the stages of "updating" Amos, see Robert B. Coote, *Amos Among the Prophets: Composition and Theology* (Philadelphia: Fortress, 1981); Wolff, *Joel and Amos*, 106–13.

[98] Harrison, *IOT*, 892.

[99] Craigie, *The Old Testament*, 183.

[100] John Barton, *Amos's Oracles Against the Nations: A Study of Amos 1.3–2.5* (Cambridge: Cambridge University Press, 1980). Barton argues that Amos condemns the nations on the basis of international conventions of peace and war.

[101] For a study on the hymnic forms, see Cullen I. K. Story, "Amos— Prophet of Praise," *VT* 30 (1980): 67–80.

[102] Childs, *IOTS*, 405.

[103] For other structural analyses, see Adri Van der Wal, "The Structure of Amos," *JSOT* 26 (1983): 107–13; Claude Coulot, "Propositions pour une structuration du livre d'Amos au niveau redactionnel," *RevScRel* 51 (1977): 169–86; and Duane A. Garrett, "The Structure of Amos as a Testimony to Its Integrity," *JETS* 27 (1984): 275–76.

[104] For a form-critical analysis of the hymns, see James L. Crenshaw, *Hymnic Affirmation of Divine Justice: The Doxologies of Amos and Related Texts in the Old Testament* (Missoula, Mont.: Scholars Press, 1975); Thomas M. McComiskey, "The Hymnic Elements of the Prophecy of Amos: A Study of Form-Critical Methodology," *JETS* 30 (1987): 139–57. Klaus Koch ("Die Rolle der hymnischen Abschnitte in der Komposition des Amos-Buches," *ZAW* 86 [1974]: 504–37) correlates the hymns with the parenetic exhortation ("hear," 4:1; 5:1; 8:4) as original markers of Amos' preaching, which were left unaltered by the editor for the canonical purpose of seeing Yahweh's lordship over the political, military, and cultic events.

[105] For the connection of the oracles against the nations with the war oracle, see Duane L. Christensen, *Transformations of the War Oracle in Old Testament Prophecy: Studies in the Oracles Against the Nations* (Missoula, Mont.: Scholars Press, 1975), 57–72.

[106] See Werner Berg, *Die sogenannten Hymnenfragmente im Amosbuch* (Bern: Herbert Lang, 1974), 121–96. Amos uses the terrestrial phenomena of earthquake and tidal waves (see B. Z. Luria, "Who Calls the Waters of the Sea and Spills Them on the Face of the Earth [Amos 5:8; 9:6]," *Beth Mikra* 30

[1984–85]: 259–62 [Hebrew]) and the celestial phenomena (Lawrence Zalcman, "Astronomical Illusions in Amos," *JBL* 100–101 [1981]: 53–58) as expressive of Yahweh's power.

[107]H. W. Wolff speaks of Yahweh's irresistible word of judgment in Amos (*Prophetische Alternativen: Entdeckungen des Neuen im Alten Testament* [Munich: Kaiser, 1982], 9–23). In his commentary, he writes, "Every future reader should recognize behind the prophetic oracles here transmitted the devastating power of Yahweh himself" (*Joel and Amos,* 126).

[108]J. L. Crenshaw concludes that the designation Lord Almighty affirms Yahweh as the Creator, Judge, and sole object of worship ("*YHWH Sᵉbā'ot Sᵉmô:* A Form-Critical Analysis," *ZAW* 81 (1969): 156–75.

[109]Koch concludes that all Amos's sayings have reference to God in and outside our world (*Prophets* 1:70–71).

[110]Barstad suggests that Amos argues creatively that Yahwism was "the fertility religion" (*Religious Polemics of Amos,* 10).

[111]Wolff, *Joel and Amos,* 333.

[112]Walter Brueggemann, "Amos' Intercessory Formula," *VT* 19 (1969): 385–99.

[113]C. van Leeuwen, "The Prophecy of the *Yôm YHWH* in Amos V 18–20," *OTS* 19 (1974): 113–34.

[114]Koch looks at history at four levels: (1) divine initiative; (2) efficacious powers; (3) human spheres of activity; and (4) the realistic level. He concludes that at each level the present and the future are linked together (*Prophets* 1:63–65).

[115]Rudolf Smend ("Das Ende ist gekommen: ein Amoswort in der Priesterschrift," in *FS Wolff,* 67–71) relates God's judgment in Amos to his judgment in the Flood, his judgment of Sodom and Gomorrah, and God's message to Ezekiel (7:2).

[116]Michael L. Barré argues persuasively that the Lord is intent on terminating the covenant relationship on the basis of an analysis of the phrase "I will not turn back my wrath" ("The Meaning of *l' 'sybnw* in Amos 1:3–2:6," *JBL* 105 [1986]: 611–31).

[117]For a study on Yahweh's power in judgment and his freedom to love, see Anders Jørgen Bjørndalen, "Yahwe in den Zukunftsaussagen des Amos," in *FS Wolff,* 181–202.

[118]Gerhard F. Hasel, *The Remnant: The History and Theology of the Remnant Idea from Genesis to Isaiah* (Berrien Springs, Mich.: Andrews University Press, 1972), 173–215.

[119]Koch observes, "It must, however, be conceded that Amos never talks as if the Israelites are going to be completely blotted out, although almost all textbooks interpret him as saying this. . . . A miserable remnant is left" (*Prophets* 1:44).

[120]Wolff views these exhortations as examples of wisdom exhortations (*Amos the Prophet,* 44–53).

[121]Jared J. Jackson interprets 5:13: "Therefore the successful/prosperous person will wail/lament at that time, for it will be a time of disaster" ("Amos 5, 13 Contextually Understood," *ZAW* 98 [1986]: 434–35).

¹²²Wolff incisively observes that "right" is a wisdom term to be contrasted with "crooked or perverse" as in Prov. 8:8–9 (*Amos the Prophet*, 57).

¹²³Wolff remarks that "the most frequently repeated key words by which Amos measures the guilt of Israel are *mišpāṭ* (justice) and *ṣᵉdāqāh (righteousness)*" (*Amos the Prophet*, 59–60). See John Sowada, "Let Justice Surge Like Water ...," *TBT* 19 (1981): 301–5. On "justice" and "righteousness" as kingdom motifs, see Koch, *Prophets* 1:56–62.

¹²⁴Many scholars date 9:11–15 to a postexilic redaction (Wolff, *Amos the Prophet*, 113; Claude J. Peifer, "Amos the Prophet: The Man and His Book," *TBT* 19 [1981]: 295–300; Peter Weimar, "Der Schluss des Amos-Buches: Ein Beitrag zur Redaktionsgeschichte des Amos-Buches," *BN* 16 [1981]: 60–100). But, see Stanley N. Rosenbaum's argument that the prophecy of reunification under David comes from Amos ("Northern Amos Revisited: Two Philological Suggestions," *HS* 18 [1977]: 132–48).

¹²⁵G. Henton Davies concludes that Amos preached the urgency of reunion of the twelve tribes as a requisite of enjoyment of the age of restoration ("Amos—The Prophet of Re-Union," *ExpT* 92 [1980–81], 196–200).

¹²⁶See Walter C. Kaiser's epochal study on Amos 9:9–15 in the light of the New Testament, "The Davidic Promise and the Inclusion of the Gentiles (Amos 9:9–15 and Acts 15:13–18): A Test Passage for Theological Systems," *JETS* 20 (1977): 97–111. Gerhard F. Hasel, *The Remnant*, 209–15. Wolff vacillates between seeing in this text a theology of "suzerainty and ownership" over the nations and the narrower postexilic limits: the city of Jerusalem (*Joel and Amos*, 353).

¹²⁷For the textual issues, see Michael A. Braun, "James' Use of Amos at the Jerusalem Council: Steps Toward a Possible Solution of the Textual and Theological Problems," *JETS* 20 (1977): 113–21. For the relation of Amos 9:11–15 with Acts 15:16–17, see O. Palmer Robertson, "Hermeneutics of Continuity," in *FS Johnson*, 89–108.

¹²⁸Dumbrell, *CCOTT*, 169–70.

¹²⁹Wolff, *Amos the Prophet*, 86.

¹³⁰Dumbrell, *CCOTT*, 168.

Chapter 5

¹There are as many as thirteen men in the Old Testament who are named Obadiah; see 1 Kings 18:3; 1 Chron. 3:21; 27:19; 2 Chron. 17:7; Ezra 8:9; Neh. 10:5; 12:25.

²The LXX and the Vulgate suggest the reading of the nominal form ʿ*ebed* ("servant") rather than the MT participial form (ʿ*ōbēd*, "worshiper").

³For a discussion, see Leslie C. Allen, *The Books of Joel, Obadiah, Jonah and Micah*, NICOT (Grand Rapids: Eerdmans, 1976), 129–33; John Calvin expressed little concern with the dating of the book in his preface to Obadiah: "I know not whether Obadiah and Jeremiah were contemporaries, and on this subject we need not bestow much labour" (*Joel, Amos & Obadiah* [1846; reprint, Edinburgh: Banner of Truth, 1986], 418–19).

⁴Allen rightly concludes, "It is unlikely that the problem may be solved. . . .

Possibly (both reflect on) . . . the community's inheritance of a venerated oracle" (*Joel, Obadiah, Jonah and Micah,* 132–33).

[5]G. Ch. Aalders advances good arguments against a lengthy redactional history. In this case his contemporaries were Jeremiah in Judah and Ezekiel in Babylon (*Obadja en Jona,* COT [Kampen: Kok, 1958], 8–12).

[6]N. K. Gottwald, "Studies in the Book of Lamentations," *SBT* 14 (1954): 88.

[7]Allen, *Joel, Obadiah, Jonah and Micah,* 129–33. For critical issues, see Harrison, *IOT,* 899–903; LaSor, *OTS,* 455–58; Childs, *IOTS,* 412–13.

[8]See Fohrer's survey, "Die Sprüche Obadjas," in *FS Vriezen,* 81–93; H. W. Wolff, *Obadja und Jona* BKAT (Neukirchen-Vluyn: Neukirchener, 1977), 5–6.

[9]Allen, *Joel, Obadiah, Jonah and Micah,* 137.

[10]Childs, *IOTS,* 415.

[11]See M. H. Woudstra, "Edom and Israel in Ezekiel," *CTJ* 3 (1968): 21–35; Aalders, *Obadja en Jona,* 58.

[12]John Calvin, *Joel, Amos & Obadiah,* 452.

[13]For the connection of the oracles against the nations (Edom) with the war oracle, see Duane L. Christensen, *Transformations of the War Oracle in Old Testament Prophecy: Studies in the Oracles Against the Nations* (Missoula, Mont.: Scholars Press, 1975), 163–66.

[14]For a list of suggested passages on the transformation of human society, man, and nature, see Donald E. Gowan, *Eschatology in the Old Testament* (Philadelphia: Fortress, 1986), 10.

[15]Childs, *IOTS,* 415.

[16]J. R. Lillie, "Obadiah—A Celebration of God's Kingdom," *CurTM* 6 (1979): 18–22.

[17]For a history of Edom, see Robert Gordis, "Edom, Israel and Amos—An Unrecognized Source for Edomite History," in *Essays on the Occasion of the Seventieth Anniversary of the Dropsie University (1909–1979),* ed. Abraham I. Katsh and Leon Nemoy (Philadelphia: Dropsie, 1979), 109–32.

[18]J. R. Bartlett, "From Edomites to Nabataeans: A Study in Continuity," *Palestine Exploration Quarterly* 111 (1979): 53–66.

[19]Josephus, *The Jewish War,* trans. G. A. Williamson (Middlesex: Penguin, 1974), 247–50.

[20]He was contemporary with Amaziah (796–767 B.C.) and Uzziah (792–740 B.C.), kings of Judah; with Jeroboam II (793–753 B.C.), king of Israel; with Adad-Nirari III (810–783 B.C.), Shalmaneser IV (782–773 B.C.), and Ashur-dan III (772–755 B.C.), kings of Assyria; with Benhadad III (806–770 B.C.), king of Aram. For dates, see Merrill, *History;* Edwin R. Thiele, *A Chronology of the Hebrew Kings* (Grand Rapids: Zondervan, 1977).

[21]See the stimulating study by Jonathan Magonet, *Form and Meaning: Studies in Literary Techniques in the Book of Jonah* (Sheffield: Almond Press, 1983).

[22]For the issues regarding Jonah, see Harrison, *IOT,* 914–18; LaSor, *OTS,* 349–53; Childs, *IOTS,* 418–21.

[23]Scholarship is divided on the issue of authorship. Some advance convincing arguments of Jonah's authorship (see E. J. Young, *An Introduction to the Old Testament* [Grand Rapids: Eerdmans, 1964], 261–63; Gleason L. Archer, Jr., *A Survey of Old Testament Introduction* [Chicago: Moody Press, 1964], 296). Others

project that a prophetic author gave us the present book, as G. Ch. Aalders, *Oud-Testamentische Kanoniek* (Kampen: Kok, 1952), 262.

[24] See David F. Payne, "Jonah from the Perspective of Its Audience," *JSOT* 13 (1979): 3–12.

[25] H. L. Ellison, "Jonah," *EBC* 7:363.

[26] Craigie, *Old Testament,* 189.

[27] Jacques Ellul, *The Judgment of Jonah,* trans. Geoffrey W. Bromiley (Grand Rapids: Eerdmans, 1971), 14–18.

[28] B. S. Childs, "Jonah: A Study in Old Testament Hermeneutics," *SJT* 11 (1958): 53–61.

[29] J. H. Stek speaks of Jonah as *"interpreted* history" ("The Message of the Book of Jonah," *CTJ* 4 [1969]: 34). For a defense of the historicity, see Donald J. Wiseman, "Jonah's Nineveh," *TB* 30 (1979): 29–51; Eugene H. Merrill, "The Sign of Jonah," *JETS* 23 (1980): 23–30; G. Ch. Aalders, *The Problem of Jonah* (London: Tyndale Press, 1948).

[30] Von Rad, *OTT* 2:289.

[31] P. R. Ackroyd, *Exile and Restoration: A Study of Hebrew Thought of the Sixth Century B.C.* (Philadelphia: Westminster, 1968), 244–45.

[32] Millar Burrows, "The Literary Category of the Book of Jonah," in *FS May,* 80–107; John C. Holbert, " 'Deliverance Belongs to Yahweh!': Satire in the Book of Jonah," *JSOT* 21 (1981): 59–81.

[33] Allen rightly criticizes this approach as too restrictive (*Joel, Obadiah, Jonah and Micah,* 180).

[34] For a discussion of these issues, see Harrison, *IOT,* 905–14; Childs, *IOTS,* 421–26.

[35] Stek looks at Jonah as representative of Israel, which was unfaithful in its mission to bring God's blessing to the Gentiles ("The Message," 40–41).

[36] Childs says that Jonah "serves as a critical prophetic judgment on Israel in line with the rest of the prophetic witnesses of the Old Testament" (*IOTS,* 426).

[37] S. R. Driver, *An Introduction to the Literature of the OT* (New York: Scribner, 1925), 325.

[38] Allen, *Joel, Obadiah, Jonah and Micah,* 178.

[39] George M. Landes, "Jonah: A Māšāl?" in *FS Terrien,* 137–58. David F. Payne, "Jonah from the Perspective of Its Audience," 3–12.

[40] Jonah's prayer was almost certainly used in the community as a thanksgiving hymn since it encourages the godly to look to Yahweh for salvation (v. 9). See von Rad, *OTT* 1:359; G. M. Landes, "The Kerygma of the Book of Jonah," *Int* 21 (1967): 3–31. For a comparison with the Psalms, see Ellison, "Jonah," 364.

[41] See the suggestions on the theological implications of the canonical approach by Brevard S. Childs in "The Canonical Shape of the Book of Jonah," in *FS LaSor,* 122–28.

[42] On the "sign of Jonah," see Stek's intriguing article, "The Message," 41–50; Claude J. Peifer, "Jonah and Jesus: The Prophet as a Sign," *TBT* 21 (1983): 377–83.

[43] Magonet, *Form and Meaning,* 112.

[44] Allan John Hauser sees the contrastive picture of Yahweh: the God of

wrath and forgiveness ("Jonah: In Pursuit of the Dove," *JBL* 104 [1985]: 21–37).

[45]Stek may well be right when he concludes that "the imperfection, weakness, and brokenness of His people's response to Him does not hinder the sovereign Lord of history in carrying out His saving purposes. . . . Yahweh will do His saving work in Israel *in spite* of her, not because of her" ("The Message," 41). But the New Testament use of the sign of Jonah should not be misconstrued as God's rejection of Israel, as may be implied by Stek (49)! There is always a hiddenness in the ways of God regarding the nations and also the Jewish people. On the issue of theodicy, see Terence E. Fretheim, "Jonah and Theodicy," *ZAW* 90 (1978): 227–37. On the place of repentance, see R. E. Clements, "The Purpose of the Book of Jonah," SVT 28 (1975): 16–28.

[46]For a survey of recent research on Micah, see Knud Jeppesen, "New Aspects of Micah Research," *JSOT* 8 (1978): 3–32.

[47]Hans Walter Wolff, *Micah the Prophet,* trans. R. D. Gehrke (Philadelphia: Fortress, 1981), 25; idem, "Micah the Moreshite—The Prophet and His Background," in *FS Terrien,* 77–84; idem, "Wie verstand Micha von Moreschet sein prophetisches Amt?" SVT 29 (1978): 403–17; for a criticism of Wolff see José Nunes Carriera, "Micha—ein Ältester von Moreschet?" *Trierer Theologische Zeitschrift* 90 (1981): 19–28.

[48]Magen Broshi, "The Expansion of Jerusalem in the Reigns of Hezekiah and Manasseh," *IEJ* 24 (1974): 21.

[49]See also chap. 9: "The Message of Isaiah: Isaiah and His Time."

[50]For the background of Micah's time, see A. S. van der Woude, *Profeet en Establishment* (Kampen: Kok, 1985), 13–24; Allen, *Joel, Obadiah, Jonah and Micah,* 239–41; B. Z. Luria, "Judah in the Days of Micah and Hezekiah," *Beth Mikra* 28 (1982–83): 6–13 (Hebrew).

[51]See Merrill, *History,* 410–12.

[52]Francis I. Anderson and David Noel Freedman, *Hosea: A New Translation with Introduction and a Commentary,* AB (Garden City: Doubleday, 1980), 60–66.

[53]For example, see *'attâ* ("you," 4:8; 5:2 [MT 5:1]; 6:14, 15) and *'attâ* ("now," 4:9, 10, 11; 5:1 [MT 4:14]; 5:4 [MT 5:3]; 7:4, 10), *sim' u* ("hear"), ("listen," 1:2; 3:1, 9; 6:1, 2, 9).

[54]For critical issues, see Allen, *Joel, Obadiah, Jonah and Micah,* 241–53; Harrison, *IOT,* 922–25; LaSor, *OTS* 356–59; Childs, *IOTS,* 429–31.

[55]A. S. van der Woude has made a significant contribution to the rhetorical analysis of Micah. *Profeet en Establishment;* idem, *Micha* (Nijkerk: Callenbach, 1977); idem, "Micah in Dispute with the Pseudo-Prophets," *VT* 19 (1969): 244–60; idem, "Deutero-Micha: ein Prophet aus Nord-Israel?" *NTT* 25 (1971): 365–78. See Edward A. Niederhiser, "Micah 2:1–11: Considerations on the Nature of the Discourse," *BTB* 11 (1981): 104–7.

[56]H. W. Wolff speaks of Micah's message against the leadership of Judah as the "unmasking" (*demaskierende*) word (*Prophetische Alternativen: Entdeckungen des Neuen im Alten Testament* [Munich: Kaiser, 1982], 40–54).

[57]For other structural analyses, see Allen, *Joel, Obadiah, Jonah and Micah,* 260–61; J. T. Willis, "The Structure of the Book of Micah," *SEÅ* 34 (1969): 5–

42; Alphonse P. Spilly, "Between Judgment and Salvation," *TBT* 20 (1982): 7–12.

[58] C. J. Labuschagne, *The Incomparability of Yahweh in the Old Testament* (Leiden: Brill, 1966).

[59] Von Rad, *OTT* 1:366.

[60] Delbert R. Hillers, *Micah,* Hermeneia (Philadelphia: Fortress, 1984), 18. See Charles S. Shaw, "Micah 1:10–16 Reconsidered," *JBL* 106 (1987), 223–29.

[61] See E. Hammershaimb, "Some Leading Ideas in the Book of Micah," in *Some Aspects of Old Testament Prophecy from Isaiah to Malachi* (Copenhagen: Rosenkilde Og Bagger, 1966), 29–41.

[62] Hammershaimb contrasts the false with the true prophets by designating the former as "the prophets of happiness" and the latter "the prophets of doom" (ibid., 30, 41).

[63] Knud Jeppesen concludes that the archaeological evidence gives a commentary on the extent of Canaanite religious influence on Jerusalem; see "Micah V 13 in the Light of Recent Archaeological Discovery," *VT* 34 (1984): 462–66.

[64] Jean M. Vincent, "Michas Gerichtswort gegen Zion (3, 12) in seinem Kontext," *ZTK* 83 (1986): 167–87. For the symbolism of wild animals (3:12) inhabiting the city, see Isa. 13:21–22; 14:23; 18:6; 34:11, 13–15; Jer. 9:11; 10:22; 49:33; 50:39; 51:37; Ezek. 14:21; Zeph. 2:14–15.

[65] Increasingly, more scholars accept the authenticity of hope: see B. Renaud, *Structure et attaches littéraires de Michée IV–V* (Paris: J. Gabalda, 1964); B. Rudolf, *Kommentar zum Alten Testament* 13, 3 (Gütersloh: Mohr, 1975).

[66] Van der Woude, *Micha,* 141–45; John T. Willis, "Micah 2:6–8 and the 'People of God' in Micah," *BZ* 14 (1970): 72–87.

[67] McComiskey writes, "We shall one day reign under the aegis of Messiah, as Micah said the remnant would (4:7). We shall experience the ultimate triumph of Christ (Mic. 2:12–13)" (*The Covenants of Promise: A Theology of the Old Testament Covenants* [Grand Rapids: Baker, 1985], 229).

[68] See chap. 12: "Living the Prophetic Word."

[69] R. P. Gordon, "Micah VII 19 and Akkadian *Kabāsu,*" *VT* 28 (1978): 355.

[70] Hillers, *Micah,* 4–8.

[71] See McComiskey's excellent treatment of the extension of the land promise: "The promise of the land is never abrogated in the covenants, and it too undergoes expansion. . . . the dominion of the people of God as extending far beyond the boundaries of Palestine to include the whole world" (*Covenants of Promise,* 172).

[72] See the challenging article by Walter Brueggemann, " 'Vine and Fig Tree': A Case Study in Imagination and Criticism," *CBQ* 43 (1981): 188–204.

[73] See McComiskey's careful analysis of "origins." He concludes that "the Davidic roots of the coming ruler are emphasized by the prophet Micah" (*Covenants of Promise,* 28).

[74] Hammershaimb connects the message of Isa. 7:14 and Mic. 5:2–4 as representative of a preexilic, royal theology ("Some Leading Ideas in the Book of Micah," 48–50).

[75] McComiskey, *Covenants of Promise,* 29.

[76] Eichrodt distinguishes between the kingdom of God as universalistic and

the messianic king as nationalistic, but is forced to admit the arbitrariness of his distinction (*TOT,* 1:484–85).

[77]Kaiser, *TOTT* 188.

[78]Wolff, *Obadja,* 39.

[79]Ibid., 50–51.

Chapter 6

[1]O. T. Allis, "Nahum, Nineveh, Elkosh," *EQ* 27 (1955): 67–80.

[2]For a recent work on reading Nahum in the exilic context, see A. S. van der Woude, "The Book of Nahum: A Letter Written in Exile," *OTS* 20 (1977): 108–26.

[3]See Ashurbanipal's account of the fall of Thebes in *ANET,* 295.

[4]For example, van der Woude, "The Book of Nahum," *OTS* 20: 108–26.

[5]As sole regent (686–642 B.C.).

[6]In favor of this position is the use of *sēper* ("the scroll") in 1:1 (see Jer. 36:2).

[7]Van der Woude, "The Book of Nahum." In support of this, D. L. Christensen writes, "The reading suggested here would indicate that this particular text was a rather finely crafted literary composition from the outset and not simply the memory of the spoken words of a prophet in ancient Israel" ("The Book of Nahum: The Question of Authorship within the Canonical Process," *JETS* 31 [1988]: 57).

[8]Several older commentators have held this view, among them A. van Hoonacker and W. Rudolph.

[9]See J. D. W. Watts, *The Books of Joel, Obadiah, Jonah, Nahum, Habakkuk, and Zephaniah,* CBC (Cambridge: Cambridge University Press, 1975).

[10]I. H. Eybers concludes that Nahum prophesied around 630 B.C. ("A Note Concerning the Date of Nahum's Prophecy," *Biblical Essays: Proceedings of the Twelfth Meeting of Die Ou-Testamentiese Werkgemeenskap in Suid-Africa,* ed. A. H. Van Zyl [Potchefstroom: Pro Rege-Pers, 1969], 9–12). See also Bernard Renaud, "La Composition du Livre de Nahum," *ZAW* 99 (1987): 198–219. Merrill prefers a setting between 640 and 627 (*History,* 454).

[11]*DOTT,* 75–76. See H. W. F. Saggs, "Nahum and the Fall of Nineveh," *JTS* 20 (1969): 220–25.

[12]For a stylistic analysis, see O. T. Allis, "Nahum, Nineveh, Elkosh," 67–80.

[13]For critical issues, see Harrison, *IOT,* 928–30; Childs, *IOTS,* 441–42.

[14]Carl E. Armerding, "Nahum," *EBC* 7:456.

[15]A. Van Selms, "The Alphabetic Hymn in Nahum 1," *Biblical Essays,* ed. A. H. Van Zyl, 33–45; S. J. De Vries, "The Acrostic of Nahum in the Jerusalem Liturgy," *VT* 16 (1966): 476–81. See also D. L. Christensen, "The Acrostic of Nahum Reconsidered," *ZAW* 87 (1975): 17–30; idem, "The Acrostic of Nahum Once Again: A Prosodic Analysis of Nahum 1, 1–10," *ZAW* 99 (1987): 409–15.

[16]In two extended metaphors he likens Nineveh to a lioness in her lair (2:11–12) and after her fall to an unwanted whore (3:4–7).

[17]G. A. Smith, *The Book of the Twelve Prophets,* 2 vols. (London: Hodder & Stoughton, 1898), 2:91.

[18] F. Charles Fensham, "Legal Activities of the Lord According to Nahum," *Biblical Essays,* ed. A. H. Van Zyl, 13–20.

[19] P. D. Miller, Jr., *The Divine Warrior in Early Israel* (Cambridge: Harvard University Press, 1973), 170–75.

[20] The Lord as the "kinsman-redeemer" (gō'ēl) is further developed by Dumbrell in his comments on Ex. 6:6 and 15:13 (*CCOTT,* 100). The motif of "holy War" has been carefully studied since von Rad's seminal work (*Der heilige Krieg im alten Israel* [Göttingen: Vandenhoeck & Ruprecht, 1969]). More recently P. D. Miller, Jr., has contributed a study on this topic (*The Divine Warrior*). See also T. Longman III, "Psalm 98: A Divine Warrior Victory Song," *JETS* 27 (1984): 267–74.

[21] See Kevin Cathcart, "The Divine Warrior and the War of Yahweh in Nahum," in *Biblical Studies in Contemporary Thought,* ed. Miriam Ward (Burlington: Trinity College Biblical Institute, 1975), 68–76; Richard A. Coggins relates the message of Nahum to Isaiah 40–55 in "An Alternative Prophetic Tradition?" in *FS Ackroyd,* 84–85.

[22] Childs, *IOTS,* 445.

[23] Renaud, "La Composition du Livre de Nahum," 214–19. For an explanation of Nineveh's doom from a covenantal background, see K. J. Cathcart, "Treaty Curses and the Book of Nahum," *CBQ* 35 (1973): 179–87.

[24] Yahweh had revealed his perfections to Israel at Mount Sinai (Ex. 20:5; 34:5–6) and Israel remembered the "theophany" with awe (see Ex. 19:16; Job 38:1; Pss. 18:7–15; 68:2, 7–8; 77:16–19; Isa. 28:2; 29:6; 66:15; Jer. 23:19; Zech. 7:14; 9:14). See also R. C. Dentan, "The Literary Affinities of Exodus XXXIV 6f," *VT* 13 (1963): 34–51; Samuel E. Loewenstamm, "The Trembling of Nature During the Theophany," in *Comparative Studies in Biblical and Ancient Oriental Literatures* (Neukirchen-Vluyn: Neukirchener, 1980), 173–89.

[25] Ralph L. Smith remarks, "This part of the psalm says that not only are the sea (chaos) and the river under Yahweh's control, but the hills, mountains, the earth and her inhabitants are also subject to the power of God" (*Micah–Malachi,* WBC [Waco, Tex.: Word, 1984], 74).

[26] J. P. J. Olivier, "The Concept Day in Nahum and Habakkuk," in *Biblical Essays,* ed. A. H. Van Zyl, 71–74.

[27] For similar promises of the phrase "never again," see Isa. 54:9; 62:8; Jer. 31:40; Ezek. 36:12; 37:22; 43:7; Joel 2:19, 26–27; 3:17; Amos 9:15; Zeph. 3:15; Zech. 14:11.

[28] For "jealousy" as divine "zeal" in Nahum, see Kaiser, *TOTT,* 221–22.

[29] George E. Mendenhall relates Yahweh's vengeance to his punishment and judgment; see "God of Vengeance, Shine Forth!" *Wittenberg Bulletin* 45 (1948): 37–42; idem, "The 'Vengeance' of Yahweh," in *The Tenth Generation* (Baltimore: Johns Hopkins University Press, 1973), 69–104.

[30] God's goodness denotes his fidelity to his covenant, as in Ps. 23:6; see F. C. Fensham, "Legal Activities of the Lord," 18. For *good* as a covenantal term, see also G. Brin, "Concerning Several Biblical Expressions using *ṭôb,*" *Beth Mikra* 31 (1985–86): 227–41 (Hebrew); Michael Fox, "*Tôb,*" as Covenant Terminology," *BASOR* 209 (1973): 41–42; Ingeborg Johag, "*ṭôb* —Terminus Technicus in Vertrags-und Bündnisformularen des Alten Orients und des Alten Testaments," in *FS Botterweck,* 3–23.

[31] Elizabeth Achtemeier, *Nahum–Malachi, Interpretation* (Atlanta: John Knox, 1986), 29.

[32] Some have tried to explain his name by etymology, "heartener" or "one who takes another to his heart and his arms," or "wrestler" (Jerome). Others take it as an Akkadian loan word for a plant.

[33] His contemporaries were among the prophets: Zephaniah and Jeremiah; the kings of Judah: Josiah (640–609 B.C.), Jehoahaz (609 B.C.), and Jehoiakim (608–598 B.C.); and the Babylonian kings: were Nabopolassar (625–605 B.C.) and Nebuchadnezzar (605–562 B.C.).

[34] Von Rad writes, "The roles seem to be reversed: the initiative lies with the prophet, for it is he who is discontented and impatient, while Yahweh is the one who is questioned" (*OTT* 2:190).

[35] E. Otto, "Die Stellung der Wehe-Worte in der Verkundigung des Propheten Habakuk," *ZAW* 89 (1977): 73–107.

[36] Habakkuk may have employed a wisdom method; for his relationship with the wisdom tradition, see D. E. Gowan, "Habakkuk and Wisdom," *Perspective* 9 (1968): 157–66.

[37] Donald E. Gowan summarizes Habakkuk in two phrases: "Woe!" and "Yet I will rejoice!" (*The Triumph of Faith in Habakkuk* [Atlanta: John Knox, 1976]).

[38] Kevin G. O'Connell, "Habakkuk—Spokesman to God," *CurTM* 6 (1979): 227–31.

[39] J. Gerald Janzen, "Eschatological Symbol and Existence in Habakkuk," *CBQ* 44 (1982): 394–414.

[40] See O. Palmer Robertson, " 'The Justified (By Faith) Shall Live by His Steadfast Trust'—Habakkuk 2:4," *Presbyterion* 9 (1983): 52–71; George J. Zemek, Jr., "Interpretive Challenges Relating to Habakkuk 2:4b," *GTJ* 1 (1980): 43–69.

[41] Koch interprets "faith" as " 'waiting for' the fulfillment of a particular prophecy" (*Prophets* 2:83).

[42] James M. Scott ("A New Approach to Habakkuk II 4–5a," *VT* 35 [1985], 330–40) rightly concludes from the *qal waḥomer* argument that Yahweh will punish all offenders, whether pagan Gentiles or apostate Judeans.

[43] Achtemeier's caution is proper: "We do not delay the Kingdom's coming; but the New Testament suggests we can hasten it (I Peter 3:12; I Cor 16:22)" (*Nahum–Malachi*, 44).

[44] For issues pertaining to chap. 3, see J. H. Eaton, "The Origin and Meaning of Habakkuk 3," *ZAW* 76 (1964): 144–71.

[45] On the significance of theophany, see von Rad, *OTT* 1:366.

[46] Walter E. Rast concludes that Habakkuk should be understood as a nascent apocalyptic eschatology ("Habakkuk and Justification by Faith," *CurTM* 10 [1983]: 169–75).

[47] See the helpful book by D. M. Lloyd-Jones, *From Fear to Faith: Studies in the Book of Habakkuk* (London: Inter Varsity, 1966).

[48] The name *Zephaniah* means "he whom Yah(weh) shelters." The superscription links him with Hezekiah's family; see Wilson (*Prophecy*, 279–80), who concludes that with the use of genealogy "the prophet placed himself solidly within the Jerusalemite royal establishment" (280). A. S. Kapelrud concludes

472

cautiously, "What is hidden in this enumeration remains hidden" (*The Message of the Prophet Zephaniah* [Oslo: Universitets Forlaget, 1975], 44).

49 Merrill, *History*, 456–57.

50 For the astral cults during Manasseh's days, see Morton Cogan, *Imperialism and Religion: Assyria, Judah and Israel in the Eighth and Seventh Centuries B.C.E.* (Missoula, Mont.: Scholars Press, 1974), 85–88.

51 Duane L. Christensen argues well in favor of Josiah's expansionist policies ("Zephaniah 2:4–15: A Theological Basis for Josiah's Program of Political Expansion," *CBQ* 46 [1984]: 669–82).

52 Kapelrud dates Zephaniah between 635 and 625 B.C. (*Zephaniah*, 42 n. 77, 115). Cogan treats Zephaniah as a reliable "eye-witness account of the cosmopolitan atmosphere in Jerusalem prior to the Josianic reforms, complementing the picture derived from extra-biblical finds" (*Imperialism and Religion*, 94).

53 Other contemporaries were Josiah (640–609 B.C.) of Judah; Ashurbanipal (668–627 B.C.) of Assyria; and Nabopolassar (625–605 B.C.) of Babylon.

54 See Kapelrud's discussion on Judah's syncretistic religion (*Zephaniah*, 78). For an evaluation of Assyrian policy and Judah's readiness to adapt to pagan cultures, including religious expressions, see Cogan, "Judah in the Orbit of Assyria," in *Imperialism and Religion*, 65–96.

55 Cogan, *Imperialism and Religion*, 96.

56 For critical issues, see Harrison, *IOT*, 940–43; Childs, *IOTS*, 458.

57 Kapelrud observes: "Zephaniah lived in the traditions of the great prophets and used them extensively. . . . Zephaniah was very moderate in his choice of images" (*Zephaniah*, 93). For literary examples, see ibid., 25.

58 G. von Rad, "The Origin of the Concept of the Day of Yahweh," *JSS* 4 (1959): 97–108; *OTT* 2:119–25. Duane L. Christensen, *Transformations of the War Oracle in Old Testament Prophecy: Studies in the Oracles Against the Nations* (Missoula, Mont.: Scholars Press, 1975), 154–63.

59 For a fuller treatment, see the section in chap. 8: "The Day of the Lord." See VanGemeren, *Progress*, 448–64.

60 Composer Thomas of Celano (ca. 1190–1260); for further discussion, see *Dictionary of Hymnology*, ed. John Julian, vol. 1 (Grand Rapids: Kregel, 1985), 295–301.

61 Michael de Roche, "Zephaniah i 2–3: The 'Sweeping' of Creation," *VT* 30 (1980): 104–9.

62 Merrill makes a good observation regarding the historical and eschatological compenetration in prophetic writing (*History*, 457).

63 For the relationship between 3:14–15 and the enthronement psalms, see A. S. Kapelrud, *Zephaniah*, 91–94.

64 There is a distinct difference in speech. He spoke to the people in the second person, and his oracles of judgment against the leaders are in the form of indirect speech.

65 Gerhard F. Hasel, *The Remnant: The History and Theology of the Remnant Idea from Genesis to Isaiah* (Berrien Springs, Mich.: Andrews University Press, 1972).

66 For a similar warning, see our Lord's teaching in Matt. 7:21–23; 25:31–33.

67The wisdom motif appears in the use of "humility" (see Prov. 15:33; 18:12; 22:4) and "fear" and "correction" (3:7; see Prov. 1:3; 8:10).

68See Kapelrud's comparison of the language of Zephaniah and Jeremiah (*Zephaniah,* 65–66). He concludes, "Both to Jeremiah and Zephaniah it was obviously significant to emphasize the importance of being guileless, without fraud and deceit. They knew what was the weakness of their own time, what they needed to attack" (66).

69Ibid., 102.

70Gowan's focus on Zion as "the center of Old Testament eschatology" presents us with a biblical emphasis on God's immediate and continuing kingship, the presence of Yahweh, and the reversal of fortune, "God's promise to make right all that has gone wrong with this world and human life, the essence of OT eschatology" (*Eschatology in the Old Testament* [Philadelphia: Fortress, 1986], 15).

71See George W. Anderson, "The Idea of the Remnant in the Book of Zephaniah," *ASTI* 11 (1977–78): 11–14.

72A preferable reading of the MT is "he will renew you with his love," supported by LXX.

73Ihromi, "Die Haufung der Verben des Jubelns in Zephanja iii 14f., 16–18: *rnn, rw', śmḥ, 'lz, śwś und gil,*" *VT* 33 (1983): 106–10.

74Von Orelli, *Old Testament Prophecy,* 326, cited by Kaiser, *TOTT,* 227.

75See W. S. Prinsloo, "Die boodskap van die Boek Habakuk," *NGTT* 20 (1979): 146–51.

76John Calvin, *Commentary on the Twelve Minor Prophets,* trans. John Owen, 4 vols. (Grand Rapids: Baker, 1979), 4:109.

Chapter 7

1On the problems pertaining to the historical reconstruction of the exilic and postexilic era, see P. R. Ackroyd, "The History of Israel in the Exilic and Post-Exilic Periods," in *Tradition and Interpretation: Essays by Members of the Society for Old Testament Study,* ed. G. W. Anderson (Oxford: Clarendon, 1979), 320–50; idem, "Faith and Its Reformulation in the Post-exilic Period," *Theology Digest* 27 (Winter 1979): 323–46.

2Usually "former prophets" designates the prophets who wrote the books Joshua through 2 Kings in the Hebrew text. The phrase "former prophets" also denotes the prophets who served the Lord in prophesying the judgment of exile (Zech. 1:4). The "former" are in contrast to "latter," the postexilic era of restoration.

3J. J. M. Roberts defines "miraculous signs" ('*ôtôt*) in Ps. 74:9 as referring to the exilic expectation of fulfillment of the prophetic word (the downfall of Babylon, the return of the temple vessels, and the inauguration of the era of restoration). The disappointment of the exilic community is an example of prophetic dissonance ("Of Signs, Prophets, and Time Limits: A Note on Ps 74:9," *CBQ* 39 [1977]: 474–81).

4See Ralph W. Klein, *Israel in Exile: A Theological Interpretation* (Philadelphia: Fortress, 1979); Merrill, *History,* 469–87; VanGemeren, *Progress,* 290–99.

5VanGemeren, *Progress,* 300–12.

[6]From the perspective of the postexilic Chronicler, the remnant consisted of all tribes, the godly remnant from the northern kingdom and the southern kingdom (H. G. M. Williamson, *Israel in the Books of Chronicles* [London: Cambridge University Press, 1977], see esp. pp. 126–40).

[7]Paul D. Hanson, "Israelite Religion in the Early Postexilic Period," in *FS Cross*, 485–508.

[8]Otto Plöger speaks of "the restoration eschatology" theology of the preexilic and early postexilic era as a *restitutio in integrum* in *Theocracy and Eschatology*, trans. S. Rudman (Richmond: John Knox, 1968), 115.

[9]Th. C. Vriezen speaks of this era as "actualizing eschatology" in "Prophecy and Eschatology," SVT 1 (1953): 227.

[10]*DOTT*, 93; Merrill, *History*, 491–93.

[11]E. Hammershaimb, "The Change in Prophecy during the Exile," in *Some Aspects of Old Testament Prophecy from Isaiah to Malachi* (Copenhagen: Rosenkilde Og Bagger, 1966), 91–112.

[12]Odil Hannes Steck, "Theological Streams of Tradition," in *Tradition and Theology in the Old Testament*, ed. Douglas A. Knight, (Philadelphia: Fortress, 1977), 207–12.

[13]Paul D. Hanson sees the development of two ideologies in the sixth century: the visionary and the realistic (*The Dawn of the Apocalyptic* [Philadelphia: Fortress, 1979], 210).

[14]Rex Mason, "The Prophets of Restoration," in *FS Ackroyd*, 145.

[15]David L. Petersen, *Late Israelite Prophecy: Studies in Deutero-Prophetic Literature and in Chronicles* (Missoula, Mont.: Scholars Press, 1977).

[16]Ibid., 97.

[17]Robert P. Carroll, *When Prophecy Failed: Cognitive Dissonance in the Prophetic Traditions of the Old Testament* (New York: Seabury, 1979).

[18]Mason, "Prophets of Restoration," 142.

[19]W. McKane writes, "They [the postexilic prophets] believed themselves to stand on the other side of the judgement which the preexilic prophets had proclaimed and that it was more comfortable than standing under that judgement" ("Prophecy and the Prophetic Literature," in *Tradition and Interpretation: Essays by Members of the Society for Old Testament Study*, ed. G. W. Anderson [Oxford: Clarendon, 1979], 187).

[20]Thomas M. Raitt, *A Theology of Exile: Judgment/Deliverance in Jeremiah and Ezekiel* (Philadelphia: Fortress, 1977), 222.

[21]Carroll, *When Prophecy Failed*, 157–83.

[22]Bruce K. Waltke, "Kingdom Promises as Spiritual," in *FS Johnson*, 284–85.

[23]Raitt, *Theology of Exile*, 220–21.

[24]I assume the fifth century dating of Ezra-Nehemiah, over against Richard J. Saley, "The Date of Nehemiah Reconsidered," in *FS LaSor*, 151–65; see also Ralph W. Klein, "Ezra and Nehemiah in Recent Studies, in *FS Wright*, 361–76.

[25]Carroll, *When Prophecy Failed*, 180–81; Kenneth Tolefson, "Nehemiah, Model for Change Agents: A Social Science Approach to Scripture," *CSR* 15 (1985): 107–24.

[26]K. Koch, "Ezra and the Origins of Judaism," *JSS* 19 (1974): 196.

[27]Wilhelm Vischer, "Nehemia, der Sonderbeauftragte und Statthalter des Königs," in *FS von Rad*, 610 (translation mine).

[28]The name *Haggai* is well-attested in the Bible and means "my feasts" or "festal." The occasion for this peculiar name is uncertain. Some conjecture that he was a priest by birth. Hanson refers to Haggai as a *hierocrat,* who had a programmatic approach to the temple cult (*Dawn of Apocalyptic,* 173–76). For a criticism, see Peter Ackroyd, "Apocalyptic in its Social Setting," *Int* 30 (1976): 412–15. His name may also express the hope for the restoration of the "feasts" (Passover, Firstfruits, Tabernacles, see 2:1).

[29]Ackroyd, "Haggai," in *Peake's Commentary on the Bible,* ed. M. Black (London: Nelson, 1962), 643–45. W. A. M. Beuken concludes to the contrary that Haggai was left in Judah and lived as a farmer during the exile in Judah (*Haggai-Sacharja 1–8* [Assen: Van Gorcum, 1967], 216–29). For an evaluation of the various views, see Pieter A. Verhoef, *The Books of Haggai and Malachi* (Grand Rapids: Eerdmans, 1987), 6–8.

[30]LaSor (*OTS,* 482) follows Richard A. Parker and Waldo H. Dubberstein in dating the oracles: oracle 1 (1:1)—August 29, 520; oracle 2 (2:1)—October 17, 520; oracle 3 (2:10)—December 18, 520; oracle 4 (2:20)—December 18, 520 (in *Babylonian Chronology 626* B.C.–A.D. *75* [Providence: Brown University Press, 1956]).

[31]On the issues raised regarding the authorship and unity, see Verhoef, *Haggai and Malachi,* 9–17.

[32]P. R. Ackroyd's "Studies in the Book of Haggai," *JSS* 2 (1951): 163–76, *JSS* 3 (1952): 1–13.

[33]Ralph L. Smith, *Micah-Malachi,* WBC (Waco, Tex.: Word, 1984), 148.

[34]R. A. Mason, "The Purpose of the 'Editorial Framework' of the Book of Haggai," *VT* 27 (1977): 413–21.

[35]Beuken, *Haggai-Sacharja 1–8,* 43.

[36]J. William Whedbee properly reinstates Haggai as a major-minor prophet, whose message is in continuity with the prophetic tradition ("A Question-Answer Schema in Haggai 1: The Form and Function of Haggai 1:9–11," in *FS LaSor,* 184–94).

[37]See Mason, "The Purpose of the 'Editorial Framework,'" 417–19.

[38]Beuken, *Haggai-Sacharja 1–8,* 57–58; Willem A. VanGemeren, "The Spirit of Restoration," *WTJ* 50 (1988): 81–102.

[39]Ibid., 33, 41.

[40]See Mason's discussion of Haggai's theological outlook. He writes that the "present fulfillment of Haggai's preaching did not exclude a greater, future hope. . . . the future outcome could be awaited with confidence and hope because of the fulfillment of them they were already experiencing in the present" ("The Purpose of the 'Editorial Framework,'" 421).

[41]Hanson, *Dawn of Apocalyptic,* 245–46.

[42]The "desired" cannot signify Jesus as "the desire of the nations" or the elect of the nations. The context clarifies that the Lord uses the material resources of the nations; see Herbert Wolf, "'The Desire of All Nations' in Haggai 2:7: Messianic or Not?" *JETS* 19 (1976): 97–102; Gerhard von Rad, *The Message of the Prophets,* trans. D. M. G. Stalker (New York: Harper & Row, 1965), 250.

[43]John A. Kessler, "The Shaking of the Nations: An Eschatological View," *JETS* 30 (1987): 159–66.

[44]Verhoef, Haggai and Malachi, 148–50.

[45] According to Ezra 4:24–6:15, Zerubbabel is the same as Sheshbazzar; see J. Lust, "The Identification of Zerubbabel with Sheshbazzar," *ETL* 63 (1987): 90–95.

[46] B. B. Warfield, "On the Post-Exilian Portion of Our Lord's Genealogy," *The Presbyterian Review* 2 (1881): 388–97.

[47] William J. Dumbrell is correct in his emphasis on the temple, but he suppresses the eschatological significance of Zerubbabel as a descendant of David (*The End of the Beginning: Revelation 21–22 and the Old Testament* [Grand Rapids: Baker, 1985], 60–61).

[48] Beuken (*Haggai–Sacharja 1–8*, 61–62) concludes that the expectation of peace associated with the temple and the Davidic dynasty was as yet fully alive. David L. Petersen stresses that Zerubbabel was a royal participant in the ritual of the rededication of the temple ("Zerubbabel and Jerusalem Temple Reconstruction," *CBQ* 36 [1974]: 366–72). Paul D. Hanson connects the royal-Zion theology tradition of the preexilic era with Haggai ("Israelite Religion in the Early Postexilic Period," in *FS Cross*, 493–96).

[49] Craigie, *Old Testament*, 202. However, Haggai was not a political activist, as P. F. Bloomhardt argued ("The Poems of Haggai," *HUCA* 5 [1928]: 153–95).

[50] G. von Rad speaks of an imminent establishment of God's kingdom (*The Message*, 247); Joachim Becker views the shift from monarchy to the people as a collective interpretation of the monarchic privilege (*Messianic Expectation in the Old Testament*, trans. David E. Green [Philadelphia: Fortress, 1980], 68–78).

[51] See Elizabeth Achtemeier's good survey of these motifs (*Nahum–Malachi*, *Interpretation* [Atlanta: John Knox, 1986], 96–98).

[52] Mason correlates the present fulfillment with the eschatological hope in Haggai's ministry ("Prophets of Restoration," 142–44).

[53] *Zechariah* means "Yah(weh) remembers." It was a popular name of some thirty different people (T. M. Mauch, "Zechariah," *IDB* 4:941–43). But David L. Petersen has put it well that the name Zechariah "resonates with his task" (*Haggai and Zechariah 1–8: A Commentary*, OTL [Philadelphia: Westminster, 1984], 110).

[54] On the problem of Berachiah, son of Iddo, see Smith, *Micah–Malachi*, 167–68; Wilson, *Prophecy*, 130–31, 288–89.

[55] Jerome, cited by Smith, *Micah–Malachi*, 166–67.

[56] Baldwin cites Saint Jerome in *Haggai, Zechariah, Malachi*, TOTC (Downers Grove, Ill.: InterVarsity Press, 1972), 59.

[57] G. E. Ladd, "Why Not Prophetic-Apocalyptic?" *JBL* 76 (1957): 192–200. It is not apocalyptic in the same sense as defined by D. S. Russell (*The Method and Message of Jewish Apocalyptic* [Philadelphia: Westminster, 1964]), but it is in that of Paul Hanson (*Dawn of Apocalyptic*, 251, see 240–62). According to Hanson, apocalyptic is a development of the prophetic, out of which apocalyptic eschatology arose. Apocalyptic eschatology denotes a genre of writing reflecting a religious perspective in which the tensions of the present and the future and of the real and the supernatural are resolved in favor of the future and the supernatural (see also his *Diversity of Scripture* [Philadelphia: Fortress, 1982], 37–62). Zechariah reveals the continuity between the prophetic and the apocalyptic, a stage that led to the apocalyptic movement of the second century B.C. For a discussion on apocalyptic, see the appendix of this book. Carroll

disagrees with Hanson and argues that apocalyptic arose because of the dissonance arising from lack of fulfillment (*When Prophecy Failed,* 204–13). For the complex issues pertaining to apocalyptic, see Smith, *Micah–Malachi,* 173–75. For a small study of apocalypticism, see Leon Morris, *Apocalyptic* (Grand Rapids: Eerdmans, 1972); Samuel Amsler, "Zacharie et l'origine de l'Apocalyptique," SVT 22 (1972): 227–31.

[58] Dumbrell, *The End of the Beginning,* 61–63.

[59] For a summary of critical opinion, see Smith, *Micah–Malachi,* 170–73; Baldwin, *Haggai, Zechariah, Malachi,* 63–66; Harrison, *IOT,* 950–56; LaSor, *OTS* 491–93; Childs, *IOTS,* 474–76.

[60] Most recently Stephen L. Portnoy and David L. Petersen, "Biblical Texts and Statistical Analysis: Zechariah and Beyond," *JBL* 103 (1984): 11–21.

[61] See Baldwin, *Haggai, Zechariah, Malachi,* 78–79; P. Lamarche, *Zacharie i–xiv: Structure, littéraire et messianisme* (Paris: Gabalda, 1961).

[62] See Walter Harrelson's critique of Lamarche in the book review section of *JBL* 82 (1963): 116–17. But Andrew E. Hill gives a linguistic analysis of Zech. 10–14 and dates these chapters to 515–475 B.C. ("Dating Second Zechariah: A Linguistic Re-examination," *HAR* 6 [1982]: 105–34).

[63] Childs, *IOTS,* 482–85.

[64] Lamarche, *Zacharie,* 8–9.

[65] For similarities between Haggai and Zechariah, see Mason, "Prophets of Restoration," 146–49.

[66] Beuken (*Haggai–Sacharja 1–8,* 90) relates 1:3–6 to 2 Chron. 30:6–9.

[67] Hanson, *Dawn of the Apocalyptic,* 249.

[68] See the intriguing study by David L. Petersen, "Zechariah's Visions: A Theological Perspective," *VT* 34 (1984): 195–206.

[69] See Petersen on the nature of prophetic visions (*Haggai and Zechariah 1–8,* 111–20).

[70] For the significance of Zerubbabel as a messianic type, see the discussion in Haggai in this chapter.

[71] For a study on the appearance of the lampstand of the *kernos* type, see Robert North, "Zechariah's Seven-Spout Lampstand," *Bib* 51 (1970): 183–206.

[72] For the correlation of Spirit and the olive trees, see Kenneth A. Strand, "The Two Olive Trees of Zechariah 4 and Revelation 11," *AUSS* 20 (1982): 257–61.

[73] G. von Rad observes that "the 'now' is characteristic of the realism" of Haggai and Zechariah about redemptive history: "The time of adversity is at an end, and blessing . . . will begin immediately . . . and has indeed begun already" (*OTT* 2:286; see Hag. 2:15–19; Zech. 8:10–12). Similarly Beuken, *Haggai–Sacharja 1–8,* 163.

[74] Zech. 9–10 presents Yahweh as the Divine Warrior. For a literary analysis, see Hanson, *Dawn of Apocalyptic,* 292–334.

[75] Hanson's analysis of Zech. 9–14 is novel and creative, but assumes that a rift had emerged between the visionary and the temple-oriented Jews early in the postexilic era, that these chapters came from another tradition than that of Zech. 1–8, and that the visionary tradition producing these chapters was close in theology to Isa. 60–62 (*Dawn of Apocalyptic,* 286–401).

[76] Carroll Stuhlmacher, "Justice Toward the Poor," *TBT* 24 (1986): 385–90.

[77] Baruch Halpern argues for the integral connection between the night visions and the temple reconstruction in "The Ritual Background of Zechariah's Temple Song," *CBQ* 40 (1978): 167–90.

[78] The gospel writers were intrigued by the prophecy of Zechariah. The early church read Zechariah with the suffering of Jesus in mind, since the gospel accounts had already made the connection between Old and New. Twenty-seven out of the seventy-one quotations of Zechariah occur in the Gospels, fourteen of which are in Matthew alone! Moreover, the book of Revelation draws heavily from Zechariah. Out of the seventy-one references to Zechariah, forty-one appear in Revelation. For a treatment on the Messiah in Zechariah, see Smith, *Micah–Malachi,* 175–81.

[79] See Matt. 21:5; John 12:15.

[80] For the connection between Zech. 9–14 and the New Testament understanding of our Lord's suffering, see F. F. Bruce, "The Book of Zechariah and the Passion Narrative," *BJRL* 43 (1960–61): 336–53; idem, "The Shepherd King," in *The New Testament Development of Old Testament Themes* (Grand Rapids: Eerdmans, 1968), 100–114; Hubert Cunliffe-Jones, *A Word for Our Time? Zechariah 9–14, the New Testament and Today* (London: Athlone, 1973).

[81] Kaiser writes, "Then history and the first aspect of the grand plan of God's salvific promise would be wrapped up in the most decisive triumph ever witnessed" (*TOTT,* 256).

[82] Some have speculated as to whether or not it is intended as a proper name. The Hebrew word may also be rendered as "my messenger" (2:7; Hag. 1:13; LXX, "his messenger"). The Targum of Jonathan ben Uzziel includes the explanatory gloss, "whose name is Ezra the scribe." Jerome observed that the Jews of his day ascribed the book to Ezra. This prophecy has also been attributed to Nehemiah and Zerubbabel.

[83] For critical issues, see Harrison, *IOT,* 960–61; Childs, *IOTS,* 489–90.

[84] Ackroyd, *Exile and Restoration,* 231.

[85] I disagree with the redating of Nehemiah to the fourth century as proposed by Richard J. Saley in "The Date of Nehemiah Reconsidered," 151–65.

[86] For the background, see Merrill, *History,* 497–515.

[87] See the intriguing article by W. J. Dumbrell, "Malachi and the Ezra-Nehemiah Reforms," *RTR* 35 (1976): 42–52.

[88] See the excellent treatise by Adrian Graffy, *A Prophet Confronts His People: The Disputation Speech in the Prophets,* Analecta Biblica 104 (Rome: Biblical Institute Press, 1984). He excludes Malachi's disputation speeches as a later variant of the original, short-lived disputation speeches, in agreement with E. Pfeiffer, "Die Disputationsworte im Buche Malachi. Ein Beitrag zur formgeschichtlichen Struktur," 19 (1959): 546–68, and Hans Jochen Boecker, "Bemerkungen zur formgeschichtlichen Terminologie des Buches Maleachi," *ZAW* 78 (1966): 78–80; contra James A. Fischer, "Notes on the Literary Form and Message of Malachi," *CBQ* 34 (1972): 315–20.

[89] Baldwin writes, "Malachi does not employ any particular literary structure in order to convey his meaning" (*Haggai, Zechariah, Malachi,* 214).

[90] This designation is most frequent in the postexilic prophets: in Haggai fourteen times, in Zechariah fifty-three times, in Malachi twenty-four times. T. N. D. Mettinger explains that with the return to Jerusalem the exiles brought

together the royal and Zion theologies and that the frequent correlation of Zerubbabel and Jeshua, Lord of Hosts and the temple reflects the consolidation of the traditions (*The Dethronement of Sabaoth: Studies in the Shem and Kabod Theologies* [Lund: Gleerup, 1982], see esp. 134). I disagree with his methodology but do not dispute the evidence of the correlation of motifs in the postexilic literature. See also J. L. Crenshaw, "*YHWH Sᵉbāʾot Sᵉmô*: A Form-Critical Analysis," *ZAW* 81 (1969): 156–75; Otto Eissfeldt, "Jahwe Zebaoth," in *Kleine Scriften,* ed. Rudolf Sellheim and Fritz Maas (Tübingen: Mohr, 1966), 3:103–23; Tryggve N. D. Mettinger, "YHWH Sabaoth—The Heavenly King on the Cherubim Throne," in *Studies in the Period of David and Solomon and Other Essays,* papers read at the International Symposium for Biblical Studies, December 1979, ed. Tomoo Ishida (Winona Lake, Ind.: Eisenbrauns, 1979), 109–38; B. N. Wambacq, *L'Epithète divine Yahvé Sébaoth* (1947); *THAT* 2:498–507; *TWOT* 2:750–51.

[91] The MT has no finite verbs, and meaning must be contextually determined. I favor the view that the Jews of the Diaspora together with the God-fearers were the object of God's commendation. It is as if God is saying to the Jews in Judea: Close the doors of the temple, because I do not need your offerings. I get the worship and honor due to me from elsewhere, i.e., "from the rising to the setting of the sun." See J. Swetnam, "Malachi 1:11: An Interpretation," *CBQ* 31 (1969): 200–209. In favor of a futuristic interpretation, see Baldwin, *Haggai, Zechariah, Malachi,* 228; so also T. C. Vriezen, "How to Understand Malachi 1:11," in *Grace upon Grace,* ed. James I. Cook (Grand Rapids: Eerdmans, 1975), 128–36.

[92] Walter C. Kaiser, Jr., *Malachi: God's Unchanging Love* (Grand Rapids: Baker, 1984), 47. For a treatment of the various exegetical options, see P. A. Verhoef, "Some Notes on Malachi 1:11," *NGTT* 21 (1980): 21–30.

[93] H. J. Boecker, "Bemerkungen zur formgeschichtlichen Terminologie des Buches Maleachi."

[94] S. D. Snyman correctly places the emphasis on Yahweh's *love* in "Haat Jahwe vir Esau ('n Verkenning van Mal. 1:3a)" *NGTT* 25 (1984): 358–62.

[95] Steven L. McKenzie and Howard N. Wallace, "Covenant Themes in Malachi," *CBQ* 45 (1983): 549–63.

[96] Verhoef, *Haggai and Malachi,* 277, 280–81.

[97] I agree with Verhoef that tithing should *not* be continued in the present age. He writes, "In connection with 'tithing' it must be clear that it belonged, in conjunction with the whole system of giving and offering, to the dispensation of shadows, and that it therefore has lost its significance as an obligation of giving under the new dispensation. . . . We are but stewards who will have to give an account of all we possess" (ibid., 311).

[98] I question the validity of the conclusion of many exegetes that Yahweh accepts the sincere Gentile worship of idols (Bruce V. Malchow, "The Prophetic Contribution to Dialogue," *BTB* 16 [1986]: 130).

[99] Verhoef interprets 4:5 as follows: "When Elijah comes he will restore the covenant relationship. . . . Fathers and children will not meet one another on the temporary or personal plane, . . . the scope of the encounter, in this process of turning to one another is the covenant relationship, . . . which forms the real basis for the restored communion with God, their Father and Creator (1:2;

2:10), and with one another" (*Haggai and Malachi,* 342–43). See also Walter C. Kaiser, Jr., "The Promise of the Arrival of Elijah in Malachi and the Gospels," *GTJ* 3 (1982): 221–33; see Dumbrell, "Malachi and the Ezra-Nehemiah Reforms," 42–52; A. Wiener, *The Prophet Elijah and the Development of Judaism: A Depth Psychological Study* (London: Kegan Paul, 1978).

[100] For the significance of *sᵉgullâ* in the Old Testament, see W. A. VanGemeren, *Progress,* 147–48; see Moshe Greenberg, "Hebrew *sᵉgullâ:* Akkadian *sikiltu,*" *JAOS* 71 (1951): 172–74.

[101] I appreciate Verhoef's approach to this difficult passage (3:13–4:3), as he comments, "The specific application of a prophecy can only be discerned in the various stages of fulfillment," including Christ's first coming and his coming again (*Haggai and Malachi,* 325).

[102] G. von Rad is right in observing that Malachi "gives less of a broad exposition of eschatological ideas than any other prophet" (*The Message,* 255). Malachi's concern lies with application in view of the eschaton rather than with the eschaton as a separate doctrine.

[103] See the implicit criticism of Hanson by Mason: "Malachi not only thus reveals a concern for the holding together of the external and internal, . . . but also holds together concern for the cultic needs of the present theocratic community and lively eschatological hope for the future. The too-absolute distinction drawn by some between 'theocratic' and 'eschatological' in postexilic Judaism is due for considerable revision" ("Prophets of Restoration," 151).

[104] Wilson posits different criteria: concern for prophetic authority and polemics with conflicting factions (*Prophecy,* 290–92).

[105] Robert F. Carroll posits that "hermeneutics" is an attempt at explaining the disparity arising out of the prediction, the nature of fulfillment, and the expectation of fulfillment (*When Prophecy Failed,* 124–28). I disagree with Carroll's exclusive use of the anthropological approach to the phenomenon of prophetism. He reveals an insufficient regard for the progressive unfolding of God's plan, for the theocentric place of the prophet, for the canonical function of God's Word in the community of faith, and for the place of the Spirit. For a salutary warning on the danger and possibility of the use of social sciences in biblical interpretation, see Bruce J. Malina, "The Social Sciences and Biblical Interpretation," *Int* 36 (1982): 229–42.

[106] William J. Dumbrell concludes, "Haggai and Zechariah are endeavors to implement the platform of Ezekiel, while Chronicles, Ezra and Nehemiah are, in their own way, attempts to realise the theology of the New Covenant expectation" (*CCOTT,* 199). The weakness of Dumbrell's argument lies in his unwillingness to recognize the significant progress of redemption and fulfillment in the postexilic era (see 201–6). Similarly, in *The End of the Beginning,* 101–3, 149–51.

[107] Beuken, *Haggai–Sacharja 1–8,* 171. See Plöger, *Theocracy and Eschatology,* 93–94.

[108] Baldwin, *Haggai, Zechariah, Malachi,* 33; the books of Chronicles present us with a reconstruction of preexilic era from the perspective of "realized eschatology" according to Hanson, *Dawn of Apocalyptic,* 278.

[109] Plöger, *Theocracy and Eschatology,* 106–17.

[110] Hanson, *Dawn of Apocalyptic,* 245–46; see also Otto Plöger, *Theocracy*

and Eschatology, 106–17. However, he is mistaken in the too-radical separation between the theocratic concerns of the postexilic prophets and the eschatological dimension of hope (see Mason, "Prophets of Restoration," 137–54; Michael A. Knibb, "Prophecy and the Emergence of Jewish Apocalypses," in *FS Ackroyd,* 155–80).

111 Mason, "Prophets of Restoration," 152.

112 Ackroyd, *Exile and Restoration,* 170.

113 Kaiser, *TOTT,* 252–53 (emphasis mine).

114 In this light the prophecy of Joel could be read as a postexilic writing in which the prophet focuses on the Spirit of God as *the* sign of God's presence with his people, even when he is judging the nations. See the treatment of Joel and the Spirit of restoration in chap. 4.

Chapter 8

1 See chap. 1: "Elijah: the Message of the Classical Prophets" and chap. 2: "The Prophetic Message."

2 See chap. 1: "Revelation and Religion."

3 See chap. 3: "Prophecy and Eschatology."

4 VanGemeren, *Progress,* 448–60.

5 S. Mowinckel, *Psalmenstudien,* 2 vols. (Amsterdam: Schippers, 1961), 2:229; *He That Cometh,* trans. G. W. Anderson (Nashville: Abingdon, 1956), 132–33.

6 G. von Rad, "The Origin of the Concept of the Day of Yahweh," *JSS* 4 (1959): 97–108. See also Frank Cross, "The Divine Warrior in Israel's Early Cult," in *Biblical Motifs,* ed. A. Altmann (Cambridge: Harvard University Press, 1966), 11–30; A. Joseph Everson, "The Days of Yahweh," *JBL* 93 (1974): 329–37. Everson concludes that eighteen texts have specific reference to the Day of the Lord, that the Day of the Lord may be past, present, and future, that five texts relate to past events, and that the prophetic tradition uses the Day of the Lord to interpret the realities of war—the memories of war or the anticipation of new occasions of war" (336). See also Gwilym H. Jones, " 'Holy War' or 'Yahweh War'?" *VT* 25 (1975): 642–58; P. C. Craigie, "Yahweh Is a Man of Wars," *SJT* 22 (1969): 183–88.

7 Von Rad, *OTT* 2:124.

8 F. Charles Fensham, "A Possible Origin of the Concept of the Day of the Lord," in *Biblical Essays* (Bepeck: Potschefstroom Herald, 1966), 90–97.

9 Meir Weiss, "The Origin of the 'Day of the Lord'—Reconsidered," HUCA 37 (1966): 29–60.

10 Ibid., 60.

11 Yair Hoffmann, "The Day of the Lord as a Concept and a Term in the Prophetic Literature," *ZAW* 93 (1981): 37–50.

12 See C. van Leeuwen, "The Prophecy of the *Yôm YHWH* in Amos V 18–20," *OTS* 19 (1974): 113–34.

13 See Martin J. Buss, *The Prophetic Word of Hosea: A Morphological Study,* BZAW 111 (Berlin: Töpelmann, 1969), 93–95.

14 See the brief analysis by A. Kapelrud, *The Message of the Prophet Zephaniah: Morphology and Ideas* (Oslo: Universitetsfor laget, 1975), 61–64, 80–87.

15 Hoffmann associates theophany and slaughter (see Isa. 13; Joel 3; Zeph. 1;

in "The Day of the Lord," 44–45). Tryggve N. D. Mettinger speaks of the divine epiphany in "Fighting the Powers of Chaos and Hell—Towards the Biblical Portrait of God," *ST* 39 (1985): 32–33. John Gray relates the Day of the Lord to Yahweh's epiphany at the autumn festival ("The Day of the Lord in Cultic Experience and Eschatological Prospect," *SEÅ* 39 [1974]: 5–37).

[16] Kapelrud observes that the emphasis on universality distinguishes the message of Zephaniah from that of other prophets (*Zephaniah,* 85–86).

[17] For example, Midian's defeat (Isa. 9:4) and Jerusalem's fall (Ezek. 13:5).

[18] Josef Scharbert, "Das Verbum PQD in der Theologie des Alten Testaments," in *Um das Prinzip der Vergeltung in Religion und Recht des Alten Testaments,* ed. Klaus Koch (Darmstadt: Wissenschaftliche Buchgesellschaft, 1972), 278–99; idem, = *Biblische Zeitschrift,* Neue Folge 4 (1960): 209–26.

[19] Underlying this concept is the doctrine of retribution. Koch has argued that the prophets teach a poetic justice (that is, actions have built-in consequences) and that sin will find out the sinner ("Is There a Doctrine of Retribution in the Old Testament?" in *Theodicy in the Old Testament,* ed. James L. Crenshaw [Philadelphia: Fortress, 1983], 57–87; for a criticism of his position, see John Barton, "Natural Law and Poetic Justice in the Old Testament," *JTS* 30 [1979]: 1–14). J. Barton and Patrick D. Miller agree that the prophets proclaimed a poetic justice in which Yahweh decrees and executes the judgment of sin through human or natural agencies (Miller, *Sin and Judgment in the Prophets: A Stylistic and Theological Analysis* [Chico: Scholars Press, 1982]; Barton, "Natural Law and Poetic Justice," 1–14). Yet Miller concludes, "There remains a mystery to this interaction of divine act and human agency behind which one cannot go, but its reality and centrality for the prophetic are always assumed" (ibid., 139).

[20] Samuel E. Loewenstamm, "The Trembling of Nature during the Theophany," in *Comparative Studies in Biblical and Ancient Oriental Literatures* (Neukirchen-Vluyn: Neukirchener, 1980), 173–89; Jörg Jeremias, *Theophanie: Die Geschichte einer alttestamentlichen Gattung* (Neukirchen-Vluyn: Neukirchener, 1977).

[21] See Kirsten Nielsen, *Yahweh as Prosecutor and Judge: An Investigation of the Prophetic Lawsuit (Rîb-Pattern),* JSOTSS 9 (Sheffield: JSOT, 1978).

[22] See Peter C. Craigie, *The Problem of War in the Old Testament* (Grand Rapids: Eerdmans, 1978); Frank Moore Cross, Jr., "The Divine Warrior in Israel's Early Cult," in *Biblical Motifs: Origins and Transformations,* ed. A. Altmann (Cambridge: Harvard University Press, 1966), 11–30; P. D. Miller, Jr., "El the Warrior," *HTR* 60 (1967): 411–431; idem, *The Divine Warrior in Early Israel* (Cambridge: Harvard University Press, 1973); Marvin E. Tate, "War and Peacemaking in the Old Testament," *RevExp* 79 (1982): 587–96; Moshe Weinfeld, "Divine Intervention in Ancient Israel and in the Ancient Near East," in *History, Historiography and Interpretation: Studies in Biblical and Cuneiform Literatures,* ed. H. Tadmor and M. Weinfeld (Leiden: Brill, 1984), 121–47; *TDOT* 2:373–77; *THAT* 1:398–402, 2:221–24, 538–43; *TWOT* 1:148–49, 169; 2:627, 652, 756, 761, 771, 871.

[23] For the wrath of God, see Samuel E. Balentine, *The Hidden God: The Hiding of the Face of God in the Old Testament* (Oxford: Oxford University Press, 1983); J. Gray, "The Wrath of God in Canaanite and Hebrew Literature,"

Journal of the Manchester University Egyptian and Oriental Society 25 (1947–53): 9–19; L. Morris, "The Wrath of God," *ExpT* 63 (1951–52): 142–45; R. V. G. Tasker, *The Biblical Doctrine of the Wrath of God* (London: Tyndale, 1951); Claus Westermann, "Boten des Zorns," in *Erträge der Forschung am Alten Testament* (Munich: Kaiser, 1984), 3:96–106; *TDNT* 5:392–418; *TDOT* 1:348–60; 3:106–11, 462–65; *THAT* 1:220–24, 581–83, 634–35, 838–42; 2:206–7, 432–60, 663–66; *TWOT* 1:58, 247, 322, 374–75, 451; 2:643–44; 808–9.

[24]David Hill, *Greek Words and Hebrew Meanings* (London: Cambridge University Press, 1967); Leon Morris, "The Idea of Redemption in the Old Testament," *RTR* 11 (1952): 94–102; Hans Heinrich Schmid, "Creation, Righteousness, and Salvation: 'Creation Theology' as a Broad Horizon of Biblical Theology," in *Creation in the Old Testament,* ed. Bernard W. Anderson (Philadelphia: Fortress, 1984), 102–17; *THAT* 785–90; *TDOT* 2:350–55; *y-š-ʿ* 3:1035–59; 4:436–41; *TWOT* 1:414–16.

[25]Thomas M. Raitt, *A Theology of Exile: Judgment/Deliverance in Jeremiah and Ezekiel* (Philadelphia: Fortress, 1977), 175–84.

[26]Weinfeld, "The Day of the Lord: Aspirations for the Kingdom of God in the Bible and Jewish Liturgy," 358–66.

[27]These events are to be interpreted as intrusive of the eschatological concept. The prophets predicted that they would happen. However, I disagree with Everson, according to whom the prophets interpreted *past* events as examples of the Day of the Lord ("The Days," 336–37).

[28]For a discussion of dissonance, see chap. 2.

[29]The only clear exception is Ezek. 13:5. For a possible explanation, see Hoffmann, "The Day of the Lord," 46, 47.

[30]Buss, *The Prophetic Word,* 132.

[31]Kapelrud, *Zephaniah,* 101–2.

[32]Raitt, *Theology of Exile,* 101.

[33]Ibid., 215.

[34]On the kingdom of God, see John Bright, *The Kingdom of God* (Nashville: Abingdon, 1953); John Gray, *The Biblical Doctrine of the Reign of God* (Edinburgh: T. & T. Clark, 1979); R. H. Hiers, "Kingdom of God," *IDBS,* 516 (up-to-date bibliography); H. Ridderbos, *The Coming of the Kingdom* (Philadelphia: Presbyterian & Reformed, 1976); Gary V. Smith, "The Concept of God/the Gods as Kings in the Ancient Near East and the Bible," *TrinJ* 3 (1982): 18–38; M. Tsevat, "King, God as," *IDBS,* 515–16; W. A. VanGemeren, "Kingship," *EDB,* forthcoming; idem, *Progress,* 460–64; *THAT* 1:908–19; *TWOT* 1:507–9.

[35]John Calvin, *Commentaries on the Book of the Prophet Jeremiah and the Lamentations* (Grand Rapids: Baker, 1979), 4:82. See also Bruce K. Waltke, "Kingdom Promises as Spiritual," in *FS Johnson,* 263–87, and from a different vantage point, Walter C. Kaiser, Jr., "Kingdom Promises as Spiritual and National," in *FS Johnson,* 289–307.

[36]John Gray, "The Kingship of God in the Prophets and Psalms," *VT* 11 (1961): 1–29; Walter Harrelson, "Nonroyal Motifs in the Royal Eschatology [Is 8, 23–9, 6; 11, 1–9; Mi 4, 14–5, 4; Sach 9, 9s]," in *FS Muilenburg,* 147–65.

[37]Wolff writes, "So we live at the same time between the covenants, or better: in the first stages of the renewal of the new covenant" ("Was ist das Neue

im neuen Bund?" in *Prophetische Alternativen: Entdeckungen des Neuen im Alten Testament* [Munich: Kaiser, 1982], 63 [translation mine]).

38There is no knowledge of God without devotion to him. The Hebrew root *y-d-'* ("know") signifies "commitment," see JPS: "devoted" and "obedient." Regrettably the NIV renders this form by "acknowledge" and "acknowledgment" (resp.).

39John Calvin was very sensitive to the principle of accommodation: "They [the prophets] describe the kingdom of Christ in a way suitable to the comprehension of a rude people, and hence they set before them external images; for when Christ's kingdom is the subject, mention is made of gold, of silver, of every kind of wealth, and also of great splendour and of great power, for we know that what is beyond and above the world cannot be immediately comprehended by the human mind" (*Commentaries on the Book of the Prophet Jeremiah and the Lamentations,* 4:82).

40See Willis Judson Beecher, *The Prophets and the Promise* (1905; reprint, Grand Rapids: Baker, 1963), 241–62, 365–86; J. Jocz, "Messiah," *ZPEB* 4:198–207; Walter C. Kaiser, Jr., *TOTT,* 152–64; idem, "The Davidic Promise and the Inclusion of the Gentiles (Amos 9:9–15 and Acts 15:13–18): A Test Passage for Theological Systems," *JETS* 20 (1977): 97–111; idem, "The Blessing of David: The Charter for Humanity," in *FS Allis,* 310–18; idem, "Messianic Prophecies in the Old Testament," in *Dreams, Visions and Oracles: The Layman's Guide to Biblical Prophecy,* ed. Carl Edwin Armerding and W. Ward Gasque (Grand Rapids: Baker, 1977), 75–88; idem, *Toward Rediscovering the Old Testament* (Grand Rapids: Zondervan, 1987), 101–20. See also Joachim Becker, *Messianic Expectation in the Old Testament,* trans. David E. Green (Philadelphia: Fortress, 1980); R. E. Clements, "Messianic Prophecy or Messianic History," *HBT* 1 (1979): 87–104; Gerhard von Rad, OTT, 1:306–54; Timo Veijola, *Verheissung in der Krise: Studien zur Literatur und Theologie der Exilszeit an hand des 89. Psalms* (Helsinki: Suomalainen Tiedeakatemia, 1982); Keith K. Whitelam, *The Just King: Monarchical Judicial Authority,* JSOTSS 12 (Sheffield: JSOT, 1979); Walther Zimmerli, "The Hope of Israel and the Hope of the World," in *The Old Testament and the World,* trans. John J. Scullion (Atlanta: John Knox, 1976), 122–50; idem, *Old Testament Theology in Outline,* trans. David E. Green (Atlanta: John Knox, 1978), 86–93. *TDOT* 9:496–509; *THAT* 1:907–20; *TWOT* 1:530–31.

41See M. Weinfeld, "The Covenant Grant in the OT and in the Ancient Near East," *JAOS* 90 (1970): 184–203.

42For the ideal of monarchy, see Keith K. Whitelam, *The Just King: Monarchical Judicial Authority.* M. Tsevat, "Studies in the Book of Samuel III. The Steadfast House: What was David promised in II Samuel 7:11b–16?" *HUCA* 34 (1963): 71–82.

43VanGemeren, *Progress,* 347–55, 460–64.

44The same holds true in the New Testament. Luke identifies the "kingdom" with "salvation" in order not to restrict its meaning to that of a political ideology or to raise unnecessary issues in the Roman Empire (see Baarlink, *Vrede op Aarde: de Messiaanse Vrede in bijbels Perspectief* [Kampen: Kok, 1985]). Similarly, Luke's use of "restoration" in Acts (see Ladd, *TNT,* 332–33).

45For a fine summary of Jesus' teaching on the kingdom, see Anthony A.

Hoekema, *The Bible and the Future* (Grand Rapids: Eerdmans, 1979), 41–54. He defines the kingdom as "the reign of God dynamically active in human history through Jesus Christ, the purpose of which is the redemption of his people from sin and from demonic powers, and the final establishment of the new heavens and the new earth" (45).

[46]VanGemeren, *Progress,* 458–60.

[47]On the correlation of the Spirit and eschatology, see Hoekema, *The Bible and the Future,* 55–67; Willem A. VanGemeren, "The Spirit of Restoration," *WTJ* 50 (1988): 81–102.

[48]Likened to the sand on the seashore (Gen. 22:17; see 1 Kings 4:20) or the dust of the earth (Gen. 13:16; 28:14; see Num. 23:10; 2 Chron. 1:9) or the stars of the sky (15:5; 22:17).

[49]Robertson correctly argues for the continuity and relevance of the Mosaic covenant in the present age (*The Christ of the Covenants* [Grand Rapids: Baker, 1980], 175–99).

[50]The Mosaic covenant cannot be defined as "an externalized summation of God's will," as Robertson does (ibid., 173).

[51]W. Zimmerli, *The Law and the Prophets: A Study of the Meaning of the Old Testament,* trans. R. E. Clements (New York: Harper & Row, 1965), 93.

[52]VanGemeren, *Progress,* 456–58.

[53]See Isa. 6:10; 30:26; 57:19.

[54]VanGemeren, *Progress,* 295–312.

[55]On Zion, see Donald E. Gowan, *Eschatology in the Old Testament* (Philadelphia: Fortress, 1986); John H. Hayes, "The Traditions of Zion's Inviolability," *JBL* 82 (1963): 419–26; Jon D. Levenson, *Sinai and Zion: An Entry into the Jewish Bible* (Minneapolis: Winston Press, 1985); Bennie Charles Ollenburger, "Zion, the City of the Great King: A Theological Investigation of Zion Symbolism in the Tradition of the Jerusalem Cult" (Ph.D. diss., Princeton Theological Seminary, 1982); J. J. M. Roberts, "The Davidic Origin of the Zion Tradition," *JBL* 92 (1973): 329–44; idem, "Zion Tradition," *IDBS,* 985–87; Gunther Wanke, *Die Zionstheologie der Korachiten in ihrem Traditionsgeschichtlichen Zusammenhang* (Berlin: Töpelmann, 1966); *TDNT* 7:292–338; *THAT* 2:498–506; *TWOT* 764–65.

[56]H. G. M. Williamson writes, "We conclude, therefore, that the Chronicler . . . achieved this by demonstrating from the history of the divided monarchy that a faithful nucleus does not exclude others, but is a representative centre to which all the children of Israel may be welcomed if they return" (*Israel in the Books of Chronicles* [London: Cambridge University Press, 1977], 140).

[57]Gerhard Hasel, *The Remnant: The History and Theology of the Remnant Idea from Genesis to Isaiah* (Berrien Springs, Mich.: Andrews University Press, 1972), 393–94.

[58]W. C. Kaiser, Jr., "The Blessing of David," 298–318.

[59]W. C. Kaiser, Jr., "The Davidic Promise and the Inclusion of the Gentiles," 103.

[60]See Kaiser's fine argument in which he correlates the inclusion of the Gentiles with the Spirit, new covenant, and the church (ibid., 104).

[61]See also O. Palmer Robertson, "Hermeneutics of Continuity," in *FS Johnson,* 89–108.

62 Ollenburger, "Zion, the City of the Great King," 286–94.

Chapter 9

1 Claude J. Peifer, "Isaiah, Man of Jerusalem," *TBT* 92 (1977): 1350–57.

2 Roland de Vaux, "Jerusalem and the Prophets," in *Interpreting the Prophetic Tradition,* ed. Harry M. Orlinsky (New York: Ktav, 1969), 275–300.

3 For a historical background, see Merrill, *History,* 393–420.

4 Ibid., 375–77.

5 Ibid., 405–7.

6 For a detailed study on Assyria, Israel, and Judah, see Morton Cogan, *Imperialism and Religion: Assyria, Judah and Israel in the Eighth and Seventh Centuries B.C.E.* (Missoula, Mont.: Scholars Press, 1974).

7 Merrill, *History,* 409–20.

8 Ibid., 412–13.

9 Ibid., 413–16.

10 *DOTT,* 67.

11 Brevard S. Childs, *Isaiah and the Assyrian Crisis,* SBT 2.3 (Naperville: Allenson, 1967). For the significance of the events surrounding 701 B.C., see Rüdiger Liwak, "Die Rettung Jerusalems im Jahr 701 v.Chr.: Zum Verhältnis historischer und theologischer Aussagen," *ZTK* 83 (1986): 137–66; Annti Leato, "Hezekiah and the Assyrian Crisis in 701 B.C.," *Scandinavian Journal of the Old Testament* (1987): 49–68.

12 *DOTT,* 67.

13 R. B. Y. Scott, "Isaiah," *IB* 5:162.

14 Jehoshua Gitay, "The Effectiveness of Isaiah's Speech," *JQR* 75 (1984): 162–72.

15 A. Graeme Auld, "Poetry, Prophecy, Hermeneutic: Recent Studies in Isaiah," *SJT* 33 (1980): 567–81.

16 I shall not enter into the debate on authorship. This matter is sufficiently dealt with in introductory works and commentaries; see John N. Oswalt, *The Book of Isaiah: Chapters 1–39,* NICOT (Grand Rapids: Eerdmans, 1986), 44–46; E. J. Young, *The Book of Isaiah,* 3 vols., NICOT (Grand Rapids: Eerdmans, 1965–72), 3:538–49; Harrison, *IOT,* 764–95; LaSor, *OTS,* 371–78.

17 Peter R. Ackroyd, "Isaiah I–XII: Presentation of a Prophet," SVT 29 (1978): 16–48.

18 John H. Eaton, "The Isaiah Tradition," in *FS Ackroyd,* 58–76; Lloyd Neve, "The Common Use of Traditions by the Author of Psalm 46 and Isaiah," *ExpT* 86 (1974–75): 243–46.

19 Joseph Jensen, "Yahweh's Plan in Isaiah and in the Rest of the Old Testament," *CBQ* 48 (1986): 443–55. This conclusion is extensively argued in his revised dissertation *The Use of tôrâ by Isaiah: His Debate with the Wisdom Tradition* (Washington: Catholic Biblical Association, 1973).

20 Robert P. Carroll explains the repetitions in chaps. 1–11 as "shifts" in meaning. It is apparent that the prophet gives clues to the inner interpretation by these so-called shifts ("Inner Tradition Shifts in Meaning in Isaiah 1–11," *ExpT* 89 [1977–78]: 301–4).

21 See the stimulating study of Othmar Keel, "Der Heilige—Jes 6, 1-4," in

Jahwe-Visionen und Siegelkunst (Stuttgart: Verlag Katholisches Bibelwerk, 1977), 46–124.

[22]Von Rad, *OTT* 1:366; for the seraphim as messengers of the theophany, see John Day, "Echoes of Baal's Seven Thunders and Lightnings in Psalm XXIX and Habakkuk III 9 and the Identity of the Seraphim in Isaiah VI," *VT* 29 (1979): 143–51.

[23]NIV "Lord Almighty" (*Yahweh Ṣᵉbā'ôt*, the Lord of Hosts); see 1:9, 24; 2:12; 3:1, 15; 5:7, 9, 16, 24; 6:3, 5; 8:13, 18; 10:16.

[24]John D. W. Watts expands Isaiah's vision of Yahweh to chaps. 1–66 in which the prophet explodes the imagery of Yahweh as the Landowner/Farmer, the Patron of Jerusalem, the Covenant God, and the Holy One of Israel in "The Characterization of Yahweh in the Vision of Isaiah," *RevExp* 83 (1986): 439–50.

[25]Th. C. Vriezen, "Essentials of the Theology of Isaiah," in *FS Muilenburg*, 131–33; Walther Eichrodt, "Prophet and Covenant: Observations on the Exegesis of Isaiah," in *FS Davies*, 167–88.

[26]A. Schoors, "Isaiah, The Minister of Royal Anointment?" *OTS* 20 (1977): 85–107. See also Henri Cazelles, "La Vocation D'Isaie (Ch. 6) et les Rites Royaux," in *Homenaje a Juan Prado: Miscelánea de Estudios bíblicos y Hebráicos,* ed. L. Alvarez Verdes and E. J. Alonso Hernández (Madrid: Consejo Superior de Investisaciones Científicas Inst., 1975), 89–108; Matitiahu Tsevat, "The Throne Vision of Isaiah," in *The Meaning of the Book of Job and Other Biblical Studies: Essays on the Literature and Religion of the Hebrew Bible* (New York: Ktav, 1980), 155–76.

[27]Christof Hardmeier explains Yahweh's commission to preach harshly to the people as a final, passionate, and loving appeal to his covenant people ("Jesajas Verkündigungsabsicht und Jahwes Verstockungsauftrag in Jes 6," in *FS Wolff,* 235–51).

[28]Hasel demonstrates that the "remnant motif" is central to Isaiah's eschatology (*The Remnant: The History and Theology of the Remnant Idea from Genesis to Isaiah* [Berrien Springs, Mich.: Andrews University Press, 1972], 233–70). G. W. Ahlström, "Isaiah VI.13," *JSS* 19 (1974): 169–72.

[29]Vriezen, "Essentials of the Theology of Isaiah," 146.

[30]See Kirsten Nielsen, "Das Bild des Gerichts (*Rîb*-Pattern) in Jes i–xii," *VT* 29 (1979): 309–24.

[31]For a special study of Isaiah's use of Torah, see Jensen, *The Use of tôrâ by Isaiah.*

[32]For the vineyard as a judicial parable, see John T. Willis, "The Genre of Isaiah 5:1–7," *JBL* 96 (1977): 337–62; Gale A. Yee, "The Form-Critical Study of Isaiah 5:1–7 as a Song and a Juridical Parable," *CBQ* 43 (1981): 30–40; Gerald T. Sheppard, "More on Isaiah 5:1–7 as a Juridical Parable," *CBQ* 44 (1982): 45–47; B. Z. Luria, "What Is the Vineyard in the Parable of Isaiah?" *Beth Mikra* 31 (1985–86): 289–92 (Hebrew). The problem of genre is clearly stated by Adrian Graffy, "The Literary Genre of Isaiah 5, 1–7," *Bib* 60 (1979): 400–409.

[33]Koch (*Prophets* 1:119) distinguishes between a theophany (Isaiah) and a visitation (Amos, Hosea).

[34]I appreciate the emphasis on Yahweh's kingship, but not the association

with the autumnal New year's festivals by Kevin J. Cathcart, "Kingship and the 'Day of YHWH,' in Isaiah 2:6–22," *Herm* 125 (1978): 48–59.

[35] See the excellent study by John Barton, "Ethics in Isaiah of Jerusalem," *JTS* 32 (1981): 1–18.

[36] Hasel, *The Remnant,* 257–64.

[37] On the issue of God's dwelling on earth, see M. Metzger, "Himmlische und Irdische Wohnstatt Jahwes," *Ugarit-Forschungen* 2 (1970): 139–58.

[38] For background, see F. C. Fensham, "Die Siro-Efraimitiese Oorlog en Jesaja-'n historiese Perspektief," *NGTT* 24 (1983): 236–46; P. A. Verhoef, "Jesaja 7:1–9:6, 'n woord vir (ons?) Krisis," *NGTT* 24 (1983): 247–54; P. R. Ackroyd, "Historians and Prophets," *SEÅ* 33 (1968): 18–54.

[39] For a good discussion of the exegetical and theological issues, see Oswalt, *Book of Isaiah,* 206–14.

[40] Gerhard F. Hasel, *The Remnant,* 274–89; idem, "Linguistic Considerations Regarding the Translation of Isaiah's Shear-Jashub: A Reassessment," *AUSS* 9 (1971): 36–46. John Day holds with R. E. Clements (*Isaiah 1–39,* NCBC, 83) that a remnant of the soldiers from Aram and Israel will return ("Shear-jashub [Isaiah vii 3] and 'The Remnant of Wrath' [Psalm lxxvi 11]," *VT* 31 [1981], 76–78). See the extensive discussion by Meir Weiss, "The Contribution of Literary Theory to Biblical Research: Illustrated by the Problem of She'ar Yashub," *SH* 31 (1986): 373–86.

[41] On the Immanuel prophecy, see J. Motyer, "Context and Content in the Interpretation of Isa. 7:14," *TB* 21 (1970): 118–25. On the dual motif of doom and hope, see Michael E. W. Thompson, "Isaiah's Sign of Immanuel," *ExpT* 95 (1983): 67–71.

[42] See Johannes Lindblom, *A Study on the Immanuel Section in Isaiah (Isa. vii.1–ix.6)* (Lund: Gleerup, 1958); Gene Rice, "A Neglected Interpretation of the Immanuel Prophecy," *ZAW* 90 (1978): 220–27; John T. Willis, "The Meaning of Isaiah 7:14 and Its Application in Matthew 1:23," *ResQ* 21 (1978): 1–18; E. Hammershaimb, "The Immanuel Sign," in *Some Aspects of Old Testament Prophecy from Isaiah to Malachi* (Copenhagen: Rosenkilde Og Bagger, 1966), 9–28. H. M. Wolff is representative of those who interpret the sign in favor of the son of Ahaz ("A Solution to the Immanuel Prophecy in Isaiah 7:14–8:22," *JBL* 91 [1972]: 449–56).

[43] Hasel, *The Remnant,* 339–48. Jensen speaks of the ideal king as "Yahweh's *alter ego,*" in *The Use of tôrâ by Isaiah,* 129.

[44] See Koch, *Prophets* 1:136–40.

[45] Ibid., 1:136. See Joseph Jensen, "The Age of Immanuel," *CBQ* 41 (1979): 220–39.

[46] Koch designates these as the throne names of the Messiah, based on the Egyptian model (*Prophets* 1:133).

[47] See the excellent study by H. Baarlink, *Vrede op Aarde: de Messiaanse Vrede in bijbels Perspektief* (Kampen: Kok, 1985), 19–47.

[48] Hasel, *The Remnant,* 264–68.

[49] B. Z. Luria argues in favor of the authenticity of this prophecy in "The Prophecy in Isa. 11:11–16 on the Gathering of the Exiles," *Beth Mikra* 26 (1981): 108–14 (Hebrew).

[50] Hasel designates Isaiah's theology as a restoration to the original condition

of Israel's election and salvation, in which the *Heilszeit* corresponds to the *Urzeit* (*The Remnant,* 257, 341).

⁵¹On the Zion theology, see R. E. Clements, *Isaiah and the Deliverance of Jerusalem: A Study in the Interpretation of Prophecy in the Old Testament,* JSOTSS 13 (Sheffield: JSOT, 1980): 72–89; Roland de Vaux, "Jerusalem and the Prophets," 277–300; Donald E. Gowan, *Eschatology in the Old Testament* (Philadelphia: Fortress, 1986); Jon D. Levenson, *Sinai and Zion: An Entry into the Jewish Bible* (Minneapolis: Winston Press, 1985); and Bennie Charles Ollenburger, "Zion, the City of the Great King. A Theological Investigation of Zion Symbolism in the Tradition of the Jerusalem Cult" (Ph.D. diss., Princeton Theological Seminary, 1982); J. B. Payne, "Zion," ZPEB 5:1063–66.

⁵²G. R. Hamborg, "Reasons for Judgement in the Oracles Against the Nations of the Prophet Isaiah," VT 31 (1981): 145–59. For the connection of the oracles against the nations with the war oracle, see Duane L. Christensen, *Transformations of the War Oracle in Old Testament Prophecy: Studies in the Oracles Against the Nations* (Missoula, Mont.: Scholars Press, 1975).

⁵³Seth Erlandsson (*The Burden of Babylon: A Study of Isaiah 13:2–14:23* [Lund: Gleerup, 1970]) studies the oracle against Babylon in the context of Isa. 13–23 and against the background of the havoc created by Assyria. He further demonstrates how Isaiah affirms Zion theology over against the lures of *Realpolitik.*

⁵⁴See chap. 8: "The Day of the Lord."

⁵⁵Hasel, *The Remnant,* 348–72. John F. A. Sawyer, " 'Blessed Be My People Egypt' (Isaiah 19.25): The Context and Meaning of a Remarkable Passage," in *FS McKane,* 57–71.

⁵⁶J. Vermeylen interprets chaps. 24–27 in relation to the prophecy as a whole, resulting in a holistic interpretation (*Du Prophète Isaïe à l'Apocalyptique: Isaïe, I–XXXV, miroir d'un demi-millénaire d'expérience religieuse en Israël,* 2 vols. [Paris: Librairie Lecoffre, 1978], 1:349–81). John Day has drawn our attention to eight parallels between Hos. 13:4–14:9. He concludes that these chapters of Isaiah reflect an original unity and are an interpretation of the earlier oracles of Hosea ("A Case of Inner Scriptural Interpretation: The Dependence of Isaiah XXVI.13–XXVII.11 on Hosea XIII.4–XIV.10 [Eng. 9] and Its Relevance to Some Theories of the Redaction of the 'Isaiah Apocalypse,' " *JTS* 31 [1980], 309–19). William R. Millar concludes that these chapters are protoapocalyptic in *Isaiah 24–27 and the Origin of Apocalyptic* (Missoula, Mont.: Scholars Press, 1976), 114; R. J. Coggins, "The Problem of Isaiah 24–27," ExpT 90 (1978–79): 328–33.

⁵⁷Vriezen, "Essentials of the Theology of Isaiah," 128–46.

⁵⁸For a Ugaritic analogy, see Marvin H. Pope, "A Divine Banquet at Ugarit," in *FS Stinespring,* 170–203; E. Lipiński, "Banquet en l'Honneur de Baal: CTA 3 (V AB): A, 4–22," *Ugarit-Forschungen* 2 (1970): 75–88; P. D. Miller, Jr., "The MRZḤ Text," in *The Claremont Ras Shamra Tablets,* ed. L. R. Fisher, Analecta Orientalia 48 (Rome: Pontifical Biblical Institute, 1971): 37–49.

⁵⁹Including the nations, whether they be troublers (as Moab, 25:10–12), oppressors, or seducers.

⁶⁰Peter Welten concludes that resurrection is not the concern of the text, rather the absence of death in the everlasting kingdom, in "Die Vernichtung des

Todes und die Königsherrschaft Gottes: eine traditionsgeschichtliche Studie zu Jes 25, 6–8; 24, 21–23 und Ex 24:9–11," *TZ* 38 (1982): 129–46.

[61] Leviathan is the Old Testament symbol of evil, of the rebellious nations (30:7; Ezek. 29:3; 32:2), and of chaos. He is likened to a serpent (Ps. 74:14) and a monster (Rev. 12; 13), and he is an agent of Satan. The motif is mythopoetic. See Cyrus H. Gordon, "Leviathan: Symbol of Evil," in *Biblical Motifs: Origins and Transformations,* ed. Alexander Altmann (Cambridge: Harvard University Press, 1966), 1–10; John Day, *God's Conflict with the Dragon and the Sea: Echoes of Canaanite Myth in the Old Testament* (Cambridge: Cambridge University Press, 1985), 141–78.

[62] See John H. Eaton, "The Isaiah Tradition," 72.

[63] Jensen, *The Use of tôrâ by Isaiah,* 124–30.

[64] See the excellent discussion by Jon D. Levenson, *Sinai and Zion,* 161–65.

[65] J. J. M. Roberts, "Isaiah 33: An Isaianic Elaboration of the Zion Tradition," in *FS Freedman,* 15–25.

[66] P. R. Ackroyd makes a convincing case of explaining chaps. 36–39 as complementary to chaps. 1–12 and esp. to Isa. 6:1–9:6 ("Isaiah 36–39: Structure and Function," in *Alter Orient und Altes Testament,* ed. Kurt Bergerhof, Manfried Dietrich, and Oswald Loretz [Neukirchen-Vluyn: Neukirchener, 1982], 3–21).

[67] For a masterful study on the prophetic forms of speech in the structuring of Isa. 40–48, see Claus Westermann, *Sprache und Struktur der Prophetie Deuterojesajas* (Stuttgart: Calwer, 1981).

[68] See Bruce D. Naidoff, "The Rhetoric of Encouragement in Isaiah 40:12–31: A Form-Critical Study," *ZAW* 93 (1981): 62–76; for a rhetorical analysis of chaps. 40–48, see Jehoshua Gitay, *Prophecy and Persuasion: A Study of Isaiah 40–48* (Bonn: Linguistica Biblica, 1981).

[69] William J. Dumbrell significantly designates chaps. 40–66 as "re-creation through the divine word—covenant renewal" in *CCOTT,* 190–92. On the place of John the Baptist, see J. L. Koole, "Zu Jesaja 40:3," in *FS van der Ploeg,* 137–42. I agree with Y. Hoffman ("Prophetic Call and Prophetic Consciousness," *Tarbiz* 53 [1983–84], 169–86 [Hebrew]) that the vocabulary of Isa. 40 does not support the contention that another prophet (Deutero–Isaiah) receives a call in the exilic situation. See also Oswald Loretz, "Die Gattung des Prologs zum Buch Deuterojesaja (Jes 40,1–11)," *ZAW* 96 (1984): 210–20.

[70] Arthur Van Seters anticipates a new and glorious creation at Yahweh's theophany ("Isaiah 40:1–11," Int 35 [1981]: 401–4). Similarly C. van Leeuwen, "De Openbaring van de Kᵉbōd JHWH in Jesaja 40:5," in *FS Koole,* 93–101.

[71] Robert W. Fisher, "The Herald of Good News in Second Isaiah," *FSS Muilenburg,* 117–32.

[72] Several passages develop an extensive apologetic against idolatry (40:12–31; 41:1–10; 44:6–22; 46:1–13) and other passages speak of the uniqueness of Yahweh (41:1–5, 22–29; 43:8–13; 44:6–8; 45:20–25); see Richard J. Clifford, "The Function of Idol Passages in Second Isaiah," *CBQ* 42 (1980): 450–64; Hans Klein, "Der Beweis der Einzigkeit Jahwes bei Deuterojesaja," *VT* 35 (1985): 267–73.

[73] For a brief survey of the disputations in 40:12–17, 18–26, 27–31, see Ralph W. Klein, *Israel in Exile: A Theological Interpretation* (Philadelphia:

Fortress, 1979), 104–5. Millard C. Lind, "Monotheism, Power, and Justice: A Study in Isaiah 40–55," *CBQ* 46 (1984): 432–46.

74 For a sense of the problem involved with the Servant Songs, see Colin G. Kruse, "The Servant Songs: Interpretive Trends Since C. R. North," *StudBT* 8 (1978): 3–27; Odil Hannes Steck, "Aspekte des Gottesknechts in Deuterojesajas 'Ebed-Jahwe Liedern,'" *ZAW* 96 (1984): 372–90.

75 Klaus Baltzer infers from the Servant Songs and the theological movement in Isa. 40–55 that the prophet looks for a continuity of the Davidic promises in the people of God ("Zur Formgeschichtlichen Bestimmung der Texte vom Gottes-Knecht im Deutero-Jesaja Buch," in *FS von Rad*, 27–43).

76 Delbert R. Hillers ("Berit 'am: 'Emancipation of the People,'" *JBL* 97 [1978], 175–82) reinterprets the phrase "covenant for the people" to "emancipation of the people"; Mark S. Smith ("*Berit 'am/Berit 'olam:* A New Proposal for the Crux of Isa. 42:6," *JBL* 100 [1981], 241–43) concludes that Isaiah addresses Israel as the "king" of the nations; he translates the idiom "a covenant for the people" as "a covenant of the nations."

77 On the Servant Songs, see Paul-Eugène Dion, "Les Chants du Serviteur de Yahweh et quelques passages apparantés d'Is. 40–55," *Bib* 51 (1970): 17–38; Barnabas Lindars, "Good Tidings to Zion: Interpreting Deutero-Isaiah Today," *BJRL* 68 (1985–86): 473–97; Norman H. Snaith, "The Servant of the Lord in Deutero-Isaiah," in *FS Robinson*, 187–200.

78 M. Dijkstra, "De koninklijke Knecht: Voorstelling en Investituur van de Knecht des Heren in Jesaja 42," in *FS Koole*, 41–52.

79 W. van der Meer, "Schepper en Schepsel in Jes 42:5," in *FS Koole*, 118–26.

80 At issue is the relationship between the phrases "a covenant for the people" and "a light for the Gentiles." There are two basic interpretations: (1) the nations will join in with the covenant, and (2) the prophet promises renewal of covenant to Israel so that they may become a light to the nations. J. J. Stamm's bibliography is most valuable ("Berît 'Am bei Deuterojesaja," in *FS von Rad*, 510–24); see Dumbrell, *CCOTT*, 192–94. The phrase occurs three times in Isaiah (42:6; 49:6; 51:4) in the context of the Servant Songs and refers to the inclusion of the Gentiles in the salvation and benefits brought about by the messianic era. See also B. J. Oosterhoff, "Tot een Licht der Volken," in *FS Koole*, 157–72.

81 See Katheryn Pfisterer Darr, "Like Warrior, like Woman: Destruction and Deliverance in Isaiah 42:10–17," *CBQ* 49 (1987): 560–71.

82 See the enlightening study of J. Kruis, "JHWH, Schepper en Formeerder in Deutero-Jesaja," in *FS Koole*, 83–92.

83 Frank Matheus, "Jesaja XLIV 9–20: Das Spottgedicht gegen die Götzen und Seine Stellung im Kontext," *VT* 37 (1987): 312–26.

84 Isaiah correlates forms of the root *ṣ-d-q* (esp. *ṣedāqâ* and *ṣedeq*, "righteousness"), *š-p-ṭ* ("judge," *mišpāṭ* ["justice"]), "salvation" (*yešû'â, yēša'*), "faithfulness" ('*emûnâ, 'emet*), "peace" (*šalôm*), "strength" ('*ōz*), "splendor" (*tip'eret*), "light" ('*ôr*), "glory" (*kābôd*), "vengeance" (*nāqām*), "zeal" (*qin'â*), and "praise" (*h-l-l, tehillâ*). For a comparison of the translation of the noun "righteousness" in English versions and of commentators on Isaiah, see John W. Olley, *"Righteousness" in the Septuagint of Isaiah: A Contextual Study* (Missoula, Mont.: Scholars Press, 1979), 133–39; Ph. B. Harner, "Creation Faith in Deutero-Isaiah," *VT*

17 (1967): 298–306; Hans Heinrich Schmid, "Creation, Righteousness, and Salvation: 'Creation Theology' as a Broad Horizon of Biblical Theology," in *Creation in the Old Testament,* ed. Bernard W. Anderson (Philadelphia: Fortress, 1984), 102–17.

[85] Bo Johnson connects Yahweh with an all-encompassing righteousness, extending to heaven and earth ("Der Bedeutungsunterschied zwischen *Sādāq* und *ṣ^edāqâ*," *ASTI* 11 [1978]: 31–39).

[86] R. Davidson argues in favor of a dialectic; the Lord continues his covenant promises as expected in traditional categories, and he uses such an unconventional instrument as Cyrus to accomplish his will for the new era ("Some Aspects of the Theological Significance of Doubt in the Old Testament," *ASTI* 7 [1970]: 49).

[87] R. E. Clements, "Isaiah 45:20–25," *Int* 40 (1986): 392–97.

[88] J. L. Crenshaw, "YHWH S^eba'ot S^emô: A Form-Critical Analysis," *ZAW* 81 (1969): 156–75.

[89] Bernard W. Anderson, "Exodus Typology in Second Isaiah," in *FS Muilenburg,* 177–207; Walther Zimmerli, "Le Nouvel 'Exode' dans le message des deux grands prophètes de l'Exil," in *FS Vischer,* 1–22.

[90] For a balanced discussion, see Willis J. Beecher, "The Servant," in *Classical Evangelical Essays in Old Testament Interpretation,* ed. Walter C. Kaiser, Jr. (Grand Rapids: Baker, 1972), 187–204. See also Hans-Jürgen Hermisson, "Der Lohn des Knechts," in *FS Wolff,* 269–87.

[91] W. A. M. Beuken relates 49:1–6 to the proclamation of 49:20–21 in "De vergeefse Moeite van de Knecht: Gedachten over de Plaats van Jesaja 49:1–6 in de Context," in *FS Koole,* 23–40.

[92] For the magnificent combination of Divine Warrior and Comforter, see Theodor Seidl, "Jahwe der Krieger—Jahwe der Tröster. Kritik und Neuinterpretation der Schöpfungsvorstellungen in Jesaja 51, 9–16," *BN* 21 (1983): 116–34.

[93] On the gospel in Isaiah, see Paul D. Hanson, "Isaiah 52:7–10," *Int* 33 (1979): 389–94.

[94] Tryggve N. D. Mettinger concludes that the creation-redemption motifs have an underlying mythopoetic structure of Yahweh, the victorious King ("In Search of the Hidden Structure: JHWH as King in Isaiah 40–55," *SEAÅ* 51–52 [1986–87]: 148–57; Bennie Charles Ollenburger correlates creation theology and Zion in "Zion, the City of the Great King," 273–95.

[95] A. S. van der Woude applies this phrase to the "exodus" from exile motif in "Hoe de Here naar Sion wederkeert . . . ; Traditiohistorische Overwegingen bij Jesaja 52:7–8," in *FS Koole,* 188–96.

[96] Roy F. Melugin treats this text as an eschatological hymn; see "Isaiah 52:7–10," *Int* 36 (1982): 176–81.

[97] For a different approach, see Robert P. Carroll, "Second Isaiah and the Failure of Prophecy," *ST* 32 (1978): 119–31.

[98] For recent treatments of this passage, see D. F. Payne, "The Servant of the Lord: Language and Interpretation," *EQ* 43 (1971): 131–43; David J. A. Clines, *I, He, We, and They: A Literary Approach to Isaiah 53,* JSOTSS 1 (Sheffield: JSOT, 1976). R. N. Whybray identifies the Suffering Servant with "Deutero-

Isaiah" (*Thanksgiving for a Liberated Prophet: An Interpretation of Isaiah Chapter 53*, JSOTSS 4 [Sheffield: JSOT, 1978]).

[99]J. P. M. van der Ploeg makes a connection with the Suffering Servant, the Psalms, and our Lord's suffering in "De Dienaar van JHWH en de Psalmen," in *FS Koole*, 173–77.

[100]For the wisdom emphasis, see James M. Ward, "The Servant's Knowledge in Isaiah 40–55," in *FS Terrien*, 121–36.

[101]John W. Olley proposes that Jews and non-Jews share in the victory (" 'The Many': How Is Is. 53, 12a to Be Understood?" *Bib* 68 [1987]: 330–56).

[102]See the study by David M. Gunn on the flood motif in Isaiah. He relates the motifs of water, covenant, word, and sign in "Deutero-Isaiah and the Flood," *JBL* 94 (1975): 493–508.

[103]Richard J. Clifford, "Isaiah 55: Invitation to a Feast," in *FS Freedman*, 27–35.

[104]See H. Williamson, " 'The Sure Mercies of David': Subjective or Objective Genitive?" *JSS* 23 (1978): 31–49. I disagree with the interpretation of John H. Eaton, according to which these words apply primarily to David (*Festal Drama in Deutero-Isaiah* [London: SPCK, 1979], 87–89).

[105]Joachim Becker views the shift from monarchy to the people as a collective interpretation of the monarchic privilege (*Messianic Expectation in the Old Testament*, trans. David E. Green [Philadelphia: Fortress, 1980], 68–78).

[106]On creation imagery, see Bernard W. Anderson, "Introduction: Mythopoetic and Theological Dimensions of Biblical Creation Faith," in *Creation in the Old Testament*, ed. Bernard W. Anderson (Philadelphia: Fortress, 1984), 1–24.

[107]J. Vermeylen interprets chaps. 56–66 in relation to the prophecy as a whole, resulting in a holistic interpretation (*Du Prophète Isaïe à l'Apocalyptique* 2:451–517); Hans-Joachim Kraus, "Die ausgebliebene Endtheophanie: Eine Studie zu Jes. 56–66," in *Biblisch-theologische Aufsätze* (Neukirchen: Neukirchener, 1972), 134–50.

[108]For the parallel usage of "righteousness" and "salvation" as expressions for the fullness of God's kingdom, see 45:8; 46:13; 51:5. Also see von Rad, *OTT* 1:370–83; idem, " 'Righteousness' and 'Life' in the Cultic Language of the Psalms," in *The Problem of the Hexateuch and Other Essays*, trans. E. W. Trueman Dicken (London: Oliver & Boyd, 1966), 243–66.

[109]M. A. Beek concludes that 56:1–8 correlates Israel's election and the extension of salvation to the Gentiles in "De Vreemdeling krijgt toegang (Jesaja 56:1–8)," in *FS Koole*, 17–22.

[110]On the universalism of Isa. 56–66, see Christopher T. Begg, "Foreigners in Third Isaiah," *TBT* 23 (1985): 98–108; Bernard Wodecki, "Der Heilsuniversalismus bei Trito-Jesaja," *VT* 32 (1982): 248–52.

[111]Matitiahu Tsevat concludes that the Sabbath sign is essentially an "acceptance of the sovereignty of God" (455) and that it was the most important festival, not being bound by the annual cycle (456–59) in "The Basic Meaning of the Biblical Sabbath," *ZAW* 84 (1972): 447–59. For a discussion on the sociological significance of the Sabbath, see Niels-Erik Andreasen, "Festival and Freedom: A Study in an Old Testament Theme," *Int* 28 (1974): 281–97.

[112]Michael Barré, "Fasting in Isaiah 58:1–12: A Reexamination," *BTB* 15 (1985): 94–97.

113Paul D. Hanson connects 57:14–21; 59:15b–19, 60–62; 66:15–16; and Zech. 9–14 with nascent apocalyptic developments in *The Dawn of the Apocalyptic* (Philadelphia: Fortress, 1979), 404.

114I have dealt with this issue more fully in IHCIP, 288–90.

115Martin Buber, *On the Bible: Eighteen Studies by Martin Buber,* ed. Nahum N. Glatzer [New York: Schocken, 1982], 164–65. On the place of Jerusalem-Zion in Isaiah, see William J. Dumbrell, "The Purpose of the Book of Isaiah," *TB* 36 (1985): 111–28.

116I agree with John Calvin: "This chapter ought, therefore, to be understood in such a sense, that Christ, who is the Head of the prophets, holds the chief place, and alone makes all these revelations; but that Isaiah, and the other prophets, and the apostles, contribute their services to Christ, and each performs his part in making known Christ's benefits" (*Commentary on the Book of the Prophet Isaiah* [Grand Rapids: Baker, 1979], 303).

117The phrase "the day of vengeance of our God" seems out of place in Isa. 61:1–7, but appears to have an eschatological thrust beyond the desolation of Babylon of which Isaiah spoke; see Odil Hannes Steck, "Der Rachetag in Jesaja LXI 2: Ein Kapitel redaktionsgeschichtlicher Kleinarbeit," *VT* 36 (1986): 323–38.

118Donald E. Gowan, "Isaiah 61:1–3, 10–11," *Int* 35 (1981): 404–9.

119Frederick Holmgren explains these verses against the background of chaps. 60–62: Yahweh is the blood avenger of his people ("Yahweh the Avenger: Isaiah 63:1–6," in *FSS Muilenburg,* 133–48).

120C. R. North, "The 'Former Things' and the 'New Things' in Deutero-Isaiah," in *FS Robinson,* 111–26.

121On the relationship between this vision and Rev. 21, see Ulrich Mauser, "Isaiah 65:17–25," *Int* 36 (1982): 181–86; Richard J. Mouw, *When the Kings Come Marching In: Isaiah and the New Jerusalem* (Grand Rapids; Eerdmans, 1983); William J. Dumbrell, *The End of the Beginning: Revelation 21–22 and the Old Testament* (Grand Rapids: Baker, 1985), 18–19.

122John Calvin, *Commentary on the Book of the Prophet Isaiah* 3:398.

123See M. Metzger, "Himmlische und Irdische Wohnstatt Jahwes," *Ugarit-Forschungen* 2 (1970): 139–58.

124Roger D. Aus explains 2 Thess. 2:6–7 on the basis of Isaiah's imagery in "God's Plan and God's Power: Isaiah 66 and the Restraining Factors of 2 Thess. 2:6–7," *JBL* 96 (1977): 537–53.

125For studies on gynomorphic imagery, see M. I. Gruber, "The Motherhood of God in Second Isaiah," *RB* 90 (1983): 351–59; Leila Leah Bronner, "Gynomorphic Imagery in Exilic Isaiah (40–66)," *Dor Le Dor* 12 (1983–84): 71–83.

126R. E. Clements, *Isaiah and the Deliverance of Jerusalem,* 107–8.

127Oswalt, *Book of Isaiah,* 54.

128See Hans-Joachim Kraus, "Schöpfung und Weltvollendung," in *Biblisch-theologische Aufsätze* (Neukirchen: Neukirchener, 1972), 151–78.

129Anderson, "Mythopoetic and Theological Dimensions of Biblical Creation Faith," 18–21.

130See the magnificent study on the eschatology of Isaiah by Dumbrell, *The End of the Beginning,* 5–22.

Chapter 10

[1] Walter Brueggemann, "The Book of Jeremiah: Portrait of the Prophet," *Int* 37 (1983): 134.

[2] For a survey of issues in modern Jeremiah research, see James L. Crenshaw, "A Living Tradition: The Book of Jeremiah in Current Research," *Int* 37 (1983): 117–29; Leo G. Perdue, "Jeremiah in Modern Research: Approaches and Issues," in *A Prophet to the Nations: Essays in Jeremiah Studies,* ed. Leo G. Perdue and Brian W. Kovacs (Winona Lake, Ind.: Eisenbrauns, 1984), 1–32; P.-M. Bogaert, ed., *Le Livre de Jérémie: le Prophète et son milieu, les oracles et leur transmission* (Leuven: Leuven University Press, 1981).

[3] Samuel Amsler concludes that the acts are as much a form of revelation as the words in "Les Prophètes et la Communication par les Actes," in *FS Westermann,* 194–201.

[4] The linen belt (13:1–11; see Charles H. Southwood, "The Spoiling of Jeremiah's Girdle" [Jer. xiii:1–11], *VT* 29 [1979]: 231–37); the wineskins (13:12–14); the clay jar (19:1–13); the yoke (27:1–22); other object lessons: the prohibition against marriage (16:1–9); the potter's clay (18:2–10); the baskets of figs (24:1–10); and the purchase of a field in Anathoth (32:6–15).

[5] Alfred Marx, "A Propos des doublets du Livre de Jérémie," in *FS Fohrer,* 106–20.

[6] For examples, see William L. Holladay, *The Architecture of Jeremiah 1–20* (Lewisburg: Bucknell University Press, 1976), 171–72.

[7] For a significant study, see W. L. Holladay, "Prototype and Copies: A New Approach to the Poetry-Prose Problem in the Book of Jeremiah," *JBL* 79 (1960): 351–67.

[8] W. L. Holladay, "Style, Irony, and Authenticity in Jeremiah," *JBL* 81 (1962): 44–54.

[9] Louis Dorn, "The Unexpected as a Speech Device: Shifts of Thematic Expectancy in Jeremiah," *Biblical Translator* 37 (1986): 216–22.

[10] T. R. Hobbs ("Some Remarks on the Composition and Structure of the Book of Jeremiah," *CBQ* 34 [1972]: 257–75) analyzes four separate tradition complexes. In another article he concludes that Jeremiah was steeped in the wisdom tradition; see "Some Proverbial Reflections in the Book of Jeremiah," *ZAW* 91 (1979): 62–72.

[11] John Bright, *Jeremiah,* AB (Garden City: Doubleday, 1965), LVII. He also calls it "an anthology of anthologies" (LXXIX).

[12] The LXX is shorter and arranges the materials differently. For further study, see introductory works, commentaries, and also specialized studies: Emanuel Tov, "Exegetical Notes on the Hebrew Vorlage of the LXX of Jeremiah 27 (34)," *ZAW* 91 (1979): 73–93; idem, "L'Incidence de la critique textuelle sur la critique littéraire dans le Livre de Jérémie," *RB* 79 (1972): 189–99; Louis Stulman, "Some Theological and Lexical Differences Between the Old Greek and the MT of the Jeremiah Prose Discourses," *HS* 25 (1984): 18–23; J. G. Janzen, *Studies in the Text of Jeremiah* (Cambridge: Harvard University Press, 1973).

[13] For criticism, see Harrison, *IOT,* 809–17; LaSor, *OTS,* 408–10; Childs, *IOTS,* 342–45.

[14] For examples of this approach, see Jack R. Lundbom, *Jeremiah: A Study in Ancient Hebrew Rhetoric* (Missoula, Mont.: Scholars Press, 1975); Holladay, *The Architecture of Jeremiah 1–20;* idem, *Jeremiah 1: A Commentary on the Prophet Jeremiah Chapters 1–25, Hermeneia* (Philadelphia: Fortress, 1986); Charles D. Isbell and Michael Jackson, "Rhetorical Criticism and Jeremiah vii 1–viii 3," *VT* 30 (1980): 20–26; Thomas W. Overholt, "Jeremiah 2 and the Problem of 'Audience Reaction,' " *CBQ* 41 (1979): 262–73; also see the review by James L. Crenshaw, "A Living Tradition," 119–20.

[15] Walter Brueggemann writes, "Texts may not be assessed any longer 'from the outside,' according to our critical control, but must be appreciated for their fullness, filled as they are with irony, subtlety, [and] incongruity" ("The 'Uncared For' Now Cared For [Jer. 30:12–17]: A Methodological Consideration," *JBL* 104 [1985]: 428).

[16] S. K. Soderlund, "Jeremiah, Book of," *ISBE* 2:988; for the older approach, see Bright, *Jeremiah,* VII–IX; idem, "The Book of Jeremiah: Its Structure, Its Problems, and Their Significance for the Interpreter," *Int* 9 (1955): 259–78.

[17] So writes J. A. Thompson, *The Book of Jeremiah,* NICOT (Grand Rapids: Eerdmans, 1980), 28. Thompson correctly posits several shorter collections within chaps. 1–25, but it remains doubtful that these chapters form one unit, given the variety of material, including a call to repentance to Israel, confessions, and oracles whose contexts are more limited in scope. G. R. Castellino observes, "The prophet is shown to be speaking in coordinated sequences and developing his themes, ideas, passions, inspiration with a mastery of the full gamut of artistic expression" ("Observations on the Literary Structure of Some Passages in Jeremiah," *VT* 30 [1980], 408).

[18] For the canonical approach, see Childs, *IOTS,* 345–54.

[19] See E. W. Nicholson's *Preaching to the Exiles; A Study of the Prose Tradition in the Book of Jeremiah* (New York: Schocken, 1970). However, he does not sufficiently consider the canonical connection between the prophet and his message.

[20] Thompson favors a both-and approach. He writes, "By stressing overmuch the special relevance . . . for the people of Judah in the post-587 B.C. period, one may miss the importance of Yahweh's word through Jeremiah to the people of Judah in the pre-587 period. Both aspects of the implications of Jeremiah's preaching are important" (*Book of Jeremiah,* 49–50).

[21] For a brief survey of the problems associated with the date, see Thompson, *Book of Jeremiah,* 50–56; Peter R. Ackroyd, "The Book of Jeremiah—Some Recent Studies," *JSOT* 28 (1984): 47–59. William L. Holladay assumes that Jeremiah was born in 627 B.C. and began his career in 615 B.C. ("The Years of Jeremiah's Preaching," *Int* 37 [1983], 146–59; idem, *Jeremiah 1,* 1).

[22] Walter Brueggemann, "The Book of Jeremiah," 130–45; André Ridouard, *Jérémie, l'épreuve de la foi,* Lire la Bible, 62 (Paris: Cerf, 1983).

[23] See Martin H. Woudstra, "A Prophet to the Nations: Reflections on Jeremiah's Call to Prophetic Office," *Vox Reformata* 18 (1972): 1–13. A. Ahuviah may well be right in his conclusion that "the nations" signify Judah and Israel (see 31:27) in "I Have Appointed You a Prophet to the Nations (Jer. 1:5)," *Beth Mikra* 29 (1983–84): 249–54 (Hebrew). W. L. Holladay writes to

the contrary, "It is a true internationalizing of the prophetic office" (*Jeremiah 1,* 34).

[24]William J. Dumbrell observes the inclusion of Jeremiah's call to be a prophet to the nations and the oracles against the nations (chaps. 46–51). Thus, the book begins and ends (not considering the appendix in chap. 52) with Jeremiah's role as a prophet to the nations (*The End of the Beginning: Revelation 21–22 and the Old Testament* [Grand Rapids: Baker, 1985], 83).

[25]Childs, *IOTS,* 347; Holladay (*Jeremiah 1,* 29–31) concludes, "We are dealing here not so much with a stereotyped structure as with a deliberate parallel with the model of Moses primarily" (30); see also Holladay, "The Background of Jeremiah's Self-Understanding: Moses, Samuel, and Psalm 22," *JBL* 83 (1964): 153–64.

[26]Stanley Brice Frost aptly observed that the prophecy of Jeremiah is a *memorial* of a childless man ("The Memorial of a Childless Man: A Study in Hebrew Thought on Immortality," *Int* 26 [1972]: 446–47).

[27]H. Cunliffe-Jones summarizes the prophetic personhood as consisting of five characteristics: (1) a deep-seated personal honesty with God; (2) courage and faithfulness; (3) a passionate hatred of immorality and idolatry; (4) a sensitivity to the suffering of his people; and (5) hope in the promised restoration (*The Book of Jeremiah* [London: SCM, 1960], 32–36). John Maclennan Berridge argues against the critical contention that the confessions of Jeremiah contain no evidence of a personal Jeremiah (*Prophet, People, and the Word of Yahweh: An Examination of Form and Content in the Proclamation of the Prophet Jeremiah* [Zürich: EVZ-Verlag, 1970]).

[28]Donald H. Wimmer likens them to Saint Augustine's as expressive of the innermost feelings ("The Confessions of Jeremiah," *TBT* 19 [1981], 93–99).

[29]See John Goldingay, *God's Prophet, God's Servant: A Study of Jeremiah and Isaiah 40–55* (Exeter: Paternoster, 1984), 30; James L. Crenshaw, "Seduction and Rape: The Confessions of Jeremiah," in *A Whirlpool of Torment: Israelite Traditions on God as an Oppressive Force* (Philadelphia: Fortress, 1984), 31–56.

[30]See Ferdinand Ahuis, *Der Klagende Gerichtsprophet* (Stuttgart: Calwer, 1982).

[31]See H. Donner, "The Confessions of Jeremiah—Their Form and Significance for the Prophet's Biography," in *Papers Read at the 24th Meeting of Die Ou-Testamentiese Werkgemeenskap in Suider-Afrika, OTWSA* 24 (1981): 55–66; Franz D. Hubmann, "Stationen einer Berufung: Die 'Konfessionen' Jeremias— eine Gesamtschau," *TPQ* 132 (1984): 25–39; Koch, *Prophets* 2:38–45.

[32]Goldingay speaks about Jeremiah's suffering as his identification with God's suffering over his people: "Yet Jeremiah suffers not merely because he is identified with *Israel,* but also because he is identified with *God*" (*God's Prophet,* 41).

[33]Childs, *IOTS,* 349–50; Norbert Ittmann concludes that the confessions have the nature of prophetic legitimation with a threefold function: (1) the freedom of God in destroying the nationalism of Jeremiah's opponents by the word of his prophet, (2) the solidarity of the prophet with the anticipated suffering of his people, and (3) the continuity of Jeremiah with the prophets of Israel (*Die Konfessionen Jeremias: Ihre Bedeutung für die Verkündigung des Propheten* [Neukirchen-Vluyn: Neukirchener, 1981], 197–98).

Notes

³⁴Sheldon H. Blank, "The Prophet as a Paradigm," in *Essays in Old Testament Ethics (J. Philip Hyatt, In Memoriam)*, ed. James L. Crenshaw and John T. Willis (New York: Ktav, 1974), 111–30.

³⁵This sense of conflict is well presented by Brueggemann in "The Book of Jeremiah," 130–45.

³⁶For an exegetical study and evaluation of the tension in Paul's life as a person between the ages, see David Wenham, "The Christian Life: A Life of Tension? A Consideration of the Nature of Christian Experience in Paul," in *Pauline Studies: Essays Presented to Professor F. F. Bruce on His 70th Birthday,* ed. Donald A. Hagner and Murray J. Harris (Exeter: Paternoster, 1980), 80–94. I appreciate Wenham's admission that he arrives at two contradictory conclusions: deliverance from distress and stress as a part of the Christian experience (88). He concludes, "The explanation of Paul's two-sided view lies, as Dunn rightly observes in Paul's eschatology: he believes that the new age has broken into history in Christ, the new Adam, especially in his resurrection and in the pouring out of the Spirit. . . . The old age confronts him in the world with its persecutions and also in his inmost being in the 'body', and the believer has to learn to follow Christ in accepting suffering and in putting sin to death through the power of the Holy Spirit" (90). For Dunn's view of the tension, see James D. G. Dunn, "Rom. 7, 14–25 in the Theology of Paul," *TZ* 31 (1975): 257–73; idem, *Jesus and the Spirit: A Study of the Religious and Charismatic Experience of Jesus and the First Christians as Reflected in the New Testament* (Philadelphia: Westminster, 1975), 312–18, 326–42.

³⁷So Childs writes, "He participated himself in the judgment of his people" (*IOTS,* 350). Ulrike Eichler sees Jeremiah's role as a mediator ("Der klagende Jeremia: Eine Untersuchung zu den Klagen Jeremias und ihrer Bedeutung zum Verstehen seines Leidens," *TLZ* 103 [1978]: 918–19). See Timothy Polk's stimulating analysis of the prophetic language of the self as a paradigm in *The Prophetic Persona: Jeremiah and the Language of the Self,* JSOTSS 32 (Sheffield: JSOT, 1984).

³⁸J. G. S. S. Thomson, "Jeremiah," *NBD,* 609.

³⁹Ittmann, *Konfessionen,* 197.

⁴⁰James L. Crenshaw, "Seduction and Rape," 31–56.

⁴¹See the study by A. R. Diamond, *The Confessions of Jeremiah in Context: Scenes of Prophetic Drama,* JSOTSS 45 (Sheffield: JSOT, 1987).

⁴²This section is by no means easy. Thompson divides this section into vv. 10–12 and vv. 15–21 (*Book of Jeremiah,* 88). But see the argument of G. V. Smith, "The Use of Quotations in Jeremiah xv 11–14," *VT* 29 (1979): 229–31.

⁴³Smith, "The Use of Quotations in Jeremiah xv 11–14," 229–31.

⁴⁴John Bright aptly concludes that Jeremiah "remained a weak mortal, and like all weak mortals who are *simul iustus simul peccator,* he experienced many occasions when he knew that repentance was needful. But the weak mortal also remained God's prophet, endowed by his God with the strength to carry on" ("A Prophet's Lament and its Answer: Jeremiah 15:10–21," *Int* 28 [1974]: 74).

⁴⁵Koch admits, "To present an iron front outwardly, whatever the turbulence within him, can have been only a very limited consolation to Jeremiah" (*Prophets* 2:41).

[46]D. J. A. Clines and D. M. Gunn, "'You tried to persuade me' and 'Violence! Outrage!' in Jeremiah XX 7–8," *VT* 28 (1978): 20–27.

[47]See J. Gerald Janzen, "Jeremiah 20:7–18," *Int* 37 (1983): 178–83; M. S. Moore, "Jeremiah's Progressive Paradox," *RB* 93 (1986): 386–414.

[48]For the function of this section in the context of the collective experience of God's people, see the stimulating article by D. J. A. Clines and D. M. Gunn, "Form, Occasion and Redaction in Jeremiah 20," *ZAW* 88 (1976): 390–409.

[49]For additional (auto)biographical materials, see chaps. 26–45, except for 30–33.

[50]Von Rad, *OTT* 2:204; idem, "The Confessions of Jeremiah," in *Theodicy in the Old Testament*, ed. James L. Crenshaw (Philadelphia: Fortress, 1983), 88–99.

[51]Georg Christian Macholz presents a magnificent portrait of Jeremiah as the prophet of prayer in the spirit of Moses and Samuel in "Jeremia in der Kontinuitat der Prophetie," in *FS von Rad*, 306–34.

[52]Holladay, "Jeremiah, the Prophet," *IDBS*, 471; idem, "The Background of Jeremiah's Self-Understanding," 153–64.

[53]Crenshaw, "Seduction and Rape," 55; Patrick D. Miller, Jr., "Trouble and Woe: Interpreting the Biblical Laments," *Int* 37 (1983): 42.

[54]See R. Davidson, "Some Aspects of the Theological Significance of Doubt in the Old Testament," *ASTI* 7 (1970): 41–52.

[55]Holladay briefly discusses the exegetical ambiguity but concludes that regardless of how one interprets the text, "the term (*ḥesed*) designates outer conduct which goes beyond the minimum necessity, so that it indicates an inner attitude of affection as well" (*Jeremiah I*, 83).

[56]Michael DeRoche, "Israel's 'Two Evils' in Jeremiah ii 13," *VT* 31 (1981): 369–72.

[57]See the thorough study by Laurent Wisser, *Jérémie, critique de la vie sociale: justice sociale et connaissance de Dieu dans le Livre de Jérémie* (Geneva: Labor et Fides, 1982); the explanation on 8:7 by Herold Weiss illustrates this point ("How Can Jeremiah Compare the Migration of Birds to Knowledge of God's Justice," *Biblical Review* 2, no. 3 [1986]: 42–45).

[58]Wisser, *Critique*, 248 (translation mine).

[59]Robert P. Carroll explains Jeremiah's crisis of self-authentication solely based on anthropological criteria in his treatment of Jer. 23:8, 22 ("A Non-Cogent Argument in Jeremiah's Oracles Against the Prophets," *ST* 30 [1976]: 43–51).

[60]Thomas W. Overholt advances the thesis of continuity on the basis of his study of the word *šeqer* ("falsehood") as a way of religious conservatism versus the new revelation, "Remarks on the Continuity of the Jeremiah Tradition," *JBL* 91 (1972): 457–62; idem, *The Threat of Falsehood: A Study in the Theology of the Book of Jeremiah*, SBT 2/16 (Naperville: Allenson, 1970).

[61]Wisser, *Critique*, 198.

[62]Jeremiah incorporates his charges in judgment oracles, exhortation (6:6–8; 21:11–12; 22:1–5), proverbs (17:11), and an oracle of salvation (23:5–6).

[63]On Jeremiah and the "false prophets," see R. P. Carroll, "A Non-Cogent Argument in Jeremiah's Oracles," 43–51; see also chap. 2: "True and False Prophets."

[64]Jonathan Paige Sisson, "Jeremiah and the Jerusalem Conception of Peace,"

JBL 105 (1986): 429–42. Jon D. Levenson, *Sinai and Zion: An Entry into the Jewish Bible* (Minneapolis: Winston Press, 1985), 165–69; see also F. K. Kumaki, "The Temple Sermon: Jeremiah's Polemic Against the Deuteronomists (Dtr¹)" (Ph.D. diss., Union Theological Seminary, 1980). John Bright concludes that "Jeremiah believed in the sure and unconditional purposes of God for his people just as firmly as (more firmly than?) his opponents did" (*Covenant and Promise: The Prophetic Understanding of the Future in Preexilic Israel* [Philadelphia: Westminster, 1976], 192).

[65] See R. E. Clements, *Isaiah and the Deliverance of Jerusalem* JSOTSS 13 (Sheffield: JSOT, 1980), 72–108.

[66] For background of Jeremiah and his time, see Merrill, *History*, 436–53, 456–67.

[67] Morton Cogan, *Imperialism and Religion: Assyria, Judah and Israel in the Eighth and Seventh Centuries B.C.E.* (Missoula, Mont.: Scholars Press, 1974), 65–96. He argues against the supposition of Assyrian imposition of religious and cultural changes and in favor of assimilation and acculturation.

[68] It may be that chaps. 1–6—with the emphasis on idolatry, apostasy, and evil in Judean society (5:1, 11–13, 23)—come from this time (Christoph Levin, "Noch einmal: die Anfänge des Propheten Jeremia," *VT* 31 [1981]: 428–40).

[69] See 25:3; 36:2. The prophetic oracles that Jeremiah wrote down were probably close in form to chaps. 1–25. Rainer Albertz limits the collection to 2:4–6:30 ("Jer. 2–6 und die Frühzeitverkündigung Jeremias," *ZAW* 94 [1982]: 20–47).

[70] Bright, *Jeremiah*, XLV, XCII–VI.

[71] For background reading, see 2 Kings 21–25; 2 Chron. 33–36; Nahum; Zephaniah; Habakkuk; and Ezekiel. The Babylonian Chronicle supplements the biblical materials, see *DOTT*, 75–83; Bright, *Jeremiah*, XXVI–LIV; Holladay, *Jeremiah I*, 1–10. LaSor provides a helpful chart of the kings, dates, and dating formulas in the prophecy of Jeremiah (*OTS*, 428–30). See also P. R. Ackroyd, "Historians and Prophets," SEÅ 33 (1968): 18–54; A. Malamat, "The Last Kings of Judah and the Fall of Jerusalem: An Historical-Chronological Study," *IEJ* 18 (1968): 137–56; idem, "The Twilight of Judah: In the Egyptian-Babylonian Maelstrom," *SVT* 28 (1975): 123–45.

[72] This reconstruction is based on A. Malamat, "The Twilight of Judah," 123–45; idem, "The Last Kings of Judah and the Fall of Jerusalem," 137–56.

[73] Or Eliakim, son of Josiah and brother of Zedekiah (1 Chron. 3:15).

[74] See 36:32: "And many similar words were added to them." W. L. Holladay attempts to identify the contents of the scrolls in "The Identification of the Two Scrolls of Jeremiah," *VT* 30 (1980): 452–67.

[75] For background on this rebellion, see H. J. Katzenstein, " 'Before Pharaoh Conquered Gaza' (Jeremiah xlvii 1)," *VT* 33 (1983): 249–51.

[76] Jeremiah had predicted the sudden end of Jehoiakim (22:18–19). There appears to be some uncertainty as to his end, and it is possible that he was exiled (see 2 Chron. 36:6–7; Dan. 1:1–2).

[77] Among them Daniel and his friends (Dan. 1:1).

[78] See the Babylonian Chronicle (*DOTT*, 75–83). Jehoiachin was released thirty-six years later (52:31–34; see 2 Kings 25:27–30).

[79] Walther Zimmerli, "Visionary Experience in Jeremiah," in *FS Ackroyd*, 95–

118. For a more comprehensive study, see Susan Niditch, *The Symbolic Vision in Biblical Tradition* (Chico: Scholars Press, 1980).

[80]Zimmerli, "Visionary Experience," 109–14.

[81]"Zedekiah's reign was marked more by weakness than by meanness" (LaSor, *OTS,* 417).

[82]For the interaction of Hananiah and Jeremiah, see chap. 2: "True and False Prophets."

[83]F. C. Fensham, "Nebukadnezzar in the Book of Jeremiah," *JNSL* 10 (1982): 53–65. K. A. D. Smelik convincingly argues that Jer. 50–51 function to counteract the false impression that Jeremiah was pro-Babylonian ("De Functie van Jeremia 50 en 51 binnen het Boek Jeremia," *NTT* 41 [1987]: 265–78).

[84]For the problem involving this account and his being thrown into a muddy cistern (38:1–13), see Thompson, *Book of Jeremiah,* 636–46.

[85]For a study on Israel's sense of "land" and covenant identity, see Walter Brueggemann, "Israel's Sense of Place in Jeremiah," in *FSS Muilenburg,* 149–65.

[86]Childs, *IOTS,* 347.

[87]For a discussion, see Bright, *Jeremiah,* 162–63, 238–39; David L. Petersen, *Haggai and Zechariah 1–8: A Commentary,* OTL (Philadelphia: Westminster, 1984), 149; Norman K. Gottwald, *All the Kingdoms of the Earth: Israelite Prophecy and International Relations in the Ancient Near East* (New York: Harper & Row, 1964), 265–66.

[88]G. Pattison, "The Moment of the Void: A Meditation on the Book of Jeremiah," *ExpT* 97 (1985–86): 132–36.

[89]Walter A. Brueggemann, "The Epistemological Crisis of Israel's Two Histories (Jer. 9:22–23)," in *FS Terrien,* 85–105.

[90]I fully agree with Kaiser that "the 'new' began with the 'old' promise made to Abraham and David. Its renewal perpetuated all those promises previously offered by the Lord and now more" ("The Old Promise and the New Covenant: Jeremiah 31:31–34," *JETS* 15 [1972]: 22), but I also would add to this the promises pertaining to creation and the Mosaic covenants. All covenants reflect and incorporate the "new" or eschatological era.

[91]See Thomas M. Raitt's study on the judgment-deliverance motif in *A Theology of Exile: Judgment/Deliverance in Jeremiah and Ezekiel* (Philadelphia: Fortress, 1977); idem, "Jeremiah's Deliverance Message to Judah," in *FSS Muilenburg,* 166–85. Walter Brueggemann writes, "Jeremiah's call is to *shatter* old worlds . . . and to *form* and evoke new worlds. . . . The shattering and forming of worlds . . . is done as a poet 'redescribes' the world, reconfigures public perception, and causes people to reexperience their experience" ("The Book of Jeremiah," 135).

[92]Levenson infers from Jer. 10:2–10 that this section is "the closest to genuine monotheism, the belief in the reality of only one deity" (*Sinai and Zion,* 68). See M. Margaliot, "Jeremiah X 1–16: A Re-Examination," *VT* 30 (1980): 295–308.

[93]Werner E. Lemke, "The Near and the Distant God: A Study of Jer. 23:23–24 in Its Biblical Theological Context," *JBL* 100 (1981): 541–55.

[94]W. L. Holladay speaks of Yahweh as being "radically innovative, never bound by the decisions of the past" ("Jeremiah the Prophet," *IDBS,* 471.)

95 Brueggemann, "The Book of Jeremiah," 139–40.

96 Norman K. Gottwald phrases this well: "Pax Babylonia is the Plan of Yahweh" (*All the Kingdoms of the Earth,* 260).

97 He, like Paul, called for a transformed way of life according to which the godly live with the vision of God's kingdom (Rom. 12:2).

98 But as von Rad admits, "Jeremiah has nothing to say of any changes in the natural world of the land where God's chosen people are to dwell; and nothing of any paradise-like fertility" (*OTT,* 2:212).

99 Prescott H. Williams, Jr., "Living toward the Acts of the Savior-Judge: A Study of Eschatology in the Book of Jeremiah," *Austin Seminary Bulletin* 94 (1978): 33.

100 William J. Dumbrell, *The End of the Beginning: Revelation 21–22 and the Old Testament* (Grand Rapids: Baker, 1985), 83–86.

101 See von Rad, *OTT,* 2:219.

102 On the new covenant, see E. W. Hengstenberg, "The New Covenant," in *Classical Evangelical Essays in Old Testament Interpretation,* ed. Walter C. Kaiser, Jr. (Grand Rapids: Baker, 1972), 237–51; Walter C. Kaiser, Jr., "The Old Promise and the New Covenant," 11–23; William J. Dumbrell, "The New Covenant: The Shape of Biblical Eschatology," *CCOTT,* 164–200; idem, "The New Covenant," in *The End of the Beginning,* 79–118; Thomas E. McComiskey, *The Covenants of Promise: A Theology of the Old Testament Covenants* (Grand Rapids: Baker, 1985), 80–89; David Petersen, "The Prophecy of the New Covenant in the Argument of Hebrews," *RTR* 38 (1979): 74–81; Bernhard W. Anderson, "The New Covenant and the Old," in *The Old Testament and Christian Faith: A Theological Discussion,* ed. Bernhard W. Anderson (New York: Harper & Row, 1963), 225–42.

103 Robert P. Carroll calls attention to the delay in fulfillment of Micah's prophecy regarding Jerusalem as an example of the importance of repentance ("Prophecy, Dissonance, and Jeremiah xxvi," in *A Prophet to the Nations: Essays on Jeremiah Studies,* ed. Leo G. Perdue and Brian W. Kovacs [Winona Lake, Ind.: Eisenbrauns, 1984], 381–91).

104 I am indebted to the study of Bernhard W. Anderson, " 'The Lord Has Created Something New': A stylistic Study of Jer. 31:15–22," *CBQ* 40 (1978): 463–78. The question as to what the "new" is may be resolved by considering its inclusionary function with v. 15, where Rachel is weeping (475). The "new" consists of a renewal of creation: "The way into the future is opened by Yahweh who, in a miracle of creation, gives the people new life by restoring them to their land and giving them a posterity, a future" (476–77).

105 Raitt concludes, "Forgiveness takes place as a very special event as one part of a decisive turning point in history" (*Theology of Exile,* 194 [emphasis his]).

106 Brueggemann, "The 'Uncared For' Now Cared For (Jer. 30:12–17): A Methodological Consideration," 428.

107 E. W. Hengstenberg concludes that the differences are "relative" ("The New Covenant," 237–51).

108 H. Weippert has demonstrated the verbal correspondence between several judgment oracles in Jeremiah and the changes effected by the new covenant ("Das Wort vom Neuen Bund in Jeremia xxxi 31–34," *VT* 29 [1979]: 336–51).

[109]M. Weinfeld, "Jeremiah and the Spiritual Metamorphosis of Israel," *ZAW* 88 (1976): 17–56.

[110]H. D. Potter, "The New Covenant in Jeremiah XXXI 31–34," *VT* 33 (1983): 347–57.

[111]Yehezkel Kaufmann sees a universal dimension in the new covenant, based on the oracles against the nations. He writes, "Jeremiah's demand that all nations willingly yield themselves to Babylon arises out of his faith that the subjection of the world was the necessary prelude to its salvation" (*The Religion of Israel*, trans. and abr. Moshe Greenberg [New York: Schocken, 1960], 426). Raitt concludes that the newness of the covenant lies in the shift from conditionality to eternality (*Theology of Exile*, 201–2).

[112]So also Werner E. Lemke, "Jeremiah 31:31–34," *Int* 37 (1983): 183–87; Dumbrell, *The End of the Beginning*, 94–95; Hans Walter Wolff, "Was ist das Neue im neuen Bund?" in *Prophetische Alternativen: Entdeckungen des Neuen im Alten Testament* (Munich: Kaiser, 1982), 55–69.

[113]. John Calvin, *Commentaries on the Book of the Prophet Jeremiah and the Lamentations* (Grand Rapids: Eerdmans, 1950), 4:62, 116–18 (emphasis mine).

[114]For the connection of Jeremiah with the war oracles, see Duane L. Christensen, *Transformations of the War Oracle in Old Testament Prophecy: Studies in the Oracles Against the Nations* (Missoula, Mont.: Scholars Press, 1975), 183–280.

[115]The LXX adds the oracles against the nations at this point.

[116]For the problems of etymology, see John M. Bracke, "*šûb šᵉbût:* A Reappraisal," *ZAW* 97 (1985): 233–244; John Gray argues in favor of "restoration" as "rehabilitation" (*The Biblical Doctrine of the Reign of God* [Edinburgh: T. & T. Clark, 1979], 110–16).

[117]Harry M. Orlinsky, "Nationalism-Universalism and Internationalism in Ancient Israel," in *FS May*, 206–36.

[118]For a discussion of the meaning of *servant*, see chap. 9: "The Message of Isaiah." The promise of exalted service is close to the message of Isaiah (see 41:8–9; 44:1–2, 21; 45:4; 48:20; 49:3).

[119]Literally "widowed." They were in a state of separation, but Yahweh never divorced his people (see Isa. 54:4, 6–7).

[120]The constant movement between judgment on Babylon and the redemption of God's people has striking parallel in the book of Revelation.

[121]This is another example of repetition in Jeremiah (see 10:12–16). The language has a strong resemblance to that of Isaiah (40:12–17), Hosea (4:1, 6), and the Psalms (16:5; 65:6; 73:26; 93:1; 119:57; 135:7).

[122]J. L. Crenshaw, "*YHWH Sᵉbā'ot Sᵉmô:* A Form-Critical Analysis," *ZAW* 81 (1969): 156–75.

[123]Bright affirms the tension inherent in the covenants, but resolves this in the light of the freedom of God in the working out of his immutable plans (*Covenant and Promise*, 196).

[124]Raitt demonstrates how the prophetic call to repentance is often combined with an oracle of judgment or an oracle of deliverance. It is an either/or: judgment or deliverance (*Theology of Exile*, 39).

Chapter 11

¹For a more extensive treatment of the last days of Judah, see the discussion of Jeremiah and his time (chap. 10).

²See Anthony D. York for a discussion of the interpretations on "the thirtieth year," in "Ezekiel 1: Inaugural and Restoration Visions?" *VT* 27 (1977): 82–98.

³See D. J. Wiseman, *Chronicles of the Chaldean Kings 626–556 B.C. in the British Museum* (London: British Museum, 1956).

⁴For an analysis of Ezek. 12:1–15; 17; 19; 21:23–37, see Bernhard Lang, *Kein Aufstand in Jerusalem: Die Politik des Propheten Ezechiel* (Stuttgart: Katholisches Bibelwerk, 1978).

⁵Ibid., 117–30.

⁶The name *Ezekiel* signifies "God [El] makes [or 'is'] strong." The book itself gives three explanations: (1) "God is strong" in overpowering Ezekiel with his divine presence (3:14), (2) "God makes strong" as the Sovereign Lord over Babylon and over the scattered sheep of his people (30:25; 34:16), and (3) "God makes hard" his prophet against the ridicule and opposition of his contemporaries (3:8).

⁷Houses were made of mud brick, a sun-dried clay, the usual material available for houses in that part of the world (12:5). Jeremiah instructed the exiles to be prepared for a long stay in exile by getting married, building houses, and resuming their occupations (Jer. 29). See Jeremiah's instructions to the new community in exile (vv. 1–23), dated to the same year of Ezekiel's exile (597 B.C.).

⁸Robert R. Wilson, "Prophecy in Crisis: The Call of Ezekiel," *Int* 38 (1984): 121–22. The date of the call has been determined to be July 31, 593 B.C.; see Richard Anthony Parker and Waldo H. Dubberstein, *Babylonian Chronology 626 B.C.–A.D. 75* (Providence: Brown University Press, 1956), 28.

⁹H. L. Ellison observes that the priest's work included "pastoral oversight" and that Ezekiel, while being "a genuine prophet, yet he is carrying out his priestly functions by so acting . . . (as a) pastoral prophet caring for the souls of the individuals" (*Ezekiel: The Man and His Message* [Grand Rapids: Eerdmans, 1956], 30).

¹⁰For the priestly aspect of Ezekiel's theology, see Walther Eichrodt, *Ezekiel: A Commentary*, OTL (Philadelphia: Westminster, 1970), 28–32.

¹¹Stephen Garfinkel, "Of Thistles and Thorns: A New Approach to Ezekiel II 6," *VT* 37 (1987): 421–37.

¹²Walther Zimmerli designates this experience as an "autodramatic element" (*Ezekiel: A Commentary on the Prophet Ezekiel Chapters 1–24*. Hermeneia [Philadelphia: Fortress, 1979], 19).

¹³W. H. Brownlee, *Ezekiel 1–19*, WBC (Waco, Tex.: Word, 1986), 50; idem, "Ezekiel's Parable of the Watchman and the Editing of Ezekiel," *VT* 28 (1978): 392–408.

¹⁴I disagree with the emphasis on Ezekiel's redemptive role, as explained by Brownlee, *Ezekiel 1–19*, 51–93. Brownlee writes, "Thus it was not just the last 190 days or so of the prophet's life which were redemptive, but his whole

prophetic career" (92). For an explanation of what he means by redemptive, see 70–74.

[15] See Samuel Amsler, "Les Prophètes et la communication par les actes," in *FS Westermann*, 194–201.

[16] Ellison observes that Ezekiel's priestly background made him very suitable for symbolic communication (*Ezekiel: The Man*, 17–18).

[17] The 390 days may symbolize (1) the period of the divided kingdom till the desolation of Jerusalem (Ellison, *Ezekiel: The Man*, 34); (2) a period of ten generations from the apostasy of Solomon till Jerusalem's fall (Aalders, *Ezechiel, 1–24*, COT [Kampen: Kok, 1955], 93). The LXX reads "190 days," which scholars take as the period from the Assyrian invasion under Tiglath-pileser III till 586 B.C. (see Eichrodt, *Ezekiel: A Commentary*, 84).

[18] Zimmerli, *Ezekiel* 1:173–74.

[19] Ellison, *Ezekiel: The Man*, 20.

[20] The sign points to Yahweh, whose word Ezekiel enacts, or in the words of Zimmerli: "The purpose of the prophet's sign-actions is set forth in a visible action the event announced by Yahweh as something already begun" (*Ezekiel*, 1:29, 54–55).

[21] Koch speaks of Ezekiel's prophetic ministry as a call "to embody the fate of the house of Israel's 'total-self' " (*Prophets* 2:86).

[22] See 13:8; 21:3; 26:3; 28:22; 29:3; 30:22; 34:10; 35:3; 38:3; 39:1. One must be careful not to read too much of the prophet's personal feelings, on account of the stylized language. See Zimmerli, *Ezekiel* 1:20–21.

[23] Norman K. Gottwald, *A Light to the Nations: An Introduction to the Old Testament* (New York: Harper & Row, 1959), 381.

[24] It occurs ninety-three times. Its use signifies "human" over against or in the presence of deity.

[25] Walther Zimmerli, "Erkenntnis Gottes Nach Dem Buche Ezechiel," in *Gottes Offenbarung* (Munich: Kaiser, 1969), 41–119.

[26] See the significant study by Zimmerli, *Ezekiel* 1:36–40.

[27] Fourteen dates (1:2; 8:1; 20:1; 24:1; 26:1; 29:1, 17; 30:20; 31:1; 32:1, 17; 33:21; 40:1; see Parker and Dubberstein, *Babylonian Chronology 626 B.C.–A.D. 75*, 27–28; K. S. Freedy and D. B. Redford, "The Dates in Ezekiel in Relation to Biblical, Babylonian and Egyptian Sources," JAOS 90 [1970]: 462–85).

[28] For critical issues, see Harrison, *IOT*, 823–32; LaSor, *OTS* 464–65; Childs, *IOTS*, 357–60.

[29] See the excellent discussion of the prophetic forms in Zimmerli, *Ezekiel* 1:25–41.

[30] See Walther Zimmerli, *Ezekiel: A Commentary on the Prophet Ezekiel*, trans. Ronald E. Clements, Hermeneia, 2 vols. (Philadelphia: Fortress, 1979), 1:1–2. He writes: "In coming from the other prophetic books, one is struck by the impression of great order in the book of Ezekiel. . . . Deviations . . . do not destroy the overall impression of good order, but appear rather to confirm the rule because they are the exception" (1:2).

[31] Ellison soberly reminds us to "avoid stressing the details" (*Ezekiel: The Man*, 76). So also he writes, "We may never in Old or New Testament stress the *subsidiary* points of allegory or parable" (95).

[32]See Susan Niditch, *The Symbolic Vision in Biblical Tradition* (Chico: Scholars Press, 1980).

[33]Zimmerli, *Ezekiel* 1:19.

[34]For a further discussion of the speech units and forms in Ezekiel, see ibid. 1:21–41.

[35]Ralph W. Klein rightly concludes from the relationship between the dating formulae and the references to Jehoiachin that he was viewed as the legitimate heir to the Davidic throne (*Israel in Exile: A Theological Interpretation* [Philadelphia: Fortress, 1979], 69–70).

[36]Moshe Greenberg ("Ezekiel's Vision: Literary and Iconographic Aspects," in *History, Historiography and Interpretation: Studies in Biblical and Cuneiform Literatures,* ed. H. Tadmor and M. Weinfeld [Jerusalem: Magnes, 1984], 159–68) looks at the iconographic aspect of Ezekiel's vision in his new cultural milieu.

[37]T. N. D. Mettinger sets the royal (Zion) theology in opposition to the name (Exodus) theology. He explains that with the Josianic reforms the emphasis shifted from the Lord "of hosts" enthroned above the cherubim to the Name who dwells in heaven and acts in redemptive history (Exodus). Ezekiel's visions may lend support to this, but the whole thesis depends on assuming that Ezekiel reflects the priestly theological perspective. See his *Dethronement of Sabaoth: Studies in the Shem and Kabod Theologies* (Lund: Gleerup, 1982).

[38]However, as Koch observes, there is no indication that the *kābôd* of Yahweh was going to remain among the exiles (*Prophets* 2:88).

[39]Greenberg, "Ezekiel's Vision," 161, 167.

[40]On the sin and judgment motif in Ezekiel, see Michael Fishbane, "Sin and Judgment in the Prophecies of Ezekiel," in *Interpreting the Prophets,* ed. James Luther Mays and Paul J. Achtemeier (Philadelphia: Fortress, 1987), 170–87.

[41]Klein, *Israel in Exile,* 74.

[42]Thomas M. Raitt correlates judgment, repentance, deliverance, and covenant renewal and argues that divine mercy does not lessen the severity of God's judgment (*A Theology of Exile: Judgment/Deliverance in Jeremiah and Ezekiel* [Philadelphia: Fortress, 1977], 122–27).

[43]See Zimmerli, *Ezekiel* 1:52. He writes, "The word of Yahweh, which the prophet has to proclaim, is not a doctrine about the essential nature of God, which can be described to men apart from any events, but an announcement of Yahweh's action towards Israel" (1:55).

[44]This formula occurs more than seventy times in one form or another.

[45]Walther Zimmerli, "Ich Bin Jahwe," in *Gottes Offenbarung* (Munich: Kaiser, 1969), 11–40.

[46]Zimmerli uses the phrase "the formula of self-introduction" (*Ezekiel* 1:37).

[47]Walther Zimmerli, "Erkenntnis Gottes Nach Dem Buche Ezechiel," 41–119.

[48]Walther Zimmerli, "Le Nouvel 'Exode' Dans le Message des Deux Grands Prophètes de L'Exil," in *FS Vischer,* 216–27 (= "Der 'Neue Exodus' in Der Verkündigung der Beiden Grossen Exilspropheten," in *Gottes Offenbarung* [Munich: Kaiser, 1969], 192–204).

[49]Raitt views the return to the homeland as Yahweh's acceptance of his people and of his establishing a new relationship with them (*Theology of Exile,*

194–95). See also R. E. Clements, "The Ezekiel Tradition: Prophecy in a Time of Crisis," in *Israel's Prophetic Tradition,* 119–36.

⁵⁰Zimmerli has observed that "Ezekiel lacks a fully-developed message about the world of the nations" (*Ezekiel* 1:66). But see also Henning Graf Reventlow, "Die Völker als Yahwes Zeugen bei Ezechiel," *ZAW* 71 (1959): 33–43.

⁵¹Norman K. Gottwald, *All the Kingdoms of the Earth: Israelite Prophecy and International Relations in the Ancient Near East* (New York: Harper & Row, 1964), 326. For the distinction between internationalism and universalism, see Harry M. Orlinsky, "Nationalism-Universalism and Internationalism in Ancient Israel," in *FS May,* 206–36.

⁵²E. Hammershaimb, "Ezekiel's View of the Monarchy," in *Some Aspects of Old Testament Prophecy from Isaiah to Malachi* (Copenhagen: Rosenkilde Og Bagger, 1966), 51–62. Klein writes, "In sum, the new exodus for Ezekiel presents the faithful God acting freely. . . . By manifesting his holiness Yahweh will produce a purified remnant as a witness to the nations" (*Israel in Exile,* 82–83).

⁵³Paul D. Hanson defines Ezekiel's visions as *protoapocalyptic* in *The Dawn of the Apocalyptic* (Philadelphia: Fortress, 1979), 235.

⁵⁴Dumbrell designates 33:21–39:29 as "Ezekiel's blue-print for the return of Israel" (*CCOTT,* 185–88).

⁵⁵Klein observes, "This faith goal, this doxological intention, puts decisive checks on any merely nationalist understanding of salvation" (*Israel in Exile,* 84).

⁵⁶Ellison, *Ezekiel: The Man,* 124–25. On the importance of the people-land relation, see Walter Brueggemann, *The Land: Place as Gift, Promise, and Challenge in Biblical Faith* (Philadelphia: Fortress, 1977).

⁵⁷The setting of the prophecy against Tyre gives no warrant for applying the oracle against Tyre (28:1–11) to Satan. Tyre represents the seductive power of greed and economic advantages. See Ellison, *Ezekiel: The Man,* 108–9. Carol A. Newsom demonstrates an appreciation for the powerful, imaginative genius of the prophet in "A Maker of Metaphors—Ezekiel's Oracles Against Tyre," *Int* 38 (1984): 151–64. For a careful study against the Canaanite-Ugaritic background, see H. J. van Dijk, *Ezekiel's Prophecy on Tyre {Ez. 26, 1–28, 19}: A New Approach* (Rome: Pontifical Biblical Institute, 1968).

⁵⁸For a similar realistic view, see Zechariah (chaps. 9–14) and Revelation (chaps. 6:1–20:15).

⁵⁹Jan Gerrit Aalders asks rhetorically, "Can Ezekiel say to Israel, 'Consider carefully! The return from exile does not mark the sudden end of trials! . . . The messianic age will not come immediately with the restoration from exile; first we must experience the history of Gog!'" (*Gog and Magog in Ezechiel* [Kampen: Kok, 1951], 135 [translation mine]).

⁶⁰Daniel I. Block, "Gog and the Pouring Out of the Spirit: Reflections on Ezekiel xxxix 21–9," *VT* 37 (1987): 257–70.

⁶¹G. Ch. Aalders, *Het Herstel van Israël volgens het Oude Testament* (Kampen: Kok, 1934), 161–78.

⁶²J. Ridderbos, *Het Godswoord der Profeten* (Kampen: Kok, 1941): 4:141–72.

⁶³Aalders, *Gog and Magog,* 164 (translation mine).

⁶⁴Yehezkel Kaufmann concludes, "While the vision of Gog has a universal setting, the dichotomy between Israel and the nations remains in full force even

after Gog's fall. The nations will continue their separate ways" (*The Religion of Israel: From Its Beginnings to the Babylonian Exile,* trans. and abr. Moshe Greenberg [New York: Schocken, 1960], 446).

[65] Aalders, *Gog and Magog,* 129–44.

[66] For differences between Leviticus and Ezekiel, see R. E. Clements, "The Ezekiel Tradition," in *FS Ackroyd,* 129–34.

[67] For Ezekiel's criticism of Zedekiah, see Bernard Lang for a stimulating discussion on Ezekiel's political message against Zedekiah (12:1–15; 17:1–10, 11–21, 22–24; 19; 21:23–37) in *Kein Aufstand in Jerusalem: Die Politik des Propheten Ezechiel* (Stuttgart: Katholisches Bibelwerk, 1983).

[68] Levenson goes so far as to conclude, "The messianic office has been absorbed into the divine office, where it yet retains some identity" (*Theology of the Program of Restoration of Ezekiel 40–48* [Missoula, Mont.: Scholars Press, 1976], 95).

[69] Levenson writes, "As Zion, the mountain of Ezekiel's vision in chaps. 40–48 is associated with kingship, both of God and of the human ruler" (ibid., 57).

[70] This was partly true under David and Solomon. Yehezkel Kaufmann observes that the King is no longer portrayed as a Warrior, but as a Shepherd (*Religion of Israel,* 442).

[71] Levenson, *Theology of the Program,* 122, citing Alfred Bertholet.

[72] Koch, *Prophets* 2:114.

[73] Levenson speaks of an intertwining of the Zion and the Eden traditions in Ezekiel (*Theology of the Program,* 161).

[74] Ibid., 163. See Klein, *Israel in Exile,* 92–95.

[75] Levenson explicates the parable of the vine as a referent to the messianic age (17:23) as he observes, "The messiah is obligated by the conditions of the covenant; the covenant includes the gift of the messianic dominion, whose human subjects are an obedient Israel and whose other subject is a marvelously renewed nature. The messiah and the burgeoning of nature are each a sign of the new relationship with God" (*Theology of the Program,* 81).

[76] Kaufmann explains the details of Ezekiel's temple as a programmatic approach to update the regulations pertaining to the tabernacle, *Religion of Israel,* 444–45. For the significance in John's vision of the New Jerusalem, see Oliver O'Donovan "The Political Thought of the Book of Revelation," *TB* 37 (1986): 92–94.

[77] R. E. Clements, "The Ezekiel Tradition," 133.

[78] Jon D. Levenson, *Sinai and Zion: An Entry into the Jewish Bible* (Minneapolis: Winston Press, 1985), 138–40. Moshe Greenberg concludes that Ezekiel's program was not put into effect in postexilic Judaism and that it remained a program for an idealized restoration ("The Design and Themes of Ezekiel's Program of Restoration," in *Interpreting the Prophets,* ed. James Luther Mays and Paul J. Achtemeier [Philadelphia: Fortress, 1987], 235–36).

[79] *Daniel* means "God is judge."

[80] Regarding the problem of the biblical evidence for the first deportation (1:1; see Jer. 25:1; 46:2) and the problem of the date, see E. J. Young, *The Prophecy of Daniel* (Grand Rapids: Eerdmans, 1949), 35; Joyce Baldwin, *Daniel: An Introduction and Commentary,* TOTC (Downers Grove, Ill.: InterVarsity, 1978), 19–21; A. R. Millard, "Daniel 1–6 and History," *EQ* 49 (1977): 68–69.

[81]On the identity of Belshazzar, see R. P. Dougherty, "Nabonidus and Belshazzar," *Yale Oriental Series* 15 (New Haven: Yale University Press, 1929), 63–80; Millard, "Daniel 1–6 and History," 72.

[82]On the problem of identifying Darius with Cyrus, see J. C. Whitcomb, *Darius the Mede: A Study in Historical Identification* (Philadelphia: Presbyterian & Reformed, 1963); Baldwin, *Daniel*, 23–28.

[83]A. R. Millard ("Daniel 1–6 and History," 72) cites approvingly the identification of the Babylonian names by P. R. Berger's article (*Zeitschrift für Assyriologie* 64 [1975]: 224–33).

[84]Young, *Prophecy of Daniel*, 44.

[85]On the problems associated with the two languages in Daniel and of the dating, see Baldwin, *Daniel*, 29–35.

[86]On the issues regarding date and authorship, see Harrison, *IOT*, 1110–27; LaSor, *OTS*, 665–66; Childs, *IOTS*, 611–22. On the problem of the canonical order, see Alexander A. Di Lella, "Introduction," in *The Book of Daniel* by Louis F. Hartman and Alexander A. Di Lella, AB (Garden City: Doubleday, 1978), 46–54. The problem of the text of Daniel presents us with additional issues (see Di Lella, "Introduction," 72–84). The LXX text differs from the MT. The MT is shorter. The Greek version contains "apocryphal" additions: namely, Prayer of Azariah, the Song of the Three Young Men, Susanna, Bel and the Dragon.

[87]Roger Beckwith, *The Old Testament Canon of the New Testament Church and Its Background in Early Judaism* (Grand Rapids: Eerdmans, 1985), 208.

[88]Klaus Koch, "Is Daniel Also Among the Prophets?" *Int* 39 (1985): 126–28.

[89]The authorship has been contested since the time of Porphyry, a third-century (A.D.) philosopher. Porphyry argued that the book reflects a second-century B.C. background, recounting in predictive style the actual historical circumstances of Antiochus Epiphanes. He denied the predictive element of prophecy and explained the book as a pious hoax. Unfortunately, this line of argument has had advocates throughout the history of interpretation. Criticism has been leveled against the book's historicity, original language, date, and interpretation. See Harrison, *IOT*, 1106–27; Young, *Daniel*, 317–20; LaSor, *OTS*, 665–68; Childs, *IOTS*, 611–13; Douglas E. Fox, "Ben Sira on OT Canon Again: The Date of Daniel," *WTJ* 49 (1987): 335–50.

[90]For a treatment of this genre, see John J. Collins, *Daniel, with an Introduction to Apocalyptic Literature*, FOTL (Grand Rapids: Eerdmans, 1984); Paul Hanson, *Dawn of Apocalyptic*; William J. Dumbrell, "Daniel 7 and the Function of Old Testament Apocalyptic," *RTR* 34 (1975): 16–23; Richard J. Bauckham, "The Rise of Apocalyptic," *Themelios* 3 (1978): 10–23. For an older treatment, see D. S. Russell, *The Method and Message of Jewish Apocalyptic* (Philadelphia: Westminster, 1964), 104–39.

[91]See "Apocalyptic" in the appendix.

[92]John J. Collins, "Daniel and His Social World," *Int* 39 (1985): 131–43.

[93]Ibid., 140–43.

[94]H. H. Rowley, "The Unity of the Book of Daniel," in *The Servant of the Lord and Other Essays on the Old Testament* (London: Luttesworth, 1952), 237–68.

[95]See Collins for a survey of critical developments (*Daniel*, 27–33).

[96] Childs, *IOTS*, 614–18.

[97] Baldwin, *Daniel*, 40.

[98] See the commentaries of Daniel by Baldwin and Young. See also Harrison, *IOT*, 1106–10; Bruce K. Waltke, "The Date of the Book of Daniel," *BibSac* 133 (1976): 319–29.

[99] J. G. Gammie, "The Classification, Stages of Growth, and Changing Intentions in the Book of Daniel," *JBL* 95 (1976): 194–204. Philip R. Davies is critical of Gammie's "unreliability" ("Eschatology in the Book of Daniel," *JSOT* 17 [1980]: 49 n. 13).

[100] Ibid., 204.

[101] Baldwin, *Daniel*, 63. She is dependent on the fine article by A. Lenglet, "La Structure littéraire de Daniel 2–7," *Bib* 53 (1972): 169–90.

[102] I am indebted to Baldwin's structural development of 2:1–7:28 and to her insight into the progressive development of the visions in chaps. 8–12 in relation to the first part of the book (ibid., 59–63).

[103] Childs, *IOTS*, 618–21.

[104] Baldwin writes, "The reinterpretation of Daniel's visions given by Jesus in Matthew 24 and 25 does not underestimate the suffering which can be expected by His followers" (*Daniel*, 177–78).

[105] See John Day, *God's Conflict with the Dragon and the Sea. Echoes of Canaanite Myth in the Old Testament* (Cambridge: Cambridge University Press, 1985), 156–57.

[106] Ibid., 188.

[107] Robert J. M. Gurney, "The Four Kingdoms of Daniel 2 and 7," *Themelios* 2 (1977): 39–45; John E. Goldingay, "The Book of Daniel: Three Issues," *Themelios* 2 (1977): 45–49.

[108] Baldwin, *Daniel*, 192.

[109] For another example of how the prophetic language compresses into one prophecy a succession of events, see the Mount Olivet Discourse, in which the destruction of Jerusalem, the persecution of the church, and the end time are compenetrated (Matt. 24:1–35; Mark 13:1–37; Luke 21:5–36).

[110] See the survey of views in Baldwin, *Daniel*, 148–54.

[111] Arthur J. Ferch concludes his extensive study with several noteworthy points: The Son of Man is "an individual, eschatological, and celestial figure with messianic characteristics. . . . he is distinct from the Ancient of Days. . . . [he is] set apart from the heavenly kings. . . . he is not one of the terrestrial saints with whom he, nevertheless, shares a perpetual kingdom or kingship and dominion" (*The Son of Man in Daniel 7*, AUSSDSS 6 [Berrien Springs, Mich.: Andrews University Press, 1979], 184).

[112] See Vern S. Poythress, "The Holy Ones of the Most High in Daniel vii," *VT* 26 (1976): 208–13.

[113] The Son of Man is distinct from the saints, contra Hartmann: "Rather, the expression [Son of Man] is nothing more or less than a symbol of 'the holy ones of the Most High,' who are, as we have seen . . . the faithful Israelites to be rewarded for their steadfastness in the face of persecution and martyrdom" (*Daniel*, 97–98).

[114] For a refutation of the "saints" as "angels," see Hartmann, *Daniel*, 95–101.

[115]See the stimulating discussion by Roger T. Beckwith, "Daniel 9 and the Date of the Messiah's Coming in Essene, Hellenistic, Pharisaic, Zealot, and Early Christian Computation," *Revue de Qumran* 40 (1981): 521–42.

[116]E. J. Young regards the seventy "sevens" as a period of time during which the salvation for which Daniel prayed will be accomplished. This salvation is to effect the end of sin and transgression and the inauguration of everlasting righteousness and the anointing of the Holy of Holies. Young divides the "unit" into periods of time of unequal length:

7 "sevens"—to the period of Ezra and Nehemiah

62 "sevens"—to the coming of Jesus Christ

1 "seven"—the life and death of the Messiah till an indefinite conclusion

Clearly, Young embraces the symbolic interpretation, as he does not want to force a specific time limit on the word *week* (*Daniel*, 111–21). Joyce Baldwin agrees with Young at this point (*Daniel*, 168–75).

[117]Thomas E. McComiskey writes, "Thus, the *šābu'îm* [weeks] are not conceived of as marking precise chronological periods in this view. . . . they (the weeks) confirm an end to the exile, but they depict a longer period of time, described as a 'troubled' time, in which Jerusalem's desolations would continue" ("The Seventy 'Weeks' of Daniel Against the Background of Ancient Near Eastern Literature," *WTJ* 47 [1985]: 41). See Baldwin (*Daniel*, 177); her focus is rightly on the first Advent and on Jesus' development of Daniel's visions in the Mount Olivet Discourse (Matt. 24; 25).

[118]See the survey by Vern Sheridan Poythress, "Hermeneutical Factors in Determining the Beginning of the Seventy Weeks (Daniel 9:25)," *TrinJ* 6 (1985): 131–49.

[119]McComiskey, "The Seventy 'Weeks' of Daniel," 25–26.

[120]McComiskey concludes that the first seven takes us from the revelation of the seventy weeks to Jeremiah to Cyrus, "the anointed one, the ruler" (v. 25); the sixty-two from Cyrus to another "anointed one," whom he identifies with Antiochus Epiphanes (v. 26; "the little horn" of 7:24–26; see 11:40, 45); the last seven relates to the events surrounding the abomination and desolation. Yet, McComiskey carefully argues that the course of events was not fulfilled in 165 B.C. and that "the seventy *šābu'îm* take their course until "the supreme Desolator has been destroyed" ("The Seventy 'Weeks' of Daniel," 41).

[121]On the nature of the covenant, see Meredith G. Kline, "The Covenant of the Seventieth Week," in *FS Allis*, 452–69. For a contrary view, see McComiskey, "The Seventy 'Weeks' of Daniel."

[122]Goldingay, "The Book of Daniel," 48.

Chapter 12

[1]See these challenging works: Jacques Ellul, *Hope in Time of Abandonment*, trans. C. Edward Hopkin (New York: Seabury, 1973); Os Guinness, *The Gravedigger File* (Downers Grove, Ill.: InterVarsity Press, 1983).

[2]I appreciate the way Simon J. De Vries develops the prophetic use of "in that day": "The day future as a new opportunity for decisive action" (*Yesterday, Today and Tomorrow: Time and History in the Old Testament* [Grand Rapids: Eerdmans, 1975], 323–31).

[3] VanGemeren, *Progress,* 465–74.

[4] Anthony Hoekema, *The Bible and the Future* (Grand Rapids: Eerdmans, 1979), 54.

[5] Günther Bornkamm, "Future and Present (Eschatology and Ethics)," in *Paul,* trans. D. M. G. Stalker (New York: Harper & Row, 1971), 196–227.

[6] For these qualities of the royal ideal, see Keith K. Whitelam, *The Just King: Monarchical Judicial Authority,* JSOTSS 12 (Sheffield: JSOT, 1979), 29–37.

[7] Yehezkel Kaufmann speaks of Israel as a "prophet-nation, 'a witness to the peoples,'" in *The Religion of Israel: From Its Beginning to the Babylonian Exile,* trans. and abr. Moshe Greenberg (New York: Schocken, 1960), 451.

[8] See the fine study by Paul D. Hanson, *The People Called: The Growth of Community in the Bible* (San Francisco: Harper & Row, 1987).

[9] J. A. Bollier, "The Righteousness of God: A Word Study," *Int* 8 (1954): 404–13; K. Hj. Fahlgren, "Die Gegensätze von ṣᵉdāqâ im Alten Testament," in *Um das Prinzip der Vergeltung in Religion und Recht des Alten Testaments,* ed. K. Koch (Darmstadt: Wissenschaftliche Buchgesellschaft, 1972), 87–129; Gerhard von Rad, *OTT* 1:370–83; idem, "'Righteousness' and 'Life' in the Cultic Language of the Psalms," in *The Problem of the Hexateuch and Other Essays,* trans. E. W. Trueman Dicken (London: Oliver & Boyd, 1966), 243–66; Hans Heinrich Schmid, "Creation, Righteousness, and Salvation: 'Creation Theology' as a Broad Horizon of Biblical Theology," in *Creation in the Old Testament,* ed. Bernard W. Anderson (Philadelphia: Fortress, 1984), 102–17; VanGemeren, "Righteousness," *EDB,* forthcoming; *TDNT* 2:212–14; *THAT* 2:507–29; *TWOT* 2:752–55.

[10] Calvin's comment on Psalm 48:10 is most insightful: "*The righteousness of God* is to be understood of his faithfulness which he observes in maintaining and defending his own people" (*Commentary on the Book of Psalms* [Grand Rapids: Baker, 1979], 2:229).

[11] H. Baarlink writes that it "is remarkable how insistently in a variety of expressions peace comes as a result of human acts" (*Vrede op Aarde: de Messiaanse Vrede in bijbels Perspectief* [Kampen: Kok, 1985], 44).

[12] John W. Olley, *"Righteousness" in the Septuagint of Isaiah: A Contextual Study* (Missoula, Mont.: Scholars Press, 1979).

[13] Ibid., 9.

[14] Ibid., 43.

[15] Ibid., 63.

[16] Ibid., 117.

[17] Ibid., 123.

[18] Ibid., 126.

[19] Ibid., 151.

[20] James Luther Mays insightfully observed that the problem in ancient Israel was not with law, but with justice ("Justice: Perspectives from the Prophetic Tradition," *Int* 37 [1983]: 5–17).

[21] I agree with Mays that the prophets "were not social reformers or political activists or revolutionaries. . . . Their concentration on the demand for change in the lives of people and their trust in the work of God in overturning the old impossibilities to make way for the new was too unrelieved" (ibid., 17).

[22] See Peter Beyerhaus, "Blessed Are the Poor in Spirit: 'The Theology of

the Poor in Biblical Perspective,' " in *God Who Is Rich in Mercy: Essays Presented to Dr. D. B. Knox,* ed. Peter T. O'Brien and David G. Peterson (Homebush West: Lancer, 1986), 153–63.

[23] See esp. the fine studies by Katherine D. Sakenfeld, *The Meaning of Ḥesed in the Hebrew Bible: A New Inquiry* (Missoula, Mont.: Scholars Press, 1978); idem, *Faithfulness in Action* (Philadelphia: Fortress, 1985). For a critical review, see C. F. Whitley, "The Semantic Range of Ḥesed," Bib 62 (1981): 519–26. For older studies, see Nelson Glueck, *Ḥesed in the Bible,* trans. Alfred Gottschalk (1967; reprint, New York: Ktav, 1975) with a survey, "Recent Studies in Ḥesed," by Gerald A. Larue (1–32); W. Lofthouse, "Ḥen and Ḥesed in the Old Testament," *ZAW* 51 (1933): 29–35; Francis I. Andersen, "Yahweh, the Kind and Sensitive God," in *God Who Is Rich in Mercy,* 41–88.

[24] L. J. Kuyper, "Grace and Truth: An Old Testament Description of God, and its Use in the Johannine Gospel," *Reformed Review* 16 (1963): 1–16; E. Perry, "The Meaning of *'emuna* in the Old Testament," *JBR* 21 (1953): 252–56; E. T. Ramsdell, "The Old Testament Understanding of Truth," *JR* 31 (1951): 264–73.

[25] Jacques Ellul argues for the necessity of relating Christian ethics to the doctrine of God, Christology, to the Spirit of God, and to eschatology (*The Ethics of Freedom,* trans. Geoffrey W. Bromiley [Grand Rapids: Eerdmans, 1976]).

[26] See the excellent study of Baarlink, *Vrede op Aarde.* He relates *shalom* to the coming of Christ and to the New Testament teaching of *shalom.* See also Hubert Frankemölle, *Friede und Schwert: Frieden schaffen nach dem Neuen Testament* (Mainz: *Matthias-Grunewald-Verlag,* 1983), 52–54.

[27] See the challenging discussion by Richard J. Mouw, *When the Kings Come Marching In: Isaiah and the New Jerusalem* (Grand Rapids: Eerdmans, 1983).

[28] This is the danger of liberation theology and of the reconstructionist movement. The danger also exists in what Mouw identifies as the "transformationalist camp," which he calls the " 'Christ transforming culture' camp" (ibid., 75).

[29] James A. Sanders, *God Has a Story Too: Sermons in Context* (Philadelphia: Fortress, 1979), 18.

[30] See the exciting study by a number of Dutch New Testament scholars, written from different eschatological and theological perspectives: *Vervulling and Voleinding: De Toekomstverwachting in het Nieuwe Testament {Fulfillment and Consummation: The Expectation of the Future in the New Testament},* ed. H. Baarlink, W. S. Duvekot, and A. Geense (Kampen: Kok, 1984). See also T. Baarda, Hans Jansen, S. J. Noorda, and J. S. Vos, *Paulus en de andere Joden: Exegetische Bijdragen en Discussie* (Delft: Meinema, 1984); Baarlink, *Vrede op Aarde.*

[31] Brevard S. Childs, "The Sensus Literalis of Scripture: An Ancient and Modern Problem," in *FS Zimmerli,* 93; idem, "The Old Testament as Scripture of the Church," *CTM* 43 (1972): 709–22.

[32] Thomas M. Raitt, *A Theology of Exile: Judgment/Deliverance in Jeremiah and Ezekiel* (Philadelphia: Fortress, 1977), 217.

[33] W. Zimmerli, *The Law and the Prophets: A Study of the Meaning of the Old Testament,* trans. R. E. Clements (New York: Harper & Row, 1965), 66.

[34]The recognition of the postexilic era as a watershed in biblical eschatology is long overdue. Too often we rush past God's work in the Exile to the coming of Jesus Christ as the eschatological event, bypassing the work of salvation in the era from 538 B.C. till the coming of our Lord. The emphasis on the one plan of God and the unity of God requires a reinstatement of the postexilic era as a stage in the eschatological fulfillment. The Exile was a process of purification and resulted in a recovery of the freedom of God to establish his covenant, his kingdom, and his purposes.

[35]W. de Greef, *Calvijn en het Oude Testament* (Amsterdam: Ton Bolland, 1984).

[36]Baarlink, *Vrede op Aarde,* 48–63.

[37]For a survey of current views, see Beverly Roberts Gaventa, "The Eschatology of Luke-Acts Revisited," *Encounter* 43 (1982): 27–42.

[38]Raymond Brown, *The Birth of the Messiah: A Commentary on the Infancy Narratives in Matthew and Luke* (Garden City: Doubleday, 1977), 499.

[39]Brevard S. Childs writes that in the coming of the Spirit "the promised eschatological time becomes a reality" (*The New Testament as Canon: An Introduction* [Philadelphia: Fortress, 1984], 108).

[40]John F. Maile concludes that the Ascension is significant in Luke–Acts for these reasons: (1) the confirmation of Christ's present and exalted lordship, (2) the continuity between Christ and the church, (3) the culmination of his resurrection appearances, (4) the prelude of the coming of the Holy Spirit, (5) the basis for missions, and (6) the pledge of the coming of Christ ("The Ascension in Luke–Acts," *TB* 37 [1986]: 29–59).

[41]Donald Guthrie, *New Testament Theology* (Downers Grove, Ill.: InterVarsity Press, 1981), 236–52; Ladd, *TNT,* 135–44; Leon Morris, *The Lord from Heaven* (Grand Rapids: Eerdmans, 1958), 29–32; James D. G. Dunn, *Unity and Diversity in the New Testament: An Inquiry into the Character of Earliest Christianity* (Philadelphia: Westminster, 1977), 41–45; S. Neill, *The Supremacy of Jesus* (Downers Grove, Ill.: InterVarsity Press, 1984), 86–100.

[42]Ladd, *TNT,* 159–72; I. H. Marshall, "The Divine Sonship of Jesus," *Int* 21 (1967): 87–103; G. Vos, *The Self-Disclosure of Jesus* (Grand Rapids: Eerdmans, 1954), 141–70; James D. G. Dunn, *Christology in the Making: A New Testament Inquiry into the Origins of the Doctrine of the Incarnation* (Philadelphia: Westminster, 1980), 12–64.

[43]Ladd, *TNT,* 146–58; Guthrie, *New Testament Theology,* 270–91; B. Lindars, *Jesus Son of Man* (Grand Rapids: Eerdmans, 1983); I. Howard Marshall, "The Synoptic Son of Man Sayings in Recent Discussion," *New Testament Studies* 12 (1965–66): 327–51; Frederick M. Wilson, "The Son of Man in Jewish Apocalyptic Literature," *StudBT* 8 (1978): 28–52; Seyoon Kim, *"The Son of Man" as the Son of God* (Grand Rapids: Eerdmans, 1985); Beasley-Murray, *Jesus and the Kingdom* (Grand Rapids: Eerdmans, 1986), 219–312.

[44]Luke presents Jesus as the incarnate "Lord" of glory. For him "Lord" signifies none other than the exalted Jesus who is seated at the right hand of the Father (Acts 2:36). Thus, the use "Lord" in the gospel of Luke presupposes this exalted connotation (Luke 7:13, 19; 10:1; 11:39; 12:42; 13:15; 17:5–6; 18:6; 19:8; 22:61). See Ladd, *TNT,* 338; Dunn, *Unity,* 50–54; Archibald M. Hunter concludes that the title "Lord" summarizes the *"essential* Christology in the New

Testament" (*The Message of the New Testament* [Philadelphia: Westminster, 1944], 48).

[45] Guthrie comments that Jesus "saw himself fulfilling the whole role including the vicarious suffering" (*New Testament Theology,* 262); R. T. France, "The Servant of the Lord in the Teaching of Jesus," *TB* 19 (1968): 26–52.

[46] John F. Maile, "The Ascension in Luke–Acts," 29–59.

[47] See the challenging study by Bo Reicke, "Positive and Negative Aspects of the World in the NT," *WTJ* 49 (1987): 351–69.

[48] Anthony A. Hoekema speaks of the signs of the kingdom in Jesus' ministry, such as the casting out of demons, the fall of Satan, miracles, the preaching of the gospel, and forgiveness of sin (*The Bible and the Future,* 41–54).

[49] Herman N. Ridderbos, *Coming of the Kingdom* (Philadelphia: Presbyterian & Reformed, 1962), 55.

[50] For a survey of interpretation on the Spirit in the theology of Acts, see M. M. B. Turner, "The Significance of Receiving the Spirit in Luke–Acts: A Survey of Modern Scholarship," *TrinJ* 2 (1981): 131–58.

[51] Willem A. VanGemeren, "The Spirit of Restoration," *WTJ* 50 (1988): 81–102.

[52] See Henry J. Cadbury, "Acts and Eschatology," in *FS Dodd,* 300–321; E. G. Selwyn, "Eschatology in I Peter," in *FS Dodd,* 394–401; C. K. Barrett, "The Eschatology of the Epistle to the Hebrews," in *FS Dodd,* 363–93; Rudolf Schnackenburg, "Die lukanische Eschatologie im Lichte von Aussagen der Apostelgeschichte," in *FS Kümmel,* 249–65.

[53] E. Earle Ellis, *Eschatology in Luke* (Philadelphia: Fortress, 1972), 14. For the place of the Ascension, see Eric Franklin, "The Ascension and the Eschatology of Luke–Acts," *SJT* 23 (1970): 191–200.

[54] Ellis, *Eschatology in Luke,* 19–20.

[55] S. G. Wilson demonstrates that Luke's eschatology is not opposed to Paul's ("Lukan Eschatology," *New Testament Studies* 16 [1969–70]: 330–47).

[56] Baarlink, *Vrede op Aarde,* 65–76.

[57] I am indebted to the exegetical study by Baarlink (ibid., 79–98).

[58] Ibid., 93 (translation mine).

[59] Ladd comments, "It is of great interest that Luke summarizes the content of Paul's preaching to the Gentiles by the utterly non-Hellenistic phrase 'the Kingdom of God'" (*TNT,* 333).

[60] Ibid., 97–98; see A. J. Mattill, Jr., *Luke and the Last Things: A Perspective for the Understanding of Lukan Thought* (Dillsboro: Western North Carolina Press, 1979), 136–45.

[61] I agree with F. Scott Spencer's criticism that Sanders has not seen the continuity between the prophets and Luke, the theologian: "Like the OT prophets, Luke pronounces judgment on a rebellious people, not as a sign of personal animosity, but as a spur to repentance" (review of J. T. Sanders, *The Jews in Luke–Acts* [London: SCM, 1987], in *WTJ* 49 [1987]: 430).

[62] Willis Judson Beecher, *The Prophets and the Promise* (1905; reprint, Grand Rapids: Baker, 1963), 193.

[63] Hendrikus Berkhof, *Christian Faith: An Introduction to the Study of Faith,* trans. Sierd Woudstra (Grand Rapids: Eerdmans, 1979), 333–34. For an

evaluation of Berkhof's view of the Spirit and structures, see H. M. Kuitert, "Vernieuwing van de Wereld: De Geest en zijn Werk aan Persoon en Structuur," in *Weerwoord: Reacties op Dr. H. Berkhof's "Christelijk Geloof"* (Nijkerk: Callenbach, 1974), 191–200).

[64] N. A. Dahl, "Christ, Creation and the Church," in *FS Dodd,* 422–43.

[65] Leopold Sabourin speaks of an actualized eschatology in the light of the gift of the Spirit and the mission to the Gentiles, ("The Eschatology of Luke," *BTB* 12 [1982]: 73–76).

[66] I fully agree here with Calvin's emphasis that the responsibility for not enjoying the benefits of Christ's kingdom lies with God's people: "But we are straitened in ourselves; hence it is, that hardly the smallest drops of God's bounty come to us" (*Commentaries on the Book of the Prophet Jeremiah and the Lamentations* [Grand Rapids: Eerdmans, 1950], 4:85).

[67] Michael Green, *I Believe in the Holy Spirit* (Grand Rapids: Eerdmans, 1975).

[68] See the challenge by Jacques Ellul on personal responsibility in *Hope in Time of Abandonment,* 126–28.

[69] Joel B. Green, *How to Read Prophecy* (Downers Grove, Ill.: InterVarsity Press, 1984), 126.

[70] On faith as an eschatological phenomenon, see John Painter, "Eschatological Faith in the Gospel of John," in *FS Morris,* 36–52.

[71] Stephen H. Travis, *Christian Hope & the Future* (Downers Grove, Ill.: InterVarsity Press, 1980), 138.

[72] Barnabas Lindars, "The Sound of the Trumpet: Paul and Eschatology," *BJRL* 67 (1984–85): 782.

[73] Heinrich Quistorp, *Calvin's Doctrine of the Last Things,* trans. Harold Knight (Richmond: John Knox, 1955), 15.

[74] See the introduction by T. F. Torrance to Quistorp's *Calvin's Doctrine of the Last Things,* 8.

[75] H. Verweij, *De Komende Messias: Wereld en Welzijn in profetisch Perspectief* (Kampen: Kok, 1971).

[76] Ibid., 11–15. Similarly Jacques Ellul writes, "Nascent Christianity not only enters completely into the desacralizing process of Hebrew thought, the secularization of the world, but carries it through to the limit" (*The Subversion of Christianity,* trans. Geoffrey W. Bromiley [Grand Rapids: Eerdmans, 1986], 59). Ellul's emphasis is on demythologization, whereas Verweij's is on secularization to the point of an immanentistic, rationalistic, and humanistic culture.

[77] Oliver O'Donovan, "The Political Thought of the Book of Revelation," *TB* 37 (1986): 67.

[78] The Dutch missiologist, A. G. Honig, Jr., recognizes the danger of demythologizing Satan in our present crisis: "The denial of the demonic powers is indeed the greatest danger that threatens mankind" (*De Kosmische Betekenis van Christus in Hedendaagse Aziatische Theologie* [Kampen: Kok, 1984], 79–81 [translation mine]).

[79] Ibid., 35.

[80] Ellul, *Subversion of Christianity,* 211.

[81] Verweij, *De Komende Messias,* 42–43, 57–59. A. G. Honig, Jr. addressed the significance of the cosmic Christ in his inaugural lecture as missiologist at the

Kampen Seminary on October 1, 1968 (*De Kosmische Betekenis van Christus* [Kampen: Kok, 1968]), and spoke of the same issue at his retirement on May 18, 1984 (*De Kosmische Betekenis van Christus in Hedendaagse Aziatische Theologie*).

[82] See Abraham Kuyper, *Calvinism: Six Stone Foundation Lectures* (Grand Rapids: Eerdmans, 1943). These lectures were originally given at Princeton Theological Seminary, October 1898.

[83] Verweij, *De Komende Messias*, 97–101.

[84] Ibid., 46–76.

[85] Ibid., 49.

[86] He defines our character as "an unhealthy me-centeredness and selfishness" (ibid., 85 [translation mine]).

[87] O. Cullmann, "Eschatology and Missions in the New Testament," in *FS Dodd*, 409–21.

[88] O'Donovan, "The Political Thought of the Book of Revelation," 90.

[89] Thomas R. Schreiner, "The Church as the New Israel and the Future of Ethnic Israel in Paul," *StudBT* 13 (1983): 17–38; T. Baarda et al., *Paulus en de andere Joden*.

[90] VanGemeren, *IHCIP*. I cannot harmonize William J. Dumbrell's magnificent treatment of the new covenant in Jeremiah with his statement "Jesus rejects the nation of Israel" (*The End of the Beginning: Revelation 21–22 and the Old Testament* [Grand Rapids: Baker, 1985], 120).

[91] Kevin Giles, "Present–Future Eschatology in the Book of Acts," *RTR* 40 (1981): 65–71; *RTR* 41 (1982): 11–18.

[92] Ivan Dugandzic writes, "These questions [in the doxology] recapitulate once more everything that has been stated about the freedom and sovereignty of God in his dealings with people" (*Das "Ja" Gottes in Christus: Eine Studie zur Bedeutung des Alten testaments für das Christusverständnis des Paulus* [Würzburg: Echter Verlag, 1977], 295 [translation mine]).

[93] For a summary of the approaches to Rom. 9–11 and a significant literary analysis, see James W. Aageson, "Scripture and Structure in the Development of the Argument in Romans 9–11," *CBQ* 48 (1986): 265–89.

[94] See Charles Hodge, *Commentary on the Epistle to the Romans* (1886; reprint, Grand Rapids: Eerdmans, 1960), 374; G. Vos, *Pauline Eschatology*, 89; John Murray, *Romans*, 2 vols. (Grand Rapids: Eerdmans, 1959, 1965), 2:99; Hendrikus Berkhof, *Christian Faith: An Introduction to the Study of the Faith*, trans. Sierd Woudstra, rev. ed. (Grand Rapids: Eerdmans, 1986), 253–70; Nils Alstrup Dahl, "The Future of Israel," in *Studies in Paul* (Minneapolis: Augsburg, 1977), 137–58.

[95] James W. Aageson writes, "Paul advances his discussion, attempts to demonstrate that God's word has not failed, and seeks to inspire among his readers a way of understanding the relationship between Jews and Gentiles in God's plan of salvation. This inspirational aspect of Romans 9–11 is too often overlooked. Paul is not writing as a dispassionate theologian to a dispassionate audience" ("Scripture and Structure in the Development of the Argument in Romans 9–11," 288). See Otfried Hofius, "Das Evangelium und Israel. Erwägungen zu Römer 9–11," *ZTK* 83 (1986): 297–324.

[96] Ladd, *TNT*, 562; Dahl writes, "Paul's scheme, which provides the

framework of his exegesis, follows the workings of God's mercy from Israel to the Gentiles, and from the Gentiles back to Israel, for the ultimate good of all" ("The Future of Israel," 156).

[97] Peter Richardson, *Israel in the Apostolic Church* (Cambridge: Cambridge University Press, 1969), 201–3. Van Buren coins the phrase "theology of displacement" (*Discerning the Way,* 61, see also 60–67, 138–44).

[98] James Atkinson's study briefly traces the tensions between Jews and Christians (*Christianity & Judaism: New Understanding, New Relationship,* Latimer Studies 17 [Oxford: Latimer House, 1984]).

[99] Berkhof, *Christian Faith,* 261. Dahl writes, "There is no Jewish problem, but there is a Christian problem" ("The Future of Israel," 158).

[100] For an appeal to dialogue with non-Christians, see Bruce V. Malchow, "The Prophetic Contribution to Dialogue," *BTB* 16 (1986): 127–31.

[101] Hans Walter Wolff, "Was ist das Neue im neuen Bund?" in *Prophetische Alternativen: Entdeckungen des Neuen im Alten Testament* (Munich: Kaiser, 1982), 55–69.

[102] Ibid., 68–69.

[103] Bennie Charles Ollenburger, "Zion, the City of the Great King: A Theological Investigation of Zion Symbolism in the Tradition of the Jerusalem Cult" (Ph.D. diss., Princeton Theological Seminary, 1982), 273–95.

[104] Hendrikus Berkhof rightly distinguishes between *futurology* and *eschatology*. Futurology is the outworking of man's plans and dreams toward an ideal society, enjoying the benefits of climate control, automation, medicine and genetic engineering, prosperity, societal and psychological transformation, and world peace (*Well-founded Hope* [Richmond: John Knox, 1969], 69–82).

[105] William McKane, *Prophets and Wise Men,* SBT 44 (London: SCM, 1965): 129.

[106] Raitt, *Theology of Exile,* 228–29.

[107] Walter Brueggemann, *The Prophetic Imagination* (Philadelphia: Fortress, 1978), 95.

[108] Berkhof, *Well-founded Hope,* 72.

[109] Ibid., 74. Jürgen Moltmann is probably correct in his mild criticism of Berkhof that the latter speaks of extrapolation from what God has given us in Christ and the Spirit, whereas it is preferable to speak of prolepsis or anticipation ("Extrapolation und Antizipation, Zur Methode in der Eschatologie," in *Weerwoord,* 201–8).

[110] J. van Genderen, *Geloofskennis en Geloofsverwachting* (Kampen: Kok, 1982), 46.

[111] Ibid., 62–66. See also Painter, "Eschatological Faith in the Gospel of John," 36–52.

[112] Berkhof, *Well-founded Hope,* 99–100.

[113] Paul D. Hanson, *The Diversity of Scripture* (Philadelphia: Fortress, 1982).

[114] Ibid., 39.

[115] I agree with Raitt that "eschatology is the search for and discovery of a frame of reference to explain events which are not understandable in terms of any previously existing tradition" (*Theology of Exile,* 215).

[116] Ellul develops three aspects of hope—waiting, prayer, and realism—in *Hope in Time of Abandonment,* 258–83.

117The prophetic vision opens up great vistas, as Jürgen Moltmann writes, "If the process of creation is to be consummated through the indwelling of God, then the unlimited possibilities open to God will indwell the new creation and glorified man will be free to participate in the unlimited freedom of God. . . . Thus time and history, future and possibility may be admitted into the kingdom of glory and, moreover, both to an unimpeded extent and in a way that is no longer ambivalent" ("Creation and Redemption," in *FS Torrance,* 130). On the freedom of God and history, see Gerhard von Rad, "The Witness of the Prophets to God's Ways in World History," in *God at Work in Israel,* trans. John H. Marks (Nashville: Abingdon, 1980), 160–75.

118David A. Hubbard, "Hope in the Old Testament," *TB* 34 (1983): 58.

119See the recent challenge by Scott J. Hafemann, "Seminary, Subjectivity, and the Centrality of Scripture: Reflections on the Current Crisis in Evangelical Seminary Education," *JETS* 31 (1988): 129–43.

120Walther Zimmerli, *The Old Testament and the World,* trans. John J. Scullion (Atlanta: John Knox, 1976), 150.

121See Luke 18:1–8, the laments psalms, the Lord's Prayer, and Rev. 22:20. J. H. Eaton, *Vision in Worship: The Relation of Prophecy and Liturgy in the Old Testament* (London: SPCK, 1981).

122Here I agree with Ellul's warning, "Thus when all Christianity is reduced to the temporal, the insertion of the eternal into the temporal has the last word, producing inversion by a reconquest of the eternal that decisively overturns the temporal" (*Subversion of Christianity,* 211). Brueggemann's study on man's establishment of his counterkingdom on earth is a move in a positive direction. He calls for a renewed investigation of the place of the church in the world and of the secularization of revelation, characterized by (1) a management mentality; (2) a legitimatizaton of an "official religion of optimism"; and (3) an annulment of the neighbor (Brueggemann, *Prophetic Imagination,* 42–43).

123See Bennie Charles Ollenburger, "Zion, the City of the Great King"; Hans Heinrich Schmid, "Creation, Righteousness, and Salvation: 'Creation Theology' as a Broad Horizon of Biblical Theology," in *Creation in the Old Testament,* ed. Bernard W. Anderson (Philadelphia: Fortress, 1984), 102–17; Joachim Becker, *Messianic Expectation in the Old Testament,* trans. David E. Green (Philadelphia: Fortress, 1980).

124Philip Edgcumbe Hughes, *A Commentary on the Epistle to the Hebrews* (Grand Rapids: Eerdmans, 1977), 580–81.

125Ellul, *Subversion of Christianity,* 13.

126Robert N. Bellah, Richard Madsen, William M. Sullivan, Ann Swidler, and Steven M. Tipton, *Habits of the Heart: Individualism and Commitment in American Life* (Berkeley: University of California Press, 1985).

127See the humanistic proposal by Bellah et al., "Transforming American Culture," in *Habits of the Heart,* 275–96.

128Ralph W. Klein, *Israel in Exile: A Theological Interpretation* (Philadelphia: Fortress, 1979), 151–54; see 149–54.

Appendix

1Huffmon's contribution comes from the wider study of the ANE treaties and legal language. He differentiates between the heavenly court, in which the gods render a verdict in which earthly and heavenly forces are brought together against the offending party, and the legal suit (*rîb*), according to which the offending party is indicted and must be judged for breaching the covenant ("The Covenant Lawsuit in the Prophets," *JBL* 78 [1959], 295).

[2] F. C. Fensham, "Maledictions and Benedictions in Ancient Near-Eastern Vassal Treaties and the Old Testament," *ZAW* 74 (1962): 1–19.

[3] D. R. Hillers, *Treaty-Curses and the Old Testament Prophets,* Biblica et Orientalia 16 (Rome: Pontifical Biblical Institute, 1964), 86–87; see F. C. Fensham, "Common Trends in the Curses of the Near Eastern and Kudurru-Inscriptions Compared with Maledictions of Amos and Isaiah," *ZAW* 75 (1963): 155–75. The criticism by W. Schottroff (*Das altisraelitische Fluchspruch,* WMANT 30 [Neukirchen-Vluyn: Neukirchener, 1969]) is well taken. He argues that the oracles are too general, lacking the specific connections with the Mosaic "curses."

[4] Cf. G. Ernest Wright, "The Lawsuit of God: A Form-Critical Study of Deuteronomy 32," in *FS Muilenburg,* 26–67; H. B. Huffmon, "The Covenant Lawsuit," 285–95; Julien Harvey, "Le 'Rib-Pattern, requisitoire prophétique sur la rupture de l'alliance," *Biblica* 43 (1962): 172–96; *Le Plaidoyer Prophétique contre Israël après la rupture de l'alliance* (Paris: Desclée de Brouwer, 1967); B. Gemser, "The Rîb- or Controversy Pattern in Hebrew Mentality," in *FS Rowley,* 120–37; James Limburg, "The Root רִיב and the Prophetic Lawsuit Speeches," *JBL* 88 (1969): 291–304.

[5] Claus Westermann, "Sprache und Struktur der Prophetie Deuterojesajas," in *Forschung am Alten Testament* (Munich: Kaiser, 1964), 92–170.

[6] H. Huffmon, "The Covenant Lawsuit," 285–95.

[7] Wright, "The Lawsuit," 52–54. For other examples, see Isa. 1; Jer. 2; Mic. 6. However, the legal presentation of the lawsuit is not limited to the prophets, as it also underlies the argument of Job 9:2–; 13:3–; cf. E. von Waldow, *Der traditionsgeschichtliche Hintergrund der prophetlichen Gerichtsreden,* BZAW 85 (Berlin: Töpelmann, 1963). A technical term for the sentence may well be *massā'* (cf. Isa. 13:1; 14:28; 15:1; 17:1; 19:1; 21:1, etc.), see J. A. Naude, "Massā' in the Old Testament with Special Reference to the Prophets," in *Biblical Essays,* ed. A. H. van Zyl (Potchefstroom: Pro Rege-Pers, 1969), 91–100.

[8] R. E. Clements, *Prophecy and Tradition* (Atlanta: John Knox, 1975), 13–21; Klaus Koch rejects the legal interpretation of the forms of prophetic speech, see *The Growth of the Biblical Tradition: The Form-Critical Method,* trans. S. M. Cupitt (New York: Scribner, 1967).

[9] See the significant study by Kirsten Nielsen, *Yahweh as Prosecutor and Judge: An Investigation of the Prophetic Lawsuit (Rîb-Pattern),* JSOTSS 9 (Sheffield: JSOT, 1978).

[10] See the excellent treatise by Adrian Graffy, *A Prophet Confronts His People: The Disputation Speech in the Prophets,* Analecta Biblica 104 (Rome: Biblical Institute Press, 1984). The former category includes Isa. 28:14–19; Jer. 8:8–9; 31:29–30; Ezek. 11:2–12, 14–17; 12:21–25; 18:1–20; 33:23–29; Hag. 1:2, 4–11. The latter includes Isa. 40:12–31; 49:14–25; Jer. 33:23–26; Ezek. 12:26–28; 20:32–44; 33:10–20; 37:11–13. Graffy excludes Malachi's disputa-

tion speeches as a later variant of the original, short-lived disputation speeches, contra J. A. Fischer, "Notes on the Literary Form and Message of Malachi," *CBQ* 34 (1972): 315–20. Antoon Schoors distinguishes between two forms of polemic genres: trial speeches and disputations (*I Am God Your Saviour. A Form-Critical Study of the Main Genres in Is. XL–LV*, SVT 24 [Leiden: Brill, 1973], 176–295).

11 Egon Pfeiffer, "Die Disputationsworte im Buche Malachi. Ein Beitrag zur formgeschichtlichen Struktur," 19 (1959): 546–68; Hans Jochen Boecker, "Bemerkungen zur formgeschichtlichen Terminologie des Buches Maleachi," *ZAW* 78 (1966): 78–80; Graffy, *A Prophet Confronts His People*, 16–17.

12 See Isa. 5:8–10, 11–14, 18–19, 20, 21, 22–24; 10:1–3; 28:1–4; 29:1–4, 15; 30:1–3; Amos 5:18–20; 6:1–7; Mic. 2:1–4; for examples in Habakkuk, Jeremiah, Ezekiel, and Zechariah, see R. J. Clifford, "The Use of HOY in the Prophets," *CBQ* 28 (1966): 458–64.

13 Koch, *The Growth,* 210–20.

14 Ibid., 193–94.

15 Claus Westermann, *Basic Forms of Prophetic Speech,* trans. H. C. White (Philadelphia: Westminster, 1967), 181–89.

16 Norman K. Gottwald, *All the Kingdoms of the Earth: Israelite Prophecy and International Relations in the Ancient Near East* (New York: Harper & Row, 1964), 49. See the criticism of Gottwald's approach by Burke O. Long, "The Social World of Ancient Israel," *Int* 36 (1982): 252–55.

17 For a summary, see Clements, *Prophecy and Tradition,* 58–72.

18 Hans-Martin Lutz, *Jahwe, Jerusalem und die Völker. Zur Vorgeschichte von Sach 12, 1–8 und 14, 1–5* (Neukirchen-Vluyn: Neukirchener, 1968), 147–204.

19 Friedrich Huber, *Jahwe, Juda und die anderen Völker beim Propheten Jesaja,* BZAW 137 (Berlin: Walter de Gruyter, 1976).

20 As in the Zion psalms (Pss. 46; 48; 76). See Clements, *Prophecy and Tradition,* 67–69.

21 Duane L. Christensen, *Transformations of the War Oracle in Old Testament Prophecy: Studies in the Oracles Against the Nations* (Missoula, Mont.: Scholars Press, 1975).

22 Thomas M. Raitt, "The Prophetic Summons to Repentance," *ZAW* 83 (1971): 30–49.

23 Antoon Schoors treats the words of salvation under the categories of oracles of salvation, proclamation of salvation in *I Am God Your Saviour: A Form-Critical Study of the Main Genres in Is. XL–LV,* 32–175.

24 Cf. Jer. 28:2–4; 32:14–15; 34:4–5; 35:18–19.

25 Cf. Isa. 41:8–13, 14–16; 43:1–4, 5–7; 44:1–5; cf. J. Begrich, "Das priesterliche Heilsorakel," *ZAW* 52 (1934): 81–92; idem, "Die priesterliche Tora," BZAW 66 (1936). Both articles are reprinted in *Gesammelte Studien zum Alten Testament* (Munich: Kaiser, 1964), 217–60; idem, *Studien zu Deuterojesaja,* BWANT 4/25 (Stuttgart: Kohlhammer, 1958).

26 Claus Westermann, *Isaiah 40–66,* OTL (1969), 13–14; cf. Isa. 41:17–20; 42:14–17; 43:16–21; 49:7–12.

27 Susan Niditch, *The Symbolic Vision in Biblical Tradition* (Chico: Scholars

Press, 1980); cf. Burke O. Long, "Reports of Visions Among the Prophets," *JBL* 95 (1976): 353–65.

28 Ibid., 248.

29 Ibid., 71.

30 Ibid., 174.

31 Ibid., 215.

32 There exists an extensive literature on this subject: Martin Buber, "Prophecy, Apocalyptic, and the Historical Hour," in *On the Bible: Eighteen Studies by Martin Buber*, ed. Nahum N. Glatzer (New York: Schocken, 1982), 172–87; Frank M. Cross, Jr., "New Directions in the Study of Apocalyptic," *Journal for Theology and the Church* 6 (1969): 157–65; John G. Gager, "The Attainment of Millennial Bliss Through Myth: The Book of Revelation," in *Visionaries and Their Apocalypses*, ed. Paul Hanson (Philadelphia: Fortress, 1983), 146–55; Paul D. Hanson, "Old Testament Apocalyptic Reexamined," *Int* 25 (1971): 454–79; idem, "Jewish Apocalyptic Against Its Near Eastern Environment," *RB* 78 (1971): 31–58 (= *Visionaries and Their Apocalypses*, 37–60); idem, *The Dawn of the Apocalyptic*, rev. ed. (Philadelphia: Fortress, 1979); K. Koch, *The Rediscovery of Apocalyptic: A Polemical Work on a Neglected Area of Biblical Studies and Its Damaging Effect on Theology and Philosophy*, SBT 2/22 (London: SCM, 1972); Otto Plöger, *Theocracy and Eschatology*, trans. S. Rudman (Richmond: John Knox, 1968). For the issues raised see James Barr, "Jewish Apocalyptic in Recent Scholarly Study," *BJRL* 58 (1975–76): 9–35; Robert P. Carroll, "Twilight of Prophecy or Dawn of Apocalyptic," *JSOT* 14 (1979): 3–35 (see Hanson's response to Carroll's criticism in "From Prophecy to Apocalyptic: Unresolved Issues," *JSOT* 15 [1980]: 3–6); John J. Collins, "The Place of Apocalypticism in the Religion of Israel," in *FS Cross*, 539–58; G. I. Davies, "Apocalyptic and Historiography," *JSOT* 5 (1978): 15–28; Rex Mason, "The Prophets of Restoration," in *FS Ackroyd*, 137–54; E. W. Nicholson, "Apocalyptic," in *Tradition and Interpretation: Essays by Members of the Society of Old Testament Study*, ed. G. W. Anderson (Oxford: Clarendon, 1979), 189–213; Norman Perrin, "Apocalyptic Christianity: The Synoptic Source of 'Q'; the Apocalyptic Discourses; the Book of Revelation," in *Visionaries and Their Apocalypses*, 121–45; Robert North, "Prophecy to Apocalyptic via Zechariah," *SVT* 22 (1972): 47–71; Michael A. Knibb, "Prophecy and the Emergence of Jewish Apocalypses," in *FS Ackroyd*, 155–80; Odil Hannes Steck, "Überlegungen zur Eigenart der spätisraelitischen Apokalyptik," in *FS Wolff*, 301–15; Stephen H. Travis, "The Value of Apocalyptic," *TB* 30 (1979): 53–69; Jonathan Z. Smith, "Wisdom and Apocalyptic," in *Visionaries and Their Apocalypses*, 101–20.

33 Plöger, *Theocracy and Eschatology*, 106–17.

34 For a criticism, see Joseph Blenkinsopp, *Prophecy and Canon: A Contribution to the Study of Jewish Origins* (Notre Dame, Ind.: University of Notre Dame Press, 1977), 114–16.

35 Koch, *Rediscovery of Apocalyptic*, 28–33.

36 Hanson, *Dawn of the Apocalyptic*, 10–11, 430–31.

37 Ibid., 11–12; idem, "Old Testament Apocalyptic Reexamined," 454–79.

38 Hanson, *Dawn of the Apocalyptic*, 12. He disagrees with Otto Plöger as too restrictive to a particular sect (Plöger, *Theocracy and Eschatology*).

[39]For recent surveys, see E. W. Nicholson, "Apocalyptic," 189–213; and Michael A. Knibb, "Prophecy and the Emergence of Jewish Apocalypses," 155–80.

[40]Koch, *The Rediscovery of Apocalyptic*, 131. See the insightful comments by Joyce Baldwin, *Daniel*, TOTC (1968), 13–17.

[41]Clements, "Patterns in the Prophetic Canon," in *Canon and Authority: Essays in Old Testament Religion and Theology*, ed. George W. Coats and Burke O. Long (Philadelphia: Fortress, 1977), 45; H. P. Müller, *Ursprünge und Strukturen alttestamentlicher Eschatologie*, BZAW 109 (Berlin: Walter de Gruyter, 1969).

[42]Hanson, *Dawn of the Apocalyptic*, 27.

[43]Stephen H. Travis, "The Value of Apocalyptic," *Tyndale Bulletin* 30 (1979), 53–76.

[44]John J. Collins, "The Place of Apocalypticism in the Religion of Israel," *FS Cross*, 539–58; Shemaryahu Talmon, "Typen der Messiaserwartung um die Zeitenwende," in *FS von Rad*, 571–88.

Subject Index

Scripture Index

542